C0-APO-770

365 Reasons WHY I BELIEVE

The Church of Jesus Christ of Latter-day Saints is the Authorized Kingdom of God on the Earth Today

Any and all profits from the sale of this book will be donated to the LDS Church for Missionary work, Humanitarian Aid, or to the Perpetual Education Fund.

Cover design by Scott Peck, Scott Peck Design

ISBN: 978-1-68222-175-4

This book is dedicated to

Justin

Becca

Sarah

Spencer

Sam

Their exceptional wives and husbands,
My grandchildren,
And our generations yet to be,

And to Fiona, who encouraged my writing,
And shares in this testimony.

ACKNOWLEDGEMENTS

I would like to acknowledge and thank the friends and professionals who have reviewed all or portions of the manuscript, and shared their insight, observations, and expertise. Your encouragement, along with that of my family, has made this book what I wanted it to be. Thank you.

TABLE OF CONTENTS

Part One
Crucial Reasons

Part Two
Doctrinal Reasons

Part Three
Foretold Reasons

Part Four
Confirming Reasons

282 There is an enthusiastic response to missionary service at the call of a Prophet.

283 The *Children's Songbook* used in Primary teaches true doctrine to young people.

284 Living the standard "Sunday School answer" will keep our testimonies bright.

285 The four Gospels are replete with evidences of God and Jesus as separate beings.

286 The power of leadership in the Church is enabled by the membership they serve.

287 The Living Christ is a testament and reminder of His victory and our hope.

288 Provident living and self-reliance are inspired counsel.

289 The Addiction Recovery Program is Christ-like and Christ-centered.

290 LDS funerals are uplifting services that teach the plan of salvation and give hope.

291 The Welfare Program of the Church is inspired of God and upheld by the faithful.

292 Financial debt can be a form of bondage that the Lord warns against.

293 It is my own belief that even prophets live by faith more often than not.

294 The Church supports the injunction, "In the sweat of thy face shalt thou eat bread."

295 The writings of Joseph Smith and the revelations of the Lord are discernibly different.

Part Five
A Summary Core Reason

PREFACE

As covenant members of The Church of Jesus Christ of Latter-day Saints, we are blessed by the comprehensive, scriptural, inclusive, fair, merciful, comforting, rational, and in many cases, intuitive doctrines and practices of the Church. Just as the writing of this book has caused me to better appreciate the harmony of such doctrines and practices, it is my hope that the reader may likewise see afresh the great things the Lord has done for His children.

Writing this book has been a very rich experience for me personally. I've very much enjoyed the research, thought, and reflection required to capture in about five hundred words for each chapter, the various tenets of why I believe. The reasons themselves were not hard to come by, but getting them on paper in such a concise format and staying true to the title of the book sometimes was.

The title of the book states that they are reasons why *I* believe. This is not an attempt to comprehensively reiterate or to list LDS doctrines. It is not an apologetic work for the faith. There are many unique doctrines and admirable practices of the Church that I accept, but they don't really move me as much as those in this book do. These 365 reasons, and more, move me. They kindle something within that continues to thrill me. They are reasons why I believe.

I hope these reasons will either re-stimulate, establish, and/or proudly confirm, your faith in the restored gospel of Jesus Christ, as has been my experience. I hope that they will serve as a reminder of the breadth and depth of the divine Plan of Salvation, the Plan of Happiness.

The book is written on the premise that God lives and that Jesus is the Resurrected Christ. I don't try to make that case, but assume we have that knowledge in common as a point of entry.

"The fundamental principles of our religion are the testimony of the Apostles and Prophets, concerning Jesus Christ, that he died, was buried, and rose again the third day, and ascended into heaven; and all other things which pertain to our religion are only appendages to it."[1]

That quote is from Joseph Smith. Joseph Smith is a pivotal figure in my testimony—the man whom the Lord called and sustained in restoring the fullness of the Gospel of Jesus Christ to the earth once again. I believe that a testimony of the Lord Jesus Christ must ultimately include a testimony that Joseph is His Prophet. Clearly that understanding is a foundational pillar to the title of this book.

In a sense, this is a choir book given to members of the choir. It will not likely recruit new members for the choir, nor convince anyone of the joy of singing. It is written to those who already believe but perhaps have lost sight of the beauty and richness of what the Lord has revealed, what He has provided, and what He has promised.

On the final day of the 2013 Campus Education week at Brigham Young University, Robert L. Millett related the following:

> "One Saturday morning, [I] received a call from Elder Neal A. Maxwell of the Quorum of the Twelve. Elder Maxwell was concerned about a book that had received a lot of attention and had gained somewhat of a cult following. He asked me if I knew about it and what I thought about it. I said, 'Elder Maxwell, frankly, it has a lot of doctrinal problems.' Elder Maxwell responded, 'It never ceases to amaze me how gullible the Latter-day Saints can be. Our lack of doctrinal sophistication makes us an easy prey for such fads.' Brother Millett then went on to explain that Latter-day Saints ought to pore over the scriptures constantly to learn the doctrines, lest they be deceived."[2]

We live in a day when the Gospel of Jesus Christ is firmly established. Much has been revealed to and clarified by those we sustain as prophets, seers, and revelators. The tools available to us today to study, learn, research, cross-reference, and then to discover truth for ourselves, is unprecedented. On three separate occasions in the Doctrine and Covenants, the Lord admonishes us to "seek learning even by study and also by faith" (D&C 88:118, 109:7, 14). To study spiritual truths without faith would be a fruitless experience, or worse, could lead to doubt, disbelief, and cynicism.

In an article entitled "Approaching Mormon Doctrine," we read, "Not every statement made by a Church leader, past or present, necessarily constitutes doctrine. A single statement made by a single leader on a single occasion often represents a personal, though well-considered, opinion, but is not meant to be officially binding for the whole Church."[3]

I have a personal bias to want to wrap everything up in a neat package and put a bow on it. It's the accountant in me, I suppose. But my observation and experience is that the Lord has not given us enough textual certainty in all the doctrines to be able to sequentially place all parts and pieces of the Plan of Salvation. Perhaps, this is to cause us to yearn, to study, and to prayerfully ponder what truths we do know so that those doctrines and principles can facilitate further understanding.

"It has been said that Jesus initiated true religion, and man invented churches. That's not exactly right, but it does reflect a crucial principal. True religion is a way of life. A Church is an institution designed to strengthen people in the exercise of that life."[4]

In other words, the Church is not the end-game. It is the vehicle. Yet its creation was at the hands of the Master when He declared to Peter that "upon this rock I will build my church" (Matthew 16:18). That gives importance to this vehicle we call the Church. Within it will be housed divine authority, the saving doctrines, administrative requirements, policies, practices, and principles.

I acknowledge that no list of reasons or corresponding supporting data can prove the gospel of Jesus Christ is true. That was never my intent for writing this book. My own faith in the gospel is founded on just that—faith. Yet that faith is founded on empirical evidence, thoughtful consideration, and (in my own estimation) rational derivations. Most convincingly on a personal level, it is the witness of the Holy Ghost that cements and re-cements my faith.

This book does not represent The Church of Jesus Christ of Latter-day Saints, nor is it endorsed by the Church. I am not an authority of or a spokesman for the Church. These are my own sincere beliefs. And they move me.

Notes:

1. Joseph Fielding Smith, comp., *Teachings of the Prophet Joseph Smith,* Salt Lake City: Deseret Book, 1976, 121.
2. www.lds.org/church/news/five-ways-to-detect-and-avoid-doctrinal-deception.
3. www.mormonnewsroom.org/article/approaching-mormon-doctrine.
4. Terryl Givens and Fiona Givens, *The Crucible of Doubt,* Salt Lake City: Deseret Book, 2014, 39.

Part One

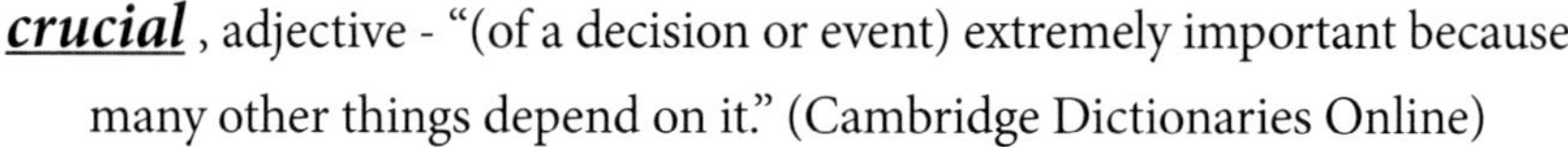

Crucial Reasons

crucial, adjective - "(of a decision or event) extremely important because many other things depend on it." (Cambridge Dictionaries Online)

1. Jesus is the Christ, the only begotten Son of God, the Messiah, the Redeemer.

Jesus Christ, who lived in the meridian of time, was mortal by his mother Mary, yet divine by his Father, God. He was and is the promised Messiah of the Old Testament. He experienced, "pains and afflictions and temptations of every kind" (Alma 7:11). He took upon himself the pains, sicknesses, infirmities, and sins of his people, "that he may know according to the flesh how to succor his people" and "that he might blot out their transgressions according to the power of his deliverance" (Alma 7:11-13).

To the woman at the well in Samaria, Jesus said, "I that speak unto thee am he [the Messiah]" (John 4:26).

"Search the scriptures; for in them ye think ye have eternal life: and they are they which testify of me" (John 5:39).

"I am the way, the truth and the life: no man cometh unto the Father, but by me" (John 14:6).

Jesus declared unto Martha, "I am the resurrection, and the life: he that believeth in me, though he were dead, yet shall he live" (John 11:25). To which Martha responded, "Yea, Lord: I believe that thou art the Christ, the Son of God, which should come into the world" (John 11:27).

While Jesus was in Nazareth on the Sabbath day, He entered into a synagogue to worship. As was the custom, He took an opportunity to read aloud from the scriptures to all in attendance. The text He chose was what we have recorded in Isaiah as Chapter 61, verses one and two, a clear reference to the promised Messiah. Concluding His reading, Jesus sat down and astounded the audience with the words, "This day is this scripture fulfilled in your ears" (Luke 4:16-21).

Even the devils acknowledged His divinity. As Jesus was about to cast them out of two men possessed, the evil spirits cried out, "What have we to do with thee, Jesus, thou Son of God" (Matthew 8:28-29)?

There are many more accounts where Jesus clearly and openly declared His divine role as the Savior and the promised Messiah, sent from God and fully authorized of the Father. As Martha made her position known, each of us needs to reconcile the Man and the mission and decide how we will respond. He either was merely an uncommon man, or He is, in fact, the only begotten Son of God, the Messiah, the Redeemer of the world. My own testimony affirms the latter. So does the Church I belong to.

2. The Book of Mormon is another testament of Jesus Christ.

An honest man, after reading the Book of Mormon, would have to conclude that it speaks of Christ. In fact, the title page states its purpose as "to the convincing of the Jew and Gentile that Jesus is the Christ" (title page, Book of Mormon). A few samples from the Book of Mormon illustrate this central purpose:

> "And we talk of Christ, we rejoice in Christ, we preach of Christ, we prophesy of Christ, and we write according to our prophecies, that our children may know to what source they may look for a remission of their sins" (2 Nephi 25:26).
>
> "My son, be faithful in Christ; and may not the things which I have written grieve thee, to weigh thee down unto death; but may Christ lift thee up, and may his sufferings and death, and the showing his body unto our fathers, and his mercy and long-suffering, and the hope of his glory and of eternal life, rest in your mind forever" (Moroni 9:25).

> "And now, my sons, remember, remember that it is upon the rock of our Redeemer, who is Christ, the Son of God, that ye must build your foundation; that when the devil shall send forth his mighty winds, yea, his shafts in the whirlwind, yea, when all his hail and his mighty storm shall beat upon you, it shall have no power over you to drag you down to the gulf of misery and endless wo, because of the rock upon which ye are built, which is a sure foundation, a foundation whereon if men build they cannot fall" (Helaman 5:12).

> "Yea, come unto Christ and be perfected in him, and deny yourselves of all ungodliness . . . that by his grace ye may be perfect in Christ" (Moroni 10:32).

The Book of Mormon is, indeed, a second witness of Jesus as the Christ. "In the mouth of two or three witnesses shall every word be established" (2 Corinthians 13:1).

"The crowning event recorded in the Book of Mormon is the personal ministry of the Lord Jesus Christ among the Nephites soon after his resurrection. It puts forth the doctrines of the gospel, outlines the plan of salvation, and tells men what they must do to gain peace in this life and eternal salvation in the life to come" (Introduction, Book of Mormon).

The Apostle John recorded many of the plain and candid words of Jesus as he declared himself "the bread of life" (John 6:35, 48), "the living bread" (John 6:51), "the light of the world" (John 8:12, John 9:5), "the door of the sheep" (John 10:7), "the good shepherd" (John 10:11), "the resurrection, and the life" (John 11:25), "the way, the truth, and the life," (John14:6), "the Son of God" (John 19:7 10:36), and the giver of "living water" (John 4:10). Knowledge and acceptance of Jesus as our personal Savior, the only way back to the Father, are perhaps the paramount purposes of scripture, including the Book of Mormon.

"Search the scriptures; for in them ye think ye have eternal life: and they are they which testify of me" (John 5:39). The Book of Mormon is, indeed, another witness to the world that Jesus is the Christ, the promised Messiah, the Savior of all mankind.

3. We must know the actual nature of God, Christ, and the Holy Ghost.

"We believe in God, the Eternal Father, and in His Son, Jesus Christ, and in the Holy Ghost" (Articles of Faith, 1).

To truly have faith, and to communicate with Deity, one must have a correct understanding of the nature of God. "Ye shall pray unto the Father in the name of Christ" (2 Nephi 32:9).

"The Father has a body of flesh and bones as tangible as man's; the Son also; but the Holy Ghost has not a body of flesh and bones, but is a personage of Spirit. Were it not so, the Holy Ghost could not dwell in us" (D&C 130:22).

When Jesus was baptized by John, we see each member of the Godhead as individual entities—Jesus being baptized, the Holy Ghost descending upon Jesus "like a dove," and the voice of God from heaven declaring, "This is my beloved Son, in whom I am well pleased" (Matthew 3:16-17).

During His mortal ministry, Jesus often spoke of "the Father which hath sent me" (John 5:30, 36, 37, 12:49, 3 Nehphi 27:13). He made clear the distinction between the two of them and their relationship as Father and Son: "The Son can do nothing of himself, but what he seeth the Father do" (John 5:19). He was personally strengthened and directed by prayers to His Heavenly Father, which occurred throughout his earthly ministry and even and especially while in agony upon the cross.

The Holy Ghost testifies of truth, particularly that Jesus is the Christ. His influence can be felt simultaneously by many, and in differing locations, because of his nature as a spirit entity. "But the Comforter, which is the Holy Ghost, whom the Father will send in my name, he shall teach you all things, and bring all things to your remembrance, whatsoever I have said unto you" (John 14:26).

Joseph Smith taught "to acquire faith unto salvation one needs a correct idea of God's character, perfections, and attributes."[1]

God is our Father, and Jesus is the Christ. They are separate, living, active, exalted beings. The Holy Ghost is the attestor or revelator. Together they comprise the Eternal Godhead and are one in purpose. In concept, they can be understood by a child, which is as it should be.

As a frame of reference, this understanding is fundamental to my worship. I believe in a personal God, a personal Savior, and a personal witness of both of them and of all truth through the influence of the Holy Spirit.

"We [I] believe in God, the Eternal Father, and in His Son, Jesus Christ, and in the Holy Ghost" (Articles of Faith, 1).

Notes:

1. *Lectures on Faith*, Salt Lake City: N.B. Lundwall, Lecture Third, 2-4.

4. Ordinances and covenants can firmly bind man to God and God to man.

Some argue that the ordinance of baptism is an unnecessary formality, but the Lord said to Nicodemus, "Except a man be born of water and of the Spirit, he cannot enter into the kingdom of God" (John 3:5).

There is power in making a personal covenant with God. It both symbolizes and enables a committed (covenant) relationship with Him. In today's world of lawful formalities and loopholes that would excuse one from his or her previously made covenant or contract, it is refreshing and empowering to commit to a course of behavior for the remainder of one's life and to honor that commitment. All covenants with God deliver to man great blessings and are of a noble, virtuous nature. They can be, in fact, exalting.

Ordinances are the rites that initiate and animate our covenants. The most important, saving ordinances, are specifically:

- Baptism and Confirmation (and by extension, partaking of the Sacrament emblems)
- Priesthood ordination
- Temple endowment
- Temple sealing

Each of these ordinances is effected under the keys of priesthood authority. It is binding on earth, and it is binding in heaven. To Peter, the Lord said, "And I will give unto thee the keys of the kingdom of heaven: and whatsoever thou shalt bind on earth shall be bound in heaven: and whatsoever thou shalt loose on earth shall be loosed in heaven" (Matthew 16:19).

"Therefore, in the ordinances thereof, the power of godliness is manifest. And without the ordinances thereof, and the authority of the priesthood, the power of godliness is not manifest unto men in the flesh" (D&C 84:20-21).

The administration of the ordinances of salvation, under the keys of priesthood authority, is made available to all mankind through The Church of Jesus Christ of Latter-day Saints. To reflect upon one's covenants and to remember the ordinances entered into, brings one back to center and aligns us to our better self, while facing us squarely to Him who is worthy of our trust. My own covenants serve this purpose, and thereby bless both me and my family.

5. Joseph Smith is a prophet of God.

John Taylor, a contemporary of Joseph Smith, and who himself became the third President of The Church of Jesus Christ of Latter-day Saints, wrote the following tribute just after the martyrdom of Joseph Smith: "Joseph Smith, the Prophet and Seer of the Lord, has done more, save Jesus only, for the salvation of men in this world, than any other man that ever lived in it" (D&C 135:3).

That is a bold statement. It is akin to Jesus' statements of His Divine Sonship and His role as the promised Messiah. It should not be treated casually, overlooked, or avoided. Either it is true, and Joseph Smith was a divinely called prophet-leader such as Enoch, Noah, Moses, and Nephi, or Joseph Smith was a hoax.

Jesus gave us the test to apply to one who claimed to be a prophet, "Beware of false prophets, which come to you in sheep's clothing, but inwardly they are ravening wolves. Ye shall know them by their fruits. Do men gather grapes of thorns, or figs of thistles? Even so every good tree bringeth forth good fruit; but a corrupt tree bringeth forth evil fruit. A good tree cannot bring forth evil fruit, neither can a corrupt tree bring forth good fruit. Every tree that bringeth not forth good fruit is hewn down, and cast into the fire. Wherefore by their fruits ye shall know them" (Matthew 7:15-20).

Listed below are some of the major contributions (fruits) that came through Joseph Smith under the direction of the Lord, unique to the Church he restored:

- He taught correct concepts about the nature of the Father, the Son, and the Holy Ghost
- He translated and published the Book of Mormon

- He was the means whereby the Aaronic and Melchizedek priesthoods were restored
- He organized the Church of Jesus Christ again upon the earth
- He restored the offices of the priesthood, e.g., elders, seventies, apostles, patriarchs
- He revealed the true meaning of Zion, its location in the last days, and its government
- He received over one hundred revelations and published them
- He worked on a translation of the Bible, restoring lost scripture, and correcting erroneous translations
- He established settlements of the Saints, teaching principles of social order and city planning
- He restored the keys and knowledge of temple ordinances for the living and for the dead
- He received keys of restoration and priesthood from John the Baptist, Moses, Elias, Peter, James and John, and Elijah
- He initiated a missionary program that became worldwide in scope, converting millions
- He explained the Telestial, the Terrestrial, and the Celestial kingdoms following the judgment
- He explained the nature and the order of the resurrection
- He restored vicarious ordinances for the dead
- He clarified the apostasy from Christ's Church and the resultant spiritual confusion
- He announced and witnessed the coming of Elijah and explained his mission

- He taught that marriage is intended to be eternal, as are family relationships
- He restored the healing of the sick by the power of the Melchizedek priesthood
- He initiated the construction of holy temples, the first such since the time of Christ
- He received revelation restoring some of the writings of Abraham
- He taught the law of common consent
- He explained more clearly the role and purpose of Satan in the Gospel plan
- He taught the nature of the atonement of Christ and its relation to justice and mercy
- He explained the meaning and procedure for sacrament covenants
- He explained the nature of spiritual gifts and the role of the Holy Ghost
- He received and taught the revelation known as the Word of Wisdom
- He instituted the law of tithing
- He introduced the law of consecration and stewardship
- He instituted the law of obedience and sacrifice

Joseph Smith was a man, yet with an extraordinary calling to restore the Lord's Church to the earth in the last days. I look forward to meeting this great man someday. He was indeed, a Prophet of God, and he retains that position today.

6. God will force no man to heaven and will compensate the disadvantaged.

We see terrible human suffering in this world in the form of oppression, abuse, neglect, hunger, ignorance, poverty, and innumerable injustices. Some suffering is self-imposed, some is suffered at the hands of others, and much comes from natural occurrences and conditions. Some people respond to these injustices and human suffering by expressing impatience with God for not delivering His children from such misery. In reality, such restraint on His part is one of life's greatest blessings. Our earthly experiences will not go uncompensated in the hereafter.

"He that is faithful in tribulation, the reward of the same is greater in the kingdom of heaven" (D&C 58:2). Furthermore, "And if they persecute you, so persecuted they the prophets and righteous men that were before you. For all this there is a reward in heaven" (D&C 127:4).

If God were to deliver us from all undesirable experiences, what earthly experience would we have? It is much like us as earthly parents, as we watch our kids learn to walk, ride a bike, or participate in any number of life's experiences that all have an element of risk. For the child who is sheltered and coddled from ever having a negative experience, much is lost in the dimension of human growth. Experience is both the teacher and the essence of our earthly sojourn. "for if they never should have bitter they could not know the sweet" (D&C 29:39).

Men are not entirely able to choose the setting and conditions of their lives, but they are free to act according to their own conscience and desires. "And now remember, remember, my brethren, that whosoever perisheth, perisheth unto himself; and whosoever doeth iniquity, doeth it unto himself; for behold, ye are free; ye are permitted to act for yourselves; for behold, God hath given unto you a knowledge and he hath made you free" (Helaman 14:30). A great leader of a people who were threatened by overthrow said, “My soul standeth fast in that liberty in the which God hath made us free” (Alma 61:9).

The freedom to choose, even when it is a choice of wickedness that affects others, is a sacred trust that God will not violate. We are not puppets of deity, but we are agents unto ourselves. “For the power is in them, wherein they are agents unto themselves. And inasmuch as men do good they shall in nowise lose their reward” (D&C 58:28).

To see human suffering must pain God most of all. The freedom to choose always walks in the presence of its fellow, consequences. Consequences, whether imposed or otherwise, can and will be painful and sometimes mortally scarring, yet also can be sweet and eternally enduring. Knowing that God allows the mortal experience, even subject to vast inequities and injustices, should be seen in light of His unwavering absolute love for His children, not as indifference.

To me, in light of an eternal existence, a loving God, and an Infinite Atonement, this agency is a rational view of growth, choice, and the human experience. And comforting is the assurance that those who suffer most the injustices of life through no fault of their own, will in the end receive the greater compensation, according to their faithfullness.

7. God speaks to man today, as in times past.

It is fundamental to realize that God is the Heavenly Father of each and every person and loves His children with a perfect love. God lives. Everyone ever born into this life has the opportunity to communicate personally with Him through prayer and to receive answers and counsel via personal revelation. On a general level, as He spoke to His children in times past, so He continues to speak to his children today, through ordained prophets, seers, and revelators, and other general and local authorities of His Church.

Revelations given to those called of God are the word of God and have universal application to all mankind. Adam received revelations from God, as did others subsequent to him, such as Moses. The inspired compilation of some of these written communications constitute the Bible today.

Some claim that the currently published Bible is the beginning and the end of the word of God to his children. They say that such is all that is needed for an individual to navigate successfully through this life. In anticipation of such claims, the Lord cautioned us:

> "And because my words shall hiss forth—many of the Gentiles shall say: A Bible! A Bible! We have got a Bible, and there cannot be any more Bible. . . . Wherefore murmur ye, because that ye shall receive more of my word? Know ye not that the testimony of two nations is a witness unto you that I am God, that I remember one nation like unto another? . . . And I do this that I may prove unto many that I am the same yesterday, today, and forever; and that I speak forth my words according to mine own pleasure. And because that I have spoken one word ye need not suppose that I cannot speak another; for my work is not yet finished; neither shall it be until the end of man, neither from that time henceforth and forever. Wherefore, because that ye have a Bible ye need not suppose that it contains all my words; neither need ye suppose that I have not caused more to be written" (2 Nephi 29:3, 8-10).

God Himself, and His designated prophets and apostles, are not limited to any particular time or place, and certainly have not ceased to exist except as allowed by man. Both personal revelation to individuals and general revelation to mankind occur today and are doctrinal underpinnings in The Church of Jesus Christ of Latter-day Saints.

8. After the apostles were martyred, a Restoration was needed.

Following the Lord's resurrection, He gave charge to the eleven apostles to "Go ye into all the world, and preach the gospel to every creature" (Mark 16:15). Judas was replaced by Matthias as a member of the Quorum of Twelve "to be a witness with us of his resurrection" (Acts 1:22). Roman leaders considered the apostles and their followers as disturbers of Roman allegiance, and one by one, they were executed by various means, and John was permanently exiled. With them, the keys and authority of the priesthood were taken from the earth.

Yet, the cause of Christ did not end. The believers spread the message and were joined by a growing band of Christians throughout the greater region. So much so, that in approximately AD 313, the Roman emperor Constantine saw an opportunity to further coalesce the Roman Empire by legitimizing Christianity. The Creed of Nicea was adopted as the fundamental explanation of the One True God. It was written by uninspired men and in language and substance as to be rendered unintelligible by many readers.

Furthermore, translations of Holy Writ resulted in much that was lost or corrupted. "Because of the many plain and precious things which have been taken out of the book, which were plain unto the understanding of the children of men, according to the plainness which is in the Lamb of God—because of these things which are taken away out of the gospel of the Lamb, an exceedingly great many do stumble" (1 Nephi 13:29).

The Apostle Paul spoke of this falling away, or apostasy, prior to the second advent of the Savior, when he wrote, "Now we beseech you, brethren, by the coming of our Lord Jesus Christ, and by our gathering together unto him, That ye be not soon shaken in mind, or be troubled, neither by spirit, nor by word, nor by letter as from us, as that the day of Christ is at hand. Let no man deceive you by any means: for that day shall not come, except there come a falling away first, and that man of sin be revealed, the son of perdition" (2 Thessalonians 2:1-3).

The European Renaissance of the fourteenth, fifteenth, and sixteenth centuries ushered in a revival of the arts, literature, science, and education. It was also during this time that "truth-seeking men and women protested against current religious practices. They recognized that many of the doctrines and ordinances of the gospel had been changed or lost. . . . Their efforts led to the organization of many Protestant churches. This Reformation resulted in an increased emphasis on religious freedom, which opened the way for the final Restoration."[1]

Because the keys and authority of the priesthood were taken from the earth at the death of the early apostles, there was a need for a full Restoration, not simply a reformation of current religious practices and mores.

In 1820, the Lord opened the dispensation that restored the priesthood and the fullness of the gospel of Jesus Christ with prophets and apostles once again to teach truth, to correct error, and to administer the kingdom, including the ordinances of salvation. This Restored Church will remain on the earth to prepare for the glorious Second Coming of the Master, as foretold by prophets.

Notes:

1. *Preach My Gospel,* Salt Lake City: Intellectual Reserve, Inc., 2004, 35.

9. All mankind will hear of Christ and will have an opportunity to make covenants.

At the birth of Jesus, an angel declared, "I bring you good tidings of great joy, which shall be to *all people*" (Luke 2:10, emphasis added).

In the whole course of history, there have been relatively few who have heard of Christ and fewer still who have received the saving ordinances of the gospel, such as baptism. Yet the fact remains, "Except a man be born of water and of the Spirit, he cannot enter into the kingdom of God" (John 3:5).

Paul addressed the practice of proxy baptism for those who have died, as he taught and testified of the reality of the resurrection, "Else what shall they do which are baptized for the dead, if the dead rise not at all? why are they then baptized for the dead" (1 Corinthians 15:29)?

Today, all the ordinances of salvation are being done in holy temples across the earth for those people who have not had the opportunity to accept and engage in these ordinances during this mortal life. That work is currently focused on the direct ancestry of faithful members of the Church, each for his or her own family lines. These individuals, by name, are taken through the saving ordinances of the gospel of Jesus Christ within the walls of the temple and then carefully recorded in family groups.

Concurrently, the Church sponsors an ambitious family history program to locate and identify the entire human family, individual by individual, in concert with other genealogical enthusiasts. "Behold, I will send you Elijah the prophet before the coming of the great and dreadful day of the Lord: And he shall turn the heart of the fathers to the children, and the heart of the children to their fathers" (Malachi 4:5-6). We believe that the saving ordinances will be vicariously done for all those who have not yet received them. Much of that vicarious work will be done during the Millennium.

By this effort, all mankind will have the opportunity to accept or to reject these physical ordinances done on their behalf. Accepting the ordinance, they will enter into that covenant relationship with God and acknowledge Jesus Christ as the Son of God, the Savior of all mankind.

This is a most ambitious effort—comprehensive and universal in scope—yet one-by-one in practice. To me, it is perhaps the most distinguishing and glorious of all the Lord's provisions for the salvation of mankind.

10. We can receive personal revelation from God.

"And when ye shall receive these things, I would exhort you that ye would ask God, the Eternal Father, in the name of Christ, if these things are not true; and if ye shall ask with a sincere heart, with real intent, having faith in Christ, he will manifest the truth of it unto you, by the power of the Holy Ghost" (Moroni 10:4).

This promise from a Prophet of God in approximately AD 421, is specifically in reference to the Book of Mormon. It is a formula for personal revelation from Heavenly Father as stated by Moroni and is a sure template for any inquiry of truth or for needed confirmation from God. From the perspective of us impatient mortals, there is no guaranteed delivery date implicit in the promise. But that it will be delivered is certain in the declarative "He will."

Applied to the Book of Mormon, a certain witness of its divine origin logically confirms that Joseph Smith is in fact a Prophet of God and that the Church he founded, including priesthood authority restored, is likewise of divine origin.

I have tested the promise made by Moroni and have found it to be true that "He will manifest the truth of it unto you, by the power of the Holy Ghost" (Moroni 10:4). I have received personal revelation from God that The Church of Jesus Christ of Latter-day Saints as restored through the Prophet Joseph Smith is true. Such a witness of truth is perhaps even more certain than sight itself, and continues to be alive in me today.

To have received such a manifestation is where my faith in the Restored Gospel of Jesus Christ begins and by which my faith is sustained.

11. The Bible is the word of God as far as it is translated correctly.

"We believe the Bible to be the word of God as far as it is translated correctly; we also believe the Book of Mormon to be the word of God" (Articles of Faith 8).

The Holy Bible has come down to our present day as preserved by God. It is a testament of many prophets that a Messiah would come, that He did come, that He was crucified, died, and was resurrected. There are many doctrines to be understood from the Old Testament, including the creation, the fall of Adam, the need for an Atonement, obedience and sacrifice, divine commandments, the Abrahamic covenant, the covenant role of the house of Israel, the fruits of faith, and the folly of disobedience. The New Testament is a priceless record of the life of Jesus Christ, his wise and timeless teachings, his love of people, the miracles He performed and is a witness of his divine Sonship by which He was qualified and enabled to effect the everlasting atonement culminating in His resurrection from death.

But all that said, and taking nothing from the preceding paragraph, the Bible is translation literature and has been subject to multiple translations and written iterations over a period of many hundreds of years from the original writings. The widely recognized King James Version of the Bible was completed in 1611.

This sequence of Biblical history is well described by the Prophet Nephi, who was in possession of one of the then-current manual versions of these sacred writings. He recorded what was told him from an angel of God on the American continent in approximately 600 BC:

> "Thou hast beheld that the book proceeded forth from the mouth of a Jew; and when it proceeded forth from the mouth of a Jew it contained the fulness of the gospel of the Lord, of whom the twelve apostles bear record. . . . Wherefore, these things go forth from the Jews in purity unto the Gentiles...

> And after they go forth by the hand of the twelve apostles of the Lamb, from the Jews unto the Gentiles . . . they have taken away from the gospel of the Lamb many parts which are plain and most precious; and also many covenants of the Lord have they taken away. . . . And after these plain and precious things were taken away it goeth forth unto all the nations of the Gentiles" (1 Nephi 13:24-29).

The Bible has been an incalculable blessing to mankind at large and to individuals throughout human history. It is indeed the word of God and should be considered as sacred writ. The clarifier, "as far as it is translated correctly," is a refreshing proviso to the inherent hand of man in its many revisions and translations and will help to explain why there are apparent inconsistencies to the nature of God and other references within its pages.

12. The reality and the results of prayer to God the Father are powerful.

The scriptural injunction to pray is perhaps second only to the commandment to live by faith. The Lord himself thought it so important, he modeled how a prayer should be offered, "After this manner therefore pray ye: Our Father which art in heaven" (Matthew 6:9).

My first prayer was on my second BYU survival trip in 1976. I had come to the logical reasoning that there must be a supreme being, given the order of the heavens, their seeming eternal nature; the complexity and wonder of the human body, brain and systems within; and the beauty, variety, and seasonal consistency of this earth. It was all too immense and too wondrous not to be of divine creation. And so, if God existed, then He must be alive, and we as his children could communicate with Him.

My first prayer was an awakening to a whole new relationship that I had not previously known. It was real, it was communication, it was genuine, it was sincere, it was refreshing, it was personal, it was stimulating, it was comforting, it was connecting. And I felt that I was invited back as often as I desired, without price. A "come-as-you-are" type of invitation.

Prayer has been a daily part of my life since that day. Some prayers have been very, very special, some have been less moving than others, some are not moving at all. I don't think God varies the distance between Him and us, but rather we vary that distance by the way we live, the places we are in, or the preparation we give to our prayers. We are taught, "And now, my beloved brethren, I perceive that ye ponder still in your hearts; and it grieveth me that I must speak concerning this thing. For if ye would hearken unto the Spirit which teacheth a man to pray ye would know that ye must pray; for the evil spirit teacheth not a man to pray, but teacheth him that he must not pray. But behold, I say unto you that ye must pray always, and not faint; that ye must not perform any thing unto the Lord save in the first place ye shall pray unto the Father in the name of Christ, that he will consecrate thy performance unto thee, that thy performance may be for the welfare of thy soul" (2 Nephi 32:8-9).

The understanding that we are children of a living God and that we can not only commune with Him, but also are invited to do so, provides access to a dynamic and infinite well of living water. Sincere prayer is a vital source for the foundation of, the preservation of, and the perpetuation of my living faith.

13. Priesthood is the authority to act in the name of God.

"Ye have not chosen me, but I have chosen you, and ordained you, that ye should go and bring forth fruit, and that your fruit should remain" (John 15:16).

"And no man taketh this honour unto himself, but he that is called of God, as was Aaron" (Hebrews 5:4).

"We believe that a man must be called of God, by prophecy, and by the laying on of hands by those who are in authority, to preach the Gospel and administer in the ordinances thereof" (Articles of Faith, 5).

It is claimed that there are more than thirty thousand different denominations of Christianity throughout the world![1] Each has its own nuance of doctrine, procedure, and interpretation of what the Lord Jesus Christ founded.

I believe God is a God of order, and that His doctrine is "the same yesterday, today, and forever" (2 Nephi 27:23). Those who bear His priesthood will receive it in the manner scripturally described above. They will be in possession of true doctrine, administer the ordinances of the gospel, and operate under His direction and as authorized administrators and shepherds of the Master.

Priesthood offices are referred to in scripture under two heads, that of the Levitical or Aaronic, which is the preparatory priesthood to administer in the outward ordinances, and that of the Melchizedek, authority to preside and officiate in all the several offices of the holy priesthood.

Priesthood is the authority and power of God. It is an eternal authority and power, by which the heavens and the earth were created and are governed. This priesthood authority was restored to the earth prior to and requisite for the establishment of the Church of Jesus Christ once again to the earth.

Priesthood administration, callings, offices, ordinances, power, and authority are attestation of an organization that can be called after the name of the Lord Jesus Christ. It is a precondition for the Authorized Kingdom of God.

Notes:

1. David B. Barrett, ed., *World Christian Encyclopedia,* 2nd edition, Oxford University Press, 2001.

14. All those who have ever lived will be resurrected to immortality.

In some circles, the following discrete truths are misunderstood:

- The resurrection shall come to all, unconditionally, because of Christ's victory over death
- Immortality is the resurrected state of living forever
- Eternal life (exaltation) is to live eternally with God and in the perfections of God
- There is a space of time between death and the resurrection

The resurrection will come to all, the righteous and the wicked, the devout and the agnostic, the informed and the ignorant, old and young, male and female. It is a free reality effected by the atonement of Jesus Christ. "For since by man came death, by man came also the resurrection of the dead. For as in Adam all die, even so in Christ shall all be made alive" (1 Corinthians 15:21-22).

The resurrection consists in the uniting of our spirit body with our newly composed immortal body of flesh and bones, never again to be separated. "The spirit and the body shall be reunited again in its perfect form; both limb and joint shall be restored to its proper frame, even as we now are at this time. . . . Now, this restoration shall come to all, both old and young, both bond and free, both male and female, both the wicked and the righteous; and even there shall not so much as a hair of their heads be lost; but every thing shall be restored to its perfect frame" (Alma 11:43-44).

Jesus demonstrated the physical reality of the resurrected state as He appeared to His disciples after his crucifixion and said, "Behold my hands and my feet, that it is I myself: handle me, and see; for a spirit hath not flesh and bones, as ye see me have. . . . He said unto them, Have ye here any meat? And they gave him a piece of a broiled fish, and of an honeycomb. And he took it, and did eat before them" (Luke 24:39-43).

That all will be resurrected and live immortally should be a game changing doctrinal understanding. It cannot be altered. For such an eventuality, it behooves us to rejoice in His infinite mercies and to prepare accordingly. All of us.

15. Fasting is a powerful source of spiritual strength, compassion, and renewal.

Prior to his public ministry, Jesus fasted for forty days and forty nights in the wilderness. Why? Certainly during this time He was communicating with his Father in Heaven, and in order to enhance and enable that communication, He utilized the power of temporary abstinence from food.

Fasting is a principle of sacrifice, of denying self for a greater purpose. That purpose may be personal, or it may be in the sincere interest of another. It may be for a specific cause, or it may be for a general influence. Often it is for personal revelation, insight, or divine direction. Always, it brings one to a clearer perspective of personal challenges and to a greater hope and outlook.

Fasting is also a principle of power. Jesus taught His disciples that faith is enhanced by fasting, when He said to them, "Howbeit this kind goeth not out but by prayer and fasting" (Matthew 17:21).

True fasting will involve sincere prayer. It is a time of seeking the Lord, fervently seeking. It is a time of receiving answers as well. "They had given themselves to much prayer and fasting; therefore they had the spirit of prophecy, and the spirit of revelation" (Alma 17:3).

I love the simplicity, the availability, and the immediate alignment that comes from fasting. It is a principle without monetary price, effected by one's own desire and self-discipline. No one who is physically able is excluded from the power and benefits that come from an honest fast.

Today, we designate the first Sunday of each month as Fast Sunday, where members of the Church fast for twenty-four hours from food and drink. On this Sunday, we gather for worship and have the opportunity to express our personal testimony of things divine. In addition, the money that would have been spent for food, or a multiple thereof, is donated for the needs of the poor via a fast offering. In that way, the local ward (congregation) can assist its own people as temporary needs arise.

Fasting is a divinely inspired practice that blesses us and others both spiritually and temporally. It has been an essential part of my personal discipleship. "Verily, this is fasting and prayer, or in other words, rejoicing and prayer" (D&C 59:14). I have found it to be so.

16. All mankind will be judged according to what they know.

As I investigated the Church, I was concerned that any one organization could be the only way to God. How about the millions of men and women who had never even heard of Christ or those who will never have the opportunity to know the fullness of the gospel? Certainly, and by an overwhelmingly wide margin, the majority of mankind fall into this condition.

Then, while I was a student at Southern Utah State College in Cedar City, Utah, sitting outside by the flagpole at the Student Union building, an acquaintance of mine shared with me this verse from the Book of Mormon, "For behold, the Lord doth grant unto all nations, of their own nation and tongue, to teach his word, yea, in wisdom, all that he seeth fit that they should have; therefore we see that the

Lord doth counsel in wisdom, according to that which is just and true" (Alma 29:8).

There it was! That made perfect sense in light of a God who was the loving Father of all mankind. All people will someday be accountable for how they lived according to what they know. As we live honestly in the light we've been endowed with (our conscience) and the highest cultural norms of our society, we shall one day have the opportunity to receive all knowledge—either in this life or in the life to come.

Meanwhile, we can view the many faiths and traditions of the world and of the ages, for the noble virtues they have contributed to the human condition. Without compromising the Lord's commandments or seeking to widen the straight and narrow way, this understanding makes provision for all people, in all times, and in all places, of our mortal existence.

That is an inclusive, just, merciful, doctrine—what you would expect from a loving Father of all mankind.

17. The doctrines and practices in the Church are consistent throughout the world.

Religious interpretation is the norm throughout many faiths including Islam, Christianity, Judaism, Hinduism, and Buddhism. For example, Buddhism has differing forms in Tibet, China, and Japan. Judaism takes on the form of Orthodox, Conservative, and Reform. Islam has no central leadership, but rather regional and national direction defining acceptable doctrines and practices. Christian churches vary widely according to the power and control of local leaders and their interpretation of general church policies, doctrines, and practices.

Ours is a world-wide, top-down leadership, Jesus Christ being the Chief Cornerstone, the Presiding High Priest. It is He who established

His doctrine, organized His Church and Kingdom, and taught correct standards of conduct. Although the many forms of Christianity today, for the most part, inspire and encourage human improvement and compassion, the apostle Paul taught, "One Lord, one faith, one baptism" (Ephesians 4:5). He went on to describe some of the offices within the church organization, and the purpose of the church:

> "And he gave some, apostles; and some, prophets; and some, evangelists; and some, pastors and teachers; For the perfecting of the saints, for the work of the ministry, for the edifying of the body of Christ: Till we all come in the unity of the faith, and of the knowledge of the Son of God, unto a perfect man, unto the measure of the stature of the fulness of Christ" (Ephesians 4:11-13).

The Church is essential for all the reasons above, including "till we all come in the unity of the faith" (Ephesians 4:13) and unto Christ.

The worldwide Church today is led by a prophet and presiding presidency and twelve apostles of the Lord Jesus Christ. Doctrines are scriptural and by revelatory pronouncement. Practices and procedures are carefully observed by local leaders as written in the handbooks of the Church. A Sunday School lesson in Seattle, Washington on a given Sunday will likely be the same lesson being taught in Frankfurt, Germany or Santiago, Chile, or Sapporo, Japan, on that same Sunday.

Church correlation and training are embedded within the Church culture to facilitate the uniformity, doctrinal purity, and inspired programs of the Church to all of God's children. Prior to the oft quoted Ephesians 4:5 above, Paul wrote, "Endeavoring to keep the unity of the Spirit . . . there is one body, and one Spirit" (Ephesians 4:3-4). Like no other I know of, The Church of Jesus Christ of Latter-day Saints preserves this unity of the Spirit under one body and under One Head throughout all the world.

18. Man is created after the image of God.

That man and woman are created after the image of God is clear in the scriptures. "And God said, Let us make man in our image, after our likeness. . . . So God created man in his own image, in the image of God created he him; male and female created he them" (Genesis 1:26-27).

Throughout human history, it has been the tendency of men to fashion their view of God after themselves or of their own creative makings, to personify or ascribe human emotions toward that god of their creation. And if not that, they conceive of a god that is without form, without passions, and without local presence. Or they combine these two concepts to produce as interesting a result as imagination and desire can deliver.

God is not created after the image of man. In the pure definition, God is not an anthropomorphic being, meaning He does not have human forms and traits. Rather, we are made in His image, have within us His nature, form and traits, and are of His physical likeness. We, like Him, are of a dual nature, both corporeal and spiritual.

The initial scene of the restoration of the gospel in these last days, as experienced by the boy Joseph Smith in 1820, confirms these truths. "I saw a pillar of light exactly over my head, above the brightness of the sun, which descended gradually until it fell upon me. . . . When the light rested upon me I saw two Personages, whose brightness and glory defy all description, standing above me in the air. One of them spake unto me, calling me by name and said, pointing to the other—This is My Beloved Son. Hear Him" (Joseph Smith History 1:16-17).

"In the image of God" (Genesis 1:27) not only refers to the physical characteristics we inherit, but also to our receiving His divine nature. The challenge of a true believer is to cultivate this divine nature.

It is certainly one of the most inspiring doctrinal truths to know that we are literal offspring of Deity, and have His divine qualities within us to develop and to call upon. That God lives as a physical, perfected being and that we are after His image and likeness are not commonly understood today. To me, it is a foundational doctrine and understanding.

19. We are all children of Heavenly parentage, of both Father and Mother.

Jesus taught us to pray to our Father in Heaven, and throughout His life He exemplified exacting obedience and deference to His Heavenly Father. If a Father, then also a Mother, as one cannot be defined without the other. Eliza R. Snow, an early member of the church, wrote the following logical and intuitive verse to the well-loved hymn "O My Father" in 1844:

> "In the heav´ns are parents single?
> No, the thought makes reason stare!
> Truth is reason; truth eternal
> Tells me I´ve a mother there.
> When I leave this frail existence,
> When I lay this mortal by,
> Father, Mother, may I meet you
> In your royal courts on high?"[1]

Confirming this doctrinal truth, in 1909 the First Presidency wrote, "Man, as a spirit, was begotten and born of heavenly parents, and reared to maturity in the eternal mansions of the Father [as an] off-spring of celestial parentage. . . . All men and women are in the similitude of the universal Father and Mother, and are literally the sons and daughters of Deity."[2]

In 1995, the First Presidency and the Council of the Twelve issued "The Family – A Proclamation To the World." In part, it says, "All human beings—male and female—are created in the image of God. Each is a beloved spirit son or daughter of heavenly parents."[3]

So why don't we outwardly worship our Heavenly Mother as we do the Father? The scriptures themselves are silent on referring to our Heavenly Mother. There must be both purpose and model to that fact. Said Pres. Gordon B. Hinckley, of the First Presidency in 1991, "Logic and reason would certainly suggest that if we have a Father in Heaven, we have a Mother in Heaven. That doctrine rests well with me. However, in light of the instruction we have received from the Lord Himself, I regard it as inappropriate for anyone in the Church to pray to our Mother in Heaven. . . . The fact that we do not pray to our Mother in Heaven in no way belittles or denigrates her. . . . None of us can add to or diminish the glory of her of whom we have no revealed knowledge."[4]

This realization of divine parentage inspires within me a deeper identity of self and the inherent endowment of what only motherhood can offer to a child. It is a sweet and candid doctrine, and it rests well with me, too.

Notes:

1. Eliza R. Snow, "O My Father," *Hymns of the Church of Jesus Christ of Latter-day Saints,* Salt Lake City: The Church of Jesus Christ of Latter-day Saints, 1985, 292.

2. First Presidency [1909], "The Origin of Man," *Ensign,* February, 2002.

3. First Presidency and The Council of the Twelve, "The Family: A Proclamation to the World," *Ensign,* November, 1995.

4. Gordon B. Hinckley, "Daughters of God," *Ensign,* November, 1991.

20. Priesthood is divine authorization to do certain things.

Once, when speaking with a minister of another faith and presenting our views on the topic of priesthood, he questioned me, "Why would I need priesthood to do good? As it is, my entire life is devoted to bringing people to Jesus, and helping them with life's challenges. And I've done all that without any priesthood." Unfortunately, I remember that I didn't have a ready answer. I think I referred to the need for order in all things, or something like that. But further contemplation on the need for priesthood has revealed greater insight that I wish I would have shared on that occasion.

Our fifth Article of Faith states, "We believe that a man must be called of God, by prophecy, and by the laying on of hands by those who are in authority, to preach the Gospel and administer in the ordinances thereof" (Articles of Faith, 5).

By ordination to the priesthood, there is divine authorization to:

- preach the Gospel
- administer in the ordinances of the Gospel
- preside over and conduct the affairs of the Kingdom on earth

"It shall not be given to anyone to go forth to preach my gospel, or to build up my church, except he be ordained by someone who has authority" (D&C 42:11). We understand this principle for those who represent a company, a university, or perhaps a government agency. Knowledge of the subject, or even a genuine passion for it, is not the equivalent of orderly authorization.

"And without the ordinances thereof, and the authority of the priesthood, the power of godliness is not manifest unto men in the flesh" (D&C 84:21). Ordinances, such as baptism, are essential and eternally valid, when performed by one who bears the priesthood of

God and does so in the manner prescribed by God. To Peter, who himself was ordained to the priesthood, the Lord said, "And whatsoever thou shalt bind on earth shall be bound in heaven" (Matthew 16:19). Priesthood authority acting under priesthood keys, is what validates that binding power

Jesus himself was ordained to His Messianic mission, certainly by virtue of His Divine Sonship, and also as Isaiah recorded, "The Lord hath anointed me to preach good tidings unto the meek; he hath sent me to bind up the brokenhearted" (Isaiah 61:1).

All people can and should go about doing good, and that requires no special authority. My pastor friend knew this, and he was, and is, a blessing to many. However, those who bear the priesthood are specifically charged with not only doing good, but authoritatively preaching, administering ordinances, and presiding over the Church. Priesthood service is a duty to attend to the requisite chores and official acts of the Kingdom of God on earth.

21. Building and properly using a temple is one of the marks of the true Church.

Many who are not members of the Church are surprised to learn that there is no Sunday worship in our beautiful temples built throughout the world. Their question then becomes, "What do you do in those buildings, and why do you build such magnificent and costly edifices?"

"A temple is literally a House of the Lord, a holy sanctuary in which sacred ceremonies and ordinances of the gospel are performed by and for the living and also in behalf of the dead. A place where the Lord may come, it is the most holy of any place of worship on the earth. Only the home can compare with the temple in sacredness."[1]

The ceremonies and ordinances of the gospel administered in temples include:

- Proxy baptism for the deceased
- Proxy conferral of the Melchizedek priesthood
- Living and proxy receipt of a personal endowment
- Living and proxy eternal marriage (sealing of husband and wife)
- Living and proxy sealing of children to parents

"Whenever the Lord has had a people on the earth who will obey his word, they have been commanded to build temples in which the ordinances of the gospel and other spiritual manifestations that pertain to exaltation and eternal life may be administered. . . . From Adam to the time of Jesus, ordinances were performed in temples for the living only. After Jesus opened the way for the gospel to be preached in the world of spirits, ceremonial work for the dead, as well as for the living, has been done in temples on the earth by faithful members of the Church."[2]

Israel carried a Tabernacle with them during their wanderings. It was, in fact, a portable temple. It was housed under a tent that contained specific furnishings that served for sacred purposes until the building of Solomon's temple.

The Temple of Solomon was built after the model of the Tabernacle, the dimensions of each part being exactly double, and the materials and workmanship were the finest available. Enormous wealth and craftsmanship were the hallmark of Solomon's temple. The sacred Ark of the Covenant was housed in this temple.

In about 586 BC, Solomon's temple was destroyed by the Babylonians. Within fifty years or so, Cyrus captured Babylon and issued a decree allowing the Jews to return to the land of Judah and rebuild the temple under the governorship of Zerubbabel. The temple reconstruction was completed under King Darius of Persia, subsequent to King Cyrus, about 515 BC and is known as the Temple of Zerubbabel. Notably, the Ark of the Covenant was absent, either lost or destroyed during the destruction of Jerusalem by the Babylonians. The Temple of Zerubabbel went through cycles of desecration and subsequent purification over several hundred years.

In 17 BC, King Herod rebuilt the temple of Zerubabbel to win popularity with the Jews over whom he governed. It became known as the Temple of Herod. It was this temple in which the Lord Jesus Christ taught frequently, watched the people cast in their alms and purified it from the moneychangers. It was the site of several other recorded events during his ministry. This Jewish temple was destroyed by the Romans in approximately 70 AD.

The first temples of our dispensation were built at tremendous cost and sacrifice. Today (2014) there are 170 temples dedicated, announced, or under construction throughout the world. Eighty-three percent of all church membership lives within two hundred miles of a temple.

Said the Lord,

> "That there may be a house built unto me for the salvation of Zion—For a place of thanksgiving for all saints, and for a place of instruction for all those who are called to the work of the ministry in all their several callings and offices; That they may be perfected in the understanding of their ministry, in theory, in principle, and in doctrine, in all things pertaining to the kingdom of God on the earth, the keys of which kingdom have been conferred upon you. And inasmuch as my people build a house unto me in the name of the Lord, and do not suffer any unclean thing to come into it, that it be not defiled, my glory shall rest upon it; Yea, and my presence shall be there, for I will come into it, and all the pure in heart that shall come into it shall see God" (D&C 97:12-16).

The ceremonies and ordinances of the temple bring us to higher ground, to be closer to the divine. They enable family relationships to continue into the eternities. They teach us of the need for and redemptive power of the Atonement of Jesus Christ, encourage obedience to God, and charge us to live moral and upright lives.

Notes:

1. LDS Bible Dictionary, "Temple."
2. LDS Bible Dictionary, "Temple."

22. An apostle is an authorized special witness of the Lord Jesus Christ to all the world.

An apostle is an office of the Melchizedek priesthood with specific duties, authorities, and geographic scope. As in the time of Christ, there are ordained apostles on the earth today. Collectively and individually, they possess all the necessary keys of the priesthood, which keys are effective under the direction of the senior tenured apostle, Jesus Christ Himself being the head thereof (Ephesians 2:20).

The calling of an apostle "is to be a special witness of the name of Jesus Christ in all the world, particularly of his divinity and of his bodily resurrection from the dead."[1]

In this dispensation, the office of Apostle was renewed on February 14, 1835. Two weeks later, the Prophet Joseph Smith recorded the following statement regarding the calling of the Apostles:

> "They are the Twelve Apostles, who are called to the office of the Traveling High Council, who are to preside over the Churches of the Saints, among the Gentiles, where there is no presidency established; and they are to travel and preach among the Gentiles, until the Lord shall command them to go to the Jews. They are to hold the keys of this ministry, to unlock the door of the Kingdom of heaven unto all nations,

> and to preach the Gospel to every creature. This is the power, authority, and virtue of their apostleship."[2]

One month later, on March 28, 1835, a revelation on priesthood was given wherein the duties of the Twelve were further specified, "The twelve traveling councilors are called to be the Twelve Apostles, or special witnesses of the name of Christ in all the world—thus differing from other officers in the church in the duties of their calling. And they form a quorum, equal in authority and power to the three presidents previously mentioned" (D&C 107:23-24).

The Quorum of the Twelve give perpetuity to the work of the ministry, by virtue of their being equal in authority to the Presidency of the Church. This was true in anticipation of the crucifixion of Christ, although by the martyrdom of the early apostles and the subsequent apostasy from true Christian doctrines, such perpetuity was short lived. And it is true today, because the apostleship will remain upon the earth at least until the Second Coming of the Lord Jesus Christ to this earth.

A Mr. M.G. Easton has laid out criteria for the apostleship, concluding that "the office of apostle ceased with its first holders."[3] Let's look at his criteria (italicized) in light of the modern-day apostles:

- *That they should have seen the Lord, and been able to testify of him and of his resurrection from personal knowledge.* I can't say whether or not the apostles have seen the Lord, but of their personal knowledge I am certain.

- *They must have been immediately called to that office by Christ.* I know that by divine revelation to the senior apostle, they have been (see Acts 1:15-26).

- *It was essential that they should be infallibly inspired, and thus secured against all error and mistake in their public teaching, whether by word or by writing.* I think that's a little strong. Currently and anciently, these are still men, and are not infallible. However, in regard to the doctrines of salvation, yes, heeding the words of the Lord's apostles will "secure [us] against all error and mistake."[4]

- *They have the power of working miracles.* That power is active and known today.

Living apostles are an integral part of "the only true and living church upon the face of the whole earth, with which I, the Lord, am well pleased" (D&C 1:30). Living apostles bespeak of the living Christ who is actively at the head of His Church. What a blessing to have living apostles who are authorized and led by the Lord Jesus Christ!

Notes:

1. LDS Bible Dictionary, "Apostle."
2. Joseph Fielding Smith, comp., *Teachings of the Prophet Joseph Smith,* Salt Lake City: Deseret Book, 1976, 74.
3. www.biblestudytools.com/dictionaries/eastons-bible-dictionary/apostle.html.
4. www.biblestudytools.com/dictionaries/eastons-bible-dictionary/apostle.html.

23. The "two destinations only" doctrine of Heaven and Hell is narrow and exclusive.

I have an acquaintance who is the Senior Pastor at a local Christian Church. One evening his Church was conducting a seminar which they titled "The Differences between Biblical Christianity and Mormonism." He invited me to come. They concluded the evening with the summary statement that "Mormons are not Christians." Given the direction and tenor of the seminar, I was not surprised at such willful ignorance.

Afterwards, I spoke to the Senior Pastor and could sense his genuine concern for me and my eternal welfare. I asked him, "John, do you really think God would send me to hell? You know I am an honest man, that I love my family. I seek to do good. I declare the Lord's divinity, and I've devoted my life to His service."

His reply, while looking me straight in the eye, was, "Yes."

As a missionary in Mexico, I heard of mothers who experienced inconsolable sorrow at the loss of an infant. To compound that, they were told by their local priest that because the infant wasn't baptized, the baby could never enter into heaven and would be consigned to a state they referred to as limbo, which is a state that comes short of salvation.

Jesus taught that "in my Father's house are many mansions" (John 14:2).

Commenting on this verse, Joseph Smith said, "I do not believe the . . . doctrine of sending honest men and noble-minded men to hell, along with the murderer and the adulterer. . . . There are mansions for those who obey a celestial law, and there are other mansions for those who come short of the law, every man in his own order."[1]

Gordon B. Hinckley, former President of the Church, stated, "In the life to come we shall not be arbitrarily divided into two fixed groups—inhabitants of heaven and hell. . . . There will be various grades and stations."[2]

A loving earthly father wills improvement upon subsequent generations. Our loving Heavenly Father has provided kingdoms of *glory*, commensurate with the development and moral worthiness of the individual.

Paul referred to these kingdoms of glory as the Celestial and the Terrestrial, with reference to a third (1 Corinthians 15:40-42). Detailed understandings of these "degrees of glory" are given in Section 76 of the Doctrine and Covenants, and there are other references in sections 78, 88, 101, 130, 131, 132, 137, 138.

There is, of course, a place in the eternities without glory, and that is where Satan and those who choose to follow him will dwell. It is aptly named hell, or more descriptively, outer darkness.

Life is difficult. But we may know with certainty that God loves His children. The Atonement of Jesus Christ will have personal, saving effect toward each of those who dwell in these states of glory, but where Satan is, it will not have a redemptive effect beyond providing a resurrected body.

These understandings of our post-judgment existences, make provision for the varieties of the human experience and testify of the merciful, generous will of our Heavenly Father and our Savior Jesus Christ. I find it infinitely more benevolent than the evolved philosophies of men.

Notes:

1. Alma P. Burton, comp., *Discourses of the Prophet Joseph Smith,* Salt Lake City: Deseret Book, 1977, 157.

2. Gordon B. Hinckley, *Teachings of Gordon B. Hinckley,* Salt Lake City: Deseret Book, 1997, 451.

24. Faith, based on what is true, is hope that inspires action.

When I returned from serving a mission in Mexico, I was eager to share the gospel with my parents whom I stayed with for a few weeks prior to going off to college. After some study in the Book of Mormon and listening to my discussions, my dad's conclusion was that he couldn't have faith, that he just couldn't make that leap.

Faith defined, is to hope for things which are not seen, but which are true. The following scriptures are very instructive:

> "Now faith is the substance of things hoped for, the evidence of things not seen" (Hebrews 11:1).
>
> "And now as I said concerning faith—faith is not to have a perfect knowledge of things; therefore if ye have faith ye hope for things which are not seen, which are true" (Alma 32:21).
>
> "I would show unto the world that faith is things which are hoped for and not seen; wherefore, dispute not because ye see not, for ye receive no witness until after the trial of your faith" (Ether 12:6).

Note that faith is based on things which are true. We exercise a form of faith by just getting out of bed in the morning. The farmer who plants corn in the spring, exercises faith in the harvest of the fall and works to that vision with confidence.

Yet, faith unto salvation must be centered in Jesus Christ—to recognize that He is the only begotten of the Father, that He atoned sufficiently for all of mankind, and that He is worthy of our adoration and the placement of our hope. To not only believe in Him, but also to literally believe Him, is demonstrated by our obedient and optimistic behavior.

The Prophet Joseph Smith taught, "Let us here observe that three things are necessary for any rational and intelligent being to exercise faith in God unto life and salvation. First, the idea that he actually exists; Secondly, a *correct* idea of his character, perfections, and attributes; Thirdly, an actual knowledge that the course of life which one is pursuing is according to His will."[1]

True faith inspires action and is a powerful force for good. Faith must be tried and tested to both confirm its worth and to establish its saving power. Again, the Prophet Joseph Smith taught, "Let us here observe that a religion that does not require the sacrifice of all things never has power sufficient to produce the faith necessary unto life and salvation."[2]

From the Book of Mormon, the Prophet Joseph Smith, and other Latter-day Prophets, we get a practical, robust view of faith which builds upon the dominant theme and call of the New Testament which is "to make thee wise unto salvation through faith which is in Christ Jesus" (2 Timothy 3:15).

To my Dad and others who struggle with faith, the words of Alma perhaps are helpful. "Now, we will compare the word unto a seed. Now, if ye give place, that a seed may be planted in your heart, behold, if it be a true seed, or a good seed, if ye do not cast it out by your unbelief, that ye will resist the Spirit of the Lord, behold, it will begin to swell within your breasts; and when you feel these swelling motions, ye will begin to say within yourselves—It must needs be that this is a good seed, or that the word is good, for it beginneth to enlarge my soul; yea, it beginneth to enlighten my understanding, yea, it beginneth to be delicious to me. Now behold, would not this increase your faith? I say unto you, Yea" (Alma 32:28-29).

Notes:

1. *Lectures on Faith*, Salt Lake City: N.B. Lundwall, Lecture Third, 2-4.
2. *Lectures on Faith*, Salt Lake City: N.B. Lundwall, Lecture Sixth, 7.

25. Understanding vicarious work—conditional and unconditional gifts.

Perhaps the most oft referenced and recognized scriptural passage within Christianity is John 3:16, "For God so loved the world, that he gave his only Begotten Son, that whosoever believeth in him should not perish, but have everlasting life." Jesus was sent to make Himself a vicarious offering for the sins of mankind. Vicarious can be defined as "suffered or done by one person as a substitute for another."[1]

Because "all have sinned, and come short of the glory of God" (Romans 3:23), Jesus has enabled our being cleansed from sin by His personal sacrifice. He paid the price for our sins. He satisfied the demands of justice. As the Son of God, His was unlike any other moment of human suffering. It was voluntary, escapable, excruciating, "blood cometh from every pore" (Mosiah 3:7), and absolutely undeserved. His Atonement was born of His divinity, His love for mankind, and His willingness to "drink the bitter cup" (D&C 19:18).

From that singular vicarious work flows to mankind the unconditional resurrection, meaning all will participate in their own personal resurrection from the dead. Equally important from that vicarious atonement is the conditional forgiveness of our personal sins and blunders, if we acknowledge Him and repent to the best of our ability.

So the very foundation of our Christian faith is based on a vicarious act.

Christ's Atonement enables us to participate in the vicarious work of providing essential physical ordinances for those who have not received them and have departed this mortal life. In fact, Christ has commanded us to perform these priesthood ordinances for all of mankind.

Baptism is one of those ordinances. Jesus made it clear that "except a man be born of water and of the Spirit, he cannot enter into the kingdom of heaven" (John 3:5). So in holy temples, we stand in as a proxy for a given individual and are baptized for and in behalf of that person who is deceased. Other vicarious priesthood ordinances are carried out in temples as well, including the sealing of husband and wife and the sealing of children to parents in family units. All of this is done by proxy participation for each single individual. It is a very personal, one-by-one work for those who have been and are being identified in personal family history records.

The work done in temples for the deceased is conditional upon their accepting the ordinance. No church membership record is created. As is the atonement of Christ, it is an offering of love and concern for the welfare of others, yet requires their acceptance for it to have effect.

By the Lord's supreme vicarious act, all will be resurrected unconditionally, and all may be saved on condition of their obedience to the commandments and their continuous repentance. What a blessing to participate with the Savior in activating His Atonement vicariously on behalf of others. Truly, as the Prophet Joseph Smith taught, it enables us "to become saviors on Mount Zion."[2]

Notes:

1. www.merriam-webster.com/dictionary/vicarious.
2. *History of the Church of Jesus Christ of Latter-day Saints,* Salt Lake City: Deseret Book, 1962, 6:184.

26. Five tests to consider whether or not Joseph Smith was a prophet of God.

Much is written about the man Joseph Smith, and much of that is negative. He is criticized for not fitting the traditional role of a prophet, which is often characterized as older, serious, not given to cheerfulness, aloof, sedentary, studious, and more. He is criticized for his doctrines—new scripture, continuous revelation, a new concept of the trinity, priesthood, restoration, and more. He is criticized for his ambition—his worldwide missionary efforts, his gathering of the saints, building extravagant temple structures, organizing and overseeing city governments, running for President of the United States, and more.

The following points are good tests of the man Joseph Smith and whether or not he was called of God to be a prophet to restore Christ's Church in the latter days:

- Test the Book of Mormon. Read the book, ponder the doctrines and truths it avows, note the emphasis on Jesus Christ, consider its origin, and then act upon Moroni 10:3-5 (the last chapter in the Book of Mormon).
- Consider the doctrines that were taught and clarified by the Prophet Joseph Smith. Begin with the Thirteen Articles of Faith.
- Look at the fruits of the religion today. Look at individual members of the Church, individual families, and the institution worldwide.
- Follow the money. From Joseph Smith to the present, self-aggrandizement has not been the motive for individual service at any level in the Church. For an organization of such wealth as the Church is, corruption will often finds its way into the fabric of that organization via colluding individuals. Take a close look at the lives and motives of those in Church leadership positions.
- Ask the living God if Joseph Smith was a prophet sent to restore the Church in the last days. Ask with a sincere heart, with real intent, and with faith in Christ.

How is it that one knows that Noah, Samuel, Elisha, or Moses were prophets? Whatever your criteria is, use the same towards Joseph Smith. He can't be explained away by the argument of irrelevance; his legacy is too bold and so much alive today. It's not intellectually honest to dismiss him as merely an oddity. And it's foolish to argue that God doesn't, or worse couldn't, interact with his children in these times as in times of old.

My simple testimony is that Jesus is the Messiah, and that Joseph is His Prophet.

27. Keys of the Priesthood constitute the right to preside over and direct priesthood actions.

The priesthood is the power or authority of God. The keys are the right to use this power or authority in specific ways, including the right to preside over and direct the Church within a jurisdiction. "The power of directing these labors constitutes the keys of the Priesthood."[1]

To Peter, the head apostle, the Lord said that He would "give unto thee the keys of the kingdom of heaven" (Matthew 16:19). Jesus did give those keys to Peter, along with the apostles James and John, on the Mount of Transfiguration (Matthew 17:1-9).[2] These keys gave presiding authority to the apostles to carry on the work after the death of the Savior.

With the subsequent period of apostasy, wherein the apostles were killed, these keys and the Melchizedek Priesthood itself were taken from the earth. It wasn't until the latter half of May, 1829, that the Lord sent Peter, James, and John to restore the Melchizedek Priesthood and the corresponding keys. "Peter, and James, and John, whom I have sent unto you, by whom I have ordained you and confirmed you to be apostles, and especial witnesses of my name, and bear the keys of your ministry and of the same things which I revealed unto them; Unto whom I have committed the keys of my kingdom" (D&C 27:12-13).

Other important keys to enable specific labors and efforts of the priesthood were restored as well:

> "Upon you my fellow servants, in the name of Messiah I confer the Priesthood of Aaron, which holds the keys of the ministering of angels, and of the gospel of repentance, and of baptism by immersion for the remission of sins" (D&C 13).

> "And Moses appeared before us, and committed unto us the keys of the gathering of Israel from the four parts of the earth" (D&C 110:11).
>
> "And also Elijah, unto whom I have committed the keys of the power of turning the hearts of the fathers to the children, and the hearts of the children to the fathers, that the whole earth may not be smitten with a curse" (D&C 27:9).

All other keys relevant to this dispensation were also restored. Mission presidents hold keys restored by Moses for the gathering of Israel, temple presidents hold keys restored by Elijah to seal families together and to effect ordinance work for the dead. Presidents of priesthood quorums hold keys of presidency. Bishops hold keys of the Priesthood of Aaron. Ordained apostles hold all the available priesthood keys. The President of the Church is the only person upon the earth who possesses and is authorized to exercise all the priesthood keys. Any use of keys by those mentioned above is done by delegation from the President of the Church.

"The keys of the kingdom of God are committed unto man on the earth, and from thence shall the gospel roll forth unto the ends of the earth, as the stone which is cut out of the mountain without hands shall roll forth, until it has filled the whole earth" (D&C 65:2).

The Priesthood and the corresponding keys to this dispensation have been restored to the earth in these latter days. The specific order, functions, requirements, players, prophetic fulfillment, and correlation are beautifully unfurled. I don't believe Joseph Smith could have known of such a sequence of events, or even of the imperative requirement for keys, if it had not been given by revelation from a divine source.

Notes:

1. Joseph F. Smith, comp., *Gospel Doctrine,* Salt Lake City: Deseret Book, 1977, 136.

2. Joseph Fielding Smith, comp., *Teachings of the Prophet Joseph Smith,* Salt Lake City: Deseret Book, 1976, 158.

28. Jesus ministered to those in ancient America as a resurrected being.

When I was learning of the LDS church and was presented with a Book of Mormon, I was told to start reading about three-quarters of the way through the book, at a chapter called Third Nephi 11. There, I would find the account of the Savior Jesus Christ actually coming to minister among those of the Americas, following His resurrection in what we now refer to as the Holy Land.

This is information of potent value. It becomes another witness that Jesus is indeed the promised Messiah, and confirms His teachings and commandments among His "other sheep" (John 10:16).

The people of the Book of Mormon, in general referred to as Nephites and Lamanites, were of Hebrew lineage and looked forward to the coming of the Messiah. By natural signs, including "his star in the east" (Matthew 2:2), these people also knew of the birth of the baby Jesus (Helaman 14:2-6, 3 Nephi 1:15-21). Thirty-three years later, when Christ was crucified in Jerusalem, the people of the Americas witnessed "a great storm, such an one as never had before been known in all the land" (3 Nephi 8:5). In its aftermath, "the face of the whole earth became deformed" (3 Nephi 8:17), and the people knew that this was a sign of the Lord's death.

Then came the voice of God from heaven, declaring the divine Sonship of Jesus and commanding the people to "hear ye him" (3 Nephi 11:7). When He had descended from the heavens, the multitude assembled and were invited to "feel the prints of the nails in my hands and in my feet, that ye may know that I am the God of Israel, and the God of the whole earth" (3 Nephi 11:14).

He remained with the people for some time, teaching as He had in the land of Judea, ordaining others with priesthood authority, healing, blessing, and loving the people. Here, unlike his ministry in Israel, He was received with faith and reverence by all the people. So great was His influence and the people's acceptance of Him as the promised Savior, that a period of peace and harmony continued for some two hundred years after His ascension. "Surely there could not be a happier people among all the people who had been created by the hand of God" (4 Nephi 1:16).

For a true and sincere believer in Christ, this is important and confirming doctrine. Consider the words and testimony of the Prophet Nephi, "And if ye shall believe in Christ ye will believe in these words, for they are the words of Christ. . . . And if they are not the words of Christ, judge ye—for Christ will show unto you, with power and great glory, that they are his words, at the last day" (2 Nephi 33:10-11).

I, too, believe that Christ Himself will one day give public endorsement to that which is written of His ministry in the Americas, as a second witness of His role as the Messiah. It is a part of the very ministry of the Savior.

29. God the Father and Jesus Christ the Son appeared to the boy Joseph Smith.

Perhaps the most significant event affecting human salvation to have occurred since the resurrection of the Lord Jesus Christ, is the appearance of the Father and the Son to Joseph Smith in 1820. That event is referred to as the First Vision. The use of the word "vision" in this case is not to be construed as a dream, but an actual visit by actual beings. Jesus used this same term when speaking of the experience with Moses and Elias on the Mount of Transfiguration, clearly an actual visit which included dialogue (Matthew 17:1-9). The use of

"First," is to distinguish this from subsequent visions experienced by Joseph Smith.

Of the prominent non Judeo-Christian world religions—Islam, Hinduism, Buddhism, Sikhism – none of their founders claim a direct visit from God as a part of their genesis. Mohammed received revelation transcribed as the Quran, but whether or not he actually saw God is still a controversy among Muslim scholars and is certainly not an essential tenet of their theology.

There are many Protestant ministers who claim their right to preach as a special call from God, often as a result of a singular experience or from a strong inner prompting. Often these beginnings will be around lifestyle and/or doctrinal themes, building a church and a following based on their interpretation of Biblical scripture.

This visit of the Father and the Son to Joseph Smith, as he related it to his contemporaries, was received by those of his day with both contempt and ridicule. It is likewise received today, excepting for a few who sincerely have asked God if it were true. Such general rejection was a source of great sorrow to the boy Joseph, yet he concluded, "It was, nevertheless, a fact that I had beheld a vision. . . . I had actually seen a light, and in the midst of that light I saw two Personages, and they did in reality speak to me; and though I was hated and persecuted for saying that I had seen a vision, yet it was true. . . . For I had seen a vision. I knew it, and I knew that God knew it, and I could not deny it, neither dared I do it; at least I knew that by so doing I would offend God and come under condemnation" (Joseph Smith History 1:23-25).

"I refer to the awesome experience of Joseph Smith when he beheld God the Father and his Son, Jesus Christ, in the spring of 1820... Those who do not believe it happened find it difficult to explain away. Too much has happened since its occurrence to summarily deny that it ever took place."[1]

This sacred event was the ushering in of the final dispensation of time to prepare for the Second Coming of the Savior and to restore all things once again to the earth for the salvation of mankind. It is a theophany of foundational importance to the story of Joseph Smith and the coming forth of The Church of Jesus Christ of Latter-day Saints. I believe that it actually occurred on that spring morning of 1820.

Notes:

1. James E. Faust, "The Magnificent Vision Near Palmyra," *Ensign*, May, 1984.

30. Prophets, seers, and revelators are found within the Church of Jesus Christ.

We of The Church of Jesus Christ of Latter-day Saints sustain and support the members of the First Presidency and the Quorum of the Twelve Apostles as prophets, seers, and revelators. Those three titles sound much the same; however, each is distinctive in its meaning and function.

Some people think of a prophet as a fortune teller of some sort, fore-telling future events and seemingly unavoidable consequences, and that can be their gift as the situation might require. Prophecies concerning the House of Israel, the first and second coming of Christ, the last days, moral corruption, and coming times of peace or calamity serve as a short list of prophetic examples. In a presiding role, prophets "act as God's messenger and make known God's will. . . . [They are], above all, a preacher of righteousness."[1] In a more general sense, in the spirit of prophecy, a prophet is one who has a testimony that Jesus is the Christ (Revelation 19:10).

A revelator is one who reveals to others. "The Holy Ghost is a revelator," said Joseph Smith, and "No man can receive the Holy Ghost without receiving revelations."[2] This speaks to revelation beginning on a personal level as a source of both guidance and insight. Revelation is from God to man through the Holy Ghost or in some instances by visitation. In the case of the presiding authority in the Church, a revelator is one who reveals truth. Confirmation of those truths to the heart of an individual constitutes revelation received. Consistent with the laws of God, one will receive revelation only for oneself personally or for those over whom they have responsibility or authority.

"A seer is a revelator and a prophet also" (Mosiah 8:16). In the order of unique significance, a seer ranks highest amongst the three titles under discussion. "But a seer can know of things which are past, and also of things which are to come, and by them shall all things be revealed, or, rather, shall secret things be made manifest, and hidden things shall come to light, and things which are not known shall be made known by them, and also things shall be made known by them which otherwise could not be known" (Mosiah 8:17). Distinctive also to a seer, is the ability to translate or interpret, using the Urim and Thummim, when necessary.

Those ordained as prophets, seers, and revelators, possess divine attribution of these three gifts and responsibilities, which are superior to any one of the three individually. Blessed is the man or woman who receives personal revelation confirming their divine callings and then heeds their counsel.

Notes:

1. LDS Bible Dictionary, "Prophet."
2. Joseph Fielding Smith, comp., *Teachings of the Prophet Joseph Smith,* Salt Lake City: Deseret Book, 1976, 328.

31. Quorums of Seventy are activated once again upon the earth.

"The Seventy are also called to preach the gospel, and to be especial witnesses unto the Gentiles and in all the world. . . . And they form a quorum. . . . And also other seventy, until seven times seventy, if the labor in the vineyard of necessity requires it" (D&C 107:25, 26, 96).

This revelation in its entirety, given less than five years after the Church was organized, has enabled the Church to grow and mature throughout the world, while preserving sound doctrine and prophetic leadership.

Following the exodus from Egypt, Moses went to the Lord and confessed, "I am not able to bear all this people alone, because it is too heavy for me." Said the Lord in response, "Gather unto me seventy men of the elders of Israel . . . and bring them unto the tabernacle of the congregation, that they may stand there with thee . . . and I will take of the spirit which is upon thee, and will put it upon them; and they shall bear the burden of the people with thee, that thou bear it not thyself alone" (Numbers 11:14, 16-17).

In addition to the Twelve Apostles, Jesus called others to assist in the ministry during his day. "After these things the Lord appointed other seventy also, and sent them two and two before his face into every city and place, whither he himself would come" (Luke 10:1). These were specifically instructed by the Lord to preach the gospel, to perform miracles, and to declare that "the kingdom of God is come nigh unto you" (Luke 10:9). They bore witness that indeed the Messiah had come and was among them.

"The Seventy are to act in the name of the Lord, under the direction of the Twelve . . . in building up the church and regulating all the affairs of the same" (D&C 107:34). The First and Second Quorums of Seventy are ordained as General Authorities throughout the world; the subsequent Quorums are ordained as Area Authorities specific to a given area. All are ordained Seventies.

Area Presidencies throughout the areas of the world (twenty-nine areas currently) are composed of members of the Seventy. President Gordon B. Hinckley, in an April 1995 session of General Conference, made the following announcement, "More recently the Presidency were inspired to call men from the Seventy to serve in Area Presidencies. As the work grows across the world, it has become necessary to decentralize administrative authority to keep General Authorities closer to the people."[1]

It's all about ministry to people. This is the broader layer of ministry that supports and trains local stakes, missions, and districts and to fulfill the charge "to bear record of my name in all the world, wherever . . . mine apostles, shall send them to prepare a way before my face" (D&C 124:139).

I'm not aware of this priesthood office named in any other religious organization today, and it stands as an evidence of the Lord's Church restored.

Notes:

1. Gordon B. Hinckley, "This Work is Concerned with People," *Ensign,* April, 1995.

32. The Ten Commandments have not been compromised or repealed by the Lord.

Some contend that our faith has too many rules and requirements. They would have a rather milder version of the Lord's commandments, a kind of "Ten Commandments Light," a version that would adapt to the times.

The Ten Commandments are the basic framework of Judeo-Christian values and ethics and should continue to stand as the core model of our belief and behavior.

1. **Have no other gods.** Not money, career, fame, power, any other person, creation, or earthly asset.

2. **Have no graven images.** We are not to fashion objects that would distract or deviate from our focal worship of the living Father God and His resurrected Son Jesus Christ.

3. **Do not take the name of the Lord in vain.** This is a gauge of our reverence for God, and whether or not we really know Him. When we reverence Him, we would never use His name in vain, nor act out of character as one who has taken upon them His name.

4. **Keep the Sabbath day holy.** Not too long ago, stores were never open on the Sabbath. Boy, has that changed! We should not compel others to have to keep the doors of retail open on Sunday. The Sabbath is a blessing when we do those things that keep us in remembrance of Him.

5. **Honor Father and Mother.** Parenting is a learn-as-you-go experience. Even a best effort merits our honor towards them.

6. **Thou shalt not kill.** Murder. The shedding of innocent blood. Abortion for convenience.

7. **Thou shalt not commit adultery.** A civil society cannot exist long if this is not in check. "Whosoever looketh on a woman to lust after her hath committed adultery with her already in his heart" (Matthew 5:28).

8. **Thou shalt not steal.** Property rights are fundamental to the rule of law. Respect for the property of others is a form of honesty.

9. **Don't bear false witness.** For competing loyalties (money often is one of them) people will lie or taint the truth. "And there shall also be many which shall say… Yea, lie a little, take the advantage of one because of his words, dig a pit for thy

neighbor; there is no harm in this" (2 Nephi 28:8). Our own agenda should not adjust our conveyance of the truth.

10. **Thou shalt not covet.** "Keeping up with the Jones'" is a sure way to ingratitude and unhappiness. It also leads to living beyond our means for the sake of appearance. Vanity, "all is vanity" (Ecclesiastes 1:2).

"And there shall also be many which shall say: Eat, drink, and be merry; nevertheless, fear God—he will justify in committing a little sin . . . and if it so be that we are guilty, God will beat us with a few stripes, and at last we shall be saved in the kingdom of God" (2 Nephi 28:8). Such a sentiment is in contrast to the requirements of a loving God, but are often rationalized in one form or another.

The commandments of God are to bless His children. They stand as a blessing to us today as they have been in times past. The Church of Jesus Christ of Latter-day Saints really seeks to honor and uphold these commandments given of the Lord.

33. Men are that they might have joy.

Joy in a gospel sense is not necessarily the happiness of the world. Worldly happiness is a marketing creation, an illusion. It is said to come from a perfect physique, complexion, and a particular wardrobe. It is the attainment of lots of money, time to travel and seek pleasure, and a boundless circle of friends and notoriety. The natural man is drawn to these allurements, and understandably so, as we seek to escape the sometimes mundane chores and requirements of mortal life.

Contrast those pursuits with the Son of God. "He is despised and rejected of men; a man of sorrows, and acquainted with grief" (Isaiah 53:3). Rather than invite us to the French Riviera on holiday,

His invitation is "If any man will come after me, let him deny himself, and take up his cross daily, and follow me" (Luke 9:23).

Said He, "Peace I leave with you, my peace I give unto you: not as the world giveth, give I unto you. Let not your heart be troubled, neither let it be afraid" (John 14:27). This inner peace, I believe, is the essence of true joy. Even in light of the Isaiah scripture above, I believe the Savior was a man who possessed the deepest of joy. Being at peace with oneself is knowing "the course of life which he is pursuing is according to his [God's] will."[1]

Sometimes we forget our identity as a disciple of Christ and contrast our situation and mood against the perky, successful, publicly cheerful, seemingly without-a-care-in-the-world types. We think there is something wrong with us because we are not that way, nor seemingly headed in that direction. We would do well to remember that a committed discipleship will keep us near to Him who has the power to save. And that renders peace, which is akin to real joy.

Joy is born of growth – learning, discovering, attaining, becoming. It is losing ourselves in the service of others. It is congruency to the will of God. It is lasting and deep, not only immediate and short lived.

> I walked a mile with Pleasure,
> She chatted all the way,
> But left me none the wiser,
> For all she had to say.
> I walked a mile with Sorrow,
> And ne'er a word she said,
> But oh! The things I learned from her,
> When sorrow walked with me.[2]

To the early pioneers, who knew much of sorrow, the Lord said, "If thou are sorrowful, call on the Lord thy God with supplication, that your souls may be joyful" (D&C 136:29). Yes, even amidst this vale of tears, we can stand independently filled with joy. In fact, "men are, that they might have joy" (2 Nephi 2:25).

It is a part of Latter-day Saint culture to understand and to hold in balance the inevitable cross of discipleship and this joy which the Lord has promised.

Notes:

1. *Lectures on Faith*, Salt Lake City: N.B. Lundwall, Lecture Third, 5.
2. Robert Browning Hamilton, "Along the Road."

34. The Thirteen Articles of Faith are truly inspired declarations.

I love the Thirteen Articles of Faith and am proud of them as a declaration of my faith. However, they are not comprehensive of our doctrine. Rather, they stand as a succinct affirmation of significant doctrines and beliefs. Easy to comprehend, doctrinally rich and diverse, they "simultaneously set standards for conduct and declare principles of faith."[1]

The source I draw from for the following information comes from an *Ensign* article by John H. Welch and David J. Whittaker. Credit for this information and all the following quotations about the Articles of Faith should be given to these authors.

In 1834, Oliver Cowdery published a short summary of the beliefs of the Church to give the Saints an assurance of the "correctness of their own system." His were seven tenets that each began with the now familiar "We believe . . ." format. Correlation is found to Articles of Faith 1, 6, 9, 10, 11 and 13.

Joseph Young, while proselyting in Boston in 1836, responded to a local editor with a written statement of the "creed, doctrines, sentiments or religious notions" of the Church. Here we find five enumerated points of doctrine. Preface to those points, he writes, and perhaps coins the phrase, "and its principal *articles of faith* are . . ." Correlation is found to Articles of Faith 1, 3, 4, 5, 7 and 10.

Orson Pratt, while serving as a missionary in Scotland in 1840, wrote another statement of the "faith and doctrine of the Church." It was over seven pages long, eloquent, and also used the lead verbiage "We believe" for several of its tenets. Brevity was not his object. He took three pages to state what Joseph Smith encapsulated into two short sentences, as Articles 2 and 3. Correlation is found to Articles of Faith 1, 2, 3, 4, 6, 7, 8 and 9.

Orson Hyde published an even more cumbersome treatise in 1842, consisting of sixteen articles, called "Articles of Faith and Points of Doctrine." Valuable indeed, yet it is more of an explanation of belief, rather than a succinct declaration of belief. Elder Hyde's focus is on the ordinances of the priesthood and related doctrines and practices.

Joseph Smith, in 1842 at the invitation of John Wentworth, the editor of the *Chicago Democrat*, wrote a letter summarizing the history of the Church. The letter closed by stating thirteen points of faith. Except for minor changes in the fourth, fifth, sixth and tenth articles, we still use these statements today as originally written.

They are remarkable, not only in substance, but also in their clarity and in their economy. They are living and open. They invite further thought. They are declarative and affirmative, making no effort to justify or defend. The fact that all of these early statements by Cowdery, Young, Pratt, and Hyde are quite similar to each other and to the final Articles of Faith, shows that the same gospel principles were consistently taught under Joseph's leadership. The thread of inspiration and revelation that brought the Articles of Faith to final form, I find as a confirmation to their divine source, culminating at the hand of a Prophet.

Notes:

1. John W. Welch and David J. Whittaker, "We Believe… Development of the Articles of Faith," *Ensign,* September 1979.

35. Jesus is the "North Star" of Church leadership.

We believe in a resurrected, living Savior and that in these latter days, He has called the man Joseph Smith to restore His Church and Kingdom to the earth. Joseph was a prophet and has since been succeeded by prophets down to this very day. To support and to amplify the work and words of the prophet, twelve apostles have been called. Of this Paul wrote, "And are built upon the foundation of the apostles and prophets, Jesus Christ himself being the chief corner stone" (Ephesians 2:20).

As members of the Church of Jesus Christ, we are to keep our eyes on the living Savior. He is our Master, our Lord, and our King. It is He whom we follow.

I'm impressed with how carefully that focus is maintained throughout the breadth of the worldwide Church. Doctrinally, procedurally, and practically, local leadership looks to the prophet for guidance and direction. Church Handbooks are approved and issued by the First Presidency and the Quorum of the Twelve as guidebooks for local and regional Church administration. These handbooks are studied carefully and implemented with the desire to do things the Lord's way.

As the one person authorized to receive revelation for the world at large, the living prophet is an instrument in the hands of the Lord to that end. He is the mouthpiece of the Lord to all the earth. "Surely the Lord God will do nothing, but he revealeth his secret unto his servants the prophets" (Amos 3:7). His emphasis and focus become prophetic priorities for regional and local Church leaders.

In a sincere discipleship born of testimony and humility, Church leaders seek to be obedient to their file leaders, who in turn follow their leaders, all the way to the prophet, and hence, the Savior. I can think of no better way to be knit together, than by such willing obedience to authority that is directly led by Jesus Christ. Personal ego and agenda become subordinate to the will of the Lord and the building of His Kingdom. Said the Lord, "Whether by mine own voice or by the voice of my servants, it is the same" (D&C 1:38).

The apostle Peter, speaking of the Savior wrote, "Behold, I lay in Sion a chief corner stone, elect, precious: and he that believeth on him shall not be confounded" (1 Peter 2:6).

I know of no other Church that so particularly seeks to vertically align itself with a central leading figure, and to do so on a worldwide level. And by the testimony of millions, that leading figure is the Lord Jesus Christ, who directs His Kingdom through ordained prophets and apostles.

36. We encourage all to worship God according to the dictates of their own conscience.

Soon after my conversion, I remember having a particular fondness for the hymn "Know This That Every Soul is Free." It was not frequently sung, nor widely even known, but I liked the doctrine it taught. It is of interest that it was hymn #1 in the original hymnal assembled by Emma Smith in 1835. The title itself is liberating and declarative.

We are free to choose the course of our lives, including the way we worship and believe, as expressed in Article of Faith 11:

> "We claim the privilege of worshiping Almighty God according to the dictates of our own conscience, and allow all men

> the same privilege, let them worship how, where, or what they may" (Articles of Faith, 11).

As aggressive as our missionary program is, it is not our aim to cause anyone to violate his or her own conscience. Ours is to present the truth so that the Spirit can testify to the soul of its veracity.

Jesus declared as acceptable the good works of those who apparently were not under the baptismal covenant, when He said to His disciple John, "For there is no man which shall do a miracle in my name, that can lightly speak evil of me. For he that is not against us is on our part" (Mark 9:39-40).

Joseph Smith is quoted as saying (in what I see as enthusiastically), "The inquiry is frequently made of me, wherein do you differ from others in your religious views? In reality and essence we do not differ so far in our religious views but that we could all drink into one principle of love. One of the grand fundamental principles of 'Mormonism' is to receive truth, let it come from whence it may. . . If I esteem mankind to be in error, shall I bear them down? No! I will lift them up and in their own way too, if I cannot persuade them my way is better; and I will not seek to compel any man to believe as I do, only by the force of reasoning, for truth will cut its own way."[1]

> "Know this, that ev'ry soul is free,
> To choose his life and what he'll be;
> For this eternal truth is giv'n:
> That God will force no man to heav'n.
>
> "He'll call, persuade, direct aright,
> And bless with wisdom, love, and light,
> In nameless ways be good and kind,
> But never force the human mind."[2]

That doctrine and allowance for personal responsibility is, to me, at the core of having respect for our fellows and living in a society of religious freedom. It is aligned perfectly with God's inviolable gift of personal agency.

Notes:

1. *History of the Church of Jesus Christ of Latter-day Saints,* Salt Lake City: Deseret Book, 1964, 5:499.

2. Anonymous, "Know This, That Every Soul is Free," *Hymns of the Church of Jesus Christ of Latter-day Saints,* Salt Lake City: The Church of Jesus Christ of Latter-day Saints, 1985, 240.

37. God the Father and His Son Jesus Christ have corporeal bodies of flesh and bones.

"The Father has a body of flesh and bones as tangible as man's; the Son also; but the Holy Ghost has not a body of flesh and bones, but is a personage of Spirit" (D&C 130:22).

The general consensus within popular Christianity, is that God is an incomprehensible spirit entity. Cited is John 4:24, which was translated to read, "God is a Spirit." The Joseph Smith Translation of this verse concurs with the previous verse 23 and reads, "For unto such hath God promised his Spirit."

We believe in the glorified, immortal, tangible personages of God the Father and His Son Jesus Christ—a God not without body, parts or passions, but a God after whose image and likeness we have been created (Genesis 1:26, D&C 20:18).

Many faiths, Christian and non-Christian, view the physical body in a negative way. We view it as a consummate blessing. With a body, we can participate in procreation, creating families. With a body we can experience appetites, pain, exhilaration, sickness, vitality, energy, exhaustion. With a body we can learn to subject the physical appetites to spiritual resolve, becoming over time our best and true self.

Significant are the questions raised by Elder Jeffrey R. Holland:

> "A related reason The Church of Jesus Christ of Latter-day Saints is excluded from the Christian category by some is because we believe, as did the ancient prophets and apostles, in an embodied—but certainly glorified—God. To those who criticize this scripturally based belief, I ask at least rhetorically: If the idea of an embodied God is repugnant, why are the central doctrines and singularly most distinguishing characteristics of all Christianity the Incarnation, the Atonement, and the physical Resurrection of the Lord Jesus Christ? If having a body is not only not needed but not desirable by Deity, why did the Redeemer of mankind redeem *His* body, redeeming it from the grasp of death and the grave, guaranteeing it would never again be separated from His spirit in time or eternity? *Any who dismiss the concept of an embodied God dismiss both the mortal and the resurrected Christ.* No one claiming to be a true Christian will want to do that."[1]

All mankind will be resurrected and will live eternally as a physical personage. God is not of another species, nor is He a great unknowable one. He is indeed our Father. We are created in His physical image. "That when he shall appear we shall be like him, for we shall see him as he is" (Moroni 7:48). That will be in the form of the resurrected Christ, who is now "standing on the right hand of God" (Acts 7:56).

Notes:

1. Jeffrey R. Holland, "The Only True God and Jesus Christ Whom He Hath Sent," *Ensign*, November, 2007.

38. The influence of the Holy Ghost creates a commonality from many diverse cultures.

It has always been interesting to me to see the uniformity of Latter-day Saints. I can almost pick them out from a crowd. Usually, that's a positive indicator, either seen in the countenance, the behaviors, the values they hold to, their families, or other positive attributes.

I remember attending BYU and realizing that on this campus there were baptized converts from different life experiences, families, and even cultures. These converts (of which there were many) didn't have the Church standards and programs to guide them as youth. Some had tread on thorny ground and had experienced the world in ways they now saw as another life, and one they had left behind for one that was infinitely better.

Yet looking at the people on campus, and associating with them, you would never know their stories unless they were to tell you. Again, there was a likeness in the students—a shared purpose, a united trust, a common ambition—in something greater than the moment and even greater than self. Particularly, it was their covenant relationship with God and the influence of the Holy Ghost upon their very natures.

My dad told me once that he had come to the conclusion that there was no God because, as he put it, "I could see a Methodist, a Catholic, and a Jew walking down the street and could distinguish no difference amongst them. If there were really a God in heaven and if there were a people who knew him, they would be markedly different because of that influence."

"Wherefore if any man be in Christ, he is a new creature: old things are passed away; behold, all things are become new" (2 Corinthians 5:17). It's a conscious yielding "to the enticing of the Holy Spirit" (Mosiah 3:19) and a committed desire to put "off the natural man" (Mosiah 3:19) that we "becometh a saint through the

Atonement of Christ the Lord" (Mosiah 3:19) and truly attain to humility, faith, and submission to God, even "as a child" (Mosiah 3:19).

In contrasting the "works of the flesh" and "the fruit of the Spirit," Paul lists those fruits as "love, joy, peace, longsuffering, gentleness, goodness, faith, meekness, temperance" (Galatians 5:22-23). This is a nice description of attitudes, outlooks, enjoyments, and behaviors that distill upon the souls of the honest keepers of their covenants.

The Gift of the Holy Ghost in my own life and in the lives of my family members has been priceless, even life changing. A righting of the ship in every significant way. One day, my dad will acknowledge the source of what has blessed our family. My family and I know from whence come such defining blessings.

39. Truth is a pearl of great price.

When I joined the Church at twenty-one years, many of my friends asked me, "Why, on earth did you join the Mormon Church?"

Probably the most common response from me was, "Because it's true."

For something to be true, by definition, it must conform to reality or fact. It must be real, genuine, authentic, legitimate, correct. It is the opposite of false, fraudulent, counterfeit, or unreal.

"True" is important enough to be scripturally used as an adjective to modify common nouns as the following:

> "the true bread" (John 6:32)
>
> "true doctrine of the Father" (2 Nephi 31:21)
>
> "the true faith" (Enos 1:14)
>
> "true and living church" (D&C 1:30)

"I am the true vine" (John 15:1)

"my record is true" (John 8:14)

"the only living and true God" (D&C 20:19)

"a true heart" (Hebrews 10:22)

"a true seed" (Alma 32:28)

"the true knowledge" (Helaman 15:13)

"the true light" (John 1:9)

Each of these references could be said without the word "true;" however, its inclusion indicates the singularity of a particular bread, doctrine, faith, or church.

Jesus, while standing before Pilate, summarized His earthly mission saying, "To this end was I born, and for this cause came I into the world, that I should bear witness unto the truth. Every one that is of the truth heareth my voice" (John 18:37). To which Pilate responded in query either as a flippant interrogative, or out of a sincere desire to know - "What is truth?"

"And truth is knowledge of things as they are, and as they were, and as they are to come" (D&C 93:24).

Unfortunately, some take the position that truth is unknowable, or worse, subject to opinion. But truth *is* knowable; in fact, it is most desirable in every case. Who wants to be lied to, or deceived, or to base a decision on incorrect information? Nobody. And especially concerning God the Father and our Savior Jesus Christ, who Himself said, "I am the way, the truth, and the life" (John 14:6).

Spiritual truths come to us through the "power of the Holy Ghost. And by the power of the Holy Ghost ye may know the truth of all things" (Moroni 10:4-5). And then comes the liberating promise that "the truth shall make you free" (John 8:32). Free from error, remorse, uncertainty, darkness, and the misguided ways of man.

I love truth. I love the fact that truth exists. Truth is connected to light (D&C 84:45). And paired together, they connect with intelligence (D&C 93:29). And intelligence is the glory of God (D&C 93:36). Truth from whichever edifying source is worthy of all our efforts to acquire.

40. The core elements of a testimony are fundamental to my faith.

We are a testimony-bearing people. We are under covenant "to stand as witnesses of God at all times and in all things, and in all places" (Mosiah 18:9). Our missionaries teach doctrines and principles and then bear personal testimony of their veracity and their source. We even have a monthly worship service devoted to the sharing of testimonies from the pulpit to strengthen our collective and our individual faith.

The oft-quoted testimony of Job is a model of our witness, when he declared "For I know that my redeemer liveth" (Job 19:25). To know is not to surmise, or to suppose, or to merely speculate. As Job, so declared Peter when asked by the Savior, "But whom say ye that I am" (Matthew 16:15)? Responded Peter, "Thou art the Christ, the Son of the living God" (Matthew 16:16). To which the Savior taught that such a certain witness was pure revelation from heaven (see Matthew 16:17).

Looking back on my own conversion, I can see a pattern to the formation of my testimony, and that pattern is rooted in at least five essential core truths:

1. There is a God in heaven, and He is my (our) Father. First, it is the most practical conclusion as I consider the eternal expanse and order of the heavens; the variety, beauty, and interconnectivity of this earth; the wonder and complexity

of our bodies; and the scope of our intellect. Second, sincere prayer reveals Him to me personally.

2. Jesus is the Christ. I was aware of other spiritual leaders—Yogananda, Khrisna, Buddha—but Jesus is the only one who said, "I am the way" (John 14:6) and who declared on multiple occasions to be the literal Son of God. I tested His own declaration, "If any man will do his will, he shall know of the doctrine, whether it be of God, or whether I speak of myself" (John 7:17). And true to the formula, I now *know* that Jesus is in fact, the Christ.

3. The Book of Mormon is the word of God. "And when ye shall receive these things, I would exhort you that ye would ask God, the Eternal Father, in the name of Christ, if these things are not true; and if ye shall ask with a sincere heart, with real intent, having faith in Christ, he will manifest the truth of it unto you, by the power of the Holy Ghost" (Moroni 10:4). Game over. I knew of its divinity by divine manifestation to my heart and soul.

4. Joseph Smith is a Prophet of God. The Book of Mormon and Joseph Smith are a package deal. Through him, the True Church has been restored to the earth in all its fullness and authority.

5. There are living prophets and apostles upon the earth today. Continuous revelation has been ongoing since the opening scenes of the restoration. Revelations received today are every bit as important to people now as the revelations received in ancient days.

These same fundamental truths comprise the core of my testimony today. Each is burned into my heart by the receipt of personal revelation, renewed on a constant basis. Such renewal still thrills me.

41. "Keep the ordinances, as I delivered them to you."

So said Paul to the Corinthians (1 Corinthians 11:2). The word "ordinances" translates in Greek as precepts, doctrines, traditions. Ordinances within the Lord's Church are specified by revelation, either scripturally fixed, or, as in the case of giving a blessing, by personal revelation. But even in the latter, there are certain requirements to be included that are consistent to the pattern of ordinances.

Isaiah described the days in which we live where we see the resultant condition of a world that has not heeded the above admonition of Paul, "The earth also is defiled under the inhabitants thereof; because they have transgressed the laws, changed the ordinance, broken the everlasting covenant" (Isaiah 24:5). In modern revelation, the Lord says, "They have strayed from mine ordinances" (D&C 1:15).

For example, there are about as many modes of Christian baptism today as there are churches. Likewise, the mode of administering the Holy Sacrament, the Eucharist, or Communion varies widely.

The wording and procedures for the saving ordinances of baptism, sacrament, priesthood ordination, and temple covenants are prescribed by the Lord and are not to be altered by man. The specific wording is concise, meaningful, and binding. Such rites place us under covenant with the Lord, and the terms of such covenants are His.

I've heard young Aaronic priesthood bearers repeat the sacrament prayer several times in sacrament meetings until they got it word perfect. That wording is given to us scripturally in both the Book of Mormon and the Doctrine and Covenants. I used to think it was a bit obsessive to have to repeat the entire sacramental prayer for the omission of a preposition or a simple pronoun. But I've come to realize that if not carefully done, a lax or sloppy administration has no limits over time and could lead to the "changing of the ordinances" (Isaiah 24:5).

The words of the baptismal ordinance are simple indeed: "David Lee Jones (the person being baptized), Having been commissioned of Jesus Christ, I baptize you in the name of the Father, and of the Son, and of the Holy Ghost" (D&C 20:73). It is directed to the person making the covenant, states by what authority it is being performed, declares the action being performed, and invokes the approval of Deity. All ordinances are of a similar base formula.

Care and seriousness is the norm in seeking to do it right and as the Lord has directed. They are "mine ordinances" and "mine everlasting covenant," said He (D&C 1:15). There is power and perpetuity in administering ordinances as prescribed by Deity. In fact, The Church of Jesus Christ of Latter-day Saints has been a worthy steward of the priesthood ordinances of the Lord.

42. Our obedience to leaders is modeled after the relationship of the Father and the Son.

"Then shall ye know that I am he [the Son of man], and that I do nothing of myself; but as my Father hath taught me, I speak these things . . . for I do always those things that please him" (John 8:28,29).

"Verily, verily, I say unto you, The Son can do nothing of himself, but what he seeth the Father do: for what things soever he doeth, these also doeth the Son likewise" (John 5:19).

"But I would have you know, that the head of every man is Christ . . . and the head of Christ is God" (1 Corinthians 11:3).

To understand the relationship between the Father and the Son is to see a model of perfect obedience. Jesus trusted his Heavenly Father and had no personal agenda but to do the will of the Father.

This doctrine is often a blurry picture for much of Christianity. As I understand it, the Trinitarian notion doesn't allow for this Father/ Son simultaneous existence. Instead, God is Jesus when on the earth, and Jesus is God when in heaven. The most perfectly framed picture of faith, duty, and humble acquiescence is lost without the understanding that Jesus truly looked to his Father as His model.

The Savior is our example in all things, and this humble, submissive, obedient and even deferential attitude of Jesus to His Father is our example of true worship.

The following parable is illustrative of an important pattern and foreshadowing:

> "There was a certain householder, which planted a vineyard . . . and let it out to husbandmen. . . . He [the householder] sent his servants to the husbandmen, that they might receive the fruits of it. And the husbandmen took his servants, and beat one, and killed another, and stoned another. Again, he sent other servants more than the first: and they did unto them likewise. But last of all he sent unto them his son, saying, They will reverence my son. But when the husbandmen saw the son, they said among themselves, This is the heir; come, let us kill him, and let us seize on his inheritance. And they caught him, and cast him out of the vineyard, and slew him" (Matthew 21:33-39).

The servants in this parable are authorized, ordained priesthood bearers, servants of God. Jesus established the acceptable pattern of allegiance by his own example. He linked significant allegiances when he said, "And also all they who receive this priesthood receive me, saith the Lord; For he that receiveth my servants receiveth me; And he that receiveth me receiveth my Father; And he that receiveth my Father receiveth my Father's kingdom; therefore all that my Father hath shall be given unto him" (D&C 84:35-38).

To emulate the Savior's pattern of obedience to and sense of mission from the Father is what drives the Latter-day Saints to follow priesthood leaders (servants). "Whether by mine own voice, or by the voice of my servants, it is the same" (D&C 1:38). Our worship is reserved for the Father of us all and for our Savior Jesus Christ. Our obedience to them is measured in part by our obedience to their servants.

43. The Book of Mormon is, indeed, the keystone of our religion.

The Prophet Joseph Smith said, "I told the brethren that the Book of Mormon was the most correct of any book on earth, and the keystone of our religion" (Introduction, Book of Mormon). This book is emblematic of our faith and culture, represented by the descriptive terms of "Mormons" and "Mormonism." The very claim that it is a volume of Holy Scripture comparable to the Bible is a line of demarcation separating believers from unbelievers.

It is a literal keystone in the arch of our faith that the Lord restored His Church to the earth through the Prophet Joseph Smith. "This book does not merely claim to be a moral treatise or theological commentary or collection of insightful writings. It claims to be the word of God."[1] By that claim, that declaration to the world, there can be no middle ground. It is of divine origin, or it is of human deception. Quoting his great grandfather, Elder Jeffrey R. Holland said, "No wicked man could write such a book as this; and no good man would write it unless it were true and he were commanded of God to do so."[2]

There seems to be an endless supply of book critics who denounce the Book of Mormon, yet many of them have never asked God of its veracity, or worse, have never even read it! Along with the Old Testament and the New Testament from the regions of the old world, the Book of Mormon is a published witness of Christ from the Americas. It was either written by a common man, or it is a translation from the writings of prophets on gold plates as we claim. Joseph Smith gave his life for the cause built up around this book, and even read from it for comfort just prior to his martyrdom. It is not reasonable that he would consult a book that he knew to be a fraud during that dark hour.[3]

The Book of Mormon puts itself to a test within the chambers of each individual heart. "Behold, I would exhort you that when ye shall read these things . . . and ponder it in your hearts . . . that ye would ask God . . . in the name of Christ, if these things are not true . . . ask with a sincere heart, with real intent, having faith in Christ [and] he will manifest the truth of it unto you" (Moroni 10:3-4).

So writes the Prophet Moroni in the final chapter of the Book of Mormon as an invitation to all who encounter this most singular and significant book. It is the keystone of our religion and stands as its own witness. It is one of the keystones of my own faith. I am a personal witness of its divinely inspired origins.

Notes:

1. Tad R. Callister, "The Book of Mormon—a Book from God," *Ensign,* November, 2011.

2. Jeffrey R. Holland, "Safety for the Soul," *Ensign,* November, 2009.

3. Holland.

44. No amount of time or circumstance can create intelligent life from inanimate forms.

Recently, I went for an early morning walk in Branson, Missouri, and came upon a little pond. Around the edges of the pond was an ample supply of green algae floating upon the surface, amplified in color by the morning sun. It was indeed a beautiful setting.

This simple life form got me to thinking of the origins of human life. Some claim that we are a product of evolution, beginning with simple cell life forms that are invisible to the eye, yet perhaps living in this very pond. In fact, there are only two proposals that I am aware of to explain the origin of human life—by adaptive evolution or by divine creation.

In Genesis is recorded what I consider the all-important differential between a living entity and a non-living entity: "And the Lord God... breathed into his nostrils the breath of life; and man became a living soul" (Genesis 2:7).

I recently read the classic, *The Origin of Species* by Charles Darwin, published in 1859, which stands as the flagship tome for the theory of evolution by natural selection (it's not an easy read for a non-biologist). Not wanting to get too bogged down in the intellectual arguments he makes, I was particularly looking for how he might explain the breath of life moment that separates intelligent life from inanimate forms. Either I missed it, or it was, in fact, not proffered within the book.

I do acknowledge that adaptive evolution takes place within a species, as a result of complicated genetics, environment, diet, and certainly many other factors influencing the species. Tacitly agreeing with another naturalist, Darwin writes in the preface to his book, "the doctrine that species, including man, are descended from other species."[1] In contrast, the Lord, speaking of the several different classifications in the animal world, uses the phrase "after their own kind" or "after his kind" not once, but seven times in just three verses of Genesis Chapter 1 (verses 21, 24, 25). If it were not so, there would be in existence a continual display of all the various gradations of these evolving creatures, which is not the case.

But the real question goes back to the breath of life requirement and how or when a simple cellular form becomes an intelligent life form. I am left with the option that "God created man in his own image" (Genesis 1:27). And I believe that. I believe that God, and only God, could animate a non-animate form. So much of explanation, purpose, identity, hope, goodness, commonality, brotherhood, and accountability flow from this fundamental truth. Many other important truths follow, perhaps most importantly, our relationship to Him who is our creator, our very Eternal Father.

Notes:

1. Charles Darwin, *The Origin of Species, by Means of Natural Selection of the Preservation of Favoured Races in the Struggle for Life,* New York: New American Library, 1958, An Historical Sketch, second paragraph.

45. The explanation of 1 Peter 3:19 and 4:6 are glorious, merciful, comprehensive, and redemptive!

Peter explained that Christ brought the gospel to "them that are dead" (1 Peter 4:6). My soul thrills by the implications and truths that flow from these two title passages written by then senior Apostle Peter. These include salvation for the dead, the preaching of the gospel "to those who had died in their sins without a knowledge of the truth, or in transgression, having rejected the prophets" (D&C 138:32). Here is provision for the countless people who have never even heard of Christ, or who had but flimsy, incomplete, or incorrect doctrinal understanding.

These passages seem to confound mainstream Christian writers. "Considering there are nearly 180 different interpretations of 1 Peter 3:18-20, we can confidently say this passage is one of the most difficult in the entire Bible."[1] Another scholar laments, "This verse (1 Peter 4:6) is one of the most difficult verses in the Bible to interpret."[2]

Not in any way wanting to disrespect these authors interpretations, yet I pull from their conclusions to show the damning and hopeless end that they portray for much of mankind. "I believe that when Jesus went and proclaimed to the spirits in prison, it was a victorious proclamation that those in both Abraham's side and Hades heard.

Those waiting in Abraham's side heard his message and followed him to heaven, whereas those waiting in Hades heard it as a means of condemnation and now await the final judgment where they'll be sentenced to hell."[3]

"The preaching took place when these 'dead ones' were still amid the living. This is the only time when preaching is effective – when we are alive physically on earth. . . . Is there a gospel of the second chance? According to this verse [4:6] – no! There is no second chance. The only time we can come to Christ is when we are alive on earth."[4]

I'm not going to comment on second chances. It's the first real opportunity that I have concern with—that all truly feel the witness of the Spirit when presented with truth and then respond as they choose. Clearly, most of mankind has not had this opportunity during the course of their mortality.

Jesus is the Savior of all of mankind. He wrought the very Atonement among the Jews, then visited, taught, and organized the work among the spirits of the dead prior to His resurrection, ministered to those on the American continent subsequent to His resurrection, and went from there to "show myself unto the lost tribes of Israel"(3 Nephi 17:4). All will have the opportunity to hear and acknowledge Jesus as their personal Savior.

Speaking again of Peter's reference to the dead, a modern day prophet gives us further light. "The Lord went not in person among the wicked and the disobedient. . . . But from among the righteous, he organized . . . them to go forth and carry the light of the gospel to them that were in darkness, even to all the spirits of men . . . and proclaim liberty to the captives who were bound, even unto all who would repent of their sins and receive the gospel" (D&C 138:29-31).

The result parallels the requirements for salvation here in mortality. "The dead who repent will be redeemed, through obedience to the ordinances of the house of God. And after they have paid the penalty of their transgressions [repentance], and are washed clean [redemption through the Atonement of Christ], shall receive a reward according to their works, for they are heirs of salvation" (D&C 138:58-59).

This is comprehensive, merciful, hopeful, inclusive doctrine! We are most fortunate to understand, to proclaim, and to enjoy the fullness of the gospel. Jesus is the Christ, God is our Father, and they love us. All of us.

Notes:

1. Pastor Mark Driscoll, www.pastormark.tv, February 2, 2012, and a variation of the same at www.markdriscoll.org/2013/03/30where-did-jesus-go-on-saturday, March 30, 2013.

2. Dr. Grant C. Richison, www.versebyversecommentary.com/1-peter/1-peter-46, November 14, 1997.

3. Pastor Mark Driscoll, "Where Did Jesus Go On Saturday?" www.markdriscoll.org/where-did-jesus-go-on-saturday, March 29, 2013.

4. Richison.

46. Read the Book of Mormon, and tell me how you feel.

In early 1977, President Spencer W. Kimball came to St. George, Utah, to speak. I had recently moved to Cedar City to attend college, and more importantly, to dive into the faith and investigate firsthand. With the President and Prophet of the Church coming to Southern Utah, I wanted to shake his hand, look him in the eye, and sincerely ask him if he were a Prophet of God.

Even as I write that, I can see how this might seem presumptuous, perhaps arrogant, or that I was challenging this good man. But none of that was so. My intent was pure and born of my desire to know.

I knew that the eyes can tell much that words can hide. If he were uncertain, or hesitant, or worse, if he just avoided the question, I would have cause to wonder. If he were matter-of-fact, declarative, genuine, that would be an important step for me. And I also knew that there was a third experience—that I would feel something at that moment.

So, a carload of friends and I travelled the few miles down to St. George for the event. I think I told them of my intentions, and my recollection is that they all snickered at my plan.

The gathering was in a large sports-like auditorium, very well attended. After the concluding prayer, I bee-lined it for the front podium, but by the time I got there, President Kimball was already gone. I looked around at the exits for him and saw one of the participants, Elder Hartman Rector Jr. and his wife, leaving the arena. I followed them off the stage and found myself alone with them. So I grabbed his hand, and then realizing that my question wouldn't fit in this scenario, I fumbled for a backup question, "Uh, how can you claim the Book of Mormon is the word of God, what about the Koran, and other sacred books of literature?"

He calmly and directly looked at me (yes, I got that eye contact I was looking for), and he said in his Southern drawl, "Look, I want you to read the Koran and then tell me what you feel. Then I want you to read the Book of Mormon, and tell me what you feel. You'll notice a marked difference. And there's your answer!" During this exchange, and for emphasis, he was actually poking my chest. And then they were gone.

He had said something that I already knew. He was right. I was looking for confirmation of the truthfulness of this work, but was not recognizing what I had already discovered. The Lord had spoken to me by "the voice of my Spirit" (D&C 97:1), both then and many times previously. I knew. And it was thrilling to know.

47. Come, bring the truths of your faith, and let us see if we can add to it.

Many, now and throughout history, have never had the opportunity to hear of their Savior or to enter into covenants with God. The conclusion of many Christian believers is that absent having a personal acceptance of Jesus Christ during one's lifetime, too bad for them! They will be sent to hell.

This is a good example of what our missionaries mean when they say, "Bring what you have in your faith that is true, and let us add to it with the fullness of the gospel of Jesus Christ." Using the above scenario, yes, it is true that "Except a man be born of water [making the baptismal covenant where we promise to follow Christ], and of the Spirit [being confirmed a member of the Church and receiving the gift of the Holy Ghost] he cannot enter into the kingdom of heaven" (John 3:7). And that declaration of the Savior is appropriately ended with a period. But it's not the end of divine provisions that have been made for the salvation of mankind. The following uniquely LDS doctrines are some of those divine provisions that apply to this apparent dilemma:

- The Spirit of Christ (our conscience) is given to all born into mortality (Moroni 7:16-17)
- Priesthood authority and keys have not always been upon the earth[1]
- There is an active missionary effort in the world of the departed prior to the resurrection (1 Peter 3:18-20, 4:6, D&C 138:29-37, 57-59)
- Baptism and other saving ordinances are performed vicariously for all who did not comply with such ordinances nor make associated covenants (1 Corinthians 15:29)
- In the Millennium, an active missionary effort will take place, as well as a vigorous effort to perform the vicarious

work referred to above, until all mankind has been accounted for

- There are many mansions in the post-mortal life, and all are realms of glory to a degree, except hell itself, where but few will be consigned (John 14:2)

- Accountability assumes capacity to understand. Children, those with retardation, or similarly unaccountable, are innocent before God, and saved by the Atonement of Christ (Moroni 8:22, D&C 137:10)

- Jesus Christ has "drunk out of that bitter cup" and "finished my preparations unto the children of men" (3 Nephi 11:11, D&C 19:19). To take full advantage of the Atonement, our job is to repent (Helaman 5:10-11)

- We believe there is truth to be found in other religions, cultures, and norms, and that people will be accountable for the truths they were taught and understood (Alma 29:8)

- Heavenly Father and Jesus Christ are merciful to unintended ignorance (D&C 76:71-75, 137:7-9)

Such divine provisions, or truths, give light to a most merciful, loving Father in Heaven, and a Savior who is "full of grace and truth" (John 1:14, 2 Nephi 2:6). This doctrine juxtaposes with a commonly held narrow doctrine that includes an abrupt condemnation to hell. The very purposes of God are captured in these two beloved scriptures:

> "For God sent not his Son into the world to condemn the world; but that the world through him might be saved" (John 3:17).
>
> "For behold, this is my work and my glory—to bring to pass the immortality and eternal life of man" (Moses 1:39).

Precious are the doctrines of the Gospel of Jesus Christ. And blessed are those who have ears to hear, "I will remember my covenant unto you, O house of Israel, and ye shall come unto the knowledge of the *fulness* of my gospel" (3 Nephi 16:1, emphasis added).

Notes:

1. LDS Bible Dictionary, "Dispensations."

48. The Church of Jesus Christ of Latter-day Saints is the only true and living church upon the face of the whole earth.

If you believe that the revelations of the Doctrine and Covenants are truly revelations from Jesus Christ through a living prophet, then this is the end-all of divine institutional endorsements. To my knowledge, it is one of only two divine institutional endorsements, the United States Constitution being the other (D&C 1:30; 101:80).

Let's look at the two descriptors, "true" and "living," in this revelation.

True: Perhaps best defined in this case as genuine, authentic. Not false, or erroneous. It is of the same divine origin, organization, and purpose as the original Church that Jesus established. He is the head of the Church, and He is the light we look to. "This restored Church is true because it is the Savior's Church; He is 'the way, the truth, and the life' (John 14:6)."[1]

Living: This is perhaps best defined by its opposite, which is not living or having an ending. The Church Jesus organized as the original church was structured to live on after His crucifixion, as evidenced by the filling of the vacancy in the Twelve with the turning away of Judas. (Acts 1:15-26). However, the Church didn't continue. The apostles were rejected, the doctrines were changed, and cultural traditions, beliefs, and politics combined to "drive the Church into the wilderness" (D&C 86:3). The living Church was no longer upon the earth.

But the Lord himself restored His *true* church to the earth in the year 1830 through the instrumentation of the Prophet Joseph Smith. And it continues to be a *living* church as priesthood keys are passed in orderly succession to living prophets. "It is a living church because of the workings and gifts of the Holy Ghost. How blessed we are to live at a time when the priesthood is upon the earth and we can receive the Holy Ghost."[2]

I have witnessed the sustaining of four Presidents of the Church, each occasioned by the passing of his predecessor. They are sustained by the membership of the Church in what is called a solemn assembly. To me, it is the essence of the living church, as faithful saints, of their own free will, solemnly sustain and thereby pledge support to the Lord's anointed. A similar sustaining takes place to replenish the Quorum of the Twelve Apostles when occasioned by death. The calling of an apostle is under the inspiration of a living God, giving continuity to His living church.

As in the meridian of time, so in these latter days, "For unto you, the Twelve, and those of the First Presidency . . . is the power of this priesthood given." But this time, the true and living Church is preparing for His *second* coming "or the last days and for the last time, in the which is the dispensation of the fulness of times" (D&C 112:30).

The Church of Jesus Christ of Latter-day Saints is true, and it is living. And it is singular in those regards. So declared the Lord.

Notes:

1. David A. Bednar, "Receive the Holy Ghost," *Ensign*, November, 2010.

2. Bednar.

49. The Lord speaks to us via feelings, impressions, and the written word.

I'm told that a denominational church marquis was posted in a community where our missionaries were having success that read, "Don't pray about the Book of Mormon. That's how they get you!"

If that is true, we couldn't have had a better marketing tool!

Prayer to God is so fundamental and essential that the Lord Jesus taught us how to pray (Matthew 6:9, 23:14). He was an example of a prayerful Son (Matthew 14:23, 26:39). He promised us that our prayers would be answered (Matthew 21:22). He commanded us that we should pray (Matthew 5:44, 26:41). Those references are just from the testament of Matthew.

How else would a living God have personal communication with His children and still preserve the matchless endowment of living by faith? What we call the witness of the Spirit is very real. Although I have never heard the audible voice of God, I have heard His voice. The Prophet Enos described it perfectly while writing of his own experience, "And there came a voice unto me, saying: Enos, thy sins are forgiven thee" (Enos 1:5). Five verses later, he refers again to that same voice, "Behold, the voice of the Lord *came into my mind again*, saying . . ." (Enos 1:10, emphasis added).

The Lord spoke to Oliver Cowdery in the same manner, "Did I not speak peace *to your mind* concerning this matter? What greater witness can you have than from God" (D&C 6:23, emphasis added)?

Communications from God are also described as touching our hearts. After Peter gave his sermon on what we now refer to as the day of Pentecost, it is recorded, "Now when they heard this, *they were pricked in their heart*, and said unto Peter and to the rest of the apostles, Men and brethren, what shall we do" (Acts 2:37, emphasis added)?

Those two fortunate disciples on the road to Emmaus, after recognizing their Lord by the breaking of bread with Him, reasoned, "*Did not our heart burn within us*, while he talked with us by the way, and while he opened to us the scriptures" (Luke 24:32, emphasis added)?

"My sheep hear my voice, and I know them, and they follow me" (John 10:27). Jesus was speaking to those of His generation and also to those who would neither see Him with their eyes nor hear Him with their ears. Encompassing both groups, Jesus explained how we would know: "And [they] should *understand with their heart*, and should be converted, and I should heal them" (Matthew 13:15, italics added).

In addition to prayerful communication, I thrill at the on-going witness of the Spirit that the Gospel of Jesus Christ is true. It comes to my heart, to my mind, and to my soul. It is indisputable, real, clear. It comes as feelings and impressions. It supports and amplifies the written words of the prophets. It is a gift. It is the Holy Ghost teaching and bearing witness of truth.

50. Four divine commandments that distinctly bind us to our baptismal covenants.

Mormons are known by strict adherence to at least the following behaviors:

- They pay ten percent of their income to the Church
- They don't drink alcoholic beverages, don't smoke, don't even drink tea or coffee
- They don't have sex before or outside of marriage
- They don't shop, eat out, or do recreational activities on Sundays

"Weird," some say. Others note the many "don'ts" and consider them too restrictive. Still others admire such adherence, acknowledging either that they are, indeed, commandments, or at least sound practices to live by. We look at them as a part of keeping our covenants made at baptism:

- To take upon us the name of Christ
- To always remember Him
- To keep His commandments

As a ready identifier, these practices brand us as members of the LDS faith. To me, it is part of taking upon us the name of Christ. Then, given the constant barrage to live contrary to these tenets, it causes us to always remember Him and our covenants with Him of which these four behaviors are a part. Finally, we manifest our obedience to His commandments, including these four, which we hold as divinely prescribed.

Look at the law of tithing. Abraham paid tithes to Melchizedek, specifically identified as ten percent (Alma 13:15, Hebrews 7:4). Within the Old and the New Testaments, reference is made to the law of tithing. It was re-instated in these latter days as a requirement of his covenant people.

What the Lord introduced as the Word of Wisdom (D&C 89:1) is perhaps the most conspicuous of the four behaviors. Most would readily agree that tobacco use is not good for anyone. But imbibing a beer or a glass of wine on a social level is pretty common. And more common is the cup of coffee in the morning or the iced tea in the afternoon. I see the Word of Wisdom as a protection from addictions, a blessing to better health, and a demonstration of our willingness to keep the covenants listed above.

By the second chapter of the book of Genesis, the Lord told Adam to "cleave unto his wife" (Genesis 2:24), and added in this dispensation, "and none else" (D&C 42:22). We can juxtapose the experience of David and Bathsheba with Joseph and Potipher's wife and see where the Lord stands on chastity and marriage.

Almost thirty percent of the Ten Commandments (by word count) refer to keeping the Sabbath day holy—specifically not to work in our usual pursuits or to cause others to work. Wrote Isaiah, "Turn . . . from doing thy pleasure on my holy day; and call the Sabbath a delight" (Isaiah 58:13).

We feel clearly that these four behaviors are commandments of the Lord. Our strict adherence to them is evidence of our always remembering Him and our willingness to take upon us His name, particularly when such practices are unheeded or diluted in the common culture. It is seen by many as our identifying badge of membership. I see them as indicators of covenant keeping.

51. The restoration of the Aaronic Priesthood, and its order, is remarkable.

I just don't see any evidence of Joseph Smith being so scripturally savvy at the age of twenty-three that he could fabricate the coming forth of the Aaronic Priesthood in these latter days and get it so right. In fact, the protestant churches of his day were decidedly against the formality of any ordained priesthood. The timing, order, manner of conferral, function of keys, the various offices, the duties of those offices, the effecting of ordinances, and the power of this priesthood all combine as testimony to the instrumentality of Joseph Smith the Prophet.

If Joseph was thinking in terms of instituting a priesthood, it likely would have been a single order, easily overlooking (for lack of understanding), the Israelite model of Aaronic and Melchizedek priesthood offices.

Section 13 of the Doctrine and Covenants is taken from the Joseph Smith History, which was written sometime between 1838 and 1842. In that history, it speaks of Joseph and Oliver seeking guidance "respecting baptism for the remission of sins that we found mentioned in the translation of the plates" (Joseph Smith History 1:68). They weren't particularly or specifically seeking to know anything about priesthood. The next recorded verse is the actual restoration of the Aaronic Priesthood.

Oliver Cowdery recorded his own recollection of this experience under the hands of John the Baptist. That was printed in the *Messenger and Advocate* earlier in 1834. His account is somewhat different from what we read in the Joseph Smith History, a very personal narrative, and can be read as an enlightening addendum to that history.

In the Church today, "The Aaronic Priesthood deals with the temporal and outward ordinances of the law and the gospel."[1]

With the Israelites anciently, "Now God himself . . . has chosen him [Aaron] for his priest. . . . He is to have the care of the altars, and to make provision for the sacrifices."[2] "At a later period the Lord chose the tribe of Levi to assist Aaron in the priestly functions."[3]

In order to get the restoration of the Aaronic Priesthood right, Joseph would have had to:

- Have it restored prior to being baptized
- Have it precede the restoration of the Melchizedek Priesthood
- Have it restored prior to the organization of the Church in 1830
- Be conferred in this dispensation by John the Baptist, who held keys

- See that it was a priesthood of temporal affairs vs. higher spiritual administration
- Follow the pattern "And no man taketh this honour unto himself, but he that is called of God, as was Aaron" (Hebrews 5:4)

And of course, all of these criteria were met, not because Joseph was aware of the order and imperative points required for the restoration of this priesthood, but because the Lord himself was reestablishing this Aaronic Priesthood authority to the earth.

Notes:

1. lds.org, *The Guide to the Scriptures*, "Aaronic Priesthood."
2. Flavius Josephus, *The Antiquities of the Jews,* Book III, 8:1.
3. James E. Talmage, *Articles of Faith,* Salt Lake City: The Church of Jesus Christ of Latter-day Saints, 1977, 204-205.

52. Jesus taught the order of prayer.

"Although prayer has a role in many religions and cultures, rarely is prayer considered to be a two-way communication between God and man."[1]

I have always considered it intuitive that real prayer was in the form of sincere, intentional, conversation with the divine. It stems from my belief that there is a living God in heaven and that we are His offspring.

But that is not the general view of prayer. Many see prayer as a recitation of something someone else has written, almost a very beautiful form of poetry. Others see the function of prayer to be reserved for those of the cloth. I've heard some public prayers that were more of a moral sermon than a humble petition to God.

There seems to be variance of whom we pray to as well, some directing their words directly to the Lord Jesus and some directly to God the Father in Heaven. When the Master taught his disciples to pray, He clearly addressed this. "After this manner therefore, pray ye: Our Father which art in heaven . . ." (Matthew 6:9). We are to pray to God the Father and do so in the attitude of reverence and awe, "Hallowed be thy name" (Matthew 6:9).

We should align ourselves with His will, pledging our obedience to His ways, "Thy kingdom come. Thy will be done in earth, as it is in heaven" (Matthew 6:10).

We should be grateful for the blessings we are blessed with—food to eat, homes to live in, employment to support our families, clothing, and even daily breath. "Give us this day our daily bread" (Matthew 6:11).

We should recognize our need for a Savior and acknowledge our faults, committing to reform, to be better disciples every day. In acknowledging our own imperfections and pleading for patience and mercy, we treat others as we hope to be treated. "And forgive us our debts, as we forgive our debtors" (Matthew 6:12).

Recognizing the carnal temptations that we relentlessly face in mortality, we plead to keep our hearts right, to keep our faces squarely toward His kingdom. "And suffer us not to be led into temptation, but deliver us from evil: For thine is the kingdom, and the power, and the glory, for ever. Amen" (JST, Matthew 6:14).

This is the model the Lord used to teach his disciples how to pray, both then and now. It is recorded by Matthew and by Luke. The Lord's teaching about prayer in the Americas is similarly recorded in 3 Nephi 13:9-13. It is the same model our missionaries use today across the world to teach people how to pray.

There is no wrong prayer, so long as the effort is sincere and humble. "Prayer is the Soul's Sincere Desire"[2] is a hymn title and an apt description. Scripturally, we see examples of praying for power, for comfort, for direction, for testimony, for knowledge, for strength, and for our fellow beings. We are even told to pray for our enemies!

Jesus utilized prayer frequently and intensely. Alone, in wilderness locations, while others slept, and sometimes for several hours. Even in His perfections, He never neglected the tutoring that prayer afforded Him while in mortality.

To actually commune with the God of the universe! That he cares about me and about you personalizes religion and opens the door to true spirituality. It is the simplest, purest form of speech, "the Christian's vital breath, the Christian's native air."[3]

Notes:

1. *Preach My Gospel,* Salt Lake City: Intellectual Reserve Inc., 2004, 39.

2. James Montgomery, "Prayer is the Soul's Sincere Desire," *Hymns of the Church of Jesus Christ of Latter-day Saints,* Salt Lake City: The Church of Jesus Christ of Latter-day Saints, 1985, 145.

3. James Montgomery.

53. This Church is a religion that requires the sacrifice of all things.

Just this week, I was out with the missionaries teaching a first discussion to a young man and his sister. Sometime into the conversation, the man remarked, "I like your Church because it doesn't have all the rules and requirements that other churches do." Where in the world did he get that message?

Joseph Smith taught a great truth, "A religion that does not require the sacrifice of all things never has power sufficient to produce the faith necessary unto life and salvation."[1]

Elder Dieter F. Uchtdorf tells the following story that illustrates life as a Latter-day Saint:

> "Once there was a man who dreamed that he was in a great hall where all the religions of the world were gathered. He realized that each religion had much that seemed desirable and worthy. He met a nice couple who represented The Church of Jesus Christ of Latter-day Saints and asked, "What do *you* require of your members?"
>
> "*We* do not require anything," they replied, "but the *Lord* asks that we consecrate all."
>
> The couple went on to explain about Church callings, home and visiting teaching, full-time missions, weekly family home evenings, temple work, welfare and humanitarian service, and assignments to teach.
>
> "Do you pay your people for all the work they do?" the man asked.
>
> "On, no," the couple explained. "They offer their time freely."
>
> "Also," the couple continued, "every six months our Church members spend a weekend attending or watching ten hours of general conference."
>
> "Ten hours of people giving talks?" the man wondered.
>
> "What about your weekly church services? How long are they?"
>
> "Three hours, every Sunday!"
>
> "Oh, my," the man said. "Do members of your church actually do what you have said?"
>
> "That and more. We haven't even mentioned family history, youth camps, devotionals, scripture study, leadership training, youth activities, early-morning seminary, maintaining Church buildings, and of course, there is the Lord's law of health, the monthly fast to help the poor, and tithing."
>
> The man said, "Now I'm confused. Why would anyone want to join such a church?"

> The couple smiled and said, "We thought you would never ask."[2]

Sacrifice has been defined as "the surrender or destruction of something prized or desirable for the sake of something considered as having a higher or more pressing claim."[3] When people think of having to make a sacrifice in their lives of time or means or personal interests, they often forget the second half of this two-part definition, the part that speaks of what we gain. When we sacrifice personal desires in obedience to divine mandates and counsel, we both sanctify our being and further the work of the Lord.

Latter-day Saints have a rich history of sacrifice. We see it as a precursor to blessings both now and in the eternities. "But lay up for yourselves treasures in heaven, where neither moth nor rust doth corrupt, and where thieves do not break through nor steal" (Matthew 6:20). And for the time being, it enriches, refines, endows, adorns, and leads us to being "the new man, which after God is created in righteousness and true holiness" (Ephesians 4:24).

Notes:

1. *Lectures on Faith*, Salt Lake City: N.B. Lundwall, Lecture Sixth, 7.
2. Dieter F. Uchtdorf, "Come Join With Us," *Ensign,* November, 2013.
3. www.dictionary.reference.com/browse/sacrifice.

54. The opportunity to attain the fullness of the Gospel will be available to all.

Our view of world civilizations begins with Adam and Eve. Unlike the theories that men evolved from brutish, ignorant, savage forms, we see the beginning of the human species as endowed with reason, compassion, intelligence and faith, governed by a willing self-discipline and an innate desire for improvement. Clearly history shows that many corrupted their God-given qualities, as we see in the years of the Patriarchs subsequent to Adam and Eve.

But all people, in all times, have had access to some truth. All can discern between right and wrong. To illustrate this, let's look at what is referred to as the Classical Period in world civilization, about 900 BC to about AD 550. Four dominant civilizations came into being during these years and continue to influence our world culture today—China, Persia, India, and the Mediterranean. Respectively, they generated major cultural belief systems—Confucianism and Taoism, Zoroastrianism, Hinduism and Buddhism, and Christianity. What follows are noble and inspired truths that each of these belief systems teach.

Confucianism places particular emphasis on the importance of the family. It encourages ethical behavior, altruism, and "the upholding of righteousness and the moral disposition to do good."[1]

Taoism philosophy claims "that there should be a mystical harmony between persons and the Tao. . . . Thus, if persons are in mystical harmony with the Tao, they can do no wrong. Their lives will flow in natural conjunction with all other things."[2] This could correlate with what we would call the Light of Christ or even the Holy Ghost.

Zoroastrianism recognizes two opposing forces, good and evil, and one Lord, Ahura Mazda (light and wisdom).

Hinduism is the father of Jainism, Buddhism, and Sikhism. Common to each of these are the belief in the role of karma and reincarnation. "Karma is the result of the balance between one's good and bad deeds from all past lives."[3] This sounds like agency and accountability, although it entirely neglects the crucial Atonement of Jesus Christ. "Reincarnation recognizes that perfection is not attainable in one lifetime."[4] We would call that eternal progression, although we retain our unique individuality.

"A goal of Buddhism is detachment from the world through an ascetic life."[5] The truth is that we should be in the world, but not of it. People should "lay up for yourselves treasures in heaven" (Matthew 6:20), not on the earth.

These philosophies represent the major thought of the Classical Period and continue among many today. My intent is to illustrate that mankind has never been devoid of some ennobling truths to quicken and school their better inclinations. This says nothing of the inequality of the human experience, only that the pathway to the fullness of truth can begin with what is at hand and what the cultural high road is for a given civilization and time in history.

"Other good and great men, not bearing the Priesthood, but possessing profundity of thought, great wisdom, and a desire to uplift their fellows, have been sent by the Almighty into many nations, to give them, not the fullness of the Gospel, but that portion of truth that they were able to receive and wisely use."[6]

Beautiful is this summary scripture from the Book of Mormon that speaks to these thoughts, "For behold, the Lord doth grant unto all nations, of their own nation and tongue, to teach his word, yea, in wisdom, all that he seeth fit that they should have; therefore we see that the Lord doth counsel in wisdom, according to that which is just and true" (Alma 29:8).

The Plan of Salvation does not exclude any of God's children from being able to attain the blessings of salvation. All will have equal opportunity to claim eternal blessings. To prepare to receive those blessings, one needs to be in harmony with divine principles. If a fullness of those principles is not available in this life, then one needs to be in harmony with the knowledge and divine truths that have been made available to them.

For me, such an understanding gives perspective and inclusion to the many noble faiths of the earth throughout time.

Notes:

1. Wikipedia, "Confucianism."
2. Roger R. Keller, *Windows of Faith - Latter-day Perspectives on World History,* Provo: Religious Studies Center, Brigham Young University, 2005, 224.
3. Roger R. Keller, 219.
4. Roger R. Keller, 219.
5. Roger R. Keller, 222.
6. Orson F. Whitney, *Conference Report*, April, 1921, 32-33.

55. We believe in a living, communicating, all-wise God and in the order of His Kingdom.

Just recently, that order is being called into question by many not of our faith and some within the faith. Just days ago, a woman was excommunicated from Church fellowship for her public solicitation of ordaining women to the priesthood.

This is not the first time the Church has been under criticism for not conforming to contemporary social orthodoxy. Polygamy in the late 1800's was a tremendous challenge to the fledgling Church. Until 1978, the Church had the longstanding policy of blacks not being able to be ordained to the priesthood. Currently, there is the growing tide of opinion that gay unions should be treated as equal to heterosexual marriage. The issue of women being ordained to the priesthood, not a new issue, is now headlining because of the case mentioned above.

Polygamy was instituted by God for a wise purpose in Him and ended by God when He so commanded. The exclusion of certain men from being ordained to the Priesthood based on race, although not clear in its origin and in stated conflict to the personal desires of some Church leaders, was only lifted when revelation from God was received.

Unlike any other worldwide organization today, but not unlike Biblical models, we believe that God the Father and Jesus Christ the Savior live, that They direct the affairs of their Church on the earth today, that Their ways are not man's ways, and that They have ordained a system of order for the Church at large, under the direction of a Prophet, his two counselors, and Twelve Apostles.

We accept this ultimate divine authority when we see it from afar, namely, in Old Testament accounts. Consider the divine decree given to Saul to "slay both man and woman, infant and suckling, ox and sheep, camel and ass" (1 Samuel 15:3). Imagine the media outrage that would take place today if such were to occur! Instead, because Saul fell short of this commandment, in apparent compassion to the Kenite people and regard for the value of useful animals, we get an analysis (from afar), "Nothing could justify such an exterminating decree but the absolute authority of God. This was given—all the reasons of it we do not know—but this we know well, The Judge of all the earth doth right."[1]

The website of the woman who was excommunicated, which advocates for ordaining women to the priesthood, concludes their mission statement as follows, "We sincerely ask our leaders to take this matter to the Lord in prayer."[2] And if the Lord says, "No," "Not yet," or "Never," could this sister and her followers accept that? Again, it goes to the heart of belief, that either God is directing his work through His prophets or it is merely another earthly organization run by a board of directors.

Many churches today are a reflection of current cultural norms, not timeless divine directives, nor contemporary commandment from on high. They are run by a board of directors.

I agree with the analysis of 1 Samuel 15 cited above, and I believe it is equally the right analysis to issues facing the Church today. "Be still, and know that I am God" (Psalms 46:10). He lives, and He is engaged. We must remember, "For as the heavens are higher than the earth, so are my ways higher than your ways, and my thoughts than your thoughts" (Isaiah 55:9). I acknowledge the Church of Jesus Christ as just that and welcome His leadership through His prophet.

Notes:

1. www.biblehub.com/commentaries/clarke/1_samuel/15.htm.

2. Mission Statement, www.ordainwomen.org/mission.

56. If I were to join another church, what would I gain and what would I lose?

A man and I were discussing the congruence and differences of our respective churches one day. In the end, he expressed his sincere desire that I would leave the LDS Church and join the more mainstream Christian movement. I guess I didn't make my case very well…

So for the rest of the evening, I thought about what my faith would look like if I were to accept his offer. What would I gain? I already have a deep faith in Jesus Christ. I have a love for the Bible. I am a part of a community of believers, in fact a world-wide community of believers. I rely on the teachings and Atonement of Jesus Christ in my daily walk. I believe that I am saved by his grace. Other than social acceptance, I'm just not sure of what I would stand to gain from such a decision.

But here are only some of the things I would have to part with:

- Abandon a personal relationship with a corporeal, living God, and adopt the worship of an undefined spirit essence who is silent.
- Abandon the resurrected Christ for a mushy concept of God the Father, Jesus the Son, and the Holy Ghost all rolled into one and the same, with no form or presence except when Jesus walked the earth.
- Abandon the merciful post-mortal understanding of various degrees of glory and accept a narrow and absolute view of either heaven or hell.
- Leave behind the merciful vicarious work for the dead because there would be no provision for those who have never heard of Christ in this life nor redemptive work for the spirits in prison. Through no fault of their own, they will be consigned to hell.
- Abandon the strict covenant relationship I have entered into with Deity and with my family. Adopt a more practical, adaptable, contemporary, relaxed, covenant style.
- Reject ordained, modern-day prophets and apostles. Forego the inspired guidance, direction and common sense they offer in an ever-changing world. Adopt Biblical interpretations by preachers I like and agree with.
- Lay aside the rich, clarifying doctrines, and the second witness of the divinity of Jesus Christ, found in scripture brought forth by the Prophet Joseph Smith. Enter into the arena of men's interpretations of the Bible, giving rise to arguments without end and never reaching an authoritative conclusion.
- Reject the clarity regarding the Creation, the Fall, and the Atonement, which includes an understanding of our premortal existence, agency, families, and eternal progression and view our first parents as sinful and ignorant.
- Reject the sealing power enacted through ordinances and corresponding covenants, that unites families and

relationships beyond the grave. Adopt the belief that marriage will be dissolved at death and will have no place in the eternities. "That same sociality . . . only it will be coupled with eternal glory" (D&C 130:2) that exists here, will not exist there.

- Abandon temple worship, temple instruction, temple ordinances, and vicarious temple work for the dead. All this saving work would be without replacement, ignoring a vast swath of humanity.

These provisions, doctrines, principles, and practices are representative of the fullness of the gospel of Jesus Christ. It is so beautiful, so comprehensive, so merciful, so filled with faith, hope, and charity! My consideration of my friend's proposal crystallized to me the richness of the blessings the Lord desires to bestow upon His children, if they will repent and "enter in at the strait gate, and continue in the way . . . until ye shall obtain eternal life" (Jacob 6:11-12).

57. The Book of Mormon personally testifies of Jesus Christ.

I think it was the summer of 1976. Steve Hobbs and I were on a search for truth. Divine truth. We wanted to know about God, what our relationship to Him was, and what our role in life was.

So we decided to embark on a ten-day water fast. We would take Steve's sailboat, head out to a lake in the desert, and give ourselves to reading, pondering, thinking, and a little sailing for diversion. I can't remember what Steve was reading, probably the Bible, as his upbringing was of good Catholic parents. For my part, I had been interested in two different kinds of thought and doctrine—The Self Realization Fellowship movement (SRF), founded by Paramahansa Yogananda, and the Mormon faith. The former was a form of Hinduism that appealed to me and was introduced to me by a close high school friend whom I admired. The latter came by a similar introduction and then more persuasively by way of the BYU survival program I had recently attended.

At this point in my spiritual journey, I had come to know that God lived and that we could communicate with Him through prayer. I found that He didn't always just give us the answers, but wanted us to seek, study, and learn for ourselves.

What I didn't know was who Jesus was. Is He really "that bread of life (John 6:35), the "living water" (John 4:10-14), the "light of the world" (John 9:5), the "good shepherd" (John 10:11), the Only Begotten Son of God, the "way, the truth, and the life" (John 14:6), and that "no man cometh unto the Father, but by me [Him]" (John 14:6)?

And so I spent much of the week reading and pondering the Book of Mormon.

We actually ended our ten-day fast on about day seven. Steve was sick and felt he needed to eat something. I was pretty supportive of that idea.

But before we left, I knelt down privately with the Book of Mormon and asked God if Jesus Christ was really the Savior of all mankind and truly His Divine Son. On that occasion, a witness and a certainty came to me that, yes, Jesus was who He declared Himself to be, and there was no other beside Him. It was very clear and very personal. It changed my life in what has become and what is becoming an infinite number of ways for good.

That certainty and testimony came from my study of the Book of Mormon.

It was a defining point in my understanding and in my quest for the truth. The Book of Mormon truly testifies of Christ—clearly, comprehensively, frequently, and powerfully.

58. Oh, it is a blessing to live under the direction of a living Prophet!

When one comes to know that a particular living man is an ordained Prophet of God, that person will never be the same again. Going forward, it will, at times, require subordination of one's personal will—perhaps painful, usually inconvenient, but always a blessing to self, family, and other people.

The day after I was baptized, I walked alone to Church on Sunday morning, since the Church was just a few quick blocks from my apartment. On the way, I still remember the joy I felt as a newly baptized member of the Church. It was the first day of May, under a clear, blue sky. I reflected on my baptism. I came to have some thoughts and internal dialogue somewhat as follows:

> "Well you're a brand new member of the Lord's Church."
>
> "Yes, it's so great!"
>
> "You now have the blessings of following a living Prophet, President Spencer W. Kimball."
>
> "Yes, what a tremendous blessing to know he is in fact a Prophet of God."
>
> "The prophet says that every young man should go on a two-year mission."
>
> "Yes, but I'm older than the young missionaries. I'm just starting my college education. I don't have the means to serve a mission. My parents wouldn't support that. Certainly, you don't expect *me* to serve. I was just baptized, isn't that enough?"

It was an uncomfortable moment for me. But then the Spirit whispered further, "You can't go for one year anyway as a new convert, so just let it work in your heart for now." And then I felt peace again. It was about three months later that I came to want to serve a mission and made that public announcement to friends, family, and to my Bishop. My belief in a living prophet had matured a few degrees.

"A prophet denounces sin and foretells its consequences. He is a preacher of righteousness. . . . His primary responsibility, however, is to bear witness of Christ."[1]

"The Lord will never permit me or any other man who stands as President of this Church to lead you astray. It is not in the program. It is not in the mind of God. If I were to attempt that, the Lord would remove me out of my place."[2]

What is the living prophet saying today? He is warning of the evils of pornography, commending large youth cultural performances, encouraging broader temple and family history work, calling for more missionaries, modeling the need to rescue our fellows, asking us to stand firm even if that means alone, preaching tolerance toward religious differences and respect in our civil discourse. He is a life-long mentor to all of us because of his ministry to the one, the lonely, the elderly, and the forgotten. He wants us all to listen to the Spirit and act on those promptings. "When God speaks and a man obeys, that man will always be right."[3]

As I said, a prophet's counsel will always be a blessing to self, family, and other people. His is a clear, steady, and secure voice in a world of conflicting and ever vacillating messages. It is a great blessing to live under the direction of a living prophet and to have a testimony of his divine call. I had that testimony then, and I have that testimony now.

Notes:

1. lds.org, *The Guide to the Scriptures,* "Prophet."
2. Wilford W. Woodruff, *Conference Report,* October, 1890.

3. Thomas S. Monson, "Constant Truths for Changing Times," *Ensign* May, 2005.

59. The Lord is not nonchalant on important behavioral issues.

I suppose the Lord is interested (because we are), but unconcerned, whether we paint the kitchen walls white or yellow or whether we prefer our eggs scrambled or fried. Many of the decisions we make throughout the days of our lives are purely preference and lend to our individuality.

Does the Lord have a position on those certain things that really matter, those that shape our character, our thoughts, and our attitudes? Yes! God the Father and Jesus Christ the Son are not dispassionate beings. They have refined and matured thoughts and ways. The Lord said through the Prophet Isaiah, "For my thoughts are not your thoughts, neither are your ways my ways, saith the Lord. For as the heavens are higher than the earth, so are my ways higher than your ways, and my thoughts than your thoughts" (Isaiah 55:8-9).

I believe most people intuitively know where Deity stands on particular issues. Would He condone vulgar, obscene language? Is promiscuous sexual activity OK? What about modest dress and grooming in contrast to the provocative or the sensual? Is there music that He would disapprove? Where does He stand on Sabbath Day observance? Would He condone and encourage us to see sexually explicit or violent movies for violence sake?

Father Lehi, discovered "a tree, whose fruit was desirable to make one happy. . . . I beheld that it was most sweet, above all that I ever before tasted. . . . It filled my soul with exceeding great joy" (1 Nephi 8:10-11). He desired "that my family should partake of it also" (1 Nephi 8:12). To arrive at this tree, there was "a strait and narrow path, which came along by the rod of iron, even to the tree" (1 Nephi 8:20).

It was not a get-there-by-whatever-route-you-choose or a good-luck-I'll-be-waiting-for-you-at-the-tree invitation. It was a defined route, giving visual, tangible, even personal encouragement and assistance to guide one safely to the tree.

I've had people bristle at some of the standards we live by in the Church. It's as if they are saying, "My God doesn't require that," or "My God doesn't care if we do that." My point is that I think He does care. I think there is a Divine point of view on matters that really matter. Heavenly Father is the best parent, the most caring parent, and is most desirous for our happiness now and forever. By His infinite, merciful wisdom, He can see the end from the beginning. He knows what is in our best interest to insure that happiness now and forever.

Our quest is to align ourselves with the Lord's prophets, and to listen to the Holy Spirit. "It is to think what he thinks, to believe what he believes, to say what he would say and do what he would do in the same situation. It is to have the mind of Christ and be one with him as he is one with the Father."[1] Such presupposes that God, indeed, has a position on issues that influence and affect our very salvation.

Notes:

1. Bruce R. McConkie, "Be Valiant in the Fight of Faith," *Ensign*, October, 1974.

60. The covenant way is the only way.

Thursday evening, I was out with the missionaries. Elder Williams and I paired off to visit and teach a young couple. They had been visiting with the missionaries for some time but were just not progressing toward baptism. After I had given what I thought was a very good explanation of the need for a restoration—Christ's Church anciently, the apostasy, priesthood, reformation, restoration—I realized by his resultant comment that I had fallen short. Our dialogue went more or less as follows:

> He said, "Different churches are like different roads, but they all lead to God. In the end, if we keep the faith, we'll all be saved."
>
> I replied, "But if what we're saying is true, that Jesus Christ Himself has restored this Church to the earth, would you then align yourself with His Church and follow its teachings?"
>
> He countered, "My family is real strong in our church, and I am comfortable where I am."

This was a young couple with a new baby boy. They were good people. They were, by common measures, religious. They were courteous, polite, and kind. Yet, if my quoted query above is true, then the only acceptable saving response must be in the affirmative! Although "strait is the gate, and narrow is the way" (Matthew 7:14), we should rejoice that we have found such an entry point!

Knowing of the Restoration of the Gospel of Jesus Christ in these latter days, being "comfortable where I am" will not suffice. The great C.S. Lewis draws a contrast between just being comfortable and being transformed as only God can envision:

> "Imagine yourself as a living house. God comes in to rebuild that house. At first, perhaps, you can understand what He is doing. He is getting the drains right and stopping the leaks in the roof and so on; you knew that those jobs needed doing and so you are not surprised. But presently He starts knocking the house about in a way that hurts abominably and does not seem to make any sense. What on earth is He up to? The explanation is that He is building quite a different house from the one you thought of—throwing out a new wing here, putting on an extra floor there, running up towers, making courtyards. You thought you were being made

> into a decent little cottage: but He is building a palace. He intends to come and live in it Himself."[1]

"Come, follow me" (Luke 18:22) includes a willingness to "take up your cross" (3 Nephi 12:30), put your "hand to the plow" and not look back (Luke 9:62), leave your "father or mother . . . or lands, for my sake, and the gospel's" (Mark 10:29), and "let the dead bury their dead" (Matthew 8:22).

I asked, "But if what we're saying is true, that Jesus Christ Himself has restored this Church to the earth, would you then align yourself with His Church and follow its teachings?" The only rational response to this question for believers is an enthusiastic "yes!" When the "But if" clause is dropped, it becomes a statement of testimony and an invitation. When we accept that invitation, then are we "in this strait and narrow path which leads to eternal life" (2 Nephi 31:18).

Notes:

1. C. S. Lewis, *Mere Christianity,* New York: MacMillan Co., 1960, 160.

Part Two

Doctrinal Reasons

doctrine , noun – "a set of ideas or beliefs that are taught or believed to be true." (Merriam-Webster Dictionary Online)

61. The Creation, the Fall, and the Atonement are foundational doctrines.

Elder Bruce R. McConkie, an apostle, taught,"There are no events that have ever occurred in all eternity, or ever will, as important to us as individuals as the Creation, the Fall, and the Atonement, and the Creation, the Fall, and the Atonement are wrapped together in one package to form what is called the Plan of Salvation."[1]

Many doctrines stem from such an understanding, including mortality juxtaposed to a pre-mortal and a post-mortal life, personal agency to choose, probationary status, sin, opposition, spiritual and temporal death, resurrection, family relationships, and a correct knowledge of the divine roles of the Father and the Son.

Each (the Creation, the Fall, the Atonement) prepares the way for the other sequentially, enabling the Father's "great plan of happiness" (Alma 42:8) for his children.

The Creation of the earth, the setting in motion of the heavens, the ordering of the plant and animal kingdoms, all were prelude to the placing of Adam and Eve in the Garden of Eden. That setting was paradisiacal. There was no opposition, no comparative yardstick, no opportunity for personal growth. "And now, behold, if Adam had not transgressed . . . they would have had no children; wherefore they would have remained in a state of innocence, having no joy, for they knew no misery; doing no good, for they knew no sin" (2 Nephi 2:22,23).

The Fall of Adam and Eve was the event that changed it all. God could not have created a sphere other than perfect because He is not the author of lesser things. Nor could He be the cause of their falling to a lesser state. It would have to be of their own choice. Adam saw the plan for mankind and exclaimed, "Blessed be the name of our God, for because of my transgression my eyes are opened" (Moses 5:10). Eve realized (apparently the first to realize), "Were it not for our transgression we never should have had seed, and never should have known good and evil, and the joy of our redemption" (Moses 5:11).

That joy of redemption is through the Savior Jesus Christ. His atoning sacrifice overcomes our passing from mortality where the body and the spirit are separated and has the power to reconcile us to the perfections of God, to one day live with Him again in a celestial realm.

The Plan of Salvation is not a cleverly crafted story of explanation. It is a cause and effect reality of law and mercy. Central to who we are, why we are here, and where we are going is to understand the purposes of the Creation, the effects of the Fall, and the need for a Divine Atonement.

Notes:

1. Bruce R. McConkie, "The Probationary Test of Mortality," University of Utah Institute of Religion, January 10, 1982.

62. The Joseph Smith Translation clarifies the privilege of seeing the Lord.

The greatest singular event in the history of mankind since the resurrection of the Lord Jesus Christ, is the appearance of the Father and the Son to the boy Joseph Smith in the year 1820. By that introduction, the marvelous restoration of the fullness of the gospel was ushered in for these latter days.

Two Bible verses have been cited as being at odds with the Joseph Smith story. In John, it says, "No man hath seen God at any time" (John 1:18). In Exodus, it is recorded that the Lord said to Moses, "Thou canst not see my face; for there shall no man see me, and live" (Exodus 33:20). Let's look at each in turn.

The Joseph Smith Translation of John 1:18 gives important clarification and completion to the verse. "No man hath seen God at any time, *except he hath borne record of the Son*" (JST, John 1:18, emphasis added). This conditional addendum confirms that indeed man has seen God.

The verse in Exodus is also made whole through a Joseph Smith Translation and teaches an important truth. Remember, it is Jesus Christ, the God of the Old Testament, who is speaking to Moses, "Thou canst not see my face *at this time, lest mine anger be kindled against thee also, and I destroy thee, and thy people;* for there shall no man *among them* see me *at this time,* and live, *for they are exceeding sinful. And no sinful man hath at any time, neither shall there be any sinful man at any time, that shall see my face and live*" (JST, Exodus 33:20, emphasis added).

Contrast that with previous verses in Exodus 24:7-12, where because of their righteousness, "All that the Lord hath said will we do, and be obedient," Moses, Aaron, Nadab, Abihu, and seventy of the elders of Israel saw the Lord.

And later in Exodus we read, "And the Lord spake unto Moses face to face, as a man speaketh unto his friend" (Exodus 33:11). That's pretty clear and convincing language to the affirmative. The Lord immediately allows Moses "to see my back parts; but my face shall not be seen" (Exodus 33:23). Leaving that verse to stand alone would be confusing in light of verse 11 where Moses and the Lord spoke face to face. Again, the Joseph Smith Translation completes that verse so it reads consistently "to see my back parts; but my face shall not be seen *as at other times; for I am angry with my people Israel*" (JST, Exodus 33:23).

The written record recording the voice and visions of God the Father are when He has born witness of the Son. Jesus as the God of the Old Testament, Jehovah, has made Himself manifest to his servants as He has felt to do so, both pre- and post-mortally.

Both of these scenarios are clarified by the Joseph Smith Translation, which clarifies otherwise contradictory scriptural language.

63. Little children have no need for baptism.

"Every spirit of man was innocent in the beginning; and God having redeemed man from the fall, men became again, in their infant state, innocent before God" (D&C 93:38).

In an over-zealous interpretation of the Savior's commandment for all to be baptized as a covenant of our faith, the practice of infant baptism has come into being. However, the required precedent action of repentance is somehow lost in the process. John, known as the Baptist, carried the message of "Repent ye; for the kingdom of heaven is at hand" (Matthew 3:2).

Little children prior to eight-years-old have no need to repent. They are pure. In fact, in their innocence, they are protected of their Maker "for power is not given unto Satan to tempt little children, until they begin to become accountable before me" (D&C 29:47). Many a parent might like to argue that point when it comes to their own seven-and-under child, but they would likely agree, in the end, that children are just children and have not come to the age of being entirely responsible for their actions.

"Little children are whole, for they are not capable of committing sin; wherefore the curse of Adam is taken from them in me," said the Savior, "and their little children need no repentance, neither baptism. . . . But little children are alive in Christ. . . . For awful is the wickedness to suppose that God saveth one child because of baptism, and the other must perish because he hath no baptism" (Moroni 8:8, 11, 12, 15).

The Lord has designated the age of eight years as the appropriate time for the baptism of children. That allows parents the opportunity to teach them "to understand the doctrine of repentance, faith in Christ the Son of the living God, and of baptism and the gift of the Holy Ghost by the laying on of the hands, when eight years old" (D&C 68:25).

Nor do we perform vicarious baptisms or vicarious endowments for children who died before the age of eight. It is just not needed, "for they are whole from the foundation of the world" (Moses 6:54).

That "little children are alive in Christ" (Moroni 8:12, 22) is a sweet and fair doctrine that should be understood by all who bring children into this world and experience that parent to child love.

64. Both faith and works have a role for a disciple of Jesus Christ.

Mormons are often criticized as relying too much on their own works for salvation. It is argued that works undermine faith in, and the grace of, Christ. We reply with clarity, "For we labor diligently to write, to persuade our children, and also our brethren, to believe in Christ, and to be reconciled to God; for we know that it is by grace that we are saved, after all we can do" (2 Nephi 25:23).

Another passage in the Book of Mormon confirms, "It is only in and through the grace of God that ye are saved" (2 Nephi 10:24).

The word "grace" is often used in the writings of Paul and refers to a divine means of help or strength.[1] This connects well with the adage, "God will help those who help themselves." To somehow divorce one's own efforts (works) from faith and grace is, to me, contrary to common sense. The New Testament is replete with admonitions, such as, "work out your own salvation with fear and trembling" (Philippians 2:12), and "faith without works is dead" (James 2:20, 26). Over and over did the Master condemn those hypocrites who said one thing and did another (or nothing). And over and over did He make reference to the need to work, to do.

"It is through the grace of the Lord that individuals . . . receive strength and assistance to do good works that they otherwise would not be able to maintain if left to their own means. This grace is an enabling power . . . after [and while] they have expended their own best efforts."[2] Such strength and assistance is a direct result of the Atonement of Jesus Christ and one's exercise of faith in Him.

Our faith is best expressed and made manifest by the efforts we expend to become like the Lord. That takes work—a lifetime of work, faith, devotion, and utilizing the enabling power of the atonement of Christ. The Apostle James succinctly stated our position when he wrote, "I will shew thee my faith by my works" (James 2:18). Works, James teaches, is what we do because of testimony and love. And as taught so pointedly in the Book of Mormon, we know that our works are made effective and even magnified by the grace of God.

Notes:

1. LDS Bible Dictionary, "Grace."
2. LDS Bible Dictionary, "Grace."

65. The law of sacrifice today is to have a broken heart and a contrite spirit.

The ancient law of sacrificing animals was a type or symbol of the atoning sacrifice of the Savior. Adam and Eve offered sacrifices, "and after many days an angel of the Lord appeared unto Adam, saying: Why dost thou offer sacrifices unto the Lord? And Adam said unto him: I know not, save the Lord commanded me. And then the angel spake, saying: This thing is a similitude of the sacrifice of the Only Begotten of the Father, which is full of grace and truth" (Moses 5:6-7).

This sacrifice of the Only Begotten of the Father in the meridian of time was the end of the law of sacrifice by the shedding of blood. It was replaced by the ordinance of the sacrament, the partaking of bread and water in remembrance of this last sacrifice. In partaking of the holy sacramental emblems, we covenant to take upon us His name, to always remember Him, and to keep His commandments. If we truly remember His atoning sacrifice on our behalf and for our sins and transgressions, we will naturally feel contrition for our sins and regret for our offenses. Our heart will be broken in our humility and willing submission to Him. Thus, this sacrifice is a state of being, an attitude toward God, a humble acknowledgement of dependence upon One far greater than self.

This is the required sacrifice for baptism. Said the Lord, "And ye shall offer for a sacrifice unto me a broken heart and a contrite spirit. And whoso cometh unto me with a broken heart and a contrite spirit, him will I baptize with fire and with the Holy Ghost" (3 Nephi 9:20).

Such a disposition will enable one to be nearer to God. "The Lord is nigh unto them that are of a broken heart; and saveth such as be of a contrite spirit" (Psalms 34:18).

Isaiah described in part the mission of the Savior "he hath sent me to bind up the brokenhearted" (Isaiah 61:1). Nephi speaks similarly in regards to those who would accept Jesus as their Savior, "Behold, he offereth himself a sacrifice for sin, to answer the ends of the law, unto all those who have a broken heart and a contrite spirit" (2 Nephi 2:7).

The commandment is, "Thou shalt offer a sacrifice unto the Lord thy God in righteousness, even that of a broken heart and a contrite spirit" (D&C 59:8).

And the promise is, "Verily I say unto you, all among them who know their hearts are honest, and are broken, and their spirits contrite, and are willing to observe their covenants by sacrifice—yea, every sacrifice which I, the Lord, shall command—they are accepted of me" (D&C 97:8).

I'm grateful for these latter-day scriptures. It un-stresses me when I remember this attitude. Immediately, the world's happy-face requirement goes away, and my own circle of concerns and weaknesses are OK. In fact, they draw me to Him. In fact, He is the best example of one who walked with a broken heart and a contrite spirit.

66. Eternity is without beginning or end.

As mortals, our minds can't very well grasp the concept of forever. We go into a sort of mental loop as we try to envision no beginning and no end. But it is so.

"My works have no end, neither beginning" (D&C 29:33).

Regarding the holy priesthood, the Lord said, "Which priesthood continueth in the church of God in all generations, and is without beginning of days or end of years" (D&C 84:17). And again touching the priesthood, "The holy priesthood after the order of the Son of God is without father or mother and has neither a beginning nor an end of days" (JST, Hebrews 7:3).

As we peer into the heavens on a clear night, we can ponder this concept of never ending and accept it on logic and reason. Could there be a ceiling out there? If so, what's on the other side of that ceiling? Or when does the thickness of that ceiling end? Then what? Of course, there can be no definite ending point. Much like counting numbers, you could always add one more to wherever you are in the process.

The elements and all matter are eternal. So declared the Lord, "The elements are eternal" (D&C 93:33). They are ordered, dis-ordered, and re-ordered into various compounds and creations. The first words to begin the Old Testament state, "In the beginning God created the heaven and the earth" (Genesis 1:1). The writings of Abraham use the words "organized and formed" in place of the verb "created" (Abraham 4:1). Prior to that passage, we read, "We will take of these materials, and we will make an earth whereon these may dwell" (Abraham 3:24).

As the heavens unarguably have no end, so it can be concluded that they have no beginning. They and all parts thereof have an eternal existence. I particularly like the words and music of the hymn "If You Could Hie to Kolob," which poetically ponders these truths:

> If you could hie to Kolob In the twinkling of an eye,
>
> And then continue onward With that same speed to fly,
>
> Do you think that you could ever, Through all eternity,
>
> Find out the generation Where Gods began to be?
>
> Or see the grand beginning, Where space did not extend?
>
> Or view the last creation, Where Gods and matter end?
>
> Me thinks the Spirit whispers, "No man has found 'pure space,'
>
> Nor seen the outside curtains, Where nothing has a place." [1]

Eternity is a concept and a truth beyond our ability to comprehend, and it is very humbling to contemplate. However, our understanding is essential for a true and actual perspective. Although to understand entirely is beyond my grasp, this understanding of eternity—eternal dimensions, eternal priesthood, eternal elements, eternal life—sets well with me.

Notes:

1. William W. Phelps, "If You Could Hie to Kolob," *Hymns of the Church of Jesus Christ of Latter-day Saints*, Salt Lake City: The Church of Jesus Christ of Latter-day Saints, 1985, 284.

67. The individual spirits of men and women are eternal.

Mortal birth is not the beginning of existence, but the acquiring of a body to house our eternal spirit. "Man was also in the beginning with God. Intelligence, or the light of truth, was not created or made, neither indeed can be" (D&C 93:29).

As God the Father is everlasting, without beginning or ending, so is the spirit component of man. Speaking to the Prophet Jeremiah, the Lord explained, "Before I formed thee in the belly I knew thee; and before thou camest forth out of the womb I sanctified thee, and I ordained thee a prophet unto the nations" (Jeremiah 1:5).

From the writings of Abraham, we have the following insight to this preexistent state prior to our mortal life, "Now the Lord had shown unto me, Abraham, the intelligences that were organized before the world was; and among all these there were many of the noble and great ones; And God saw these souls that they were good, and he stood in the midst of them, and he said: These I will make my rulers; for he stood among those that were spirits, and he saw that they were good; and he said unto me: Abraham, thou art one of them; thou wast chosen before thou wast born" (Abraham 3:23).

To Moses, the Lord said, "And I, the Lord God, had created all the children of men; and not yet a man to till the ground; for in heaven created I them; and there was not yet flesh upon the earth" (Moses 3:5).

To Adam, he spoke similarly, "I am God; I made the world, and men before they were in the flesh" (Moses 6:51).

God is our Father in Heaven, the Father of our spirits. We are begotten of Him, from some existing form of intelligence to a unique spiritual individual. We receive physical bodies from our earthly parents and will someday lay that body by through the inevitability of death. Then, because of the Atonement of Jesus Christ, all will be resurrected and will take up that body in its glorified state and live forever.

The spirit and the purposes of man are of an eternal nature. The Lord said, in what could be seen as a declaration of purpose, "For behold, this is my work and my glory—to bring to pass the immortality and eternal life of man" (Moses 1:39).

Man existed in a premortal realm, followed by this earthly existence, and will yet exist in the future and forever in an immortal state. Man is an eternal being. To me, such an understanding coincides with eternity itself.

68. Where does the soul of man go after death and prior to the resurrection?

At the death of a loved one, or at the later stages of one's own life, this is the great question to which we seek an answer. I know of no clearer or more comforting scripture in this time of need than that recorded by the Prophet Alma to his son Corianton. "Now, concerning the state of the soul between death and the resurrection—Behold, it has been made known unto me by an angel, that the spirits of all men, as soon as they are departed from this mortal body, yea, the spirits of all men, whether they be good or evil, are taken home to that God who gave them life. And then shall it come to pass, that the spirits of those who are righteous are received into a state of happiness, which is called paradise, a state of rest, a state of peace, where they shall rest from all their troubles and from all care, and sorrow" (Alma 40:11-12).

Subsequent verses describe the state of the wicked. They reside in a spirit prison which is in stark contrast to the description of spirit paradise.

The apostle Peter wrote, "For Christ also hath once suffered for sins, the just for the unjust, that he might bring us to God, being put to death in the flesh, but quickened by the Spirit: By which also he went and preached unto the spirits in prison; Which sometime were disobedient" (1 Peter 3:18-20) And further on Peter wrote, "For this cause was the gospel preached also to them that are dead, that they might be judged according to men in the flesh, but live according to God in the spirit" (1 Peter 4:6).

All men will be resurrected. Prior to that glorious event, the physical body will lay in the earth, and the spirit of man will dwell in this state of spirit paradise or spirit prison. "And there he preached unto them the everlasting gospel. . . . Thus was the gospel preached to those who had died in their sins, without a knowledge of the truth, or in transgression, having rejected the prophets" (D&C 138:19, 32).

In other words, the work of salvation will continue on after this life and prior to the final judgment. Although death is a mortal moment of sorrow for the living, we can be comforted by understanding that "there is a state of the soul between death and the resurrection" (Alma 40:11). There people will experience a state of happiness, rest, and peace, or they will have the opportunity to have the gospel preached to them and to accept the saving grace of Jesus Christ. This is sweet and merciful doctrine!

69. Adversity is a vital component of growth and eternal development.

Consider those we would associate with in the highest realms of eternity—Adam, Abraham, Moses, Nephi, Abinadi, Moroni, Joseph Smith, and even the Savior Jesus Christ. Common to all of these men is that their lives were difficult. Abraham was called upon to be willing to sacrifice his only son Isaac. Moses wandered in the desert for forty years. Abinadi suffered death by fire for his testimony. Joseph Smith was forever persecuted as were his people, and he was ultimately martyred at a young age. Jesus was "despised and rejected of men; a man of sorrows, and acquainted with grief" (Isaiah 53:3).

When we are in our most trying moments, we are most likely to reach out for divine assistance and acknowledge our own mortal shortcomings. The Prophet Ether said, "And if men come unto me I will show unto them their weakness. I give unto men weakness that they may be humble; and my grace is sufficient for all men that humble themselves before me" (Ether 12:27).

The apostle Paul suffered much and yet counseled us to be "patient in tribulation" (Romans 12:12). In lamenting one of his own personal struggles, he was told of the Lord, "My grace is sufficient for thee; for my strength is made perfect in weakness" (2 Corinthians 12:9). To which Paul concluded, "Therefore, I take pleasure in infirmities, in reproaches, in necessities, in persecutions, in distresses for Christ's sake; for when I am weak, then am I made strong" (2 Corinthians 12:10).

A very tender exchange is recorded as revelation to the Prophet Joseph Smith when he was unjustly imprisoned for several months in Liberty, Missouri. We can all find comfort in their words:

> "O God, where art thou? How long shall thy hand be stayed? Yea, O Lord, how long shall they [the Saints] suffer these wrongs and unlawful oppressions" (D&C 121:1-3)?
>
> "My son," answered the Lord, "peace be unto thy soul; thine adversity and thine afflictions shall be but a small moment. And then if thou endure it well, God shall exalt thee on high" (D&C 121:7-8).

And further, while in that same Liberty jail, this powerful realization was given to Joseph. "If thou shouldst be cast into the pit, or into the hands of murderers, and the sentence of death passed upon thee; if thou be cast into the deep; if the billowing surge conspire against thee; if fierce winds become thine enemy; if the heavens gather blackness, and all the elements combine to hedge up the way; and above all, if the very jaws of hell shall gape open the mouth wide after thee, know thou, my son, that all these things shall give thee experience, and shall be for thy good. The Son of Man hath descended below them all. Art thou greater than he" (D&C 122:7-8)?

We need not seek out adversity, but rather spiritually understand its inherent part in our mortal sojourn and endure it well, rejoicing in the opportunity to be refined and molded by the hand of the Master. Such an understanding can be seen in the lives of the faithful throughout the scriptures and by the early Saints in this dispensation. For me, it gives context and scope to what otherwise could be seen as life's undeserved difficulties.

70. Obedience is the first law of heaven.

"We believe that through the Atonement of Christ, all mankind may be saved, by obedience to the laws and ordinances of the Gospel" (Articles of Faith 3).

I really enjoy getting out in nature to experience the grandeur of mountains, the expanse of the oceans, the stark beauty of the deserts. There is a peace that I feel when I am away from the press of crowds and schedules. I believe that that peace exists because all things, both living and nonliving, are existing in perfect harmony and obedience to the purpose of their creation.

Man is endowed with agency to choose and to act for himself. To choose God and His righteousness, which is a life of service and sacrifice for the good of others, is not the natural inclination of most of us. Therefore, the continuous call of the Lord is to "obey my voice," and "walk in my statutes" (Jeremiah 7:23, Ezekiel 11:20, and others). Individual obedience is an alignment to who we really are, to our best self. Broad societal obedience to God will create harmony and cooperation.

Obedience enables us to become like God and to receive His blessings. "And when we obtain any blessing from God, it is by obedience to that law upon which it is predicated" (D&C 130:21).

So important is obedience to the happiness of man, we are taught, "And my people must needs be chastened until they learn obedience, if it must needs be, by the things which they suffer" (D&C 105:6). Our suffering on the way to obedience is both for the wrong choices we make and for staying the course within the strait and narrow way. Even Jesus had to learn obedience, although his suffering was entirely within the strait and narrow way. "Though he were a Son, yet learned he obedience by the things which he suffered" (Hebrews 5:8).

The children of Israel had to first wander in the wilderness for forty years to learn obedience prior to entering into the Promised Land. The Law of Moses "was our schoolmaster to bring us unto Christ" (Galatians 3:24). Our young missionaries today are taught strict obedience to mission rules first and foremost, so that they may have a full measure of the spirit, be instruments in the hands of the Lord, and go on to love ever more surely.

Simple and honest obedience is of greater value than pompous programs or an elaborate showing of devotion. "Behold, to obey is better than sacrifice, and to hearken than the fat of rams" (1 Samuel 15:22). Obedience is taught in the Church as the first law of heaven and is a precursor to the sustained blessings of the Lord.

71. Mortality is an opportunity to prove and to test our faith and devotion.

This existence can only be understood correctly by knowing of the eternal nature of man—that we lived prior to this earthly experience and that we will live beyond this earthly experience.

In the premortal life, all those who have been born on the earth chose to follow the Savior's plan of salvation. Each would be born into a physical body, experience joy and sorrow, goodwill and sin, health and sickness, victories and defeats. Some of these experiences would come as a result of our own choices, others would be imposed upon us, and still others would be the result of natural causes beyond our control.

A cornerstone to this earthly existence, is that we have no clear recollection of our antemortal existence. That absence of memory requires us to attain and to live by faith. Paul said, "For now we see through a glass, darkly; but then face to face" (1 Corinthians 13:12). Such faith is ultimately founded in Christ and His teachings and Atonement.

The Lord has endowed each person with a compass, our conscience, which will guide us to right actions and choices. "For behold, the Spirit of Christ is given to every man, that he may know good from evil" (Moroni 7:16). Yet we also know that "the natural man is an enemy to God" (Mosiah 3:19). We reconcile these two conditions by our freedom to choose our responses to life's challenges. "Wherefore men are free according to the flesh. . . . And they are free to choose liberty and eternal life, through the great Mediator of all men, or to choose captivity and death, according to the captivity and power of the devil" (2 Nephi 2:27).

God will not impose His will upon us. We are not mere puppets. But He will grant us according to our desires.

Heavenly Father, in company with the Savior said, "And we will prove them herewith, to see if they will do all things whatsoever the Lord their God shall command them" (Abraham 3:25). And as always, to the end that we may be blessed of the Lord with his richest blessings, He said, "That you may prove yourselves unto me that ye are faithful in all things whatsoever I command you, that I may bless you, and crown you with honor, immortality, and eternal life" (D&C 124:55).

In truth, God already knows our propensities and dispositions. Perhaps the real test is to prove to ourselves that we are willing to "bind yourselves to act in all holiness before me" (D&C 43:9). I believe, that in the wisdom of God, mortality is an opportunity to test and to prove our faith and devotion in Him. For which, and by which, we can acquire His holy attributes.

72. The payment of tithing is a commandment of God.

Tithing is one of the Lord's fundamental laws as a means of funding His earthly Kingdom. It is an equitable law for all, being defined as "one tenth of all their interest annually" (D&C 119:4).

Contrast that understandable revenue code with the complex, convoluted U.S. national tax code of many thousands of pages. A child can understand the concept of ten percent.

The ancient Prophet Malachi asked the question, "Will a man rob God?" (Malachi 3:8) and then went on to teach the law of tithing as a requirement of the faithful, "that there may be meat in mine house" (Malachi 3:10).

The payment of an honest tithe is a freewill offering and is privately paid. It is not collected in public or raised because of a requirement. It is between an individual or couple and the Lord. Each year, each member of the Church has the opportunity to declare to the Bishop their tithing faithfulness, an accounting before the Lord's authorized servant of their stewardship.

To really understand the law of tithing, we must understand that stewardship is the proper view of our earthly possessions. We realize that all things are first the Lord's, and we are really stewards of the resources, creations, and material attainments in this life. We enter this life with none of them, and we leave this life with the same.

Inherent to this principle of stewardship is gratitude for the material blessings we receive.

Those who pay an honest tithe can attest to the promise of the Lord for keeping this commandment, "and prove me now herewith, saith the Lord of hosts, if I will not open you the windows of heaven, and pour you out a blessing, that there shall not be room enough to receive it" (Malachi 3:10). Tithing is a principle that both blesses the Church at large and blesses the giver.

The law of tithing in the Church is fair, fixed, confidential, and ultimately voluntary. And it is a commandment of the Lord. It is, and will remain, "a standing law unto them [the Saints] forever" (D&C 119:4).

73. Essential requirements for the proper mode of baptism are shown in Jesus' example.

There are many forms of baptism in the world today. This is an odd outcome, indeed, when the Savior gave us an example of the proper mode of baptism. His baptism in the River Jordan included at least six vital components:

- He was of age
- He came prepared
- He was baptized of his own will and decision
- He was baptized by one who had Priesthood authority to do so
- He was immersed
- The Holy Ghost bore witness to his divinity, "descending like a dove, and lighting upon him" (Matthew 3:16).

Jesus was baptized at thirty years of age according to the customs of his day. In latter-day revelation we learn that the Lord has set the age of eight years as the time when a person begins to become accountable and can be baptized (D&C 68:25).

Although Jesus came to John as the sinless Son of God, when we come prepared to be baptized, we must have sincerely repented of our sins. We must also be willing to "take upon us the name of Christ, and always remember him, and to keep his commandments" (Moroni 4:3). Additionally, we must be "willing to mourn with those that mourn, and comfort those that stand in need of comfort, and to stand as a witness of God" (Mosiah 18:8-9).

Baptism, to be eternally binding, must be performed by one who bears the Holy Priesthood and is authorized to perform the ordinance. Such was John the Baptist who bore the Aaronic Priesthood.

Baptism symbolizes death, burial, and resurrection, and can only be acceptable when done by immersion and followed by receiving the Gift of the Holy Ghost. In this way, we become a new person, born again.

The Master taught Nicodemus the need for baptism, when he said, "Verily, verily, I say unto thee, Except a man be born of water and of the Spirit, he cannot enter into the kingdom of God." (John 3:5). We can conclude then that the valid ordinance of baptism is essential for personal salvation.

All of the vital components we learn from the baptism of the Savior are also essential practices and requirements for the ordinance of baptism in The Church of Jesus Christ of Latter-day Saints. It is after the example and authority of the Master.

74. Worlds without number have I created.

To gaze into a clear night sky is to see into forever. Can anyone argue that there is a final point of ending, a boundary of sorts? What may exist beyond the boundary? Although our minds are finite in their current capacity to understand, intellectually, we must agree that the heavens stretch forth forever without end.

To some, it is unspeakable to suppose that there are other worlds or creations of God. But in the context of an eternal expanse, it is both egocentric and unlikely that this earth would be the only planet of human habitation.

"Up to 80 percent of the stars in the galaxy are thought to be red dwarfs. If 6 percent have an Earth-like planet, that means the galaxy could host between 9.6 billion and 19.2 billion potentially-habitable Earths around these stars alone."[1]

And that is only within our own galaxy. "Our Solar System is just one member of a vast Milky Way galaxy with 200 to 400 billion stars. But how many galaxies are there in the entire universe? The most current estimates guess that there are 100 to 200 billion galaxies in the Universe, each of which has hundreds of billions of stars. A recent German supercomputer simulation put that number even higher: 500 billion."[2]

Stunning. Incomprehensible.

The Lord said to Moses,

> "And worlds without number have I created; and I also created them for mine own purpose; and by the Son I created them, which is mine Only Begotten. And the first man of all men have I called Adam, which is many. But only an account of this earth, and the inhabitants thereof, give I unto you. For behold, there are many worlds that have passed away by the word of my power. And there are many that now stand, and innumerable are they unto man; but all things are numbered

> unto me, for they are mine and I know them. . . . And the Lord God spake unto Moses, saying: The heavens, they are many, and they cannot be numbered unto man; but they are numbered unto me, for they are mine" (Moses 1:33-37).

We cannot comprehend all that God comprehends.

For our mortal life, the Lord has not given us to know the particulars of any other worlds or earths other than our own. He has shared with us that they exist. Someday we will have a comprehension of the eternal and will see beyond this earthly existence to the infinite creations of an omnipotent God. It settles well with me that we are not the single, centric point of existence in a never-ending expanse of eternity.

Notes:

1. Pete Spotts, "Earth-like planets next door? Prospect could point to 9.6 billion more," *Christian Science Monitor*, Feb 6, 2013, www.csmonitor.com/USA/2013/0206/Earth-like-planets-next-door-Prospect-could-point-to-9.6-billion-more.
2. Fraser Cain, "How Many Galaxies in the Universe," *Universe Today*, May 4, 2009, www.universetoday.com/30305/how-many-galaxies-in-the-universe.

75. Learning, or gaining knowledge, is a lifelong pursuit that enables our progression.

The Lord's own declarations on the importance and eminence of education are of themselves enlightening:

> "The glory of God is intelligence, or, in other words, light and truth" (D&C 93:36).

> "Whatever principle of intelligence we attain unto in this life, it will rise with us in the resurrection. And if a person gains

more knowledge and intelligence in this life through his diligence and obedience than another, he will have so much the advantage in the world to come" (D&C 130:18-19).

> "And as all have not faith, seek ye diligently and teach one another words of wisdom; yea, seek ye out of the best books words of wisdom; seek learning, even by study and also by faith" (D&C 88:118).

The very gulf between God and man is His very state of omniscience and His perfect understanding and adherence to all truth and to all knowledge. Intelligence.

Early on in the founding of the Church in these latter days, the brethren began what they called the School of the Prophets, where they studied Latin, Hebrew, astronomy, and scripture. Brigham Young established a college in Salt Lake City soon after arriving in the West. Towards the end of his life, a school bearing his name was established in Provo. Today, there are four Church colleges and universities and at least seventeen elementary and preparatory schools around the world. The Church Educational System includes seminaries and institutes in some 140 countries of the world for youth and adults.

"Education and literacy are keys to personal growth, preparation for employment, building strong families, service in the Church, and making a meaningful contribution to the society in which we live."[1]

That God encourages us to learn of things both secular and spiritual enables us to grow, expand our enjoyments, and reason more effectively.

"The glory of God is intelligence" (D&C 93:36) is a doctrinal summation of why education is an important emphasis in the Restored Church of Jesus Christ. Such inspired counsel has indeed expanded my enjoyments in this mortal journey.

Notes:

1. "Lifelong Learning: Education and Literacy," www.mormon.org/values/learning.

76. Remission of sin through the Atonement of Christ is operative only to the repentant.

Consider the following two scriptures:

> "Behold, I have come unto the world to bring redemption unto the world, to save the world from sin" (3 Nephi 9:21).

> "Who is he that shall come? Is it the Son of God? And he said unto him, Yea. And Zeezrom said again: Shall he save his people in their sins? And Amulek answered and said unto him: I say unto you he shall not, for it is impossible for him to deny his word. . . . I say unto you again that he cannot save them in their sins; for I cannot deny his word, and he hath said that no unclean thing can inherit the kingdom of heaven; therefore, how can ye be saved, except ye inherit the kingdom of heaven? Therefore, ye cannot be saved in your sins" (Alma 11:32-37).

It is imperative to understand that Jesus saves us *from* our sins, but not *in* our sins. The point here is that we can't be unrepentant and wanton sinners and expect Jesus to just deal with it. His divine Sonship, His perfect Atonement, and His infinite love are all sufficient for the sins and sufferings of mankind and satisfy the demands of justice where justice must be met. Personal redemption, though, the application of the Atonement in one's own life, is made effective "because of repentance" (Helaman 5:11).

Repentance includes the acknowledgement of our need for a divine Redeemer and the recognition of "a more excellent way" (Ether 12:11).

The apostle Paul cautioned us to be not deceived by false doctrines and taught, "Know ye not that the unrighteous shall not inherit the kingdom of God" (1 Corinthians 6:9)?

Jesus is the very Son of God, the Savior of all mankind, the promised Messiah. His sacrifice for all of God's children excludes no one. Only we ourselves can, in fact, exclude ourselves from the incomparable blessings of the Atonement.

"For behold, I, God, have suffered these things for all, that they might not suffer if they would repent; But if they would not repent, they must suffer even as I" (D&C 19:16-17).

"But if any man sin *and repent*, we have an advocate with the Father, Jesus Christ the righteous" (JST, 1 John 2:1).

No man can contribute to Christ's divine power to save. That we must be willing participants in our discipleship toward salvation just makes sense.

77. The Atonement is seen in Gethsemane, Golgotha, and Crowning Emmaus.

Central to Heavenly Father's plan of salvation, or the plan of happiness, is Jesus Christ's Atonement. "For God so loved the world, that he gave his only begotten Son . . . that the world through him might be saved" (John 3:16-17).

The fulfillment of the Atonement began in the Garden of Gethsemane where Jesus took upon himself the pains, sicknesses, temptations, afflictions, and infirmities of us all (Alma 7:11-12). Luke records the awful reality of that experience, which only the very Son of God could or would endure, and only by whom a perfect atonement for others could be made. "Father, if thou be willing, remove this cup from me: nevertheless not my will, but thine, be done. And being in an agony he prayed more earnestly: and his sweat was as it were great drops of blood falling down to the ground" (Luke 22:42, 44).

This act of infinite mercy for all men, was immediately followed by the wholly undeserved sacrifice of His life by crucifixion on Golgotha. As the Son of God, Jesus had the power to save Himself from this cruel treatment, "Nevertheless, glory be to the Father, and I partook and finished my preparations unto the children of men" (D&C 19:19). From the time of Adam down to this sinless sacrifice for sin by the Son of God, all ancient rites of animal sacrifice have been but a type and a foreshadowing of Christ's sacrifice (see Moses 5:5-8).

But the miracle of Christ did not end with His crucifixion. Subsequent to His burial, an angel at the tomb declared, "He is risen" (Matthew 28:6). Mary, the apostles, and scores of others testified that Jesus who once was dead, now lived. The glorious resurrection for all mankind was ushered in by the victory over death wrought by the Son of God.

The Atonement included His suffering in the Garden of Gethsemane and His suffering and death on the cross. "His rising from death on the third day crowned the Atonement."[1] Thus, did Jesus triumph over spiritual death (sin which would keep us from God's presence) and physical death.

The Crucifixion is the focal act of Christian worship, but not to include a reverent understanding of what Jesus actually did for our salvation in the Garden of Gethsemane is to greatly err. And to not see His resurrection as the capstone of His divine mission of salvation would be to disconnect from the full understanding of His Atonement.

"Behold, I say unto you that ye shall have hope through the atonement of Christ and the power of his resurrection, to be raised unto life eternal" (Moroni 7:41).

Such hope is perfectly placed.

Notes:

1. Bruce R. McConkie, "The Purifying Power of Gethsemane," *Ensign*, May, 1985.

78. There must be opposition in all things.

As the Prophet Lehi instructed his son Jacob concerning "redemption [which] cometh in and through the Holy Messiah" (2 Nephi 2:6), it was necessary to explain the law of "opposition in all things" (2 Nephi 2:11). This beautiful and lucid doctrine helps us to endure trials, to recognize the seductive influence of evil, and to enable the joy and happiness which comes from contrast and experience.

"For it must needs be, that there is an opposition in all things. If not so, my first-born in the wilderness, righteousness could not be brought to pass, neither wickedness, neither holiness nor misery, neither good nor bad. Wherefore, all things must needs be a compound in one; wherefore, if it should be one body it must needs remain as dead, having no life neither death, nor corruption nor incorruption, happiness nor misery, neither sense nor insensibility" (2 Nephi 2:11).

Lehi then gave this very logical argument, "Wherefore, it must needs have been created for a thing of naught; wherefore there would have been no purpose in the end of its creation. . . . And if ye shall say there is no law, ye shall also say there is no sin. If ye shall say there is no sin, ye shall also say there is no righteousness. And if there be no righteousness there be no happiness. And if there be no righteousness nor happiness there be no punishment nor misery. And if these things are not there is no God. And if there is no God we are not, neither the earth; for there could have been no creation of things, neither to act nor to be acted upon; wherefore, all things must have vanished away" (2 Nephi 2:12-13).

Lehi explained that man is given to act for himself but could not do so unless he were "enticed by the one or the other" (2 Nephi 2:16). He told of how Satan became the devil and seeks the misery of all men. The temptation of Mother Eve is highlighted with its inherent consequences and then contrasted with the merciful redemption wrought by the Messiah. Finally, in summary, Lehi concluded with a plea to "look to the great Mediator, and hearken to his great commandments" (2 Nephi 2:28).

One of my personal favorite scriptures on our mortal condition and the law of opposite influences is when Lehi taught: "Wherefore, men are free according to the flesh; and all things are given them which are expedient unto man. And they are free to choose liberty and eternal life, through the great Mediator of all men, or to choose captivity and death, according to the captivity and power of the devil; for he seeketh that all men might be miserable like unto himself" (2 Nephi 2:27).

To understand the law of opposites and the reality of good and evil help us to conduct ourselves with a discerning spirit, a careful outlook, and a patient understanding. This Book of Mormon father to son exchange is, I believe, a priceless gem to help us on our mortal journey.

79. The commandment to be perfect has not been rescinded, nor is it unattainable.

After delivering the equivalent of the Sermon on the Mount to the Nephites, Jesus instructed them, and all of us, "Therefore I would that ye should be perfect even as I, or your Father who in heaven is perfect" (3 Nephi 12:48). Later in his ministry to the Nephites, he asked and answered, "Therefore, what manner of men ought ye to be? Verily I say unto you, even as I am" (3 Nephi 27:27).

The pursuit of such a lofty end is in itself a process. A football team works on fundamentals over and over in the hope of playing a game with zero mistakes. Inevitably, when the game is played, the team still makes mistakes. But the frequency of those mistakes is minimized and the potential for success is maximized by the very diligence given to the pursuit of excellence, or perfection.

As mortals, we will not attain perfection in all its forms while in this earthly sojourn. But we can envision it, and then desire it. These are the first steps towards such an end. As with all things, this desire must be tempered by the reality of our condition and the need for a Redeemer to "putteth off the natural man and becometh a saint through the atonement of Christ the Lord" (Mosiah 3:19).

Let us not forget that perfection can be attained in some forms while in this life. For example, we can be perfect in not using vulgar or profane language, perfect as a tithe payer, and perfect in our observance of the Word of Wisdom. We can conduct ourselves in perfect honesty, chastity, or attending Sunday worship services. Perfect obedience to these commandments provide immediate blessings to those who so live.

The contrary argument to the invitation and mandate of the Lord to "be ye therefore perfect" (Matthew 5:48) is, in my view, a side-step from personal responsibility and the hard work of becoming like the Master. To develop and cultivate a "broken heart and a contrite spirit" (D&C 59:8, 97:8) is never going to be the cover story of popular magazines. To only partially define the gospel use of "mercy" and "grace," as solely being acted upon, will leave us short of the most intimate, refining opportunity to prayerfully come to know the Lord and seek to truly emulate him. Such emulation of a Divine Being will eventually yield those perfect behaviors.

I'm grateful for a Church that encourages this process of continuous improvement, that recognizes the ultimate role of the grace of Christ, and that tempers to reality that we "should not run faster than we have strength" (Mosiah 4:27). The Church keeps our vision squarely on a Perfect Master.

80. Angels are real beings who minister to mankind.

Angels seem plausible to many people when spoken of in a time and place removed, but few will acknowledge their personal ministry in the present. We declare that angels continue to minister to man and that much of the work of restoring the Church to the earth in these latter days was done by angels.

Angels are messengers from the realm of God to minister to mankind on the earth. They are manifest in bodily form (resurrected) or in unembodied form (in spirit state). Elder Jeffrey R. Holland has written the following as illustrative of the work of angels:

> "When the time for the Savior's advent was at hand, an angel was sent to announce to Mary that she was to be the mother of the Son of God (Luke 1:26-38). Then a host of angels was commissioned to sing on the night the baby Jesus was born (Luke 2:8-14). Shortly thereafter an angel would announce to Joseph that the newborn baby was in danger and that this little family must flee to Egypt for safety (Matthew 2:13-15). When it was safe to return, an angel conveyed that information to the family, and the three returned to the land of their heritage (Matthew 2:19-23)."[1]

Elder Holland went on to point out, "From the beginning down through the dispensations, God has used angels as His emissaries in conveying love and concern for His children."[2]

After the sacred theophany experienced by Joseph Smith in 1820, the subsequent unfolding of the Restoration of the Gospel took place through heavenly messengers. Moroni, John the Baptist, Peter, James, John, Moses, Elijah, and Elias all ministered to Joseph Smith as angels.[3] They brought priesthood and priesthood keys to the earth once again, delivered up the plates containing the Book of Mormon, and conveyed important instructions and understanding to the Prophet Joseph Smith. "Has the day of miracles ceased? Or have angels ceased to appear unto the children of men? Or has he withheld the power of the Holy Ghost from them? Or will he, so long as time shall last, or the earth shall stand, or there shall be one man upon the face thereof to be saved? Behold I say unto you, Nay; for . . . it is by faith that angels appear and minister unto men. . . . For behold, they are subject unto [Christ], to minister according to the word of his command, showing themselves unto them of strong faith and a firm mind in every form of godliness" (Moroni 7:35-37, 30).

We believe in the role and reality of angels anciently and that God continues that ministering pattern today.

Notes:

1. Jeffrey R. Holland, "The Ministry of Angels," *Ensign,* November, 2008.
2. Jeffrey R. Holland.
3. LDS Bible Dictionary, "Angels."

81. All people, throughout history, share common human conditions and experiences.

Our missionaries go into all the world, among various religions, cultures, educational and economic levels, political systems, and social norms. Their message is consistent and uniform in its application to the human experience. Among other truths, we teach that:

- God is our Heavenly Father, and all people are his spirit offspring (Genesis 1:27)
- Jesus Christ is the Son of God, the Savior of all mankind (John 14:6)

- All have lived pre-mortally as spirits, and all will be physically resurrected to live immortally
- Prayer and personal revelation are inherent opportunities to those who humbly seek
- Joseph Smith is a prophet in a long line of prophets who have walked the earth
- The Book of Mormon is another testament of Jesus Christ
- There are living prophets and apostles on the earth today
- Each individual is responsible for his or her own responses, choices, actions, and behaviors
- This life is the time for men to prepare to meet God (Alma 34:32-34)
- Covenants with God are essential to bring us back to His presence (John 3:5)

Some argue that there are no absolute truths that span the human condition in all the world and in all times. They would argue that there could be no universal set of expectations that would apply to human happiness, no common sense of morality. Yet, as spirit children of the same Heavenly Father, unique as we each are, we indeed share some very fundamental similarities, yearnings, and sense of decency.

As testament to the acceptance of eternal truths, the Church today has members in some 165 countries of the world, which is approximately eighty-three percent of all sovereign nations. Converts come from all walks of life: the humble conditions of the Philippines, the isolation of Mongolia, the isles of the South Pacific, metropolitan Hong Kong, developing Africa and India, Japan, South America, and Australia. The message of the restored gospel is one of universal application to human happiness. Jesus Christ is indeed the Savior of all mankind.

As diverse as we are by race, nationality, culture, time, and place, yet we, in fact, share our divine heritage and, therefore, our divinely placed attributes. The success of our missionary program speaks well of the brotherhood of man and of universal human yearnings.

82. Man is not inherently evil but is endowed with the Spirit of Christ.

Many take the position that man is inherently evil from birth, either because of original sin or because of the nature of this world. But the apostle John spoke of "the true Light (Christ), which lighteth every man that cometh into the world" (John 1:9).

It is true that the nature of this world will influence the natural man to choose evil, but it still remains a choice. "For behold, the Spirit of Christ is given to every man, that he may know good from evil" (Moroni 7:16).

"Wherefore, men are free according to the flesh; and all things are given them which are expedient unto man. And they are free to choose liberty and eternal life, through the great Mediator of all men, or to choose captivity and death, according to the captivity and power of the devil; for he seeketh that all men might be miserable like unto himself" (2 Nephi 2:27).

Each person is given the Spirit of Christ, which is light. We can refer to this as our conscience. "This light of Christ is just what the words imply: enlightenment, knowledge, and an uplifting, ennobling, persevering influence that comes upon mankind because of Jesus Christ."[1]

This light, or influence of Christ, is not the same as the Holy Ghost. The Holy Ghost is a personage of spirit whose influence and companionship can be confirmed upon an individual as a gift (following the ordinance of baptism) or can be felt as a power (usually as a witness to truth).

Perhaps the most convincing evidence that man is not born inherently evil is in the form of a baby or a child. Even the most crusty of men are for a moment made soft by a one-on-one encounter with a young child.

"Every spirit of man was innocent in the beginning; and God having redeemed man from the fall, men became again, in their infant state, innocent before God" (D&C 93:38). Truly, man is born in innocence and acquires the traits and character of his chosen habits. By this knowledge, The Church of Jesus Christ of Latter-day Saints teaches us to see our fellows as inherently good and to inspire and/or reclaim that goodness, as the case may be.

Notes:

1. LDS Bible Dictionary, "Light of Christ."

83. Anointing with consecrated oil is done to administer a blessing to the sick.

An anointment to the sick is done under the authority of the priesthood, using holy consecrated olive oil. Jesus sent forth the twelve apostles, and among other charges, they were to "anoint with oil many that were sick, and heal them" (Mark 6:13).

James wrote, "Is any sick among you? Let him call for the elders of the church; and let them pray over him, anointing him with oil in the name of the Lord. And the prayer of faith shall save the sick" (James 5:14-15).

Anointing is used scripturally as a sign of hospitality (Luke 7:46), routine grooming (2 Samuel 12:20), setting apart to an office (Exodus 30:30, 1 Samuel 10:1), and to sanctify and set apart certain religious emblems (Exodus 30:25-29). Jesus himself was referred to as being anointed "to preach good tidings unto the meek" (Isaiah 61:1).

But anointing the sick is a priesthood administration that requires a separate sealing of the anointing and allows for words of blessing, all through the laying on of hands by one or more priesthood bearers. It is subject to "the prayer of faith" (James 5:15), and ultimately, will align with the will of the Lord. Jesus repeated to those who were healed on several occasions throughout his ministry, "Thy faith hath made thee whole" (Mark 5:34, Luke 17:19, Mark 10:52, Luke 8:48, Matthew 9:22, Enos 1:8).

Regarding the will of the Lord, Elder Dallin H. Oaks, an apostle, teaches, "We learn that even the servants of the Lord, exercising His divine power in a circumstance where there is sufficient faith to be healed, cannot give a priesthood blessing that will cause a person to be healed if that healing is not the will of the Lord."[1] He also said, "When elders anoint a sick person and seal the anointing, they open the windows of heaven for the Lord to pour forth the blessing He wills for the person afflicted."[2]

Anointing the sick is a demonstration of faith in the priesthood and of trust in the Lord. It enables and can facilitate the healing that is so desired. It is a priesthood ordinance that blesses both the giver and the receiver and is ordained of God.

Notes:

1. Dallin H. Oaks, "Healing the Sick," *Ensign,* May, 2010.
2. Dallin H. Oaks.

84. Elohim is the exalted Hebrew name-title used to denote God the Father.

Although familiar to us as Latter-day Saints, the name-title of Elohim is not found in the King James version of the Bible.

"El" is the Hebrew word for God (singular) and Elohim (or Eloheim), constitutes the plural form. Such plural usage is correctly used in reference to the Creation, as we know that Jesus is the Creator, under the direction of God the Father. "Jesus Christ, whom we also know as Jehovah, was the executive of the father, Elohim, in the work of creation."[1] "Elohim" in its plural form also connotes God the Father's supremacy and omnipotence.[2]

Similarly, T.E. McComiskey has written, "When God is presented in relation to his creation and to the peoples of the earth in the Pentateuch, the name Elohim is the name most often used. It is for this reason that Elohim occurs consistently in the creation account of Gen. 1:1-2:42 and in the genealogies of Genesis."[3]

Significant is our doctrinal understanding that God the Father and Jesus Christ the Messiah are separate and distinct individuals, yet one in purpose, objective, and desire.

In 1916, under the administration of Joseph F. Smith, the First Presidency and the Quorum of the Twelve felt it was necessary to clarify the doctrine of the Father and the Son. This 4,189 word document defines the roles, titles, and relationships of Heavenly Father and Jesus Christ. In that document is stated our belief regarding Elohim, "God the Father, whom we designate by the exalted name-title of 'Elohim.'"[4]

From that authoritative declaration to the present, our understanding of Elohim, meaning God the Father, has not been in question.

I am less interested in all of the semantics (although I do find them important to understand as it relates to our espoused doctrine), as I am in the actual, personal relationship we have with our Heavenly Father. He is the object of our prayers. He lives. He loves all of His children. And by formal name, He is Elohim.

Notes:

1. "The Father and the Son: A Doctrinal Exposition by the First Presidency and the Quorum of the Twelve Apostles," *Improvement Era,* August, 1916, reprinted *Ensign,* April, 2002

2. Bruce R. McConkie, *Mormon Doctrine,* "Elohim," Salt Lake City: Bookcraft, 2nd ed, 1966, 224.

3. T.E. McComiskey, "Names of God: The Theological Significance of Divine Names: Elohim," www.mb-soft.com/believe/txh/namesgod.htm.

4. "The Father and the Son: A Doctrinal Exposition by the First Presidency and the Quorum of the Twelve Apostles."

85. Lucifer became the devil, called Satan.

Satan was not created evil, but by his own choices and hard-headed positioning, he "rebelled against [God] and sought to destroy the agency of man" (Moses 4:3). The Prophet Lehi said, "That an angel of God, according to that which is written, had fallen from heaven; wherefore, he became a devil, having sought that which was evil before God" (2 Nephi 2:17).

Prior to the peopling of the earth and revolving on the need of mortal man to have a Savior, the following dialogue reveals motives, both selfish and sublime:

> "And I the Lord God, spake unto Moses, saying: That Satan . . . is the same which was from the beginning, and he came before me, saying—Behold, here am I, send me, I will be thy son, and I will redeem all mankind, that one soul shall not be lost, and surely I will do it; wherefore give me thine honor.
>
> But, behold, my Beloved Son, which was my Beloved and Chosen from the beginning, said unto me—Father, thy will be done, and the glory be thine forever.
>
> Wherefore, because that Satan rebelled against me, and sought to destroy the agency of man, which I, the Lord God, had given him, and also, that I should give unto him mine

> own power; by the power of mine Only Begotten, I caused that he should be cast down; And he became Satan, yea, even the devil, the father of all lies, to deceive and to blind men, and to lead them captive at his will, even as many as would not hearken unto my voice" (Moses 4:1-4).

Satan, no doubt by his sophistry, did not go out alone. "And there was a war in heaven; Michael and his angels fought against the dragon; and the dragon fought and his angels, and prevailed not. . . . He was cast out into the earth, and his angels were cast out with him" (Revelation 12:7-9). For a perspective on the number of the devil's angels, the Lord said, "For he rebelled against me, saying, Give me thine honor, which is my power; and also a third part of the hosts of heaven turned he away from me because of their agency; And they were thrust down, and thus came the devil and his angels" (D&C 29:36-37).

A summary of the above is recorded in the book of Abraham, "And the Lord said: Whom shall I send? And one answered like unto the Son of Man: Here am I, send me. And another answered and said: Here am I, send me. And the Lord said: I will send the first. And the second was angry, and kept not his first estate; and, at that day, many followed after him" (Abraham 3:27-28).

And in apparent astonishment, Isaiah declared, "How thou art fallen from heaven, O Lucifer, son of the morning" (Isaiah 14:12)!

Lucifer became the devil, in large part, by his purely selfish desires, his disregard for the agency of man to choose for themselves, his wanting to control and manipulate mankind, and his refusal to allow any risk of failure or imperfection.

God could never create evil. Instead, it had to be a falling from grace, by Lucifer's own choices. Latter-day scripture gives much needed understanding of the scriptural references to Lucifer and the dragon found in Isaiah and the Book of Revelation.

86. All things were created spiritually before they were created physically.

"The Lord God made the earth and the heavens, And every plant of the field before it was in the earth, and every herb of the field before it grew" (Genesis 2:4-5). Another scripture further clarifies, "And every plant of the field before it was in the earth, and every herb of the field before it grew. For I, the Lord God, created all things, of which I have spoken, spiritually, before they were naturally upon the face of the earth" (Moses 3:5). Man also was created under this divine pattern, as the same verse goes on to state, "And I, the Lord God, had created all the children of men; and not yet a man to till the ground; for in heaven created I them; and there was not yet flesh upon the earth, neither in the water, neither in the air" (Moses 3:5).

All forms of living things—man, animals, and vegetation—existed as individual spirits, before any form of life existed upon the earth. In this spiritual state, that "form" is in the likeness of the physical entity.

"And the Gods [God the Father and Jesus Christ] formed man from the dust of the ground, and took his spirit [that is, the man's spirit], and put it into him; and breathed into his nostrils the breath of life, and man became a living soul" (Abraham 5:7).

The following truths lend much to our understanding:

> "There is no such thing as immaterial matter. All spirit is matter, but it is more fine or pure, and can only be discerned by purer eyes; We cannot see it; but when our bodies are purified we shall see that it is all matter" (D&C 131:7).
>
> "For by the power of my Spirit created I them; yea, all things both spiritual and temporal— First spiritual, secondly temporal" (D&C 29:31-32).

To me, this is an important understanding of how the Lord works—how spiritual form took place before physical form, and that spiritual form is actually a material matter, as well. It may not be a saving doctrine, but latter-day scripture clarifies the opening verses of Genesis as quoted above. Our Heavenly Father is the Master Architect.

87. When God the Father has spoken publicly, it has been to bear record of the Son.

Jesus Christ is the God of the Old Testament, and it is He who is referenced when Abraham, Jacob, Moses, the Elders of Israel, Job, Manoah and his wife, and others are recorded as seeing God. The Joseph Smith Translation may help with this. "And no man hath seen God at any time, except he hath borne record of the Son; for except it is through him no man can be saved" (JST, John 1:18).

Who hath borne record of the Son? An individual who has seen God or God the Father? I don't know the answer to that, but if the latter, it is in harmony with a pattern of introduction and approval throughout the scriptures.

That pattern holds true in each of the recorded instances I know of that refer to the Father's manifestation to His children by audible voice or in vision. These instances are:

- When Jesus was baptized. Then, came the "voice from heaven, saying, This is my beloved Son, in whom I am well pleased" (Matthew 3:17).
- On the mountain of the transfiguration of Jesus before Peter, James, and John. "And while he (Peter) yet spake, behold, a bright cloud overshadowed them; and behold a voice out of the cloud, which said, "This is my beloved Son, in whom I am well pleased; hear ye him" (Matthew 17:5).
- Speaking of his impending Sacrifice, Jesus pleaded with the Father to "glorify thy name. Then came a voice from heaven, saying, I have both glorified it, and will glorify

it again. . . . Jesus answered [the people] and said, This voice came not because of me, but for your sakes" (John 12:28, 30).

- When Jesus appeared to the people in the Americas. "And they did look steadfastly towards heaven, from whence the sound came . . . and it said unto them: "Behold my Beloved Son, in whom I am well pleased, in whom I have glorified my name—hear ye him" (3 Nephi 11:7).

- To Nephi. "And I heard a voice from the Father, saying; Yea, the words of my Beloved are true and faithful" (2 Nephi 31:15).

- To the Prophet Joseph Smith in the year 1820. "When the light rested upon me I saw two Personages, whose brightness and glory defy all description, standing above me in the air. One of them spake unto me, calling me by name and said, pointing to the other—This is My Beloved Son. Hear Him" (Joseph Smith History 1:17)!

- In an 1832 vision to Joseph Smith and Sidney Rigdon. "For we saw him, even on the right hand of God; and we heard the voice bearing record that he is the Only Begotten of the Father" (D&C 76:20, 23).

The pattern of God the Father introducing His Son to mortal beings is a consistent and insightful understanding recorded in each of the four standard works of scripture. He is clearly commending, and pointing us toward, our personal Savior.

88. Adam and Eve exercised choice but did not sin against God in the Garden of Eden.

It is an unfortunate and sorry misunderstanding of the purposes and perfections of God, to attribute the fall of Adam to a sinful act. The Garden of Eden was a place of perfect, immortal status, "And all things which were created must have remained in the same state in which they were after they were created; and they must have remained forever, and had no end" (2 Nephi 2:22).

God, being perfect, would not and could not, command Adam and Eve to descend from their immortal state to a lesser mortal state. Such a transition from a paradisiacal existence to a mortal existence must be brought about by their own doing. In the wisdom of a loving Father, God gave two commandments to our first parents, which appear to be in conflict with one another: 1) not to partake of the fruit of the tree of knowledge of good and evil, and 2) to multiply and replenish (fill) the earth. While in the Garden, they did not have the capacity for procreation, which apparently was a condition of mortality. "And now, behold, if Adam had not transgressed he would not have fallen, but he would have remained in the Garden of Eden. . . . And they would have had no children" (2 Nephi 2:22-23).

The choice of Eve to partake of the fruit of the tree of knowledge of good and evil, I believe, was born of her intuition and selfless desire to enable the human race. It is scripturally recorded that she subsequently "was glad," saying, "Were it not for our transgressions we never should have had seed, and never should have known good and evil, and the joy of our redemption, and the eternal life which God giveth unto all the obedient" (Moses 5:11). Adam said, "Blessed be the name of God, for because of my transgression my eyes are opened, and in this life I shall have joy, and again in the flesh I shall see God" (Moses 5:10).

To have remained in the Garden would have frustrated the entire Plan of Salvation. There would be no need for an atonement, no need for a Savior, no opportunity to choose between good and evil, no mortal experience for mankind. "Wherefore they would have remained in a state of innocence, having no joy, for they knew no misery; doing no good, for they knew no sin. But behold, all things have been done in the wisdom of him who knoweth all things. Adam fell that men might be; and men are, that they might have joy" (2 Nephi 2:23-25).

Adam and Eve are to be held in honor for their role in the opening scene of mortality. It was they who activated the very plan of God, which would enable all succeeding generations of mankind and result in eventual joy. The Church of Jesus Christ of Latter-day Saints holds Adam and Eve in the highest regard for their selfless, courageous role as our first parents.

89. The observance of the Sabbath day brings delight.

The commandment to "Remember the Sabbath day, to keep it holy" (Exodus 20:8) is not taken very seriously in the world today. Sunday has become a day of sports, political analysis, shopping, mowing the yard, boating, camping, recreation, and more. While all of these activities are worthy of our attention and engagement, they crowd out and frustrate the purpose of the Sabbath day as the Lord has provided for His children.

Verses nine and ten of Exodus specifically command us not to work on Sunday. To support that command, the Church teaches us not to shop on the Sabbath. That act causes others to work. Sabbath observance used to be understood and widely kept, and for many years it was a common business practice among retailers not to open on Sunday.

It is wisdom in the Lord that there be set aside a day each week for man to rest from his temporal labors, to ponder and refresh in the spiritual realities, and to assemble for public worship.

We learn from the early Jewish experience of the Sabbath, that while casual observance is not true worship, neither is ritualistic over-governance by defined rules. Jesus demonstrated this to the lawfully rigid Pharisees, knowing that He would draw their condemnation when His disciples picked ears of corn, presumably to assuage their hunger. Jesus furthered this lesson, by immediately entering into a synagogue and healing a man with a withered hand, also on the same Sabbath day. On another occasion, the Savior taught, "Which of you shall have an ass or an ox fallen into a pit, and will not straightway pull him out on the Sabbath day" (Luke 14:5)? The summation of these lessons is that "the Sabbath was made for man, and not man for the Sabbath" (Mark 2:24-27, 3:1-6).

Isaiah observed that we would "call the Sabbath a delight" if we would not seek "from doing thy pleasure on my holy day," and "not doing thine own ways, nor finding thine own pleasure, nor speaking thine own words" (Isaiah 58:13).

"And that thou mayest more fully keep thyself unspotted from the world, thou shalt go to the house of prayer and offer up thy sacraments upon my holy day; For verily this is a day appointed unto you to rest from your labors, and to pay thy devotions unto the Most High. . . Verily, this is fasting and prayer, or in other words, rejoicing and prayer" (D&C 59:9-10, 14).

My family and I have benefitted greatly from trying to follow the commandment to keep the Sabbath Day holy. In practice, I have found it to be more about our heart and worshipful attitude than it is about our rigid compliance. I'm grateful for the teachings of the Church that highlight and make the Sabbath Day a priority. I can honestly call the Sabbath a delight.

90. Charity prevents a multitude of sins.

The King James version of the New Testament states, "And above all things have fervent charity among yourselves: for charity shall cover the multitude of sins" (1 Peter 4:8). Significantly, the Joseph Smith Translation is written, "For charity *preventeth* a multitude of sins" (JST, 1 Peter 4:8, emphasis added).

The judgment bar will not be a weights and balance mechanism where good works offset the bad one-for-one. Rather, what will determine how we exercised our stewardship here in mortality will be by what we have become.

Charity edifieth (1 Corinthians 8:1). Charity is the pure love of Christ (Moroni 7:47). Charity is inextricably linked with faith and hope (Moroni 7:42-44). Charity brings confidence, understanding, knowledge, the Holy Ghost, and authority (D&C 121:45). Charity is essential to be saved in the kingdom of God (Moroni 10:21). Charity never faileth (1 Corinthians 13:8). And if that isn't enough material to build a noble character, then add these ideas, "And charity suffereth long, and is kind, and envieth not, and is not puffed up, seeketh not her own, is not easily provoked, thinketh no evil, and rejoiceth not in iniquity but rejoiceth in the truth, beareth all things, believeth all things, hopeth all things, endureth all things" (Moroni 7:45). Paul adds, "Charity vaunteth not itself . . . does not behave itself unseemly" (1 Corinthians 13:4-5).

Such conduct will indeed prevent a multitude of sins, as we become a new creature in Christ (2 Corinthians 5:17). It is not the desire of a true disciple to cover or hide his sins, but rather to overcome them, to lay them aside, to "have the gates of hell be shut continually before him" (2 Nephi 4:32). Such a life will eventually bring us to where "we shall be like him" (Moroni 7:48).

Avoiding sin is the best course. Preventing it from coming into our lives is pro-active. Charity is a vital component in that prevention. The Joseph Smith Translation contains powerful counsel to enable us to avert the woes of sin and to turn ourselves to more Christ-like behavior.

91. The Lord will not lead us into temptation or to the devil's influence.

"Then was Jesus led up of the Spirit into the wilderness to be tempted of the devil" (Matthew 4:1). The Joseph Smith Translation corrects the last six words to read "to be with God." (JST, Matthew 4:1).

This is a very significant correction and understanding. Jesus, always under the influence of the Holy Spirit, would not seek out the devil, and worse, seek to place Himself to be subject to the devil's tempting influences.

Usually, the scriptural use of tempting or temptation is in the context of wickedness. There are also recorded instances of faithless individuals who tempt the Lord God, or challenge Him, wanting to test or prove His power. Christ was tempted of both the devil and his surrogates, who tried through their carefully crafted questions to get Him to take the bait. Although the devil knew him as the Christ, his surrogates knew not with whom they dealt.

Jesus' tutorial on the manner and form of prayer includes, "Lead us not into temptation, but deliver us from evil" (Matthew 6:13). Recognizing that the Lord would never lead us into temptation, the Joseph Smith Translation of that same verse reads, "And suffer us not to be led into temptation" (JST, Matthew 6:13). In the oft-repeated Psalm 23 we read where the Lord will always lead us, "He leadeth me in the paths of righteousness for his name's sake" (Psalms 23:3).

In the course of life, we will encounter temptations which are inherent to this world in which we live. "And it must needs be that the devil should tempt the children of men, or they could not be agents unto themselves; for if they never should have bitter they could not know the sweet (D&C 29:39).

Heavenly Father allows us to be tempted, "but God will not suffer us to be tempted above that which we can bear." Not that He will forcibly deliver us, but "will with the temptation, also make a way to escape, that we may be able to bear it" (1 Corinthians 10:13).

We also have the assurance that "the Lord knoweth how to deliver the godly out of temptations" (2 Peter 2:9).

It is powerful knowledge to know from where come the temptations that can have harmful effects upon us and also to know to whom we should look for deliverance from those temptations. The Joseph Smith Translation consistently teaches that it is not the Lord who brings us temptation, but it is His work to deliver us out of temptations.

92. The infrequent Biblical use of the name Jehovah is clarified by latter-day revelation.

The LDS understanding that Jesus is the God of the Old Testament, the God of Israel, Jehovah, seems to draw some debate among our brothers and sisters. Understandably so, if the Bible is to be taken alone as divine canon. Latter-day prophets, the Book of Mormon, and the Book of Abraham, make clear that "Jehovah is the premortal Jesus Christ, and came to earth being born of Mary."[1]

There are only four explicit references to the proper name Jehovah in the Bible, all in the Old Testament. Additionally in Psalms, David tells us to extol JAH, which is clarified as Jesus Christ, Jehovah, in the footnotes. The four are as follows:

> "That men may know that thou, whose name alone is Jehovah, art the most high over all the earth" (Psalms 83:18).
>
> "Behold, God is my salvation; I will trust, and not be afraid: for the Lord Jehovah is my strength and my song; he also is become my salvation" (Isaiah 12:2).
>
> "Trust ye in the Lord for ever: for in the Lord Jehovah is everlasting strength" (Isaiah 26:4).
>
> "And I appeared unto Abraham, unto Isaac, and unto Jacob, by *the name of* God Almighty, but by my name Jehovah was I not known to them" (Exodus 6:3).

The Joseph Smith Translation of this verse in Exodus sheds important light and proper context. "And I appeared unto Abraham, unto Isaac, and unto Jacob. I am the Lord God Almighty; the

Lord Jehovah. And was not my name known unto them" (JST, Exodus 6:3)?

In fact, we know the name of Jehovah *was* known to those prior to Moses' time (Abraham 1:16, 2:8). The writings of Paul to the Corinthians support an understanding that Jesus was the God of Israel, the Jehovah of the Old Testament (see 1 Corinthians 10:1-4).

Living prophets and apostles teach that "He [Jesus] was the Great Jehovah of the Old Testament, the Messiah of the New."[2]

When Joseph and Oliver saw the resurrected Lord in the Kirtland Temple, it was "the voice of Jehovah" (D&C 110:3-4) that declared Himself as our advocate with the Father.

We believe that God the Father and the Lord Jesus Christ are two separate and distinct beings. That doctrine is uncommon or perhaps unique in Christian theology. We further believe each is known by His covenant or proper name – Elohim and Jehovah.

Jesus is the Savior of all mankind. It is He who led His people and gave counsel and commandments from Adam to the present day. He is the referenced Jehovah. We are fortunate to have prophetic understanding of the Great Jehovah and His mission as the God of Israel.

Notes:

1. LDS Bible Dictionary, "Jehovah."
2. *The Living Christ: the Testimony of the Apostles,* The Church of Jesus Christ of Latter-day Saints, January 1, 2000.

93. Sin is inherent to our mortal experience.

Sin is and will be a constant of our lives. To minimize the frequency of and/or the repetitive patterns of sinful thoughts, actions, and attitudes is the quest of a devoted disciple. This liberating course leads to deeper joy and satisfaction, both now and in eternity.

"If we say that we have no sin, we deceive ourselves, and the truth is not in us" (1 John 1:8). John also defines sin very simply when he wrote, "For sin is the transgression of the law" (1 John 3:4). In other words, it is the transgression of the commandments of God and/or the laws of the universe. Elder James E. Talmage wrote, "Sin is any condition, whether omission of things required, or in commission of acts forbidden, that tends to prevent or hinder the development of the human soul."[1]

In the book of First John, the Joseph Smith Translation gives consistent clarity to what otherwise might be misunderstood in light of 1 John 1:8 quoted above. Here are two verses as they are written in First John, with the Joseph Smith translation in italics to the right:

1 John 3:9, King James Bible	1 John 3:9, Joseph Smith Translation
"Whosoever is born of God doth not commit sin; for his seed remaineth in him: and he cannot sin, because he is born of God.	*Whosoever is born of God doth not continue in sin; for the Spirit of God remaineth in him; and he cannot continue in sin, because he is born of God, having received that holy Spirit of promise."*

1 John 5:18, King James Bible	1 John 5:18, Joseph Smith Translation
"We know that whosoever is born of God sinneth not; but he that is begotten of God keepeth himself, and that wicked one toucheth him not." (1 John 5:18)	*"We know that whosoever is born of God continueth not in sin; but he that is begotten of God and keepeth himself, that wicked one overcometh him not."*

Disciples of Christ will not seek to *continue* in sin. Our attitude will be as the experience of the people of King Benjamin when they were converted to Christ. "Because of the Spirit of the Lord Omnipotent, which has wrought a mighty change in us, or in our hearts, that we have no more disposition to do evil, but to do good continually" (Mosiah 5:2).

Faith on the Lord Jesus Christ and His Atonement and repentance keep us from continuing in sin. The same book of John says, "If we confess our sins, he is faithful and just to forgive us our sins, and to cleanse us from all unrighteousness" (1 John 1:9).

"My little children, these things write I unto you, that ye sin not. And if any man sin *and repent*, we have an advocate with the Father, Jesus Christ the righteous" (JST, 1 John 2:1, emphasis added).

I grew up in a world that adopted the saying, "If it feels good, do it." Those advocates would argue that there is no sin, that such classification of behavior is too subjective, too narrow, and that there is no universal moral code.

I believe there is a universal moral code. Prophets ancient and modern counsel us to live within this moral code. The understanding of sin and our ability to turn away by degree over the course of a lifetime and to be forgiven is empowering doctrine.

Notes:

1. James E. Talmage, *Articles of Faith,* Salt Lake City: The Church of Jesus Christ of Latter-day Saints, 1977, 52.

94. Under the direction of the Father, Jesus Christ created the heavens and the earth.

This truth is best understood in light of the following:

- God the Father and his Son Jesus Christ are separate and distinct beings
- Jesus is the God of the Old Testament

- The relationship of the Father and the Son include delegation, accountability, priesthood power, and complete unity

Scripturally, it is clear that the creation of the paradisiacal earth (and after the Fall, this telestial earth) and its attendant heavens was done by the pre-mortal Christ. I will cite some of those scriptures:

> "And he shall be called Jesus Christ, the Son of God, the Father of heaven and earth, the Creator of all things from the beginning; and his mother shall be called Mary" (Mosiah 3:8).
>
> "In the beginning was the Word . . . and the Word was with God. . . . All things were made by him" (John 1:1-3).
>
> "Which from the beginning of the world hath been hid in God, who created all things by Jesus Christ" (Ephesians 3:9).
>
> "I am the Beginning and the End, the Almighty God; by mine Only Begotten I created these things; yea, in the beginning I created the heaven, and the earth upon which thou standest" (Moses 2:1).
>
> "We will go down, for there is space there, and we will take of these materials, and we will make an earth whereon these may dwell" (Abraham 3:24).

The Lord has given at least three accounts of the Creation, each complementary and in harmony to the others—the Mosaic, the Abrahamic, and a part of the temple endowment. In addition, important doctrinal clarity is found in the New Testament and in the Doctrine and Covenants.

Elder Bruce R. McConkie answers the question of why this is important to understand:

> "An understanding of the doctrine of creation is essential to salvation. . . . This doctrine is that the Lord Jesus Christ is both the Creator and the Redeemer of this earth and all that on it is, save only man. It is that the Lord God himself, the Father of us all, came down and created man, male and female, in his own image and likeness. It is that the earth and all else were created

> in a paradisiacal state so there could be a fall. It is that the Great Creator became the Redeemer so he could ransom men from the effects of the Fall, thereby bringing to pass the immortality and eternal life of man. It is that the Creation, the Fall, and the Atonement are the three pillars of eternity. It is that all who accept him as both the Creator and the Redeemer have power to become joint-heirs with him and thereby inherit all that his Father hath."[1]

This role of Jesus as the Creator, under the direction of the Father, enlarges our understanding and deepens our worship. I agree with Elder McConkie. It is a truth essential to our salvation.

Notes:

1. Bruce R. McConkie, "Christ and the Creation," *Ensign*, June, 1982.

95. The work of the Lord and the work of man are clearly defined.

For all the effort, all the talk, all the expense, all the blood, sweat, and tears that are expended towards the subject of religion and personal religious faith, it would be wise to ask, "So what's the bottom line?" Why has such tremendous personal and collective energy been spent and to what end? Perhaps the question could better be presented in two parts:

1. What divine objective is God seeking?
2. What is the responsibility of man toward God?

The Lord's simple yet comprehensive answers to these questions are stated clearly and in various contexts throughout the scriptures. Elder David A. Bednar[1] has noted the following two verses as succinct summary statements found in the book of Moses and the Doctrine and Covenants:

"For behold, this is *my work* and my glory—to bring to pass the immortality and eternal life of man" (Moses 1:39, emphasis added).

"Behold, this is *your work*, to keep my commandments, yea with all your might, mind and strength" (D&C 11:20, emphasis added).

Immortality for all of God's children has been made a reality because of the Atonement of Jesus Christ. All will be resurrected and pass from this mortal state to an immortal state, unconditionally and unavoidably.

Eternal life (the quality of life that our Eternal Father lives, which includes the continuation of the family), in contrast, is conditional upon man's choices and behavior. Yet it is universal and unconditional in the fact that it is available to all of God's children, again, because of the Atonement of Christ.

These two summary statements of purpose (*my* work and *your* work) become circular and complementary by the Lord's promise, also found in the Doctrine and Covenants: "And, *if you keep my commandments* and endure to the end *you shall have eternal life*, which gift is the greatest of all the gifts of God" (D&C 14:7, emphasis added).

We then can become partners with God in bringing about his divine purposes. And the beneficiaries! Said King Benjamin, "He doth require that ye should do as he hath commanded you; for which if ye do, he doth immediately bless you; and therefore he hath paid you. And ye are still indebted unto him, and are, and will be, forever and ever; therefore, of what have ye to boast" (Mosiah 2:24)?

This then, becomes the ultimate Win/Win arrangement. Foolish is the man who won't take this deal.

Notes:

1. David A. Bednar, "The Tender Mercies of the Lord," *Ensign*, April, 2005.

96. The order of post-mortal life enlightens our understanding.

A universal yearning of the human soul is to understand what takes place after this mortal life. No one who has experienced birth will avoid the inevitability of the grave.

I like the title of a book that speaks about this inevitability, *The Birth We Call Death* by Paul H. Dunn and Richard M. Eyre because the title is, in reality, a very succinct nugget of truth. Sometimes, because there is so much conflict and differing dogma on this subject, some will conclude, as a last resort, that there is no post-mortal life at all.

To understand the sequence of events that will take place after passing from this life is both comforting and inspiring. To me, death is not something to be feared, but rather something to anticipate like the conclusion to a great contest with the score heavily in your favor.

The following sequence of events is confirmed and made clear through the prophets, both ancient and modern. It is only an overview, with selected moments and scriptural passages:

1. Death is the separation of the mortal body and the immortal spirit.

2. The human spirit goes to either paradise or prison (hell), a temporary first judgment (Alma 40:11-21).

3. The Millennium begins when Christ comes again (Revelation 20:4, D&C 29:11).

4. The resurrection will resume at Christ's coming (Matthew 27:52-53, 1 Corinthians 15:22-23, Revelation 20:1-6).

5. Celestial and Terrestrial worthy people will dwell on the earth during the Millennium (D&C 88:97-99).

6. The earth will be restored to its paradisiacal state during the Millennium (Articles of Faith, 10).

7. Missionary work (for the early years) and temple work will be a focus of the Millennium.[1]

8. The resurrection will recommence at the end of the Millennium for those then in the spirit world. (D&C 88:100-101, Mosiah 15:26).

9. Final judgment will then take place for all, to "be judged according to their works" (Revelation 20:11-15).

Death came into the world by the fall of Adam and Eve. Salvation, or deliverance from death, comes by the Atonement of Jesus Christ, the Son of God. Essential ordinances and associated covenants provide a means for our willing compliance and submission to the Lord's ways, thereby demonstrating our acceptance of the Atonement through our repentance and obedience.

These truths are more than just another plausible explanation of life after death. They are unchanging, eternal verities. And the Lord has seen fit in this final dispensation to give a sequence and an understanding to these final scenes that tie together the knowledge of all past dispensations.

Notes:

1. Joseph Fielding Smith, *Doctrines of Salvation,* vol. III, Salt Lake City: Bookcraft, 1956, 58, 64, 65.

97. Repentance can continue after death and prior to the final judgment.

God is not eager to consign us to hell, but rather by the mercy and grace of his Son, He has provided a way for our return to his presence. And if not to that exalted realm, to realms of lesser glories, but glories nonetheless. Prior to the Final Judgment, all who have ever lived in mortality will have had the opportunity to hear the Gospel of Jesus Christ and to show their obedience to it or their indifference or rejection of it. Their level of obedience and valiance to eternal truth will determine what they have become in totality.

The opportunity to hear the Gospel, in concert with the witness of the Holy Ghost, will be in this life, in the spirit world while awaiting the resurrection, or in the millennial period.

"We believe in a heaven or paradise and a hell following mortal life, but to us that two-part division of the righteous and the wicked is merely temporary, while the spirits of the dead await their resurrections and final judgments."[1]

During the time in the spirit world prior to the resurrection, the gospel will be preached by the righteous. Jesus initiated this, as recorded in 1 Peter, "By which also he went and preached unto the spirits in prison . . . that they might be judged according to men in the flesh, but live according to God in the spirit" (1 Peter 4:6).

By this preaching, "The dead who repent will be redeemed, through obedience to the ordinances of the house of God" (D&C 138:58).

"One of the greatest [truths] is that to hell [spirit prison] there is an exit as well as an entrance. Hell [spirit prison] is no place to which a vindictive judge sends prisoners to suffer and to be punished principally for his glory; But it is a place prepared for the teaching, the disciplining of those who failed to learn here upon the earth what they should have learned. . . . No man will be kept in hell [spirit prison] longer than is necessary to bring him to a fitness for something better. When he reaches that stage the prison doors will open and there will be rejoicing among the hosts who welcome him into a better state."[2]

Man will be given ample opportunity to "become the servants of righteousness" (Romans 6:16-18) whether in this life or in the life to come. But Alma cautions us, "This life is the time for men to prepare to meet God. . . . Do not procrastinate the day of your repentance. . . for that same spirit which doth possess your bodies at the time that ye go out of this life, that same spirit will have power to possess your body in that eternal world" (Alma 34:32-34).

James E. Talmage also gave such a caution, "To suppose that the soul who has willfully rejected the opportunity of repentance in this life will find it easy to repent there is contrary to reason. To procrastinate the day of repentance is to deliberately place ourselves in the power of the adversary."[3]

In other words, we only become a "new creature" in Christ (Galatians 6:15) when we avail ourselves of repentance, and the sooner the better.

How broad and comprehensive is the great Plan of Salvation, and how merciful and long-suffering is our Heavenly Father!

Notes:

1. Dallin H. Oaks, "Apostasy and Restoration," *Ensign,* May, 1995.
2. James E. Talmage, *Conference Report,* April, 1930, 97.
3. James E. Talmage, *Articles of Faith,* Salt Lake City: The Church of Jesus Christ of Latter-day Saints, 1977, 115.

98. The Resurrection will take place during at least five different periods of time.

Without exception, all who have ever lived on this earth will be resurrected. It is fundamental to my testimony of the divinity of Jesus Christ to know that He, in fact, rose from the dead and was the first to ever be resurrected.

"Now, there is a death which is called a temporal death; and the death of Christ shall loose the bands of this temporal death, that all shall be raised from this temporal death" (Alma 11:42).

"But now is Christ risen from the dead, and become the firstfruits of them that that slept. . . . But every man in his own order: Christ the firstfruits; afterward they that are Christ's at his coming" (1 Corinthians 15:20, 23).

This order of the resurrection will take place in two major resurrections, one for the just (numbers 1-4 below) and one for the unjust (numbers 5-6 below) including, but not limited to, the following:

1. The resurrection of Christ and those resurrected at that time- After Jesus was resurrected, it is recorded, "And the graves were opened; and many bodies of the saints which slept arose, And came out of the graves after his resurrection" (Matthew 27:52-53). "These were the righteous saints who had lived from the days of Adam to the time of his crucifixion."[1]

2. Those who will be resurrected at his Second Coming- When Christ comes again, He will come in glory, and those of a celestial nature will be resurrected at the time of His coming. This is referred to as the morning of the first resurrection. (see 1 Thessalonians 4:16-17, D&C 88:97-98, 29:13, 43:18)

3. Those resurrected at the beginning of the Millennium- "And after this another angel shall sound, which is the second trump" (D&C 88:99). "This is the afternoon of the first resurrection; it takes place after our Lord has ushered in the millennium. Those coming forth at that time do so with terrestrial bodies and are thus destined to inherit a terrestrial glory in eternity."[2]

4. Those living at the time of Christ's Second Coming, and those born during the Millennium, shall not die, but "shall be changed in the twinkling of an eye." (D&C 63:50-51).

5. Those resurrected at the end of the Millennium-

"But the rest of the dead lived not again until the thousand years [Millennium] were finished" (Revelation 20:5). These are those who inherit a telestial glory.

6. Those resurrected last, to have no part in eternal glory- The last resurrection will be for those who will be cast out to live with the unembodied devil, those who will not enjoy any degree of glory, those upon whom will pass the second death, and who "remain filthy still" (D&C 88:102).

As the resurrection to an immortal state is a reality for all of us, the Lord has given many particulars as to what we may expect and how to attain to the greatest happiness in the hereafter. To align ourselves with His greatest blessings yields both happiness in this life and security for the next.

Notes:

1. Joseph Fielding Smith, *Doctrines of Salvation,* vol. II, Salt Lake City: Bookcraft, 1955, 260.

2. Bruce R. McConkie, *Mormon Doctrine, 2nd ed.,* Salt Lake City: Bookcraft, 1966, 640.

99. The purposes for and the conditions of the Millennium are revealed.

We have received quite a bit of information from the prophets concerning the thousand years referred to as the Millennium. This period will begin at the Second Coming of Christ, and He personally, as the Savior of all mankind, will reign upon the earth. The earth itself will be renewed and returned to its paradisiacal state, as it was at the time of Adam.

At His coming, the Lord will cleanse the earth of "every corruptible thing" (D&C 101:24) and "the enmity of man, and the enmity of beasts, yea, the enmity of all flesh, shall cease from before my face" (D&C 101:26). "And Satan shall be bound, that he shall have no place in the hearts of the children of men" (D&C 45:55). People, as mortals, who are of a celestial and a terrestrial nature will dwell on the earth during the Millennium without the demeaning influences of Satan. Mortals will continue to have children and raise them in families as now. Immortal, resurrected beings will visit the earth and participate in the government and other work. Hence, the Millennium will be a period of peace and industry.

"In many ways, life will be much as it is now, except that everything will be done in righteousness. People will eat and drink and will wear clothing.[1] People will continue to plant and harvest crops and build houses[2] (Isaiah 65:21). To maintain a sound social order, there will of necessity be industry and commerce. Education will be pure and correct, and the Lord will "reveal all things" (D&C 101:32).

Of particular importance will be the work of teaching the gospel to those who have not yet received the ordinances of the gospel. This missionary effort will likely be short-lived though, because Christ will be in their midst, and "they shall all know me, from the least of them unto the greatest of them" (Jeremiah 31:34). The righteous of the earth, I expect, will readily seek participation and compliance with the first principles and ordinances of the gospel of Jesus Christ.

The other companion work of the Millennium will be to perform vicarious ordinances in the temples for those yet to be resurrected, those residing in spirit prison. We have been charged to set in order the saving ordinances for all mankind, and although our efforts here in mortality are impressive, we will be far short of the stated goal. Immortal beings will help in this work, and records will be made available, corrections made, families identified and sealed together by priesthood ordinances, thus, enabling individual covenants with God.

This understanding of millennial life is given through modern-day revelation, in harmony with Old and New Testament prophecies. It is entirely consistent with the Lord's work of salvation for his children, bringing them to a personal covenant relationship with Him and sealing family units in His way.

Notes:

1. See *Teachings of the Presidents of the Church: Brigham Young*, 1997, 333.

2. "The Millennium," *Gospel Principles,* Salt Lake City: The Church of Jesus Christ of Latter-day Saints, 2009, 266-267.

100. Jesus Christ is the firstborn of the Father.

"Jesus Christ is the firstborn of the spirit children of our Heavenly Father, the Only Begotten of the Father in the flesh, and the first to rise from the dead in the resurrection."[1]

These truths can only be understood if one understands the nature of the relationship within the Godhead, the reality of pre-mortal life, and the order of the resurrection.

Two notable Bible scriptures that refer to this issue are the following:

"Who is the image of the invisible God, the firstborn of every creature" (Colossians 1:15).

"To the general assembly and church of the firstborn, which are written in heaven" (Hebrews 12:23).

John 1:1 is another good reference, "In the beginning was the Word, and the Word was with God, and the Word was God. The same was in the beginning with God." In Moses, it is similarly recorded, "And I, God, said unto mine Only Begotten which was with me from the beginning" (Moses 2:26).

Modern-day prophets have clearly taught that "among the spirit children of Elohim [Heavenly Father] the firstborn was and is Jehovah or Jesus Christ to whom all others are juniors."[2]

Without the comprehensive understanding that the gospel of Jesus Christ gives to us, the scriptural references to firstborn status could be thought to apply to the unique begotten nature of Jesus in the flesh or to be explained in terms of rank or priority.

To understand the role of Jesus Christ in relation to all others is to better understand "that in all things he might have the preeminence" (Colossians 1:18). Whether or not this is a saving doctrine, this truth is nonetheless important to understand—that He is the firstborn of our Heavenly Father, the only begotten into mortality, and the first to be resurrected from the dead.

Notes:

1. LDS Bible Dictionary, "Firstborn."
2. "The Father and the Son: A Doctrinal Exposition by the First Presidency and the Quorum of the Twelve Apostles," *Improvement Era,* August, 1916, reprinted *Ensign,* April, 2002.

101. The birthright, mission, and significance of the tribe of Ephraim are revealed.

The complete blessings of the Abrahamic covenant flow through Isaac, Jacob, and his twelve sons who are known collectively as the House of Israel. Joseph, the youngest of those twelve sons, is father to Manasseh and Ephraim. Jacob, their grandfather, adopted Manasseh and Ephraim when he declared "they shall be mine" (Genesis 48:5). Jacob then gave these two grandsons a blessing, wherein the younger Ephraim was set before Manasseh and received the greater blessing (Genesis 48:14-20).

"Ephraim was given the birthright in Israel (1 Chronicles 5:1-2, Jeremiah 31:9), and in the last days, it has been the tribe of Ephraim's privilege first to bear the message of the Restoration of the gospel to the world and to gather scattered Israel."[1] "It is essential in this dispensation that Ephraim stand in his place at the head, exercising the birthright in Israel which was given to him by direct revelation. Therefore, *Ephraim must be gathered first to prepare the way.*"[2] Much of that gathering came from the peoples of Europe among whom the Ephraimites were scattered. "Ephraim, he hath mixed himself among the people; Ephraim is a cake not turned" (Hosea 7:8). The early converts to the Church in this dispensation were largely Ephraimites.[3] Joseph Smith himself was from the tribe of Ephraim, "a pure Ephraimite."[4]

From Book of Mormon genealogy, Lehi was a descendant of Manasseh, and Ishmael was a descendant of Ephraim[5] (Alma 10:3). It is through these branches of the tribe of Joseph that at least two significant prophecies are fulfilled:

- "Joseph is a fruitful bough, even a fruitful bough by a well; whose branches run over the wall" (Genesis 49:22). This was the blessing given to Joseph by Jacob and finds particular fulfillment in the coming to the Americas by the families of Lehi and Ishmael, as well as the early American settlers.

- "Moreover, thou son of man, take thee one stick, and write upon it, For Judah, and for the children of Israel his companions: then take another stick, and write upon it, For Joseph, the stick of Ephraim, and for all the house of Israel his companions: And join them one to another into one stick; and they shall become one in thine hand" (Ezekiel 37:16). This is a direct reference to the Bible and to the Book of Mormon (D&C 27:5).

Today, missionaries, many with Ephraimite lineage by blood or adoption, fan out across the world to declare that the gospel of Jesus

Christ was restored to the earth through the Prophet Joseph Smith. They carry with them the stick of Judah and the stick of Ephraim.

That Ephraim received the birthright over his older brother Manasseh and was also given firstborn status over Jacob's firstborn Reuben is very significant. The promises given to Joseph that would flow through Ephraim and the role of Ephraim's natural or adopted posterity to gather scattered Israel are thrilling to behold as they unfold today.

Notes:

1. LDS Bible Dictionary, "Ephraim."
2. Joseph Fielding Smith, *Doctrines of Salvation,* vol. III, Salt Lake City: Bookcraft, 1956, 252.
3. Joseph Fielding Smith, *Doctrines of Salvation,* vol. III, 252.
4. Joseph Fielding Smith, *Doctrines of Salvation,* vol. III, 253.
5. Erastus Snow, "God's Peculiar People, Etc.," delivered at Logan, Utah, May 6, 1882, reported by Geo. F. Gibbs, *Journal of Discourses, vol. 23,* 184.

102. A blessing received under the hands of an ordained Patriarch is very special.

Any blessing received under the hands of the priesthood is a very personal experience, but the singular receipt of a patriarchal blessing is particularly both personal and intimate. The blessing is received once in a person's life, in an appropriate environment, usually in the select company of a spouse or parents, and often in the spirit of fasting.

"A patriarchal blessing is a revelation to the recipient, even a white line down the middle of the road to protect, inspire, and motivate activity and righteousness. A patriarchal blessing literally contains chapters from your book of eternal possibilities. I say eternal, for just as life is eternal, so is a patriarchal blessing."[1]

"Patriarchal blessings contain admonitions, promises, and assurances. They tell of our spiritual gifts, talents, and sometimes callings."[2]

The First Presidency said, "Patriarchal blessings [are] an inspired declaration of the lineage of the recipient, and also, where so moved upon by the Spirit, an inspired and prophetic statement of the life mission of the recipient, together with such blessings, cautions, and admonitions as the patriarch may be prompted to give. . . . The realization of all promised blessings is conditioned upon faithfulness to the gospel of our Lord."[3]

The declaration of lineage from the House of Israel is important. Such becomes both our claim to the promises given to Father Abraham and an understanding of our responsibilities as a member of the House of Israel. "It does not matter if a person's lineage in the house of Israel is through bloodlines or by adoption. Church members are counted as a descendant of Abraham and an heir to all the promises and blessings contained in the Abrahamic covenant."[4]

My own patriarchal blessing has been a source of direction, confidence, and confirmation to me. It confirms that, indeed, God lives as our Father in Heaven and knows me as His son. I can see the fulfillment of some things said and the possibility of those unfolding still. What a grand part of the fullness of the gospel, to be able to receive a patriarchal blessing at the hands of an ordained Patriarch!

Notes:

1. Thomas S. Monson, "Your Patriarchal Blessing: A Liahona of Light," *Ensign*, November, 1986, 66.

2. "Gaining Strength through Patriarchal Blessings," *Ensign*, June, 1994.

3. First Presidency Letter to Stake Presidents, 28 June, 1957.

4. "Patriarchal Blessings," www.lds.org/topics/patriarchal-blessings

103. Men will be punished for their own sins and not for Adam's transgression.

It is true that all of mankind is subject to this mortal, telestial world as a result of Adam's transgression, in contrast to the Garden of Eden where Adam and Eve began. However, in the eternal scope of things, that is a blessing of primary significance, enabling the plan of salvation, individual character growth, physical development, and most importantly, the creation of eternal families.

Some teach the doctrine of original sin, meaning both that Adam's transgression was in fact the first sin, and that there exists "the hereditary stain with which we are born on account of our origin or descent from Adam."[1] Neither of these two proposals is entirely accurate. Sin is "to willfully disobey God's commandments or to fail to act righteously despite a knowledge of the truth" (James 4:17).[2] It was precisely because of Adam and Eve's nascent knowledge of the truth, that they chose to transgress, thereby setting in motion the greater good, namely, the plan of our Heavenly Father for His children. Nor is it true to assume that each new baby born into this world carries some inherent stain of sin because of what Father Adam did or didn't do. We are not accountable for the actions of anyone else other than our own. Again, we can and are *affected* by the actions of others, but in the sense of judgment, we are not culpable.

"The Son of God hath atoned for original guilt, wherein the sins of the parents cannot be answered upon the heads of the children, for they are whole from the foundation of the world" (Moses 6:54).

In fact, the very concept of a lingering, hereditary sin is contrary to the nature and the purposes of the Atonement of Jesus Christ. Paul and others taught, "Wherefore, my beloved . . . work out your own salvation with fear and trembling" (Philippians 2:12).

What liberating doctrine it is to understand that although we are born into a sinful world, we are not born in sin. Nor will we be accountable for the sins of our fathers or mothers or any of our ancestry. Nor will our children and posterity be accountable for our sins. By and through the atonement of Jesus Christ, we can repent of our own misdeeds, receive forgiveness, and be constantly renewed.

Notes:

1. Catholic Encyclopedia, *Original Sin,* www.newadvent.org/cathen/11312a.htm.
2. www.lds.org/topics/sin.

104. Repentance is much more than just acknowledging wrong doings.

When Jesus sent out the apostles two by two, their message was simple and direct. "They went out, and preached that men should repent" (Mark 6:12).

The preeminent position of repentance in the life of a disciple follows closely behind the prominent injunctions to have faith in the Lord Jesus Christ and to pray. In fact, true faith in the Savior will cause us to want to repent. It is only through sincere and continuous repentance that the very Atonement relieves us of our sins. "For he shall save his people *from* their sins" (Matthew 1:21). "Therefore, ye cannot be saved *in* your sins" (Alma 11:37).

Repentance, properly understood, is a positive process or event. "[It] denotes a change of mind, i.e., a fresh view about God, about oneself, and about the world . . . a turning of the heart and will to God, and a renunciation of sin."[1] The sixteenth century reformer John Calvin said that repentance is "consisting in the mortification of the flesh and of the old man, and in the vivification of the Spirit."[2] I like the use of the word "vivification," because it denotes an invigorating course towards progress and purpose.

Scriptures and living prophets have given us a clear outline to the steps of true and complete repentance:

- Feel a godly sorrow for our sins
- Confess our sins to God (and to our Bishop if the sin is of such a magnitude)
- Make restitution to the offended, as possible
- Forsake the sinful behavior
- Ask forgiveness of God and those we've offended
- Turn to God and live the commandments with full purpose of heart

Such a course enables us to move forward, to make progress, to be at peace. "Sincere repentance is manifested when the same temptation to sin, under the same conditions, is ever after resolutely resisted.[3] The Lord said it succinctly, "By this ye may know if a man repenteth of his sins—behold, he will confess them and forsake them" (D&C 58:43). And then comes the great blessing, "Behold, he who has repented of his sins, the same is forgiven, and I, the Lord, remember them no more" (D&C 58:42).

Repentance and the Atonement of Christ are inextricable. The Atonement will both enable our repentance and will sanctify our experience. It will cleanse us by vicariously satisfying the demands of justice.

Such an understanding of true repentance is an invitation to a fuller life of peace, personal progress, and a compassionate outlook towards our fellows.

Notes:

1. LDS Bible Dictionary, "Repentance."
2. John Calvin, *Institutes of the Christian Religion,* Edinburgh: 1537, Book Third, Chapter III.5.
3. *Jewish Encyclopedia,* "Repentance – Rabbinical View," 1906, www.jewishencyclopedia.com/articles/12680-repentance.

105. The Lord's law of health invites and enables the Holy Ghost to be with us.

To feel active, alive, interested, and to be able to move about, work, play, have stamina and strength, all bring joy and dimension to our lives. When we are feeling healthy, we have a sense of well-being.

Doctrine and Covenants Section 89, known as the Word of Wisdom, is both a practical code for good health and also an identifying behavior of the Lord's covenant people in the latter days. It is "given for a principle with promise" (D&C 89:3). The revelation concludes with that promise in two parts: First, a promise of physical health and mental acuity, where they "shall receive health in their navel and marrow in their bones. And shall find wisdom, and great treasures of knowledge . . . And shall run and not be weary, and shall walk and not faint" (D&C 89:18-20). Second, a promise of protection to the obedient, "that the destroying angel shall pass by them, as the children of Israel, and not slay them" (D&C 89:21).

The body we have is the body we will occupy throughout the eternities. Comforting is the doctrine that it will be restored to its perfect frame in the resurrection, but during mortality, we have the responsibility for its care. "What? know ye not that your body is the temple of the Holy Ghost which is in you? . . . For ye are bought with a price: therefore glorify God in your body, and in your spirit" (1 Corinthians

6:19-20). We must provide a clean and a fit habitation for the Holy Ghost to dwell with us as our constant companion.

To live the Word of Wisdom as given of the Lord is within the reach and ability of all men. It is "adapted to the capacity of the weak and the weakest of all saints, who are or can be called saints" (D&C 89:3). It does require discipline and effort, but that is to be expected within our discipleship. We, as a people, are very familiar with the things specified in the revelation from which we refrain. There is also inspired counsel of what we can and should do to bring about good health and fitness.

Coupled with the timeless wisdom of moderation in all things, the Lord has given this revelation for our good health and as a part of our covenant relationship with Him. Adherence to the Word of Wisdom is a blessing that will enable the Holy Ghost to be our constant companion as we walk in obedience to all the commandments of the Lord. I have found this to be true.

106. Both before and after marriage, sexual purity is a commandment of God.

"Do not, my young friends, expect the world to esteem the seventh commandment—chastity before marriage and fidelity after. . . . We will have to keep the seventh commandment because it is spiritually correct, not because we will get much support from society's other institutions."[1]

Perhaps it has always been, but it seems that there is an increasing obsession with sex, without regard for its divine intentions or the inherent consequences. Popular opinion makers on television, in movies, on magazine covers and within print media, bombard us with appeals to the natural man. The internet has become the new Pied Piper for those who would be lulled into the hell that pornography creates.

Within my lifetime, I've seen accepted standards in media go from the "I Love Lucy" show, where Lucy and Ricky had separate single beds in the bedroom, to live scenes of steamy intercourse by unmarried couples.

The problem with this unbridled public and private fixation is at least three-fold:

1. It violates the command of God.
2. It diminishes intended divine purposes.
3. It is rooted in selfishness, the opposite of love.

The high standard of a true disciple of Christ regarding this code of conduct is stated by the Master himself, "But I say unto you, That whosoever looketh on a woman to lust after her hath committed adultery with her already in his heart" (Matthew 5:28). We must reject Satan's deceitful enticing that come to us packaged as acceptable norms. We must even flee from the enticement, as did Joseph from Potiphar's wife, if occasion so requires.

"[A] distinctive characteristic of the gospel is the adherence to the Lord's law of chastity. From ancient times to the present, the Lord has commanded his people to obey the law. Such strict morality may seem peculiar or outdated in our day when the media portrays pornography and immorality as being normal and fully acceptable. Remember, the Lord has never revoked the law of chastity."[2]

I am a personal witness of the protection and the personal confidence that come from bridling the baser inclinations regarding morality. I am grateful to belong to a Church that stands firm and uncompromising in defending and upholding the Lord's law of chastity.

Notes:

1. Elder Neal A. Maxwell, "The Pathway of Discipleship," address given at Brigham Young University, January 4, 1998.

2. Joseph B. Wirthlin, "Fruits of the Restored Gospel of Jesus Christ," *Ensign,* November, 1991.

107. An all-male priesthood is in the wisdom of the Lord.

I can only offer my own musings on why the Lord has decreed that the priesthood only be conferred upon and exercised in office, by worthy male members of the Church. As a preface, I offer no apology for what I consider to be divine wisdom in the order of responsibility given to His children.

Priesthood chores and duties are rooted in charity. "No power or influence can or ought to be maintained by virtue of the priesthood, only by persuasion, by long-suffering, by gentleness and meekness, and by love unfeigned" (D&C 121:41). These characteristics are not always identified with the male image, whereas females often seem to be inherently endowed with such qualities. To be "partakers of the divine nature" as Peter spoke of (2 Peter 1:4), we must attain charity, which Peter listed as the culminating virtue (see 2 Peter 1:7). To exercise the priesthood on behalf of our families and others at large, a man must get out of the recliner and take an active role—first in the family and also among his fellow men and women (I acknowledge that that is an over-simplified general statement). The Prophet Joseph Smith said, "Love is one of the leading characteristics of Deity, and ought to be manifested by those who aspire to be the sons of God. A man filled with the love of God is not content with blessing his family alone but ranges through the world, anxious to bless the whole of the human family."[1]

It's certainly not that women are somehow incapable or unworthy of bearing the priesthood. That is not argued by anyone. Nor is it a matter of men making all the rules. We believe this is a divine delegation of duty.

Whereas women have primary nurturing responsibility towards their children, men in the Church have been given responsibility to preside, administer, and effectuate the work of the Church, including overseeing the ordinances of the gospel. These are very distinct roles, yet have overlapping, supporting, and participating synergy. "Although the authority of the priesthood is bestowed only on worthy male members of the Church, the blessings of the priesthood are available to all—men, women, and children. We all benefit from the influence of righteous priesthood leadership, and we all have the privilege of receiving the saving ordinances of the priesthood."[2]

Priesthood responsibility, properly understood and exercised, will make men better husbands, better fathers, better providers, and better citizens. These qualities infused into the male segment of our society, can do much to alleviate the otherwise deteriorating family structure and to bless mankind.

Whatever the Lord's reason for setting up roles and responsibilities as He has, I have no qualm with it. I am satisfied to know that priesthood authority is upon the earth, there is order in the Kingdom, and the ordinances of salvation are available to all.

Notes:

1. Joseph Fielding Smith, comp., *Teachings of the Prophet Joseph Smith*, Salt Lake City: Deseret Book, 1976, 174.
2. *True to the Faith*, "Priesthood," 2004, www.lds.org/manual/true-to-the-faith/priesthood.

108. Vain pride is a destructive, deceptive attribute.

To be proud of your kids, your spouse, your country, your Church, your parents, or a myriad other worthy objects of our delight, is well placed and wholesome. It should always be balanced with recognizing the blessings that enable us, including the role of other people and especially Heavenly Father and our Savior Jesus Christ. It's when we attribute gain or privilege to our own efforts entirely and consider ourselves above others, that pride crosses the line from wholesome to unhealthy.

The Book of Mormon prophets wrote frequently about the spiritually corrosive influence of selfish pride taking root in our hearts. In fact, the whole history of the various peoples of the Book of Mormon is a recurring chronicle of forgetting God, exhibiting pride over others, suffering wars and contention, then repenting and seeking God anew. This cycle is repeated over and over throughout the book. Following are some statements of the prophetic counsel that warns against pride:

> "O the vainness, and the frailties, and the foolishness of men! When they are learned they think they are wise, and they hearken not unto the counsel of God" (2 Nephi 9:28).
>
> "Let not this pride of your hearts destroy your souls" (Jacob 2:16)!
>
> "Behold, are ye stripped of pride? I say unto you, if ye are not ye are not prepared to meet God" (Alma 5:28).

While President of the Church, Ezra Taft Benson spoke on several occasions of the sin of pride. In General Conference in 1989, he gave a masterful talk entitled "Beware of Pride." Among other things, he said, "The central feature of pride is enmity—enmity toward God and enmity toward our fellowmen. . . . The proud cannot accept the authority of God giving direction to their lives. . . . We are tempted daily to elevate ourselves above others and diminish them. "[1]

C.S. Lewis wrote "Pride gets no pleasure out of having something, only out of having more of it than the next man. . . . It is the comparison that makes you proud: the pleasure of being above the rest."[2]

The Old Testament repeatedly denounces the proud. The Savior declared the polar fate of both the proud and the humble when He said, "And whosoever shall exalt himself shall be abased; and he that shall humble himself shall be exalted" (Matthew 23:12).

The sin of pride has been clearly exposed, and we have received ample warning in these last days. Said President Benson in 1989, "Pride is the great stumbling block to Zion. I repeat: Pride *is* the great stumbling block to Zion."[3] When a prophet speaks, we should listen. And in this case, conduct a self-examination.

Notes:

1. Ezra Taft Benson, "Beware of Pride," *Ensign,* May, 1989.
2. C. S. Lewis, *Mere Christianity,* New York: Touchstone, 1996, 109-112.
3. Ezra Taft Benson.

109. The office of a bishop is a blessing to the saints and to the community.

A bishop is an ordained office in the Aaronic Priesthood, best characterized as an overseer or shepherd of a ward (congregation). Paul listed the partial qualifications of a bishop while writing to Timothy, "A bishop then must be blameless, the husband of one wife, vigilant, sober, of good behaviour, given to hospitality, apt to teach; Not given to wine, no striker, not greedy of filthy lucre; but patient, not a brawler, not covetous; One that ruleth well his own house, having his children in subjection with all gravity . . . Not a novice . . . Moreover he must have a good report of them which are without" (1 Timothy 3:1-7).

Bishops are men of testimony and faith. They love those they serve. They make themselves available to counsel their ward members, to pray with them, to assist them in aligning their lives with their better inclinations. They encourage faith in Christ, activity in the kingdom, strong families, and community involvement. They guide the youth, attend to the administration of the ward, seek out and assist the poor, preside at meetings, and oversee the work of the priesthood at the ward level. They stand as the bishop of a given geography to all, both members of the Church and those who are not members, and seek to spread the restored gospel through missionary effort.

It is a remarkable thing to witness the mantle of a bishop. When a bishop is called, sustained by his ward, and set apart by the Stake President, he then is on his own for the most part. The stake presidency will likely give an hour or so of instruction at the outset, and a handbook is distributed to the new bishop, and then his work begins. But in fact, he is not without prior training, as his life to this point has been preparing him in faith for this important calling. He is not left entirely on his own because the Holy Ghost is his guide and inspiration. He is to represent the Lord among the people. Love for those he serves and love for the Lord will be his motivation.

All this is in addition to his full-time employment. He receives no monetary remuneration. Yet, bishops serve cheerfully and faithfully, usually for five or so years. It is a testament to the sense of responsibility and duty that flow from the fountain of faith and testimony of this great latter-day work. Bishops are a blessing to the people they serve and to the Church at large.

110. In the mid to late 1800's, plural marriage was a divine decree for a season.

My testimony of the Prophet Joseph Smith and his divine mandate to form and establish the Church of Jesus Christ in these latter days causes me to agree with the title of this chapter. However, I appropriately harbor neither desire nor tolerance for the practice today. Rather, I see that it was an important part of the "restitution of all things" (Acts 3:21) in this, "the dispensation of the fullness of times" (Ephesians 1:10), as declared by Paul.

Judeo-Christians seem to have no problem with the polygamous lives of Father Abraham, Jacob, Gideon, Elkanah, and surely others who engaged in this then acceptable practice. No one can argue the favor which Abraham and Jacob found with God that indicated their righteousness and purity.

David and Solomon are Old Testament examples of the abuse of this practice. Said the Lord, "For they seek to excuse themselves in committing whoredoms. . . . Behold, David and Solomon truly had many wives and concubines, which thing was abominable before me, saith the Lord" (Jacob 2:23-24). Either without the sanction of the Lord, or by selfish abuse, or by adultery in David's case, these leaders of Judah were not right with God.

Only by divine decree is the practice of plural marriage acceptable. "For if I will, saith the Lord of Hosts, raise up seed unto me, I will command my people; otherwise they shall hearken unto these things [monogamy]" (Jacob 2:30). In obedience to direction from God, Latter-day Saints followed the practice of polygamy for about fifty years, formally ending the contracting of plural marriages in 1890.

Certainly, there were abuses of the practice, as there can be found terrible abuses today within some traditional marriages. However, the tender care which Joseph F. Smith (an example of many) extended to his wives and children, and the harmony and family cooperation within that polygamous family, is indicative of the love and respect that existed in their relationships. As in any family, placing God first gave the balancing dynamic to enable such harmony and happiness.

If Joseph Smith wanted to find favor with the world for the acceptance and expansion of this new Church, introducing the practice of plural marriage would not have been a smart idea. Nor was it a mechanism to give license to his baser inclinations, as some would argue, for Joseph did not fall out of favor with God. In fact, it was contrary to his own internal constitution, and the Lord had to command him on several occasions and over several years to institute this practice.

As a historic result, the Church has reaped tremendous generational blessings of faith, industry, cooperation, obedience, and wholesome family legacies. That this provocative practice could ever have taken root in these times required a Prophet of God, and the ratification of the Holy Ghost to the hearts of the people that, indeed, he was a prophet and that God had so commanded. I accept that part of our history on those terms as well.

111. We believe in the literal gathering of Israel and in the restoration of the Ten Tribes.

The twelve tribes of Israel have been the Lord's covenant people, through which flows the promises of the Abrahamic Covenant. It is not only a lineage of birthright, but also inclusive by way of adoption to all of Heavenly Father's children from the time of Adam and Eve.

The work of "gathering Israel" has meaning on several levels:

- "For, lo, the days come, saith the Lord, that I will bring again the captivity of my people Israel and Judah, saith the Lord: and I will cause them to return to the land that I gave to their fathers, and they shall possess it" (Jeremiah 30:3). This includes the Ten Tribes and refers to a given geography to which they (Israel and Judah) will be gathered.
- "Thou shalt preach the fulness of my gospel, which I have sent forth in these last days, the covenant which I have sent forth to recover my people, which are of the house of Israel" (D&C 39:11). Across the globe, our missionaries are gathering those who hear the Master's voice, through the covenant of baptism.

- In the early part of this dispensation, gathering meant to assemble the saints in a common body, culminating with the great gathering to the west under the direction of Brigham Young
- Today, the Lord gathers His people Israel when they accept Him and keep His commandments, without any particular or specific geographic location

The gathering of Israel in these latter days is effected under the keys given to Joseph Smith and Oliver Cowdery while in the Kirtland Temple on April 3, 1836. "The heavens were again opened unto us; and Moses appeared before us, and committed unto us the keys of the gathering of Israel from the four parts of the earth, and the leading of the ten tribes from the land of the north" (D&C 110:11).

This understanding of our duty to gather the Lord's people in these latter days, motivates us in our labors as a Church to share the gospel. "And he gathereth his children from the four quarters of the earth; and he numbereth his sheep, and they know him; and there shall be one fold and one shepherd; and he shall feed his sheep, and in him they shall find pasture" (1 Nephi 22:25). Such a picture of unity and peace bespeaks the brotherhood of mankind and the opportunity for all to gather to His fold. It is an active and on-going gathering process, remarkable in its scope and in its inevitable fulfillment. As a covenant member of the Church, I sense that mission of gathering Israel and find it to be an inspiring influence.

112. Only the Lord can forgive sins, but we are commanded to forgive trespasses against us.

In the Doctrine and Covenants Section 64, a significant distinction is made that an uninspired hand might have missed. As it is, the Lord teaches an important truth. Said He, "I, the Lord, forgive sins" (D&C 64:7), and "ye ought to forgive . . . (your) brother his trespasses" (D&C 64:9).

Only the Lord Jesus Christ and God the Father can forgive us of our sins. That communication comes as a personal revelation to the fully repentant. Bishops, Stake Presidents, and Mission Presidents, as judges in Israel, help members to overcome transgression through repentance, which may require Church discipline. They can forgive on behalf of the Church, but they cannot pronounce forgiveness of the sin.

Those of us without those keys of authority on behalf of the Church, are under the above charge to simply forgive those who have wronged us. Though the sin remains and is to be dealt with by that individual, ours is not to forgive the sin, but to forgive the sinner.

On several occasions, Jesus made a simple, unequivocal declaration to individuals, "Thy sins are forgiven thee." The following are a few examples:

- To the man sick of the palsy, in spite of the scribes (Matthew 9:2-8)
- To the woman who washed and anointed His feet with her tears (Luke 7:47)
- To Enos as a voice from heaven (Enos 1:5)

In the Doctrine and Covenants, Section 64, the Lord forgives the sins of several collectively as He addresses the elders of the Church, "I have forgiven you your sins" (D&C 64:1-3).

Notably, when the sin was committed against him personally, Jesus pled with the Father to grant forgiveness to the offenders, "Father, forgive them; for they know not what they do" (Luke 23:34).

Forgiveness is a divine attribute. To receive forgiveness is liberating. To grant it is also liberating. The one frees us from guilt and self-condemnation, the other from bitterness and grudge. It is the Lord who can forgive sins, we are to forgive the sinner and those trespasses we experience. The consistent doctrine of forgiveness from the Lord to us, and from us to our fellows, is another witness of the source of the revelations given to the Prophet Joseph Smith.

113. The Gift of the Holy Ghost comes by the laying on of hands by those in authority.

When we enter the waters of baptism through repentance, we demonstrate our willingness and desire to follow the Savior. We covenant to take upon us His name, to always remember Him, and to keep His commandments. As a part of that ordinance, the Lord gives us the sublime Gift of the Holy Ghost, which will be a guide, a revelator, a sanctifying influence, and a comforter to us.

This Gift of the Holy Ghost is the right to have the companionship or influence of a member of the very Godhead! Truly, "the Holy Ghost, whom the Father will send in my name, he shall teach you all things, and bring all things to your remembrance, whatsoever I have said unto you" (John 14:26). It is interesting that Jesus indicates in this verse that the Holy Ghost (as a constant companion) will yet be sent, that it was still future.

While Jesus ministered among men, the *Gift* of the Holy Ghost was apparently not necessary (John 7:39, 16:7). Jesus Himself was the teacher; He was in person "the way, the truth, and the life." Yet the *power* of the Holy Ghost was operative in the hearts of the believers, as evidenced when Elizabeth "heard the salutation of Mary" (Luke 1:41), also with child, and she "was filled with the Holy Ghost" (Luke 1:41).

As a resurrected being, Jesus came to his disciples and said to them, "Receive ye the Holy Ghost" (John 20:22). This is the same language used today when one is confirmed a member of the Church following baptism and is given the Gift of the Holy Ghost. It is done in the same manner that Paul performed among the Ephesians, "Paul had laid his hands upon them, and the Holy Ghost came on them" (Acts

19:6). The bestowal of the Gift of the Holy Ghost is the oft referenced baptism of fire, which speaks to the sanctifying influence of this gift.

To have the constant influence of deity is above any other consideration. Think of it! Such an influence is a moral compass, a fountain of truth, a refiner of character, and a source of solace without equal. It is available to all who will so receive in the order and the manner the Lord has prescribed, in connection with the ordinance of baptism.

114. Only the Savior can blot out my transgressions.

Recently, I had a long conversation with a brother who is investigating the Church. By his own admission, his religious understanding to date had been an amalgamation of different philosophies, without any real anchor or clear objective.

As our conversation continued, our focus came to the LDS doctrines regarding God the Father and the Savior Jesus Christ. "Why was it necessary," he asked, "that Christ should have to answer the demands of Justice when we had repented and learned from our sins and transgressions? Was it not those very lessons of life that cause us to be better people? And if the result of a lifetime was to have become a better person, even god-like, why would there still be a score to settle? Had we not, from our own efforts, become what God had hoped we would become?"

We discussed briefly the enabling power of Christ and His Atonement in our quest for improvement. We then looked at Alma 7:11-13 to examine the breadth of the Atonement and what it is that Jesus suffered and why. We readily agreed that His divine Atonement overcame death and provided for the universal resurrection, which we could not have achieved on our own. We could understand that through His suffering pains, afflictions, temptations, sicknesses, and infirmities, He would absolutely understand the human condition and be able to succor his people with empathy.

But particularly regarding the remission of sins, the apostle John wrote, "The blood of Jesus Christ his Son cleanseth us from all sin" (1 John 1:7). Throughout the scriptures, it is written variously of this third party arrangement:

"laid on him the iniquity of us all" (Isaiah 53:6)

"gave his life a ransom" (Matthew 20:28)

"for the remission of sins" (Matthew 26:28, Acts 2:38, Hebrews 9:22, and more)

"to bear the sins of many" (Hebrews 9:28)

"to take away our sins" (1 John 3:5)

"offereth himself a sacrifice for sin" (2 Nephi 2:7)

"slain for the sins of the world" (3 Nephi 11:14)

We repent of our sins, overcome them, put them behind us, and become better people. To be harrowed up with the memory of those sins would be to keep current the guilt, shame, and embarrassment that would even intensify as we distance ourselves from such behavior and then see it for what it was. Alma records that he would "take upon him the sins of his people, that he might *blot out their transgressions*" (Alma 7:13, emphasis added). The Lord has mercifully promised, "Behold, he who has repented of his sins, the same is forgiven, and I, the Lord, *remember them no more*" (D&C 58:42, emphasis added).

"Repent ye therefore, and be converted, *that your sins may be blotted out*, when the times of refreshing shall come from the presence of the Lord" (Acts 3:19, emphasis added).

We may rise above our personal weaknesses and sins and even do so in large part of our own doing. But only the Savior, the Son of God, alone was qualified in His perfection to atone for our sins, and He alone could thereby blot them out.

It is requisite for us to live with peace in this life and to someday dwell comfortably in the presence of God, to know that our repented sins have been blotted out, even from the memory of heaven. I have personally experienced this heavenly mercy. Latter-day scripture has lent much to this generous understanding. "Thanks be unto God for his unspeakable gift" (2 Corinthians 9:15).

115. The word "Zion" has rich meanings.

Zion is a term used in each of the four books of scripture, and carries at least the following meanings and usages:

- As a reference to the city of Enoch (Moses 7:18-21)
- As a reference to the ancient city of Jerusalem (2 Samuel 5:6-7, 1 Kings 8:1)
- As a reference to the New Jerusalem (D&C 45:66-67, 57:1-3, Articles of Faith, 10)
- As a reference to The Church of Jesus Christ of Latter-day Saints (D&C 82:14)
- As the pure in heart (D&C 97:21)

Zion is commonly used today as a metaphor by people longing for a homeland, for relief, or the sense of community. The so-called Zionist Movement, first coined at the end of the nineteenth century, came to initial fruition with the creation of Israel as a Jewish homeland in 1948. The Jews are most commonly associated in the worldly vernacular with having an interest in the cause of Zion.

When the Church was restored, Zion became a familiar term particularly for the gathering of the Saints. By comparative frequency, Zion is found some 155 times in the Old Testament and in the Doctrine and Covenants, more than 190 times. The early

Church sought to establish Zion as a community of Saints—in Kirtland, Independence, Far West, Nauvoo, and Salt Lake City. Converts converged to these particular gathering points from Canada, England, the Eastern United States, and wherever they were found. They were gathering to Zion. It is estimated that ninety-one thousand members from Europe heeded the call to gather to Zion by 1900.

"For Zion must increase in beauty, and in holiness; her borders must be enlarged; her stakes must be strengthened; yea, verily I say unto you, Zion must arise and put on her beautiful garments" (D&C 82:14).

In the early days of this dispensation, gathering was to a central location, to provide foundational strength. Today, as the Church has spread across the globe, the Saints are encouraged to remain in their countries and to build the kingdom where they reside.

"We are building up the strength of Zion—her cords or stakes—throughout the world. Therefore, we counsel our people to remain in their native lands and gather out the elect of God and teach them the ways of the Lord. There temples are being built and the saints will be blessed wherever they live in all the world."[1]

Zion can be a designated place, but truly becomes Zion as it is occupied by the pure in heart. Thus, as the Church gains converts throughout the world, Zion is therein established one heart at a time, and collectively thereafter.

Zion is a term dear to the hearts of Latter-day Saints, and of itself, is a rallying cry for the faith. It moves me as well in that way.

Notes:

1. Spencer W. Kimball, "The Fruit of Our Welfare Services Labors," *Ensign,* November, 1978.

116. Scriptures tell of prophets, dispensations, and the latter days.

In a broad context, prophets have declared the word of God and witnessed of Christ at various times in human history. We are familiar with the prophets of the Old Testament—Isaiah, Jeremiah, Ezekiel, Daniel, Hosea, and many others. These men were called of God to testify of the coming of the Messiah and to preach repentance to the people. No doubt, they stood in stark contrast to the common affairs taking place during their time.

There have also been *dispensational* prophets who have had particular priesthood responsibility to initiate, preside over, administer the ordinances of, and oversee the Church and Kingdom of God on the earth.

"A dispensation of the gospel is a period of time in which the Lord has at least one authorized servant on the earth who bears the holy priesthood and the keys, and who has a divine commission to dispense the gospel to the inhabitants of the earth. . . . There have been many gospel dispensations since the beginning."[1]

Father Adam certainly headed a dispensation of time, as did Enoch, Noah, Abraham, and Moses. In the meridian of time, Jesus presided as the promised Messiah. This last dispensation, ushered in under the Prophet Joseph Smith, will prepare the world for the second advent of the Savior, and is known as "the dispensation of the fulness of times" (Ephesians 1:10).

"In addition there were dispensations of the gospel among the Nephites, the Jaredites, and the Lost Tribes of Israel. Melchizedek could also be included, as well as John the Baptist, since they truly held the priesthood and taught the word of the Lord to the people and were unique in their time. There are many other prophets who have had the priesthood and a knowledge of the gospel. Perhaps if more were revealed to us, we would learn that they too should be spoken of as having a dispensation. These could include, among others, Abel, Esaias, Gad, Jeremy, Elihu, Caleb, Jethro, Zenock, and Zenos."[2]

During this last dispensation, the keys of the priesthood have been passed unbroken through a line of prophetic leadership and will do so until the coming of Christ (D&C 27:13, 128:18-21). Said the Lord to the Prophet Joseph Smith, "Therefore, the keys of this dispensation are committed into your hands" (D&C 110:16).

To recognize the role of prophets and dispensational prophets and to consider the days in which we live will cause us to thrill in the great latter-day work of the restoration through the Prophet Joseph Smith. This is, indeed, the final dispensation, which will culminate in the glorious Second Coming of the Lord Jesus Christ.

Notes:

1. LDS Bible Dictionary, "Dispensations."
2. Bible Dictionary, "Dispensations."

117. Hope is a powerful doctrine of the Gospel of Jesus Christ.

Hope is a companion to faith. Moroni said, "How is it that ye can attain unto faith, save ye shall have hope" (Moroni 7:40)? And then he went on to say what it is we should hope for, "Behold I say unto you that ye shall have hope through the atonement of Christ and the power of his resurrection, to be raised unto life eternal, and this because of your faith in him according to the promise" (Moroni 7:41).

Hope is most notably aligned with positive expectations. I've always been impressed with the general leadership of the Church and their positive outlook. They have a clear expectation of good things to come, "that all these things shall give thee experience, and shall be for thy good" (D&C 122:7).

President Gordon B. Hinckley is quoted frequently in the hopeful and faithful affirmation that "things will work out. Keep trying. Be believing. Be happy. Don't get discouraged. Things will work out."[1]

President Hinckley's attitude on life is the very dictionary definition of hope, "the feeling that what is wanted can be had or that events will turn out for the best."[2]

The hope of a child is inextricably tied to the faith of certain fulfillment. Such pure certainty brings enthusiasm for the future, joy in the anticipation, eagerness for tomorrow, and happiness today. Hope is a partner of faith, each enabling and encouraging the other.

Nephi wrote that we should walk "having a perfect brightness of hope" (2 Nephi 31:20). That is a beautiful and illustrative mandate for living a life of faith and optimism.

Moroni taught of the connection of faith, hope, and its resultant behavioral trait of charity, "the pure love of Christ" (Moroni 7:47).

Hope can bridge the gap of uncertainty, loneliness, doubt, remorse, failure, sickness, abuse, and oppression. It is centered in Christ and His resurrection, and the "hope of eternal life" (Titus 1:2). It is a principle and a doctrine well exercised in The Church of Jesus Christ of Latter-day Saints.

Notes:

1. Gordon B. Hinckley, quoted by Jeffrey R. Holland, "President Gordon B. Hinckley: Stalwart and Brave He Stands," *Ensign,* June, 1995.

2. www.dictionary.reference.com/browse/hope.

118. The family is central to the Creator's plan for the eternal destiny of His children.

So reads a portion of the opening sentence in the 1995 "The Family: A Proclamation to the World,"[1] which was issued by the First Presidency and the Quorum of the Twelve. That statement for the centrality of the family encompasses at least the following:

- The human race is perpetuated by committed family relationships
- The deepest joys and securities can be felt within a loving family
- The family is the fundamental unit of society
- Each of us is inextricably linked to past generations
- The family is the best laboratory to learn and to exercise God-like attributes

The very word "family" connotes feelings of warmth, love, refuge, and enjoyment. Of teaching and learning, service and support, understanding and acceptance, laughing and crying. It is a fundamental yearning to belong to a family and a virtuous natural instinct to be loyal to family relationships.

The Prophet Moroni made significant enhancements (italicized) to the words found in Malachi chapter 4 when he said to the Prophet Joseph Smith, "Behold, I will reveal unto you *the Priesthood, by the hand of* Elijah the prophet. . . . And he shall plant in the hearts of the children the promises made to the fathers, and the hearts of the children shall turn to their fathers. *If it were not so, the whole earth would be utterly wasted at his coming*" (D&C 2:1-3, emphasis added).

Family relationships are intended to continue beyond the grave. In light of the Creator's plan, families are bound together through covenants, which enable and establish eternal family bonds. Hence, "If it were not so, the whole earth would be utterly wasted at his coming"

(D&C 2:3). In other words, the very purposes of God would come to naught if our hearts were not turned (sealed) to our ancestry.

Prophets in this dispensation have said:

> "No other success in life can compensate for failure in the home."[2]
>
> "The greatest work you will ever do will be within the walls of your own home."[3]

Family life is the most fulfilling social engagement available. It should be no wonder that the Church puts so much emphasis on the family unit. It both meets our deepest innate desires, and at the same time, fulfills the purposes and designs of our loving Heavenly Father.

I will be forever grateful for my family, both living and deceased, and the enjoyments we have shared, we do now share, and those we will yet share together.

Notes:

1. First Presidency and The Council of the Twelve, "The Family: A Proclamation to the World," *Ensign,* November, 1995.
2. David O. McKay, *Conference Report*, April, 1964, 3-7.
3. Harold B. Lee, *Strengthening the Home*, Salt Lake City: Church of Jesus Christ of Latter-day Saints, 1973.

119. Even God is subject to natural laws that give men a solid floor for their choices.

The recent Harry Potter phenomenon has included some fun make-believe, including screaming root plants, shifting staircases, and floating candles. Much of the appeal of this series is the unpredictable, the surprise, the other-worldly experiences of Harry and his friends. Yet to live under these circumstances would be to live in constant apprehension of "What's next?"

Many throughout the earth have the mistaken idea that the Lord operates at will and by magic. At will, yes, his perfect will. "There is nothing that the Lord thy God shall take in his heart to do but what he will do it" (Abraham 3:17). But it is not by some arbitrary magic. Rather, because He understands all things, has all knowledge, and can harness such knowledge, He can do amazing things. Omniscient is the state He lives in—of things past, present, and future.

Two hundred years ago, to think that one could speak into a device held in his hand and be heard by someone on another continent as though he were in the same room would have been seen as fiction. To transport people and cargo to and from anywhere in the world within twenty-four hours would have likewise made good fictional material. There are countless other discoveries and applied knowledge that first amazed us, but have since become commonplace to our familiar world.

In the classic children's stories that C.S. Lewis wrote to teach of Christ, Lucy reads from a book an incantation to make invisible things visible. In doing so, Aslan (Christ) appears to her. Their exchange is as follows:

> "Oh Aslan," said she, "it was kind of you to come."
>
> "I have been here all the time," said he. "But you have just made me visible."
>
> "Aslan," said Lucy almost a little reproachfully, "don't make fun of me. As if anything *I* could do would make you visible!"
>
> "Indeed," said Aslan, "do you think I wouldn't obey my own rules?"[1]

The Lord is the great Creator. All of the elements have been given a particular mix of character, form, property, quality, attribute, life cycle, and other characteristics. Furthermore, "And again, verily I say unto you, he hath given a law unto all things, by which they move in their times and their seasons; and their courses are fixed" (D&C 88:42-43).

That there is order in the universe, and reason to all eventualities, as opposed to having a capricious, fickle being or beings of power, is settling doctrine. We can play the game when we understand the rules and know that those rules are fixed. Even for the Lord. The glory of God certainly is intelligence (D&C 93:36).

Notes:

1. C. S. Lewis, *The Voyage of the Dawn Treader*, New York: HarperCollins, 1952, 158, 159.

120. Christ has brought to pass the bodily resurrection of every living thing.

Living in the country, we have had our share of cats, dogs, rabbits, fish, cows, and even a snake that got loose and may still exist somewhere in the back room. We have some sweet memories and photos of not a few puppy litters. And we have buried several cats and rabbits and beloved dogs at various locations on the property.

So will there be animals after the resurrection? In fact, yes. It is through the irrevocable Atonement and resurrection of Jesus Christ that every living thing will experience a bodily resurrection.

"Every creature on the earth, whether it be man, animal, fish, fowl, or other creature, that the Lord has created, is redeemed from death on the same terms that man is redeemed. These creatures are not responsible for death coming into the world any more than we were, and since they have been created by the Father, they are entitled to their redemption and eternal duration."[1]

Yet the judgment will be a different matter. Animals, unlike man, are not governed by a conscience (truth be said, some men aren't either!). Better stated, animals have no conscience. They cannot sin, they cannot repent, for they have no sense of right and wrong: they are governed entirely by their nature and instinct. They are truly pure in the realm of their existence, although we may characterize some of the more violent animals as mean and even murderous.

What about those favorite pets? Will animals be with their owners in the hereafter? "There is no revealed word on the subject. Reason would tell us that a rancher or farmer may not want all of the cattle he has owned during his life. On the other hand, emotional ties may be honored and family pets may well be restored to their owners in the resurrection. Elder Orson F. Whitney wrote that Joseph Smith expected to have his favorite horse in eternity."[2]

The resurrection is the uniting of the spirit and the body in immortality. "The spirit of man in the likeness of his person, as also the spirit of the beast, and every other creature which God has created" (D&C 77:2). Animals qualify as possessing both body and spirit for the wonder of the resurrection. Such doctrine can give deeper dimension to the relationships we have with cherished pets and animals.

Notes:

1. Joseph Fielding Smith, *Doctrines of Salvation,* vol. II, Salt Lake City: Bookcraft, 1956, 281.

2. Gerald E. Jones, "I Have a Question – Where do animals fit in the eternal plan of things?" *Ensign,* March, 1977.

121. The popular doctrine of the Trinity is man-made.

That the Father and the Son are two separate and distinct living beings was without question during the life of the Lord Jesus Christ. The recorded instances of Jesus praying to His Father are many. At both His baptism and upon the Mount of Transfiguration, Jesus and His disciples distinctly heard the approving voice of God. Stephen "saw the glory of God, and Jesus standing on the right hand of God" (Acts 7:55). And if that's not clear enough, Jesus said, "For I came down from heaven, not to do mine own will, but the will of him that sent me" (John 6:38).

The notion of the Trinity is rooted in the Nicene Creed of AD 325 and subsequent iterations of the same in AD 381, 431 and 451. The original Ecumenical Council of Nicene was to settle the growing rift between the factions championed by Arius and by Athanasius. Arius taught that the Son of God came after God the Father in time and substance and implied that there are two Gods separate from each other. The Council of Nicene sustained the Athanasians, resulting in the one God, one substance, one person, three persons doctrine of the Trinity. These doctrines were formed in the fourth and fifth century after Christ!

In 1646, the Westminster Confession of Faith was drawn up as a Reformed confession of faith for the Church of England. It includes doctrines common to most of Christendom today, including the Trinity concept. The Trinity doctrine teaches that "there is only one God. . . . This means that there are three persons in one God and not three Gods. The persons are known as the Father, the Son, and the Holy Spirit; and they have always existed as three distinct persons."[1]

"Theologians admit that the word "person" is not the perfect word to use because it carries with it the idea of individuals who are different beings . . . and this is one of the problems with using the term 'person' when describing the Father, the Son, and the Holy Spirit."[2]

That seems to be the dilemma that they can't resolve. The insistence in the false Trinitarian notion of the Godhead force them into this uninspired position and preclude the separate existence of Jesus as the divine Son of God.

God is my Father, and to Him I pray and receive inspiration and revelation. Jesus is my Savior, my Exemplar, and my Master. It is not incorrect to refer to Him as my God as well, as He is the God of the Old Testament, the God of Israel, and the Head of the Restored Church today that bears His name. I am ever so grateful for the witness of the Holy Ghost of these foundational truths regarding the Father, the Son, and the Holy Ghost.

Notes:

1. Matt Slick, "The Trinity," Christian Apologetics & Research Ministry, www.carm.org/dictionary-trinity.
2. Matt Slick, "Does the Trinity really teach that there are three gods?" Christian Apologetics & Research Ministry, www.carm.org/does-the-trinity-really-teach-there-are-three-gods.

122. There is a formula for overcoming the natural man tendencies in all of us.

"For the natural man is an enemy to God, and has been from the fall of Adam, and will be, forever and ever, unless he yields to the enticings of the Holy Spirit, and putteth off the natural man and becometh a saint through the atonement of Christ the Lord, and becometh as a child, submissive, meek, humble, patient, full of love, willing to submit to all things which the Lord seeth fit to inflict upon him, even as a child doth submit to his father" (Mosiah 3:19).

I think most people would agree that there is a huge gap between us as mortals and God as an immortal, perfect being. Yet, that does not discourage the true disciple of Christ from seeking to obtain this "divine nature" (2 Peter 1:1-8) as Peter wrote about to the faithful.

Let's examine this inspired scriptural formula, given to close the gap between us and God. "For the natural man is an enemy to God" (Mosiah 3:19). Unchecked, our natural tendencies will lead us to some combination of selfishness, greed, lust, laziness, irreverence, intolerance, indulgence, and a host of other human weaknesses and excesses. First, on this climb to higher ground is the recognition that "unless he yields to the enticings of the Holy Spirit" and has a desire "to put(teth) off the natural man" (Mosiah 3:19), true course correction will not occur. I like the word "enticings" when referring to the Holy Ghost. He will not yell at us, nor compel us, but we can choose to yield to His gentle and sweet influence.

Next, is the essential acceptance of the Atonement of Jesus Christ, without which we could not attain the presence of God. He is our Redeemer from sin and error. We have, and will, commit sin and error of judgment in our mortal experience. He not only redeems us from sin (which is enough!) but enables us along our earthly sojourn.

Finally, we must become like a child, "submissive, meek, humble, patient, full of love, willing to submit to all things" (Mosiah 3:19). All of this implies faith, a deep trust in the Lord and in his plan, an attitude such that the Lord can work with us, as the potter molds the clay.

The resulting creature (not to be completed in this life) is one that takes upon him the name of Christ, and truly "becometh a saint through the Atonement of Christ the Lord" (Mosiah 3:19).

This is a scriptural verse of truth, power, hope, and motivation. It is a reminder of the course we are on. It has brought me back to center on many occasions, and I consider it to be loving counsel through an inspired prophet of God.

123. Through the Atonement of Jesus Christ, we gain vision and hope.

The Prophet Alma recorded perhaps the most inclusive and whole view of the Atonement's breadth, summarized in three consecutive verses which I will abbreviate:

"And he shall go forth, suffering *pains* and *afflictions* and *temptations* of every kind . . . and the *sicknesses* of his people. And he will take upon him *death* . . . and he will take upon him their *infirmities* . . . that he might take upon him the *sins* of his people" (Alma 7:11-13, emphasis added).

Most of the Christian world would acknowledge that the fundamental work of the Savior is to redeem us from sin and from death. So what does it mean that He took upon Him our pains, afflictions, temptations, sicknesses, and infirmities? Do we somehow transfer those to Him? Not any more than we could transfer to Him the experience of death. We cannot. Each will leave this life through the process of death. But we have the certain knowledge that His death and subsequent resurrection will "loose the bands of death which bind his people" (Alma 7:12).

It is, likewise, with sin. We cannot entirely escape the transgressions inherent to this mortal life "for all have sinned, and come short of the glory of God" (Romans 3:23). Yet, like the promise of the resurrection in answer to the dilemma of death, "though your sins be as scarlet, they shall be as white as snow; though they be red like crimson, they shall be as wool" (Isaiah 1:18).

In other words, we have the hope and assurance that ultimately sin and death will be overcome. In the end, they will hold no sway to the truly penitent (Alma 42:23-24).

By experiencing the farthest extremity of human pain, affliction, infirmity, sickness, and temptation, "his bowels may be filled with mercy . . . that he may know according to the flesh how to succor his people" (Alma 7:12, see also Hebrews 2:18). Truly, Christ's willingness to take upon Himself these conditions so that He would know our mortal plight is mercy defined.

In addition to this empathetic selflessness, Christ taking upon Himself these experiences also argues favorably for His overcoming them. Like sin and death, through Jesus and His atoning sacrifice, someday all pains, afflictions, sickness, infirmities and even temptations, will be no longer. This vision makes the present bearable, even giving us the hope to "be of good cheer" (John 16:33), for someday, "we shall be like him" (Moroni 7:48).

To apply the Atonement in our lives, we gain a hope for delivery from our temporary earthly afflictions. It is to see beyond the moment. It is to know that "The Son of Man hath descended below them all" (D&C 121:8). "These things I have spoken unto you, that in me ye might have peace. In the world ye shall have tribulation: but be of good cheer; I have overcome the world" (John 16:33). The Book of Mormon gives us priceless insight into the breadth and depth of the atoning sacrifice of the Lord Jesus Christ.

124. Signs shall follow them that believe.

"And Jesus went about all Galilee, teaching in their synagogues, and preaching the gospel of the kingdom, and healing all manner of sickness and all manner of disease among the people" (Matthew 4:23). The Joseph Smith Translation adds this addendum, "which believed on his name," to the verse above. In other words, even the healing work of the Savior required the believing heart of the recipient.

This is important to understand. Unlike the fictional waving of a wand to change scenarios, faith in the divine Sonship of Jesus is necessary as an enabler to effect miracles in the lives of others. There is power in this kind of faith.

Casual recognition of Jesus has not the power to do mighty work as was illustrated while Jesus was in his own country. There He was seen as "the carpenter, the son of Mary" (Mark 6:3), even though He astonished them by His powerful teaching in the synagogue. It was there that He declared, "A prophet is not without honour, but in his own country, and among his own kin, and in his own house. . . . And he could there do no mighty work. . . . And he marvelled because of their unbelief" (Mark 6:1-6).

"Signs [miracles, healings, tongues, and others] shall follow them that believe," is a consistent phrase in the New Testament, the Book of Mormon, and the Doctrine and Covenants. For example, "And these signs shall follow them that believe; In my name shall they cast out devils; they shall speak with new tongues; They shall take up serpents; and if they drink any deadly thing, it shall not hurt them: they shall lay hands on the sick, and they shall recover" (Mark 16:17-18). Similar language is used in Mormon 9:24 and D&C 84:65-72.

Many look for a sign as the proof they claim to need in order to convince them to embrace faith. However, that is entirely backward and often disingenuous. "But, behold, faith cometh not by signs, but signs follow those that believe" (D&C 63:9). And to those who believe, the signs that follow become sweet confirmation of their faith in the Resurrected Lord (Mark 16:20).

This ordering of faith first as a gateway to attendant blessings and marvelous works is consistently taught in the New Testament and in Latter-day scripture. That Joseph Smith would make this inspired addendum to Matthew 4:23 gives significant clarity to this doctrinal truth.

125. The Holy Sacrament is an ordinance that is linked to baptism.

When we are baptized, we covenant to do at least three things:

- Take upon us the name of Christ
- Always remember Him
- Keep His commandments

The revealed sacramental prayers, offered in preparing the emblems of the sacrament to be partaken of, include language that corresponds to our baptismal covenants:

- "willing to take upon them the name of thy Son" (D&C 20:77)
- "and always remember Him" (D&C 20:77, 79)
- "and keep His commandments which He has given them" (D&C 20:77)

Just as baptism is preceded by repentance, so effectively partaking of the sacrament requires preparation which involves a humble attitude, a submissive spirit, and real intent to more fully align ourselves with the Spirit of the Lord.

Prior to going out to the Mount of Olives and then on to Gethsemane, Jesus instituted the sacramental emblems to his apostles. Over the bread, He commanded them to "Take, eat: this is my body" (Mark 14:22). Then, of the wine, He said, "Drink ye all of it; For this is my blood of the new testament, which is shed for many for the remission of sins" (Mark 14:23-24).

In Roman Catholic theology, it is taught that there is a "transition of the entire substance of the bread and wine into that of the Body and Blood of Christ."[1] Although we do not believe in that changing of organic form, there is like symbolism to the fact that we ingest the bread and the wine (water). Symbolically, we take into us the Christ, are nourished by Him, and re-commit ourselves to become like Him. The bread and water are *emblems* of the flesh and blood of Christ (D&C 20:40).

Baptism brings a fresh new awareness and a hopeful beginning to one's soul, even a re-birth. The worthy participation in the ordinance of the sacrament, or the Lord's Supper as referred to by Paul, promises us that we will "always have his Spirit to be with [us]" (D&C 20:77). Such a renewal and a promise is indeed a hopeful beginning at any point in our life! It is a welcome refreshment as we journey through this mortal experience as imperfect beings.

Jesus initiated the manner and the purposes of the sacramental ordinance to be administered in His absence and in remembrance of Him. Such administration was restored in 1830 and continues today as the focus of our Sabbath worship.

Notes:

1. Catholic Encyclopedia, *The Real Presence of Christ in the Eucharist; Transubstantiation a) paragraph 2,* www.newadvent.org/cathen/05573a.htm#section3.

126. Families can be together forever and live in celestial glory.

Common language in wedding ceremonies include the words, "till death do you part" or "legally and lawfully wedded for the period of your mortal lives." That is entirely commensurate and appropriate to the authority of the person officiating. To wed a couple beyond the confines of this mortal sphere requires priesthood authority from God and specific delegation of sealing power. That is, indeed, what God has provided and what He desires for His children.

Those who have experienced love and those who long for such an experience, intuitively believe that such love and association will not end with our mortal death and that husband and wife, children, and siblings will continue to enjoy a special relationship we call family.

"The divine plan of happiness enables family relationships to be perpetuated beyond the grave. Sacred ordinances and covenants available in holy temples make it possible for individuals to return to the presence of God and for families to be united eternally."[1]

Of course, children grow up and marry as well, so the celestial family circle will be composed of individuals, all of whom are sealed to a companion, and bound through the family lines of each spouse. But the family relationships we develop, the experiences we have shared, the memories, the associations—those defining bonds of love—will always remain. The Prophet Joseph Smith taught, "And that same sociality which exists among us here will exist among us there, only it will be coupled with eternal glory, which glory we do not now enjoy" (D&C 130:2).

Marriage is a prerequisite to celestial life, and the Lord has called it an "everlasting covenant of marriage" (D&C 131:2).

"In the resurrection there will be no marrying nor giving in marriage; for all questions of marital status must be settled before that time, under the authority of the Holy Priesthood, which holds the power to seal in marriage for both time and eternity."[2] Those not bound (sealed) under this authority, "are appointed [as] angels in heaven" (D&C 132:16). This is what the Savior taught, when confronted with the question of marriage in the hereafter (see Matthew 22:23-33). He further taught, "For this cause shall a man leave father and mother, and shall cleave to his wife; and they twain shall be one flesh. . . . What therefore God hath joined together, let not man put asunder" (Matthew 19:4-6).

"Let it be remembered that the first marriage on this earth was made before there was any death. In that day the Lord said, 'It is not good for man to be alone.' Therefore he gave him a wife. This marriage was not intended to be broken, and the idea of death and an eternal separation never entered into it."[3]

I thank God for my family. As children, spouses, and grandchildren expand that circle of love and enjoyment, happy is the man and woman who can look forward to those wonderful bonds of family togetherness forever. "Which [celestial] glory shall be a fullness and a continuation of the seeds forever and ever" (D&C 132:19).

Notes:

1. First Presidency and The Council of the Twelve, "The Family: A Proclamation to the World," *Ensign*, November, 1995.
2. James E. Talmage, *Jesus the Christ,* Salt Lake City: Deseret Book, 1977, 548.
3. Joseph Fielding Smith, *Answers to Gospel Questions*, Salt Lake City: Deseret Book, 1957, 2:120, 4:146.

127. Jesus is the Begotten Son of God the Father, not the incarnate of Him.

The notion of the Incarnation of Christ begins with the doctrine of the Trinity and is widely held in Christendom today. It is in essence "that the second person of the Trinity, also known as God the Son . . . became flesh by being conceived in the womb of Mary. . . . The Incarnation, then, [is that] Jesus Christ is fully God and fully human."[1]

This incarnation of Christ as seen under the doctrine of the Trinity is conflicting. From what is known as the Nicene Creed, originating from the First Council of Nicaea in 325, Jesus is said to be "one substance with the Father."[2] Some iterations of the creed use the word consubstantial - regarded as identical in substance or essence though different in aspect. They say that God the Father exists as an omnipresent spirit, and at the same time, as the embodied Son of God in mortality. Yet, that would be two concurrent aspects or manifestations of God, contrary to what the Trinity doctrine allows by its own definition of a monotheistic core.

The truth is that they are separate and distinct individuals. Jesus is literally the Son of God. He is not a transmutation of the Father. Unlike the common religious use and intent of the incarnation, we see Jesus rather as the Only Begotten of God the Father, not a substitute form of God the Father.

However, it can be said that Christ *is* the Incarnate God in one sense. He alone was born into this world of divine parentage. The oneness of the Father and the Son in purpose and action are evident in the following declarations made by Jesus: "And that I am in the Father, and the Father in me, and the Father and I are one—The Father because he gave me of his fulness, and the Son because I was in the world and made flesh my tabernacle, and dwelt among the sons of men" (D&C 93:3-4). "And he that sent me is with me: the Father hath not left me alone; for I do always those things that please him" (John 8:29).

There should be no blurring of identities as the common notion of the incarnation proposes. "And this is life eternal, that they might know thee the only true God, and Jesus Christ, whom thou hast sent" (John 17:3).

Notes:

1. Incarnation (Christianity), *Wikipedia*, www.en.wikipedia.org/wiki/incarnation_%28Christianity%29, February, 2015.
2. *Creed of Nicaea – Agreed at the Council in 325*, www.earlychurchtexts.com/public/creed_of_nicaea_325.htm.

128. Inspiration from God is not limited to baptized members of the Church.

There is a joke told of a man who died and went to heaven. Upon arrival, St. Peter took him around to meet the other fortunate souls. "John, these are the Baptists. Everyone say hello to John!" Whereupon the Baptists greeted John heartily. They proceeded on, where they were met by the Presbyterians, and a similar introduction took place. Further on, they met the Catholics, the Methodists, and people of other churches, all extending the same welcoming hand. Then, some distance off, were seen a group of people dressed in white, whereupon John asked, "And who are those people?"

"Shhhhh, those are the Mormons. They think they're the only ones here!"

Although the joke is on us, the fact is that we actually believe that the millennial period will be populated with those of many faiths. Ultimately, "every knee shall bow, and every tongue shall confess" that Jesus is the Christ (D&C 88:104). With that confession and knowledge, most will willingly comply with the ordinances required of the Lord for Salvation.

Until that time (speaking of "that time" for each individual), Heavenly Father is not exclusive in giving light to those who will magnify that light and talent for the betterment of humanity. For example, regarding the founding of the United States and particularly the drafting of the Constitution, the Lord said, "And for this purpose have I established the Constitution of this land, by the hands of wise men whom I raised up unto this very purpose" (D&C 101:80).

We, as a people, are commanded to "seek ye diligently . . . yea, seek ye out of the best books words of wisdom" (D&C 88:118). At the top of my list of best books would be the Book of Mormon, prophetically termed "the most correct of any book on earth" (Introduction, Book of Mormon). Included in those best books would have to be the human dramas of Shakespeare, the mastery of language by Hawthorne, the weaver's pen of Hugo, and the call to action of Stowe or Sinclair. Of course, this is only a fractional representation of these best books.

We are to "seek learning, even by study" (D&C 88:118, 109:7, 14). We marvel at the genius of Beethoven, Socrates, Edison, Churchill, Michelangelo, Copernicus, and innumerable other musicians, philosophers, inventors, statesmen, artists, astronomers, and great thinkers and creators of human history. Such genius, generously deposited upon the mortal experience, is inspired of God.

I believe that these great thinkers, although not of our faith in this life, will yet align themselves fully with the truth when it is presented to them. Meanwhile, we are indebted to them for the contribution they left as an expression of their God-given gifts and talents.

129. Humans are not puppets of divine decree, but they are free to choose their own course.

When I served as a missionary in Mexico, I often heard the qualifying clause, "Si Dios quiere," meaning, "if God be willing." That is ultimately good and true, except when the phrase is used as a release from personal responsibility and decision making.

The Joseph Smith Translation of Matthew 13:12 is a consistent clarification of a truth. The italicized words that follow are the corrected text, from the parentheticals as it reads in the King James version. "For whosoever (hath) *receiveth,* to him shall be given, and he shall have more abundance; but whosoever (hath not) *continueth not to receive*, from him shall be taken away even that he hath" (Matthew 13:12).

God has not placed us on this earth to exercise his arbitrary will, manipulating us like pawns on a chess board! He has given us the power to choose, to pursue, to behave, to think, and to reason. In the process and progress of life, He desires that we would choose Him above all else. Hence, the usage of the verb "receive" animates what otherwise could be read as merely being acted upon.

When the gift of the Holy Ghost is conferred upon a new member of the Church, the authoritative verbiage used is to "*receive* the Holy Ghost."[1] It is an invitation, and at the same time, a commandment. Receiving the companionship of the Holy Ghost greatly enhances the course of life we will choose. Nephi taught "that if ye will enter in by the way, and receive the Holy Ghost, it will show unto you all things what ye should do" (2 Nephi 32:5). Implicit in this gift is the guidance to choose.

Priesthood covenants have similar scriptural language requiring our pro-active choice, "And also all they who *receive* this priesthood *receive* me, saith the Lord; For he that *receiveth* my servants *receiveth* me; And he that *receiveth* me *receiveth* my Father; And he that *receiveth* my Father *receiveth* my Father's kingdom; therefore all that my Father hath shall be given unto him" (D&C 84:35-38, emphasis added).

All men can change and come unto Christ, if they will so choose, and thereby, they will receive him. His Atoning Sacrifice is broad enough for all.

My personal choice of discipleship is so much the sweeter because I am not compelled, but gently persuaded by "the enticings of the Holy Spirit" (Mosiah 3:19). I rejoice in the freedom to act, to choose, and to become.

Notes:

1. *Handbook 2 Administering the Church*, Salt Lake City: The Church of Jesus Christ of Latter-day Saints, 2010, 20.3.9, also see D&C 20:41.

130. Be ye therefore perfect; however, do not run faster than you have strength.

The New Testament scriptural conclusion to Matthew chapter 5 is a summary statement to the rich teachings of the Savior known as the

Sermon on the Mount. "Be ye therefore perfect, even as your Father which is in heaven is perfect" (Matthew 5:48).

Such a mandate is immediately unattainable in its entirety, and on its own, could lead to frustration, or worse, to abandon the path of faith. Yet, it is the Savior's vision for each of us.

In the Book of Mormon, King Benjamin teaches the people to have faith in Jesus Christ and His Atonement, to serve others, to care for the poor, and many other eternal values. Toward the conclusion of his sermon, he tempers all the list of to-do's and not-to-do's with this gem, "And see that all these things are done in wisdom and order; for it is not requisite that a man should run faster than he has strength. And again, it is expedient that he should be diligent, that thereby he might win the prize; therefore, all things must be done in order" (Mosiah 4:27).

This then becomes a formula to attain to the perfection that the Savior unequivocally commanded! It is a companion truth to the command to be perfect. It is the balance to the eventuality and the sometimes painfully slow journey.

Although this is distinctly LDS doctrine, the counsel of King Benjamin is not broadly taken to heart as a balm for our inevitable human shortcomings and limitations. I see too many members of the Church berating themselves for their coming short of the perfections they seek. There must be a balance between the ideal (which we will keep firmly as our end) and the journey.

Recently, I attended my first yoga class with Justin and Rachel. I was surprised at how demanding and difficult it was. We went through twenty-six poses while an instructor called out the positioning, purposes, and nuances of each pose. "Touch your head to your knee.... There should be no gap between your biceps and your ears.... Lock your leg and extend it straight out.... Concentrate and balance....

And . . ." I couldn't attain to the ideal of any of the poses, although I tried to do so. I fell short in all my efforts.

On the next session, I realized that this was going to take time to master and that I would go at a reasonable yet challenging pace. I finished that class having made progress, and just as importantly, having enjoyed the session so that I wanted to return to make more progress.

This comforting doctrine of pace and tempo from the Book of Mormon, gives perspective to eternal pursuits. Coupled with the power, grace, and mercy of the Lord, we can indeed "do all things through Christ" (Philippians 4:13). Only with such perspective can we fulfill the Second Great Commandment to "love thy neighbour as thyself" (Matthew 22:39). Patience with self, not to run faster than we have strength, will bring greater peace, enjoyment, and stamina. We are to endure to the end, not to get it all done just perfectly today.

131. Damnation is a result of personal choice.

For many years this word has been used negatively and usually inappropriately. I have to agree though, it is not a word connoting anything positive. For me, the best illustration of its correct use is in visualizing a dam that is constructed to hold back water. There ends the course of the water. It can go no further. It is dammed. To be damned spiritually is similar, but more expressly in regard to our eternal attainments.

The Bible dictionary defines damnation, "Damnation is the opposite of salvation, and exists in varying degrees. All who do not obtain the fullness of celestial exaltation will to some degree be limited in their progress and privileges, and hence be damned to that extent."[1] This definition is unique to LDS understanding. Whereas most would equate damnation with a singular, ultimate destination called hell, damnation is in fact by degrees.

Jesus warned some of a "greater damnation" (Mark 12:40, Luke 20:47, Matthew 23:14) which also demonstrates that there are indeed various degrees of this limitation or damnation.

It's my observation that many in our society also see damnation as a divine invective. On their own, they want to command God to use it on their behalf, kind of like shooting arrows at the guilty.

But damnation is what we do to ourselves. It is the very purpose and objective of God to keep us from damning ourselves. Christ came to make possible the Father's intentions "to bring to pass the immortality and eternal life of man" (Moses 1:39).

It is interesting to me that I don't see the word "damn" or "damnation" at all in the Old Testament. In other scripture citations, its variations are used most (at least eight times) regarding noncompliance with the ordinance of baptism. Mark 16:16 is a succinct example: "He that believeth and is baptized shall be saved; but he that believeth not [and is not baptized] shall be damned." That is in alignment with our definition of damnation being a result of our personal course.

In a way that is closely associated with the covenant of baptism, we are cautioned to avoid damnation by not partaking of the sacrament emblems unworthily (1 Corinthians 11:29, 3 Nephi 18:29). Other damning behaviors are hypocrisy, public piety, taking advantage of the poor and the widows (Matthew 23:14), blasphemy, denying the Holy Ghost (Mark 3:29, D&C 132:27) resisting the ordinances of the gospel (Romans 13:2), slothfulness, doubt (D&C 58:29), and not accepting or keeping essential covenants (D&C 132:4,6). All of these are brought on by our personal choices. None of them are hurled at us by a vindictive God.

Damnation occurs when we halt our progress, defer or abandon our discipleship, disregard our covenants, break the commandments, or any number of other ungodly behaviors. It is the opposite of Heavenly Father's program to bring salvation to His children.

Notes:

1. LDS Bible Dictionary, "Damnation."

132. Hell is a real place.

Hell is commonly held to be a single destination immediately following death, where the devil resides, and where the evil and the unbelievers will live eternally. In more casual language, people use it as a make-believe place to send their foes when they get ticked off. The former is accurate in part; the latter is not our prerogative.

The first sentence above is accurate in part, but it doesn't occur immediately following death. There is a "state of the soul between death and the resurrection" (Alma 40:11). This temporary state is divided into paradise and hell (also known as a spirit prison). Those sent to this temporary hell include those who "have no part nor portion of the Spirit of the Lord; for behold, they chose evil works rather than good; therefore the spirit of the devil did enter into them, and take possession of their house" (Alma 40:13). It also includes those "who received not the gospel of Christ, neither the testimony of Jesus" (D&C 76:82), and significantly, "who deny not the Holy Spirit" (D&C 76:83).

At the end of the millennium, "death and hell delivered up the dead that were in them: and they were judged every man according to their works" (Revelation 20:13). "Hell must deliver up its captive spirits" (2 Nephi 9:12). Thus, those in this hell (spirit prison) will come forth for the resurrection and then the final judgment.

This final judgment will consign these resurrected souls to either a degree of glory through the redemption made by Jesus Christ, or to dwell with the devil in "hell, that he may reign over you in his own kingdom" (2 Nephi 2:29). That hell, where the devil dwells, is a final eternal destination. The following scripture describes who qualifies for that judgment and the conditions of hell: "These are they who are the sons of perdition . . . with the devil and his angels in eternity; Concerning whom I have said there is no forgiveness in this world nor in the world to come—Having denied the Holy Spirit after having received it, and having denied the Only Begotten Son of the Father, having . . . put him to an open shame. These are they who shall go away into the lake of fire and brimstone . . . And the only ones on whom the second death shall have any power . . . the only ones who shall not be redeemed" (D&C 76:32-38).

For those not redeemed, hell is every bit of its traditional definition as "the fire that shall never be quenched" (Mark 9:43, Isaiah 66:24, Mosiah 2:38, Jacob 6:10, D&C 43:33) and "where there is weeping, and wailing, and gnashing of teeth" (D&C 133:73).

The Lord has provided every opportunity for man to avoid this ultimate hell through His merciful, redeeming Atonement. There will be time and teaching both here and beyond the veil. Ours is to accept the gospel of Jesus Christ, to repent, and to show our obedience. In fact, we believe that there will be relatively few who won't accept, repent, and obey. Church doctrine has a very generous view of the inherent goodness of mankind and the power of the Atonement to successfully entice men to accept, repent, and obey.

But for those who will not, there is a place for them, which is to dwell with the devil in hell.

133. Not all will be saved by the Atonement of Christ, but all may if they will.

I want to make immediate clarification to the above title. Jesus will save us from death—all will be resurrected unconditionally—all people will, to that extent, be saved by the Atonement of Christ.

The second clarification, to be "saved" by the Atonement of Christ as it pertains to our sins, is not a simple two-part existence of either heaven or hell. Hell will be hell, where the devil reigns and where there is no redemption claimed on the Atonement of Jesus Christ. But all other realms are to exist in some degree of glory and enjoyment, the highest in the very presence of God the Father and our Lord Jesus Christ, enjoying family relationships and linked associations.

Now, to the title of this writing.

My son-in-law called me this week regarding an exchange they had in a Sunday School class recently. The instructor stated that the suffering and atoning sacrifice of Jesus was just enough for those sins that we repent of, but it did not cover all the sins of mankind. This is an erroneous conclusion.

I think it stemmed from our doctrine (likely unique to our faith) that the Atonement of Christ will redeem us, will even blot out, those sins that we repent of, and those that we are unaccountable for. "And mercy claimeth the penitent, and mercy cometh because of the atonement" (Alma 42:23). "And he hath power given unto him from the Father to redeem them from their sins because of repentance" (Helaman 5:11, see 5:10).

Inseparably connected to this doctrine, is that those sins we don't repent of, are thusly dealt with, "But if they would not repent they must suffer even as I" (D&C 19:17).

We must remember that the breadth of the Atonement is independently infinite in its scope. It is sufficient to redeem all mankind.

"There was no partial drinking of the cup, no selective discrimination in absorbing certain sins and not others; he would take upon him, as the scriptures said, 'the sins of the whole world' (1 John 2:2). Nothing would be left on the table. . . . It would even include the suffering of those who chose not to repent. In other words, the

Savior suffered not only for those whom he knew would repent, but even for those who would choose never to embrace his sacrificial offering."[1]

Salvation is claimed by many differing doctrines: the belief in universal reconciliation or that all will be reconciled to God (Christian Universalism), predestination and a limited atonement (Calvinism), or by being "born again" (Evangelical). These are a few examples of those saving beliefs, although I realize that I am not doing them justice by such brevity.

Our doctrine holds that the Atonement is broad enough and available for all, but we must choose to avail ourselves of its redeeming power. In summary, "We believe that through the Atonement of Christ, all mankind may be saved, by obedience to the laws and ordinances of the Gospel" (Articles of Faith, 3). To me, that is fair, merciful, and sound doctrine.

Notes:

1. Tad R. Callister, *The Infinite Atonement,* Salt Lake City: Deseret Book, Illustrated Edition, 2013, Chapter 13, 105-106.

134. The Plan of Salvation is a huge success.

As Latter-day Saints, we are accustomed to seeing ourselves as a small minority, yet possessing the very keys of eternal life. Perhaps it is an overlay of that view that some also see the Celestial world as sparsely populated. And coupled with our own self-judgment, many unnecessarily deny themselves the hope of personal salvation, narrowing even more that population in their mind.

Such an outlook and conclusion would characterize the Plan of Salvation and the very Atonement of Jesus Christ as largely a failure measured by the numbers. This is just not so.

The Plan of Salvation is merciful, infinite, universal, comprehensive, fair, and divine. It is conceived and designed to overcome death and sin, to refine our very natures, and to provide for eternal happiness. For you and for me and for all of mankind.

To the Prophet Joseph in the Kirtland temple in 1836, "Thus came the voice of the Lord unto me, saying; All who have died without a knowledge of this gospel [also all who shall die henceforth without a knowledge of it] who would have received it if they had been permitted to tarry, shall be heirs of the celestial kingdom of God; For I, the Lord, will judge all men according to their works, according to the desire of their hearts. And I also beheld that all children who die before they arrive at the years of accountability are saved in the celestial kingdom of heaven" (D&C 137:7-10).

A listing of those who will attain to Celestial life include the following:

- Those who die without ever hearing the gospel, who would have received it and will receive it prior to the final judgment
- All children who die before the age of eight years
- All those unaccountable for reasons of mental or physical deficiency
- Those spirits born during the Millennium
- Translated beings
- Those mortals throughout history who have lived faithful to their priesthood covenants

Alonzo L. Gaskill has written that the spirit world will be "the realm where most of His children will be introduced to the truths of Christ's Atonement and the restoration of his gospel. . . . In the April 1894 general conference, President Wilford Woodruff stated: 'There will be very few, if any, [in the spirit world] who will not accept the gospel.'"[1]

In an attempt to quantify the number of children who have died before the age of accountability, and are "alive in Christ" (Moroni 8:22), the estimates from various studies range somewhere between thirty and fifty plus percent of the whole human family! The Prophet Joseph Smith said, "The Lord takes many away, even in infancy, that they may escape the envy of man, and the sorrows and evils of this present world; they were too pure, too lovely, to live on earth."[2]

Additionally, "all those billions of people who will be born during the millennium, when Satan is bound, 'shall grow up without sin unto salvation' (D&C 45:58) and therefore will not be tested."[3] Elder McConkie is also of the opinion that "It is not unreasonable to suppose that more people will live on earth during the millennial era than in all the six millenniums that preceded it combined."[4]

Add to those numbers those who are unaccountable by mental or physical handicaps, translated beings, and those of us who are "work[ing] out your own salvation" (Philippians 2:12), and we begin to see a large segment of the human family who will achieve ultimate salvation.

This is entirely consistent with a loving Father in heaven; a loving, merciful Savior; and a divine plan to enable eternal felicity.

Notes:

1. Alonzo L. Gaskill, *Odds Are You're Going to Be Exalted,* Salt Lake City: Deseret Book, 2010, 36-37.

2. Joseph Fielding Smith, comp., *Teachings of the Prophet Joseph Smith,* Salt Lake City: Deseret Book, 1976, 196-197.

3. Bruce R. McConkie, "The Salvation of Little Children," *Ensign,* April, 1977.

4. Bruce R. McConkie, *The Millennial Messiah*, Salt Lake City: Deseret Book, 1982, 671.

135. The devil has no power over us except as we permit him.

In the early 1970's, the beloved comedian Flip Wilson introduced us to the character of Geraldine Jones, a sassy woman of the times. Geraldine coined a line that became a national catchphrase when she would excuse her impulsive actions by concluding, "The devil made me do it."

It's a cute line, and in some ways has made it into the fabric of people's belief as a convenient excuse for behavior they know is not right. As if we of ourselves had no control over certain aspects of our behavior. Its sister line would be, "It's not my fault."

Joseph Smith taught an important doctrinal truth, "The devil has no power over us only as we permit him. The moment we revolt at anything which comes from God, the devil takes power."[1]

From the days when Adam and Eve were in the garden, Satan has been the great tempter. Our challenge is to resist his temptations, even as the Lord modeled to us prior to His public ministry and following His forty-day fast. In fact, He modeled such behavior throughout His perfect life, "For we have not an high priest which cannot be touched with the feeling of our infirmities; but was in all points tempted like as we are, yet without sin" (Hebrews 4:15).

There are three intelligent powers in the universe—God, man, and Satan—and the power of God is the greatest of all. The devil is given the power to lay before us temptations (3 Nephi 28:39, D&C 101:28), but we are given power to rise above and overcome such temptations (D&C 10:5, Ephesians 6:10-13).

Understanding that the power is in us to overcome evil and temptations that would distance us from God is a correct understanding that empowers us. Rather than see ourselves as victims of an evil will, we can recognize temptation for what it is and not succumb to it. We can resolutely turn to face God, realizing that the power is in us to reject or to embrace the power of the devil. That firm stance toward God brings us this grand promise, "If ye continue in my word, then are ye my disciples indeed; And ye shall know the truth, and the truth shall make you free" (John 8:31-32). Therein is true and absolute freedom, regardless of our circumstances.

Notes:

1. Joseph Fielding Smith, comp., *Teachings of the Prophet Joseph Smith,* Salt Lake City: Deseret Book, 1976, 181.

136. The doctrine of eternal marriage confirms our yearnings and intuitive beliefs.

"For in the resurrection they neither marry, nor are given in marriage, but are as the angels of God in heaven" (Matthew 22:30, Mark 12:25).

Jesus' statement does not preclude the postmortal institution of marriage, but rather the performance of marriage in the realm of the hereafter. Elder James E. Talmage explains, "In the resurrection there will be no marrying nor giving in marriage; for all questions of marital status must be settled before that time, under the authority of the Holy Priesthood, which holds the power to seal in marriage for both time and eternity."[1] This sealing work is taking place and will continue to take place in temples for both the living and the dead now and throughout the millennium and prior to the final judgment.

"Therefore, if a man marry him a wife in the world, and he marry her not by me nor by my word, and he covenant with her so long as he is in the world and she with him, their covenant and marriage are not of force when they are dead. . . . Therefore, when they are out of the world they neither marry nor are given in marriage; but are appointed angels in heaven. . . . For these angels did not abide my law; therefore, they cannot be enlarged, but remain separately and singly, without exaltation" (D&C 132:15-17). They may be in states of glory (heaven), but not as exalted beings.

Fundamental, and to my knowledge unique, is the LDS doctrine that declares, "The divine plan of happiness enables family relationships to be perpetuated beyond the grave."[2] Our sweetest sociality is that of family life.

It was God who commanded the man and the woman to be "one flesh" (Genesis 2:24), and what "God hath joined together, let not man put asunder" (Matthew 19:5-6).

Robert L. Millet tells of a personal experience with a friend from another faith who questioned the need for temples that we hold so dear. Particularly in light of Matthew 22:30 and Mark 12:25. Their abbreviated conversation follows:

> "Your wife Debbie – do you love her?"
>
> "Well, of course, I love her. She's my wife."
>
> "I know she's your wife, but do you love her?"
>
> "Yes, I love her!"
>
> "Those four children you have—what are their names?"
>
> He named them off.
>
> "Do you love them?"
>
> He said, "This is getting juvenile."
>
> "No, it's not, do you love them?"
>
> "I do!"
>
> "Do you really love them?"

> "Of course I do!"
>
> "Now I want you to answer a question not from your intellect, but from your soul."
>
> He saw that I was very serious about this, and he said, "I'll try to do that."
>
> I said, "You really do believe that following death you will be with that woman and those four children in the life to come, don't you?"
>
> He stared at me, then became misty, and said, "Yes, I do."[3]

It's not only a yearning to continue the relationships with our loved ones, it is an intuitive belief that we will. And as Brother Millet pointed out to his friend, "In temples, we formalize and provide authority for the thing you already know in your heart of hearts to be true."[4]

In isolation, Matthew 22:30 and Mark 12:25 can be and have been interpreted to be in conflict with other divine decrees. And such an interpretation is in conflict with the intuition of the human soul. But as clarified and expanded by latter-day prophets, deep is the hope that fills our hearts, and sweet is the doctrine of an eternal marriage relationship.

Notes:

1. James E. Talmage, *Jesus the Christ,* Salt Lake City: Deseret Book, 1977, 548.

2. First Presidency and The Council of the Twelve, "The Family: A Proclamation to the World," *Ensign,* November, 1995.

3. Robert L. Millett, "Doctrines, Covenants, and Sweet Consolation," in Richard Neitzel Holzapfel, editor, *Joseph Smith's Prophetic Ministry - 1843,* Salt Lake City: Deseret Book, 2009, audio CD.

4. Robert L. Millet.

137. "The days of our probation" is scripturally unique to LDS understanding.

I've known several people who have ended up in jail for a time and later are released and begin a defined period of what is called probation. During this time of probation, they are being tested to see if their conduct, character, associations, and ambitions are in alignment with imposed norms of civil behavior. Having proved themselves true to the terms of their probation, they are once again given their full freedoms.

The Book of Mormon and the Doctrine and Covenants are unique in their scriptural use of the term "probation." The Bible often speaks of our need to endure and to overcome the inevitable trials of this mortal life. Adversity, afflictions, trials, tribulations, temptations, opposition, testing, trying, and proving are all scriptural terms from the Bible to describe the various experiences that will test and strengthen our faith. In a sense, all of these words are a part of how we would characterize mortality, which the Prophet Alma referred to as "a probationary state" (Alma 12:24).

Nephi, Lehi, Alma, Samuel the Lamanite, and Moroni all wrote of the days of probation as a reference to this life. Describing the mortal state immediately following the fall of Adam and Eve, Lehi taught his son Jacob, "And the days of the children of men were prolonged, according to the will of God, that they might repent while in the flesh; wherefore, their state became a state of probation" (2 Nephi 2:21).

"Probation is defined as the testing or trial of a person's conduct, character, and qualifications."[1] In the context of our mortal life, this definition implies a previous existence, one in which we defined our conduct and to some degree developed our character. The experience in this fallen world then becomes the perfect testing ground of our soul, of who we really are, and of who we are willing to become. In the end, perhaps it is as much a test to prove to ourselves who we really are, as it is to God who already knows our dispositions so well.

The doctrinal understanding of a premortal existence, coming to earth to live by faith, and then living post-mortally without end, gives a correct view and estimation of this mortal sphere. It is indeed a probationary state, to see if we will hearken to the voice of the Good Shepherd and keep His commandments. "And we will prove them herewith, to see if they will do all things whatsoever the Lord their God shall command them" (Abraham 3:25). It is a temporary state, but one of such infinite consequences.

Notes:

1. www.dictionary.reference.com/browse/probation.

138. "Returning to live with our Heavenly Father" is a commonly used, doctrinally profound statement.

Attend any LDS Sunday worship meeting, and chances are good that you will hear the above phrase spoken as a kind of statement of purpose. You may hear it in sacrament meeting, in youth classes, in the Primary, in the Relief Society, and in priesthood meetings. Attending other Christian denominations, LDS members would notice the conspicuous absence of the verb "return" when speaking of life with God.

Much doctrine is tied to this declaration:

- "The spirit shall return unto God who gave it" (Ecclesiastes 12:7). We know that we are spirit children of Heavenly parentage. To return implies we were once there, in the presence of God.
- We existed in the pre-mortal realm as spirit entities. Now, our physical bodies are of mortal elements, "for dust thou art" (Genesis 3:19), then to be buried "and unto dust shalt thou return," awaiting the resurrection (Genesis 3:19). Later, we will become immortal because of the Atonement of Christ and His

conquering of death, bringing a universal resurrection to all mankind.

- Our spirit is housed within this body, and we are learning in this life to control physical appetites with spiritual resolve. We are but children in this exercise and lived only as spirits in our pre-mortal life.

- We are returning home. Home implies someplace where we are comfortable, someplace familiar. A place where we can truly be ourselves, without pretense, surrounded by those who love us and whom we love, a time and a place of pure enjoyment.

- Realizing that we are returning to live with our Heavenly Father inspires us to seek higher standards of conduct, a more God-like character. At the same time, we know that we were once in His holy presence and who we really are.

- "The glory of God is intelligence" (D&C 93:36). We have much to learn. So very much. "Seek learning, even by study and also by faith" (D&C 88:118). "Whatsoever principle of intelligence we attain unto in this life, it will rise with us in the resurrection" (D&C 130:18). Returning to live with God, we will take with us knowledge and experience that could only have been learned here in mortality.

- This life is a testing time to see if we will live by faith and endure in faith to the end. It is a time to make covenants with God, clinging to our faith and demonstrating our commitment by complying with outward ordinances and commandments as prescribed by God.

To hear a child speak of returning home to live with their Father in Heaven carries with it all these doctrines and more. It is matter-of-fact. It gives laser focus to who we are, why we are here, and to where we are going.

139. Enoch was a mighty Old Testament prophet, and this is the rest of the story.

The Biblical references to the ancient Prophet Enoch are scant, but distinctive. In the recorded genealogy of Father Adam's literal descendants, there is a three-part pattern in Chapter 5 of Genesis:

1. X lived so many years, and begat Y.
2. And X lived after he begat Y so many years.
3. And all the days of X were so many years and he died.

This pattern, following the early "order of the priesthood," (D&C 107:40-41) continues by description for the first five generations after Adam. In the sixth lineal generation, through Enoch, after fathering Methuselah, it is recorded that Enoch "walked with God" (Genesis 5:22, 24), as perhaps an intended contrast to the common "and X lived." Enoch's was a holy existence. And then "he was not; for God took him" (Genesis 5:24).

The apostle Paul wrote of Enoch and gave clarity to his being taken by God, "that he should not see death" (Hebrews 11:5), coining and defining the state of translation that Enoch experienced.

Jude makes reference to Enoch's prophecy of the Second Coming (Jude 1:14), which is a clear indication that there was more to be known of Enoch than is available in the Bible as we have it today.

Through the Prophet Joseph Smith, the Lord has revealed much about Enoch and his ministry. He was ordained under the hand of Adam when twenty-five-years-old. He received a special blessing from Adam when he was sixty-five-years-old, and from that time "he saw the Lord, and he walked with him, and was before his face continually" (D&C 107:48, 49). In the valley of Adam-ondi-Ahman, Father Adam bestowed upon the righteous his last blessing, "and the Lord appeared unto them". Enoch was there and recorded these sacred events (D&C 107:53, 54, 57).

An inspired translation of the Bible by the Prophet Joseph, brought forth selections from what is called the Book of Moses, where we have two long chapters describing great details of Enoch, his life, and his relationship with God. He was a preacher of righteousness. He taught of the fall, death, agency, repentance, baptism, atonement, immortality, the Holy Ghost, and the plan of salvation. He conversed and reasoned at length with the Lord, witnessed and marveled at the weeping of God, beheld angels descending from heaven, saw Satan in his mocking attitude, gazed upon all the inhabitants of the earth, saw the salvation of his posterity through his great grandson Noah, and beheld the yet-to-occur crucifixion of the Savior. And much more. (see Moses 6 & 7)

We learn that Enoch not only walked with God, but also "Enoch and all his people walked with God" (Moses 7:69). Enoch "built a city that was called the City of Holiness, even Zion" (Moses 7:19). We learn "that not only Enoch, but also his entire city was translated."[1] In the last days, Zion will again exist, even a New Jerusalem, and "Then shalt thou and all thy city meet them there. . . . And there shall be mine abode, and it shall be Zion" (Moses 7:69, 62-64).

Rich and poignant are these writings of the life and ministry of Enoch. They span from the ancient to the present and into the millennium. What a blessing to have them once again through the revelations of a living prophet.

Notes:

1. LDS Bible Dictionary, "Enoch."

140. "One Lord, one faith, one baptism" speaks well for the restoration.

This simple declaration by Paul to the Ephesians (Ephesians 4:5) makes a great case for the Church of Jesus Christ being restored to the earth through the Prophet Joseph Smith. Categorically, this scripture gives focus to the Godhead, to the Church, and to authorized ordinances.

"Christ is the one Lord, the gospel plan taught by him is the one faith, and his baptism by immersion is the one baptism."[1]

That this verse in Ephesians is referring to Jesus Christ is made clear by the subsequent verses, where Paul identifies the Father, "One God and Father of all, who is above all, and through all, and in you all" (Ephesians 4:6). The One Lord Paul is referring to is the Lord Jesus Christ as our Savior (Ephesians 4:7), Him to whom we must look for redemption, He who stands on the right hand of God, and who is the author of our salvation (see Acts 7:55-56, Hebrews 5:9).

Jesus is the author of our salvation by the infinite Atonement He wrought and by the plan of salvation He taught and teaches today. The vehicle for this one faith is His Church as He established it while in the flesh and as He restored it in these latter days. "For God is not the author of confusion, but of peace, as in all churches of the saints" (1 Corinthians 14:33). What did Paul mean by "all churches of the saints?" Certainly, he was referring to the one Church that Christ established. At that point, the churches were founded upon the apostolic authority and were being formed in places like Corinth, Rome, Galatia, Ephesia, and other cities. The entire ministry of Paul, Peter, and the other apostles was to teach a common doctrine of "Jesus Christ, and him crucified" (1 Corinthians 2:2) and to set in order the Church by establishing, correcting, clarifying, even instituting (as in the case of Peter's vision in Acts 10) correct doctrine—one faith.

Jesus made clear the necessity of ordinances when he said, "Except a man be born of water and of the Spirit, he cannot enter into the kingdom of God" (John 3:5). And he gave the example of how that was to be. Paul pleaded with the Corinthians that they would "keep the ordinances as I delivered them to you" (1 Corinthians 11:2). They are not to be altered by man. And those ordinances are to be performed under "the keys of the kingdom of heaven: and whatsoever thou shalt bind on earth shall be bound in heaven" (Matthew 16:19). Jesus modeled the one correct manner of baptism as an example of eternally binding ordinances.

One Lord, one faith, one baptism. And one human family, which can be "knit together in love and unto all riches of the full assurance of understanding" (Colossians 2:2). "Till we all come in the unity of the faith, and of the knowledge of the Son of God, unto a perfect man, unto the measure of the stature of the fulness of Christ" (Ephesians 4:13).

I stand with the apostle Paul. I believe there is one Lord (Jesus Christ), one faith (the Church He established anciently, and restored in these latter days), and one baptism (ordinances administered under the keys of priesthood).

Notes:

1. Delbert L. Stapley, "The Path to Eternal Life," *Conference Report,* October, 1973.

141. Enduring to the end is founded on faith in Christ and a promise.

When I was first baptized, I used to think it was odd that we would hear so much over the pulpit of the need to endure to the end. What is there to endure? This is sweet! To me, that was like bemoaning having to endure a day at the beach.

I have since grown up. And grown up in the gospel. It is, indeed, a paradox to speak of the joy of the saints, and at the same time, hope that we can endure all things. I understand now that those are not necessarily contradictory statements and that the latter indeed leads to the former.

Scripturally, we are to endure:

- The cross (Hebrews 12:2)
- Chastening (Hebrews 12:7, D&C 101:5)
- Hardness (2 Timothy 2:3)
- Affliction (2 Timothy 4:5, 3:11, D&C 24:8)
- Persecution (Mark 4:17, 2 Thessalonians 1:4, 2 Timothy 3:11, D&C 101:35)
- Hatred (Mark 13:13)
- Suffering (2 Corinthians 1:6)
- Tribulations (2 Thessalonians 1:4)
- Grief (1 Peter 2:19)

Enduring has a promise and a purpose: "But he that shall endure unto the end, *the same shall be saved*" (Matthew 24:13, emphasis added).

Do a scriptural search on "endure to the end" and you'll find in every instance, it connects with being saved, or having eternal life. Scriptural endurance isn't just to make it through, but to "endure in faith on his name [Jesus Christ] to the end" (D&C 20:29).

Each of the following behavioral admonitions also include the counsel to endure to the end and then promises the resultant salvation or eternal life. Note the richness of LDS scripture, and the foundation in Jesus Christ:

- Repent (D&C 20:29, 2 Nephi 9:24)
- Believe in Christ (D&C 20:25, 29, 2 Nephi 9:24, 33:4)
- Come unto Christ (Omni 1:26)
- Look unto Christ (3 Nephi 15:9)
- Follow the example of Christ (2 Nephi 31:16)

- Be baptized as was Christ (D&C 20:25, 9:24, Mormon 9:29, D&C 18:22)
- Partake of the sacrament worthily in the name of Christ (Mormon 9:29)
- Feast upon the words of Christ (2 Nephi 31:20)
- Keep the commandments of Christ (1 Nephi 22:31, D&C 14:7)
- Offer our whole souls to Christ (Omni 1:26)
- Seek to bring forth Zion (1 Nephi 13:37)
- Continue in fasting and prayer (Omni 1:26)
- Worship the Father in the name of Christ (D&C 20:29)

These could be seen as sequential steps on our way to eternal life, and perhaps they do have some ordered chronology. But more importantly they are on-going habits and characteristics of those who are truly enduring to the end.

Latter-day Saints speak often of enduring to the end, indicating a correct understanding and an important aspect of our faith. We hope to be among those "who have endured valiantly for the gospel of Jesus Christ" (D&C 121:29), to the same end that Abraham secured for himself "after he had patiently endured, he obtained the promise" (Hebrews 6:15). That promise is salvation.

142. To die in the faith is to complete our time of probation.

I'm not going to lie—there have been times in my life that I've thought the requirements of gospel living have been onerous. I look at those who come home from work, do some labor in their well-tended garden, have dinner with the family, then settle in to a good book, or watch their favorite programs piped in on one of the many cable channels. They have Saturday and Sunday completely clear to travel, camp, or pursue hobbies.

But then I recall that the designs of God are to fashion us to be like Him, and that transformation can only occur when His ways become our ways and His thoughts our thoughts (Isaiah 55:7-9). We must be "willing to submit to all things which the Lord seeth fit to inflict upon him" (Mosiah 3:19). We must "be submissive and gentle; easy to be entreated" (Alma 7:23).

This life is a time of testing our resolve, our discipleship, our willingness to be transformed. "And we will prove them herewith, to see if they will do all things whatsoever the Lord their God shall command them" (Abraham 3:25).

The good news is that for the faithful saints of God, the testing will end with this life. Elder Bruce R. McConkie taught the following at the funeral of S. Dilworth Young:

> "If we die in the faith, that is the same thing as saying that our calling and election has been made sure, and that we will go on to eternal reward hereafter. As far as faithful members of the church are concerned, they have charted a course leading to eternal life. This life is the time that is appointed as a probationary state for men to prepare to meet God, and as far as faithful people are concerned, *if they are in the line of their duty, if they've done what they ought to do, although they may not have been perfect in this sphere, their probation is ended.* Now there will be some probation for some other people hereafter, *but for the faithful Saints of God, now is the time and the day, and their probation is ended with their death, and they will not thereafter depart from the path.*"[1]

There is advantage to faithfully adhering to the gospel life while in mortality. For those ignorant of gospel truths, or those who for various reasons have not embraced gospel covenants, their time of testing will be beyond the grave.

"But blessed are they who are faithful and endure, whether in life or in death, for they shall inherit eternal life" (D&C 50:5). All those who will inherit eternal life must pass through that refining fire that transforms the human desires and appetites to characteristics of the divine.

Common, ordinary, faithful Saints, living the best they can, should live with the hope that eventually all their efforts to follow the Master will one day be no effort at all. "Beloved, now are we the sons of God, and it doth not yet appear what we shall be; but we know that, when he shall appear, we shall be like him" (1 John 3:2).

To die firmly in the faith, is to complete our time of probation, having endured to the end.

Notes:

1. Bruce R. McConkie, address given at the funeral of Elder S. Dilworth Young, July 13, 1981.

143. All men and women are spiritually brothers and sisters.

In the Church, we have a few appellations that we use in addressing one another, such as Bishop, President, Elder, Brother, and Sister. I have served in positions that carried the title of Elder, Bishop, and President. But my favorite is to be known as Brother Rogers. I find it warm, personal, descriptive, even familial. It is a reminder of a great truth—that we are indeed brothers and sisters of a common Father in Heaven, spiritually begotten prior to our mortal birth. We are in this together, and we are our brother's keeper.

Paul and other New Testament writers frequently use the expression of brother as they refer to fellow servants in Christ. The book of Philemon is a good example of this. "Not now as a servant, but above a servant, a brother" (Philemon 1:16). Jesus made a similar conditional, familial description when he said, "For whosoever shall do the will of God, the same is my brother, and my sister, and mother" (Mark 3:35).

But the more common usage by Jesus throughout his ministry is the general reference to our fellows as our brothers (and by extension, our sisters). Not just brothers in a cause, or brothers by similar behavior, but brothers, in fact. We are not to fixate on the mote in our brother's eye, we are to have compassion when we see a brother in need, we must not create a stumbling block in our brother's way, we are not to be angry with our brother, we are to forgive the brother who trespasses against us.

"And this commandment have we from him, That he who loveth God love his brother also" (1 John 4:21). This is another rendering of the great commandment that Jesus gave when he said, "Thou shalt love the Lord thy God with all thy heart. . . . Thou shalt love they neighbour as thyself" (Matthew 22:37, 39). And to give clarity to whom our neighbour might be, Jesus gave the parable of the Good Samaritan, describing the good works of a fellow traveler to a complete stranger. I imagine this Samaritan knew that the brotherhood of man is greater than national or tribal distinctions and that such a brotherhood is founded on our being sons and daughters of Almighty God.

I've always liked the fact that in the Church we continue to refer to one another as Brother or Sister So-and-So. It is both a reminder of a great truth and, at once, a warm and inclusive reference to another. And it's also a great crutch when you just can't remember someone's name!

144. Lo, children are an heritage of the Lord.

Looking up the word "heritage," I conclude that the scripture that says that "children are an heritage of the Lord" (Psalms 127:3) refers to the birth of a child as a gift from God. We know that all gifts from

God are given to bless His children. A subsequent verse says just that, "Happy is the man that hath his quiver full of them" (Psalms 127:5). There is no determined quantity to constitute a full quiver in this life. It could be one child for this family and any number for another. "The decision as to how many children to have . . . is extremely intimate and private and should be left between the couple and the Lord."[1]

That being said, LDS people are known for having larger than average families. There is a reason, which is embedded within the doctrines we hold dear. It is primarily the doctrine of our eternal spirits and the coming to this world from a pre-mortal existence. LDS parents know that they are actually creating earthly tabernacles for spirit children of our Father in Heaven. "We know that every spirit assigned to this earth will come."[2] Elder Benson then spoke of the doctrinal understanding of parenthood, "The first commandment given to man was to multiply and replenish the earth with children (Gen. 1:28). That commandment has never been altered, modified, or canceled. The Lord did not say to multiply and replenish the earth if it is convenient, or if you are wealthy, or after you have gotten your schooling, or when there is peace on earth, or until you have four children. . . . We believe God is glorified by having numerous children and a program of perfection for them."[3]

Sister Cheryl A. Esplin gave a concise doctrinal lesson when she said, "What a sacred responsibility Heavenly Father places upon us as parents to partner with Him in helping His choice spirits become what He knows they can become."[4] This is the unique understanding of LDS moms and dads. The Lord said, "Ye will teach them to walk in the ways of truth and soberness; ye will teach them to love one another, and to serve one another (Mosiah 4:15).

"When a wrong wants righting, or a truth wants preaching, or a continent wants discovering, God sends a baby into the world to do it."[5]

Bringing children into this world is not first about enhancing the marital relationship, achieving a norm, or creating special bonds to fill their own void, although each of these come to pass within a family. It's the understanding of enabling the spirits in heaven to come to this earth and experience mortality in a family. Our family. Your family. Their family.

Notes:

1. *Handbook 2 Administering the Church,* Salt Lake City: The Church of Jesus Christ of Latter-day Saints, 2010, 21.4.4.
2. Ezra Taft Benson, "To the Humble Followers of Christ," *Conference Report,* April, 1969, 10-15.
3. Ezra Taft Benson.
4. Cheryl A. Esplin, "Teaching Our Children to Understand," *Ensign,* May, 2012.
5. F.M Bareham, as quoted by Spencer W. Kimball, "A Prophet is Born," *Conference Report,* April, 1960, 83-86.

145. The name, term, and person of Elias is used in several contexts in the scriptures.

Judging from the questions posed to Jesus relative to the person and mission of Elias, the Jewish leaders and even the disciples of Christ had only a partial understanding. The fact that Jesus referred to the name or term of Elias on at least three occasions and that He was in the presence of Elias on another gives importance to our understanding the mission and use of this name.

The easy explanation is that Elias is the Greek form of the Hebrew name Elijah. Elias is not used in the Hebrew Old Testament, nor is Elijah used in the Greek New Testament. Elijah was a commanding figure from the Old Testament, so much so, that Malachi closed out his record by recording, “Behold, I will send you Elijah the prophet before the coming of the great and dreadful day of the Lord” (Malachi 4:5).

Most of the references in the New Testament to Elias are clearly references to Elijah of the Old Testament. However, the Savior also referred to John the Baptist as an Elias, “Behold, I will send my messenger before thy face, which shall prepare the way before thee. . . . there hath not risen a greater than John the Baptist. . . . And if ye will receive it, this is Elias, which was for to come” (Matthew 11:10, 11, 14).

Following the experience on the Mount of Transfiguration, where Elias (Elijah) was a participant, the disciples were confused. As their scriptures recorded (Matthew 11:10, 11, 14), Elijah was to come *before* the Lord, and there on the mount they had seen him *after* the Lord Jesus was manifest. Again, Jesus made reference to John the Baptist as an Elias, “Elias truly shall first come, and restore all things. But I say unto you, That Elias is come already, and they knew him not. . . . Then the disciples understood that he spake unto them of John the Baptist” (Matthew 17:11-13). The Joseph Smith Translation of Verse 13 adds, “and also of another who should come and restore all things, as it is written by the prophets” (JST, Matthew 17:13). This is a significant addition, as we shall see.

Jesus was not saying that John the Baptist was Elijah who was to return. John himself made this clear when the priests and Levites asked him, “Art thou Elias (Elijah)?” He answered flatly, “I am not” (John 1:21).

John the Baptist was a forerunner, a preparer of the way. This, then, is another meaning of the term Elias. Hence, I’ve inserted “an” as a designation used rather than a proper name used three paragraphs above. The Joseph Smith Translation and revelations in the Doctrine and Covenants expand this meaning to include one who will restore all things. John the Revelator (D&C 77:9, 14), Gabriel, who is Noah

(D&C 27:6-7, Luke 1:11-19), and Christ Himself (JST, John 1:21-28) are all referred to as Elias, in addition to John the Baptist.

But we're not done yet. "A man called Elias apparently lived in mortality in the days of Abraham, who committed the dispensation of the gospel of Abraham to Joseph Smith and Oliver Cowdery in the Kirtland Temple on April 3, 1836 (D&C 110:12). We have no specific information as to the details of his mortal life or ministry."[1]

In summary, Elias is used after the times of the Old Testament in at least the following contexts:

- As the Greek form of Elijah, the ancient prophet of the Old Testament
- As one who is sent by God to prepare or to restore
- As an important keyholder named Elias

Latter-day revelation has given much light to an otherwise fragmented use of the name Elias. But to those who will hear, it is light indeed. Jesus himself recognized that not all would understand, when he said on two occasions, "And if ye will receive it, this is Elias" (Matthew 11:14 D&C 77:9).

Notes:

1. LDS Bible Dictionary, "Elias."

146. Section 137 of the Doctrine and Covenants gives profound doctrinal instruction that surprised the Prophet Joseph.

Section 137 came as a vision to the Prophet Joseph Smith in the Kirtland temple two months prior to its actual dedication. "The heavens were opened upon us, and I beheld the celestial kingdom of God, and the glory thereof" (D&C 137:1). It was a vision of a future time, given to illustrate an important doctrine that Joseph had heretofore not known and likely had not even considered.

In the vision of the celestial kingdom, Joseph saw his brother Alvin, who had died in 1823, almost seven years before the priesthood and the Church were restored to the earth. William Smith, the Prophet's brother, later recalled the funeral service for Alvin, wherein the Reverend Benjamin Stockton "intimated very strongly that he [Alvin] had gone to hell, for Alvin was not a church member."[1]

Up to this time there was no saving doctrinal provision for those who did not accept Christ and the required ordinance of baptism while in mortality. Hard as it was to swallow, Joseph likely tacitly agreed with the reverend's conclusion.

The prevailing Protestant conundrum at the time was the conflict of three truths:[2]

- A loving God desires the salvation of his children
- Salvation comes only through one's acceptance of Christ and His atonement and manifesting that acceptance through baptism
- Innumerable are God's children who have lived and died without an opportunity to accept Christ and His atonement, nor could be baptized

How could those truths be reconciled? When the answer came, apparently even Joseph "marveled" (D&C 137:6). "All who have died without a knowledge of this gospel, who would have received it if they had been permitted to tarry, shall be heirs of the celestial kingdom of God. Also all that shall die henceforth without a knowledge of it, who would have received it with all their hearts, shall be heirs of that kingdom. For I the Lord will judge all men according to their works, according to the desires of their hearts" (D&C 137:7-9).

These verses bring profound hope and fairness to the hearts of those who truly love and have concern for their fellow travelers on this earth. It allows for the three truths above to stand, and instead of contraction regarding the possibility of salvation for mankind, provides for an expansion for God's children to be saved.

The Lord later revealed the ordinance of baptism for the dead, which both enables and brings into compliance and harmony the above truths.

The Lord revealed this doctrine of salvation even to the surprise and wonder of the Prophet Joseph Smith. It is not only an inclusive and merciful doctrine, but also it illustrates well that Joseph was ever learning from the source of all truth. This is not the church of Joseph, nor is it limited by the contemporary practices and beliefs of his time. Even he, as student, "marveled how it was" (D&C 137:6).

Notes:

1. William Smith, interview by E.C. Briggs and J.W. Peterson, October or November 1893, originally published in *Zion's Ensign,* reprinted in *Deseret Evening News,* January 20, 1894.

2. Steven C. Harper, "Joseph and the Kirtland Temple Experience," in Richard Neitzel Holzapfel, editor, *Joseph Smith's Prophetic Ministry - 1836*, Salt Lake City: Deseret Book, 2009, audio CD.

147. Eternal realms of glory are glorious doctrines indeed.

When I was a missionary in Mexico, I had only been a member of the Church for about two years. As with most missionaries, the preaching of the gospel caused me to think deeply of doctrines and their implication to my own life. For the most part, the implications were welcome, comforting, and expansive. But there was something I couldn't reconcile in my mind, and it was this: How could I be happy in the eternities if my own non-believing family would be in a different state of glory than I?

So I decided to ask my mission president at the next round of interviews we were to have. "President Marshall, we speak of and we long for this celestial realm of being in God's presence and having a continuation of families. Of course, it is conditioned on the individual faithfulness of each member. Such would be the highest attainment of happiness and joy. But how could it be entirely joyful if my own family, whom I dearly love, would not be there?"

At the time, I remember his answer did not fully assuage my concerns. As best as I can remember, he said our lives are like going into a room full of riches and treasures of various values and being allowed to gather up what we could in a certain time. Upon leaving with those items of our own choosing, we would be very happy for both the opportunity and for the newly acquired wealth that we then had ownership of. In other words, my family members would be happy in the next life.

Actually, I'm sure the explanation that Pres. Marshall gave me was better than what I just wrote, but that is what I remember. The point, though, was that my question and concern was not put to bed. I still felt that my own happiness would be less than full, given such a separation.

What I know now is that I was looking at it from my own perspective and desires. What about their desires? And if, in fact, I knew they were happy, wouldn't that make me happy?

One of the beautiful doctrines of the restoration is that of the degrees of glory after this life. Glory. Not just degrees of existence, but degrees of glory. Even the least degree of glory is described as "surpasses all understanding" (D&C 76:89). That sounds pretty elevated from the world we now live in.

Every person will be consigned to a kingdom in which they will be comfortable and among those they have come to be like. Said another way, they will go to where they most want to go. For the people I know, that will always be hyphenated with the word "glory" which connotes good things.

We will only rise to what we become, or in a very real sense, to what we choose to take from that room full of riches and treasures.

President Marshall's analogous explanation was a good one.

148. It's OK to be labeled by Evangelicals as different in our forms of Christianity.

Richard Land, a noted evangelical leader, recently was asked at a religious diversity conference at Princeton that if the LDS faith is not a cult, what is it? "I would describe it as a fourth Abrahamic religion . . . a religion based upon the Old and New Testaments . . . but with an additional revelation—in the case of the LDS Church, the Book of Mormon . . . that seems to communicate what I think evangelicals want to communicate."[1]

Because we believe we belong to the very Church Christ established, I can agree with Brother Land's characterization, but would instead place the LDS Church as the one to occupy the position as one of the three Abrahamic religions, and all other Christian movements and organizations to fall into a fourth category. And I'm OK with that distinction, for there certainly are important doctrinal differences.

At the least, the following truths illustrate some of the unique doctrinal scaffolding of the LDS Christian faith, not widely held by other Christian faiths:

- An understanding of the Plan of Salvation: "All human beings . . . [are] a beloved son or daughter of heavenly parents. . . . In the premortal realm, spirit sons and daughters . . . accepted His [God's] plan by which His children could obtain a physical body and gain earthly experiences to progress toward perfection."[2]

- The concept of God, Jesus Christ, and the Holy Ghost: God is our divine Father whom we address in prayer. Jesus is His only begotten Son in the flesh, the Savior of the world, our advocate, our model and example in all things. He sits on the right hand of God. The Holy Ghost is an unembodied spirit, the testator of truth, the comforter, our companion in righteousness.

- The fall of Adam and Eve: "The most tragic predicaments in which we find ourselves are those that require a choice between competing Goods, not Good and Evil. The author of Genesis frames Eve's choice as just such a dilemma, a choice between the safety and security of the Garden and the goodness, beauty, and wisdom that comes at the price—and only at the price—of painful lived experience. Her decision is more worthy of admiration for its courage and initiative, than reproach for its rebellion."[3] This is a vital understanding in order to construct the truth of the beginning of mankind and our very noble heritage.

- The saving Atonement of Jesus Christ: First, "the Lord surely should come to redeem his people, but that he should not come to redeem them in their sins, but to redeem them from their sins, . . . to redeem them from their sins because of repentance . . . which bringeth unto the power of the Redeemer, unto the salvation of their souls" (Helaman 5:10, 11). We must accept Christ, keep his commandments, and repent. Second, "for we know that it is by grace that we are saved, after all we can do" (2 Nephi 25:23). "After all we can do" refers to our discipleship born of our love for Him. It does not imply diminishing or setting aside the intrinsic blood of Christ.

- Priesthood authority and continuing revelation: First, we believe that there is a required line of authority to

> officiate in the name of the Lord and to bind on earth so that such will be bound in heaven (Matthew 16:19). Second, we believe God has called living prophets and apostles in these latter days, designating organized quorums of divine leadership for all the world.

All of the above (and many others that could be listed) are unique doctrines and understandings to the Church of Jesus Christ of Latter-day Saints.

Common to all of us as Christians is our faith in Jesus Christ as the Savior of all mankind. We do not see our fellow Christian friends as an adversarial entity. Rather, as Jesus counseled his apostles, "for he that is not against us is for us" (Luke 9:50). The Spirit of Jesus Christ has been, and is, a powerful influence for good across the earth, and most of that has been built and founded in the faith and works of those Christians not of our faith. Christian influence existed long before 1820 and has continued to elevate the human condition outside the Restored Gospel since 1820. Concurring in this recognition of similarities, Mr. Land went on to say, "I think that evangelicals have got to accept the fact that the LDS Church is a tremendous ally and fellow combatant against the things that are most threatening to us in America."[4]

Our message to all the world, including our Christian friends, is that the Gospel of Jesus Christ in all its fullness has been restored to the earth through a prophet. We see it as original Christianity in its pure form, brought forth in these latter days, by Him whose name we take upon us as Christians.

Notes:

1. Richard D. Land, interview with Matthew Brown, *Deseret News – Faith Section*, Sept. 15, 2013.

2. First Presidency and The Council of the Twelve, "The Family: A Proclamation to the World," *Ensign,* November, 1995.

3. Terryl L. Givens and Fiona Givens, *The God Who Weeps,* Salt Lake City: Ensign Peak, October, 2012, 57.

4. Richard D. Land.

149. Salvation applies to little children who die before the age of accountability.

"In his day [early 1800's] the fiery evangelists of Christendom were thundering from their pulpits that the road to hell is paved with the skulls of infants not a span long because careless parents had neglected to have their offspring baptized. Joseph Smith's statements, as recorded in the Book of Mormon and latter-day revelation, came as a refreshing breeze of pure truth: *little children shall be saved.*"[1]

"Salvation means eternal life; the two terms are synonymous; they mean exactly the same thing."[2]

Abinadi, a prophet in his own day, taught, "Little children also have eternal life" (Mosiah 15:25).

The Lord gave this understanding to the Prophet Joseph Smith, while in the Kirtland Temple, "I also beheld that all children who die before they arrive at the years of accountability are saved in the celestial kingdom of heaven" (D&C 137:10).

Eternal life. Saved. Celestial Kingdom.

These spirits will pass from this life in their innocence, will wait in paradise for the resurrection, and will be resurrected at the Second Coming of the Savior to a millennial realm with a celestial body. "Will these children ever be tested? Absolutely not! Any idea that they will be tested in paradise or during the millennium or after the millennium is pure fantasy. Why would a resurrected being, who has already come forth from the grave with a celestial body and whose salvation is guaranteed, be tested?"[3]

Further enlightening doctrine is, "Joseph Smith taught the doctrine that the infant child that was laid away in death would come up in the resurrection as a child; and, pointing to the mother of a lifeless child, he said to her: 'You will have the joy, the pleasure, and satisfaction of nurturing this child, after its resurrection, until it reaches the full stature of its spirit.' There is restitution, there is growth, there is development, after the resurrection from death."[4]

"The bodies of little children will grow after the resurrection to the full stature of the spirit, and all the blessings will be theirs through their obedience, the same as if they had lived to maturity and received them on the earth."[5]

"But as the child dies, so shall it rise from the dead. . . . It will never grow [in the grave]; it will still be the child, in the same precise form [when it rises] as it appeared before it died out of its mother's arms."[6]

"Little children are redeemed from the foundation of the world through mine Only Begotten" (D&C 29:46). And if they die in infancy or childhood, that redemption will make them inviolable, securing to them the blessings of salvation, eternal life. These must be special spirits indeed. What exquisite, magnificent, merciful, consoling doctrine this is!

Notes:

1. Bruce R. McConkie, "The Salvation of Little Children," *Ensign,* April, 1977.

2. Bruce R. McConkie.

3. Bruce R. McConkie.

4. Joseph F. Smith, comp., *Gospel Doctrine,* Salt Lake City: Deseret Book, 1977, 455-456.

5. Joseph Fielding Smith, *Doctrines of Salvation,* vol. II, Salt Lake City: Bookcraft, 1956, 54.

6. Alma P. Burton, comp., *Discourses of the Prophet Joseph Smith,* Salt Lake City: Deseret Book, 1977, 138-139.

150. The spirit of man is in the likeness of the physical body.

Unique to LDS doctrine is that when we refer to man in their pre-mortal or immediate post-mortal experience, we see each unique individual in the same likeness as the physical body. In contrast, I have never been able to endorse the notion that our spirit, or soul, is somehow without form or substance.

Addressing his remarks to children, Elder Boyd K. Packer gave this very simple, yet very illustrative teaching of this truth, "Pretend, my little friends, that my hand represents your spirit. It is alive. It can move by itself. Suppose that this glove represents your mortal body. It cannot move. When the spirit enters into your mortal body, then it can move and act and live. . . . When I separate them, the glove, which represents your body, is taken away from your spirit; it cannot move anymore. . . . But your spirit is still alive."[1]

Elder Packer is teaching that it's actually the hand (representing the spirit) that gives shape, or requisite shape, for the body. Not the other way around. The body houses, or conforms to, the spirit.

Nephi was "caught away in the Spirit of the Lord, [The Lord] spake unto him as a man speaketh; for I beheld that he was in the form of a man; yet nevertheless, I knew that it was the Spirit of the Lord; and he spake unto me as a man speaketh to another" (1 Nephi 11:1).

The Lord Jesus Christ showed his spirit body to the very faithful brother of Jared during a divine exchange, "Behold this body, which ye now behold is the body of my spirit; and man have I created after the body of my spirit; and even as I appear into thee to be in the spirit will I appear unto my people in the flesh" (Ether 3:16).

In 1832, the Lord confirmed to the Prophet Joseph Smith, "The spirit of man [is] in the likeness of his person" (D&C 77:2).

Brent Top, in his study of near-death-experiences, finds frequent confirmation of this LDS-held belief of the spirit of man. "For example, one woman who had a near-death experience stated that when her spirit left her body, she was surprised to find that 'I still had hands, and feet, and a body, for I had always regarded the soul as a something without shape and void. . . . I was surprised to find, that though I was 'dead' I still had form, [that] was new to me."[2] He quotes others who wrote, "Quadriplegics are no longer paralyzed, multiple sclerosis patients who have been in wheelchairs for years say that when they were out of their bodies, they were able to sing and dance; . . . people who had been blind from birth—never had any vision whatsoever—who had near-death encounters with the other side reported being able to clearly see."[3]

Physical impairments, imperfections, decrepitness—are all unknown to our spirits.

Although "we cannot see it," (D&C 131:8) it is true that "all spirit is matter" (D&C 131:7), and therefore, has shape. We are made in the image and likeness of God (Genesis 1:26), first spiritually and then mortally. Our bodies, although now imperfect, are the contour of our eternal spirits.

Notes:

1. Boyd K. Packer, "Behold Your Little Ones," *Conference Report,* April, 1973.

2. Brent Top, *What's on the Other Side?* Salt Lake City: Deseret Book, 2012, 6.

3. Brent Top, 9.

151. "This is my gospel," and "this is my doctrine."

Such declarations by the Son of God should grab our attention and stimulate our interest to hear and understand the completion of these statements. It is also of interest to me to see the consistent scriptural thread given at various times, connecting these declarations to what we refer to as the first principles and ordinances of the gospel.

In about 550 BC, the Prophet Nephi taught "concerning the doctrine of Christ" (2 Nephi 31:2) and dedicated an entire chapter to this most important subject. He begins by speaking of the baptism of Jesus as an example we must follow, adding the need for our repentance. Broad highlights of the chapter are captured as follows: "For the gate by which ye should enter is repentance and baptism by water; and then cometh a remission of your sins . . . and ye have received the Holy Ghost, which witnesses of the Father and the Son. . . . And now, behold, this is the doctrine of Christ, and the only true doctrine of the Father, and of the Son, and of the Holy Ghost" (2 Nephi 31:17, 18, 21).

About AD 34, Jesus came and ministered to the people of Nephi (3 Nephi 11). Immediately following His miraculous appearance and after the people recognized him as "the God of Israel" (3 Nephi 11:14-15), the Lord called and ordained men with "power that ye shall baptize this people when I am again ascended into heaven" (3 Nephi 11:21). He then taught them the correct manner to effect the ordinance of baptism. "And this is my doctrine...that the Father commandeth all men, everywhere, to repent and believe in me. And whoso believeth in me, and is baptized, the same shall be saved... and unto him will the Father bear record of me, for he will visit him with fire and with the Holy Ghost. . . . Verily, verily, I say unto you, that this is my doctrine, and whoso buildeth upon this buildeth upon my rock" (3 Nephi 11:32, 33, 35, 39).

In January 1831, came the revelation of Jesus Christ through Joseph Smith, "And this is my gospel—repentance and baptism by water, and then cometh the baptism of fire and the Holy Ghost, even the Comforter, which showeth all things, and teacheth the peaceable things of the kingdom" (D&C 39:6).

A tenet of our faith is, "We believe that the first principles and ordinances of the Gospel are: first, Faith in the Lord Jesus Christ; second, Repentance; third, Baptism by immersion for the remission of sins; fourth, Laying on of hands for the gift of the Holy Ghost" (Articles of Faith, 4).

The Gospel is the Plan of Salvation and includes all eternal truth, laws, ordinances, and associated covenants.[1] To fully appreciate and participate in gospel covenants, we must qualify and enter into "this strait and narrow path [baptism] which leads to eternal life" (2 Nephi 31:18) and receive the Gift of the Holy Ghost. Therein is His gospel and His doctrine that will lead us to eternal life, if we will thereafter endure to the end.

Notes:

1. lds.org, *The Guide to the Scriptures*, "Gospel."

152. Doctrinal clarity is given to scriptural references of Jesus as both the Father and the Son.

In the first four verses of Mosiah Chapter 15, the Prophet Abinadi speaks of Jesus Christ as God Himself, a redeemer, an obedient begotten Son of God, and as the Father. He then says, "And they are one God, yea, the very Eternal Father of heaven and of earth" (Mosiah 15:4).

In 1916, the First Presidency and the Quorum of the Twelve issued a doctrinal exposition titled "*The Father and the Son,*" written "to clarify the meaning of certain scriptures where Jesus Christ, or Jehovah, is designated as the Father."[1] In this exposition, there are four contexts in which Jesus is appropriately referred to as our Father:

1. Jesus declared to the brother of Jared, well before His earthly advent, "Behold I am Jesus Christ. I am the Father and the Son" (Ether 3:14). As the only begotten son of God in mortality, Jesus is uniquely qualified to acknowledge his literal kinship to God. "I am come in my Father's name" (John 5:43). He is the Son of God both spiritually and as bodily offspring. In a manner of speaking, He alone can claim the surname of Father.

2. Zeezrom, a lawyer seeking to trip the Prophet Amulek by his cunning, posed the question, "Is the Son of God the very Eternal Father" (Alma 11:38)? To which Amulek responded, "Yea, he is the very Eternal Father of heaven and of earth, and all things which in them are" (Alma 11:39). A second scriptural meaning of "Father" is that of Creator. Jesus Christ organized this physical world, or in essence, fathered the creation.

3. "For verily I say unto you, all those who receive my gospel are sons and daughters in my kingdom" (D&C 25:1). Joseph Fielding Smith explained, "What is a father? One who begets or gives life. What did our Savior do? He begot us, or gave us life from death. . . . He [Jesus Christ] became a father to us because he gave us immortality or eternal life through his death and sacrifice upon the cross. I think we have a perfect right to speak of him as Father."[2]

   King Benjamin added another dimension when he said, "And now, because of the covenant which ye have made ye shall be called the children of Christ, his sons, and his daughters; for behold, this day he hath spiritually begotten you; for ye say that your hearts are changed through faith on his name; therefore, ye are born of him and have become his sons and his daughters" (Mosiah 5:7).

Joseph Fielding Smith further explained, "The Son of God has a perfect right to call us his children, spiritually begotten, and we have a perfect right to look on him as our father who spiritually begot us."[3]

4. "I and my Father are one" (John 10:30, 17:11, 22). Jesus Christ is the Father by divine investiture of authority. "For I came down from heaven, not to do mine own will, but the will of him that sent me" (John 6:38).

By divine lineage into mortality, as the Creator of heaven and earth and all things which in them are, as our Redeemer, and as the authorized emissary of God the Father, Jesus can and has assumed the title of Father.

Abinadi concludes his divinely inspired message, which we can now read with greater understanding, "Teach them that redemption cometh through Christ the Lord, who is the very Eternal Father. Amen" (Mosiah 16:15).

Notes:

1. "The Father and the Son: A Doctrinal Exposition by the First Presidency and the Quorum of the Twelve Apostles," *Improvement Era,* August, 1916, reprinted *Ensign,* April, 2002.

2. Joseph Fielding Smith, "Book of Mormon Critics Refuted," *Conference Report,* October, 1962, 20-22.

3. Joseph Fielding Smith.

153. When we pray for our fellows, we neither seize their agency, nor alert God.

"And whatsoever ye shall ask the Father in my name, which is right, believing that ye shall receive, behold it shall be given unto you" (3 Nephi 18:20).

But what about when we pray for an outcome in the life of another human being? Do we take from them their freedom to choose, or do we override the consequences of their choices? Furthermore, is God not already aware of their needs and wouldn't He already be poised to mercifully bless His children independent of our pleadings?

We should keep these four truths in mind:

- God is all-knowing, loves his children, does not sleep, is filled with love and mercy, and has the power to right all wrongs
- Man cannot compel another without physical force, and God will not
- We are by nature selfish, "unless he yields to the enticings of the Holy Spirit" (Mosiah 3:19)
- We are commanded to pray for others

Jesus made what we refer to as intercessory prayers to the Father on behalf of His disciples. "I pray for them," He said simply in one prayer (John 17:9). In the Garden of Gethsemane, Jesus pled for and atoned for all of mankind. Later in the Americas, he pled for those people, saying, "And now Father, I pray unto thee for them" (3 Nephi 19:23). Jesus both prayed for and worked on behalf of all men.

"The effectual fervent prayer of a righteous man availeth much" (James 5:16).

"For them that honour me I will honour, and they that despise me shall be lightly esteemed" (1 Samuel 2:30).

Righteousness seems to be an effectual power. Righteous Alma prayed "with much faith" (Mosiah 27:14) for his wayward son. As a result, the Lord sent an angel to Alma the younger "that the prayers of his servants might be answered according to their faith" (Mosiah 27:14). Ammon was spared the sword because of the promise given his righteous father Mosiah "according to thy faith" (Alma 19:23).

There is another truth we should keep in mind. "For your Father knoweth what things ye have need of, before ye ask him" (Matthew 6:8). In fact, He knows the needs of all His children, at all times.

From the example of Jesus as He interceded and continues to intercede on our behalf, we know that we, too, must pray for our fellow beings. The power and influence of those prayers will have greatest effect when we ourselves are living righteously, when our petitions are fervent, such as Enos, "I did pour out my whole soul unto God for them" (Enos 1:9), and when those petitions are in alignment with God's will. That power and influence will not compel or override the agency of anyone, but it does become a contributing factor, a very real influence, in the blessings and opportunities that can then be available.

Perhaps, it is so that we can be drawn into this work of mercy and redemption by our own participation, that we are commanded to pray for those in need, and even for those "which despitefully use you, and persecute you" (Matthew 5:44). In doing so, we will refine our very natures, align ourselves with the Spirit, and be contributors to the divine powers that bless mankind. All the while, we understand the omniscience of God and the agency of man.

154. How do we activate and access the blessings of the Atonement in our lives?

We talk about the Atonement of Jesus Christ a lot in the Church, and that is as it should be. We talk of what a great blessing it is to us, and it is. We talk of utilizing the Atonement in our daily lives, and we should.

None of us have a perfect understanding of how it is, nor how impactful it is. Nor do I pretend to have some special insight to write about. The Atonement has some profound effects to all of mankind and some very personal effects to those who seek that influence. I write about my personal observations and experiences regarding activating and accessing the blessings of the Atonement and include insights unique to our faith.

There is nothing we can do to activate the Atonement as a redeeming act of God. It is done. "I have drunk out of that bitter cup" (3 Nephi 11:11), said Jesus, and "partook and finished my preparations unto the children of men" (D&C 19:19). Because of this supernal act, all mankind will be resurrected, and the redemption required by justice for the sins of mankind is sufficient. The resurrection is an unconditional gift to us. To be redeemed requires our obedience to the laws and ordinances of the Gospel.

Elder David A. Bednar speaks also of another power of the Atonement, "the strengthening and enabling power."[1] To access that empowerment, I have my own personal, yet partial list. Yours no doubt may be different to some degree.

- Be humble, teachable, submissive, childlike: "And my grace is sufficient for all men that humble themselves before me" (Ether 12:27). The Bible dictionary defines the main idea of grace as "divine means of help or strength."[2] Elder Bednar says he inserts the term "enabling power" whenever he encounters the word "grace."[3] So reread the above scripture substituting "enabling power" for the word "grace." We get back to the Atonement.

- Be baptized, receive the Gift of the Holy Ghost, and all other saving ordinances and covenants: "And be baptized in my name, that ye may be sanctified by the reception of the Holy Ghost, that ye may stand spotless before me at the last day" (3 Nephi 27:20). Baptism presupposes repentance, and sanctification can only be possible because of the Atonement. Continuous sanctification comes from continuous repentance, because of a continuous atonement.

- Obtain the virtues of charity: Charity "is the pure love of Christ . . . which he hath bestowed upon all who are true followers of his Son, Jesus Christ . . . that we may be purified even as he is pure" (Moroni 7:47-48).

- Plead prayerfully: "And now it came to pass that the burdens which were laid upon Alma and his brethren were made light; yea, the Lord did strengthen them that they could bear up their burdens with ease, and they did submit cheerfully and with patience to all the will of the Lord" (Mosiah 24:15).

- Receive the Lord's prophets and servants: "For he that receiveth my servants receiveth me" (D&C 84:36). We are in the mainstream of the Lord's enabling power if we are in alignment with his servants the prophets.

Because of the Atonement of Jesus Christ, I feel approved, forgiven, encouraged, confident, and hopeful. All of life's yearnings for "if only" – are addressed. Death and sin are overcome, and by His grace and mercy, I am enabled and empowered.

Notes:

1. David A. Bednar, "The Atonement and the Journey of Mortality," *Ensign*, April, 2012.

2. LDS Bible dictionary, "Grace."

3. David A. Bednar.

155. Evil does not and cannot emanate from God.

When Samuel the Prophet anointed David to be King of Israel (because the Lord rejected Saul), it is recorded that "the Spirit of the Lord came upon David from that day forward" (1 Samuel 16: 13). The very next verse says, "But the Spirit of the Lord departed from Saul, and an evil spirit from the Lord troubled him. And Saul's servants said unto him, Behold now, an evil spirit from God troubleth thee" (1 Samuel 16:14-15).

Can God be the source or author of an evil spirit? No! It is fundamentally contrary to his character, perfections, and attributes. "For I the Lord cannot look upon sin [evil] with the least degree of allowance" (D&C 1:31). Evil influences derive from the Evil One himself, the Prince of Darkness, Lucifer. As an important part of our mortal experience, Heavenly Father allows Lucifer to work his schemes, but never as a joint partnership.

The above scripture in Samuel has been more correctly recorded in the Joseph Smith Translation, which reads, "But the Spirit of the Lord departed from Saul, and an evil spirit *which was not of the Lord,* troubled him. And Saul's servants said unto him, Behold now, an evil spirit *which is not of God,* troubleth thee" (JST, 1 Samuel16: 14-15, emphasis added).

This consistent correction is also made in 1 Samuel 16:16, 23; 18:10; and 19:9; giving better clarity and alignment to the crucial and opposing nature of good and evil.

We see this needed correction in the book of Matthew, Chapter 4 when it records, "Then was Jesus led up of the Spirit into the wilderness to be tempted of the devil" (Matthew 4:1). The Spirit of the Lord would never lead Jesus to spend time with the devil. Rather, the Joseph Smith Translation reads, "Then was Jesus led up of the Spirit into the wilderness to be *with* God" (JST, Matthew 4:1). The subsequent presence of the devil on this occasion is better viewed as an uninvited presence, albeit allowed by God to bring about His purposes. "Though he were a Son, yet learned he obedience by the things which he suffered" (Hebrews 5:8).

The clearest formula I'm aware of to recognize good and evil and their corresponding rival sources, is recorded in the Book of Mormon. "For every thing which inviteth to do good, and to persuade to believe in Christ, is sent forth by the power and gift of Christ; wherefore ye may know with a perfect knowledge it is of God. But whatsoever thing persuadeth men to do evil, and believe not in Christ, and deny him, and serve not God, then ye may know with a perfect knowledge it is of the devil" (Moroni 7:16-17).

Knowing that God will never be the author of the evils we experience and seeing evil for what it is and where it originates are important baselines of understanding. We are blessed by these corrections to scriptural verse that properly ascribe evil influence to Evil himself.

156. Broad salvation is made available through Jesus Christ.

A simple dictionary definition of Christian salvation is "to be saved (delivered) from sin and its consequences, brought about by faith in Jesus Christ."[1] In a two-dimensional after life, the opposite would not to be saved (delivered) from sin and its consequences. It's either one or the other for everyone.

But the doctrine of salvation through Jesus Christ, or LDS soteriology, is much deeper. It manifests more broadly the grace of Christ, providing for the "many mansions" (John 14:2) Jesus spoke of. "Salvation.... in its most pure and perfect definition, it is a synonym for exaltation."[2] This word "exaltation" is unique to latter-day scripture.

Salvation can be defined on two counts—saved from physical death and saved from spiritual death. It is by the death and resurrection of Jesus Christ and the grace of God, that all people will be saved from their physical death via a universal resurrection.

Spiritual death, at the Final Judgment, is to be cut off in any way from the presence and kind of life that God and Jesus Christ enjoy. At its worse, that would mean being consigned to hell to dwell with Lucifer and his ilk and have no part in the blessings or influence of the Father or the Son except the reality of the resurrection. That fate, also called the second death, "will come to very few."[3] (see also D&C 76:31-37, 40-45)

Now is where it really gets exciting. If one does not experience the very presence and life of God the Father and the Lord Jesus Christ, there are many mansions that have been prepared by, or under the direction of, the Savior Himself, all of which extend various degrees of salvation, glory, and divine influence. Telestial, Terrestrial, and lower realms of the Celestial world are scripturally classified as these kingdoms.

Salvation then, through the Atonement of Jesus Christ, applies in some degree to all but those few that will be subject to the second death, or spiritual death (although even they will experience the resurrection).

Exaltation is to live in the presence of God the Father and the Lord Jesus Christ, being a part of His family, joint-heirs, continuing our family relationships. It includes a continuation of the seed, meaning eternal family increase.

Salvation without exaltation is damnation to some degree. However, by the mercy of God, it is salvation still to all but those few who will dwell with the devil in hell.

The very Plan of Salvation is intended to bring us back to the presence of God, to enjoy the highest state of happiness with our families, to culminate a lifetime of discipleship and to "be like him" (1 John 3:2, Moroni 7:48). It is to enjoy exaltation, to actually be exalted. Exaltation is the most complete and purest definition for salvation. However, "almost every person who has ever lived on the earth is assured [some form of] salvation."[4]

This is indeed merciful doctrine from a most merciful God.

Notes:

1. www.oxforddictionaries.com/us/definition/american_english/salvation.
2. Bruce R. McConkie, *Mormon Doctrine,* 2nd ed., Salt Lake City: Bookcraft, 1966, 257.
3. *True to the Faith*, Salt Lake City: The Church of Jesus Christ of Latter-day Saints, 2004, 153.
4. *True to the Faith,* 153.

157. Predestination and foreordination are not the same.

Personally, I've never been comfortable when people give divine attribution to every single act of our lives, that whatsoever happens is the will of the Lord. I'll admit that I've probably used this acceptable language on occasion, but honestly, I was being a bit disingenuous in my expression if I have. If everything that happens in this life is God's will, and more pointedly, if it is all a predetermined script, then in reality, we have no choice. To take that to an eternal view, then some are predestined to eternal life and some to damnation. By what criteria we know not, nor could we affect. Yet the truth of the matter is as Paul wrote, "He [Jesus] became the author of eternal salvation unto all them that obey him" (Hebrews 5:9). For that truth, the resurrected Lord's charge to his ordained servants is to "Go ye into all the world, and preach the gospel to every creature. He that believeth and is baptized shall be saved" (Mark 16:15-16).

We believe in what we call foreordination, and it is rooted in the fact that we lived a pre-mortal life and that all born into this world already chose to follow the Son of God. When the Lord called Jeremiah as a prophet, He instructed him of his identity, "Before I formed thee in the belly I knew thee; and before thou camest forth out of the womb I sanctified thee, and I ordained thee a prophet unto the nations" (Jeremiah 1:5).

"Foreordination is the premortal selection of individuals to come forth in mortality at specific times, under certain conditions, and to fulfill predesignated responsibilities."[1] Our faithful performance or dereliction of those responsibilities is up to us. "Foreordination is like any other blessing—it is a conditional bestowal subject to our faithfulness."[2]

The Lord is omniscient, "and I know the end from the beginning" (Abraham 2:8). However, "He foresees, but does not fix the outcome."[3]

It is inconceivable to suppose that God is an arbitrary, impulsive, or capricious God. Yet predestination without pre-qualification, would be just that. And more so predestination after having developed a premortal resumé, would frustrate the very purposes of our mortal experience.

Foreordination is a positive, hopeful doctrine. "We believe that through the Atonement of Christ, all mankind may be saved, by obedience to the laws and ordinances of the Gospel." (Articles of Faith, 3) All mankind! "For behold, ye are free; ye are permitted to act for yourselves; for behold, God hath given unto you a knowledge and he hath made you free" (Helaman 14:30).

Jesus, while addressing the doubters of his day, said, "My sheep hear my voice, and I know them, and they follow me" (John 10:27). And furthermore, "he that will hear my voice shall be my sheep" (Mosiah 26:21). He was speaking of believers. The power is within us all to rise to the stature of our foreordination and be believers.

Notes:

1. Brent L. Top, *LDS Beliefs, A Doctrinal Reference,* Salt Lake City: 2011, 233.
2. Neal A. Maxwell, "A More Determined Discipleship," *Ensign,* February, 1979.
3. Brent L. Top, 233.

158. From the time of Adam, ordinances and covenants have been administered.

"We believe that through the Atonement of Christ, all mankind may be saved, by obedience to the laws and ordinances of the Gospel.

"We believe that the first principles and ordinances of the Gospel are: first, Faith in the Lord Jesus Christ; second, Repentance; third, Baptism by immersion for the remission of sins; fourth, Laying on of hands for the gift of the Holy Ghost.

"We believe that a man must be called of God, by prophecy, and by the laying on of hands by those who are in authority, to preach the Gospel and administer in the ordinances thereof." (Articles of Faith, 3-5)

These truths and requirements are universal to all mankind. Adam and Eve were the first to observe and practice them. At some point in our mortal or immortal experience, they will be made available to all who have or will be born into this world.

Let's look at the ordinance of baptism. Many would argue that baptism began with John the Baptist who came baptizing unto repentance. It appears that this was not a foreign concept to the people who came to John to be baptized. Nor was it to Jesus, who came to John to be baptized "to fulfil all righteousness" (Matthew 3:15).

The valid ordinance of baptism is essential for personal salvation. Jesus made that clear to Nicodemus in uncompromising language (John 3:5). It is an ordinance for those who accept the need for a Savior and desire to trust Him as their Redeemer. It is relevant in all ages.

Although there is no reference to the word "baptism" in the Old Testament, latter-day scripture gives indispensable light on the subject:

After the Lord commanded Adam to be baptized, Adam inquired, "Why is it that men must repent and be baptized in water? . . . All men, everywhere, must repent, or they can in nowise inherit the kingdom of God. . . . Even so ye must be born again into the kingdom of heaven . . . And he [Adam] was caught away by the Spirit of the Lord, and was carried down into the water, and was laid under the water, and was brought forth out of the water. And thus he was baptized" (Moses 6:53, 57, 59, 64, 65).

Isaiah speaks of Israel who "are come forth out of the waters of Judah" (Isaiah 48:1). That same verse, taken from the Brass Plates by Nephi, says, "Are come forth out of the waters of Judah, or out of the waters of baptism" (1 Nephi 20:1).

Lehi taught of baptism, as did Nephi, Jacob, Alma, Ammon, Helaman, and others in the new world prior to the coming of Jesus in the flesh.

The ordinance of baptism is an example of the timeless, saving ordinances of the Gospel of Jesus Christ. These ordinances are a blessing to mankind, either received in the flesh, or received vicariously. They have been taught and administered in dispensations since the time of Adam and Eve. No one will be denied the ordinances and associated covenants of the gospel as commanded by the Lord Jesus Christ.

159. Much of LDS doctrine and behavior stems from obtaining a physical body.

The following statement from "The Family, A Proclamation to the World" is rich in doctrine and LDS understanding, and expands on the title to this chapter. "In the premortal realm, spirit sons and daughters knew and worshipped God as their Eternal Father and accepted His plan by which His children could obtain a physical body and gain earthly experience to progress toward perfection and ultimately realize their divine destiny as heirs of eternal life."[1]

Some of the profound doctrines and understandings from that statement follow:

- We are eternal beings, having come to this earth from a premortal life as spirit beings
- God is the Father of our spirits, and He is our God
- As His spirit children, we lived with Him, associated with Him, and agreed to come to earth
- We came to earth to obtain a physical body to house our spirit and to gain mortal experience
- Our destiny is to become like Him, and to live eternally like Him and with Him

Elder David A. Bednar commented on the Proclamation in a Church Educational System fireside address on May 3, 2009, "Please note the primary importance of obtaining a physical body in the process of progressing toward our divine destiny. . . . the body and the spirit constitute our reality and identity. When body and spirit are inseparably connected, we can receive a fulness of joy; when they are separated, we cannot receive a fulness of joy." (D&C 93:33-34).[2]

Elder Bednar then referenced a quote from the Prophet Joseph Smith wherein he taught with clarity the importance of our physical bodies: "We came to this earth that we might have a body and present it pure before God in the celestial kingdom. The great principle of happiness consists in having a body. The devil has no body, and herein is his punishment. He is pleased when he can obtain the tabernacle of man, and when cast out by the Savior he asked to go into the herd of swine, showing that he would prefer a swine's body to having none. All beings who have bodies have power over those who have not. . . . The devil has no power over us only as we permit him; the moment we revolt at anything which comes from God, the devil takes power."[3]

Elder Bednar then makes the point of our unique doctrinal understanding, "Lucifer seeks to frustrate our progression by tempting us to use our bodies improperly. . . . By violating the law of chastity, by using drugs and addictive substances, by disfiguring or defacing themselves, or by worshipping the false idol of body image, whether their own or that of others to minimize the importance of their physical bodies."[4]

So it's not just a seemingly strict set of rules and behaviors within the Church. It is a recognition of who we are and of whom we are up against. "For we wrestle not against flesh and blood, but . . . against powers . . . against spiritual wickedness in high places" (Ephesians

6:12). We fight against him who is insanely jealous of having a physical body and who is bent on having us misuse our own unique and individual dwelling place. It is about enabling ourselves and others of that personal fullness of joy.

This understanding of mortal life has given me a proper regard for our physical bodies, including our stewardship toward and the purposes of such a marvelous gift.

Notes:

1. First Presidency and The Council of the Twelve, "The Family: A Proclamation to the World," *Ensign*, November, 1995.
2. David A. Bednar, "Things as They Really Are," *Ensign*, June, 2010.
3. *Teachings of the Presidents of the Church: Joseph Smith*, Salt Lake City: The Church of Jesus Christ of Latter-day Saints, 2007, 211.
4. David A. Bednar.

160. Being saved by Jesus Christ is the greatest provision for mankind ever made.

I am reading a book by Tad R. Callister titled *The Infinite Atonement.*[1] I have been moved by his insight and thoughtful study of the scriptures on this central doctrinal topic. Much of what I will now write is drawn from his insight.

In truth, there are different gradations of being saved. Saved from what? Saved from the negative consequences of the fall of Adam and Eve and saved from the negative consequences of our own behavior. In the case of being saved from the consequences of the fall of Adam and Eve, all mankind will be saved unconditionally. Being saved from our own sins is conditional on our faith, our repentance, and our accountability.

Prior to the Fall, Adam and Eve lived in the presence of God, and they were not subject to death. These were two favorable conditions. Yet they "would have had no children . . . [being] in a state of innocence, having no joy, for they knew no misery; doing no good, for they knew no sin" (2 Nephi 2:23). These were two unfavorable conditions. Listed, they are as follows:

Prior to the Fall

Positive conditions

- Man lived in the presence of God (Genesis 3:8, Moses 4:14)
- There was no death (Genesis 2:17)

Negative conditions

- Man did not have a knowledge of good and evil and was innocent (2 Nephi 2:22-23)
- There was no opportunity to have children and create families (2 Nephi 2:20, 23, 25)

These positive and negative conditions are swapped because of the Fall of Adam:

After the Fall

Negative conditions

- Man does not live in the presence of God (Genesis 3:23-24, Helaman 14:16)
- Death is an inevitable condition of mortality

Positive conditions

- Man has a knowledge of good and evil and is responsible (2 Nephi 2:26-27, Alma 42:3)

- Children are born into mortality in order to create families (Moses 5:11, 2 Nephi 2:19-20)

Now watch the miracle of divine math, which can make everything positive:

Effects of the Atonement of Jesus Christ

Positive unconditional conditions

- All men will return to God's presence for judgment purposes (2 Nephi 2:10, 2 Nephi 9:38, Alma 12:15, Helaman 14:15-18, Mormon 9:12-14)

- All men will be resurrected from the dead (1 Corinthians 15:20-22)

Positive conditions conditional upon our faithfulness and repentance

- Man has the potential for unlimited knowledge of good and evil

- Families can continue forever, including "a continuation of the seeds" (D&C 132:19)

- We can live in the presence of God and Jesus Christ forever (D&C 88:15-20)

I believe the Lord wants us to deeply contemplate and understand what He has done for us and what He has made available to us. Such rich doctrinal understanding of what flows from the Fall of Adam, the need for a Savior, and the resultant provisions of the Atonement is a precious gift that we would do well to receive. The implications of our choices and behavior take on an implicit importance in light of the Atonement.

It is the Atonement that makes possible eternal life. "For God so loved the world, that he gave his only begotten Son, that whosoever believeth in him should not perish, but have everlasting life" (John 3:16). It is the Atonement that makes possible the purposes of God "to bring to pass the immortality [unconditional] and eternal life [conditional] of man" (Moses 1:39). It is the Atonement that overcomes the consequences of Adam's transgression and is the power to redeem us from our sins.

The understanding of this preeminent Christian doctrine is worthy of a lifetime of study, and latter-day scripture and the words of living prophets have contributed abundantly to that study.

Notes:

1. Tad R. Callister, "*The Infinite Atonement*," Salt Lake City: Deseret Book, 2000.

Part Three

Foretold Reasons

foretell, verb – "to tell beforehand; predict; prophesy." (Dictionary.com)

161. The coming forth of the Book of Mormon is a fulfillment of prophecy.

"Moreover, thou son of man, take thee one stick, and write upon it, For Judah, and for the children of Israel his companions: then take another stick, and write upon it, For Joseph, the stick of Ephraim, and for all the house of Israel his companions: And join them one to another into one stick; and they shall become one in thine hand" (Ezekiel 37:16-17).

The record of Judah is, of course, the Bible, written in the old world. The record of Joseph is the Book of Mormon, written in the Americas. It was Jacob who prophesied of Joseph's intercontinental destiny when he said, "Joseph is a fruitful bough, even a fruitful bough by a well; whose branches run over the wall" (Genesis 49:22).

A similar passage, written around 580 BC in the Americas, states, "Wherefore, the fruit of thy loins shall write; and the fruit of the loins of Judah shall write; and that which shall be written by the fruit of thy loins, and also that which shall be written by the fruit of the loins of Judah, shall grow together, unto the confounding of false doctrines and laying down of contentions, and establishing peace among the fruit of thy loins, and bringing them to the knowledge of their fathers in the latter days, and also to the knowledge of my covenants, saith the Lord" (2 Nephi 3:12).

The plates of the Book of Mormon were buried in the earth by the Prophet Moroni about four hundred years after the coming of Christ. Joseph Smith was led by the now resurrected angel Moroni to retrieve the plates from their buried location for the purpose of translation and publication. "Truth shall spring out of the earth" (Psalms 85:11). "It shall be brought out of the earth, and it shall shine forth out of darkness . . . and it shall be done by the power of God" (Mormon 8:16).

"In the mouth of two or three witnesses shall every word be established" (2 Corinthians 13:1). "These last records, which thou hast seen among the Gentiles, shall establish the truth of the first, which are of the twelve apostles of the Lamb, and shall make known the plain and precious things which have been taken away from them; and shall make known to all kindreds, tongues, and people, that the Lamb of God is the Son of the Eternal Father, and the Savior of the world; and that all men must come unto him, or they cannot be saved" (1 Nephi 13:40). What a powerful witness of the book which has come through the Gentiles, namely Joseph Smith, to establish truth!

The general response to the Book of Mormon has also been accurately prophesied, as well as the Lord's rejoinder,

"And because my words shall hiss forth—many of the Gentiles shall say: A Bible! A Bible! We have got a Bible, and there cannot be any more Bible. . . . Know ye not that there are more nations than one? Know ye not that I, the Lord your God, have created all men, and that I remember those who are upon the isles of the sea; and that I rule in the heavens above and in the earth beneath; and I bring forth my word unto the children of men, yea, even upon all the nations of the earth? Wherefore murmur ye, because that ye shall receive more of my word? Know ye not that the testimony of two nations is a witness unto you that I am God, that I remember one nation like unto another? Wherefore, I speak the same words unto one nation like unto another. And when the two nations shall run together the testimony of the two nations shall run together also" (2 Nephi 29:3, 7, 8).

Jesus taught, "And other sheep I have, which are not of this fold: them also I must bring, and they shall hear my voice; and there shall be one fold, and one shepherd" (John 10:16). The Book of Mormon is a record of some of those other sheep, those who lived on the American continent(s). It exists as a testament that Jesus is the Christ and that Joseph Smith was a prophet. This book has been a great blessing to me and to millions of others as a companion scripture to the Holy Bible, an inspired record of God. Its existence today has come about as prophets have written.

162. The role of the Gentiles is being fulfilled by the Restored Church.

There are several scriptural uses of *Gentiles,* including those "people of non-Jewish lineage," or more broadly, "people of non-Israelite lineage," and particularly in the Book of Mormon and the Doctrine and Covenants, "nations that are without the gospel, even though there may be some Israelite blood among the people."[1] A good general explanation of the use of the word Gentile is given by Daniel Ludlow: "The basic meaning of the word *Gentile* is 'foreign,' 'other,' or 'non.' Thus to a Hebrew, a Gentile is a non-Hebrew; to an Israelite, a Gentile is a non-Israelite, and to a Jew, a Gentile is a non-Jew . . . [one] might be called a Gentile in a political or geographical sense because he lives in a land or nation that is primarily Gentile, or non-Israelitish."[2]

By the work of the gathering, and the ordinance of baptism, "The Gentiles shall be blessed and numbered among the house of Israel" (2 Nephi 10:18).

The gospel of Jesus Christ being restored through the Gentiles on the American continent was recorded some six hundred years before the birth of Christ and was to be the hope of Israel. "And after the house of Israel should be scattered they should be gathered together again; or, in fine, after the Gentiles had received the fulness of the Gospel. . . . The remnants of the house of Israel, should . . . come to the knowledge of the true Messiah, their Lord and their Redeemer" (1 Nephi 10:14).

The coming forth of the Holy Bible, the record of the Jews, was a necessary step in this restoration through the Gentiles:

> "And I beheld a book, and it was carried forth among them. . . . Behold, it proceedeth out of the mouth of a Jew. . . . They contain the covenants of the Lord, which he hath made unto the house of Israel; wherefore, they are of great worth unto the Gentiles" (1 Nephi 13:23).

The Gentiles would also be the custodians of the coming forth of the Book of Mormon. That was a prophetic requirement of the restoration. In this instance, Gentiles refer to those of a non-Israelite nation:

> "I will be merciful unto the Gentiles in that day, insomuch that I will bring forth unto them, in mine own power, much of my gospel, which shall be plain and precious, saith the Lamb. . . . Behold, these things shall be hid up, to come forth unto the Gentiles, by the gift and power of the Lamb. . . . These last records, which thou hast seen among the Gentiles, shall establish the truth of the first . . . and shall make known the plain and precious things which have been taken away from them; and shall make known to all kindreds, tongues, and people, that the Lamb of God is the Son of the Eternal Father, and the Savior of the world; and that all men must come unto him, or they cannot be saved" (1 Nephi 13:34-40).

The Church today is being taken to all the world, including to the house of Israel by way of the Gentiles in this dispensation. Given that the tribe of Ephraim holds the firstborn status in the House of Israel (Genesis 48:15-20, 1 Chronicles 5:1-2, Jeremiah 31:9), and the corresponding charge "to bear the message of the Restoration of the gospel to the world and to gather scattered Israel,"[3] the Gentiles in this sense are those from Gentile nations. "In our day, the gospel was delivered first to Joseph Smith and the Latter-day Saints, those of us who are 'identified with the Gentiles' (D&C 109:60), that is, those who are Israelite by descent (see D&C 52:2, 86:8-10) and Gentile by culture."[4]

The foundational moral document of the Gentiles in America was the record of the Jews, which they brought with them from Europe.

The Book of Mormon, spread forth by the Gentiles, confirms that record. We are seeing the literal fulfillment of these prophetic events in these latter days in the restoration of the Gospel through the Prophet Joseph Smith, and the gathering of scattered Israel.

Notes:

1. lds.org, *The Guide to the Scriptures*, "Gentiles."
2. Daniel H. Ludlow, "Of the House of Israel," *Ensign,* January, 1991.
3. LDS Bible Dictionary, "Ephraim."
4. Robert L. Millet, *Living in the Millennium*, Salt Lake City: Deseret Book, 2014, Chapter 4.

163. Elijah the ancient Jewish prophet, came on Easter Sunday 1836 to a temple.

It is of particular interest that the prophetic utterance of Malachi has been placed at the end of the Old Testament. "Behold, I will send you Elijah the prophet before the great and dreadful day of the Lord. And he shall turn the heart of the fathers to the children, and the heart of the children to their fathers, lest I come and smite the earth with a curse" (Malachi 4:5-6.). This great and dreadful day is in reference to the Second Coming of the Lord.

I am told that for centuries in the tradition of the Jewish Passover and during the meal known as the Seder, a setting is made at the table for the return of Elijah as an invited guest. The front door is left open, among other reasons, to welcome Elijah into the home, with the hope that he will mark the coming of the Messiah.

We have a recorded visit of Elijah upon the earth subsequent to the prophecy given in Malachi. That was his appearance at the Mount to a transfigured Christ, and to Peter, James, and John (Matthew 17:3).

This occasion could not be what Malachi referred to, since it did not occur in connection to the Second Coming - "before the great and dreadful day of the Lord [His Second Coming]" (Malachi 4:5).

We also have a recorded visit of Elijah to the only dedicated temple then on the earth, which was situated in Kirtland, Ohio. The date was April 3, 1836. On that occasion, Elijah said to Joseph Smith and Oliver Cowdery, "The keys of this dispensation are committed into your hands; and by this ye may know that the great and dreadful day of the Lord is near, even at the doors" (D&C 110:16).

The third day of April in 1836 was Easter Sunday, and this same weekend was the Jewish Passover. I don't think Joseph Smith could have premeditated or orchestrated this event. I doubt that he knew of all the scriptural particulars and implications that would be required for its authenticity. It is recorded as a portion of Section 110 in the Doctrine and Covenants. That section also records several other heavenly messengers bringing and restoring necessary keys of the Priesthood to effect the work of the latter-days.

It is most significant that on this specific date—Easter Sunday, 1836, Passover weekend— Elijah presented himself in a holy temple to his fellow prophet, Joseph Smith, in fulfillment of both Jewish tradition and Biblical prophecy. It thrills my soul to see the very fulfillment of this most important prophesied event and to ponder its significance.

164. The work of the Lord will be brought about by the simple of the world.

Speaking to his son Helaman, regarding the impact of the records they had in their possession (scriptures on brass plates), the Prophet Alma declared, "Now ye may suppose that this is foolishness in me; but behold I say unto you, that by small and simple things are great things brought to pass; and small means in many instances doth confound the wise. And the Lord God doth work by means to bring about his great and eternal purposes; and by very small means the Lord doth confound the wise and bringeth about the salvation of many souls" (Alma 37:6-7).

"But God hath chosen the foolish things of the world to confound the wise; and God hath chosen the weak things of the world to confound the things which are mighty" (1 Corinthians 1:27).

"To prepare the weak for those things which are coming on the earth, and for the Lord's errand in the day when the weak shall confound the wise. . . . And by the weak things of the earth the Lord shall thrash the nations by the power of his Spirit" (D&C 133:58-59).

The early converts to the Church were not the rich and powerful of the world, but in large measure, the weak and simple, and for the most part, the poor. These converts built the foundation of the Kingdom in places like Kirtland, Far West, Nauvoo, and Salt Lake City. They went on to establish the Church throughout the western United States, in Northern Mexico, Canada, and England, establishing a legacy of faith and industry that is a part of our culture today.

The Church continues to grow by and among the simple of the earth. Young missionaries eighteen and nineteen years of age preach and baptize throughout the world. Their strength is not their erudite manners but their sincere testimony that what they teach is true. Local leaders of the Church throughout the world are not trained in a seminary prior to their service, but as a lay ministry, they are given tremendous authority and responsibility, trusting in the Holy Ghost to guide and to teach them.

"God hath chosen the weak things of the world to confound the things which are mighty" (1 Corinthians 1:27). These are weak and simple by the measures of the world yet humble and teachable toward the Lord. Such were the disciples in the meridian of time, and such are his disciples today.

165. Paul described the conditions of the times in which we live.

Paul wrote 2 Timothy towards the end of his life and while he was imprisoned in Rome. It has been said that it is a distillation of his experience and wisdom and his formula for one to build a lasting spirituality. He knew that the work of the Savior was not a parochial movement, but it would include the return of the Son of God in the latter days and was of import and impact to all mankind.

"This know also, that in the last days perilous times shall come. For men shall be lovers of their own selves, covetous, boasters, proud, blasphemers, disobedient to parents, unthankful, unholy, Without natural affection, trucebreakers, false accusers, incontinent, fierce, despisers of those that are good, Traitors, heady, highminded, lovers of pleasures more than lovers of God; Having a form of godliness, but denying the power thereof: from such turn away . . . Ever learning, and never able to come to the knowledge of the truth" (2 Timothy 3:1-5, 7). This statement could probably apply to many eras in the history of civilization, but it is specifically identified with the last days. Each of the accusing titles above could be evidenced by contemporary examples. It speaks of man's baser instincts, his disregard for the Sabbath day, the rejection of the priesthood, and the study of vain and man-made doctrines.

"For the time will come when they will not endure sound doctrine; but after their own lusts shall they heap to themselves teachers, having itching ears; And they shall turn away their ears from the truth, and shall be turned unto fables" (2 Timothy 4:3-4).

People today often shop their churches to find a pastor or a social setting in which they are comfortable with the doctrines being taught. But remember, sound doctrine is pure truth. Truth and its attendant doctrine are not subject to the opinions and fancies of men. It is incumbent upon each of us to discover and conform to truth, and as Paul cautioned, not to seek after (our) own lusts.

"For he is the same yesterday, today, and forever" (1 Nephi 10:18).

These are the last days, preparatory to the coming of the Lord. These days have been prophesied, characterized, and singled out so that we may recognize this historic time. The Lord's Church has been restored and will house the pure, sound doctrine as taught by Christ and his apostles.

166. The covenants made with Father Abraham are available to all people.

We are fortunate that the Lord has given further understanding of the Abrahamic Covenant, and most particularly how one can be heir to such covenant blessings. In summary, the Abrahamic Covenant from the Old and the New Testament includes:

- Abraham's posterity shall be numerous "as the stars of the heaven" (Genesis 22:17) and "known among all nations" (JST, Genesis 17:9)
- Certain lands will be given to Abraham's posterity for "an everlasting possession" (Genesis 17:8)
- The Messiah, Christ, would come through his lineage (Galatians 3:16, 29)

From the writings of Abraham, brought forth by the Prophet Joseph Smith, further insight is given to the blessings and responsibilities of this numerous posterity:

- Abraham's descendants would receive the gospel and bear the priesthood (Abraham 2:9)
- Through the ministry of his seed, "all the families of the earth [will] be blessed, even with the blessings of the Gospel, which are the blessings of salvation, even of life eternal" (Abraham 2:11, also Genesis 12:3, 22:18)

When people worthily enter into the covenant of baptism, they are either by blood a lineal descendant of Abraham (through one of the twelve sons of Israel), or they are thereby adopted into the house of Israel, making them of the seed of Abraham. Baptism is a covenant of salvation, made effective by the Atonement of Jesus Christ.

Covenant Church members, as the seed of Abraham, are heirs to the blessings and responsibilities of the Abrahamic covenant. When we say that we are heir to the covenants made to Abraham, we are saying that these promises are made to us as they were to Abraham (except Christ coming through his lineage, which is, of course, a singular occurrence). To enable receipt of all these blessings, it is necessary to enter into the order of celestial marriage in the House of the Lord. Celestial marriage is the covenant of exaltation.

We see the fulfillment of these blessings and the carrying out of these responsibilities in the generations of the faithful even today, as families send out missionaries to bless all the families of the earth.

To understand the Abrahamic covenant and to see its application and continuance in our own lives, our posterity, and ancestry gives a powerful sense of identity and purpose. The restored gospel, which includes additional scripture written by Father Abraham and the enabling ordinances of the priesthood, is essential to the understanding and fulfillment of the Abrahamic covenant.

167. The prophet Moroni plays a significant part in restoring the everlasting gospel to the earth.

"And I saw another angel fly in the midst of heaven, having the everlasting gospel to preach unto them that dwell on the earth, and to every nation, and kindred, and tongue, and people, Saying with a loud voice, Fear God, and give glory to him; for the hour of his judgment is come: and worship him that made heaven, and earth, and the sea, and the fountains of waters" (Revelation 14:6-7).

This significant revelation to the apostle John speaks in large part of the coming of the prophet Moroni to the boy Joseph Smith, which took place on several occasions, and plays a conspicuous role in the restoration of the fullness of the gospel in these latter days.

Moroni wrote the concluding chapters of what we now have as the Book of Mormon and was among the last surviving Nephites of faith. He was the one who sealed up the gold plates in the Hill Cumorah to come forth as the Book of Mormon under the hands of Joseph Smith. Some of his final words etched on the gold plates clearly highlight his character and mission, "Yea, come unto Christ, and be perfected in him" (Moroni 10:32).

In partial fulfillment of this revelation to John, Moroni as a resurrected being, came to young Joseph to teach and prepare him for the work yet to unfold—the restoration of the everlasting gospel of Jesus Christ. It was Moroni who told Joseph "that God had a work for me to do" (Joseph Smith History 1:33). Moroni also declared that "there was a book deposited, written upon gold plates . . . that the fulness of the everlasting Gospel was contained in it" (Joseph Smith History 1:34). It was Moroni who tutored Joseph at least annually for four years until the actual time came to take possession of the plates for the purpose of translation.

"Listen to the voice of Jesus Christ, your Lord, your God, and your Redeemer. . . . Moroni, whom I have sent unto you to reveal the Book of Mormon, containing the fulness of my everlasting gospel, to whom I have committed the keys of the record of the stick of Ephraim" (D&C 27:1, 5). Such is the significance of the mission of Moroni.

It is thrilling to live in the days so prophesied and to witness the unfolding of this great latter-day work that will go "to every nation, and kindred, and tongue, and people" (Revelation 14:6).

168. In 1832, the Lord revealed to Joseph Smith the particulars of the US Civil War.

As a matter of history, the great Civil War began on April 12, 1861, when General Beauregard ordered the first shot to be fired against the Union at Fort Sumter, South Carolina.

Twenty eight and one half years previous to this watershed event, on Christmas Day 1832, Section 87 of the Doctrine and Covenants was given. This section gives remarkable detail regarding the war. The following prophetic declarations are now recorded history:

- "wars . . . beginning at the rebellion of South Carolina"
- "which will eventually terminate in the death and misery of many souls"
- "the Southern states shall be divided against the Northern states"
- "the Southern states will call on . . . Great Britain . . . and other nations"
- "and then war shall be poured out upon all nations"
- "slaves shall rise up against their masters"

The early 1830's saw fissures between the North and the South on the issue of tariffs and other concerns. South Carolina had declared in late 1832 to abrogate itself from the Tariff Acts of 1828 and 1832. However, this wouldn't be the fundamental issue resulting in the Civil War. Over ten years later in 1843, still eighteen years prior to the actual outbreak of the war, the Prophet Joseph Smith said, "It may probably arise through the slave question" (D&C 130:13).

It has been estimated that some 2.3 to 3.2 million soldiers served in the cause of the Civil War, suffering casualties of 620 to 850 thousand dead and another 500,000 wounded. Truly resulting "in the death and misery of many souls," (D&C 87:1) in both absolute numbers and by percentage of population.

That "war shall be poured out upon all nations" (D&C 87:3) is to place the Civil War as the prelude to inevitable world conflicts. Elder Joseph Wirthlin observed, "The Civil War came in 1861 [and ended in 1865]; the war between Denmark and Prussia in 1864; Italy and Austria in 1865 and 1866; Austria and Prussia in 1866; Russia and Turkey in 1877; China and Japan in 1894 and 1895; Spanish-American in 1898; Japan and Russia in 1904 and 1905; World War I in 1914—1918. . . . Then, the World War just passed [World War II] and, of course, the Korean War."[1] Since 1958 there have been, among numerous other wars, the Vietnam War in Southeast Asia, the war in Angola, the Six-Day and Yom Kippur wars in the Holy Land, the Persian Gulf War, Operation Iraqi Freedom, war on terrorism in Afghanistan.

Doctrine and Covenants Section 87 and Section 130:12-13 are stunning prophecies of future events from our current vantage point of actual history.

Notes:

1. Joseph L. Wirthlin, "In Consequence of Evils and Designs," *Conference Report,* October, 1958, 33.

169. Turning the hearts of the children to their fathers is happening now.

The family history program of the Church is known throughout the world as the premier repository of genealogical records available anywhere. Thousands of people are contributing to, and drawing from, the vast database of family records. We call this the Spirit of Elijah, felt throughout the world in the hearts of Church members and non-members alike. It is working in the hearts of the human family.

About three and a half years after Joseph Smith experienced the opening scene of the restoration as a fourteen-year-old boy, he was visited by the Prophet Moroni, "a messenger sent from the presence of God" (Joseph Smith History 1:33). Moroni laid out the work Joseph was called to do, and included the foundational purposes, including, "And he shall plant in the hearts of the children the promises made to the fathers, and the hearts of the children shall turn to their fathers. If it were not so, the whole earth would be utterly wasted at his coming" (Joseph Smith History 1:39). Compare this to the last verse in the book of Malachi, and we see some enlightening differences.

Why would the whole earth be utterly wasted at the Lord's second coming if the hearts of the children do not turn to their fathers? Because the gospel of Jesus Christ is fundamentally designed to qualify the children of a loving Heavenly Father to live with Him again, in an immortal, glorified existence. It would be a familial existence, born of obedience to ordinances and covenants and a love and longing for a celestial order of the kind God enjoys. This familial existence, as well as the qualifying ordinances, are established and sealed by the manner prescribed of the Lord.

"The keys of the priesthood were restored and the sealing authority revealed and temples built to tie the generations together."[1] It was in Kirtland, Ohio on April 3, 1836, that the prophecy in Malachi 4:5 was fulfilled by the coming of Elijah: "For Elijah the prophet, who was taken to heaven without tasting death, stood before us, and said: Behold, the time has fully come, which was spoken of by the mouth of Malachi—testifying that he [Elijah] should be sent, before the great and dreadful day of the Lord come—To turn the hearts of the fathers to the children, and the children to the fathers, lest the whole earth be smitten with a curse—Therefore, the keys of this dispensation are committed into your hands " (D&C 110:13-16).

It is especially significant that Moroni would include the reference to Malachi's prophecy in his initial tutoring of the young prophet Joseph Smith at the opening of this dispensation. Probably the full importance and context of those words were not then understood—certainly not in terms of the scope and influence that they would have on the human family.

The ambitious work of collecting, validating, organizing, and preserving family history creates family units and family trees. It is turning the hearts of the children to their fathers. It is the Spirit of Elijah, which is the Spirit of the Holy Ghost. It is the fulfilling of ancient prophecy.

Notes:

1. Boyd K. Packer, "The Golden Years," *Ensign,* May, 2003.

170. Persecution has, and always will be, the lot of those who are disciples of Jesus Christ.

"When Christianity becomes woven in the social fabric, it becomes easier to ignore and take for granted. . . . Christianity especially has always thrived under persecution. For then it has no lukewarm professors."[1]

Certainly, in the early days of the Church in this dispensation, the Saints were persecuted both individually and collectively. The product of that persecution and contempt has been to establish the Church ever more strongly in the hearts of the faithful.

As prologue to the experience of His then current and future disciples, the Lord said, "Blessed are ye, when men shall hate you, and when they shall separate you from their company, and shall reproach you, and cast out your name as evil, for the Son of man's sake" (Luke 6:22).

Even today, and among otherwise educated people, Mormons are sometimes separated from mainstream religious circles because of their faith. In the recent political arena, we had a Mormon running for the office of President of the United States, and a good number of the political pundits wrote of his faith as a liability. Fundamentally, that faith is centered and anchored in Christ. Ironically, it was those who profess Christian faith who made such claims of asserted liability.

Persecution is a blessing if it turns us to God for help and comfort. His allowance of persecution is not indifferent forbearance, but rather loving forbearance. It must have been a source of grief and pain for Him to see the Saints suffer so at the hands of Missouri mobs, entirely undeserved, and heaped upon such children of faith. Yet He who is Omnipotent stayed His hand. "They shall be a scourge unto thy seed, to stir them up in the ways of remembrance" (1 Nephi 2:24).

The Lord said to those who endure such reproach in his name, "Rejoice ye in that day, and leap for joy: for, behold, your reward is great in heaven: for in the like manner did their fathers unto the prophets" (Luke 6:23).

Such a response builds, strengthens, comforts and steels the very faith in Christ that will bless an individual and a people. All Christian believers will suffer persecution and challenge to their faith in some form or fashion. For the LDS people as a whole, it has only served to strengthen and deepen their faith in Christ and His Church restored.

Notes:

1. Eric Metaxes, *Amazing Grace: William Wilberforce and the Heroic Campaign to End Slavery,*" New York: HarperOne, 2007, 170.

171. Moroni vividly describes the latter days and the restoration of the Gospel.

Moroni, the son of Mormon, played a significant role in the wrapping up of the Nephite record, and in the restoration of the Gospel in this dispensation. He abridged and included the record of the Jaredites just prior to his closing the Book of Mormon and then wrote a book under his own name. Prior to that abridgement, he wrote two chapters as "commanded by my father" (Mormon 8:1), which we have today as Mormon Chapters eight and nine.

Moroni tells about the "saints who have gone before me, who have possessed this land" (Mormon 8:23) and "their prayers were also in behalf of him that the Lord should suffer to bring these things forth" (Mormon 8:25). He speaks of the coming forth of the Book of Mormon. "It shall be brought out of the earth, and it shall shine forth out of darkness" (Mormon 8:16). He speaks of the Prophet Joseph Smith and his divine mission to "bring this thing to light" (Mormon 8:16).

For a description of the times when Joseph Smith would establish this work, Moroni wrote, "It shall come in a day when it shall be said that miracles are done away; and . . . in a day when the power of God shall be denied" (Mormon 8:26, 28). While Joseph was yet very young, just after experiencing the First Vision, he was told by a mainstream minister "that there were no such things as visions or revelations in these days; that all such things had ceased with the apostles, and that there would never be any more of them" (Joseph Smith History 1:21). This mainstream minister seems to be emblematic of this vision of the latter days as described by Moroni.

Moroni described the churches of Joseph's day and of this dispensation. "Yea, it shall come in a day . . . when leaders of churches and teachers shall rise in the pride of their hearts . . . and shall say: Come unto me, and for your money you shall be forgiven of your sins" (Moroni 8:28, 32). That attitude and practice is institutionalized in some churches of these days and to a lesser extent in others.

Furthermore, we see the signs of these times that Moroni wrote about. "Yea, it shall come in a day when there shall be heard of fires, and tempests . . . of wars, rumors of wars, and earthquakes in divers places . . . when there shall be great pollutions upon the face of the earth; there shall be murders, and robbing, and lying and deceivings, and whoredoms, and all manner of abominations" (Mormon 8:29-31). Certainly, these latter conditions are timeless in their existence within the human experience, but collectively, Moroni describes well this particular dispensation of time. "Behold, I speak unto you as if ye were present, and yet ye are not. But behold, Jesus Christ hath shown you unto me, and I know your doing" (Mormon 8:35).

These latter times are days foreseen and days yearned for, not necessarily for their conditions, but for their timing in the whole course of human events. The restoration through the Prophet Joseph Smith is the final dispensation prior to the Second Coming of the Lord Jesus Christ. And Moroni so prophesied some 1,400 years prior to the opening scenes of the restoration. What a blessing to experience these days and this work!

172. The "stone cut out of the mountain without hands" spoken of in Daniel is this great latter-day work.

What a thrill it must have been for the early Saints of this dispensation to read in the second chapter of the book of Daniel, a prophetic description of the work that was then unfolding. Now, almost two hundred years later, I feel that same thrill as I read of "what shall be in the latter days" (Daniel 2:28).

Daniel recounted and then interpreted King Nebuchadnezzar's dream, after having "the secret revealed unto Daniel in a night vision" (Daniel 2:19).

I'll quote some of what I consider the most salient points of what is written and share comments on the italicized portions:

> "Thou, O king, sawest, and behold a great image. . . . This image's head was of fine gold, his breast and his arms of

silver, his belly and his thighs of brass, his legs of iron, his feet part of iron and part of clay . . . *a stone was cut out without hands,* which smote the image upon his feet that were of iron and clay, and brake them to pieces . . . that no place was found for them; and the stone that smote the image became a great mountain, and filled the whole earth. . . . Thou [Nebuchadnezzar] art this head of gold. And after thee shall arise another kingdom inferior to thee, and another third kingdom of brass. . . . And the fourth kingdom shall be strong as iron . . . and subdueth all things . . . the feet and toes . . . shall be divided . . . partly strong and partly broken. . . . *And in the days of these kings* shall the God of heaven set up a kingdom, which shall never be destroyed; and the kingdom shall not be left to other people, but it shall break in pieces and consume all these kingdoms, *and it shall stand for ever.* Forasmuch as thou sawest that the stone was cut out of the mountain without hands, and that it brake in pieces the iron, the brass, the clay, the silver, and the gold; the great God hath made known to the king what shall come to pass hereafter; *and the dream is certain, and the interpretation thereof sure*" (Daniel 2:31-45).

"'*Cut out of the mountain without hands,*' means that it was begun through the intervention of God. It is not just another human institution. What other organizations or churches ascribe their founding to the declaration that messengers have come to human beings from the God of heaven with authority and power to restore ordinances and keys lost by apostasy?"[1]

"The interpretation included the domination of other kingdoms [following the kingdom of Nebuchadnezzar]. Cyrus the great, with his Medes and Persians, would be replaced by the Greek or Macedonian kingdom under Philip and Alexander; and that world power would be replaced by the Roman Empire; and Rome would be replaced by a group of nations of Europe represented by the toes of the image . . . *And in the days of these kings [that is, the group of European nations].*"[2]

Remember the opening declaration by Daniel that gives chronology to this prophecy, "what shall be in the latter days" (Daniel 2:28). The latter days is given clarity in scriptures such as Isaiah 2:2, Job 19:25, and D&C 4:1. Nebuchadnezzar's dream was not in reference to the meridian of time. Following an apostasy, the Lord restored his Church *"and it shall stand for ever"* (Daniel 2:44) means, at least, until the coming of the Son of God to the earth the second time.

The Church of Jesus Christ of Latter-day Saints is the fulfillment of that great dream recorded in Daniel Chapter two: *"And the dream is certain, and the interpretation thereof sure"* (Daniel 2:45). As King Nebuchadnezzar expressed sheer delight upon receiving this understanding and then acknowledging the God of heaven, I so feel likewise to be a part of this great work in these latter days.

Notes:

1. Ezra Taft Benson, "A Marvelous Work and a Wonder," *Ensign,* May, 1980.

2. Spencer W. Kimball, "The Stone Cut Without Hands," *Ensign,* May, 1976.

173. These latter days are frequently referred to throughout the scriptures.

On the corner of Foothill Boulevard and Fanuel Street in San Diego was the ward meetinghouse within blocks of my home as a teenager. Not a member of the Church, I puzzled at the name on the building "The Church . . . of Latter-Day Saints." In my mind I always thought it was "later" day saints, and couldn't for the life of me see its utility in the naming of a church.

However, now I see it as an inspired name, making a distinction between the original Church Jesus Christ established and that same Church restored in these *latter* days.

Scripturally, the latter days or last days, indeed refer to this time in which we live in preparation for the Second Coming of the Savior Jesus Christ. Jacob (Israel) gathered his twelve sons together and gave voice to his prophetic vision of their future lineage, and particularly of that "which shall befall you in the last days" (Genesis 49:1). Moses, Job, Isaiah, Ezekiel, Daniel, Joel, Malachi, John, Jude, Paul, Nephi, and the Savior himself, all are on scriptural record referring to the latter days.

The contextual use of "latter days" or "last days" in scripture, include the following:

- The temporal and political conditions at the Second Coming of the Lord Jesus Christ
- The moral conditions leading up to the Second Coming
- The restoration of the Church to the earth prior to the Second Coming
- The resurrection and the Day of Judgment

That these are, indeed, those latter days is made clear by many scriptural prophecies:

> "Daniel, who foresaw and foretold the establishment of the kingdom of God in the *latter days*, never again to be destroyed nor given to other people" (D&C 138:44, Daniel 2:44, emphasis added).

> "That in the *latter days*, when our seed shall have dwindled in unbelief . . . then shall the fulness of the gospel of the Messiah come unto the Gentiles, and from the Gentiles unto the remnant of our seed" (1 Nephi 15:13, emphasis added).

> "Pointing to the covenant which should be fulfilled in the latter days; which covenant the Lord made to our father Abraham, saying: In thy seed shall all the kindreds of the earth be blessed." (1 Nephi 15:18).

> "For I know *that* my redeemer liveth, and *that* he shall stand at the *latter day* upon the earth" (Job 19:25, emphasis added).
>
> "And it shall come to pass in the *last days*, *that* the mountain of the Lord's house shall be established in the top of the mountains, and shall be exalted above the hills; and all nations shall flow unto it" (Isaiah 2:2, emphasis added).
>
> "This know also, that in the *last days* perilous times shall come. For men shall be lovers of their own selves . . . lovers of pleasures more than lovers of God . . . from such turn away" (2 Timothy 3:1-5, emphasis added).

Moroni quoted to the Prophet Joseph Smith the eleventh chapter of Isaiah in one of the opening scenes of the restoration. Almost fifteen years later, the Lord said the "root of Jesse" spoken of in the tenth verse of Isaiah 11, "It is a descendant of Jesse, as well as of Joseph, unto whom rightly belongs the priesthood, and the keys of the kingdom, for an ensign, and for the gathering of my people in the *last days*" (D&C 113:6, emphasis added).

It is a thrill and a singular responsibility to live in these last days as a participant in the work so prophesied as the capstone period of human existence. These are the very days leading up to the Lord's Second Coming to the earth, scripturally written of as the last or latter days.

174. In the latter days, the Church will be in all the world but will be small in number.

The Church that Jesus Christ organized was small in number and confined to a fairly local world stage. Bold indeed was the charge Jesus gave to his apostles to "Go ye therefore, and teach all nations, baptizing them in the name of the Father, and of the Son, and of the

Holy Ghost" (Matthew 28:19). The apostles and disciples took this charge to heart and fanned out across much of the Mediterranean world, yet winning relatively few converts in the dominant Roman world of paganism.

Speaking of the last days, and in the form of an allegory, Jacob said, "And it came to pass that the Lord of the vineyard sent his servant; and the servant went and did as the Lord had commanded him, and brought other servants; and they were few" (Jacob 5:70).

Today, there are some fifteen million members of the Church worldwide. Given an approximate world population of seven billion, that works out to about one fifth of one percent, or one member for every 467 people in the world.

Looking at the breadth of that distribution, of the 193 or so sovereign nations in the world today, the church has membership and/or missionary presence in approximately 161 of them, or eighty-three percent of the nations of the world. Together, those statistics speak to a broad distribution of membership, yet of very small numbers.

So it was prophesied to be, "And it came to pass that I beheld the church of the Lamb of God, and its numbers were few . . . nevertheless, I beheld that the church of the Lamb, who were the saints of God, were also upon all the face of the earth; and their dominions upon the face of the earth were small" (1 Nephi 14:12).

Jesus said, "Because strait is the gate, and narrow is the way, which leadeth unto life, and few there be that find it" (Matthew 7:14).

The restored Church in these latter days reflects the prophecies of its existence regarding geographic scope and membership numbers.

175. The settling of the saints in Salt Lake City was seen by the prophets.

"And it shall come to pass in the last days, that the mountain of the Lord's house shall be established in the top of the mountains, and shall be exalted above the hills; and all nations shall flow unto it. And many people shall go and say, Come ye, and let us go up to the mountain of the Lord, to the house of the God of Jacob; and he will teach us of his ways, and we will walk in his paths: for out of Zion shall go forth the law, and the word of the Lord from Jerusalem" (Isaiah 2:2-3, Micah 4:1-2).

Temples are the houses of the Lord. The Salt Lake Temple stands today as a beacon to the world and is probably the site most associated with Salt Lake City, Utah. It was forty years in construction. The Salt Lake Valley is truly on the top of the mountains, since it sits approximately 4,300 feet above sea level.

People come from all over the world to Salt Lake City, but most particularly, saints come from all over the world to settle there. They come that "he will teach us of his ways, and we will walk in his paths" (Isaiah 2:2-3, Micah 4:1-2).

It is a fulfillment of prophecy that the Church headquarters are established in the mountains of Utah in these latter days and that, indeed, all nations shall flow unto it.

176. Professor Charles Anthon unwittingly fulfilled the words of Isaiah.

In September of 1827, Joseph Smith received the gold plates from which he later translated the Book of Mormon. His initial translation efforts in late 1827 and early 1828 were comprised of "copying the characters off the plates. I copied a considerable number of them, and by means of the Urim and Thummim I translated some of them, which I did between the time I arrived at the house of my wife's father, in the month of December, and the February following" (Joseph Smith History 1:62).

Martin Harris, who was helping in the translation effort, took a copy of the written characters with the intention of verifying their authenticity in February 1828. His account is as follows:

> "I went to the city of New York, and presented the characters which had been translated, with the translation thereof, to Professor Charles Anthon, a gentleman celebrated for his literary attainments. Professor Anthon stated that the translation was correct, more so than any he had before seen translated from the Egyptian. I then showed him those which were not yet translated, and he said that they were Egyptian, Chaldaic, Assyriac, and Arabic; and he said they were true characters. He gave me a certificate, certifying to the people of Palmyra that they were true characters, and that the translation of such of them as had been translated was also correct. I took the certificate and put it into my pocket, and was just leaving the house, when Mr. Anthon called me back, and asked me how the young man found out that there were gold plates in the place where he found them. I answered that an angel of God had revealed it unto him. He then said to me, 'Let me see that certificate.' I accordingly took it out of my pocket and gave it to him, when he took it and tore it to pieces, saying that there was no such thing now as ministering of angels, and that if I would bring the plates to him he would translate them. I informed him that part of the plates were sealed, and that I was forbidden to bring them. He replied, 'I cannot read a sealed book.' I left him and went to Dr. Mitchell, who sanctioned what Professor Anthon had said respecting both the characters and the translation" (Joseph Smith History 1:64-65).

This remarkable, unrehearsed exchange, is a direct fulfillment of words written by Isaiah in the Old Testament, "And the vision of all is become unto you as the words of a book that is sealed, which men deliver to one that is learned, saying, Read this, I pray thee: and he saith, I cannot; for it is sealed" (Isaiah 29:11).

I just don't believe Martin and Joseph knew of this Isaiah prophecy and then colluded to play into it. In fact, a little over a year later, Martin mortgaged a portion of his farm for the publication of the then translated Book of Mormon. That speaks highly for the confirming impression the above experience had upon Martin Harris. I think it's an amazing prophetic fulfillment.

177. Isaiah prophesied that out of Zion shall go forth the law, and the word of the Lord from Jerusalem.

The above scripture from Isaiah 2:3 (see also Micah 4:2-3, 2 Nephi 12:3) is to be fulfilled during the Millennium when Christ will reign personally upon the earth. It speaks of two capital centers to be on the earth, each with its respective functions. Isaiah made further references to and distinctions between Zion and Jerusalem in Isaiah 40:9. The Prophet Joel said it this way, "The Lord also shall roar out of Zion, and utter his voice from Jerusalem" (Joel 3:16).

"We believe . . . that Zion (the New Jerusalem) will be built upon the American continent" (Articles of Faith, 10).

Joseph Fielding Smith has written, "Zion and Jerusalem: Two World Capitals. When Joseph Smith translated the Book of Mormon, he learned that America is the land of Zion which was given to Joseph and his children, and that on this land the City Zion, or New Jerusalem, is to be built.. He also learned that Jerusalem in Palestine is to be rebuilt and become a holy city. These two cities, one in the land of Zion and one in Palestine, are to become capitals for the kingdom of God during the millennium."[1]

Zion, or the New Jerusalem on the American continent, will be the seat of government while Jesus reigns during the millennium. From there will go the law, because there will still be need of an organized, lawful society to insure the peace and freedom of individuals. The Lord has revealed the location of this New Jerusalem, or Zion, to be Independence, Missouri (D&C 57:1-3, D&C 45:66-67).

Jerusalem, in the old world, will be the ecclesiastical seat of governance.

I believe in this future millennial scenario because I believe in living prophets. Living prophets have made this understanding of millennial governance clear. To declare that Independence, Missouri will someday have blessed status like Rome or Jerusalem seems a bit peculiar or random perhaps. But I think that's because Independence, Missouri is just so familiar, it's just Anytown, USA, to most of us.

This clarification of a future community gives insight and understanding of the Lord's millennial plan. It provides structure to the prophecy given by Isaiah and others as they looked into the future. It is a visionary understanding, unique to LDS beliefs.

Notes:

1. Joseph Fielding Smith, *Doctrines of Salvation,* vol. III, Salt Lake City: Bookcraft, 1956, 66-72. See also Ether 13:4-5 and 3 Nephi 20:22.

178. We see "falling away," "itching ears," spiritual "famine," and a need for a "restitution."

The scriptural basis necessitating the restoration of the gospel to the earth in the latter days is, I think, pretty clear. Whereas other inspired men sought to reform what they saw as corrupted, a restoration, not a reformation of the gospel, was required. Why?

"Priesthood authority did not continue in an unbroken line of succession from the Apostle Peter. To reform is to change what already exists; to restore is to bring back something in its original form. Thus, restoration of priesthood authority through divine messengers was the only possible way."[1]

In writing to the Churches of Galatia, Paul lamented for those in the early Church who easily accepted deviations and doctrinal perversions, "I marvel that ye are so soon removed from him that called you into the grace of Christ unto another gospel: Which is not another; but there be some that trouble you, and would pervert the gospel of Christ" (Galatians 1:6-7).

But it was not only a problem for the Galatians. Paul saw it as a precursor to the times yet future. "For the time will come when they will not endure sound doctrine; but after their own lusts shall they heap to themselves teachers, having itching ears; And they shall turn away their ears from the truth, and shall be turned unto fables" (2 Timothy 4:3-4).

On another occasion, Paul wrote, "Let no man deceive you by any means: for that day shall not come [the Second Coming of Christ], except there come a falling away first" (2 Thessalonians 2:3).

That falling away is a reference to falling away from the pure doctrines of Jesus Christ, including the absence of priesthood authority, corruption of church organization, changing of the saving ordinances, uninspired scriptural interpretation, and diminished standards of worthiness.

The Old Testament Prophet Amos described the period after the martyrdom of the apostles and prior to the restoration in this way, "Behold, the days come, saith the Lord God that I will send a famine in the land, not a famine of bread, nor a thirst for water, but of hearing the words of the Lord: And they shall wander from sea to sea, and from the north even to the east, they shall run to and fro to seek the word of the Lord, and shall not find it" (Amos 8:11-12).

But then comes the glorious promise, "Whom [Jesus Christ] the heaven must receive until the times of restitution of all things, which God hath spoken by the mouth of all his holy prophets since the world began" (Acts 3:21).

The restitution of all things is found in the restored Church of Jesus Christ. It is as its name implies. The Church at the time of Christ and His apostles was lost through wickedness and is once again actively authorized upon the earth today. The scriptural basis for this sequence of historical events is indeed compelling.

Notes:

1. *Preach My Gospel,* Salt Lake City: Intellectual Reserve, Inc., 2004, 36.

179. The work of the Church in Communist East Germany was led by the hand of God.

In 1961, the infamous Berlin Wall was built to keep people from emigrating from communist East Germany to the West. There were less than five thousand members of the Church in East Germany at that time. Their Church heritage spanned clear back to 1855 and included the German convert Karl G. Maeser, who became the principal of Brigham Young Academy. In 1968, Elder Thomas S. Monson, a young apostle forty-one-years-old, received the apostolic assignment to supervise the European missions of Germany, Italy, Austria, and Switzerland. His first visit with the Saints behind the iron curtain was in November, 1968.

The Gorlitz meeting place was a dilapidated, war ravaged, abandoned factory building. There, Elder Monson made a promise to the 235 assembled saints, "If you will remain true and faithful to the commandments of God, every blessing any member of the Church enjoys in any other country will be yours."[1] From his own journal entry of that day, Elder Monson recorded, "This evening in my hotel room, as I realized the full impact of the promise I had made at Gorlitz earlier today, I dropped to my knees and said to my Heavenly Father, 'Father, I am on Thy errand; this is Thy Church. I have spoken words that came not from me, but from Thee and Thy Son. Wilt Thou, therefore, fulfill the promise in the lives of this noble people.' There coursed through my mind the words from the Psalm, "Be still and know that I am God."[2]

At the time, there were no wards or stakes in Eastern Germany. There were almost no written manuals or materials, just the standard works. The people were poor by western standards. Because of Church membership, they were discriminated against by the government from opportunities. They had no patriarch, no dedicated meetinghouse, and no temple. Their opportunity to travel to Switzerland to receive temple blessings was costly, and permission was arbitrarily decided by government officials. All meetings were carefully monitored and watched by the ruling authorities. Nevertheless, the faithful saints believed the promise that an apostle of the Lord had given them.

"We believe in being subject to kings, presidents, rulers, and magistrates, in obeying, honoring, and sustaining the law" (Articles of Faith, 12). In 1975, Elder Spencer W. Kimball counseled the leader of the saints in Eastern Germany to "have a change of heart," and to "befriend the Communists . . . and not hold any grudges against them."[3] Difficult as that was to befriend those who had labeled you as "an enemy of the state,"[4] the long process of working within the system and building bridges was begun.

Over the years, Elder Monson built that same trust and respect in his associations with government officials. In a country hostile to all religions, permission was granted in 1979 for the Church to construct five chapels and, miracle of miracles, a temple in Freiberg! In a meeting with Chairman Erich Honecker in 1988, permission was granted, without precedent, to allow our missionaries to both come into and to go out from Eastern Germany!

It was only a year later that the Berlin wall came down in a groundswell movement for freedom. I believe that in the providence of Almighty God, these events were an important prelude to this historic revolution and a fulfillment of an apostolic promise given in the dark days of 1968 to a faithful people.

Notes:

1. Thomas S. Monson, *Faith Rewarded: A Personal Account of Prophetic Promises to the East German Saints,* Salt Lake City: Deseret Book, 1996, recorded under the date of Sunday, November 10, 1968, 5.

2. Thomas S. Monson, 7.

3. Heidi S. Swinton, *To the Rescue: The Biography of Thomas S. Monson,* Salt Lake City: Deseret Book, 2010, 308.

4. Heidi S. Swinton, 308.

180. Ward and stake divisions fulfill Isaiah's prophecy to "strengthen thy stakes."

In these days of mega-churches, the Lord's Church stands in marked contrast. Although it is truly one big mega-Church in the fact that we are centrally led by a Prophet, each ward and stake is an independent unit of the Church. In fact, when a ward or stake reaches a certain population within a given geographic area and with a given demography, that ward or stake is divided to create new units of the Church.

My wife and I have lived all our married life in the same small city now for thirty years. Initially, we belonged to the first ward in an adjoining city. From that beginning, and within the geography it then occupied, there are now four additional stakes, and some forty plus wards! That means at least forty Bishops, forty Relief Society Presidents, forty Elders Quorum Presidents, and a whole lot of teachers, clerks, ward missionaries, and on and on.

To create new wards and stakes gives broader opportunity to participate in the Lord's Kingdom in various capacities. Such participation is a service to the Lord and to our fellows, both members and those who are not members of the Church. What did Isaiah mean when he gave the formula that would "strengthen thy stakes" (Isaiah 54:2)?

"Enlarge the place of thy tent, and let them stretch forth the curtains of thy habitations; spare not, lengthen thy cords, strengthen thy stakes" (Isaiah 54:2).

My own opinion is that the strengthening of stakes is not merely in the creation of stakes, but more so, in the devotion and obedience of its members. Such devotion and obedience is best learned and nurtured when we are involved in the work of the Lord and depend upon His guidance, wisdom, correction, and inspiration. It is pure genius to have the lay membership at large run the church at the local level. It is a blessing to the humble and a source of strengthening, confirming, even renewing, one's personal testimony of truth.

When Isaiah recorded to "let them" (Isaiah 54:2), I wonder if it means to let the presiding authority make those oftentimes uncomfortable changes to our wards and stakes. The Stake President has the presiding authority to recommend ward creations, and General Authorities have presiding authority to create new stakes. Perhaps this clause has reference to the sustaining of presiding authorities, and if so, we alone have such a priesthood structure and priesthood authority to fulfill this scriptural injunction.

The Lord's Church has and is spreading across all the earth. There are some three thousand stakes and about thirty thousand wards and branches today. Taken as a whole, that is one mega-mega church! It is indeed led by one preacher, the very Messiah; however, He calls ordinary people of faith to minister to the needs of God's children in the stakes and wards of Zion.

What a blessing and a privilege to participate in the strengthening of the Lord's Kingdom in these latter days, not as a bystander, but as authorized participants!

181. The "fulness of times" is a scriptural description of these days.

The Apostle Paul wrote to the Ephesians, "That in the dispensation of the fulness of times he might gather together in one all things in Christ, both which are in heaven, and which are on earth; even in him" (Ephesians 1:10).

That fullness of times is now. The Prophet Joseph Smith wrote to the Church at large, "For it is necessary in the ushering in of the dispensation of the fulness of times, which dispensation is now beginning to usher in, that a whole and complete and perfect union, and welding together of dispensations, and keys, and powers, and glories should take place, and be revealed from the days of Adam even to the present time. And not only this, but those things which never have been revealed from the foundation of the world, but have been kept hid from the wise and prudent, shall be revealed unto babes and sucklings in this, the dispensation of the fulness of times" (D&C 128:18).

What a time to be alive!

Both Paul and Nephi wrote of the role of the Gentiles in the latter days (Romans 11:11-25, 1 Nephi 15:12, 13), that was ushered in by the visit of the Father and the Son to the boy Joseph Smith, "Because he stood at the head of the dispensation of the fullness of times."[1]

Elder Bruce R. McConkie eloquently spoke of this dispensation:

> "*We see* Moroni flying through the midst of heaven, sounding the trump of God, and revealing the book which whispers from the dust with a familiar spirit (see Revelations 14:6).
>
> *We see* other angelic ministrants come, bringing keys and powers and authorities until all of the keys of the kingdom of God are committed unto man on the earth.
>
> *We see* the little stone cut from the mountain without hands beginning to roll forth toward that coming day when it shall smite the Babylonian image, break in pieces the kingdoms of men, and fill the whole earth (see Daniel 2:34–35).
>
> *We see* the elders [and sisters]of the kingdom going forth to many nations, crying repentance, gathering Israel, and assembling the faithful in the tops of the mountains where stands the house of the Lord (see 2 Nephi 12:2).
>
> *We see* converts and stakes and temples. Gifts and signs and miracles abound. The sick are healed and the dead are raised by the power of God, and the work of the Lord goes forward.
>
> *We see* prophet follow prophet as the faithful seek to prepare a people for the Second Coming of him whose witnesses they are."[2]

Included in these enumerations defining the fullness of times are the ordinances of the temple. "That I may reveal mine ordinances therein unto my people; For I deign to reveal unto my church things which have been kept hid from before the foundation of the world, things that pertain to the dispensation of the fulness of times" (D&C 124:40, 41).

I like the summary statement given by Elder Dean L. Larsen speaking of the fullness of times: "It is the period during which the Lord and his servants will make the final great effort to take the message of truth to all the peoples of the earth and to reclaim the descendants of ancient Israel who have lost their true identity."[3]

What a time to be alive and to be a covenant member of The Church of Jesus Christ of Latter-day Saints!

Notes:

1. John Taylor, *Journal of Discourses*, vol. 18, Joseph F. Smith, ed., London: Latter-day Saints' Book Depot, 1877, 326.
2. Bruce R. McConkie, "The Coming Tests and Trials and Glory," *Ensign*, May, 1980.
3. Dean L. Larsen, "A Royal Generation," *Ensign*, May, 1983.

182. We are witnessing the unfolding of a prophetic utterance given in 1833.

"For it shall come to pass in that day, that every man shall hear the fulness of the gospel in his own tongue, and in his own language, through those who are ordained unto this power, by the administration of the Comforter, shed forth upon them for the revelation of Jesus Christ" (D&C 90:11).

When this revelation was given, there were less than 3,500 members of the Church. Yet the words speak of a future time when every man in his own language would hear the fullness of the gospel.

Section 90 of the Doctrine and Covenants is a continuing step in the formation of the First Presidency of the Church, which would be and continue as the presiding quorum of the Church. It states that "through your administration, [the First Presidency] the word may go forth unto the ends of the earth. . . . And then cometh the day when the arm of the Lord shall be revealed in power" (D&C 90:9-10).

This is that day. It is occurring on at least two fronts.

On January 3, 1972, the First Presidency organized a new Department of Internal Communications, which held worldwide responsibility for the publication and distribution of all Church instructional materials, magazines, and administrative manuals. Elder J. Thomas Fyans, the first Director of this new department, commented, "The inspiration of the First Presidency in bringing together in one organization the responsibilities of internal communications has made possible . . . an important move toward the fulfillment of this scripture [D&C 90:11]."[1]

At the end of 2012, the Church offered varying amounts of Church materials in 108 languages. In addition to the ten prevalent languages of the earth, these include the more local languages such as Bislama (Vanuatu), Cesky (Czech Republic), Efik (Nigeria), Cakchiquel (Guatemala), Bahasa (Malaysia, Indonesia), and Eesti (Estonia).

The Book of Mormon has been translated and distributed in eighty-two languages and another twenty-five languages of selected passages as of 2012.

The other fulfillment of this early prophecy is the obvious missionary force of the Church. Of the approximately 88,000 proselyting missionaries serving throughout the earth in over 155 countries, "fifty percent of all missionaries serve in their own homeland."[2] The fullness of the gospel is being taken to the inhabitants of the world in their own tongue, and in their own language.

The call of a missionary always comes from the President of the Church, and by that call, or "through your administration [the office of the First Presidency]" (D&C 90:9), they are "ordained unto this power, by administration of the Comforter" (D&C 90:11), which is revelation.

It is a thrill to see this revelation that was given some 185 years ago, come to such fruition today as the gospel in its fullness spreads across the earth, to be heard and received in native tongues. And all "for the revelation [testimony] of Jesus Christ" (Galatians 1:12).

Notes:

1. J. Thomas Fyans, "The Fullness of the Gospel in Each Man's Language," *Conference Report,* April, 1972.
2. Elder Neil L. Anderson, "Preparing the World for the Second Coming," *Ensign,* May, 2011

183. The gospel is sent unto every nation, and kindred, and tongue, and people.

We are witnessing in our day the fulfillment of prophetic utterances as recorded in scripture:

> "Go ye therefore, and teach all nations" (Matthew 28:19).
>
> "And again, this Gospel of the Kingdom shall be preached in all the world, for a witness unto all nations" (Joseph Smith Matthew 1:31).
>
> "Ye shall be witnesses unto me both in Jerusalem, and in all Judea, and in Samaria, and unto the uttermost part of the earth" (Acts 1:8).
>
> "This gospel shall be preached unto every nation, and kindred, and tongue, and people" (D&C 133:37).
>
> "And I saw another angel fly in the midst of heaven, having the everlasting gospel to preach unto them that dwell on the earth, and to every nation, and kindred, and tongue, and people" (Revelation 14:6).

Joseph Smith declared, "The Standard of Truth has been erected; no unhallowed hand can stop the work from progressing; persecutions may rage, mobs may combine, armies may assemble, calumny may defame, but the truth of God will go forth boldly, nobly, and independent, till it has penetrated every continent, visited every clime, swept every country, and sounded in every ear, till the purposes of God shall be accomplished, and the great Jehovah shall say the work is done."[1]

This is a remarkably bold declaration, particularly in light of the size and geographic scope of the Church at the time it was recorded. The early apostles and believers at the time of Christ and at the time of the restoration held dear such declarations that rested on their faith. We live in a time where we are actual witnesses of their eventual fulfillment.

The Church is in Cape Verde, Madagascar, Ethiopia, Central African Republic, Namibia, Croatia, Russia, Mongolia, Kazakhstan, Sri Lanka, Cambodia, Hong Kong, Papua New Guinea, Uruguay, and Haiti. You can find the Church from the cold northern reaches of Norway and Finland, down to equatorial Kenya and Gabon, to the far southern hemisphere of Chile, and across the isles of the Pacific and Indian Oceans. In Asia, Africa, North America, South America, Europe, and Australia, Latter-day Saints reside, preach the gospel, and are legally organized.

When we look at a map of the world, those countries where we have not yet been able to organize the Church are most noticeably in Northern Africa, the Middle Eastern countries, and most of the "Stans"—Pakistan, Afghanistan, Turkmenistan, Uzbekistan, Kyrgyzstan, and so on. China is another large country where we have not yet received legal status. However, Hong Kong, Macau, and Taiwan do recognize and allow our members to assemble and to proselyte.

"Somehow, brethren, I feel that when we have done all in our power that the Lord will find a way to open doors. That is my faith."[2] The footprint of the Lord's Church throughout the earth is large and firmly planted. It is truly approaching every continent, every clime, every nation, and every kindred, tongue and people. And it will continue to do so until "the great Jehovah shall say the work is done."[3]

Notes:

1. Joseph Smith, Jun., *History of the Church of Jesus Christ of Latter-day Saints,* Salt Lake City: Deseret Book, 1960, 4:540.
2. Spencer W. Kimball, "When the World Will be Converted," *Ensign,* October, 1974.
3. Joseph Smith, Jun., 4:540.

184. Hyrum Smith's family legacy fulfills prophecy.

In Section 23 of the Doctrine and Covenants, the Lord speaks to Oliver Cowdery, Hyrum Smith, Samuel Smith, Joseph Smith Sr., and Joseph Knight regarding their respective duties just days after the Church was formally organized. The counsel to each is very similar. But uniquely to Hyrum, the Lord said, "Wherefore thy duty is unto the church forever, and this because of thy family" (D&C 23:3).

That clause regarding his family could refer to his belonging to the Joseph and Lucy Smith family, although no such verbiage is used when addressing Joseph Sr. in the same revelation. I believe it was a forward statement, referring to his faithful posterity.

No other Smith family line carries the faithful legacy of Church leadership more so than Hyrum Smith. Hyrum served as the Presiding Patriarch of the Church upon the death of his father, Joseph Smith, Sr. A Presiding Patriarch was ordained as a prophet, seer, and revelator, as are the members of the First Presidency and the Quorum of the Twelve. Hyrum's oldest son, John Smith, served as the Presiding

Patriarch of the church between the years of 1855 and 1911. Subsequently, two great-grandsons of Hyrum served in this office. Eldred G. Smith, a great-great-grandson of Hyrum held this position from 1947 until his death in 2013.

Joseph F. Smith, not yet six years old when his Father Hyrum was martyred, went West with the Saints and became an orphan at thirteen years old. At age fifteen, he was called to serve a mission in the remote Hawaiian Islands. His service to the Church from that point forward has become legendary, culminating in his serving as President of the Church from 1901 to 1918. He left a legacy of doctrinal understanding and family love, and was known as a deeply spiritual man, a devoted disciple of the Lord Jesus Christ.

His eldest son, Hyrum Mack Smith, a grandson of Hyrum Smith, served as an apostle from 1901 to 1918. He died prematurely at forty-five years of age in Salt Lake City.

Another son, Joseph Fielding Smith, also a grandson of Hyrum Smith, served as the tenth President of the Church in this dispensation. Prior to that he served as the Church Historian, President of the Genealogical Society, and President of the Salt Lake City Temple. He was a noted scholar of Church history and doctrine, and the Church today is beneficiary of his thoughtful and prayerful writings.

M. Russell Ballard serves today as a member of the Quorum of the Twelve Apostles, and is a great-great-grandson of Hyrum Smith. He continues the long legacy of faithful service to the Church. He has been a strong voice for sharing the gospel and for remembering our pioneer heritage.

"Wherefore thy duty is unto the church forever, and this because of thy family" (D&C 23:3). "His name [Hyrum] may be had in honorable remembrance from generation to generation, forever and ever" (D&C 124:96). These early declarations of the Lord to Hyrum have come to fruition. It is a remarkable prophetic family legacy.

185. By this shall all men know that ye are my disciples, if ye have love one to another.

This is the distinguishing characteristic of a true disciple of Jesus Christ.

In 1977, I went to Cedar City to attend Southern Utah State College. I was not a member of the Church, but I felt a remarkably warm and inclusive outpouring from many within the Church. I remember visiting a friend's family in Panguitch one weekend. It was almost magical to me. They were an incredibly close, loving family—we prayed together, sang together, laughed, played games, read scriptures, and shared family meals together. Without consciously noting it, I was experiencing the scripture above. These were committed disciples and had a home of love one to another.

Jesus said a lot about love:

> "If ye love me, keep my commandments" (John 14:15).
>
> "This is my commandment, that ye love one another as I have loved you" (John 15:12).
>
> "Thou shalt love the Lord they God with all thy heart, and with all thy soul, and with all thy mind. . . . Thou shalt love thy neighbor as thyself" (Matthew 22:37, 39).

As I've observed the Saints over many years now, I see a people who have been, and are now, a loving people. I see that love prioritized as written in Matthew above.

More important than the pursuit for worldly praise and acceptance, and in spite of sometimes social discrimination, Latter-day Saints are first and foremost true to the witness they've received from God. That love toward our living Heavenly Father is confirmed and steadied by our covenants. That love is what causes us to want to be obedient to His will and to His prophets. I've experienced times when actions or expressions from local Church leaders may seem harsh, yet when peeled back, it is because of that leader's love of God and reverence for His ways that prompt him to take an apparently difficult position.

It would be a much easier course to simply be members of this great Church and keep the blessings to ourselves. We could simply enjoy the gift of the Holy Ghost and have the hope of our eternal families. We could simply bask in the teachings and resources available to help us on this mortal journey, including living prophets and additional Holy Scripture. We could simply understand and benefit from the nature and nearness of Deity. Instead, Latter-day Saints reach out in love to their fellows because they see doing that as a part of their discipleship. It is a part of our culture to sacrifice our time and resources to the service of others through our callings, our personal ministries, our global ministry, and our humanitarian efforts worldwide. It is a labor of love. It is what we do.

Some people who are not members of the Church misinterpret, misunderstand, or teach out of context, the doctrines of the LDS Church. Most who have a professional, working, or neighborly friendship with an LDS member will feel the love and goodness that is genuinely manifested. Some will make that connection to the voice of the Master when He said, "By this shall all men know that ye are my disciples, if ye have love one to another" (John 13:35). We see that in others as well.

186. This Church restored is the "marvelous work and a wonder" Isaiah referred to.

Isaiah chapter 29 is a thrilling chapter prophesying of the apostasy that would follow the time of Christ, the restoration in the latter days, the coming forth of the Book of Mormon, and the light of pure doctrine so that those "that erred in spirit shall come to understanding" (Isaiah 29:24). Verse 13 gives prologue explanation to verse 14, wherein the Lord states "Therefore, behold, I will proceed to do a marvelous work among this people, even a marvelous work and a wonder" (Isaiah 29:14).

Elder LeGrand Richards wrote a book entitled *A Marvelous Work and a Wonder* which I read while I investigated the Church back in 1976 and 1977. In this book, Elder Richards makes a compelling case for just how marvelous and just how wonderful this restored gospel truly is. Below is a listing of selected chapters from the Table of Contents:

- The Personality of the Father and the Son
- False Doctrines and Universal Apostasy
- The Coming Forth of the Book of Mormon [prophesied]
- Restoration of Priesthood Authority
- The Ordinance of Baptism
- The Mission of the Holy Ghost
- The Mission of Elijah
- Marriage for Time and for All Eternity
- The Gathering of Israel
- Israel in the Latter Days
- Differences between Salvation and Exaltation
- Whence Cometh Man?
- Why is Man Here?
- Where is Man Going?
- The Sabbath Day
- The Word of Wisdom
- The Law of Tithing

Those are just some of the chapter titles and restored truths that Elder Richards expounds upon.

I am sure that we don't fully appreciate the comprehensive, inclusive, prophetically precise, merciful, saving doctrines, and principles that the Lord has revealed to His children through prophets. Through the written word of scripture, the living words of prophets, the personal witness of the Spirit, by exercising our intelligence and rational deduction, by obedience to divine direction, and by mighty prayer, we have access to an unlimited source of understanding and truth.

Joseph Smith is eminent among a long line of prophets. More saving doctrine has been revealed in these latter days through Joseph Smith than at any time in human history. Additional scripture, living prophets, the gift of the Holy Ghost, priesthood leadership, the practice of ordinances and covenants, the gathering of Israel once again—It truly is a marvelous work and a wonder taking place across the earth, as foretold by the prophet Isaiah!

187. There is a distinct scriptural kinship between Jewish and LDS doctrine.

First of all, a brief refresher. The Abrahamic covenant came through Father Abraham, to Isaac his son, and to Jacob his son. Jacob (whose name was changed by God to Israel) had twelve sons, whose lineage we now call the House of Israel. Prominent to the twelve tribes of Israel was the tribe of Judah and the tribe of Joseph. Joseph had two sons, Ephraim and Manasseh, and it was Ephraim who was given the birthright status over Jacob's eldest, Reuben. All but Benjamin, Judah, "and the strangers with them out of Ephraim and Manasseh, and out of Simeon" (2 Chronicles 15:9) were carried away captive into Assyria in about 721 BC. Those carried away are now known as the Lost Tribes of Israel. Those who remained in the Southern Kingdom took the name of Judah. It is this people, the Jews, who have had such a rich, difficult, prophetic, and Messianic history. It is this people whom we (Christians and Jews) recognize as the covenant people of the Lord, a modern day remnant of the House of Israel.

In the last days, it has been the privilege of the tribe of Ephraim first to bear the message of the Restoration of the gospel to the world and to gather scattered Israel, including the Jews.[1]

"In the latter days . . . then shall the fulness of the gospel of the Messiah come unto the Gentiles, and from the Gentiles unto the remnant of our seed" (1 Nephi 15:13).

"Behold, I will lift up mine hand to the Gentiles, and set up my standard to the people" (Isaiah 49:22).

"After the Gentiles had received the fulness of the Gospel . . . the remnants of the house of Israel, should be grafted in, or come to the knowledge of the true Messiah, their Lord and their Redeemer" (1 Nephi 10:14).

These scriptures highlight the role of the Gentiles in taking the gospel to the world and gathering scattered Israel. Since we know that the tribe of Ephraim will lead this gathering effort in the last days, the Gentiles in this sense are those from Gentile (non-Israelite) nations.

"Ours is the responsibility to help fulfill the Abrahamic covenant... This is the appointed day when the gospel is to be taken to the kindreds of the earth. This is the time of the promised gathering of Israel."[2]

Israel! Do You Know? is the title of a book written by Elder LeGrand Richards of the Quorum of the Twelve. To the descendants of Judah, Elder Richards pleads, "Look up, O House of Judah! The divine promises which God made to your fathers Abraham, Isaac, and Jacob have spanned the centuries and their blessed fulfillment are upon you."[3]

"For behold, the Lord will remember his covenant which he hath made unto his people of the House of Israel" (3 Nephi 29:3). That covenant light will come to the Jews by way of the Gentile, just as Nephi foresaw that light coming to his seed in the latter days, "through the fullness of the Gentiles . . . they shall come to the knowledge of their Redeemer and the very points of his doctrine, that they may know how to come unto him and be saved" (1 Nephi 15:13, 14).

Notes:

1. LDS Bible Dictionary, "Ephraim."
2. Elder Russell M. Nelson, "Covenants," *Ensign,* November, 2011.
3. LeGrande Richards, *Israel! Do You Know?* Salt Lake City: Deseret Book, 1954, preface.

188. The Book of Mormon prophesies of the discovery of the Americas by Columbus.

About 2,100 years in advance of Christopher Columbus' coming upon the Americas, the Prophet Nephi saw it in vision and recorded, "And I looked and beheld a man among the Gentiles, who was separated from the seed of my brethren by the many waters; and I beheld the Spirit of God, that it came down and wrought upon the man; and he went forth upon the many waters, even unto the seed of my brethren, who were in the promised land" (1 Nephi 13:12).

"We interpret that [1 Nephi 13:12] to refer to Columbus. It is interesting to note that the Spirit of God wrought upon him. . . . I have no doubt that Christopher Columbus was a man of faith, as well as a man of indomitable determination."[1]

I, too, find it interesting to note that here we have recorded confirmation that the hand of the Lord was clearly upon Christopher Columbus and this most important and historical mission. This was a step toward the gentiles peopling the Americas and all that led up to the restoration of the Gospel in the state of New York some 328 years later.

It is also significant to note the spirituality and motives of Christopher Columbus. From a biography titled "*Admiral of the Ocean Sea*" by Dr. Samuel Eliot Morison, Elder Hinckley notes, "But it was he who in faith lighted a lamp to look for a new way to China and who in the process discovered America. . . . In his reports to the sovereigns of Spain, Columbus repeatedly asserted that his voyage was for the glory of God and the spread of the Christian faith."[2]

In a letter to the Spanish hierarchy, Columbus himself wrote, "Our Lord unlocked my mind, sent me upon the sea, and gave me fire for the deed. Those who heard of my emprise called it foolish, mocked me, and laughed. But who can doubt that the Holy Ghost inspired me?"[3]

"I'm sure that he [the Lord] inspired a little boy, Christopher Columbus, to stand on the quays in Genoa, Italy, and yearn for the sea. He was filled with the desire to sail the seas, and he fulfilled a great prophecy (1 Nephi 13:12) made long, long, ago, that this land, chosen above all other lands, should be discovered. And so, when he was mature, opportunity was granted to him to brave the unknown seas, to find this land."[4]

I believe that many of the great discoveries that push back the frontiers of knowledge or geography are inspired of God, but here we have a direct recognition of that influence and errand. It is particularly momentous to Latter-day Saints in light of the restoration on the American continent. It is a remarkable prophecy.

Notes:

1. Gordon B. Hinckley, "Building Your Tabernacle," *Ensign*, November, 1992.
2. Gordon B. Hinckley.

3. Mark E. Peterson, *The Great Prologue,* Salt Lake City: Deseret Book, 1975, 26.

4. Spencer W. Kimball, "The Work Among the Lamanites," *Conference Report,* October, 1950, 63.

189. Nephi saw the American Revolutionary War some 2,370 years prior to its occurrence.

In Chapter 13 of the First Book of Nephi in the Book of Mormon, Nephi saw in vision the discovery, peopling, and early foundations of what he called the promised land, [the Americas] and then more specifically, what was to become the United States of America.

As a part of that chronology and those events is the prophetic reference to the future engagement of their mother country (Britain) in a war for independence by the American colonies, "And it came to pass that I, Nephi, beheld that the Gentiles who had gone forth out of captivity did humble themselves before the Lord; and the power of the Lord was with them. And I beheld that their mother Gentiles were gathered together upon the waters, and upon the land also, to battle against them. And I beheld that the power of God was with them, and also that the wrath of God was upon all those that were gathered together against them to battle. And I, Nephi, beheld that the Gentiles that had gone out of captivity were delivered by the power of God out of the hands of all other nations" (1 Nephi 13:16-19).

Many believe that the founding of the United States of America was divinely inspired, while others would say that is an arrogant or colored assumption. Here we have published to the world that, indeed, the founding of this great country was by the power of God for specific purposes and future influences which would bless nations and indeed the entire human family.

"Thus the American colonies attained their independence and set up the government of the United States, all under the divine intervention of God in preparing this land for its divine destiny."[1]

We often see the hand of God in history as we glance back at what has become a matter of record. Many are the recorded journals, letters, articles, and remembrances that ascribe the defeat of the British monarchy by the rag-tag colonists as divinely inspired and divinely intended. Not only do we have recorded a prophecy that the war for independence would occur, but also the prophecy confirming the outcome of that war.

To know that the United States was founded and sanctioned by direct intervention of the Almighty gives us perspective to its purposes and noble expectations.

Notes:

1. Nathan E. Tanner, "If They Will But Serve the God of the Land," *Ensign,* May, 1976.

190. The Church is an ensign to all the world.

"And even so I have sent mine everlasting covenant into the world, to be a light to the world, and to be a standard for my people, and for the Gentiles to seek to it, and to be a messenger before my face to prepare the way before me" (D&C 45:9).

We see this "standard for my people" as a great ensign in the latter days, an ensign to rally around, to gather to, to be a beacon to all nations. It is to be lifted up as "an ensign of peace . . . unto the ends of the earth" (D&C 105:39).

Isaiah made several references to this idea of an ensign being raised in the latter days:

> "And he will lift up an ensign to the nations from far, and will hiss unto them from the end of the earth: and behold, they shall come with speed swiftly" (Isaiah 5:26).
>
> "All ye inhabitants of the world, and dwellers on the earth, see ye [pay attention!], when he lifteth up an ensign on the mountains" (Isaiah 18:3).

Isaiah Chapter 11 is so significant to the work Joseph Smith was called to that in September 1823, Moroni quoted it to Joseph saying, "it was about to be fulfilled" (Joseph Smith History 1:40). Within that chapter are these verses, "And it shall come to pass in that day, that the Lord shall set his hand again the second time to recover the remnant of his people. . . . And he shall set up an ensign for the nations, and shall assemble the outcasts of Israel, and gather together the dispersed of Judah from the four corners of the earth" (Isaiah 11:11-12).

Joseph F. Smith gave a very particular understanding to the above scripture when he said, "In the little town of Fayette, Seneca County, New York, the Lord set up an ensign to the nations. It was in fulfillment of the prediction made by the Prophet Isaiah, which I have read (above). That ensign was the Church of Jesus Christ of Latter-day Saints, which was established for the last time, never again to be destroyed or given to other people."[1] That is certainly part of what Moroni meant when he said to Joseph that it was about to be fulfilled.

And another Isaiah reference says, "There shall be a root [descendant] of Jesse, which shall stand for an ensign of the people; to it shall the Gentiles seek" (Isaiah 11:10). Further light is given to this passage when the Lord said of this descendant of Jesse, "unto whom rightly belongs the priesthood, and the keys of the kingdom, for an ensign, and for the gathering of my people in the last days" (D&C 113:6).

Along with the Church as this ensign to all nations, the Book of Mormon is also an ensign to all the world. Nephi wrote that it will "hiss forth unto the ends of the earth, for a standard unto my people, which are of the House of Israel" (2 Nephi 29:2).

"The Book of Mormon and the Church of Jesus Christ are symbolic ensigns to all nations of the earth."[2] I, along with millions of others including ancient and modern prophets, declare that these are those times when the ensign has been raised to all the world.

Notes:

1. Joseph Fielding Smith, *Doctrines of Salvation,* vol. III, Salt Lake City: Bookcraft, 1956, 254-255.
2. lds.org, *The Guide to the Scriptures,* "Ensign."

191. The prophecies in the Book of Mormon foretell the peopling of America.

I'm not a historian, nor am I familiar with all the theories of how and from where the peoples of North and South America came to be. But as a part of that peopling, the Lord has given us much insight and understanding of origins, purposes, chronology, and conditions through the Book of Mormon.

Lehi prophesied that those who would subsequently come to America "should be led out of other countries by the hand of the Lord" (2 Nephi 1:5) and that this land "shall be a land of liberty unto them" (2 Nephi 1:7).

In about 595 BC, the prophet Nephi received in vision the beginnings of what would become a great Gentile nation, referring to the coming of the pilgrims to North America, "and it came to pass that I beheld the Spirit of God, that it wrought upon other Gentiles [subsequent to Columbus]; and they went forth out of captivity upon the many waters" (1 Nephi 13:13).

"I have a firm conviction that the Lord led the Pilgrims and the Puritans (1 Nephi 13:13) across the ocean, perhaps permitted the persecutions that would bring them here, so that when they came to the American shores with their righteous blood and their high ideals and standards, they would form the basis of a nation which would make possible the restoration of the gospel."[1]

"And it came to pass that I beheld many multitudes of the Gentiles upon the land of promise . . . [and they] did humble themselves before the Lord; and the power of the Lord was with them" (1 Nephi 13:14, 16).

Ezra Taft Benson gives a historical sketch of these pilgrims:

> "Our history clearly records that the early peoples who did come were humble, God-fearing men and women. Bradford records that their first act upon arriving here upon [North] American soil was to go upon their knees in humble prayer and bless the God of heaven. The impelling force in their hearts it seems to me, was a love for basic ideals and principles, which were dearer to them than life itself. Among these were their love of God, faith in his divine purposes, their love of freedom, industry, thrift, decency, and honor. Yes, this nation had its beginnings in a high-minded manner. The rules of conduct established by the early colonists and our founding fathers were taken from the scriptures. They were embodied in the Decalogue and in the gospel. The Sabbath was set aside as a sacred day. Profanity and other vices were condemned, and gambling was forbidden. People were encouraged to keep good company and to repeat no grievances. They emphasized the spiritual virtues."[2]

That the Gentiles "did prosper and obtain the land for their inheritance" (1 Nephi 13:15) is now a matter of record as American history. These are powerful prophecies laid out in the Book of Mormon more than two thousand years prior to their actuality. They have been marvelously fulfilled.

Notes:

1. Spencer W. Kimball, "The Work Among the Lamanites," *Conference Report,* October, 1950, 63.

2. Ezra Taft Benson, "America – What of the Future?" *Conference Report,* April, 1952, 57-58.

192. Through His prophets, the Lord prepared for the gathering of the Jews to Palestine.

Some would argue that to assert that the Latter-day Saints had any influence toward the gathering of the Jews to their homeland and the establishment of the modern State of Israel is an egocentric position. However, the historical chronology of events through the Lord's prophets appear as prologue to some of the significant beginnings leading to what we see today as sovereign Israel, a modern Jewish homeland. Much of the following information comes from an article titled "The Birth of Modern Israel" by W. Cleon Skousen, published in the May, 1972, *Ensign.*[1]

During the Passover season of 1836, in the dedicatory prayer for the Kirtland Temple, Joseph Smith petitioned the Lord, "Have mercy on the children of Jacob, that Jerusalem, from this hour, may begin to be redeemed; . . . and the children of Judah may begin to return to the lands which thou didst give to Abraham, their father" (D&C 109:62, 64).

At that time in history, there was not yet an organized Zionist movement, and Palestine was ruled by Ottoman Egypt. Even earlier, in 1831, Joseph Smith gave a blessing to Orson Hyde stating, "In due time thou shalt go to Jerusalem, the land of thy fathers . . . which shall prepare the way and greatly facilitate the gathering together of that people."[2]

In 1839, the wealthy Italian-English Jew, Moses Montefiore, visited Palestine and felt a tremendous urge to start the gathering. He felt practical steps should be taken to set up Jewish settlements in Palestine.

It was during the April Conference of 1840 that Elder Hyde was called to fulfill the prophetic blessing of 1831 and given the charge to dedicate the land of Palestine for the gathering of the House of Israel. He did so on Sunday morning, October 24, 1841, upon the Mount of Olives. The land at this time was described as barren, unproductive, and desolate.

Then in 1845, the Council of the Twelve, under the leadership of Brigham Young, issued a proclamation which included, "The Jews among all nations are hereby commanded, in the name of the Messiah, to prepare to return to Jerusalem in Palestine; and to rebuild that city and temple unto the Lord: And also to organize and establish their own political government. . . . For be it known unto them that we now hold the keys of the priesthood and kingdom which is soon to be restored unto them."[3]

By 1856, a small trickle of Jewish immigration encouraged Moses Montefiore to set up a Jewish owned orange grove near Jaffa. He hoped that it would encourage more Jewish immigration.

In 1868, Karl Netter, a Jew living in France, founded the Alliance Israelite Universelle, to build global unity among Jewish people and "to fight against hate and prejudice."[4] He too, established a modern Jewish agricultural settlement in the land of Palestine.

In 1873, Brigham Young sent George Albert Smith of the First Presidency, and Elders Lorenzo Snow and Albert Carrington of the Council of the Twelve, on a special mission to Palestine to dedicate the land a second time. They were also told to bless the land "with fruitfulness, preparatory to the return of the Jews."[5]

In 1884, Zionism, or the idea of building a Jewish homeland in Palestine, received official impetus when Dr. Leo Pinsker held an all-Jewish congress in Poland. Then in 1896, Theodore Herzl published "*Der Judenstaat*," (The Jewish State) outlining reasons for European Jews to establish a Jewish homeland, a political structure, and a culture of their own. At a Zionist Congress in Switzerland in 1897, Herzl and others created the basic framework for a Jewish homeland, including plans for a university, a Jewish world bank to finance colonization, even a blue and white flag and a national anthem. All that for a country that didn't yet exist!

In 1914, at the start of World War I, there were approximately eighty-five thousand Jews in Palestine. On November 2, 1917, the famous Balfour declaration was made by Great Britain that they would "favour the establishment in Palestine of a national home for the Jewish people."[6] In 1948, the state of Israel as a Jewish homeland was recognized by the United Nations General Assembly.

That the tribe of Judah has been restored to the land of Palestine is a fulfillment of prophecy that thrills my soul. It is a modern miracle amid the cultural, political, economic, and general prejudices that the Jewish people were up against. Yet prophets, both ancient and modern, have been bold in their vision, proclamations, and dedications to usher in this gathering in the last days. It is, indeed, the work of the Lord.

Notes:

1. W. Cleon Skousen, "The Birth of Modern Israel," *Ensign,* May, 1972.

2. *History of the Church of Jesus Christ of Latter-day Saints,* Salt Lake City: Deseret Book, 1960, 4:375.

3. *Proclamation of the Twelve Apostles or the Church of Jesus Christ of Latter-day Saints,* New York, April 6, 1845.

4. Wikepedia, "Charles Netter," www.wikipedia.org/wiki/Charles_Netter.

5. Letter from Brigham Young and Daniel H. Wells to George A. Smith, October 15, 1872; Edward William Tullidge, *Tullidge's Histories,* vol. 2, Salt Lake: The Press of the Juvenile Instructor, 1889, 17.

6. Arthur James Balfour, *The Balfour Declaration,* November 2, 1917, an official letter from British Foreign Secretary Arthur James Balfour to Lord Rothschild.

193. The Lamanites shall blossom as the rose.

The Lamanites are "a group of people in the Book of Mormon, many of whom were descendants of Laman, the eldest son of Lehi."[1] Initially, they rejected the teachings of the gospel their Father Lehi taught them. "However, shortly before the birth of Jesus Christ, the Lamanites accepted the gospel and were more righteous than the [heretofore righteous] Nephites. Two hundred years after Christ visited the Americas, both the Lamanites and the Nephites became wicked and began to wage war against each other. Around AD 400, the Lamanites completely destroyed the Nephite nation."[2]

The Book of Mormon was "written to the Lamanites, who are a remnant of the house of Israel; and also to Jew and Gentile . . . that they may know the covenants of the Lord" (Title Page, Book of Mormon). The Lamanite lineage in the House of Israel came through Father Lehi, and from the house of Ishmael, who were both of the tribe of Joseph.

The Lamanites are likely included in Isaiah's promise that "Israel shall blossom and bud, and fill the face of the world with fruit [the blessings of salvation]" (Isaiah 27:6). A few chapters later, Isaiah records that in the day of restoration, "the desert shall rejoice, and blossom as the rose. It shall blossom abundantly" (Isaiah 35:1-2).

That brings us to the prophecy specifically regarding the Lamanites. That prophecy uses the same language given to Isaiah. "But before the great day of the Lord shall come, Jacob [Israel] shall flourish in the wilderness, and the Lamanites shall blossom as the rose" (D&C 49:24).

This prophecy was given in early 1831, and I believe it refers to the conversion of the indigenous people of North and South America to the Church of Jesus Christ of Latter-day Saints. Today, approximately thirty-eight percent of total Church membership resides from Mexico south to the southern tip of Chile. By far, most of that growth has been within the last sixty years or the most recent third of Church history. Truly, it has seemed as a blossoming of the rose. A further fulfillment that the Lamanites will be restored to a knowledge of their forefathers and of the Gospel of Jesus Christ (2 Nephi 30:3-6).

It is acknowledged that certainly not all of the native people residing in that area are direct descendants of the Lamanites, nor could a percentage be accurately ascertained. However, whether it be by blood, culture, or geography, we generally consider these people the Lamanite people, heirs of the scriptural promises to the "remnant of the House of Israel" (Title Page, Book of Mormon).

These people have become a strong and a faithful people in the Lord's Kingdom on earth. They are humble, obedient, energetic, reverent, and full of love. They serve in the presiding councils and organizational presidencies of the worldwide Church.

A flower is said to bloom when its buds open, whereas a tree or a plant producing fruit is said to blossom. It is an apt description of the work of the Lord among the Lamanite people in this the final dispensation.

Notes:

1. lds.org, *The Guide to the Scriptures*, "Lamanites."
2. lds.org, *The Guide to the Scriptures*, "Lamanites."

194. "Choice above all other lands" is a Book of Mormon reference to America.

"For members of The Church of Jesus Christ of Latter-day Saints . . . a belief in the special heavenly endowment and the special mission of America is a basic concept of their religion. Both the prophets of the Book of Mormon and the prophets of the latter days have declared that America is a choice land. It is the land designated by God for the restoration of His Church and gospel, as well as the land from which the Church and gospel would spread forth across the earth."[1]

In what way is America to be a choice land above all other lands? In the October, 1958 General Conference of the Church, Milton R. Hunter gave as his opinion the following four purposes for such a designation:

1. In the latter days, the Savior would restore his gospel and establish his Church and Kingdom through a prophet whom the Lord would raise up in the United States of America.

2. The fulfilling of covenants made by the Lord with the children of Israel would occur when the Jews would be restored to Palestine; the Gentiles or Ephraimites, [from Europe] would occupy North America; and the Lamanites would not be "utterly destroyed" (1 Nephi 10:3, 13:30).

3. The Book of Mormon would be published by the prophet in the United States (2 Nephi 29:1-2).

4. The Book of Mormon and the gospel would go to all the inhabitants of the earth from this choice land through the seed of Ephraim, or as Nephi stated, through the Gentiles (2 Nephi 30:3-8).[2]

All of these purposes have come to pass or are in some stage of being carried out.

There are also conditional promises of liberty and prosperity given to those who possess this choice land; "Behold, this is a choice land, and whatsoever nation shall possess it shall be free from bondage, and from captivity, and from all other nations under heaven, if they will but serve the God of the land, who is Jesus Christ" (Ether 2:12).

"And he hath said that: inasmuch as ye shall keep my commandments ye shall prosper in the land; but inasmuch as ye will not keep my commandments ye shall be cut off from my presence" (2 Nephi 1:20, see also 1 Nephi 2:20 , 4:4, Jarom 1:9, Omni 1:6, Alma 9:13, 36:1, 36:30, 38:1, 50:20).

The blessings of liberty and prosperity attached to this choice land, specifically the United States of America, are evident in our history to date but are not permanently secured. When "ye are fully ripe ye shall be cut off from the presence of the Lord" (Ether 2:15). Apparently, this has not yet occurred; however, it could be argued that our course is toward that awful state.

America is referred to repeatedly in the Book of Mormon as a choice land, and furthermore, choice above all other lands. Knowing of such covenant promises, gives hope in the Lord's purposes, a love of freedom and opportunity, and a deep love for this choice land.

Notes:

1. Luis B. Cardon, "Champion of Freedom in the Modern World," in Roy A. Prete, ed., *Windows of Faith,* Provo: Religious Studies Center, Brigham Young University, 2005, 385.

2. Milton R. Hunter, "A Marvelous Work and a Wonder," *Conference Report,* October, 1958, 26-30.

Part Four

Confirming Reasons

confirm, verb – "to make firm or more firm; add strength to; settle or establish firmly." (Dictionary.com)

195. The Church's focus on Jesus Christ is central, broad, and substantive.

A friend of mine was on business travel over a weekend and was free on Sunday. Not able to locate an LDS meetinghouse anywhere nearby, he tuned into a religion channel, hoping for some spiritual uplift on the Sabbath. He noted early on, that preacher after preacher, with a more than normal level of energy and volume, delivered essentially the same message, over and over, "Jesus is Lord, sing praises to the Lord."

Not that this is bad or even incorrect, but the shallowness of their ability to teach doctrine or to expound on the life and ministry of Jesus Christ was striking.

In the LDS edition of the scriptures, there are fully eighteen plus pages of scriptural references relating to the life and mission of the Lord Jesus Christ, divided into fifty-six subtitles. Each subtitle begins with "Jesus Christ" and is then appended with a particular topic. Some of those appending topics are the following:

- Antemortal Existence of
- Prophecies about
- Creator
- Condescension of
- Jehovah
- Divine Sonship, Only Begotten Son
- Relationship with the Father
- Teaching Mode of
- Baptism of
- Atonement through
- Death and Crucifixion of

- Resurrection of
- Second Coming of
- Millennial Reign
- Judge

In addition are topics that identify his roles and responsibilities, including:

- Firstborn
- Messiah
- Savior
- Redeemer
- Lord
- Lamb of God
- Bread of Life
- Light of the World
- Advocate/Mediator
- Good Shepherd
- Second Comforter
- Son of Man
- Exemplar
- Rock
- King

The teachings of the Master are so profound as never to be fully exhausted in our understanding and implementation. These teachings truly embody the living water from which we "shall never thirst,"

(John 4:14) and which shall be to us "a well of water springing up into everlasting life" (John 4:14).

In addition, we accept the Book of Mormon as "Another Testament of Jesus Christ" (Title Page, Book of Mormon). Anyone who reads the book with a sincere heart and with real intent, having faith in Christ, and is willing to ask the Living God to know of its truthfulness will receive the witness of the Holy Ghost that it is, indeed, a record inspired of God. It is another testament of Jesus Christ.

Jesus Christ is alive and is the head of this Church today. He speaks through His Prophets for the Church at large. He is our example in all things, He is "the way, the truth and the life" (John 14:6). Practical and comprehensive are the doctrines and teachings He has given us. I am grateful for the leadership of the Church that stays focused on, completely deferential towards, and dependent upon, the Son of God.

196. The Presidents of this wealthy Church live in humble, common circumstances.

In 1976, I was travelling through Utah to see friends. In route to their home, the person I was with asked if I'd like to see where President Spencer W. Kimball lived since we were in the area. I said, "Yes," since I knew he was the leader of the LDS Church and that the Church was a very wealthy enterprise. I was pleasantly surprised to see that this powerful and influential man lived in a small one-story frame house with a very well-kept yard and ivy growing on the exterior to frame the windows. The home was probably 1,500 square feet by my estimate.

I joined the Church in 1977 and have now had many years intimately involved with local operations of the Church, including leadership responsibility for its growth and management. I can honestly say that I cannot recall any decision being made with the intent to enrich financially any individual member of the Church. Financial considerations at the local level are made prudently in order to be wise stewards over the tithing funds of the Church, but there is no thought of individual or institutional financial enrichment.

Contrary to critics of the faith, the leading councils of the Church do not sit around and conspire on how they can take in more money. The simple and equitable law of the tithe, as commanded of God, is the requirement of the faithful. There is no compulsion to comply with this commandment, only persuasion and encouragement, as it would be with any of the Lord's commandments.

It is accurately said that if you follow the money trail, you will eventually get to the driving force of an organization or an individual's true motive. In the case of the Church, that motive is not financial at all.

197. The voluntary personnel structure in the Church is driven by personal testimony.

The work of the ministry throughout the world at the local level is performed by average members, on a "called to serve" basis, without any monetary remuneration. There is no campaigning for position, no antecedent training requirement, and no sequential progression of importance to a particular calling. Perhaps eighty percent of all active members of the church have a formal Church calling. Also the speakers (preachers) in the weekly sacrament service are from the general congregation, which includes youth. Financial collections and disbursements, maintenance of buildings, and self-performed audits are, likewise, accomplished within this structure.

In addition to the local workings, the Church currently has some 88,000 missionaries throughout the world serving at their own expense. My son is serving in New York right now for two years. He earned $6,000 on his own to pay toward the $11,000 cost, and we, the family, picked up the rest. Additionally, there are countless volunteers serving throughout the world on humanitarian, welfare, temple, historical, genealogy, academic, and public relations missions, all at their own expense.

What would drive a nineteen-year-old boy or girl to take a hiatus from the normal course of college and courtship or senior folks to leave grandkids and established homes and serve for an extended period of time as they are called to strange lands, climes, and cultures—at their own expense? Or what would drive a seminary teacher to teach scripture classes to the youth each day at 6 am, while maintaining the demands of his employment, family, and other commitments? Even more remarkable, what drives the youth to wake up so early and attend a scripture class before school?

The driving reason, the motivation to serve and to participate, is our faith in Christ, the influence of the Holy Ghost, conscious covenants we have made with God, and love for our fellows. Jesus said, "Thou shalt love the Lord thy God with all thy heart, and with all thy soul, and with all thy mind. This is the first and great commandment. And the second is like unto it, Thou shalt love thy neighbour as thyself" (Matthew 22:37-39).

The voluntary contribution of time and resources certainly speaks louder than words and stands as a witness through the lives of millions the world over. The Spirit and influence of Christ is real and abiding in this, His restored Church.

198. Correct principles is the governing ingredient for order in the Church.

On November 15, 1851 the Millennial Star printed this statement by President John Taylor, "Some years ago, in Nauvoo, a gentleman in my hearing, a member of the Legislature, asked Joseph Smith how it was that he was enabled to govern so many people, and to preserve such perfect order. . . . Mr. Smith remarked that it was very easy to do. . . . 'How?' responded the gentleman; 'to us it is very difficult.' Mr. Smith replied, 'I teach them correct principles, and they govern themselves.'"[1]

Throughout history, there have been many ways of governing groups of people, and most have been negative, based in the self-interest of a few. Royal decree, controlling complexity, brute force, exploitation, ignorance, cultural class distinctions, and straight-forward deception are some of the most common.

Religion has been another form of governance, used for both good and evil. In either case, it is an appeal to man's better nature, at the hands of the well-intended or the self-serving.

Compulsion and inordinate selfish motivation have never been correct principles. Latter-day Saints don't pay tithing because they are publicly shamed into doing so, but because they want to contribute to the building of the Kingdom of God. They don't serve two- and three-year missions at their own expense because of future reward but rather out of love for their fellows, love of God, and an active testimony of truth.

The early Saints were an amalgamation of European and Canadian immigrants and early generation Americans. They were rich and poor, educated and simple, male and female, skilled and unskilled. Yet they received a common witness that God had restored His Church and priesthood authority through the Prophet Joseph Smith.

Priesthood, which in part is the authority to preside, is held generally throughout the Church. In other words, governance is broad. There is no seminary to train Bishops or Stake Presidents or Relief Society presidents. Correct principles, based in the scriptures and words of the living prophets and confirmed by the Holy Spirit, guide and govern the Latter-day Saints.

Freedom and self-direction breathe life and motivation into the framework of the Church of Jesus Christ of Latter-day Saints. Correct principles and unchanging truths are at the core.

Notes:

1. John Taylor, "The Organization of the Church," *Millennial Star*, Nov. 15, 1851, 13 no. 22.

199. The translation of the Book of Mormon is an amazing reality.

The Book of Mormon is 531 pages of text in English, coins over two hundred unique names and words, introduces an exchange system, a measuring standard, animals, and building materials, speaks of three distinct groups of individuals who came to the Americas from the old world, and weaves together an intricate history of these peoples over a span of approximately one thousand years.

More importantly, it is another testament of the Lord Jesus Christ as the Savior of the world and agrees and concurs with both the Old Testament and the New Testament. The book of Isaiah is referenced extensively, usually with minor or no textual differences. Adam, Abraham, Isaac, Jacob, Elijah, Jeremiah, Malachi, Moses, all Old Testament prophets, are cited in the Book of Mormon.

The translation occurred from April 7 through about June 30, 1829. The copyright was filed for on June 11. This indicates an astounding pace of translation. Emma, Joseph's wife and occasional scribe in the translation process, said, "When my husband was translating the Book of Mormon, I wrote a part of it, as he dictated each sentence, word for word, and when he came to proper names he could not pronounce, or long words, he spelled them out, and while I was writing them, if I made a mistake in spelling, he would stop me and correct my spelling, although it was impossible for him to see how I was writing them down at the time."[1]

There is no indication of re-drafting, or proofing the manuscript, it was pure dictation. "A stream of consciousness" is how Steven C. Harper describes the process. "[Joseph] would dictate to me for hour after hour; and when returning after meals, or after interruptions, he would at once begin where he had left off, without seeing the manuscript or having any portion of it read to him."[2] There is no evidence of fleshing out the story with Oliver Cowdery, chief scribe, or anyone else. Interestingly, it appears that many Book of Mormon scholars agree that after the loss of the 116 pages, it was the books of Mosiah to Moroni that were translated first (the Larger Plates) and then First Nephi through Omni (the Smaller Plates) were translated.

Joseph was twenty-three-years-old and not an educated man at this point in his life. When the Lord called him, he was a young man, unlearned, simple, and very ordinary in the eyes of the world. This, though, was of the pattern described by Paul when he said, "But God hath chosen the foolish things of the world to confound the wise; and God hath chosen the weak things of the world to confound the things which are mighty" (1 Corinthians 1:27).

The existence of the Book of Mormon, and the setting, circumstance, and elapsed time of its translation stand as a witness to the divine intervention Joseph Smith received in bringing forth this sacred volume of scripture. I have read it, studied it, and taught from it, and I am another witness to the divine intervention that brought forth this sacred volume of scripture.

Notes:

1. Edmund C. Briggs, "A Visit to Nauvoo in 1856," *Journal of History 9,* (January 1916), 454.

2. Joseph Smith III, "Last Testimony of Sister Emma," *Saints' Advocate 2/4,* (October 1879), 50-52; *Saints' Herald 26/19* (1 October 1879), 289-290.

200. The poor have the gospel preached to them.

In large measure, it is not the influential and the powerful, the academics, the rich, or those of stature who are being baptized into the Church today. It is often the common, the average, the humble, the poor. Yet, it is those who respond to the spirit, those whose hearts are open to the truth, and as Alma wrote, "Their afflictions had truly humbled them, and that they were in a preparation to hear the word . . . who were truly penitent, and . . . that ye are brought to a lowliness of heart; for ye are necessarily brought to be humble" (Alma 32:6-12).

It was the same in the time of Christ. His disciples were not of the influential Sadducees and Pharisees, not the ruling class or the self-described learned men of the day, but rather humble fishermen, a despised tax collector, and others of simple lives. Certainly, there were some of influence who hearkened to Jesus' call to "come, follow me" (Luke 18:22), but as today, His followers were not primarily from those of status and privilege.

When John the Baptist asked two of his disciples to query the Lord as to whether or not He were the Christ (which John already knew for himself), Jesus responded by saying, "Go and shew John again those things which ye do hear and see: The blind receive their sight, and the lame walk, the lepers are cleansed, and the deaf hear, the dead are raised up, and the poor have the gospel preached to them" (Matthew 11:4-5). Jesus was showing fulfillment of Messianic prophecy, leaving no doubt in the mind of His hearers who He was. His was a prophesied ministry to the disabled and to the poor.

Our missionaries throughout the world today, teach anyone who will listen to their message of the restoration. They tract, street contact, seek referrals, invite, and labor among and within all strata of society. However, not often enough do we see the leading citizens of a community or of nations accept their message. So it was at the time of Christ, and so it is today.

201. The gift of tongues is in practical use among the missionaries of the Church today.

"We believe in the gift of tongues, prophecy, revelation, visions, healing, interpretation of tongues, and so forth" (Articles of Faith, 4).

The scriptural use of the word "tongues" is most often associated with regional, cultural and national languages, "nations, kindreds, tongues and people" (See Revelation 10:11, 11:9, 13:7, 1 Nephi 19:17, Mosiah 3:13, 27:25, Alma 9:20, D&C 7:3, 88:103, 98:33, etc.).

The oft-referenced scene at the day of Pentecost as recorded in the book of Acts, does not speak of unintelligible pronunciations, but rather of speaking in known languages, understood by those who were native to that language, "every man heard them speak in his own language" (Acts 2:6). The apostle Peter stood up on that occasion and declared it to be the very thing prophesied by Joel in the Old Testament, "But this is that which was spoken by the Prophet Joel; And it shall come to pass in the last days, saith God, I will pour out of my Spirit upon all flesh: and your sons and your daughters shall prophesy, and your young men shall see visions, and your old men shall dream dreams" (Acts 2:16-17). That which took place on that day of Pentecost was the same experience that would come to pass in the last days. When Moroni came to young Joseph Smith, this very scripture from the book of Joel was quoted to Joseph, "He [Moroni] also said that this was not yet fulfilled, but was soon to be" (Joseph Smith History 1:41).

Today, we witness the miracle of our sons and daughters preaching the gospel in all parts of the world, among all nations, kindreds, tongues, and people as the missionary force of the Church. When called to foreign lands, they are given about two months of intense language training, and within a very short time of weeks or months after arriving in their field of labor, they are speaking in the native tongue of that land. It truly is a miracle. It is a gift of the spirit, "for the benefit of the children of God" (D&C 46:26).

In the final verses of the book of Mark, the Savior says that "signs shall follow them that believe . . . they shall speak with new tongues" (Mark 16:17). In fact, by the exercise of faith, we see the gospel taught in over eighty-nine official languages, by otherwise ordinary eighteen to twenty-five year-old young people. They are instruments in the hands of the Lord, communicating in the native tongues of God's children. It is a literal witness of the gift of tongues in practice.

202. The Joseph Smith Translation of Genesis 19:5-10 vindicates Lot.

Lot was the nephew of Abraham, and travelled with Abraham to the land of Canaan. There, they agreed to part ways to accommodate their large herds. Lot chose the Plains of Jordan to the East, and Abraham went into Hebron.

The King James Bible records the following incident that is a disturbing account of the man Lot:

> "And they called unto Lot, and said unto him, Where *are* the men which came in to thee this night? bring them out unto us, that we may know them. And Lot went out at the door unto them, and shut the door after him, And said, I pray you, brethren, do not so wickedly. Behold now, I have two daughters which have not known man; let me, I pray you, bring them out unto you, and do ye to them as *is* good in your eyes: only unto these men do nothing; for therefore came they under the shadow of my roof. And they said, Stand back. And they said *again,* This one *fellow* came in to sojourn, and he will needs be a judge: now will we deal worse with thee, than with them. And they pressed sore upon the man, *even* Lot, and came near to break the door. But the men put forth their hand, and pulled Lot into the house to them, and shut to the door" (Genesis 19:5-10).

This paints Lot as a selfish, immoral, weak man. However, the corrected version reads as follows:

> "*And they said unto him, Stand back. And they were angry with him. And they said among themselves, This one man came in to sojourn among us, and he will needs now make himself to be a judge; now we will deal worse with him than with them. Wherefore they said unto the man, We will have the men, and thy daughters also; and we will do with them as seemeth us good. Now this was after the wickedness of Sodom.* And Lot said, Behold now, I have two daughters which have not known man; let me, I pray you, *plead with my brethren that I may not* bring them out unto you; and ye shall *not* do unto them as seemeth good in your eyes; *For God will not justify his servant in this thing; wherefore, let me plead with my brethren, this once only, that* unto these men ye do nothing, *that they may have peace in my house*; for therefore came they under the shadow of my roof. *And they were angry with Lot* and came near to break the door, but the *angels of God, which were holy men*, put forth their hand and pulled Lot into the house unto them, and shut the door" (JST, Genesis 19:5-10).

Although Lot made the very poor decision to pitch his tent toward Sodom, he was not the weak, immoral man one would have to conclude from the erroneous translation of the Bible. The Joseph Smith Translation of this incident provides important corrections and understanding.

203. Blessed are the poor in spirit *who come unto me.*

"Blessed are the poor in spirit: for theirs is the kingdom of heaven" (Matthew 5:3). This promise is expanded as recorded of the Savior's visit to the Americas. "Yea, blessed are the poor in spirit *who come unto me*, for theirs is the kingdom of heaven" (3 Nephi 12:33, emphasis added).

Being poor in spirit isn't of itself a virtue. The word "poor" can refer to a state of poverty, but it also speaks of those who are poor in pride, and those who are humble in spirit. While the latter two definitions of poor are usually associated with virtuous behavior, unless those attitudes are born of conscious acknowledgement and willful submission to God, they can describe mere hopeless souls.

There is power and growth when we come unto the Savior. We can actually be transformed "and putteth off the natural man and becometh a saint through the atonement of Christ the Lord" (Mosiah 3:19).

The benefits of willful humility before God are beautifully stated by the Lord to the Prophet Moroni. "And if men come unto me I will show unto them their weakness. I give unto men weakness that they may be humble; and my grace is sufficient for all men that humble themselves before me; for if they humble themselves before me, and have faith in me, then will I make weak things become strong unto them" (Ether 12:27).

Many in the world live out their mortal existence in a state of oppression, fear, and/or low self-esteem. Their lot is hard and often miserable. To them, and to all, the Savior beckons a way of hope, self-confidence, patience, love, and many other traits and gifts that yield a joy that can transcend circumstances.

"Yea, come unto Christ, and be perfected in him, and deny yourselves of all ungodliness; and if ye shall deny yourselves of all ungodliness, and love God with all your might, mind and strength, then is his grace sufficient for you, that by his grace ye may be perfect in Christ; and if by the grace of God ye are perfect in Christ, ye can in nowise deny the power of God" (Moroni 10:32).

The more complete scriptural record found in the Book of Mormon shows hope and context to the Savior's declaration to the poor in spirit and deepens its dimension tremendously.

204. The Lord delights in sacred music.

Music is a powerful form of expression and communication that is of a universal language. Particularly in its religious use, the Lord has commended it in the personal revelation given to Emma Smith, the wife of Joseph Smith, "For my soul delighteth in the song of the heart; yea, the song of the righteous is a prayer unto me, and it shall be answered with a blessing upon their heads" (D&C 25:12).

In the book of Luke, we read that angels sang praises at the birth of Jesus (Luke 2:13-14) and in Matthew we read that Jesus and his twelve disciples sang a hymn after the Last Supper and prior to His experience in the Garden of Gethsemane (Matthew 26:30). There must have been tremendous spiritual strength derived from the hymn sung as prelude to the awful and unimaginable intensity of what then took place in Gethsemane.

Just five years after the Church was organized in 1830, the first collection of hymns was published, containing a total of ninety hymns. About thirty-five of these were written by Latter-day Saints; the remainder were Protestant hymns.

During the difficult journey of pioneers crossing the plains to the valley of the Great Salt Lake, music became a source of invigoration, hope, and a declaration and affirmation of their faith. Great latter day hymns were written during this time such as "Come, Come Ye Saints,"[1] a tribute to the courage, faith, and doctrine of the LDS pioneers.

It was soon after the arrival of Brigham Young in the Salt Lake Valley in 1847 that the beginnings of the famed Mormon Tabernacle Choir was formed. Since that time, the Choir has represented the Church and is known broadly for its musical excellence. To date, its weekly radio program of music and inspiration is the longest continuously running radio broadcast in history.

As a part of the Primary program of the Church for children, music is an important component in order to teach basic doctrines, instill a love of the Savior, teach values, and experience pure enjoyment. It is a location close to heaven to hear young voices express their faith through fervent song.

I personally love the hymns of the Church. They lift my spirit, confirm my faith, and become an expression of my own testimony. I thank God for sacred, uplifting music, and for the prominent place it occupies in the Church and in the homes of the Saints today.

Notes:

1. William Clayton, "Come Come, Ye Saints," *Hymns of The Church of Jesus Christ of Latter-day Saints*, Salt Lake City: The Church of Jesus Christ of Latter-day Saints, 1985, 30.

205. Family Home Evening is an inspired activity.

The setting aside of Monday nights for family time is evidence of Church doctrine in practice. "The family is ordained of God."[1]

It's ironic that with all the labor saving devices, the efficiencies built into our lives, and the increased prosperity of this generation that time is the hardest commodity to come by. Parents are rushing to work, to kids' activities, and to a myriad of daily requirements. The kids are off to school, extra-curricular activities, and with friends more and more as they grow up. Much of our family association occurs in passing.

Fortunate is the family who holds firm to the family dinner hour. Studies have shown this to be perhaps the single most important activity in building strong families and well adjusted, well informed children. Other than the family dinner time, or better, in addition to the family gathering each day for the evening meal, the observance of Monday nights for family time is of great worth to a family.

The Family Home Evening program was initiated many years ago with this statement:

> "We advise and urge the inauguration of a 'Home Evening' throughout the church, at which time fathers and mothers may gather their boys and girls about them in the home and teach them the word of the Lord. . . . 'Home Evening' should be devoted to prayer, singing hymns, songs, instrumental music, scripture-reading, family topics and specific instruction on the principles of the gospel, and on the ethical problems of life, as well as the duties and obligations of children to parents, the home, the Church, society and the nation. For the smaller children appropriate recitations, songs, stories and games may be introduced. Light refreshments of such a nature as may be largely prepared in the home might be served. . . . If the Saints obey this counsel, we promise that great blessings will result. Love at home and obedience to parents will increase. Faith will be developed in the hearts of the youth of Israel, and they will gain power to combat the evil influence and temptations which beset them."[2]

A more current endorsement states, "Monday nights are reserved throughout the Church for family home evenings. We encourage members to set aside this time to strengthen family ties and teach the gospel in their homes. . . . Church buildings and facilities should be closed on Monday evenings. No ward or stake activities should be planned, and other interruptions to family home evenings should be avoided."[3]

There are many inspired activities in the Church, all designed to strengthen families and to build faith in Jesus Christ. The Family Home Evening program clearly focuses on both of these objectives most effectively.

Notes:

1. First Presidency and The Council of the Twelve, "The Family: A Proclamation to the World," *Ensign,* November, 1995.

2. James R. Clark, comp., *Messages of the First Presidency of the Church of Jesus Christ of Latter-day Saints,* Salt Lake City: Bookcraft, 1965-1975, 4:337-339; Letter dated April 27, 1915, Joseph F. Smith, Anthon H. Lund, Charles W. Penrose.

3. *Letter from the First Presidency,* dated October 4, 1999, Gordon B. Hinckley, Thomas S. Monson, and James E. Faust; *Ensign,* June, 2000.

206. Knowledge and use of the Urim and Thummim are restored.

Reference is made in several places in the scriptures of the use of a Urim and Thummim in Old Testament times:

- Abraham received intelligence from the Lord through the Urim and Thummim (Abraham 3:1-4)
- Aaron used it as a part of his priestly garments, worn over his heart in a "breastplate of judgment" (Exodus 28:30)
- Moses set Joshua before Eleazar the priest "who shall ask counsel for him after the judgment of Urim [and Thummim] before the Lord" (Numbers 27:21)
- Just prior to his passing, Moses blessed the children of Israel by tribe. To the tribe of Levi, and by the Urim and Thummim, "They shall teach Jacob thy judgments, and Israel thy law" (Deuteronomy 33:8, 10)
- Saul, when faced with the host of Philistines arrayed in battle against Israel, received not immediate answer to his prayers, "neither by dreams, nor by Urim [and Thummim], nor by prophets" (1 Samuel 28:6)
- And when the Jews were allowed by King Cyrus of Persia to go back to Jerusalem, those Jews whose genealogy was lost were put from the priesthood, "till there stood

up a priest with Urim and Thummim" (Ezra 2:61-63, Nehemiah 7:63-65)

Use of a Urim and Thummim in these Old Testament contexts, convey its usefulness to give judgment, insight, counsel, direction, knowledge, and restoration of that which was lost. In summary, it assists in the obtaining of revelation.

In the Book of Mormon, it is particularly used as an instrument of language translation, as interpreters of sacred writings. Ammon assured King Limhi that indeed King Mosiah could translate the records they discovered "for he has wherewith that he can look, and translate all records that are of ancient date . . . and the things are called interpreters" (Mosiah 8:13). In the book of Ether, the brother of Jared was given "two stones" (Ether 3:22-24) for the purpose of future translation of their writings. This particular Urim and Thummim used by the Jaredites was included in what Moroni buried in the Hill Cumorah along with the gold plates at the end of his ministry (D&C 17:1).

It is by this and other means that Joseph was enabled to translate the plates. Oliver Cowdery described the events: "Day after day I continued, uninterrupted, to write from his mouth, as he translated with the Urim and Thummim, or, as the Nephites would have said, 'Interpreters,' the history or record called 'The Book of Mormon.'"[1]

This tool of revelation and translation (of which there is not only one) could be seen as an obscure reference in scripture but, in fact, is an important revelatory tool of both the ancient and modern work of the Lord. I believe Joseph Smith's explanation of his use of a Urim and Thummim in translating the Book of Mormon would have been beyond his own knowledge of Biblical practices.

Notes:

1. Appended to the Joseph Smith – History, *The Pearl of Great Price,* 1981, 58.

207. Blessed is the man who resists temptation.

The Joseph Smith Translation uses the word "resisteth" in place of the King James Version use of "endureth" in James 1:12. This teaches a powerful lesson and is wise counsel.

When Jesus was tempted of the devil in the desert, He did not endure the temptation but resisted and then rebuffed the very source. It is noteworthy that He recognized the source of these debilitating temptations as the devil himself. He did not see them as idle or random thoughts, and thereby suffer the inclination to rationalize and argue their merits. Certainly, after such a prolonged fast, He could have rationalized the need for bread. The issue wasn't hunger. It was winning the very core matter of whether He (Christ) would abdicate to the devil's persuasion, or if He would recognize His personal identity and retain control of His actions. In each of the three temptations—testing His resolve in the arenas of physical appetite, personal identity, and worldly power—Jesus responded in the language of the scriptures, and cast out the devil in the name of God. By such resolve and such an approach, "the devil leaveth him, and, behold, angels came and ministered unto him" (Matthew 4:1-11).

It is always the best course to resist temptation, and as Jesus demonstrated above, to confront it for what it is. Not all temptations go away speedily, though. Indeed, there are times when we are subject to long periods of incessant temptation. The worldly course is often to give in to such persistent temptation, thereby alleviating the weight of continued resistance. Immodest dress, immoral entertainment, Sabbath day un-observance, profane language, selfish lifestyles, unearned receipt of goods and services, and on and on, all have a lure of their own upon the human condition. We don't seek to endure them but rather to resist them, to disassociate from them.

"Though he were a Son, yet learned he obedience by the things which he suffered" (Hebrews 5:8). Yes, we will be tried, temptations will be our lot in life, and so it was even with the Son of God. But we can resist and rebuff those temptations and minimize our encounters with them in large measure. This is, indeed, wise and insightful counsel from the inspired Joseph Smith Translation.

208. Jesus never compromised to win popularity or acclaim.

It would be difficult to argue that Jesus lived to gain the approval or popularity of the masses. Knowing that He was indeed the promised Messiah and seeking only to do the will of His Father, His doctrine was true, eternal, and divine. It would cut its own way. It was not tailored to win over the prominent of the day, or the wealthy who could support His work, or to appease and ingratiate Himself to the religious class. He did not come as a warrior or a powerful military deliverer as the Jews had envisioned. His teachings were just the opposite: "Love your enemies, do good to them which hate you, Bless them that curse you, and pray for them which despitefully use you" (Luke 6:27-28).

"Because strait is the gate, and narrow is the way, which leadeth unto life, and few there be that find it" (Matthew 7:14). The Lord has commanded us to do things His way. Some of His ways are baptism by immersion by one holding Priesthood authority; observance of the Sabbath Day; leaving father and mother (if necessary); turning not back even to bury our dead, giving our time, talents and means to His work and kingdom; keeping family and marital covenants; taking the gospel to all the world; healing the sick; honoring the temple; and more.

The Lord's Church will never cater to the popular, the trendy, or the convenient. It is not first a "big tent" and second, founded upon eternal principles. It has never been, nor ever will be, a general collection of ideas to attract the masses. Rather, it will stand firmly on eternal principles and values common to the human experience in all places and at all times. Fundamentally, it will be founded upon "the Rock of our Redeemer who is Christ, the Son of God" (Helaman 5:12).

209. Brigham Young was a modern day Moses in leading the Saints westward.

There are significant parallels between the children of Israel being led out of slavery in Egypt to the Promised Land and the modern Latter-day Saints being led out of their persecutions to the Salt Lake Valley. Both were inspired of God, both included tremendous hardship, and both prepared a people to dwell with a firm faith in God.

The leadership of Moses and Brigham Young is not common among men. These were men raised up of faith and good judgment who inspired their people. Neither knew the exact destination to where they were heading, but each knew that God would be their guide.

Why did the children of Israel wander in the desert for forty years prior to entering the Promised Land? Perhaps, some of the reasons were to learn the very commandments of God, to exercise faith in him, to administer the ordinances of the gospel, and to be obedient. They needed to learn firm obedience and always to trust in God and in His servants. They learned this by witnessing the parting of the Red Sea, receiving the Ten Commandments, observing the rites of the portable tabernacle, the daily receipt of manna from heaven, water from dry rocks, and other heavenly manifestations. They needed this show of miracles to be convinced once again of the power of God, having been in slavery for so many generations. Understanding and obedience came slowly, perhaps giving reason for prolonging the wandering for forty years.

In the case of the modern-day children of Israel, some have wondered why the Lord would not have tempered the elements, or otherwise have made easier the plight of His Pioneer Saints. The following account is testimony of the eternal purposes that were realized from such trying conditions:

> "Some years after the Martin company made their journey to Salt Lake City, a teacher in a Church class commented how foolish it was for the Martin company to come across the plains when it did. The teacher criticized the Church leaders for allowing a company to make such a journey without more supplies and protection.
>
> An old man sitting in the classroom listened for a few moments and then spoke out, asking that the criticism be stopped. He said, "Mistake to send the Handcart Company out so late in the season? Yes. But I was in that company and my wife was in it. . . . We suffered beyond anything you can imagine and many died of exposure and starvation, but did you ever hear a survivor of that company utter a word of criticism? *Not one of that company ever apostatized or left the Church, because everyone of us came through with the absolute knowledge that God lives for we became acquainted with him in our extremities.*
>
> "Was I sorry that I chose to come by handcart? No. Neither then nor any minute of my life since. *The price we paid to become acquainted with God was a privilege to pay, and I am thankful that I was privileged to come in the Martin Handcart Company*"[1]

The Lord will have a faithful people. "My people must be tried in all things, that they may be prepared to receive the glory that I have for them, even the glory of Zion; and he that will not bear chastisement is not worthy of my kingdom" (D&C 136:31). The parallel experiences of the ancient Exodus and the modern trek westward did produce the faith necessary to establish Israel both then and now. Both experiences, in the wisdom of God and led by a prophet, embedded faith into the very culture of Hebrew and LDS life through to the present day.

Notes:

1. William Palmer, quoted in David O. McKay, "Pioneer Women," *Relief Society Magazine,"* January, 1948, 8 (emphasis in original).

210. The peace found in nature is truly a forerunner of heaven.

I will be forever grateful that my parents instilled within me a love of the great outdoors. Growing up in San Diego near the beach, we used to go tide-pooling as a family after dinner, watching the sunset, strolling along, and seeing what sea life we could find in the rock formations exposed by the lowing tide.

The shoreline always seemed to be the edge of the earth to me. Man's encroachment had an end. Mountains seem to have that same dividing line between the disorder of human activity and the absolute order of nature. To me, nature has always been a refreshing, even spiritually conducive environment.

I have felt that the peace found in natural settings is the result of all things living in harmony with their intended purpose. Unlike man—vegetation, animal life, and the inanimate—all are doing what they should be doing, for lack of a better way of saying it.

Then, I read what the Lord said to the Prophet Joseph Smith in 1832, "And again, verily I say unto you, the earth abideth the law of a celestial kingdom, for it filleth the measure of its creation, and transgresseth not the law" (D&C 88:25).

So my intuition was right! Abiding according to celestial law would mean exact obedience, harmony, unity. Absent would be discord, doubt, and deceit. Yes, we witness what we consider gory truths in seeing one animal take down another, but it is within the order of nature, and fills the measure of its creation, certainly not transgressing the law.

The ability to feel the Holy Spirit in the quiet and secluded beauty of the outdoors is a rich experience. My very first prayers were in such places. Jesus went into the wilderness to be with God following his baptism. It was on a mountain top which we now refer to as the Mount of Transfiguration where sacred and significant events occurred with his disciples. On another of doubtless many occasions, "He went up into a mountain apart to pray: and when the evening was come, he was there alone" (Matthew 14:23).

Moses went to Mount Sinai to receive the Ten Commandments. Enos gained a testimony while in the forests. Alma preached at the waters of Mormon. Joseph Smith's first prayer was in a grove of trees, a place we now call Sacred.

The greatest state of peace we, as offspring of God, can attain to is to live in harmony with God's way of living, a celestial existence. This is the ultimate measure of our own creation. It is who we really are.

Until that ultimate attainment, and for all those who will experience it, a bit of heaven is right here among us for our enjoyment and refreshment.

211. We become most like the Master when we can teach and serve as He did.

It is unique to this Church that the general membership conduct, teach, preach, and serve in the various required positions within the several organizations at the local level in contrast to having a paid, professional leadership structure. We are all familiar with the aphorisms that "the teacher learns more than the student," and "if you want to really understand something, teach it to someone else."

Joseph Smith did not establish the Church with absolute authority taken to himself or as a charismatic and singular preacher. In fact, the priesthood authority was distributed broadly, and preaching was done by no one in particular. Missionaries were sent around the world with authority, and branches of the Church were established in many cities and several countries. Even the important task of choosing of the original Twelve Apostles in these latter-days was delegated to others.

For most of us, it's just not in our makeup to step up and do what we are not naturally fitted for. Recognizing the gap between who we are and who we want to become helps us to appreciate the need to serve as He did and to seek to emulate the very nature and demeanor of the Master. This does not come from a life of self-serving or self-indulgence. "For whosoever will save his life shall lose it; but whosoever shall lose his life for my sake and the gospel's, the same shall save it" (Mark 8:35).

There is personal, spiritual growth in standing before others to give a talk on faith or to teach a class on a chapter from Luke. It requires prayer, communication to seek the will of the Lord and his inspiration, digging in the scriptures, pondering, organizing, even conducting ourselves on a higher standard, and realizing the need to receive divine assistance. Such growth and opportunity cannot come from passive observance, but rather from active participation, even when, and most particularly when, it requires us to stretch beyond our seeming natural abilities.

To become like Jesus, we are certainly required to leave our comfort zone. As an active member of the Church, those opportunities for growth will ever be available. It was a merciful design that enabled the broad concept of member involvement and responsibility in the work of the Lord.

212. Lehi's vision of the Tree of Life is relevant to current conditions in the world.

I love the vision that Father Lehi had, recorded in 1 Nephi chapters 8, 11, 12, and 15. It is full of vivid parallels to contemporary life and gives valuable insight to our mortal sojourn. I believe it to be yet another of the many compelling narratives contained in the Book of Mormon that attest to its divinity. (Italics in the following narrative are my emphasis of important elements of the vision.)

Lehi, as the patriarch of his family, is led through a *dark and dreary waste*, which he comes through only by the *tender mercies* of the Lord, into a *large and spacious field.* There he came to a tree laden with fruit. Lehi partook of the fruit and found it to be absolutely delicious, *most sweet above all,* and in fact had such a quality as to *make one happy.* It was a metaphor for the love of God, as manifested in his Son, Jesus Christ. As he was enjoying the fruit, and feeling such *exceeding joy*, he looked around for his family, desirous that they too, might come to the tree and enjoy the fruit.

Leading to the tree was a straight *rod of iron* (the scriptures and words of the prophets), which served as a guide to navigate through *an exceedingly great mist of darkness*. Apparently, the fruit of the tree was known to be really good, and many wanted to have access to it, but those who let go of the iron rod, got lost in the mist of darkness and never made it to the tree. Only those who were wise enough to recognize that the rod of iron was their best hope and held on to it made it to the tree. And they enjoyed the fruit.

But then a very peculiar thing happened. *After they had partaken of the fruit*, still in enjoyment from the joy it brought, they *"cast [their] eyes round about, and beheld, on the other side of the river of water, a great and spacious building . . . and it was filled with people . . . in the attitude of mocking and pointing their fingers towards those who had come at and were partaking of the fruit"* (1 Nephi 8:26-27, emphasis added). Such ridicule caused the people to be ashamed, and they left the tree and its fruit, *and they fell away into forbidden paths and were lost!*

Why would someone leave something that brings them such joy because someone else makes fun of them? Yet this happens, particularly among our youth. That big building and its occupants represent the *vain imaginations and the pride of the world. And great was the multitude that did enter into that strange building.*

Being able to stand tall when it isn't popular to do so, to follow wise counsel to obtain joy, and to not let anyone rob us of our true happiness by their unbelief or ignorance, are lessons we can apply each and every day. Lehi's vision is a great blessing to see clearly what we face in this world as disciples of Jesus Christ.

213. Joseph Smith acted like a man of Godly vision.

We see the formation of many churches, and generally they are singular enterprises that seek to grow within the local reach. Sometimes, they will multiply within a region. There are few who extend their franchise across a continent and fewer who can claim international membership.

When Joseph Smith founded the Church on April 6, 1830, it was formally organized with six charter members. Four years later, with all the priesthood of the Kirtland area gathered in one small log cabin, Joseph gave a prophetic vision of the destiny of this work, "It is only a little handful of Priesthood you see here tonight, but this Church will fill North and South America—it will fill the world."[1]

Bold! Yet Joseph proceeded to administer the fledgling Church in absolute confidence of the above declaration. He sent missionaries to Canada, to Great Britain and other countries in Europe, to the South Pacific Islands, to Chile, and all across the then known United States. He commissioned Elder Orson Hyde to go to Palestine and there dedicate that land for the return of the Jewish people. When the Book of Mormon was printed, it was an ambitious print job of five thousand copies, with no pre-sold commitments!

And the results? Estimates are that some thirty thousand converts emigrated from Europe to join the saints in America prior to 1860. The Jews did return to Palestine and declared the state of Israel in 1948. Cumulatively, over 130 million copies of the Book of Mormon have now been published. In South and Central America including Mexico, there are over five million members of the Church.[2] Canada, the United States and the islands of the Caribbean account for another approximately seven million.

Said the Prophet Joseph Smith, "The Standard of Truth has been erected; no unhallowed hand can stop the work from progressing; persecutions may rage, mobs may combine, armies may assemble, calumny may defame, but the truth of God will go forth boldly, nobly, and independent, till it has penetrated every continent, visited every clime, swept every country, and sounded in every ear, till the purposes of God shall be accomplished, and the Great Jehovah shall say the work is done."[3] Those sound like the confident words of a prophet of God to me.

Today, we see the literal fulfillment of these prophecies and can see the vindication of Joseph Smith's confident, even certain, vision of the Church and Kingdom he was given to found. It is the Lord's work, and it is for all of God's children, and it is, in fact, the Church of Jesus Christ.

Notes:

1. Wilford Woodruff, *Conference Report,* 1898, 57.
2. 2010 Church Almanac, 2009 Membership Statistics, Salt Lake City: Deseret News, 2010, 181-187.
3. *History of the Church of Jesus Christ of Latter-day Saints,* Salt Lake City: Deseret Book, 1960, 4:540.

214. We are the "peculiar people" of these latter days.

It is interesting that we humans have dual yet conflicting desires, to stand out as unique, and yet at the same time, to fit in, to be a part of the crowd. As a Church, it is readily acknowledged that we satisfy the former, yet we also long for acceptance by our mainstream Christian brothers and sisters. Ecumenical efforts that require the compromise or departure from doctrines will never be acceptable to us as Latter-day Saints because the doctrines are not of our own making. The commandments of the Lord are, in fact, commandments of the Lord.

When the word "peculiar" (emphasis added below) is used in scripture to describe the Lord's people, it refers favorably to a group that one would want to be a part of:

"Now therefore, if ye will obey my voice indeed, and keep my covenant, then ye shall be a *peculiar* treasure unto me above all people" (Exodus 19:5).

"For thou art an holy people unto the Lord thy God, and the Lord hath chosen thee to be a *peculiar* people unto himself, above all the nations that are upon the earth" (Deuteronomy 14:2).

"And the Lord hath avouched thee this day to be his *peculiar* people, as he hath promised thee, and that thou shouldest keep all his commandments" (Deuteronomy 26:18).

"For the Lord hath chosen Jacob unto himself, and Israel for his *peculiar* treasure" (Psalms 135:4).

"Who gave himself for us, that he might redeem us from all iniquity, and purify unto himself a *peculiar* people, zealous of good works" (Titus 2:14).

"But ye are a chosen generation, a royal priesthood, an holy nation, a *peculiar* people; that ye should shew forth the praises of him who hath called you out of darkness into his marvelous light" (1 Peter 2:9).

The house of Israel, and specifically the Levites in ancient Israel, were the authorized stewards over the Lord's kingdom on the earth, performing ordinances and rites of worship as prescribed by the Lord.

Today, it is the priesthood responsibility of the Latter-day Saints to conduct the affairs of the kingdom and to administer the ordinances of the gospel. As a lifestyle, this includes attending a three-hour block of Sunday worship, paying an honest tithe, giving hours of service during the week, sending sons or daughters on missions for two years, participating in temple work, sharing the gospel with others—all of which, and by many other measures—are seen by others as somewhat peculiar.

Reviewing the above scriptures indicates that the Lord's peculiar people will be obedient to him, keep his commandments, enter into covenants with him, and be zealous of doing good works. In turn, those people will be his treasure, holy, chosen, purified, and will bear his priesthood and enjoy marvelous light. That's the team I want to be on.

215. Just as latter-day revelation is rejected today, so it was with Jesus.

"And as Jesus passed by, he saw a man which was blind from his birth" (John 9:1). It was the Sabbath day. Certainly born of compassion, Jesus anointed the man's eyes with clay, and instructed him to go and wash in the pool of Siloam. He returned "and came seeing" (John 9:7). Word spread among neighbors and family, such that he was brought to tell his story to the Pharisees. Their quick assessment of the situation concluded that the healing of the blind man couldn't be of God because it had been done on the Sabbath. Clearly their interest was not in the miracle itself, nor in the means nor power by which it was effected, but rather to discredit the worker of the miracle.

The man who had newly received his sight had a more practical assessment of the experience, "Whether he be a sinner or no, I know not: one thing I know, that, whereas I was blind, now I see" (John 9:25). He went on to declare his discipleship to this man Jesus and invited the Pharisees to do likewise. Their response was a self-righteous, self-justifying, "Thou art his disciple; but we are Moses' disciples" (John 9:25, 27-28). And then they cast him out from their religious circle.

Jesus declared that in Him was the Law of Moses fulfilled and that a higher law of love was now the rule (Galatians 3:24-25, Luke 5:36-39, Matthew 22:36-40). His was a new revelation, a prophesied evolution for the House of Israel. Wrote Elder James E. Talmage, "The recreant Jews rejected the Savior because He came to them with a new revelation. Had they not Moses and the prophets to guide them, and what more could they need? . . . So called Christian sects of the day are practically a unit in declaring that direct revelation ceased with the apostles . . . that further communication from the heavens is unnecessary; and that to expect such is unscriptural."[1]

Frequently to justify such a position, the concluding words to the book of Revelation are cited as though they were the last words God ever uttered to man (Revelation 22:18-19). True as the scripture says, that no *man* shall add to, or take from, but certainly God could do as he deems prudent. As the historical pattern has been, when speaking generally to his children, He will call a prophet. In fact, "Surely the Lord God will do nothing, but he revealeth his secret unto his servants the prophets" (Amos 3:7).

Jesus, the hoped-for Messiah, was rejected by His own because of the rigid, self-serving, and impersonal form of worship that was more of a cultural phenomenon than a religious one. Today, living prophets, apostles, and scriptural increase are also rejected by some, when, in fact, it is being delivered to the world by the Master himself.

Notes:

1. James E. Talmage, *Articles of Faith,* Salt Lake City: The Church of Jesus Christ of Latter-day Saints, 1977, 308.

216. Worldwide conferences and training sessions are opportunities to hear the Lord.

Other than governments disseminating information to the populace, or perhaps commercial marketing campaigns, I don't know of any organization that communicates more effectively with its worldwide membership than does The Church of Jesus Christ of Latter-day Saints. The general conferences of the Church are opportunities for the leadership to convey the will of the Lord generally to the Church and for members to assemble in faith and testimony to be instructed. "Wherefore, he that preacheth and he that receiveth, understand one another, and both are edified and rejoice together" (D&C 50:22).

"One Lord, one faith, one baptism," wrote the apostle Paul (Ephesians 4:5). "There shall be one fold, and one shepherd" (John 10:16). Jesus speaking of the people while addressing the Father, "that they may be one, as we are" (John 17:11).

"And the multitude of them that believed were of one heart and of one soul" (Acts 4:32).

"And hath made of one blood all nations" (Acts 17:26).

"So we, being many, are one body in Christ, and every one members one of another." (Romans 12:5).

"For both he that sanctifieth and they who are sanctified are all of one" (Hebrews 2:11).

"They were of one heart and one mind" (Moses 7:18).

"With one mind striving together for the faith of the gospel" (Philippians 1:27).

"Till we all come in the unity of the faith, and of the knowledge of the Son of God, unto a perfect man, unto the measure of the stature of the fullness of Christ" (Ephesians 4:13).

The above scriptures describe the purposes and the spirit of these general conferences. In addition to counsel given to all the world, each member of the Church is given the opportunity to sustain the leadership of the Church. Announcements are made including the locations for new temple projects, ratifying revelations as new scriptural canon, and formal proclamations to the world. Church statistics are read. An independent audit report is stated concerning the integrity of the financial policies and procedures of the Church.

The Lord is one voice, and to send that generally to all the worldwide membership of his Church is marvelous to behold. The Church delivers the broadcast to eighty-three countries transmitting to over 5,700 Church facilities and airing over 18 television and 1700 cable stations. Volunteer language professionals translate the sermons into over eighty languages live during the simulcast, meaning that ninety-eight percent of Church members can listen to general conference in their native language.

Unprecedented and unparalleled, these semi-annual conferences and other training sessions, cement the faith and works of the LDS people worldwide. "Whether by mine own voice or by the voice of my servants, it is the same" (D&C 1:38).

217. Abstinence before marriage is a standard by which our youth live.

The standard of not having sex before marriage, I believe, is well understood by most everyone. The standard seems to be built into our conscience. Yet because of advertising, media, conversation, relaxed norms, and even pressures to violate this standard, many youth go against their better selves in favor of the perceived normal behavior for adolescents. Once violated, frequency can and does diminish the warning signs of a good conscience.

I have been able to work closely with hundreds of youth in the Church for many years now and am happy to report that, by far and away, the majority of our youth do keep themselves clean and choose abstinence until marriage. In an age when public agencies are handing out condoms and teaching young people that they might as well give in to the inevitable, our youth stand in stark contrast to what has become the norm in high school behavior.

Our youth are taught from an early age, "The sacred powers of procreation are to be employed only between man and woman, lawfully wedded as husband and wife."[1] They are taught to understand and to expect the hormonal changes they will experience as they mature and to keep those under control by avoiding that which would arouse those powerful emotions. Dating is discouraged until age sixteen and thereafter encouraged to be in groups or double dates. They are taught to "Stay in areas of safety where you can easily control your physical feelings."[2]

What most causes our youth to keep this high standard of morality are the covenants they have made and the Spirit of the Lord that they carry as the Gift of the Holy Ghost. They are committed to their faith. They are committed to the Lord. They have positive peer association within the Church and with other youth of like mind and commitment. They renew their covenants each week as they partake of the sacrament. It is meaningful to them.

"Let no man despise thy youth; but be thou an example of the believers, in word, in conversation, in charity, in spirit, in faith, in *purity* (1 Timothy 4:12, emphasis added).

Our youth are exemplary in a world that desperately needs good examples. It is a collective example that abstinence is indeed a workable policy and the best policy—best for those who live by it and best for society at large.

Notes:

1. First Presidency and The Council of the Twelve, "The Family: A Proclamation to the World," *Ensign*, November, 1995.

2. "Sexual Purity," *For the Strength of Youth: Fulfilling Our Duty to God*, Salt Lake City: The Church of Jesus Christ of Latter-day Saints, 2001.

218. Conversion to the Gospel of Jesus Christ is done one heart and one mind at a time.

Baptism is the ordinance that is an outward demonstration of our conversion to the Gospel of Jesus Christ. It is not a group or family ordinance, but it is an individual ordinance.

True conversion is not a momentary, off-the-cuff decision or experience. It is not often done en masse. Nor is it attained without understanding, personal prayer, study of the scriptures, or a witness of the Spirit.

I think it is significant that each person who comes into the Church through the gate of baptism as a convert, sits down with the full-time missionaries and evaluates his or her own readiness for this ordinance. That is true for each individual person throughout all the world! That interview will gauge testimony of Jesus as the Christ, the Holy Messiah and their personal Savior. It will inquire into the depth of one's prayers. It will invite a declaration of receiving the witness of the Spirit as to the truthfulness of the restoration, the Book of Mormon, and that Joseph Smith is indeed a prophet of God. The interview will determine one's personal worthiness to be baptized, evidenced by keeping the commandments and recent alignment of his or her life with the Gospel of Jesus Christ.

With few exceptions, those who are converts to the Church have been taught by the full-time missionaries a series of lessons and discussions that teach the basic doctrines they now embrace. I was out with the missionaries this week, and we taught a single lady by the name of Tara. We spent a little over an hour with her (a bit long), and introduced her to the restored gospel, teaching of Jesus, God the Father, the organization of the Church that Jesus established, the apostasy, and the glorious First Vision to the young boy Joseph Smith. The missionaries adeptly tailored the discussion to her concerns and needs, always sensitive to her understanding of the concepts and principles they were teaching. They were patient and genuine in their concern for her personally. They then set an appointment to return and to resume the lessons. Assuming she progresses to baptism, she will have another five or so of these lessons. And each lesson will be to and for her personally.

"Remember the worth of souls is great in the sight of God (D&C 18:10). The missionary work of the Church is not first about quantity, but about individuals and about conversion of the heart. I believe that is how Jesus influenced his converts.

219. The order of conversion occurs first things first.

"We believe that the first principles and ordinances of the Gospel are: *first, Faith* in the Lord Jesus Christ; *second, Repentance*; *third, Baptism* by immersion for the remission of sins; *fourth, Laying on of hands* for the gift of the Holy Ghost" (Articles of Faith, 4, emphasis added).

Without consciously setting out to follow such a mapped course, my own conversion included each of these principles and ordinances and in the order prescribed. That period of my life was an exhilarating, growing, discovering, joyous adventure that I will always look back on with fondness.

The adventure lies in attaining and exercising faith in the Lord Jesus Christ and changing the course of one's life to be in conformity with the commandments of God. These are the principles. The ordinances are the crowning manifestation of these attainments and include a supernal gift from God, the Gift of the Holy Ghost.

Faith in Christ unto salvation is deeper than a sudden impulse or emotion. Such stirrings though can be the beginning of a faith yet to be germinated (Alma 32:27-28). Jesus taught that "he that heareth the word, and understandeth it; which also beareth fruit, and bringeth forth" (Matthew 13:23) are the truly converted. In the same parable, he warned about the faith that is not yet matured to stand in "tribulation or persecution," (Matthew 13:21) or to ignore the lure of "the care of this world" (Matthew 13:22) evidencing that they "understandeth it not" (Matthew 13:19). True faith is a principle of action. We act with confidence in the wisdom of God exercised on our behalf, and knowing that such a course is acceptable of God.

Such faith in the divinity of the Savior leads us on to follow His perfect example in purity, kindness, love, faith, obedience, temperance, patience, humility, diligence, and other of his modeled qualities. Therein springs the desire to change from our natural man ways (Mosiah 3:19) and "seek for the things of a better" (D&C 25:10). The acquisition of Christ-like qualities and a commitment to them for a lifetime and beyond, is the manifestation of true repentance. It is not to be perfect but to be perfectly resolved to strive to keep his commandments.

Then is one ready to enter into the waters of baptism, as a demonstration of the "new creature" (2 Corinthians 5:17) and for the remission of sins. Subsequent to our obedient compliance with this ordinance, we are confirmed a member of his Church, and enjoined to "receive the Holy Ghost" (D&C 84:64).[1]

Such a sequence of conversion will most likely parallel the words of the Master – "But other fell into good ground, and brought forth fruit, some an hundredfold, some sixtyfold, some thirtyfold" (Matthew 13:8). I have experienced this course and have seen others do likewise. It is a divinely inspired course.

Notes:

1. *Handbook 2 Administering the Church*, Salt Lake City: The Church of Jesus Christ of Latter-day Saints, 2010, 20.3.9. See also D&C 20:41.

220. The local financial procedures of the Church are administered by lay members.

Fraud for personal gain is a constant to guard against wherever there is money to be transacted. The care and even reverence with which the funds of the Church are handled is an anomaly among large corporations. Sure, there is fraud even within the Church, but I can say that in my nearly forty years working at many local levels within the Church, I've never seen it happen, not even on a small scale or by singular occurrence.

It's interesting how the Church operates financially. Essentially, each ward and branch is a separate storefront of the Church, collecting and disbursing funds from and for the membership it serves. Currently, there are about thirty thousand wards and branches throughout the world, each a stand-alone entity for financial purposes. By contrast, there are approximately 8,500 Wal-Mart and Sam's Club stores worldwide, although the difference by inventory, employees and complexity is understood. Within the United States (and maybe worldwide, I don't know), each ward or branch makes deposits to a local bank, and those funds are swept to the general Church bank account at least each week. All checks written at the local level are drawn on the general Church bank account.

Each stake and district is then allotted a budget amount based on quarterly attendance figures, which, in turn, is allocated to the wards and branches. This is what each unit operates within. These budget amounts are from the general tithing donations of the faithful saints.

Each unit has a financial clerk. When donations are received via sealed envelope, they are opened and prepared for deposit by the financial clerk and a member of the ward or branch leadership. Together, they make the deposit at a local bank each Sunday. Financial clerks also write checks, with supporting documentation, as authorized by the Bishop or Branch President.

Stakes have an audit committee to audit the units at least annually, checking for compliance with approved procedures. The auditors follow a written audit program.

All of this is done by non-financial, common members of the Church. The opportunity for collusion and fraud is certainly available. Yet, because of the individual testimonies of the members that the funds they are administering are sacred tithing funds and other freewill offerings, the system works. At the local level, there is never any concern for the profitability of the ward or branch, rather the concern is to manage within the allotted budgets.

The integrity to which this financial system operates is a testament to the faithfulness and testimony of the common members of the Church and that financial motives are not a factor whatsoever in the local administration of the Church.

221. The Book of Mormon includes three separate migrations from the Old World.

Let's see if I can get this straight . . .

The Jaredites are an ancient people who "came out from the tower, at the time the Lord confounded the language of the people" (Omni 1:22, see also Ether 1:33 and Genesis 11:1-9), which refers to the tower of Babel about 2500 BC. They became a "great nation" (Ether

1:43) on the American continent, "And there shall be none greater than the nation which I will raise up unto me of thy seed, upon all the face of the earth" (Ether 1:43).

The families of Lehi and Ishmael, along with Zoram, came to the Americas about six hundred years before Christ. It was during the early reign of Zedekiah, the last king of Judah prior to the Babylonian captivity (1 Nephi 1:4). Lehi and Ishmael were descendants of the tribe of Joseph (Alma 10:3). These families settled in "the land south" (Helaman 6:10).

The Mulekites came to the Americas about twelve years after the Lehites, establishing Zarahemla in "the land north" (Helaman 6:10). Mulek, the groups namesake, was a surviving son of King Zedekiah (Helaman 6:10), from the tribe of Judah.

What is noteworthy to me is the consistent integrity of the interplay of these three groups of people throughout the Book of Mormon. Both the Jaredites and the Mulekites are referenced by Amaleki, a direct descendant of Lehi, (Omni 1:20-22). Under the direction of the Lord, Mosiah led a group of the Lehites to "depart out of the land with him, into the wilderness" (Omni 1:12) whereupon they discovered the people of Zarahemla, the Mulekites. Amaleki was born in the days of Mosiah and was the keeper of the plates of Nephi (Omni 1:12-14, 23).

It was Ether who wrote the record of the Jaredite people, and it was Moroni who abridged that record as the book of Ether that we have today. Moroni includes commentary that Ether hid the record "in a manner that the people of Limhi did find them" (Ether 15:33). King Limhi was a Mulekite who served as the King of the Nephites (Mosiah 7:9). It was an expedition of men under King Limhi who discovered the remains of the self-destroyed nation of the Jaredites.

Hard to follow? I wrote it as clearly as I could. In addition, in the final scenes of the Jaredite history, Ether warns King Coriantumr that if he would not repent, "every soul should be destroyed save it were Coriantumr" (Ether 13:21) and that Coriantumr should receive a burial at the hands of "another people receiving the land for their inheritance" (Ether 13:21). In fact, Amaleki records that the people of Zarahemla discovered Coriantumr, and he dwelt with them and died in Zarahemla. (Omni 1:21).

This is an abbreviated view of the intertwining of some of the peoples in the Americas. It is consistent with Biblical moments, and it is consistent through various authors and time frames in the Book of Mormon. In my estimation, it is far too complex of a story line for Joseph Smith to devise in three months. It is another evidence to me of the divinity of the Book of Mormon.

222. The Bishop's Storehouse is a grocery store without cash registers.

Some years ago, other urban cowboys and I headed down to the Welfare farm in Southeast Dallas on a given Saturday to do the chores required of a cattle ranching operation. We hauled hay bales to the barn, fixed fences, ground feed, put out salt blocks, cleaned quonset huts, repaired cattle gates, and completed many other tasks. It was hard work, yet great fellowship. I carry a scar on my right wrist from a gash I received while working there and look upon it with quite fond remembrances.

The cattle from the Dallas operation went into a larger system of commodities across the country, and even internationally to some degree. Beef from Dallas, tuna from San Diego, peaches from Georgia, peanut butter from Houston, and apples from Washington are examples of Church-owned welfare operations. There are about sixty-four welfare farms owned and operated by the Church.

These commodities are shipped to one of approximately 123 processing centers and canneries owned by the Church in the United States,

Canada, and Mexico, They are then shipped as packaged product to the approximately 125 Bishop's Storehouses, which are essentially grocery stores of goods without price. From these storehouses, a local Bishop can see that the needy among his flock are provided with the essential food and household items they may need, so that they may conserve their cash for housing, utilities, gas and other necessary bills.

Such assistance is expected to be short term, and an opportunity to work or give service by the recipient is inherent to the transaction. This helps to preserve the dignity of the recipient, while enshrining the nobility of work. "Thou shalt not be idle; for he that is idle shall not eat the bread nor wear the garments of the laborer" (D&C 42:42).

What a beautiful system to care for our own! Yet the system is not only for Church members. Here in our small town some years ago, the Church sent an entire semi-truck load of foodstuffs to the Food Pantry by request of our local liaison with the Pantry. No charge, delivered.

"And behold, thou wilt remember the poor, and consecrate of thy properties for their support. . . . Therefore, the residue shall be kept in my storehouse, to administer to the poor and the needy" (D&C 42:30, 34).

By the volunteer effort of a faithful membership worldwide, the Bishop's Storehouse is a safety net for those in need. We are, indeed, our brother's keeper and believe of a truth, "Inasmuch as ye have done it unto one of the least of these my brethren, ye have done it unto me" (Matthew 25:40). It is an ambitious, inspired plan.

223. The Relief Society for women is a divinely inspired organization.

On March, 17, 1842, in Nauvoo, Illinois, the Prophet Joseph Smith established the Relief Society for the women of the Church. On that occasion there were twenty sisters present, and Sister Emma Smith was called as the president. She suggested two counselors and a secretary to serve with her. Today, it is the largest women's organization on earth, with over six million members in approximately 160 countries.

The purpose of this organization parallels the mission of the Church at large—to provide for "the relief of the poor, the destitute, the widow and the orphan, and for the exercise of all benevolent purposes. . . [and] to save souls."[1] "Charity Never Faileth" is the motto for Relief Society, taken from Paul's writings on the qualities of charity in 1 Corinthians 13.

These purposes and the Relief Society motto are captured in three overarching responsibilities of each member of the organization:

- Increase faith and personal righteousness
- Strengthen families and homes
- Serve the Lord and his children

Part of the program of Relief Society is the visiting teaching program, a network of sister-to-sister care and concern. Each sister is assigned to watch out for and visit other sisters each month. They bring a spiritual message relevant to the sister and her needs and make themselves available as needs may require. This is a marvelous program in order to see that everyone has personal attention, care, and a feeling of belonging.

The women called to lead the local and general Relief Societies have presiding authority within their jurisdiction. "Under the priesthood authority of the bishop, the president of a ward Relief Society presides over and directs the activities of the Relief Society in the ward. A stake Relief Society president presides and exercises authority over the function to which she has been called."[2]

The First Presidency has said, "In the work of the Relief Society are intellectual, cultural, and spiritual values found in no other organization and sufficient for all general needs of its members."[3] Truly the breadth of the Relief Society is well captured in the Thirteenth Article of Faith, which states, "We believe in being honest, true, chaste, benevolent, virtuous, and in doing good to all men . . . If there is anything virtuous, lovely, or of good report or praiseworthy, we seek after these things" (Articles of Faith 13).

Relief Society is a knitting together of young mothers and grandmothers, married and single, educated and seeking to be educated, rich and poor, generational member and recent convert. Each one is a vital participant. It is a worldwide sisterhood. It is the largest organization of its kind in the world. It was founded under divine providence.

Notes:

1. *History of the Church of Jesus Christ of Latter-day Saints,* Salt Lake City: Deseret Book, 1960, 4:567, 1964, 5:25.
2. Dallin H. Oakes, "The Relief Society and the Church," *Ensign*, May, 1992.
3. *A Centenary of Relief Society,* Salt Lake City: General Board of Relief Society, 1942, 7.

224. The fast offering is a simple practice to care for the poor.

Jesus spoke often of and for the poor. One of the characteristics of His earthly mission, by which the disciples of John the Baptist recognized him, was that through Him would be fulfilled the scriptural account, "And the poor have the gospel preached to them" (Matthew 11:5). To the rich young ruler, Jesus said, "If thou wilt be perfect, go and sell that thou hast, and give to the poor" (Matthew 19:21).

To give to the poor blesses both parties, giver and receiver. We not only have a Christian responsibility to the poor and the less fortunate, but also a civic responsibility if we are to claim ours as a civil society.

In an attempt to fulfill that civic responsibility to the poor, well-intended government programs take root and have become bureaucracies unto themselves. They are not freewill charitable offerings of one to another, but rather mandated redistribution through legislated programs that define the rules and the recipients. Ultimately, they are not sustainable because the bureaucracy encourages broad participation and dependence. This dependence often becomes generational. The cost of the bureaucracy significantly diminishes the actual distribution to the poor.

Contrast that with the Lord's way of caring for the poor among us. My family and I fast for two meals once a month and contribute the money we would have spent for food (or a multiple thereof) to our Bishop so that he may use the money to help the poor. It helps them pay their utilities, buy gas to get to work, and maybe pay rent for a few months while they get back on their feet. One hundred percent of our contribution goes to help the poor! There is no cost of administration whatsoever. The money does not go to Church headquarters to be allocated back to the ward and its needs. It is to alleviate local needs. If a significant surplus builds up, that can and should be forwarded on to the general Church fund to help the poor in other parts of the world.

In addition, each recipient of temporary assistance is given an opportunity to serve in some way to feel the satisfaction of working for what they receive. Assistance is given to help that person or family become self-sustaining and independent through employment or the marketing of their talents.

This simple practice, honored by the saints in each ward or branch throughout the world, amply meets the needs of those poor among us. It complies with the Lord's injunction, "I would that ye should impart of your substance to the poor, every man according to that which he hath" (Mosiah 4:26).

What a beautiful manner to care one for another! What inspired direction!

225. The power of godliness is distinct from the form of godliness.

From the visit of the Father and the Son to Joseph Smith in what we now refer to as the First Vision, we get a glimpse into the state of the prevailing sects of his day. Joseph's purpose in going to the grove that spring morning was "to inquire of the Lord . . . which of all the sects was right, that I might know which to join" (Joseph Smith History 1:18).

In the unanticipated answer to his question, the Lord gave no endorsement to any of the prevailing churches. He flatly declared that "they were all wrong" (Joseph Smith History 1:19). Their creeds, their professors, their doctrines and teachings, were not of Him. In fact, "he again forbade me to join with any of them" (Joseph Smith History 1:20).

He said to Joseph that the existing churches had "a form of godliness, but they deny the power thereof" (Joseph Smith History 1:19.) What does that mean? It is interesting that Paul used the same language in describing the same time period, and then warned, "From such turn away" (2 Timothy 3:1-5).

Perhaps, this is what it means. In 1832, the Lord gave a revelation to Joseph Smith on the Priesthood, in which He said, "Therefore, in the ordinances thereof, the power of godliness is manifest. And without the ordinances thereof, and the authority of the priesthood, the power of godliness is not manifest unto men in the flesh" (D&C 84:20-21).

The power of godliness, then, is made evident by the authority of priesthood and in the exercise of sacred ordinances. Religion and its attendant trappings are a form of godliness, but without power—priesthood power. Ordinances or sacraments performed under the sanction of a board of directors, a council of bishops, or by individual decree are in the form of godliness. But "the rights of the priesthood are inseparably connected with the powers of heaven" (D&C 121:36).

Religious form can and does cause godliness in the conduct of a believer, but it cannot promise blessings beyond this life. It has not the power that was given to Peter by the Savior that "whatsoever thou shalt bind on earth shall be bound in heaven: and whatsoever thou shalt loose on earth shall be loosed in heaven" (Matthew 16:19).

The First Vision was experienced by Joseph Smith in 1820 and written as an official history in 1838. Doctrine and Covenants Section 84 was received in 1832. I find it confirming and consistent doctrinal teaching to read of the power of godliness so clearly defined in both the conditions of its presence and the conditions of its absence. It is another confirmation of the source of clear and insightful doctrinal teaching.

226. Priesthood authority functions either in Catholicism or Mormonism.

There's a joke I've heard that goes like this: The secretary to the Pope comes in to the Papal office, and breathlessly announces to the Pontiff that he has both good news and bad news. "The good news is that Jesus Christ has come to earth, and He wants to speak to you on the phone! The bad news is that He's calling from Salt Lake City, Utah."

Certainly, in Catholic circles this could be told in reverse with similar tongue-in-cheek intention. It is true though that only Catholics and Mormons could be the subjects in this joke. Both claim to have divine authority to preside and officiate as the authorized Kingdom of God on the earth. Both claim to have received that authority from original apostles of Jesus Christ. Both claim unbroken succession of that authority.

All other Protestant Christian denominations originated in protest to (Protestant) the dominant Roman Catholic Church, or the later born Anglican Church. Derivations based on specific doctrines and Biblical interpretations (or in the more recent generic forms of non-denominational churches) have given rise to countless Christian churches and a concept of the priesthood of all believers, going back to the sixteenth century and Martin Luther.[1]

Interesting is the following observation of one not of our faith, as related by Elder Orson F. Whitney:

> "Many years ago a learned man, a member of the Roman Catholic Church, came to Utah and spoke from the stand of the Salt Lake Tabernacle. A great scholar, with perhaps a dozen languages at his tongue's end, he seemed to know all about theology, law, literature, science and philosophy. One day he said to me: 'You Mormons are all ignoramuses. You don't even know the strength of your own position. It is so strong that there is only one other tenable in the whole Christian world, and that is the position of the Catholic Church. The issue is between Catholicism and Mormonism. If we are right, you are wrong; if you are right, we are wrong; and that's all there is to it. The Protestants haven't a leg to stand on. For, if we are wrong, they are wrong with us, since they were a part of us and went out from us; while if we are right, they are apostates whom we cut off long ago. If we have the apostolic succession from St. Peter, as we claim, there is no need of Joseph Smith and Mormonism; but if we have

> not that succession, then such a man as Joseph Smith was necessary, and Mormonism's attitude is the only consistent one. It is either the perpetuation of the gospel from ancient times, or the restoration of the gospel in latter days.'"[2]

It begs us to consider carefully such a dichotomy in position of something as important as priesthood authority from God. I have. My position is a secret to no one. So have my Catholic friends, and I certainly respect their conclusions. Even so, after the issue is finally settled, I am sure we will continue to work shoulder to shoulder according to the faith.

Notes:

1. Martin Luther, *The Epistles of St. Peter and St. Jude: Preached and Explained,* New York: Anson D.F. Randolph, 1859, 106.
2. Orson F. Whitney as quoted by LeGrand Richards, *A Marvelous Work and a Wonder,* Salt Lake City: Deseret Book, 1978, 3.

227. The Church doesn't look to create profit centers or for-fee services.

Look in the official monthly Church magazines, and you'll not see one sponsoring advertisement. Go out to the Church website, and likewise, you'll not see one commercial advertisement.

Recently, our stake sponsored an institute class for adults. It is an extension program of Brigham Young University. They will meet weekly for class for a term of fifteen weeks, or a common semester. The teacher was supplied by the Church Educational System, someone already administering the Seminaries and Institutes for this region. The cost to each student was $22.50, or about $1.50 per class! It would be easy and even understandable if the Church were to see this as a profit-center and charge on a tuition fee basis or some reasonable factor thereof. But they don't.

Similarly, Church DVD's, scriptures, family teaching materials, manuals, handbooks of administration are all sold at, or near cost, or are free. The Church magazines, with a much smaller audience than, say, *Reader's Digest*, comes to our home for $12 per year. They contain beautiful, color photographs, art and text, are usually some ninety pages, arrive monthly, and have no advertisements.

Four of our kids are married, and we held their wedding receptions at the Church building, using the kitchen facilities and available tables and chairs, decorating as we wanted to. We entertained some 250 people at each reception at no cost for the use of the building.

Bishops counsel, oversee baptisms, ordinations, worship services, youth programs, they minister to the poor, and provide a myriad of other services for their flock. None of these have fees attached.

Faithful members of the Church can attend holy temples with no entrance fee. Again, it would be easy to charge a small fee for entrance to offset maintenance costs.

The Church doesn't market logos, t-shirts, hats, pens, or any other common source of revenue pitched on its brand or mission.

The Prophet Isaiah beautifully said, "Ho, every one that thirsteth, come ye to the waters, and he that hath no money; come ye, buy, and eat; yea, come, buy wine and milk without money and without price. . . . Hearken diligently unto me, and eat ye that which is good, and let your soul delight itself in fatness" (Isaiah 55:1-2).

The mission of the Church could be summed up as to bring all unto Christ. It is not a business first, but a vehicle for the salvation of the human family.

228. "Inasmuch as ye have done it unto one of the least of these" is a foundational belief.

The Christian imperative to care for the poor and to actively seek out and administer to the needy is well known and scripturally replete.

At one point in the Savior's ministry, He promised the faithful that they would inherit "the kingdom prepared for you" (Matthew 25:34). Then, He described the qualifying behavior for such a reward, that of feeding the hungry, clothing the naked, taking in the stranger, visiting the sick or the imprisoned, and more. The righteous, wondering, asked, "Lord, when saw we thee an hungered, and fed thee? or thirsty, and gave thee drink? When saw we thee a stranger, and took thee in? or naked, and clothed thee? Or when saw we thee sick, or in prison, and came unto thee? And the King shall answer and say unto them, Verily I say unto you, Inasmuch as ye have done it unto one of the least of these my brethren, ye have done it unto me" (Matthew 25:34-40).

King Benjamin gave similar light to human service and kindness when he declared, "And behold, I tell you these things that ye may learn wisdom; that ye may learn that when ye are in the service of your fellow beings ye are only in the service of your God" (Mosiah 2:17).

During a sample period of twenty-five years from 1985 to 2010, the Church sent humanitarian aid around the world, including:

- Total cash and commodities assistance - $1,115,900,000
- Countries served – 167

- Food – 61,308 tons
- Medical supplies – 12,829 tons
- Clothing – 84,681 tons
- Hygiene, newborn, and school kits – 8,600,000

Major responses to emergencies include:

2010 – Haiti earthquake, Chile earthquake, Pakistan floods

2009 – Samoan/Tongan earthquake, Philippines typhoon

2008 – China earthquake, Ethiopia famine

2007 – Peru earthquake, California wildfires

2006 – Indonesia earthquake, Lebanon war relief

2005 – U.S. hurricanes Katrina and Rita, Pakistan earthquake

2004-2007 – South Asia tsunami

2004 – Florida and Caribbean hurricanes

2003 – Africa floods and famine, Iraq and Liberia war relief

2002 – Europe and Chile flooding

2001 – El Salvador and Peru earthquakes, Afghanistan war relief

2000 – Mozambique and Brazil flooding, Belize hurricane

1999 – Kosovo war relief

1998 – Central America hurricane

1997 – U.S. Midwest flooding, North Korea crop failure

1996 – Bosnia, Croatia, Serbia war relief

1995 – Japan earthquake

1994 – Rwanda war relief[1]

Much of this relief is accompanied by Church volunteers on the ground, and usually, if not always, in concert with other relief organizations. It is administered according to need. Membership in the

Church not a necessary determinant. In fact, in several of the above locations, the Church has no members or presence.

This humanitarian effort is funded in part from the tithing donations and from other free-will offerings made by members and friends to relieve the suffering of the world. "One hundred percent of every dollar donated [to Humanitarian Services] is used to help those in need without regard to race, religion, or ethnic origin."[2]

We believe the heart of a Christian life is to fulfill the two great commandments to love God and to love our neighbor. You likely won't read about the Church's relief efforts because they are not widely publicized, nor is it tainted by a desire to be recognized. Simply, yes, we are our brother's keeper, and "Inasmuch as ye have done it unto one of the least of these my brethren, ye have done it unto me [the Lord]" (Matthew 25:40).

Notes:

1. 2010 Church Almanac, 2009 Membership Statistics, Salt Lake City: Deseret News, 2010, 30-31.
2. www.ldsphilanthropies.org/humanitarian-services/funds/humanitarian-general-fund.html.

229. For forty days in the wilderness, Jesus communed with and was taught by God.

When Jesus set out for forty days in the wilderness, he went out "to be with God," not "to be tempted of the devil" (JST, Matthew 4:1 and Matthew 4:1).

Another important clarification/correction is found in the translation of Luke 4:2, which helps us understand the nature and the quality of the experience the Lord had while in the wilderness for those forty days. The King James Version of the Bible says, "Being forty days tempted of the devil" (Luke 4:2). The Joseph Smith Translation reads, "And *after forty days*, the devil came unto him, to tempt him" (JST, Luke 4:2).

And similarly in Mark 1:13, "And he was there in the wilderness forty days, tempted of Satan". Whereas, the Joseph Smith Translation indicates an apparent barrier to Satan during such a sacred time as this was. "And he was there in the wilderness forty days, Satan *seeking* to tempt him" (JST, Mark 1:11).

In Luke, it is even written that entering into the wilderness experience, "Jesus being full of the Holy Ghost . . . was led by the Spirit" (Luke 4:1). This speaks of the attitude and readiness with which Jesus approached God the Father. I don't believe Satan had a ticket to this glorious, intimate tutoring event.

It was after the forty days, as stated above, that Jesus experienced the three temptations that we are so familiar with from the scriptures. The strength derived during those forty days of communion with the divine, certainly enabled his resistance and confounding of those broadly inclusive temptations common to man.

As testimony to the effectiveness of such communion, Luke records the almost immediate declaration of his Messiahship within the synagogue of Nazareth. We know that Jesus knew of His divinity prior to the forty days in the wilderness, but perhaps He knew it even more deeply subsequent to that experience.

Such insight to the nature and purpose of that wilderness experience at the beginning of the Savior's public ministry is to see hallowed ground for what it is. Perhaps for us, it is to seek like experiences through prayer, to enable our resistance to the temptations of Satan and his servants, and to better understand our true identity.

Clearly, these are just my personal meditations, but they seem to be supported by the consistent adjustments that Joseph Smith made to the several recordings of this wilderness event. I think Joseph

Smith's work of translation sheds important light on this very sacred experience.

230. "And you must wait yet a little while, for ye are not yet ordained."

Joseph Smith was clearly told of his unique mission when Moroni made known to him "that God had a work for me to do" (Joseph Smith History 1:33). Moroni also quoted to Joseph from Malachi 4:5, with additional insight on Elijah's mission: "Behold, I will reveal unto you the Priesthood, by the hand of Elijah the prophet" (Joseph Smith History 1:38).

Young Joseph was seventeen-years-old at the time of this visitation from the Prophet Moroni. It would be another six and a half years until the Church was formally organized. That Joseph would have understood the importance of priesthood authority is not likely at this point of his life.

It was during the translation of the Book of Mormon when he found mention therein of baptism and the remission of sins, that Joseph and his scribe Oliver Cowdery retired to the woods to inquire of the Lord concerning baptism. Certainly to their amazement, John the Baptist came and conferred the Aaronic Priesthood upon them. That this was entirely unexpected is shown in the fact that John had to introduce himself and explain his mission. This significant event occurred on May 15, 1829.

Prior to this experience, a revelation given to Joseph Smith significantly made mention of this future priesthood ordination. "For hereafter you shall be ordained and go forth and deliver my words unto the children of men" (D&C 5:6). In the same revelation, Joseph Smith was told, "And you must wait yet a little while, for ye are not yet ordained" (D&C 5:17). This revelation was given sometime in March of 1829.

I find it a consistent point of order that reference is made to an ordination yet to occur two months hence. In my mind, it is evidence of a divinely ordered choreography that young Joseph just wouldn't have known to make reference to.

231. Home Teaching brings spiritual and material help into the home of every member.

"Home teaching is the priesthood way of watching over the Saints and accomplishing the mission of the Church."[1]

In a ward, or any other religious community, how is it that the bishop or the lead pastor is able to minister to the large and diverse flock he is given to shepherd? Moses was confronted with a similar charge that was beyond his singular capacity to accomplish. "Moses sat to judge the people . . . from the morning unto the evening" (Exodus 18:13). Jethro, his father-in-law, saw that "The thing that thou doest is not good. Thou wilt surely wear away, both thou, and this people that is with thee: for this thing is too heavy for thee; thou art not able to perform it thyself alone" (Exodus 18:17-18). Jethro went on to counsel Moses to "chose able men" (Exodus 18:21) and give them responsibility and authority to minister to the people, thus delegating the work of the ministry (Exodus 18:13-26).

The Lord has charged those who bear the priesthood to "visit the house of each member, and exhort them to pray vocally and in secret and attend to all family duties. . . . And see that there is no iniquity in the church, neither hardness with each other, neither lying, backbiting, nor evil speaking" (D&C 20:47, 54). Home teachers represent the Lord, the bishop, and quorum or group leaders. That makes their responsibility and charge very special, worthy of their attention and diligence.

It is a remarkable outreach to each individual member of the Church, done in his or her own home. Over time, trust and friendship are developed, and genuine love seems to go both ways. As is the case with the Lord's work, both the giver and the receiver are blessed.

The Lord Himself was a constant minister to the needs of others. He didn't sit in a palace or on a mountain top expecting those in need to seek Him out, but rather he walked with them, was in their homes, and went to them. He saw the man infirm at the pool of Bethesda, and Zacchaeus whom he called down from the tree, then went to his home. He answered the plea of a ruler to come to his home and raise his daughter from death. He sat with Mary in her home while Martha made preparations for dinner. Rich are the examples in His ministry.

It is humbling to consider that one is on the Lord's errand. I believe that is precisely what is at the heart of the Home Teaching program. It is a means of ministering to the spiritual and temporal welfare of individuals and families. My family and I have been blessed by good home teachers over the years, and we will be forever grateful.

Notes:

1. Ezra Taft Benson, "To the Home Teachers of the Church," *Ensign,* May, 1987.

232. Wards operate on a very frugal budget, relying on spiritual substance instead.

There is a billboard south of town that over the years has advertised for one of the large local Churches. They change the sign fairly often, and each seems to be announcing a new program or performance or other reason to attend or join their community of believers.

That same church also has a marvelous facility, including a bowling alley and other recreational amusements. Some years ago, there were musings among several of our youth leaders to see if we could combine with them and other Churches to allow our youth to have some of these "fun and entertaining" experiences. In the end, it was decided that that is not within the primary objectives of what we really want to teach and accomplish with our youth.

It is related that in an early morning seminary class, the teachers decided to offer breakfast as an incentive to increase attendance among the youth. Initially, it had that effect, but very soon thereafter, attendance actually dropped off from where it had been previous to this innovation. The youth were coming for the spiritual food, not what could be purchased at McDonald's. Although they may have appeared inattentive or even disinterested at that early hour, in actuality, they brought their cups to be filled.

Certainly, there is a desirable balance, which includes entertainment and activity. The Especially For Youth program models this exceptionally well. The youth come away from those week-long experiences with glowing enthusiasm and reverent testimonies.

A typical ward will operate on an annual budget of approximately $45 per person! That amount will have to suffice for all of the following activities (and the list is not comprehensive):

- About 288 individual weekly youth group activities
- Twelve combined youth nights
- A portion of the cost of girls camp for one week
- A portion of the cost of High Adventure camp for boys
- Sponsorship of a Cub Scout pack
- Participation in a Twilight camp for cubs
- Three or four ward parties
- Elders Quorum budget
- High Priest Group budget
- Relief Society budget

- Copier/library supplies
- Sunday program costs, forty-eight weeks

"Most activities should be simple and have little or no cost."[1]

In reality, how nice it is not to have a sales and marketing budget to manage with its attendant purposes at the local level of administration. The work of a ward is to "exhort you that ye would come unto Christ" (Moroni 10:30). This non-reliance on extravagant programs and relying on the sweetness and certain witness of the spirit is truly refreshing. And it works.

Notes:

1. *Handbook 2 Administering the Church*, Salt Lake City: The Church of Jesus Christ of Latter-day Saints, 2010, 13.2.8.

233. Divine accuracy is seen in the recording of the Lord's visit to the brother of Jared.

In the Book of Mormon, specifically the book of Ether, one of the principal characters is referred to as the brother of Jared, and we are left with that impersonal naming throughout the book. The brother of Jared was "a man highly favored of the Lord" (Ether 1:34), which indicates his obedience and devotion to the Lord's ways. He was no stranger to the Lord and communicated often and freely in prayer, receiving divine instruction for him and his people.

It was during one of these times of counsel and prayerful communication, that it is recorded that the brother of Jared saw the Lord Jesus Christ. The record, in part, follows:

> "And it came to pass that when the brother of Jared had said these words, behold, the Lord stretched forth his hand and touched the stones one by one with his finger. And the veil was taken from off the eyes of the brother of Jared, and he saw the finger of the Lord; and it was as the finger of a man,

> like unto flesh and blood . . . for I knew not that the Lord had flesh and blood. And the Lord said unto him: Because of thy faith thou hast seen that I shall take upon me flesh and blood. . . Lord, show thyself unto me. . . And when he had said these words, behold, the Lord showed himself unto him. . . Behold, I am he who was prepared from the foundation of the world to redeem my people. Behold, I am Jesus Christ . . . Behold, this body, which ye now behold, is the body of my spirit; and man have I created after the body of my spirit; and even as I appear unto thee to be in the spirit will I appear unto my people in the flesh. And now, as I, Moroni, said I could not make a full account of these things which are written, therefore it sufficeth me to say that Jesus showed himself unto this man in the spirit, even after the manner and in the likeness of the same body even as he showed himself unto the Nephites" (Ether 3:6, 8, 9, 10, 13, 14, 16, 17).

It would have been an easy oversight for the uninspired not to have recognized and distinguished between the unembodied Savior and the resurrected Savior. A further truth employed is that our spirit entities are of bodily shape and form. "There is no such thing as immaterial matter. All spirit is matter, but it is more fine or pure, and can only be discerned by purer eyes" (D&C 131:7).

The Lord's visit to the brother of Jared is consistent with revealed truth. It is both chronologically accurate and wholly enlightening.

234. The announcement of the Perpetual Education Fund is visionary.

While I served as a missionary in Mexico, most of my assigned fields of labor were among the very poor. I appreciated their purity of faith, their depth of commitment to their covenants, and their love of the gospel. Tremendous sacrifices were made to attend distant temples and to support sons and daughters in serving missions. Upon returning from missions faithfully served, now well grounded in the gospel and filled with the spirit, many would resume the hopeless, grinding course of poverty from which they left. It was clear to see that such poverty was the result of a lack of educational opportunity, not a lack of industry.

In April of 2001, President Gordon B. Hinckley announced the creation of the Perpetual Education Fund, designed to make loans for education to those who otherwise wouldn't have that opportunity.

> "The Church is establishing a fund largely from the contributions of faithful Latter-day Saints who have and will contribute for this purpose. . . . We shall call it the Perpetual Education Fund. It entails no new organization, no new personnel except a volunteer director and secretary. It will cost essentially nothing to administer. With good employment skills, these young men and women can rise out of the poverty they and generations before them have known. They will better provide for their families. They will serve in the Church and grow in leadership and responsibility. The beneficiaries will repay the money, and when they do so, they will enjoy a wonderful sense of freedom because they have improved their lives not through a grant or gift, but through borrowing and then repaying. They can hold their heads high in a spirit of independence. The likelihood of their remaining faithful and active throughout their lives will be very high."[1]

Through 2013, there were over sixty countries where the program was operative, and over 61,000 have participated in the program. The average participant increases his or her earning potential three to four times.[2]

The Lord would have us care for the poor. That is a clear mandate. But to raise the poor from being generational recipients to being generational contributors is truly noble and far reaching.

I believe that countries of poverty will see the Latter-day Saints rise to positions of leadership within communities, corporations, and government because of the PEF. The influence of such leadership will help lift their respective communities, and even countries, out of the grip of ignorance and its attendant poverty.

It absolutely thrills me to see this inspired program and the resultant blessings to the world.

Notes:

1. Gordon B. Hinckley, "The Perpetual Education Fund," *Ensign,* May, 2001.
2. Perpetual Education Fund website, *About PEF.*

235. Alma 32 has helped countless people identify and nurture the witness of the Spirit.

I remember what I consider to be one of the earliest encounters with the Spirit (particularly as a witness of truth) around a campfire on a thirty-day outdoor survival course. We had just completed a long overnight hike and were pleasantly exhausted. Judy Burris brought out her Book of Mormon and wanted me to read the promise given by Moroni at the conclusion of that book (Moroni 10:3-5). I knew her intent. She wanted me to consider the Mormon faith. I agreed to read those passages, and did so right there on the spot. The promise made by Moroni seemed to me to be honest, fair, and verifiable. I would take his challenge. Now looking back, I can see that my consenting to read those passages blessed my life forever.

Alma gave an analogy to the journey I would begin, "But behold, if ye will awake and arouse your faculties, even to an experiment upon my words, and exercise a particle of faith . . . that ye can give place for a portion of my words . . . that a seed may be planted in your heart" (Alma 32:27-28).

Alma goes on to describe perfectly the conversion process that most, if not all, experience as the gospel is being taught to them. "If ye do not cast it [the seed] out by your unbelief, . . . behold, it will begin to swell within your breasts . . . it beginneth to enlighten my understanding, yea, it beginneth to be delicious to me" (Alma 32:28).

Such was my experience. "And now, behold, is your knowledge perfect? Yea, your knowledge is perfect in that thing, and your faith is dormant; and this because you know" (Alma 32:34). To know the gospel is true, and all that it includes, is a personal experience. "O then, is not this real? I say unto you, Yea, because it is light . . . because it is discernible . . . and now behold . . . ye have tasted of this light" (Alma 32:35).

Alma continues and pleads with us that "as the tree beginneth to grow . . . Let us nourish it with great care, that it may get root . . . and bring forth fruit" (Alma 32:37). He cautions us of the alternative course of neglecting the tree, which will cause it to "wither away . . . not because the seed was not good, . . . but it is because . . . ye will not nourish the tree" (Alma 32:38-39).

Like any living thing, a testimony must be nourished. Daily drawing from the words of the prophets, faithful activity in the kingdom, humble reliance on the Lord Jesus Christ, love of our fellows, keeping the commandments—all of these firm and form our testimony. Alma Chapter 32 is a model of the conversion process and the nurturing of faith over a lifetime. It has helped many to understand the new and exciting course they now experience. It is the model that I have personally experienced. It is truly inspired and inspiring.

236. Nephi nails the shallow religious stance of false and vain and foolish doctrines.

I'm told that in Australia, you just don't talk about religion, you confine your conversation to sports, weather, and politics. It is much the same throughout Europe, they say, and Canada, as well. Perhaps to a lesser extent, regions of America either exclude such meaningful dialogue or conform to a mere tacit acknowledgment. Religion is just not something that is taken seriously by many people nowadays. I know these are broad generalizations, but to an extent, such an attitude has been with mankind throughout history.

Nephi described this attitude well when he wrote specifically of attitudes in the last days, "Yea, and there shall be many which shall say; Eat, drink, and be merry, for tomorrow we die; and it shall be well with us. And there shall also be many which shall say: Eat, drink, and be merry; nevertheless, fear God—He will justify in committing a little sin; yea, lie a little, take the advantage of one because of his words, dig a pit for thy neighbor; there is no harm in this; and do all these things, for tomorrow we die; and if it so be that we are guilty, God will beat us with a few stripes, and at last we shall be saved in the kingdom of God. Yea, and there shall be many which shall teach after this manner, false and vain and foolish doctrines, and shall be puffed up in their hearts, and shall seek deep to hide their counsels from the Lord; and their works shall be in the dark" (2 Nephi 28:7-9).

God is merciful, kind, loving, and quick to forgive the penitent. But to shirk our own personal responsibility to "work out your own salvation with fear and trembling" (Philippians 2:12) is a mistake. An attitude of humility, dependence, repentance, reverence, coupled with a love and respect of our fellow travelers, enables spiritual growth. There is no approaching the Divine when we view the Divine casually.

"I am left to mourn because of the unbelief, and the wickedness, and the ignorance, and the stiffneckednesss of men; for they will not search knowledge, nor understand great knowledge, when it is given unto them in plainness, even as plain as word can be" (2 Nephi 32:7). Nephi really saw our day.

237. The Church's position on same-gender attraction is Christlike and timeless.

For whatever reason one is decidedly homosexual, be it learned, inherited, DNA, or other factors, that person is still, first and foremost, a child of God. Jesus' Atonement is applicable to all of God's children, and His and Heavenly Father's love are unconditional.

Is homosexuality a sin? Said Elder Dallin H. Oaks, "The distinction between feelings or inclinations on the one hand, and behavior on the other hand, is very clear. It's no sin to have inclinations that if yielded to would produce behavior that would be a transgression. The sin is in yielding to temptation. Temptation is not unique. Even the Savior was tempted. . . . Homosexual is not a noun that describes a condition. It's an adjective that describes feelings or behavior. . . . The line of sin is between the feelings and the behavior. The line of prudence is between the susceptibility and the feelings."[1]

Furthermore, as doctrinal clarity, a statement issued by the First Presidency in 1991 says, "The Lord's law of moral conduct is abstinence outside of lawful marriage and fidelity within marriage. Sexual relations are proper only between husband and wife, appropriately expressed within the bonds of marriage. Any other sexual conduct, including fornication, adultery, and homosexual and lesbian behavior is sinful. Those who persist in such practices or influence others to do so are subject to Church discipline."[2]

There are many temptations and challenges that characterize this mortal existence. Whereas some might have a propensity to anger, or alcoholism, or stealing, others will have an entirely different set of mortal weaknesses. Whatever our individual challenges, we are to conform to the commandments of God and seek to tame those impulses that are inconsistent with the commandments. Comforting is the truth that "the answer is that same-gender attraction did not exist in the pre-earth life and neither will it exist in the next life. It is a circumstance that for whatever reason or reasons seems to apply right now in mortality, in this nano-second of our eternal existence."[3]

Jesus said that "for this cause shall a man leave his father and mother, and cleave to his wife; and they twain shall be one flesh. . . . What therefore God has joined together, let not man put asunder" (Mark 10:7-9). Regarding the current political winds, Elder Oaks notes that "the Parliament in Canada and the Congress in Washington do not have the authority to revoke the commandments of God, or to modify or amend them in any way."[4]

In a conference address on this same subject, President Gordon B. Hinckley said, "I desire now to say with emphasis that our concern for the bitter fruit of sin is coupled with the Christlike sympathy for its victims, innocent or culpable. We advocate the example of the Lord, who condemned the sin, yet loved the sinner. We should reach out with kindness and comfort to the afflicted, ministering to their needs and assisting them with their problems."[5]

Regardless of how the world characterizes the position of the Church on this issue, stated above are clear doctrines and principles in the light of compassion, tolerance, and eternal verities and purposes.

Notes:

1. Dallin H. Oaks, lds.org, Mormon Newsroom "*Interview With Elder Dallin H. Oaks and Elder Lance B. Wickman: 'Same-Gender Attraction'*", 2006.

2. Dallin H. Oaks, during above interview, quoting from a First Presidency statement given in 1991.

3. Lance B. Wickman, lds.org, Mormon Newsroom interview through LDS Public Affairs, *Same-Gender Attraction*, 2006.

4. Dallin H. Oaks.

5. Gordon B. Hinckley, "Reverence and Morality," *Ensign*, May, 1987.

238. In the quiet hours of the morning, when all is at peace, I feel certainty of truth anew.

Sometimes in the thick of everyday life, doubts can creep into our minds—doubts of the Lord's divine plan, questions of leadership, even doubts of our own divine origin and capabilities. Recently, there seems to be a steady stream of publishing that seeks to discredit or diminish the truly divine role of the Savior and the historical context of the Gospels. As Latter-day Saints, our beliefs are often under attack, so we end up defending not only New Testament Christianity, but also the refulgent doctrines of the Gospel of Jesus Christ restored through the Prophet Joseph Smith.

I find it a point of logic that one is entirely unable to prove that there is no God in heaven, yet the personal witness of His existence in one's heart cannot be overturned. The Lord said, "Behold, I will tell you in your mind and in your heart, by the Holy Ghost, which shall come upon you and which shall dwell in your heart. Now, behold, this is the spirit of revelation" (D&C 8:2-3).

Revelation is personal, in the instance that it is received. It is clear, unmistakable, moving. Another wonderful piece of instruction regarding personal revelation and our participation in the process to learn of truth states "But, behold, I say unto you, that you must study it out in your mind; then you must ask me if it be right, and if it is right I will cause that your bosom shall burn within you; therefore, you shall feel that it is right. But if it be not right you shall have no such feelings, but you shall have a stupor of thought that shall cause you to forget the thing which is wrong" (D&C 9:8-9).

When all is quiet, when the din of the world is shut out, and when one is left to his or her own enjoyment, those moments are perhaps our most genuine, particularly when they are coupled with humble prayer, giving thanks, and seeking direction from our Heavenly Father. It is in these moments that I can realign, take a deep breath, feel once again at peace, and reinvigorate my desire to actively participate in the Lord's work to my fellows.

"Be still, and know that I am God" (Psalms 46:10, D&C 101:16). I have received that counsel, and it has given me great faith, hope, and certainty anew.

239. The evolution of teaching practices for full-time missionaries is rooted in faith.

When I was a missionary in the late 1970's, we actually memorized a series of six or so lessons to present the doctrines of the Church to investigators. As a new missionary in the field, the lesson presentation itself, to be close to word perfect, would sometimes become the objective. A more experienced, more astute missionary would come to realize that the Spirit is the real teacher and know that to be governed by the Spirit makes all the difference.

Over many years now, I have watched as the delivery platform for our missionaries has evolved and continues to evolve from the rote format we used as a basis in my day, to a much heavier emphasis on relying upon the Spirit to guide the discussions.

This methodology requires faith—faith that, indeed, the Spirit will communicate, or witness, of the truths that are being taught and faith in Moroni's promise, "And by the power of the Holy Ghost ye may know the truth of all things" (Moroni 10:5). It gives place for an active role to be played by a member of the Godhead, the spirit entity we call the Holy Ghost or the Holy Spirit.

This personal spiritual witness is what was experienced by the two disciples on the road to Emmaus when they had listened to the Savior as their traveling companion, "Did not our heart burn within us, while he talked with us by the way, and while he opened to us the scriptures" (Luke 24:32)?

Our missionaries are taught to ask questions, to listen for understanding, and to tailor a lesson to an individual's particular needs. "Good questions will help you understand interests, concerns, or questions that others have. They can enhance your teaching, invite the Spirit, and help your investigators learn."[1]

"More important than speaking is listening. . . . Be genuine. Reach out sincerely. Ask these friends what matters most to *them*. And then listen."[2]

"Wherefore, he that preacheth and he that receiveth, understand one another, and both are edified and rejoice together" (D&C 50:22).

To send out nineteen-year-old young men and women to teach by the Spirit and to believe that the Lord will literally team up with them as their faithful companion is to really believe in Him. It is not to merely dispense information and hope to convert by the power of our persuasion. It is to enable the Spirit to testify of truth. It is confidence that the Spirit *will* testify of the truths being taught by our missionaries.

Notes:

1. *Preach My Gospel*, Salt Lake City: Intellectual Reserve, Inc., 2004, 183.
2. Elder Jeffrey R. Holland, "Witnesses Unto Me," *Ensign*, May, 2001.

240. The revelations on the Constitution were way ahead of their time.

Today, with the benefit of historical context, the wisdom of the United States Constitution is generally held without dispute. But in the early 1830's such historical perspective was still developing. The test of time was not yet matured nor was it yet compelling.

Less than fifty years into the American constitutional experiment, during the years of 1833-1836, the Lord spoke through the Prophet Joseph Smith and made such bold declarations as, "And that law of the land which is constitutional, supporting that principle of freedom in maintaining rights and privileges, belongs to all mankind, and is justifiable before me" (D&C 98:5).

"According to the laws and constitution of the people, which I have suffered to be established, and should be maintained for the rights and protection of all flesh, according to just and holy principles; That every man may act in doctrine and principle pertaining to futurity, according to the moral agency which I have given unto him. . . . And for this purpose have I established the Constitution of this land, by the hands of wise men whom I raised up unto this very purpose" (D&C 101:77-80).

That last statement confirms what many people have long believed when considering the caliber of men that drafted, engaged in intelligent argument for, and then as representatives of the people, signed.

To put it in its marvelous context, Elder Dallin H. Oaks said, "In 1833, when almost all people in the world were still ruled by kings or tyrants, few could see how the infant United States Constitution could be divinely designed 'for the rights and protection of all flesh.' Today, 176 years after that revelation, almost every nation in the world has adopted a written constitution, and the United States Constitution profoundly influenced all of them. Truly, this nation's most important export is its constitution, whose great principles stand as a model 'for the rights and protection of all flesh.'"[1]

Furthermore, the following is a sample of an 1835 "declaration of belief regarding governments and laws in general," (Section Heading, D&C 134) adopted by the Church. It is as fundamental to American life as apple pie. "We believe that governments were instituted of God for the benefit of man. . . . We believe that no government can exist in peace, except such laws are framed and held inviolate as will secure to each individual the free exercise of conscience, the right and control of property, and the protection of life" (D&C 134:1-2).

These revelations on the adherence to law, of loyalty to country, and of the visionary view of a just government, were given at a time when the Church was under increasing persecution and denied many of its own constitutional rights. Yet, the Lord said, "Therefore, I, the Lord, justify you, and your brethren of my church, in befriending that law which is the constitutional law of the land" (D&C 98:6).

While yet nascent in the 1830's, the Lord knew of the profound influence the United States Constitution would have on the unfolding history of the world and the restoration of the gospel, which began just three decades after the Bill of Rights was ratified. Truly, the revelations received regarding the Constitution were inspired declarations.

Notes:

1. Elder Dallin. H. Oaks, *BYUI Devotional*, "Religious Freedom," October 13, 2009.

241. But it must needs be done in mine own way.

When I was a teenager and not a member of the Church, I had (and still have) a dear friend, Mark Jensen, who lived just up the street from us in San Diego. He was LDS. All of the boys in the neighborhood were avid surfers. We lived to surf. On several occasions, I tried to convince Mrs. Jensen that to go surfing on a Sunday would bring Mark closer to God than anything, arguing for the purity of nature, and on and on.

There are many who make the argument that they don't need to go to Church to worship God or that there is no need to receive the priesthood to preach the Gospel and administer in the ordinances thereof. They claim that baptism is unnecessary. Too many today believe that chastity before marriage is an outdated Puritanical view.

Others believe that tithing is to be paid when a family can finally afford it. They propose that helping the poor is feeding them each day, neglecting to impart hope and the opportunity for self-sufficiency within the framework of stewardship.

Abraham is an example of one who recognized from a young age the blessings of conforming to the Lord's ways. "And, finding there was greater happiness and peace and rest for me, I sought for the blessings of the fathers, and the right whereunto I should be ordained to administer the same . . . and desiring to receive instructions, and to keep the commandments of God, I became a rightful heir" (Abraham 1:2).

Abraham knew the source and the sure pattern, "And when we obtain any blessing from God, it is by obedience to that law upon which it is predicated" (D&C 130:21).

I believe it is the Lord's intention to bless his children. Who knows best how to make us eligible to receive those blessings than He Himself? Here are some words of the Lord where I can sense His longing to be able to bless us:

> "And Zion cannot be built up unless it is by the principles of the law of the celestial kingdom; otherwise I cannot receive her unto myself" (D&C 105:5).
>
> "I the Lord, am bound when ye do what I say; but when ye do not what I say, ye have no promise" (D&C 82:10).

Cherry picking the laws and ordinances of the gospel to fit our own desires and timetable leaves blessings unclaimed. The Frank Sinatra song, "I Did it My Way," has been wildly popular, and I actually like it in the context of a confident approach to life. However, regarding our relationship to Deity, that song title could be the antithesis of discipleship.

I am grateful that the Lord is clear in describing and delineating the "strait and narrow path which leads to eternal life" (2 Nephi 31:18).

I am grateful that His doctrine and commandments are not squishy, regional, or interpretive. I am grateful to know that He loves us and only wants to bless us on an eternal scale. Therefore, I know there is value in seeking to know and to comport with His ways. Like Abraham, I can testify that as a result in my own life, I have been blessed with greater happiness and peace.

In the end, I have to concede that Mrs. Jensen had the better argument.

242. The Law of Consecration and Stewardship is a unique system for social order.

About nine months after the Church was organized, the Lord revealed to the Prophet Joseph Smith that the Church was under obligation to care for the poor (D&C 38). In that same revelation, Joseph was told that the Lord's way of doing that would be revealed to him after he had arrived in Ohio. That very next month of February 1831, Joseph having arrived in Ohio, the Lord revealed the Law of Consecration and Stewardship, later referred to as the United Order, or The Order (D&C 42:30-39).

In this introductory revelation, new terms were introduced, such as, consecration of properties, deed, steward over his own property, family sufficiency, storehouse, and bishop's council. In practice, one would completely divest himself of all of his property, conveying all by covenant and by deed to the Church of his own free will. This would be the consecration part. Then he would receive back property and goods sufficient for his needs, of which he would have private ownership, and would manage both for his own welfare and to contribute surplus profits to the storehouse for the care of the poor. This would be the stewardship part. Indeed, this was a bold and an ambitious social contract.

Some contend that this system is of the same character as socialism, or worse, communism. There are several stark differences: 1) Whereas socialism is implemented by external force, the power of the state, the Lord's way is voluntary and based in a belief in God and acceptance of him as Lord of the earth. 2) Private ownership of property is abolished under pure socialism, but the Lord's way retains private ownership and personal management of property. 3) The spirit of socialism is "We're going to take." The spirit of the Lord's way is "We're going to give."[1]

Although we have not generally become the Christ-like people that would be needed to live under such a social economic system, there is nothing that prohibits any of us from choosing to consecrate our increase to the Lord's work. And we would do well to properly view our earthly property as a stewardship while living in this mortal sphere, and to have "as much as is sufficient for himself and family" (D&C 42:32). Such an attitude would be a mutual blessing to both the storehouse and to the steward. In truth, did not the Savior live that way? He gave both His time and His talents to the work of His Father, even His life.

If we are to become a Zion people, we must be "of one heart and one mind, and dwelt in righteousness; and there was no poor among them" (Moses 7:18). The Lord's unprecedented law of Consecration and Stewardship as revealed to the Prophet Joseph Smith is the model for that Zion society.

Notes:

1. Thoughts taken from Marion G. Romney, "Socialism and the United Order Compared," *Ensign,* April, 1966, 95-101.

243. The pamphlet "For the Strength of Youth" sets forth Christ-like standards.

Our youth often hear the comments, "Your Church has too many rules. You guys can't do anything!" Typically, they are referring to the fact that our youth don't smoke, drink, cuss, watch R-rated movies, engage in sex, or break the Sabbath day. A good question to ask is, "Which one of those LDS behaviors would the Savior not approve of?"

Briefly, yet very effectively, twenty standards of behavior, including Dress and Appearance, Entertainment, Music and Dancing, Dating, Language, and more are addressed in the "For the Strength of Youth" pamphlet. All of them suggest conduct that is of high-bred caliber and would make any responsible parent proud. At the same time, they insure to our youth a feeling of confidence and purity and serve as a protection from vice and regret.

Recently, a friend of mine was explaining these standards to another man, a dad, and the value they had been in the raising of his own kids. The other dad was first amazed that youth would abide by such lofty standards. "How did you get your kids to live by these rules?" His answer was, "We taught them since they were young, and they associate with others of like standards to help them keep their commitments." Additionally, such standards are intuitive. The still, small voice within us tells us that they are right. Then responded the questioning Dad, "I wish I would have had these when I was raising my kids."

Like encouraging words from the Lord himself, the First Presidency introduces the pamphlet which includes the language, "Your Heavenly father wants your life to be joyful and to lead you back into His presence. . . . Because the Lord loves you, He has given you commandments and the words of the prophets to guide you on your journey. . . . You will feel good about yourself and will be a positive influence in the lives of others."[1]

In a time when standards are seen as repressive and society is trending toward ever-greater permissiveness, the fact remains that young people need standards for behavior. Such expectations confirm to the youth the love of their parents who truly care for them and for their future happiness and of a loving Father in Heaven.

That the youth of the Church by-and-large live to these standards across the world, by their own self-governance, is a wonder to many. Yet, would anyone argue that these standards are too high for one who professes to be a disciple of Christ? Certainly not. Or, moreover, are they not in harmony with Him who is holy and pure and has given these inspired standards for the benefit of His children? Indeed, they are. They stand as a blessing to the rising generation and to all who seek to follow the Master.

Notes:

1. "Sexual Purity," *For the Strength of Youth: Fulfilling Our Duty to God,* Salt Lake City: The Church of Jesus Christ of Latter-day Saints, 2001.

244. The prominent prophetic writings of Isaiah are treasured by the LDS faith.

"If we are to comprehend the writings of Isaiah, we cannot overstate or overstress the plain, blunt reality that he is in fact the prophet of the restoration."[1]

Fully one third of the book of Isaiah is recorded by the prophets in the Book of Mormon. When Jesus came to the Americas, He specifically approved the words of Isaiah, "And now, behold, I say unto you, that ye ought to search these things. Yea, a commandment I give unto you that ye search these things diligently; for great are the words of Isaiah. For surely he spake as touching all things concerning my people which are of the house of Israel; therefore it must needs be that he must speak also to the Gentiles. And all things that he spake have been and shall be, even according to the words which he spake" (3 Nephi 23:1-3).

The Book of Mormon was written for our day as a second witness that Jesus is the Christ. Of this, Isaiah testifies beautifully (Isaiah 5:26, 29:4, 9-18). The Book of Mormon is also written "to show unto the remnant of the House of Israel what great things the Lord hath done for their fathers; and that they may know the covenants of the Lord" (Title Page, Book of Mormon). Isaiah speaks conspicuously of the House of Israel, including its mission, and its destiny.

Isaiah's chief doctrinal contributions fall into at least seven categories:[2]

1. Restoration of the gospel in the latter days through Joseph Smith

2. Latter-day gathering of Israel and her final triumph in glory

3. Coming forth of the Book of Mormon as another witness of Christ and the total revolution it will eventually bring to the doctrinal understanding of men

4. Apostate conditions of the nations of the world in the latter days

5. Messianic prophecies relative to our Lord's first coming

6. Second coming of Christ and the Millennial reign

7. Historical data and prophetic utterances relative to his own day

When Moroni came to Joseph Smith in 1823, he quoted the eleventh chapter of Isaiah, saying it was about to be fulfilled. In the Doctrine and Covenants, there are approximately one hundred instances in which latter-day revelation specifically quotes, paraphrases, or interprets language used by Isaiah. He is quoted at least fifty-seven times in the New Testament.

Although most would argue that Isaiah is difficult to understand, those who apply themselves in faith to conscientious, prayerful study will gain foundational gospel understanding. The Lord would not have commanded us to search these things diligently were there not great value in doing so. As Latter-day Saints, we have a particular interest and relevance in the writings of the Prophet Isaiah.

Notes:

1. Bruce R. McConkie, "Ten Keys to Understanding Isaiah," *Ensign,* October, 1973, 81.
2. Randal S. Chase, *Old Testament Study Guide, Pt. 3: The Old Testament Prophets,* Plain and Precious Publishing, 2012, 41

245. Man has a stewardship to care for and humanely treat the animal kingdom.

Just a year or so after I was baptized, I was sitting in a stake center in Cedar City, Utah during the Priesthood session of General Conference as President Spencer W. Kimball was speaking. His talk became known as "Don't Kill the Little Birds."[1] He spoke of the needless and thoughtless killing of animals and that it should not be, except for use as food. I saw several men squirm in their chairs on that occasion, since I was clearly in a place where hunting was an activity often engaged in from childhood, and sometimes for sheer sport.

The Lord has said, "The beasts of the field and the fowls of the air... [are] ordained for the use of man for food and for raiment" (D&C 49:19). He went on to say, "And wo be unto man that sheddeth blood or that wasteth flesh and hath no need" (D&C 49:21).

I like a particular editorial written almost one hundred years ago in the April 1918 *Juvenile Instructor.* "What is it to be humane to the beasts of the fields and birds of the air? It is more than to be considerate of the animal life entrusted to our care. It is a grateful appreciation of God's creations. It is the lesson of divine love. To Him all life is a sacred creation for the use of His children. Do we stand beside Him in our tender regard for life? . . . Men cannot worship the Creator and look with careless indifference upon his creations."[2]

I've heard it said that criminals convicted of violent behavior toward their fellows often began such cruelty by abusing animals in various sordid ways. Such activity, to embark on a road of calculated mistreatment of living things, dulls the spirit within us. It diminishes what we should be nurturing—a reverence for life.

Of note is that even animals, represented by the plural noun "cattle," are to be given rest on the Sabbath day (Exodus 20:10). Throughout the Old Testament, there are several admonitions of showing care for, and even kindness toward, the beasts of the earth (Exodus 23:4-5, Deuteronomy 22:6-7, 10, 25:4, Proverbs 12:10).

A love of animals seems to be innate within most children. We would do well to emulate that childlike characteristic and to see our relationship to animals as a stewardship rather than as an oppressor. In 1951, as President of the Church, David O. McKay commented in General Conference that "a true Latter-day Saint is kind to animals, is kind to every created thing, for God created all."[3] Such is our position as a Church and as a people.

Notes:

1. Spencer W. Kimball, "Fundamental Principles to Ponder and Live," *Ensign,* October, 1978.

2. Editorial, *Improvement Era,* April, 1918, and reprinted April, 1927.

3. David O. McKay, *Conference Report,* October, 1951, 180.

246. The "Words of Mormon" is an unexpected, divine insertion in the Book of Mormon.

The Book of Mormon begins with the writings of Nephi, which he inscribed on plates of gold leaf. These writings were then given to Nephi's brother Jacob, and he became steward of the plates. Jacob and each of seven succeeding descendants had stewardship over the plates and also added their own first-person writings to the record. For the most part, a father-son transfer of responsibility for the plates and their content continued from Jacob through Amaleki. These plates are referred to as the Small Plates of Nephi.

Then all of a sudden, "The Words of Mormon" are inserted, where we are introduced to Mormon, and we fast forward about six hundred years. We come to realize that Mormon, living several hundred years after the coming of Christ, is actually compiling the records of the above mentioned writers and adding an abridgment of the next six hundred years or so. From the book of Mosiah through Fourth Nephi, Mormon writes in the third person, taking his words from what is referred to as the Large Plates of Nephi.

I find it a literary surprise to take this turn as the Book of Mormon is unfolding. If it were a book written by Joseph or a contemporary, such an inclusion would not likely have been made. Mormon takes this opportunity to segue from the previous nine authors and caretakers of the record, to a more detailed account narrated by his own hand, which begins in the land of Zarahemla.

Mormon also introduces us to his son, Moroni, who is the last writer in the Book of Mormon. It is Moroni who had the distinct honor of bringing the Prophet Joseph Smith to the gold plates and to instruct him of his duties. For Joseph to have woven in the events surrounding the appearance of Moroni as early as 1823, to a chronologically correct placement of his role in the Book of Mormon published almost seven years later, is of particular note to me.

The Book of Mormon is translation of a divinely inspired record, covering some one thousand years on the American continents. It is the compiling and abridging of the inscribed records of many by the noble Prophet Mormon. Our first introduction to Mormon in what is titled "The Words of Mormon," is, indeed, a compelling moment for the veracity of the book which bears his name.

247. Be ye therefore perfect.

In the Bible, this mandate from the Savior is written as, "Be ye therefore perfect, even as your Father which is in heaven is perfect" (Matthew 5:48). At that point, Jesus had not yet finished his mortal ministry.

As a resurrected being on the American continent, Jesus taught the people by saying, "Therefore I would that ye should be perfect even as I, or your Father who is in heaven is perfect" (3 Nephi 12:48). Having completed His mission on the earth and having overcome all things, Jesus now had attained this state of perfection as had God, His and our Father.

None of us will attain to the perfection that Christ attained to in this life. Remember, that He was born into this world mortal by Mary and immortal by God. In fact, the word perfect is best seen in this sense as complete, finished, or fully developed.

The difference in the two passages of scripture above in light of their chronology, and in the context of Jesus' mortal and then immortal state, is an important observation. One that could very easily have been missed if written by a man or men. It stands as one of the many witnesses to me of the divine veracity of the Book of Mormon.

248. LDS disciples of Christ will not always be accepted by mainstream religionists.

"I came unto my own, and my own received me not" (3 Nephi 9:16).

When Jesus came in the meridian of time among the Jews, religious practices were a dominant feature of the Jewish culture. The Mosaic law was supreme. Probably well-meaning rabbis had expanded the law to define and address even the most trivial of daily experiences. Yet, they missed the very heart of the Mosaic law, "Wherefore the law was our schoolmaster to bring us unto Christ" (Galatians 3:24).

Prominent schools of thought, or the prominent religious groups of that time, were the Pharisees and the Sadducees. Among them were Pharisean or Sadducean Scribes, who were sometimes referred to as lawyers and whose function was to develop the Mosaic law in detail.

Jesus collided with the popular religious bodies of his day. He condemned their motivations and practices. "And when thou prayest, thou shalt not be as the hypocrites are: for they love to pray standing in the synagogues and in the corners of the streets, that they may be seen of men" (Matthew 6:5). "But all their works they do for to be seen of men: they make broad their phylacteries, and enlarge the borders of their garments" (Matthew 23:5). Repeatedly, the Lord said, "Wo unto you, scribes and Pharisees, hypocrites" (Matthew 23)! So fearful of losing their base of power and control, even when Jesus clearly declared His divinity and evidenced it by miraculous manifestation, their reaction was to discredit or to seek lawful pretense against Him.

In these days, the Latter-day Saints have never been fully accepted as a Christian faith by some of the prominent Christian Churches and Christian movements. In fact, in the early days of this dispensation, members were viciously attacked and maligned. Joseph Smith was hunted, arraigned, driven, misrepresented, and misunderstood.

Hence, his lifelong question to those who opposed him, "Why persecute me for telling the truth" (Joseph Smith History 1:25)?

We believe in the Only Begotten Son of God, born of the virgin Mary, of Davidic descent, who fulfilled all prophecies of the coming of a Messiah, the Savior of the world. He healed the sick, gave sight to the blind, caused the lame to walk, cleansed lepers, gave hearing to the deaf, raised the dead, and preached the gospel to the poor (Matthew 11:5). We declare that He suffered temptations so that He could succor us empathetically, yet lived a sinless life. Mortal by Mary, divine by God, He took upon himself the sins, pains, afflictions, infirmities, and sickness of all mankind (Alma 7:11-12), causing Him to bleed from every pore in the Garden of Gethsemane, and to willingly give His life to the brutal torment of crucifixion. Yet that was not the end. We testify that He was resurrected from the dead and that He lives today, glorified and standing on the right hand of God the Father. His motivation has always been love for His Heavenly Father, and love for all of mankind, individually.

In reality, such a testimony is not at all antithetic to mainstream Christianity. Puzzling it is to see the reaction of some modern-day Christians to conclude that we somehow worship a different Christ. Likewise though it was at the meridian of time in the reaction of the Jews to the true Savior of all mankind.

249. The Lord knows and keeps His missionaries throughout the world.

Approximately 86,000 missionaries are fanned out across the globe, and ninety-five percent of those are young people eighteen- to twenty-four-years-old, both male and female. Unlike embassies, corporate compounds, or other expatriate communities, missionaries live among the people. Missionaries eat their food, live in their housing, walk their streets, and freely associate among them. Missionaries are often many miles or perhaps even time zones from their Mission President, who is charged with their safety and training. For many of these young missionaries, this is the first time they have been on their own and away from their families.

Think of it! Two young Americans dressed in black shoes, white shirt, tie, and often donning a suit coat. Sisters wear dresses or skirts, always modest and attractive. They have the appearance of being well off and important. Take that to the poorer neighborhoods of the world, where many of our missionaries labor daily, and you might be rightly concerned for their welfare.

One of our sons served in the Los Angeles Spanish-speaking mission some years ago. His areas of service were not the kind he would normally frequent. We have heard from others that the gang members in some of these barrios actually protect the missionaries. They look at them as men of God, preachers, and they respect that. (For which we are grateful.)

Another young man is serving in the Tonga mission and currently is on an island without electricity or running water. Each day the missionaries must fish or farm for their own food. He and his companion sleep on the ground on mats and have no communication with anyone off the island. Their Mission President is several plane hops and a boat ride away.

When I served in Mexico, we were concerned for the sister missionaries who would be out at night in poor neighborhoods, just the two of them. When I talked to the sisters, they were not afraid at all. They knew they were on the Lord's errand and felt His guiding and protective hand.

And so it is throughout this world of such varied cultures, climates, politics, languages, terrains, and people. It is nothing short of miraculous that our missionaries are as safe as they are. It is true that on occasion, a missionary will be killed in an auto accident, at the hand of a lunatic, or by some other means. I do not know if these instances are accidental or if the Lord is calling them to the other side of the veil. But I do know that when they are taken, they were most recently in the very service of the Lord.

The protection afforded our missionaries on such a worldwide scope, and while so embedded among the Lord's children, is remarkable indeed. "Go ye into all the world" and "teach all nations" (Mark 16:15, Matthew 28:19). Surely, the Lord supports those who seek to fulfill this charge.

250. The Church's stance on abortion is rational, firm, and positive.

Perhaps no other issue causes more division in the United States than the issue of abortion. Estimates are that in 2011, over 2,900 abortions were performed each day, 1.06 million each year.[1] And that's just in the United States. The United States represents only about five to six percent of the worldwide abortions performed.[2]

On both sides of the debate, we see a wide pendulum position of fierce and inflexible rhetoric. Pro-choice voices contend vigorously that the woman carrying the child has the right to decide whether to carry it to term or not. Pro-life voices believe passionately that once conceived, the child should be protected and allowed to be born.

Recognizing procreation as a sacred blessing, the Lord's Church weighs in on the side of life. The official Church policy concerning abortion is:

> "The Lord commanded, 'Thou shalt not . . . kill, nor do anything like unto it' (D&C 59:6). The Church opposes elective abortion for personal or social convenience. Members must not submit to, perform, arrange for, pay for, consent to, or encourage an abortion. The only possible exceptions are when:

1. Pregnancy resulted from forcible rape or incest.

2. A competent physician determines that the life or health of the mother is in serious jeopardy.

3. A competent physician determines that the fetus has severe defects that will not allow the baby to survive beyond birth.

> Even these exceptions do not justify abortion automatically. Abortion is a most serious matter and should be considered only after the persons responsible have consulted with their bishops and received divine confirmation through prayer. Church members who submit to, perform, arrange for, pay for, consent to, or encourage an abortion may be subject to Church discipline."[3]

In addition to that very thoughtful position, those who have participated in abortions and later acknowledge its wrongful practice have hope through the concluding sentence of this same policy, "As far as has been revealed, a person may repent and be forgiven for the sin of abortion."[4] Such apparent mercy is made available through the Atonement of Christ, who alone can forgive and make right such regrettable behavior for all parties involved, including the innocent.

The position of the Church on the issue of abortion is clear, yet not extreme. It is measured. It is a position that addresses both the mother and the child, weighing in on the side of life.

Notes

1. The Alan Guttmacher Institute, *Abortion in the United States, Media Kit, Quick Stats.*

2. www.johnstonarchive.net/policy/abortion/wrjp3313.html.

3. *Handbook 2 Administering the Church*, Salt Lake City: The Church of Jesus Christ of Latter-day Saints, 2010, 21.4.1, 195.

4. *Handbook 2 Administering the Church,* 195.

251. The spiritual maturation of those who serve a full-time mission is remarkable.

Almost without exception, when a missionary returns from the mission field, we have two immediate comments, "I can't believe it's been two years already," (or eighteen months in the case of a sister), and "Wow, they've grown so much!" The latter comment is not in reference to their height, but rather to their spiritual growth, their gaining of confidence and poise, their deep love of their Heavenly Father and Jesus Christ, and their general happiness and peace. It is a transforming experience that is unique.

How does such a transformation occur? I would say it is rooted in the truism, "He that loseth his life for my sake shall find it" (Matthew 10:39). Serving a mission is entirely about losing ourselves in the service of others under the direction of the Master. There is no remuneration to be received; in fact, missionaries earn their own support prior to serving. There is no personal agenda taken to the field. Missionaries are taught to be strictly obedient to mission rules and work hard each and every day, with a portion of one day a week to do personal chores and to refresh.

It is also the activities in which they are immersed that bring about such profound change. Their activities school the heart and are vitally connected to and dependent upon communication with the Holy Ghost.

When I left on a mission to Mexico, one of my early letters home related how we spent at least two hours each morning, studying the Bible, the Book of Mormon, and other scriptures. Dad wrote me back that he was pleased to see that we were studying these source materials. I could read between the lines that he was glad that we weren't just re-packaging what we'd been told, but rather we were studying it out for ourselves. Such would lead us to our own convictions and conclusions, particularly because at that point, I myself was a relatively new convert to the faith.

Missionaries pray personally and publicly throughout each day and in earnest. Usually, their prayers express genuine gratitude for the opportunity to serve, petition for continued divine assistance, and always include pleadings on behalf of those whom they are teaching. This continuous, sincere, personal communication is to be in partnership with Him whose labor they are performing.

It is a testament to the truthfulness of the Restored Gospel, that when immersed 24/7 in the prayerful study of it, teaching it, testifying of it, conversing about it, and living it "with an eye single to the glory of God" (D&C 4:5), such a spiritual maturation and rock solid faith are developed in the lives of our young returned missionaries. It is truly a joyous wonder to behold.

252. The LDS colonization of the late 1800's is testament to the reality of the Holy Ghost.

When the Saints arrived in the Salt Lake Valley in 1847, it appeared to be a final gathering place for the Church, one from which they could practice their religion unmolested. It would seem that the task at hand of taming an untamed land would require the best collective effort of all the Saints. Yet, the Lord through His Prophet Brigham Young saw wisdom in sending out groups of Latter-day Saints to colonize and effectually spread the influence and geographical scope of the Church throughout the Western United States.

I've heard it said that some 360 known towns and cities today throughout Arizona, Nevada, Utah, Idaho, Wyoming, and surrounding states were founded by LDS colonizers during the mid to late 1800's. Additionally, settlements in Mexico and Canada were begun and continue to thrive today.

What's interesting to me is that even separated from the central leadership of the Church in Salt Lake City and without the communication we have today, the Church held together. The doctrine, purposes, and culture of the faith seemed equally embedded in Kanab, Utah, as it was in Safford, Arizona, and Rigby, Idaho. That the leading personalities of these founding communities didn't take power and doctrinal interpretation to themselves is remarkable. Perhaps unparalleled. That the people didn't lose focus on the faith in their day-to-day struggle to survive in various harsh untested lands is a common thread that merits our examination.

There was at least one settlement that did lose its focus on the faith and did not share in this common culture of belief. Samuel Brannan led a group of Saints to San Francisco, California in 1846. Under his leadership, the Church and its mission were not given priority over the easy money and business opportunities of the California gold rush. But this experience seemed to be the exception in the very ambitious colonization effort of Brigham Young.

What is that common thread that gave uniformity to the Mormon experience throughout hundreds of settlements in the West? I believe it was the covenant relationship that each Latter-day Saint had entered into with God and the resultant Gift of the Holy Ghost that then directed their conduct. It was a willing submission to authority, order, and divine sequence. It was a desire to sacrifice for a cause greater than self and seek to establish the very Kingdom of God.

That these pioneers didn't lose sight of the faith in their struggle to settle unsettled lands, and that the doctrines, practices, and culture of the Church were preserved so uniformly across such a wide geography is truly remarkable. I believe it is a testament of the reality and influence of the Gift of the Holy Ghost.

253. Latter-day Saints serve when, where, and to whom the Lord will send them.

Last week in a doctors' office, I was left in a third floor corner room for longer than I wanted, so I picked up a local magazine which was a monthly profile of the great city where this office was located. In the magazine were articles of successful community leaders, leading admirable and good lives, who often openly attributed their success and motives to being disciples of Christ. These were people who were educated, well off, socially gifted, healthy, ambitious, and service oriented. As I read the pages, I felt a twinge of envy, that I wanted to be a part of this inner circle of vibrant, pretty people.

That evening, I was scheduled to go out with one of our Priesthood leaders to visit the homes of Church members in the area. I had asked him to prayerfully select whom we would visit. We wanted to go out as servants of the Lord to lift, encourage, and to minister.

We visited two homes that evening. The first was a brother who had been through surgery for a long standing illness and was now home recovering. His was a family of quiet, steady faith, yet not of worldly recognition or status. We had our light conversation, and then we shared scriptural encouragement and joined in prayer.

The second visit was to a brother who was firm in the faith, yet struggled with alcoholism. He was what would have to be considered as uneducated, of poor health, and with very little personal ambition. It was difficult to converse with him because his speech was clumsy and his enunciation was unclear at times. Yet, we felt his conviction that the Church was true and the hope he had in Christ. We likewise shared with him an appropriate scripture of faith and concluded with prayer together.

At the end of the evening, as I got in my car to drive home, I thought to myself, as servants of the Lord, of all the homes and families we could have been directed to that night, we ended up visiting those of simple faith, the most humble, those without worldly acclaim or prominence. And much of the Savior's ministry was likewise.

The work of those good community leaders in the magazine is a similar work—promoting high ideals and Christian virtues and seeking to serve others. To that end, we applaud them as fellow laborers for Christ, and we would add the performance of Priesthood ordinances as so authorized and charged. I should be content in my lot to serve those whom the Lord will direct me to serve.

"Father, where shall I work today?"
And my love flowed warm and free.
Then he pointed out a tiny spot
And said, "Tend that for me."
I answered quickly, "Oh no, not that!
Why, no one would ever see,
No matter how well my work was done.
Not that little place for me."
And the word he spoke, it was not stern;
"Art thou working for them or for me?
Nazareth was a little place,
And so was Galilee."[1]

I consider that poem to be correct Christian doctrine and gratefully accept the opportunities given me to serve the Master. It is an honor to serve the Lord by serving our fellows. I've yet to meet anyone who was not a son or daughter of the Living God.

Notes:

1. Meade MacGuire, "Father, Where Shall I Work Today?" in *Best-Loved Poems of the LDS People,* comp. Jack M. Lyon and others, 1996, 152.

254. Joseph Smith was not the only witness of heavenly manifestations received.

"One of the striking things about the revelations of Joseph Smith is that many of them were shared with others. . . . Isaiah's and Ezekiel's visions were shared with nobody else, the Buddha's enlightenment was very personal, and Muhammad's revelatory experiences were his alone."[1]

It is noteworthy to the earnest seeker of truth, that Joseph Smith is not alone in his claim of divine restoration. Nevertheless, the First Vision and Moroni's early visits were, indeed, his alone. The burden must have been tremendous to a young boy being challenged on these experiences by the religious voices of his locale.

Then came the experience of Oliver Cowdery, David Whitmer, and Martin Harris "that an angel of God [Moroni] came down from heaven, and . . . we beheld and saw the plates, and the engravings thereon" (The Testimony of the Three Witnesses, Book of Mormon). Immediately following this experience, Joseph arrived home and exulted, "Father, Mother, you do not know how happy I am! The Lord has now caused the plates to be shown to three more besides myself. They have seen an angel who has testified to them and they will have to bear witness to the truth of what I have said. For now they know for themselves that I do not go about to deceive the people. I feel as if I was relieved of a burden that was almost too heavy for me to bear."[2]

This was followed by a like experience of eight more persons, all eleven having inscribed their witness to the preface of the Book of Mormon.

In May 1829, Oliver Cowdery and Joseph Smith were ordained to the Aaronic Priesthood under "the hands of an angel, who announced himself as John, the same that is called John the Baptist" (Preface, D&C 13). Later, these two would receive the Melchizedek Priesthood under the hands of the original apostles, Peter, James, and John. Then in 1836, Oliver and Joseph, in the newly dedicated Kirtland Temple, were visited by the Savior Himself (D&C 110). On that same occasion, to restore Priesthood keys to the earth, Moses, Elias, and Elijah also appeared to Oliver and Joseph.

Sidney Rigdon and Joseph Smith together shared the glorious revelatory experience of Section 76 in the Doctrine and Covenants, where they record their testimony of the Savior's presence. "Further, as many as 12 other men may have been in the room at the same time. One of them, Philo Dibble, later said that, although he himself did not see the vision, he 'saw the glory and felt the power' and that he and the others listened as Joseph and Sidney described what they were seeing."[3]

Neither were the revelations recorded in the Doctrine and Covenants transcribed by Joseph Smith, but in almost every case, Joseph was voice, and they were recorded by others, in the presence of others.

Many other heavenly manifestations were received by the early Saints at large, such as at the general sessions of the temple dedication in Kirtland. Such divine experiences were necessary to restore authority and keys, to teach doctrine, and to establish the Church in the hearts of the faithful.

That Joseph welcomed the sharing of these revelatory experiences with those he associated with, speaks to the integrity and the reality of these heavenly manifestations. "In the mouth of two or three witnesses shall every word be established" (2 Corinthians 13:1).

Notes:

1. Daniel C. Peterson, "Defending the Faith: Many of Prophet's Revelations were Shared Experiences," *Deseret News*, February 24, 2011.

2. Lucy Mack Smith, *History of Joseph Smith by his Mother*, Salt Lake City: Bookcraft, 1958, 152.

3. Daniel C. Peterson.

255. The required interviews to enter the holy temples are meaningful and personal.

To receive a recommend (an entrance pass) to attend the temple, a member will interview with a member of his or her Bishopric and a member of the Stake Presidency. In those interviews, the member will be asked a series of questions - designated questions - that are the same in each interview. The questions are designed to assess testimony, moral cleanliness, honesty, family conduct, and adherence to covenants. Additionally, they provide an opportunity to utilize the Atonement of Christ and/or to recognize the great blessing the Atonement is in their life.

I have had the opportunity to both receive a temple recommend and to issue temple recommends, the latter several hundred times. You would think that asking the same questions over and over would get old, but my experience is anything but that. It is a deeply personal communication of those things that are close to the heart. It is direct eye contact. It is an accounting of our personal worthiness to an authorized Priesthood leader. It is a declaration of testimony. It is a confirmation and reminder of things that are most important.

We go to the temple to participate in ordinance work for ourselves first and then subsequently for the deceased—baptisms, ordinations, confirmations, endowments, marriages and family sealings of children to parents. These are eternal, essential, ordinances for all who desire to attain the presence of our Heavenly Father. It enables our covenant relationship with Him. For this reason, the environment of the temple needs to be conducive to the Spirit of the Lord, even to be in preparation for the Lord Himself, should He occasion to visit His temple. A standard of commitment, faith, morality, integrity, and personal cleanliness by those who attend the temple are what invites the Spirit and creates harmony.

The temple recommend interview is so deeply meaningful to individuals, that often I witness their feelings of emotion in the way of tears as they declare their faith and testimony. The level of seriousness and thoughtful, deliberate, response are an indication of the value attached to these core questions.

The final question of the interview is asking members if they consider themselves worthy to enter the Lord's house and participate in these temple ordinances. That is the question most are too humble to acknowledge. But those that recognize the work of the Savior and our imperfect mortal existence, respond with a grateful "yes." We go to the temple by way of open invitation. It is a sacred work. The interview process lifts our vision and commitment and points us to Jesus Christ who is both our model and our Savior.

256. The early morning seminary program for youth is truly remarkable.

At our home, an alarm goes off at 4:30 am, Monday through Friday, and it isn't in the parents' bedroom. It's in Sam's room, our fifteen-year-old sophomore in high school. On his own, he gets up to bathe, breakfast, dress, pray, and whatever else he does to get ready for his day. First stop: Seminary at the Church building at 6:00 am.

There he unites with about ninety other high school youth from the three local high schools and studies under one of several capable teachers. They take the scriptures as their text. Class is about forty-five minutes long. Over the course of four years, he will have studied the Old Testament, the New Testament, the Book of Mormon, and the Doctrine and Covenants.

Each year they are encouraged to memorize twenty-five scriptures, read from the scriptures daily, and to attend seminary at least eighty percent of the time.

This is occurring all over the world. Today, seminary classes are held in every state in the United States and in over 170 countries.[1]

The objective of the Seminary Program "is to help youth understand and rely on the teachings and Atonement of Jesus Christ, qualify for the blessings of the temple, and prepare themselves, their families, and others for eternal life with their Father in Heaven."[2]

There are some nights when Sam is up late for some reason (it should be homework but usually isn't), and I say to him, "Sam, just sleep in tomorrow. It's too late, and you need the sleep." You'd think that would meet with an immediate agreement, but it doesn't. He wants to go to seminary. Part of the lure is the sociality of peers, but part is the spiritual food received that goes to his heart.

Said Elder J. Reuben Clark, Jr. as a charge to seminary teachers in 1938, "The youth of the Church are hungry for things of the spirit; they are eager to learn the Gospel, and they want it straight, undiluted."[3]

The seminary program is impressive on many points: That the next generation can be schooled from the scriptures and the words of the prophets; that young people would come at that time of the morning; that teachers would teach before work or home responsibilities and prepare a forty-five-minute lesson each day; that it has been implemented throughout the world; and that it is voluntary. It is the truths taught and discussed and the Spirit felt that give life to the seminary program.

Notes:

1. Seminary.lds.org/about.
2. Seminary.lds.org/about.
3. J. Reuben Clark, Jr., *The Charted Course of the Church in Education,* Address to seminary and institute of religion leaders at the Brigham Young University summer school in Aspen Grove, Utah, 8 August 1938.

257. The building of the BYU Jerusalem Center in the Holy Land is a miracle.

In 1968, Brigham Young University began a study abroad program in Israel, in order to study the history, culture, nations, and the people of Israel and the Middle East, with a major focus on the life and teachings of Jesus Christ and his Apostles. As the program grew, it became apparent that the building of a permanent facility was needed.

Elder Jeffrey R. Holland, was then commissioner of the Church Educational System, and in September of 1980 was installed as the ninth President of Brigham Young University. He tells of an early experience in 1979 at the outset of this very unlikely project:

> "We found one little, burned out building—a home that was now open to sheep and goats. And we thought maybe we had a chance to buy that, and when President Kimball and President Tanner were over for the dedication of the Orson Hyde Garden, we took them up to see this property. . . . Pres. Tanner walked up with us . . . . and he was monumentally unimpressed. . . . And so he just kept walking, walking up this little path that curved around on the brow of a hill out on what was then open property and stood out looking over the old city of Jerusalem. A stunning view over the Temple mount. There was the wall, and in every direction you could see the hallmark locations of Jerusalem. And he turned to us and said, "This is the piece, get this piece!" Well, you know, he might as well have said "get Times Square," or you know, "get Hyde Park" in London. We launched into all the reasons that this was not doable - political, economic, governmental, religious, archeological, reasons that this was not possible. Anybody, everybody wanted this piece, this piece wasn't supposed to be in the conversation. And so as gently as we could say it, "Pres. Tanner, this wasn't the piece we came to show you. . . ." (When) we were through, (he) said, "Don't tell me your problems, just get the property." And that is the very site upon which the building stands."[1]

That location is Mount Scopus, on the northern end of the Mount of Olives, situated not far from the Hebrew University. "We were told over and over again by Israelis in real estate and government positions that it was impossible to get that site. Everyone wanted it."[2]

Ultimately, BYU was granted a forty-nine year lease for the coveted plot of land with an option to renew. In 1984, when the bulldozers started to carve up the mountain side, so began a controversy that would continue throughout the construction over the next four years.

It was characterized by opponents as a "Mormon Missionary Center." "People wondered how we got permission to build on such a site," [David B.] Galbraith recalls. "Who signed off on this? How could it be that one of the last, most beautiful sites in all Jerusalem would go to a Christian group – and of all groups, the 'Mormons,' who are a proselytizing faith?"[3] It became a worldwide controversy, involving Jewish leaders, former President Gerald Ford, and a joint letter of support from the US Congress, CNN, and other major news outlets. It was so hotly contested that the Israeli government faced internal no-confidence votes on three separate occasions. Meanwhile, the construction continued.

Of the many hurdles, and one beyond anyone's control, was the oversight of the Department of Antiquities. If any relics or ruins were discovered in the excavation, the project would be halted immediately.

"The entire Mount of Olives is filled with tombs," says Galbraith, "Hebrew University encountered many tombs during their construction process."[4] Remarkably, no tombs were found on this site. "It was yet another miracle."[5] "There is no reason that site shouldn't have been peppered with tombs," recalls Dr. Kelly Ogden, "it's as though the Lord had preserved that site for us."[6]

Today the BYU Jerusalem Center stands in harmony with its Jewish hosts, and provides a venue for cultural academics, the arts, and religious studies. Given its panoramic view of Jerusalem, and its distinctive regional architecture, Elder James E. Faust referred to it as "the jewel of the Holy City."[7] I believe its very existence, at once wholly improbable, and by some even impossible, is because of divine intervention.

Notes:

1. Sheri Dew, interview with Elder and Sister Holland, *Conversations,* Episode 22, www.mormonchannel.org/listen/series/conversations-audio/elder-holland-episode-22.
2. Jamie Lawson, "A Jewel of Jerusalem," quote by David B. Galbraith, resident director at the time for the BYU study abroad program, *LDS Living Magazine,* May 15, 2009.
3. Jamie Lawson, "A Jewel of Jerusalem," quote by David B. Galbraith.
4. Jamie Lawson, "A Jewel of Jerusalem," quote by David B. Galbraith.
5. Jamie Lawson, "A Jewel of Jerusalem," quote by David B. Galbraith.
6. Jamie Lawson, "A Jewel of Jerusalem," quote by D. Kelly Ogden, administrative assistant at the time for BYU in Jerusalem.
7. Jamie Lawson, "A Jewel of Jerusalem," a comment by Elder James E. Faust recorded in the journal of D. Kelly Ogden.

258. Brigham Young University is a Disciple Preparation Center first and foremost.

No one would argue with the fact that Brigham Young University Provo is a top tier academic institution. Their Accounting program has been among the top three in the nation for many years running, and both the School of Business and the School of Law are ranked number thirty-three and number thirty-four respectively of said schools in the United States.[1] Academic excellence is achieved through credentialed and industry-active professors, along with the support of the board of directors, who continue this quest for providing high quality education.

Brigham Young University Idaho, within recent years was granted University status. It is, likewise, seeking to improve and distinguish itself academically. In the coming years, we will likely see national recognition for its various programs and colleges. And then, there is Brigham Young University Hawaii, a smaller campus of which I am not too familiar, but which provides well for its international student body.

In August of 2004, then President of BYU Idaho, David A. Bednar said, "Let me suggest that in Rexburg, Idaho, we are in the process of creating not a missionary training center (MTC), but a Disciple Preparation Center—a DPC. In this special and sacred and set apart place, you and I have access to unparalleled spiritual resources that can assist us in developing and deepening our devotion as disciples of the Lord Jesus Christ. That is the primary and most important reason for the existence of Brigham Young University-Idaho and for its sponsorship by and affiliation with The Church of Jesus Christ of Latter-day Saints."[2]

Look at the makeup of the BYUI student body—seventy-nine percent of males have served two year missions, and seventeen percent of the females are likewise returned missionaries.[3] These young people are committed to the Lord, familiar with obedience, scriptural admonition, service, hard work, and sacrifice. They pray daily, shun addictive substances, and live so as to enjoy the guidance of the Holy Ghost. Required classes include scripture study from canonized works and living prophets. Professors are all equally committed disciples of Jesus Christ and serve as mentors as well as teachers.

Perhaps coveted only to its recipient, BYU Provo has been dubbed the Number One "Stone Cold Sober" campus in the country for seventeen years running.[4] This is in contrast to the free flowing beer parties and oftentimes immoral behavior celebrated at other university campuses. Yet even so designated, a more cheerful, optimistic, and socially active environment would be hard to find than in a BYU setting.

This concept as a Disciple Preparation Center is what one would expect from a university sponsored by the Lord's Church. Although certainly not without exceptions, the commitment to high standards and noble ideals, even to a deepening discipleship to the Savior Jesus Christ, is at the core of these University programs and founding principles.

Notes:

1. U.S. News & World Report: Education, *College Ranking Lists,* 2015.
2. David A. Bednar, "Brigham Young University Idaho: A Disciple Preparation Center (DPC)," *Brigham Young University Idaho Devotional,* 31 August, 2004.
3. BYUI website, *Official Enrollment Statistics,* Fall 2014.
4. "Stone Cold Sober Schools," *The Princeton Review*, College Rankings, 2014.

259. There is a distinguishable light in the countenance of a faithful Latter-day Saint.

Paul Harvey, a famous news commentator, visited one of our Church school campuses some years ago. Later he observed, "Each . . . young face mirrored a sort of . . . sublime assurance. These days many young eyes are prematurely old from countless compromises with conscience. But [these young people] have that enviable headstart which derives from discipline, dedication, and consecration."[1] That is quite an observation and quite a compliment as well.

A similar observation took place in the 1980's while the Church was negotiating the lease for the Brigham Young Jerusalem Center. As one of the final requirements of the Israeli government to allow the construction of this beautiful facility, the Church had to sign an agreement not to proselyte in Israel. Elder James E. Faust tells of a conversation he had during these negotiations. "After the lease had been signed, one of our friends insightfully remarked, 'Oh, we know that you are not going to proselyte, but what are you going to do about the light that is in their eyes?' He was referring to our students who were studying in Israel."[2]

There are many scriptural references to light. The following are just a few:

"Let your light so shine before men" (Matthew 5:16).

"Christ shall give thee light" (Ephesians 5:14).

"Ye are all the children of light" (1 Thessalonians 5:5).

"I [Jesus Christ] am the true light that is in you" (D&C 88:50).

The Prophet Alma spoke of this lighted countenance when he queried, "And now behold, I ask of you, my brethren of the church, have ye spiritually been born of God? Have ye received his image in your countenances? . . . I say unto you, can you look up, having the image of God engraven upon your countenances" (Alma 5:14, 19)?

You would expect light in the face of one who carries and lives worthy of the companionship of the Holy Ghost. Born of faith, rooted to covenant commitments, inspired by the teachings of the Savior, and with a love of all men, this optimistic outlook can supersede the temporary disappointments of our mortal journey.

My own experience isn't one hundred percent in picking out of a crowd those who are LDS, but quite often there is a noticeable something about them. In some instances it is dress, mannerisms, words used, or behavior. But more often than not, it is the more ineffable something in the very countenance that perhaps is best described as optimism, trust, belief, enthusiasm, and yes—light.

Notes:

1. Paul Harvey, News broadcast, December 8, 1967, typescript, 1.
2. James E. Faust, "The Light in Their Eyes," *Ensign,* November, 2005.

260. The several recorded accounts of Joseph Smith's First Vision confirm its actuality.

If you search the internet on this topic, the overwhelming volume of sites are written to prove or to conclude the very opposite of what I've stated above. So, I write this chapter in the posture of an apologist and from the firm conviction that this is, in fact, the actual opening scene of the Latter-day restoration.

On at least four different occasions, Joseph Smith either wrote or dictated accounts of his personal First Vision experience. Each was to a different audience, emphasizing different aspects of the experience and with unique constraints on length. The four are:

1. 1832 – A handwritten account by Joseph Smith in his journal as an attempt at a first draft of compiling his history.
2. 1835 – A journal entry under the hand of Warren Parrish, of the Prophet relating to Robert Matthews of his earliest visionary experiences.
3. 1838 – The dictation by Joseph of a carefully considered Church history first published in 1842, which is now the Joseph Smith History in the Pearl of Great Price.
4. 1842 – A response to an inquiry by a newspaper editor, John Wentworth, on the rise of the Church.

There are at least four other written accounts, the first published in Scotland in 1840 by Orson Pratt, another published in Germany by Orson Hyde in 1842. Both are in the form of pamphlets on the doctrines of the Church. Additionally, an interview with Joseph Smith was published by a newspaper editor of the *Pittsburgh Gazette* in 1843. We also have a good account from the journal of Alexander Neibaur in 1844 from a conversation with the Prophet at the Prophet's home.

Furthermore, we have the journal entry of Edward Stevenson recorded in 1834, "The Prophet testified with great power concerning the visit of the Father and the Son, and the conversation he had with them. Never before did I feel such power as was manifested on these occasions."[1]

The first printed account of the First Vision was by Orson Pratt in 1840 and indicates that Joseph had taught of his First Vision experience at least to those who were close to him.

Milton V. Backman Jr., makes an observation against the uniformity the critics are looking for - "In an important way, the existence of these different accounts helps support the integrity of the Latter-day Saint Prophet. It indicates that Joseph did not deliberately create a memorized version which he related to everyone."[2]

I've read the eight written accounts referred to and see no material conflict in the substance of the experience. Each one of them confirms the following, with exceptions as noted:

- Joseph was confused by the religionists of his day and concerned for his soul
- He was inspired of the Bible to pray for an answer to know the truth
- He retired to a secluded place in the woods to pray

- A bright light descended upon him (Orson Hyde account, "enwrapped in a heavenly vision . . . glorious personages")

- He saw two personages in the light (1832 account, "the Lord opened the heavens . . . I saw the Lord and he spake unto me")

- The current religious creeds were not of God (1835 account, not stated)

It is of note that six of the eight accounts include that he must not join any of the churches then in existence. Five record the opposition he encountered while attempting to pray. Four of them tell of his being persecuted for his story. Three make reference to the introduction of the Son by the Father, and two note that he was addressed by name.

Each of the several accounts, related under different circumstances, and to different audiences, corroborate the glorious fact that Joseph saw and communicated with Deity as the opening scene of the Gospel restored to the earth. Joseph's own life corroborates this fact evidenced by his sure and purposeful conduct subsequent to this experience.

I believe Joseph Smith was and is a Prophet of the Lord. Fundamental to that knowledge is that God the Father and His Son Jesus Christ appeared to the boy Joseph to begin this great work of the latter days. I have received, and do receive, a distinct feeling of peace and confidence that comes from this knowledge and personal witness.

Notes:

1. Joseph Grant Stevenson, "The Life of Edward Stevenson," M.A. thesis, BYU, 1955, 19-20.

2. Milton V. Backman, Jr., "Joseph Smith's Recitals of the First Vision," *Ensign*, January, 1985.

261. The first principles and ordinances of the gospel are modeled in the Restoration.

Of our thirteen Articles of Faith, Number Four reads, "We believe that the first principles and ordinances of the Gospel are: first, Faith in the Lord Jesus Christ; second, Repentance; third, Baptism by immersion for the remission of sins; fourth, Laying on of hands for the gift of the Holy Ghost" (Articles of Faith, 4).

The Prophet Nephi refers to this four step process as "the doctrine of Christ" (2 Nephi 31:2), the "strait and narrow path" (2 Nephi 31:18), the "gate" (2 Nephi 31:18) by which we enter.

John the Baptist preached this formula as he prepared the people for the coming of the Lord. "Repent ye: for the kingdom of heaven is at hand. . . . And were baptized of him in Jordan, . . . he shall baptize you with the Holy Ghost, and with fire" (Matthew 3:2, 6, 11).

Richard E. Bennett, a professor of Church History and Doctrine at BYU, shows how this same four-part pattern characterized the opening scenes of the Restoration. He spoke about Joseph Smith and how the Fourth Article of Faith is a universal gate, "the message of the Gospel would have to be lived by the messenger of the Gospel. The integrity of the Restoration would require nothing less."[1] The following is from his lecture in *Joseph Smith's Prophetic Ministry.*

The model of Faith

The whole course of events leading to the restoration of the fullness of the gospel in these latter days began with an act of faith. "I was one day reading the Epistle of James, first chapter and fifth verse, which reads: If any of you lack wisdom, let him ask of God, that giveth to all men liberally, and upbraideth not; and it shall be given him." Joseph's entrance into the grove in 1820 was a sincere act of faith that he would receive as James so promised.

The model of Repentance

Three and one half years after the First Vision, Joseph was visited by the angel Moroni, a resurrected prophet. Moroni instructed Joseph of his forthcoming mission, including revealing the plates upon which the Book of Mormon was written. Joseph and Moroni met annually over a four-year period, through which Joseph "received instruction and intelligence from him at each of our interviews" (Joseph Smith History 1:54). No doubt this four-year period was a time of maturation, of refinement, of preparation, of repentance. In fact, one of the very purposes of angels is "to call men unto repentance" (Moroni 7:31).

The model of Baptism

As Jesus was baptized of John under priesthood authority, so that same authority was conferred upon Joseph Smith and Oliver Cowdery in May of 1829. They were baptized by one another immediately thereafter.

The model of receiving the Gift of the Holy Ghost

John the Baptist "said this Aaronic Priesthood had not the power of laying on hands for the gift of the Holy Ghost, but that this should be conferred on us hereafter" (Joseph Smith History 1:70). And it was, under the hands of the original Apostles Peter, James, and John, enabling them to be "made partakers of the Holy Ghost" (Hebrews 6:4).

Said Jesus to the Nephites "Repent . . . and come unto me and be baptized in my name, that ye may be sanctified by the reception of the Holy Ghost" (3 Nephi 27:20). This is the pattern that each disciple of the Master must follow. It is a sequential progression, placing us firmly "into this strait and narrow path" (2 Nephi 31:19). It is the doctrine of Christ, and it is the pattern that ushered in the Restoration.

Notes:

1. Richard E. Bennett, "Joseph Smith and the First Principles of the Gospel," in Richard Neitzel Holzapfel, editor, *Joseph*

Smith's Prophetic Ministry – 1820-1829, Salt Lake City: Deseret Book, 2009, audio CD, Lecture 2.

262. The pioneering work of the gospel in Africa is an inspiring story.

In June of 1978, President Spencer W. Kimball announced a revelation extending priesthood and temple blessings to all worthy male members of the Church:

> "Aware of the promises made by the prophets and presidents of the Church who have preceded us that at some time, in God's eternal plan, all of our brethren who are worthy may receive the priesthood, and witnessing the faithfulness of those from whom the priesthood has been withheld . . . by revelation [the Lord] has confirmed that the long-promised day has come when every faithful, worthy man in the Church may receive the holy priesthood, with power to exercise its divine authority, and enjoy with his loved ones every blessing that flows therefrom, including the blessings of the temple. Accordingly, all worthy male members of the Church may be ordained to the priesthood without regard for race or color" (Official Declaration – 2).

An address that portrays the growth of the gospel in Africa was given by E. Dale LeBaron at Ricks College, April 3, 2001. That speech is summarized and paraphrased below.[1]

As early as the 1950's, the spirit of the Lord was working in the hearts of the people of Africa in preparation for this revelation. By the 1960's, there were more letters requesting Church literature received from Nigeria and Ghana at Church headquarters than from all the rest of the world combined. In fact, it was reported that in the 1960's, there were over sixty congregations in Nigeria and Ghana, with more than 16,000 participants, none of whom were baptized!

The first missionaries were sent to Africa in late 1978. Anthony Obinna, who had waited for thirteen years for the church to come to Africa and had organized a congregation, was the first to be baptized. That day he was set apart as the first black African branch president and his wife as the first Relief Society president. In one twenty-four-hour period, 149 converts were baptized. Within one year, there were 1,700 members in thirty-five branches. In less than ten years, Elder Neal A. Maxwell organized the Aba Nigeria Stake in which all priesthood leaders were native Africans.

Joseph William Billy Johnson, a preacher, obtained a Book of Mormon in 1964. "As I read the Book of Mormon I became convinced that it was really the word of God, and sometimes while reading I would burst into tears."[2] For fourteen long years prior to 1978, Brother Johnson helped organize ten congregations with over a thousand unbaptized followers. His son may be the only young man in Ghana named Brigham! Twelve years after his own baptism and after several missions, he was ordained a patriarch.

During the first twenty-two years after the revelation of 1978, African membership exploded to 150,000. During the year 2000, sacrament meeting attendance in the West Africa Area was fifty-four percent, second only to the Utah South Area. Elder James A. Mason, a former Africa Area President, tells of a stake conference in West Africa which was attended by 110 percent of the stake membership and there were only eight cars in the parking lot! Africa is the only area of the Church where there are more male members than sisters, providing a strong base of priesthood leadership.

President Gordon B. Hinckley has said that, "the strength of this church lies in the hearts of its people, in the individual testimony and conviction of the truth of this work."[3] The sure witness that Jesus is the Christ, the knowledge of the gospel restored through the Prophet Joseph Smith, the tangible record of the Book of Mormon, and the sustaining of living prophets and apostles form that testimony that burns in the heart of each member. That familiar heartfelt testimony is firmly planted in the unfolding work of the Gospel spreading throughout Africa.

Notes:

1. E. Dale LeBaron, "The Inspiring Story of the Gospel Going to Black Africa," *Ricks College Devotional,* 3 April, 2001.
2. E. Dale LeBaron.
3. Gordon B. Hinckley, "The True Strength of the Church," *Conference Report,* April, 1973.

263. Prophets, apostles, and believers have been imprisoned for their faith.

The apostle Paul gloried in his suffering for Christ, "In labours more abundant, in stripes above measure, in prisons more frequent . . . If I must needs glory, I will glory of the things which concern mine infirmities" (2 Corinthians 11:23, 30).

Throughout the scriptures we read of the faithful who were arrested and/or imprisoned because of their faith and the practice of that faith. A list would include Peter, Paul, "the apostles" (Acts 5), John the Baptist, believers "both men and women" (Acts 22:4), Aaron, Muloki, Ammah, Alma, Amulek, Nephi, the disciples of Jesus, Abinadi, Jeremiah, Joseph, Zedekiah, Daniel, Shadrach, Meshach, Abed-nego, and Joseph Smith and his close associates.

Some may call it lawful persecution, although in many instances it wasn't even within prescribed lawful procedure. Alma and Amulek were arrested "because they had testified so plainly against their wickedness" (Alma 14:3). The ancient apostles were seen as a threat to the Roman status quo. Daniel was arrested for praying, which sprung the trap laid for him by lesser men consumed by jealously (Daniel 6:1-16). Shadrach, Meshach, and

Abed-nego, three youths, stood on principle and refused to "worship the golden image" (Daniel 3:12-18) in lieu of the living God.

Throughout Jesus' public life, the ruling class and religionists of His day continually sought how they might arrest Him and put an end to His teachings. He was a threat to their livelihood. He exposed their disingenuous behavior. He condemned their hypocrisy. He challenged their doctrines. All the while, He ministered to the poor and to the common. He performed miracles among the people—healing the sick, the blind, the lame, even restoring the dead to life. He communed with the heavens, controlled the elements, received the ministry of angels, and openly declared his Divine Sonship.

In the end, Jesus too was imprisoned, ending his mortality by cruel crucifixion on the hill Calvary. Ironically, that was under the charge of blasphemy.

Joseph Smith was also seen as a threat to predominant religious and political leaders of his day. He too was the object of intolerance, ignorance, and cruelty. He was arrested about forty times, tarred and feathered, poisoned, and falsely imprisoned, at one point for over five months. He was finally martyred, along with his brother Hyrum, by a mob while they were held in Carthage Jail in Illinois.

The parallel experiences of Joseph Smith, the faithful saints in scripture, persecutions of Christians through the ages, and even the Savior himself, are consistent with false legal charges and even imprisonment. When we consider the source of such vehement stirrings, we see the devil himself at the helm. We can see who and what cause is of most interest to his diabolical desires to dismantle and to destroy the Kingdom of God.

264. The cheerful and optimistic outlook of Joseph Smith is testament to his genuineness.

If Joseph were a fraud, he had a lot to cover up, such as the visit of the Father and the Son to him as a fourteen-year-old boy and the Angel Moroni instructing him on the work of the latter days and leading him to gold plates buried in the hill Cumorah. He would have had to have collusion with eleven other men who gave written testimony to having seen the actual gold plates from which the Book of Mormon was translated. The revelations he received and which are written were received in the presence of others, as was the vision of Jesus Christ while with Sidney Rigdon (D&C 76). The coming of the resurrected John the Baptist to restore priesthood authority by the laying on of hands was to both Joseph Smith and Oliver Cowdery. After which, they "went and were baptized. I baptized him [Oliver] first, and afterwards he baptized me" (Joseph Smith History 1:71). He would have had to fake the harrowing experience of the night he received the plates when he was followed and accosted in actuality. The printing of the Book of Mormon, an ambitious first printing by current standards, would have been subject to the "real" author coming forward to charge plagiarism. Or if written by Joseph, we would have seen indications in the other contemporaneous writings of Joseph Smith with the literary style he used. What we do see is a young man who wrote with poor spelling and very unpolished construction.

And these represent only a small part of the story of the restoration Joseph would have had to manage and keep in concert.

Certainly, the way the Church unfolded over the years could not have been according to what Joseph had expected. It was anything but an easy ride. Joseph never attained riches. He was constantly persecuted and saw his closest friends waver and abandon the faith. He and his followers wandered as an unwelcome people through four states.

Joseph experienced those who believed in him die at the hands of mobsters, disease, and extreme hardship.

Such a heavy price would have even weighed upon the mind of a fraud. And colluding souls would have come clean to recant previous claims.

But Joseph was cheerful throughout all the pressures and burdens he was saddled with. He was a man quite comfortable in his own skin. He was a visionary leader because he received visions. His perseverance was born of factual encounters. BYU Professor Mark D. Ogletree has written, "Moreover, the Prophet understood that God was his partner, and if he failed, or the work failed, it meant that God had failed. Since God does not fail, Joseph understood that neither he nor this work would fail."[1] To Joseph, it was just that simple. And just that pure.

Joseph's optimistic and even cheerful outlook amid overwhelming challenges is truly remarkable. It is rooted in personal experience with the divine and the resultant submissive, obedient, trusting relationship towards God and his Son, developed from a very young age. To me, it stands as an historical signature, that he was who he said he was.

Notes:

1. Mark D. Ogletree, "Joseph Smith and the Spirit of Optimism," in *Religious Educator* 13, no. 2, 2012, 161-183.

265. The Missionary Training Centers are oases of the Spirit.

Every Wednesday, new missionaries are dropped off at the curbside of the MTC, kiss their families goodbye for two years, and march forward into the unfamiliar world of intense missionary preparation. And every Wednesday night, prayers of gratitude, humility, and devotion go up to God for the beginning of this marvelous experience.

Think of the interest the Lord must have in this portion of his vineyard. In Provo, there are about 3,500 young men and young women, recently declared worthy of the very high standards of required conduct by their Bishops and Stake Presidents, willing to pay probably all that they've saved up to this point of their lives (usually thousands of dollars), eager to serve, and obedient to their call and to their charge. At the MTC, Apostles and Seventies will visit them weekly to teach and train them. Missionaries will participate in temple ordinances weekly, and they will lay aside the cares of the world to be missionaries 24/7.

Here they will learn from the scriptures and *Preach My Gospel*. They will pray frequently throughout the days. They will practice listening to and acting upon the promptings of the Spirit, and they will even practice memorization while exercising.

These young men and young women are on fire with enthusiasm and interest in what they are doing. How is it that young adolescents willingly wear suits and ties, dresses and dress shoes, practice language and teaching skills ten to twelve hours a day, and have no cell phones or Facebook? It is because of the Spirit of the Lord that is present in the MTC and that the missionaries feel that influence.

It is the influence of love—love of the Lord, and by extension, love of their fellows. As Enos in the Book of Mormon related after his own personal conversion, "I began to feel a desire for the welfare of my brethren, the Nephites; wherefore, I did pour out my whole soul unto God for them" (Enos 1:9).

The Lord said, "He that findeth his life shall lose it: and he that loseth his life for my sake shall find it" (Matthew 10:39). Truly, this is lived out in the Missionary Training Center experience. The anticipation of entering their field of labor to help others to receive the restored gospel of Jesus Christ is selfless and motivating. The structure of the entire experience is unparalleled anywhere in the world or in any preceding generation.

There are fifteen missionary training centers throughout the world in North, Central, and South America, Europe, Africa, New Zealand, Dominican Republic, and the Philippines.

In a world of increasing focus on self, personal recognition, and personal advantage, we see these MTC models as fresh and unique. As the world hastens towards self-absorption, the yield of happiness is increasingly diminished. In contrast, those preparing to serve at the Missionary Training Centers throughout the earth are living their dream and experiencing a joy that can only come from obedience to God and a commitment of selfless service to their fellowmen. It is a sustaining witness of the divine work in which they are engaged.

266. The ward is a unique unit of the Lord's worldwide Church and Kingdom.

Unlike other churches, who compete within a given market for attendees, there is no advertising budget, mailers, or special lecture series events that are designed to attract someone to a given ward or stake within the Church.

In fact, a baptized member of the Church is automatically a member of the ward or branch in which they geographically reside. When arriving in a new locale, there is no shopping for a church family or a likable preacher. It's not necessary to find a comfortable doctrine or a convenient meeting schedule.

"Now therefore ye are no more strangers and foreigners, but fellow-citizens with the saints, and of the household of God" (Ephesians 2:19).

This fellowship is worldwide. "One Lord, one faith, one baptism" (Ephesians 4:5).

Following the baptismal ordinance I attended a few weeks back, the last speaker on the program was the local Bishop who welcomed the new convert into the ward. At the baptism, were many from the ward that this new member would be folded into. The Bishop spoke of the ward family that this new member now belonged to, and in using that familiar word, made an accurate characterization.

A ward is a community of believers. Believers are obedient to the will of the Lord, love and serve one another, and sacrifice for the building of the Kingdom of God on the earth. Believers follow a common shepherd, the Bishop, who is ordained of God to this unsought-after position. Believers seek not their own, but are willing to "lift from where they are standing"[1] and create the very community that contributes to the larger worldwide Church community.

Serving in the capacity of a Bishop some years ago, I knew a young family who was fellowshipped into the Church by some friends they had from across town. After they were baptized, because of the geographical boundaries, they actually resided in a different ward than did their friends. Their Church records automatically were created in the ward where they lived. At first, they had a difficult time understanding why they couldn't just continue to attend the ward in which their friends attended and where they had begun to establish new friends.

I called them into my office and tried to explain how the Lord's Church is organized. I was concerned that they might not like the way He has so arranged things. But to my relief, and delight, they saw their new ward as where the Lord would have them be and eagerly got involved and made new and additional relationships.

The wards and stakes of Zion are the gathering places for the house of Israel in these last days. "I'll go where you want me to go, dear

Lord"[2] is more than words to a hymn for Latter-day Saints. It refers to where in the Lord's vineyard we might labor for Him. There, we are shoulder to shoulder with our brothers and sisters, serving in our ward family.

Notes:

1. Dieter F. Uchtdorf, "Lift Where You Stand," *Ensign,* October, 2008.

2. Mary Brown, "I'll Go Where You Want Me to Go," *Hymns of the Church of Jesus Christ of Latter-day Saints*, Salt Lake City: The Church of Jesus Christ of Latter-day Saints, 1985, 270.

267. Regarding Blacks and the Priesthood, the faithful have waited on the Lord.

In 1978, a revelation was given to President Spencer W. Kimball, "that the long-promised day has come when every faithful, worthy man in the Church may receive the holy priesthood" (Official Declaration - 2).

To understand why black people could not be ordained to the priesthood previous to 1978 is inconclusive. We know that Joseph Smith ordained at least one black man, Elijah Abel to the priesthood. Others were ordained during that time period and subsequent to that, as well. Even during Joseph Smith's lifetime, it was not clear as to the doctrine of blacks and the priesthood. After his martyrdom, it never got much clearer.

However the priesthood ban began, it was in the wisdom of God, albeit unexplainable by man. Many tried to retrofit the practice to the scriptures, citing the "mark of Cain" (Genesis 4:15) and the curse of Ham (Genesis 9:18-25), but in reality those arguments were Protestant means to Biblically justify slavery. It should be noted that the early beginnings of this Church were contemporary to this attitude and prevailing Christian outlook, although the Church was always anti-slavery in its position.

Here's what we do know and the reason for my including this as a tenet of my faith. During the super-charged civil rights movement of the 1960's, the First Presidency and the Quorum of the Twelve issued a position statement "with regard to the Negro"[1] dated December 15, 1969, to the leadership of the Church. Rather than cave to intense public pressure, they reaffirmed a doctrinal underpinning of our theology: "The Church of Jesus Christ of Latter-day Saints owes its origin, its existence, and its hope for the future to the principle of continuous revelation. . . . Until God reveals His will in this matter, to him we sustain as a prophet, we are bound by that same will."[2] Even amid uncertain origins, intense public pressure, and personal struggles some of the leading brethren had with the position on Blacks and the priesthood, the Church remained patient on the Lord to reveal His will.

President David O. McKay said that "he had pleaded and pleaded with the Lord, but had not had the answer he sought."[3]

Elder Jeffrey R. Holland expressed his pre-1978 feelings, "There's no issue in all my life that I had prayed more regarding—praying that it would change. . . . I was loyal to the position and the brethren and the whole concept, but there was nothing about which I had anguished more or about which I had prayed more."[4]

In that same interview, Elder Holland said, "One clear-cut position is that the folklore must never be perpetuated. . . . I have to concede to my earlier colleagues. . . . They, I'm sure, in their own way, were doing the best they knew to give shape to [the policy], to give context for it, to give even history to it. All I can say is however well intended the explanations were, I think almost all of them were inadequate and or wrong. . . . We simply do not know why that practice, that policy, that doctrine was in place."[5]

Similarly, we have only conjecture why the Savior commanded his disciples in their preaching to "Go not into the way of the Gentiles, and into any city of the Samaritans enter ye not" (Matthew 10:5). But they accepted it on faith. It was faith in His infinite wisdom, faith that God loves his children, faith that He "sent not his Son into the world to condemn the world; but that the world through him might be saved" (John 3:17). In time, we see that the restriction to the Gentiles and the Samaritans was lifted (Acts 10).

When God speaks, man will always be the intended beneficiary. And eternally speaking, all blessings will be available to all of His children—In His way, in His time, and according to His eternal view. We believe in ongoing revelation from God.

Notes:

1. *First Presidency Statement,* December 15, 1969.
2. *First Presidency Statement,* December 15, 1969.
3. David O. McKay as told to Marion D. Hanks, recorded in Spencer W. Kimball, *Lengthen Your Stride,* Salt Lake City: Deseret Book, 2005, chapter 20 working draft, 13.
4. PBS, "The Mormons: Interview with Jeffrey Holland," March 4, 2006, www.pbs.org/mormons/interviews/holland.html.
5. PBS.

268. Church discipline is both responsible and compassionate.

In the first eleven verses of John Chapter 8, we see the contrast between the judgment of men and the judgment of God. The scribes and Pharisees, in all their self-righteousness, brought a woman taken in adultery and asked Jesus if he agreed with the law of Moses that she should be stoned. Theirs was a desire for punishment, lawful justice, and public humiliation. Jesus cared more about the sinner and turning from transgression. His comment to the woman to "Go, and sin no more" (John 8:11), if indeed heeded, accomplished this and more.

Clearly, the Lord has given scriptural injunction to a code of righteous behavior, the willful violation of which puts us out of harmony with God. Many of our transgressions involve another person or persons, and thereby, create innocent victims. As an institution, those actions of the members of the Church that would impair the good name or the moral influence of the Church must be dealt with.

I have sat in on several occasions of both formal and informal Church discipline councils. In each instance, I cannot ever remember feeling anger or a desire for Church or personal retribution. Rather, there were feelings of love and compassion, a collective desire of those present to help and to give hope, pointing to the Savior and His Atoning sacrifice for sin.

In practice, and in fact, the stated purposes of Church discipline are:

- To save the souls of the transgressors
- To protect the innocent
- To safeguard the purity, integrity, and good name of the Church

By revelation, the procedure for fair review of a case at the stake level, is recorded in Doctrine and Covenants Section 102. Of the fifteen men present, six represent the accused, and six represent the interests of the Church. Depending on the difficulty of the case, and after the evidence has been presented and discussed, up to three persons will speak on behalf of the accused and up to three on behalf of the Church. The entire process to this point includes the participation and candid comments of the person for which the council was convened. A spouse or others who may lend support or information may also be invited to attend.

Outcomes of Church discipline can be informal probation (between a bishop and a member), formal probation, disfellowshipment, or excommunication (the result of a disciplinary council). Excommunication relieves a person from his or her covenants going forward, as well as the enjoyment of any privileges of Church membership.

It is a personal responsibility of Bishops and Stake Presidents to help members overcome transgression through faith in Jesus Christ and sincere repentance. True repentance requires time and genuine contrition. The fruits of true repentance are a greater commitment to the commandments of the Lord, full fellowship with the saints, peace with God, and a deep gratitude for the Savior. These blessings cannot be received by casual or instantaneous assent.

Church discipline can be a tremendous, eternal blessing to all those involved. It is an exercise of love and responsible shepherding by those given that authority of the Lord.

269. Child or spouse abuse is neither kept confidential nor passively dealt with.

Just months after I was called to serve as a Bishop, a young man tearfully confessed to me that he had been involved with an older man in the ward in acts of sexual perversion and the viewing of pornography. Clearly this young man had been led into this behavior by the older man and was now the victim.

My initial reaction was to confront this man and to deal with him personally as his Bishop. I was afraid that if this became public, it could be damaging to the Church. I called our Stake President to confer on the matter, and he, without further discussion, insisted that I call the Church Headquarters help line for cases of abuse and report it. They would then direct me on how to proceed.

So I made the call. Immediately, they took control of the situation. They told me that this would have to be reported to Texas Child Protective Services and to the local authorities. I balked, saying that I did not want this to be made public, particularly within our city. I mentioned the rights of clergy to hold in confidence matters of confession and matters of a personal nature. They firmly counseled me that this was not an optional decision, and if I refused, I would be released as a Bishop without delay, and they would pursue the case with the proper authorities.

"The Church's position is that abuse cannot be tolerated in any form. . . . All members . . . are encouraged to be alert and diligent and do all they can to protect children and others against abuse and neglect."[1]

The Church has created a DVD entitled "Protect the Child: Responding to Child Abuse" and encourages all ward leaders to view this DVD and to discuss it. All those called to work with Young Men in the Scouting program are required to take similar training, "Youth Protection," and to have a background check prior to serving.

Members who have abused others are subject to Church discipline. The first responsibility of the Church is to help those who have been abused and to protect those who may be vulnerable to future abuse.

"But whoso shall offend one of these little ones which believe in me, it were better for him that a millstone were hanged about his neck, and that he were drowned in the depth of the sea" (Matthew 18:6).

In a world where child abuse and spousal abuse is on the rise, and with seeming reticence to confront it head on, the Church has a solid procedure in place to deal with even suspected situations of abuse and to involve proper authorities according to law and prudence. And rightly so.

Notes:

1. *Handbook 2 Administering the Church*, Salt Lake City: The Church of Jesus Christ of Latter-day Saints, 2010, 21.4.2.

270. Fast and Testimony Meetings bless both the testator and the hearer.

For a long time, I wondered why we go to such great lengths to see that we have an opportunity for Fast and Testimony Sacrament Meetings twelve times per year. Normally, the meetings occur on the first Sunday of each month. General Conference falls on those Sundays twice a year, and sometimes Stake Conferences do likewise. But in those cases, Fast and Testimony Sunday is moved to a Sunday either prior to, or subsequent to the conference. It is rarely, if at all, dispensed with until the next month.

"For members of the Church of Jesus Christ of Latter-day Saints, the term *testimony* is a warm and familiar word in our religious expressions. It is tender and sweet. It has always a certain sacredness about it. When we talk about testimony, we refer to feelings of our heart and mind rather than an accumulation of logical, sterile facts. It is a gift of the Spirit, a witness from the Holy Ghost that certain concepts are true."[1]

"Neither is man capable to make them known [the mysteries of the kingdom], for they are only to be seen and understood by the power of the Holy Spirit, which God bestows on those who love him, and purify themselves before him; To whom he grants this privilege of seeing and knowing for themselves" (D&C 76:116-117).

To know for oneself is a personal testimony of truth. "And by the power of the Holy Ghost ye may know the truth of all things" (Moroni 10:5).

When we share our testimonies, as in Fast and Testimony meetings, the Holy Ghost is able to confirm those truths to our own heart and to the hearts of the listeners, "that all may be edified" (D&C 84:110, 88:122).

At times, some may sit in a Fast and Testimony meeting and feel like, "Oh no, not again," or "It's all the same thing. I know the Church is true..." Yet each expression is personal and heartfelt. Each is an opening and a sharing of one's soul, of the innermost feelings. Thus each is a sacrosanct experience for the individual bearing testimony.

As with the giving of a gift, both the giver and the receiver are blessed in the expression of a genuine testimony. How beautiful are these choice meetings of sharing testimony, particularly while in the attitude of fasting. Such meetings strengthen, ennoble, encourage, refresh, renew, and spawn feelings of gratitude, devotion, and unity. They are spiritual occasions. It is a hallmark of Latter-day Saint believers and inspired by an all-wise Heavenly Father.

Notes:

1. 1. Dieter F. Uchtdorf, "The Power of a Personal Testimony," *Ensign,* November, 2006.

271. Sections 121, 122, and 123 of the Doctrine and Covenants were bought at a high price.

The year was 1838, and it was a troubled time of open persecution toward the Church, and for Joseph Smith, most particularly. Unjustly jailed with six other men, their rough stone dungeon measured fourteen by fourteen feet, with a ceiling height of six feet. Dirt, stones, and some straw made their floor and served as their bed. The period of incarceration was in the dead of winter, December 1 through early April. They were ill prepared for such temperatures. Two small barred windows allowed both minimal light and the free flow of cold winds. The food they were given was so filthy that one of the prisoners said they "could not eat it until [they] were driven to it by hunger."[1] Joseph recorded that the entire experience was a "hell, surrounded with demons . . . where we are compelled to hear nothing but blasphemous oaths, and witness a scene of blasphemy, and drunkenness and hypocrisy, and debaucheries of every description."[2]

"Our souls have been bowed down,"[3] and "my nerve trembles from long confinement."[4]

Yet it was during that bleak time that Joseph penned some of the most sublime verses in all of scripture, received as revelation and given as counsel to the Saints. The following are a sample of these treasured three sections from the Doctrine and Covenants:

> "My son, peace be unto thy soul; thine adversity and thine afflictions shall be but a small moment" (D&C 121:7).
>
> "No power or influence can or ought to be maintained by virtue of the priesthood, only by persuasion, by long-suffering, by gentleness and meekness, and by love unfeigned; By kindness and pure knowledge, which shall greatly enlarge the soul without hypocrisy, and without guile" (D&C 121:41, 42).
>
> "Let thy bowels be full of charity to all men . . . and let virtue garnish thy thoughts unceasingly" (D&C 121:45).
>
> "And if thou shouldst be cast into the pit . . . if the very jaws of hell shall gape open the mouth wide after thee, know thou, my son, that all these things shall give thee experience, and shall be for thy good. The Son of Man hath descended below them all. Art thou greater than he" (D&C 122:7-8)?
>
> "Therefore . . . let us cheerfully do all things that lie in our power; and then may we stand still, with the utmost assurance, to see the salvation of God, and for his arm to be revealed" (D&C 123:17).

Such calming perspective, charitable entreaty, and cheerful optimism flow to and from a man of virtuous character. "He certainly turned adversity into blessing in giving us those sacred writings and reflections, so pure, noble, and Christian in both tone and content, yet produced in such an impure, ignoble, and unchristian setting."[5]

Like Job of the Old Testament, who said, "For I know that my Redeemer liveth" (Job 19:25) and Nephi in the Americas, who said,

"Nevertheless, I know in whom I have trusted" (2 Nephi 4:19), Joseph was a man of guileless, unshakable faith. He was and is a Prophet of God.

Notes:

1. As cited in Dean C. Jessee, "Walls, Gates, and Screeking Iron Doors: The Prison Experience of Mormon Leaders in Missouri, 1838-1839," in Davis Bitton and Maureen Ursenbach Beecher, New Views of Mormon History: A Collection of Essays in Honor of Leonard J. Arrington, Salt Lake City: University of Utah Press, 1987, 27.

2. *History of the Church of Jesus Christ of Latter-day Saints,* Salt Lake City: Deseret Book, 1964, 3:290.

3. Joseph Smith, Jr., "Communications," Times and Seasons 1, no. 6, April 1840, 85.

4. Joseph Smith, Jr., Letter to Emma Smith, March 21, 1839.

5. Jeffrey R. Holland, "Lessons from Liberty Jail," *Ensign,* September, 2009.

272. Charisma is not a criteria for local or general Church leadership.

A friend of mine shared a recent experience that he and his wife had at a restaurant. At the table next to them were four men sharing ideas on how to increase attendance for their congregation. Interested, this couple listened in. Much was discussed regarding the caliber of the pastor who preached the sermon on Sunday. Should he be replaced with a more dynamic speaker? Was he attracting new parishioners? Do they have the right preacher to grow their church?

What would that conversation have been like if four of our bishops were seated and having a similarly themed conversation? The focus would be on helping the membership feel of the Spirit, engage in more consistent personal worship, draw nearer to the Savior, reject evil worldly influences, and embrace the wholesome. The conversation would be centered around helping the members learn to fish for themselves, rather than providing an increasingly attractive and enticing array of common seafood.

When a bishop in the Church is chosen, the criteria given to make that selection is in part summarized by Timothy in the New Testament, "A bishop then must be blameless, the husband of one wife, vigilant, sober, of good behaviour, given to hospitality, apt to teach; Not given to wine, no striker, not greedy of filthy lucre; but patient, not a brawler, not covetous; One that ruleth well his own house, having his children in subjection with all gravity . . . Not a novice. . . . He must have a good report of them which are without" (1 Timothy 3:1-7).

Worthiness to serve is a further summation of the criteria for Church service and leadership—not effectiveness, not energy, not education, not stature. Worthiness is measured by firm discipleship to the Lord and a humble, teachable heart.

Of those worthy to serve, the Lord makes the call through revelation to his servants, just as described in the choosing of King David by Samuel. After presenting the most likely candidate of Jesse's seven sons, we read, "But the Lord said unto Samuel, Look not on his countenance, or on the height of his stature; because I have refused him: for the Lord seeth not as man seeth; for man looketh on the outward appearance, but the Lord looketh on the heart" (1 Samuel 16:7).

Finally, the youngest son, and the least likely candidate, was presented, "And the Lord said, Arise, anoint him: for this is he" (1 Samuel 16:12).

Selecting leadership in the Church is an inspired process. It is not deliberated over by a board of directors. It is not in view of profit.

It is not according to charisma. It is not by personal preference. It is entirely "For the perfecting of the saints, for the work of the ministry, for the edifying of the body of Christ" (Ephesians 4:12). It is rooted in faith that the Lord continues to inspire his servants according to the pattern described, "Arise, anoint him; for this is he" (1 Samuel 16:12).

273. The official name of the Church is by divine decree.

"For thus shall my church be called in the last days, even The Church of Jesus Christ of Latter-day Saints" (D&C 115:4). This definitive naming of the Church occurred in April of 1838, fully eight years after the church was organized by lawful charter.

The Church was originally registered under that charter simply as "The Church of Christ" and was referenced as such in sections 20, 21, 42, 102, and 107 of the Doctrine and Covenants, all chronologically prior to the above declaration of the Lord. Paul referred to the early churches as geographically organized, and collectively spoken of as "the churches of Christ" (Romans 16:16).

In May of 1834, Joseph Smith changed the name of the Church to "The Church of the Latter Day Saints," likely to distinguish its unique mission as a restored church, a restoration of the original Church from the time of Christ.

The Lord's naming of his church in section 115 is arguably long in conversation but clear and complete as a doctrinal statement.

To the Nephites, the resurrected Lord settled their disputes as to the naming of the Church with this recorded dialogue, "And they said unto him: Lord, we will that thou wouldst tell us the name whereby we shall call this Church; for there are disputations among the people concerning this matter. And the Lord said unto them: . . . ye shall call the Church in my name . . . And how be it my Church save it be called in my name? For if a Church be called in Moses' name then it be Moses' Church; or if it be called in the name of a man then it be the Church of a man; but if it be called in my name then it is my Church, if it so be that they are built upon my gospel" (3 Nephi 27:3-8).

Churches are variously named for their peculiar methods (Methodist, Christian Scientist), an adopted patron saint (St. Thomas Aquinas Episcopal), a locale, a particular claim to Biblical moorings, or a host of other name bases.

Churches are also sometimes named after their founders—Lutheran (Martin Luther), Amish (Jacob Ammann), and Calvinist (John Calvin). The Church of Jesus Christ of Latter-day Saints is named after its founder as well, as declared by His own mouth, and stands as His duly authorized Kingdom on earth today.

274. Oliver Cowdery was a faithful witness to many key scenes of the Restoration.

If the Prophet Joseph Smith were a fake, Oliver Cowdery would be the one credible voice to step forward to make that claim. Known as the Second Elder of the Church, it was he who assisted as scribe in the translation of the Book of Mormon and then was given oversight of its publishing. It was he who knelt in the presence of John the Baptist and received the Aaronic Priesthood along with Joseph and later the Melchizedek Priesthood under the resurrected hands of Peter, James, and John. Oliver is the first signer as a witness to see the actual plates from which the Book of Mormon was translated and testify that the occasion was at the hands of an angel sent from God. His belief in the revelations received by Joseph Smith is demonstrated by his editing and seeing to the publication of the Doctrine and Covenants in 1835. Oliver was such a significant player in the opening scenes of the Restoration that his name is referred to in at least twenty-three of the 112 sections (revelations) received prior to March of 1838. That is one in five sections. One of those revelations is the account of Joseph and Oliver in the Kirtland temple, where they "saw the Lord standing upon the breastwork of the pulpit" (D&C 110:2). On that same sacred occasion, Joseph received vital priesthood keys from Moses, Elias, and Elijah, to which Oliver was witness.

Yet in spite of all these unique and magnificent experiences, Oliver left the Church in March of 1838. His reasons were various, including disagreement with the direction of the Church in temporal matters and his own financial troubles which were intertwined with his Church affiliation.

With all the persecution of the Church during this time, one could only imagine the clamor from those opposed to the Church to convert Oliver Cowdery into an expert witness against the founding claims of Joseph Smith. Yet that never occurred. In his ten years outside the Church, there is no direct evidence that Oliver ever denied his testimony.

And then in 1848, Oliver returned to be with the Saints and was rebaptized into the Church. He died two years later, firm in the faith. Just before rejoining the Church, he penned his inner hopes to fellow witness David Whitmer, "Let the Lord vindicate our characters, and cause our testimony to shine, and then will men be saved in his kingdom."[1]

Oliver Cowdery played a key role in the unfolding of the Lord's work in these latter days. Although for a season he was unable to reconcile his own personal agenda with that of the Lord's Kingdom, yet he remained true to the trust placed in him and proved to be a faithful witness of the restoration through the Prophet Joseph Smith.

Notes:

1. Oliver Cowdery to David Whitmer, July 28, 1847, *Ensign of Liberty*, 1:92, as quoted by Richard Lloyd Anderson.

275. People do leave the Church, but they often do not lose their testimonies.

The Lord set the highest of standards when he declared, "Therefore I would that ye should be perfect even as I, or your Father who is in heaven is perfect" (3 Nephi 12:48). Compare that absolute standard with this prevalent attitude of many: "Eat, drink, and be merry; nevertheless, fear God—he will justify in committing a little sin; yea, lie a little, take the advantage of one because of his words, dig a pit for thy neighbor; there is no harm in this; and do all these things, for tomorrow we die; and if it so be that we are guilty, God will beat us with a few stripes, and at last we shall be saved in the kingdom of God" (2 Nephi 28:7-8).

Which would be the easier doctrine to follow? Which would cause the least feelings for self-examination or even constructive guilt? Which approach has the power to bring us back to the presence of God "that ye may become the sons of God; that when he shall appear we shall be like him" (Moroni 7:48)?

The doctrines of the Church are often described as familiar, or intuitive, to those being taught by our missionaries. For example, the fact that we existed prior to this life, that we are spirit children of a living God, that families are eternal, that each individual chooses the course of his or her own life, that we sin and cannot resolve that on our own, that scripture is inspired, and that we are accountable for our actions.

When people leave the faith, it is often the case that they don't stop believing the doctrine, but they stop living the commandments. Perhaps, they decide it is just too hard, and they lose sight of the grace of the Savior to make up the difference "after all we can do" (2 Nephi 25:23). Or they just get entangled in the things of this world and crowd out the need for spiritual maintenance.

Interestingly, I've observed that among most of our inactive members, there is still a belief residing in their hearts. Although they may not live their faith in practice, they still retain a belief that God lives, Jesus is the Christ, Joseph Smith was their prophet, the Book of Mormon is true, and that we have a prophet on the earth today.

Truly, the way is strait and narrow, but for those who persevere, it is the path "which leadeth unto life" (Matthew 7:14). It is a testimony to the power of the Spirit, that once a witness is received, "he will manifest the truth of it unto you, by the power of the Holy Ghost" (Moroni 10:4), it is often an indelible experience.

276. The Church is leading the way in gathering family history information.

Joseph Smith alluded to the restored doctrine of performing baptisms for the dead in 1836 and 1838, but it was at his preaching of an August, 1840 funeral sermon for Seymour Brunson (a bodyguard of the prophet) that the doctrine was first made public in Nauvoo.[1] Early revelations on the work of baptisms for the dead were given in January 1841 (D&C 124) and September 1842 (D&C 127 and 128). Wilford Woodruff commented on these revelations, "I remember well the first time I read the revelation given through the Prophet Joseph concerning the redemption of the dead—one of the most glorious principles I had ever become acquainted with on earth. . . . Never did I read a revelation with greater joy than I did that revelation."[2]

The early Saints responded with such enthusiasm and joy, that they waded into the Mississippi River and performed baptisms on behalf of their deceased ancestors, with Joseph Smith leading the way.[3] Letters were sent to relatives seeking family history information, such as this request from Jonah Ball, "I want you to send me a list of fathers relations his parents & Uncles & their names, also Mothers. I am determined to do all I can to redeem those I am permitted to."[4]

This doctrine of vicarious ordinances for the dead is something that we continue to take seriously and has given birth to the ambitious work of Family History, or genealogical, research. So important is this work to the human family, that people throughout the world, both members of the Church and those not of our faith, are participating in ever increasing numbers and zeal. The classic book, *Roots: The Saga of an American Family*, by Alex Haley, published in 1976, seemed to be a catalyst to what could be called a revolution in genealogical interest across the earth.

The extent of our interest in Family History as a Church is impressive and is leading and facilitating the efforts of people across the earth who get involved with seeking out their own roots. The Church has over 4,500 local family history centers in over seventy countries, all staffed by volunteers, all free of charge to the public. There are currently approximately two hundred camera projects on locations digitizing census, birth, death, marriage, and other individual and family documentation in over forty-five countries. Currently, the Church owns some 2.4 million rolls of genealogical microfilm, totaling some fifteen billion records that are being indexed and entered into the searchable on-line data base provided and maintained by the Church. Countless other physical records exist throughout the world. Housed in Salt Lake City is the largest Family History Library in the world, containing records from over 110 countries, including books, film, periodicals, microfiche, microfilm, and electronic resources. Over two thousand people visit the library each day from various parts of the world. The library is staffed by about eight hundred people; seven hundred are volunteers.

Yes, we take seriously the charge to seek out our kindred dead and are witnessing the prophecy of Malachi (which was quoted to the Prophet Joseph Smith by Moroni) that "he shall plant in the hearts of the children the promises made to the fathers, and the hearts of the children shall turn to their fathers" (Joseph Smith History, 1:39, see Malachi 4:6, 3 Nephi 25:6). Joseph Smith taught that "neither can we without our dead be made perfect" (D&C 128:15).

So we labor to identify our ancestors, place them in family groups, know of their lives and their character, and perform the saving ordinances on their behalf. It has become an impassioned, awe-inspiring effort, based on sound doctrine concerning the human families of the earth.

Notes:

1. *History of the Church of Jesus Christ of Latter-day Saints,* Salt Lake City: Deseret Book, 1960, 4:231.
2. Wilford Woodruff, *Journal*, April 6, 1891, Archives of The Church of Jesus Christ of Latter-day Saints, Salt Lake City.
3. Wilford Woodruff as recorded in *Deseret Weekly,* 25 April 1891, 554
4. Jonah Ball, letter to relatives, May 19, 1843, in Bishop, "What Has Become of Our Fathers?" 93.

277. Prophets are known by their fruits.

A prophet is one raised up by God "to act as God's messenger and [to] make known God's will."[1] A true prophet will warn of impending dangers and the cunning of men, as well as lead and preach of righteousness to bring people to God and His Son, Jesus Christ.

It is no small claim to be a prophet. At its worst, men have feigned the title for personal aggrandizement or glorification, usually deceiving even themselves by such a pronouncement. Prophets were certainly a part of the Hebrew history that Jesus frequently cited. So much so, in fact, the Master felt it was important to caution against false prophets and taught how to distinguish them from true prophets. "Beware of false prophets, which come to you in sheep's clothing, but inwardly they are ravening wolves. Ye shall know them by their fruits. Do men gather grapes of thorns, or figs of thistles? Even so every good tree bringeth forth good fruit; but a corrupt tree bringeth forth evil fruit. A good tree cannot bring forth evil fruit, neither can a corrupt tree bring forth good fruit. Every tree that bringeth not forth good fruit is hewn down, and cast into the fire. Wherefore by their fruits ye shall know them" (Matthew 7:15-20).

Jesus employed this same test when he responded to the disciples of John the Baptist to confirm that, in fact, He was the promised Messiah. "Go and shew John again those things which ye do hear and see: The blind receive their sight, and the lame walk, the lepers are cleansed, and the deaf hear, the dead are raised up, and the poor have the gospel preached unto them" (Matthew 11:4-5). He was pointing them to His works, the fruits of His ministry, and the very fulfillment of prophetic utterances.

Jesus himself was accused of doing miracles of healing "by Beelzebub the prince of devils" (Matthew 12:22-30). Jesus condemned such shallow logic in the same line of reasoning as above, precisely that a corrupt tree cannot bring forth good fruit.

That Jesus spoke of how to identify true prophets is attestation that there would be true prophets for us to be looking for. Sadly, the prophets of these latter days are all too often dismissed out of hand. Ancient prophets carry a mythical proportion, and thereby, are validated by the many. Jesus in "his own country" (Matthew 13:57) found the people without faith. He concluded, "A prophet is not without honour, save in his own country, and in his own house" (Matthew 13:53-58). Yes, familiarity often does breed contempt or disregard.

The fruits of the Church worldwide are impressive—humanitarian efforts, volunteerism, education, discipleship, temple building, strong families, scripture and doctrine, missionary work, "And faith, hope, charity and love, with an eye single to the glory of God" (D&C 4:5). Such actions and virtues flow from the leadership of true prophets of God.

Notes:

1. LDS Bible Dictionary, "Prophet."

278. Just as Jesus was not allowed to have the title of Christ, so Mormons are not always included as Christians.

Regardless of what the Jews thought of Jesus the man, I believe He was and is the Son of God, the very Christ. And regardless of what some current religious leaders say of The Church of Jesus Christ of Latter-day Saints, I believe it is the Church of Jesus Christ, and its members are therefore Christians.

In the Gospel of John alone, Jesus clearly declared His being the very Christ, or of His Divine Sonship, on at least thirty recorded occasions. He was unambiguous. Yet, the mainstream religious leaders of the day wouldn't have it. To counteract His authenticity and to stem the tide of believers, the religious and political leaders accused Him of breaking the Mosaic law and the secular law. They sought to characterize him as being mad, unstable, and irrelevant. They even labeled Him as a servant of the devil to the people. They felt it was a violation of their vaunted social position to be so openly condemned by this Jesus.

They were particularly at a loss to explain away or undermine the indisputable evidence of prophetic identification, "that the blind see, the lame walk, the lepers are cleansed, the deaf hear, the dead are raised, [and] to the poor the gospel is preached" (Luke 7:22). Even after raising Lazarus from confirmed death (which should have been convincing and compelling to all), the chief priests looked beyond the miracle and sought to take His life because "many of the Jews went away, and believed on Jesus" (John 12:11). His ministry was seen as a threat to the status quo of contemporary religiosity.

There is a parallel. Today, members of Christ's restored Church are sometimes excluded from the mainstream recognition of being referred to as Christians. As with Jesus, we are often accused of not adhering to the law, somehow in part because we believe in a second testament of the Lord Jesus Christ. We are portrayed as being different, weird, (I like "peculiar"), out of step. We too, are labeled by some as a devilish organization. They, too, often feel it is a violation of their social correctness to claim that God lives and speaks today and that Jesus is the literal Son of God and the Atoning One, sent by the Father.

Jesus was finally convicted on the accusation of blasphemy. There was no question as to what He claimed. Nor can one fail to know the core of our beliefs today by quoting even the very name of the Church.

It is truly an irony that He who was sent by God as the spiritual leader of all mankind was rejected by the religious leadership of His time in favor of waiting for another. It is, likewise, an irony that the very Church that Jesus Christ has restored to the earth is often rejected by the very people who have given their hearts and lives to Him.

Even so, Jesus is the Christ, Joseph Smith is His prophet, the church he restored is the Church of Jesus Christ, and its members are Christians. Those truths stand in ordered array, and they stand together.

279. Doctrine and Covenants Section 134 contains parallels to the founding documents of America.

In 1835, at a general assembly of Church leaders held in Kirtland and at a time of considerable lawful abuse against the Church and its leaders, a declaration was put into writing about governments and their laws. "That our belief with regard to earthly governments and laws in general may not be misinterpreted nor misunderstood, we have thought proper to present at the close of this volume [Doctrine & Covenants] our opinion concerning the same" (Header, D&C 134).

The three documents that brought forth and broadly defined the United States of America were the Declaration of Independence in 1776, the Constitution of the United States in 1787, and the subsequent Bill of Rights ratified in 1791.

Each of these documents begins with a similar declaration of purpose.

The Declaration of Independence states, "That to secure these rights, [Life, Liberty and the pursuit of Happiness] Governments are instituted among Men, deriving their just powers from the consent of the governed."[1]

The Preamble to the Constitution of the United States declares, "We the People of the United States, in Order to form a more perfect Union, establish Justice, insure domestic Tranquility, provide for the common defense, promote the general Welfare, and secure the Blessings of Liberty to ourselves and our Posterity, do ordain and establish this Constitution for the United States of America."[2]

James Madison prepared a series of seventeen amendments incorporating British precedents concerning personal liberty in an American context. Of these, ten were eventually ratified.[3] Their purpose as amendments to the Constitution was stated in the Preamble, "In order to prevent misconstruction or abuse of its powers, that further declaratory and restrictive clauses should be added: And as extending the ground of public confidence in the Government, will best ensure the beneficent ends of its institution."[4]

Section 134 begins similarly, "We believe that governments were instituted of God for the benefit of man; and that he holds men accountable for their acts in relation to them, both in making laws and administering them, for the good and safety of society . . . as will secure to each individual the free exercise of conscience, the right and control of property, and the protection of life" (D&C 134:1-2).

First Amendment rights thread throughout Section 134, as do specific parallel positions concerning individual liberty, subjection to law, the right of self-defense, separation of religious influence and civil government, loyalty to one's respective government, and respect for personal property.

Church leaders have consistently been staunch advocates and defenders of our founding documents. They are, in fact, divinely inspired as "supporting that principle of freedom in maintaining rights and privileges" (D&C 98:5).

Notes:

1. The Declaration of Independence, July 4, 1776, "the unanimous Declaration of the thirteen united states of America."
2. The Constitution of the United States, Preamble, September 17, 1787.
3. *Great American Documents,* London England: Quercus Publishing, 2007, 59.
4. *Great American Documents,* 61.

280. They were hearing Him and asking Him questions.

When Joseph and Mary returned home from Jerusalem, it is recorded that they experienced their own "Home Alone"[1] moment when they realized that their son Jesus was not in the company with their kinfolk or friends. Three sorrowful days later, and to their great relief, they discovered him in the temple.

It is recorded in the Gospel of Luke that "they found him in the temple, sitting in the midst of the doctors, *both hearing them, and asking them questions*" (Luke 2:46, emphasis added). The Joseph Smith Translation of the italicized portion of this same verse reads, "*and they were hearing him, and asking him questions*" (JST, Luke 2:46).

The former is striking as we consider Jesus was a mere twelve-years-old at the time and was fully participating with the learned men of the day in group dialogue as if He were their peer. The Joseph Smith Translation makes clear that in fact He was not their peer, but their superior. His understanding and insight held them captive, and His wisdom was being sought. Not only in striking contrast to his young age, but also in striking contrast to social norms of stature and curried position. Jesus came to this conversation with none of the prerequisites for such respect and inclusion.

But He was the Son of God. He was of a Divine Father. And He knew it already at twelve years of age. "Wist ye not that I must be about my Father's business?" He said to his parents upon their questioning Him why He wasn't in the return company to Nazareth (Luke 2:49).

Similarly, to the Elders of this dispensation, the Lord said, "Again I say, hearken ye elders of my church, whom I have appointed: Ye are not sent forth to be taught, but to teach the children of men the things which I have put into your hands by the power of my Spirit; And ye are to be taught from on high. Sanctify yourselves and ye shall be endowed with power, that ye may give even as I have spoken" (D&C 43:15-16).

Jesus was clearly taught from on high, to have such a clear understanding of His being the embodied fulfillment of all the hopes of Old Testament prophets. He knew He was to teach and that no man could teach Him wisdom or understanding above what He already possessed.

I find the Joseph Smith Translation of this verse both insightful and accurate. It places the Savior of the world in proper context and aspect and conveys the situation as it really was.

Notes:

1. A 1990 American Christmas comedy film.

281. A calling in the Church is both common and extraordinary.

It is no small claim to say that one has been called of God for a particular purpose. Certainly, those who have made significant contributions to the advancement and betterment of mankind were indeed prepared, raised up, enabled, and hence called of God. The Founding Fathers of this free nation were of this definition. The Lord explicitly said of them, "I established the Constitution of this land, by the hands of wise men whom I raised up unto this very purpose" (D&C 101:80).

Abraham Lincoln, Winston Churchill, Mahatma Ghandi, Albert Einstein, Louis Pasteur, just to name a few, all made contributions far beyond their time and place. And it's my belief that they were prepared, raised up, enabled, and called of God to play out their lives as they did.

When we speak of the ministry, we speak of being called of God for a particular role in the Church and Kingdom. Called of God to declare, teach, model, and invite all to come unto Christ. As a necessary component of this work of the ministry is the administration of His Church.

I have issued calls to scores of people in my Church experience, both to men and to women. I have personally been called to serve tens of times with corresponding releases along the way. Impressive to me is the willingness, even eagerness of members of the Church to be called to serve even though it requires time and effort. A call from God is always extraordinary, yet for a covenant member of the Lord's Church, it is also quite common.

We believe that God is active in His Church, that men are "called of God to preach the gospel, and administer in the ordinances thereof" (Articles of Faith, 5). Each of us has the individual opportunity to manifest our sustaining of those who are called of God to preside. As a consequence of that sustaining action, we respond affirmatively when called to serve.

Tomorrow morning early, I have an appointment with a brother to extend to him a call to serve. I already know how he will respond. Regardless of what the call may be, how heavy or seeming trivial it might be, whether on a broad stage, or in the corner largely unseen, he will accept the call to serve. He will see it as fulfillment of the truth "whether by mine own voice, or by the voice of my servants, it is the same" (D&C 1:38).

Such is the makeup and the heart of a covenant member of the Lord's Church. Such is the order of the Kingdom, a divine series of calls to serve with the understanding and remembrance that we have already agreed to do whatever the Lord asks of us.

282. There is an enthusiastic response to missionary service at the call of a Prophet.

In 2010, President Thomas S. Monson made a plea for more to enter the mission field, and "since that time we have seen a rather spectacular increase across the board. We're up six percent for our young elders, twelve percent for sisters, and eighteen percent for couples."[1]

Then at the October 2012 General Conference, President Monson announced, "I am pleased to announce that effective immediately all worthy and able young men who have graduated from high school or its equivalent, regardless of where they live, will have the opportunity of being recommended for missionary service beginning at the age of 18, instead of the age of 19. . . . Worthy young women who have the desire to serve may be recommended for missionary service beginning at age 19, instead of age 21."[2]

Within two weeks of this announcement, Church spokesman Michael Purdy said that while seven hundred new applicants for missionary service are typically started each week, during the last two weeks "that number has increased to approximately 4,000."[3] Slightly more than half of those were young women.

The Church has had a fairly consistent missionary force of about 55,000 serving throughout the world for the past fifteen years leading up to this announcement. Now, two years later, that force has increased by sixty percent to 88,000!

To see such an enthusiastic response from the youth, in particular, to the call of a prophet, is thrilling. There is a purity and energy in that response. Referring to the young women of the Church and the impact of this lower missionary entrance age, Sister Elaine Dalton commented, "Now, as never before, is the time to flood the earth with their virtue, their strong spirits and light."[4]

Following the announcement in general conference and directing his remarks to the young men and women of the Church, Elder Jeffrey Holland said, "God is hastening His work, and He needs more and more willing and worthy missionaries to spread the light of the truth and the hope and the salvation of the gospel of Jesus Christ to an often dark and fearful world. . . . This isn't about you. It is about the sweet and pure message you are being asked to bear."[5]

We have been and are being asked to bear that message in various iterations of "Go ye into all the world, and preach the gospel to every creature" (Mark 16:15). It is a divine mandate, and we're seeing a faithful response.

Notes:

1. Comment made by Elder Jeffrey R. Holland in early 2012 at a news conference.
2. Thomas S. Monson, "Welcome to Conference," *Ensign,* November, 2012.
3. Joseph Walker quoting Michael Purdy, "LDS Missionary Applications Jump 471 Percent," *Deseret News,* October 22, 2012.
4. Elaine Dalton, *LDS Church News* interview, "Young Women Prepare for Option of Missionary Service," December 13, 2012.
5. Jeffrey R. Holland, "Press Conference for New Missionary Service Age Requirements," October 6, 2012.

283. The *Children's Songbook* used in Primary teaches true doctrine to young people.

While on a BYU survival course prior to my baptism, the entire company gathered around and began to sing the Primary song, "I Am a Child of God." It was the first time I had ever heard it. As it unfolded, I could tell it was a children's song, and after a few lines, I left the circle because I felt it was beneath me to sing such a childish song. I have since sung it well more than a hundred times and do so as my personal testimony. It speaks of a fundamental truth.

The Primary organization in the Church serves an awesome role in the planting of testimony and true doctrine in the hearts of our children. It is the support organization to parents in raising their children, or in some rarer instances, the primary source of truth for some children. Music and singing play a most important role in this process.

For the very young, a very short attention span is about all that can be expected. The lecture format certainly has no place among children, but they love to sing. "Music is a language that everyone can understand. Children all over the world sing these same songs."[1]

Here is a sampling of doctrines that go deeply to the hearts of Primary age children as they sing with pure faith and belief:

> "Pray, he is there;
> Speak, he is listening.
> You are his child."[2] (A Child's Prayer)
>
> "Through the gospel I learn to be prayerful,
> To have faith, to repent, to obey,
> And I know if I live by his teachings,
> I will truly be happy each day."[3] (Choose the Right Way)
>
> "Faith is knowing I lived with God before my mortal birth,
> Faith is knowing I can return when my life ends on earth.
> Faith is trust in God above;
> In Christ, who showed the way.
> Faith is strengthened; I feel it grow
> Whenever I obey."[4] (Faith)
>
> "Families can be together forever
> Through Heavenly Father's plan.
> I always want to be with my own family,
> And the Lord has shown me how I can."[5] (Families Can Be Together Forever)
>
> "Now we have a world where people are confused.

If you don't believe it, go and watch the news.

We can get direction all along the way,

If we heed the prophets—follow what they say."[6] (Follow the Prophet)

"At times I am tempted to make a wrong choice,

But I try to listen [to] the still small voice."[7] (I'm Trying to Be Like Jesus)

It's been my experience that when truth is expressed, the Holy Ghost confirms to our souls it is true and good. I believe that is what takes place in the hearts of our young people as they sing the songs of Primary, and are, thereby, taught the simple doctrines, principles, and values of the gospel of Jesus Christ.

Notes:

1. "Preface," *Children's Songbook*, Salt Lake City: The Church of Jesus Christ of Latter-day Saints.
2. "A Child's Prayer," *Children's Songbook*, Salt Lake City: The Church of Jesus Christ of Latter-day Saints, 1989, 12.
3. "Choose the Right Way," 160.
4. "Faith," 96.
5. "Families Can Be Together Forever," 188.
6. "Follow the Prophet," 110.
7. "I'm Trying to Be Like Jesus," 78.

284. Living the standard "Sunday School answer" will keep our testimonies bright.

The standing joke among our youth is that if you are ever called on in class, and either were not paying attention, or don't really understand the question, just say, "Study the scriptures, say your prayers, and attend church." And more likely than not, that is indeed a good answer.

When I served as a Bishop, there were several Saints who fell away from the faith during those years. Usually, I had opportunity to counsel with them, and I observed a common, almost universal pattern. They had slowly over time, neglected their sincere, meaningful prayers, stopped reading/studying their scriptures with faith, and now wanted to discontinue their Church attendance and service. During this slide from faith, often sin or neglect of other commandments was also a companion to this downward journey.

I purposely used qualifiers for each of the above activities. Let's look at each one individually.

Prayer: Jesus is the model of prayer to our Father. His was as simple as giving thanks for bread, as far reaching as seeking inspiration/confirmation of whom to call as his apostles and as infinite as pleading for us all in the Garden of Gethsemane. His prayers varied in length as was needed, and on occasion, that was a long time. I think we would agree, that Jesus always had a prayer in his heart—the conscious, decided, humble desire to do the will of His Father.

In five verses, Jesus taught, "After this manner therefore pray ye" (Matthew 6:9-13). From His example, this partial list outlines how we should pray:

- Humbly approach God the Father
- Acknowledge his omnipotence
- Show deference
- Seek to align our will with His will
- Ask for essential needs

- Be humble and forgiving to others
- Recognize dependence on Him

Sincere, meaningful, prayer. Mighty prayer. Sometimes getting beyond the common phrases will take time. Connection with Deity is the object and beginning of our prayers.

Scriptures: "Search the scriptures . . . and they are they which testify of me" (John 5:39). That verse underscores the need to study the scriptures with *faith*. Seek to strengthen faith in Christ. The Holy Ghost is the testator of truth and will reveal to us what we need to understand and know.

I have seen a man wrestle with the scriptures, not with faith, but with doubt. His approach included studying from the writings of naysayers and precluded his receiving revelation, confirmation, and inspiration. To this day, he struggles to align his study with the faith that was so carefully planted in his childhood and youth. His is not built on "a sure foundation" (Helaman 5:12) and therefore has no divine guarantee.

Church Service: As people pull away from Church activity, they give up their calling to serve in the kingdom. Both they and those who would have received their unique service suffer for such a course.

Seeking to bring all unto Christ, leaders at the local and general level of the Church usually play these same keys of prayer, scripture, and activity, along with a few others, because they are grounding practices to the gospel of Jesus Christ. Such sincere habits animate our faith, liberate our souls, energize our lives, and bind us to God the Father, our Savior Jesus Christ, and to His Church.

285. The four Gospels are replete with evidences of God and Jesus as separate beings.

I knew the doctrine that Jesus is the Only Begotten Son of God the Father and that they are not one and the same. It makes sense. Perhaps the most quoted scripture of Christianity is John 3:16. "For God so loved the world, that he gave his only begotten Son, that whosoever believeth in him should not perish, but have everlasting life" (John 3:16).

So, I wondered how the Christian world had arrived at their Biblical Trinity doctrine that says, "There is only one God, made up of three distinct Persons who exist in co-equal, co-eternal communion as the Father, Son and Holy Spirit."[1] Another says, "The Father is not the same person as the Son; the Son is not the same person as the Holy Spirit; and the Holy Spirit is not the same person as the Father. They are not three gods and not three beings. They are three distinct persons; yet, they are all the one God."[2]

Just what does the Bible say about this? I purchased a paperback Bible and went through the four Gospels. I highlighted all verses that distinctly demonstrate the individuality of each member of the Godhead and highlighted in a different color those verses that could be construed to support the Trinity concept.

I was amazed. Of 179 pages, fully 124 pages have verses that support the fact that God and his Son are separate and individual beings. By verse count—345! Looking for verses that could give rise to the Trinity doctrine, I found nine. All of those nine were in the book of John, and all of those I believe were actually showing the oneness of heart and purpose that God the Father and His beloved Son share. Read them for yourself, and prayerfully see what you think they mean. (John 1:1, 10:30, 10:38, 12:45, 14:7, 9-11, 13)

Overwhelmingly, we read of:

- Hearing the voice of God while Jesus was in the presence of others
- Jesus being designated as the Son of God or the only Begotten of the Father
- Jesus speaking of God the Father as a separate being
- Jesus speaking of God as his Father
- Satan acknowledging Jesus as the Son of God
- Jesus praying, or directing others to pray to God the Father
- Old Testament quotations referring to Jesus as the Son of God
- Jesus speaking of being sent by the Father
- Jesus declaring His own divine Sonship
- Referring to God and Jesus as separate individuals
- Referring to God and Jesus being present together
- Jesus declaring His obedience to His Father

I highlight the voice of God on three separate occasions in the New Testament while Jesus was in the presence of others—at the baptism of Jesus (Matthew 3:17) , on the Mount of Transfiguration (Matthew 17:5), and as recorded by John just days prior to Jesus' final Passover feast (John 12:27-30). Then, there were the many prayers offered by Jesus to the Father, clearly more of dialogue than of mere yearning. Jesus addressed His Father directly, and received counsel, direction, power, and support.

I conclude with the recorded state in which God the Father and the risen Lord now exist, "So then after the Lord had spoken unto them, he was received up into heaven, and sat on the right hand of God" (Mark 16:19).

And the vision of Stephen just prior to his martyrdom "But he, being full of the Holy Ghost, looked up stedfastly into heaven, and saw the glory of God, and Jesus standing on the right hand of God. And said, Behold, I see the heavens opened, and the Son of man standing on the right hand of God" (Acts 7:55, 56).

Such is fundamental true doctrine, enabling faith in Divine Beings as they really exist.

Notes:

1. www.christianity.about.com/od/christiandoctrines/tp/deny-trinity.htm.
2. Matt Slick, *Christian Apologetics & Research Ministry*, "The Trinity," www.carm.org/trinity.

286. The power of leadership in the Church is enabled by the membership they serve.

I am being released this week from serving the past five and one half years as a counselor in our stake presidency. It has been a demanding, challenging, rich, and rewarding opportunity. There has been a recognition that many of our faithful members—children, youth, and adults—have placed trust in me and the decisions of our presidency.

This trust is very humbling. It is activated in the hearts of our members by their understanding of the order of the Kingdom and their desire to be obedient to the Lord. They really do believe that calls to leadership are from God through inspiration. They want to be in harmony with those called of God. I believe likewise.

If the membership looked casually upon those called to lead or if they saw it as purely a necessary administrative feature of the Church, the ability of those called to lead, to effect change, and to minister would be greatly diminished.

I have sat one-on-one with well over five hundred of our most faithful members and interviewed them to renew their recommends to gain access to the holy temples across the earth. It always involves direct eye contact, almost a longing on their part to be transparent. They believe they are sitting across from a priesthood leader who has authority to ask these questions and to measure their answers. I believe likewise.

It has been amazing to me to see the willingness of our members to respond to the inconvenient call to serve, wherever that may take them, or whatever that may entail. They respond in faith, "if the Lord has called me, then I accept the call." No cajoling, no making deals, no talking them into it.

I have said to my wife on several occasions that the Saints are more kind to me than I deserve. They are respectful of the position I have occupied, and I'm aware of that. President Dieter Uchtdorf related what Elder James E. Faust taught him about being a new General Authority in the Church. He said of the members, "They will treat you very kindly. They will say nice things about you. He laughed a little and then said, Dieter, be thankful for this. But don't you ever inhale it!"[1]

Truth be told, I have inhaled it a few times. But I know as they know, this is the Lord's work and the glory be His.

Moses followed the counsel of his father-in-law Jethro and "chose able men out of all Israel, and made them heads over the people, rulers of thousands, rulers of hundreds, rulers of fifties, and rulers of tens" (Exodus 18:25). Yet it was the faith of those who believed these men of Israel could "teach them ordinances and laws" (Exodus 18:20) that made it work.

President Hinckley once said that the symbol of our faith is in the lives of our members.[2] It has been my honor to witness the faith, sacrifice, love, purity, and goodness of these covenant members and to be recipient of the power that comes to a leader when the people follow in obedience to their covenants.

Notes:

1. Deiter F. Uchtdorf, "Pride and the Priesthood," *Ensign*, November, 2010.

2. Gordon B. Hinckley, "The Symbol of Our Faith," *Ensign*, April, 2005.

287. The Living Christ is a testament and reminder of His victory and our hope.

"The cross is the symbol of the dying Christ, while our message is a declaration of the Living Christ."[1]

That statement shouldn't be offensive to anyone. It merely states why the Church, in its more recent history, has chosen not to adopt the cross or the crucifix as an outward symbol of the faith. Nor is it intended to be intolerant or to take a swipe at the symbol held sacred by other faiths.

Moreover, it in no way diminishes the crucifixion of the Savior. We firmly believe "that he was lifted up upon the cross and slain for the sins of the world" (1 Nephi 11:33).

Some churches prefer to use the crucifix form with a figure of the dying Christ affixed (Anglican, Lutheran, Roman Catholic) while others, usually protestant Churches, prefer the empty cross form, which calls their attention to the death and subsequent resurrection of the Savior.

Subsequent to the time of Christ, the cross was not altogether absent as a symbol, but it likely was not as prevalent as it is today among Christians. "During the first two centuries of Christianity, the cross may have been rare in Christian iconography, as it depicts a purposely painful and gruesome method of public execution and Christians were reluctant to use it."[2]

"The extensive adoption of the cross as Christian iconographic symbol arose from the 4th century."[3]

Someone has fondly written the following concerning the Christian use of the cross, "They venerate it not as a material object seen in isolation, but as the symbol of the sacrifice by which Christ saved them, as the instrument of Christ's triumph, and the instrument of God's saving love."[4] To those who can claim that statement as their own, it is nicely put.

At the time of the restoration in the 1800's, the cross wasn't widely used among non-Catholic Churches. So it wasn't an issue that Joseph Smith or other early Church leaders really had to take into consideration. There is good evidence that the cross was used as a symbol by some of its individual members within the Church for many years, if not overtly by the Church. Likely, that was a non-issue right up until the opening of the twentieth century or into the mid twentieth century.

I find it entirely correct that the Church would not want to blend in to the larger homogenous Christian movement. Homogenous indicates common origins. Ours is uniquely a restoration story. So, if by design and directive we don't use the cross on or in our buildings, or around our necks, it serves well to highlight the fact that we are different.

However, we do believe in symbols. Symbols have powerful appeal to our emotions and to bring us to remembrance. The symbol that we feel is paramount to keep us in remembrance of Jesus—His life, teachings, divinity, love, crucifixion, atonement, resurrection—are the emblems of the sacrament. Regarding the partaking of the sacrament emblems, the Lord Himself said, "And it shall be a testimony unto the Father that ye do always remember me" (3 Nephi 18:7, 11).

We will always remember and reverence the fact that Christ died for us. We will always remember that He was resurrected from death and that He lives today. Therein is our complete hope, and a significant part of our covenant, that we "do always remember him" (D&C 20:79).

Notes:

1. Gordon B. Hinckley, "The Symbol of Our Faith," *Ensign*, April, 2005.
2. Alister E. McGrath, *Christianity: An Introduction*, Malden: Blackwell Publishing, 2006, 321-323.
3. Skarsaune, Oskar, Jewish Believers in Jesus The Early Centuries, Grand Rapids: Baker Academic, 715.
4. Unknown – widely used on various internet sites regarding the cross.

288. Provident living and self-reliance are inspired counsel.

As a young teenager long before I joined the Church, we visited my step-mom's parents in Richland, Washington. We affectionately called them Papper and Grandma. Papper was a faithful member of the Church, having been converted in his mid-forties. Grandma never joined, but Papper was faithful and enthusiastic about his membership to the day he died. Unfortunately, that was about three years before I joined the Church.

During this particular visit, Papper, Dad, Uncle Hank, and I drove over to a storage facility and spent the morning moving heavy cans of wheat, large bottles of honey, and other commodities from one unit to another. I guess Papper was downsizing the storage unit to save on the storage cost. To me, it was weird that he was storing food. My experience was that food belonged in the house and was short-term, as needed. This was my very first introduction to LDS food storage.

The principles of self-reliance are timeless. Great satisfaction, peace of mind, increased capacity, and a sense of confidence flow from being prepared and self-reliant. Here is a great summary quote of what the Church teaches regarding areas of self-reliance: "We become self-reliant through obtaining sufficient knowledge, education, and literacy; by managing money and resources wisely, being spiritually strong, preparing for emergencies and eventualities; and by having physical health and social and emotional well-being."[1]

The seven categories of preparedness and self-reliance that the Church teaches are

- Employment
- Finances
- Food Storage
- Emergency Preparedness
- Physical Health
- Education
- Gardening

Gardening? Yes! I have a recollection of a story told of Nathan Eldon Tanner, then serving as a counselor to President Spencer W. Kimball, who was an advocate for sprucing up our yards and properties and having a vegetable garden. President Tanner brought with him a nice ripe tomato to show President Kimball, and in doing so, dubbed it "the $2 tomato" he grew in his garden! Usually we'll enjoy a favorable economic result for gardening, but if not, like President Tanner, we'll reap other blessings of working in the earth and growing something.

"Planting a garden, even a small one, allows for a greater degree of self-reliance. With the right information and a little practice, individuals and entire families can enjoy the many benefits of planting and tending a garden."[2]

To assume such personal responsibility for self and family brings a tremendous measure of satisfaction, peace, and enjoyment. The Lord said, "If ye are prepared ye shall not fear" (D&C 38:30). In a time when many are looking to shift personal responsibility to government, corporations, hospitals, doctors, or any entity other than themselves, it is refreshing to hear the call to step up and to take well-rounded measures to be prepared and to make it happen.

Notes:

1. Julie B. Beck, "The Welfare Responsibilities of the Relief Society President," *Basic Principles of Welfare and Self-Reliance,* 2009, 4-6.

2. lds.org/topics/gardening.

289. The Addiction Recovery Program is Christ-like and Christ-centered.

With the advent of the internet, pornography addiction has exploded in recent years. Unlike alcoholism, where breath and behavior can't lie, an addiction such as pornography can create a double life, no doubt torturous to the addicted and heartbreaking to family members. Both substances and behaviors can create powerful addictions.

"So, if it's ruining your life, stop doing it!" Such used to be my very simplistic response. The Church has been on the leading edge of a more compassionate, patient, practical, broader, Christ-like, and Christ-centered approach to healing. It is on the leading edge, not by the program (which is an adaptation of the 12-step *Alcoholics Anonymous* program), but by its implementation as an institution.

In an area of my mission in Mexico, we were teaching a brother who was a long-term alcoholic. He attended Alcoholics Anonymous meetings and invited us to come to a meeting, so we did. I remember the crowd was not one we usually associated with—somewhat slovenly dressed, smoke in the air, colorful language—a fairly rough bunch as I remember it. But I also remember the spirit of humility, of those recognizing that they couldn't do it on their own, and that were of a broken heart and a contrite spirit that we have been commanded to acquire. They were supportive of one another, non-judgmental, and encouraging in a positive way.

Those who arrive at Step One, Honesty, of the 12 Steps, are teachable. "And he beheld with great joy; for he beheld that their afflictions had truly humbled them, and that they were in a preparation to hear the word . . . who were truly penitent and . . . lowly in heart" (Alma 32:6-8).

The Lord's Church has a high standard of morality for its members. It would be easy to conclude that those who engage in addictive Word of Wisdom violations or who mock the law of chastity through pornographic voyeurism should be cut off. Kind of like "you know the rules, either play or go home." I have been impressed and schooled by the more compassionate and substantive response of our Church leaders, as they have been inspired of the Lord to help rather than to cast off.

The Church has organized local support meetings in many of the stakes of the Church across the world. This particularly helps to bring it into the open, to deal with it, to acknowledge it. All is done with appropriate anonymity. Attendance is not shared with ecclesiastical leaders.

The front cover of the Addiction Recovery Manual, published by the Church, says, "A Guide to Addiction Recovery and Healing, Written with support from Church leaders and counseling professionals by those who have suffered from addiction and who have experienced the miracle of recovery through the Atonement of Jesus Christ."[1]

That is the miracle we all should experience, whatever flavor, fashion, or form our sins may be.

Notes:

1. *LDS Family Services: Addiction Recovery Program, A Guide to Addiction Recovery and Healing,* Salt Lake City: The Church of Jesus Christ of Latter-day Saints, 2005.

290. LDS funerals are uplifting services that teach the plan of salvation and give hope.

When Joseph Smith's brother Alvin died at twenty-five years of age in 1823 (prior to the organization of the Church), the family asked a Presbyterian minister in Palmyra, New York, to officiate at his funeral. As Alvin had not been a member of the minister's congregation, the clergyman asserted in his sermon that Alvin could not be saved. William Smith, Joseph's younger brother recalled, "[The minister] . . . intimated very strongly that [Alvin] had gone to hell, for Alvin was not a church member."[1]

I've attended funeral services where the minister, as the minister in Palmyra, takes it upon himself to pass judgment on the deceased, albeit usually saying what the bereaved would want to hear. Some of these services are so consumed with the grief of death that they send a message of hopelessness. We leave such services more saddened than when we arrived.

The eternal perspective that the Gospel of Jesus Christ provides brings a certain measure of joy in the hope that is within us, even in the event of death. Covenants and compliance with ordinances insure eternal bonds based upon our faithfulness.

An LDS funeral is a mix of looking back to remember and looking forward to divine preparations made by the Lord himself. "In my Father's house are many mansions: if it were not so, I would have told you. I go to prepare a place for you" (John 14:2). The services are dignified, solemn, and intended to be a spiritual experience for all who attend.

I've always felt that a funeral service was for us to show respect and honor to the deceased, as well as to provide support for the bereaved. Perhaps, the most significant memorial we could provide to a faithful Latter-day Saint is to share and reaffirm the testimony of the deceased with friends and family. It is an opportunity to teach the gospel and testify of the plan of salvation when attendees are open to the spirit, pondering life, death, and the purpose of life.

When we do, we are lifted in hope and eager anticipation for what God and His Son Jesus Christ have done for us. We are reminded of God's love for us, His imperfect children, and of the mercy, grace, and the saving Atonement of the Lord Jesus Christ, and of being "received into a state of happiness . . . a state of rest, a state of peace, where they shall rest from all their troubles and from all care and sorrow" (Alma 40:12). We are taught of a resurrection where "not so much as a hair of their heads be lost; but every thing shall be restored to its perfect frame" (Alma 11:44), even coming back into the presence of our Eternal Father. If obedient, we will enjoy family and other relationships nurtured in mortality. "And that same sociality which exists among us here will exist among us there, only it will be coupled with eternal glory, which glory we do not now enjoy" (D&C 130:2).

LDS funerals provide an important opportunity to teach the gospel and testify of the plan of salvation. Therein is offered the greatest hope and healing to those who are left behind in this mortal sphere. And therein the funeral becomes a standing memorial to the faithful deceased.

Notes:

1. William Smith, interview by E.C. Briggs and J.W. Peterson, October or November 1893, originally published in *Zion's Ensign,* reprinted in *Deseret Evening News,* January 20, 1894, 2.

291. The Welfare Program of the Church is inspired of God and upheld by the faithful.

Following the stock market crash of 1929, which ushered in the Great Depression, several stakes in the Salt Lake Valley formed the Deseret Employment Bureau to seek work for their members.

As early as 1930, the Church began to draw on the resources of the Deseret Employment Bureau and formed a committee to study and propose solutions to the unemployment problem. In 1936, based on the lessons learned during these early efforts, the Church inaugurated the Church Security Plan (renamed the Welfare Program in 1937). On its inaugural day, David O. McKay, then serving in the First Presidency said, "[The welfare program] is established by divine revelation, and there is nothing else in all the world that can so effectively take care of its members."[1]

Then Church President Heber J. Grant laid out the vision that would undergird the Welfare program from that time forward, "Our primary purpose was to set up in so far as it might be possible, a system under which the curse of idleness would be done away with, the evils of a dole abolished and independence, industry, thrift and self-respect be once more established among our people. The aim of the Church is to help the people to help themselves. Work is to be re-enthroned as the ruling principle of the lives of our Church membership."[2]

Since that time to the present, the Welfare Program has grown to include farms, ranches, orchards, dairies, canneries, grain silos, clothing mills, storehouses, fuel, trucks, trailers and heavy equipment. All of this is spread across international boundaries. The recently opened Bishop's Central Storehouse facility in Salt Lake City is situated on thirty-five acres, has a footprint of 570,000 square feet (with plans to add another 100,000). The total planned capacity of the building is 65,000 pallets. It stocks hundreds of different foods, from corn, beans, and cereals to cheese, ice cream, and peanut butter, as well as toiletries, tools, and electric generators. It has its own trucking company, complete with nearly fifty tractors and one hundred trailers, in addition to a one-year supply of fuel, parts, and tires for the vehicles. The facility has even been built to withstand a 7.5-magnitude earthquake. From this Central Storehouse, food and supplies are shipped to central storehouses in five other regions of the United States and Canada, which in turn distribute to more than two hundred smaller bishop's storehouses for local use.[3]

Contributions of faithful members in time and money are what make the Welfare Program possible. This is the unique ingredient, the genius that makes it work. Generous donations above and beyond the tithe and countless volunteer hours given at the local level in working the farms, ranches, canneries, and other facilities greatly minimize the cost to run such operations.

The Welfare Program of the Church is religion in action, an embodiment of Isaiah's words to "draw out thy soul to the hungry, and satisfy the afflicted soul" (Isaiah 58:10). And in the process, both the giver and the receiver are blessed. It is an inspired effort.

Notes:

1. David O. McKay, "The Church Welfare Plan," in Henry D. Taylor, 1984, 26.
2. Heber J. Grant, *Conference Report,* October, 1936, 3.
3. Naomi Schaefer Riley, "A Welfare System That Works," *Philanthropy Magazine: Philanthropy Roundtable,* Fall, 2012.

292. Financial debt can be a form of bondage that the Lord warns against.

Ever since I joined the Church in 1977, I have heard the Brethren counsel against incurring unnecessary debt. I have welcomed that counsel, and it has been a blessing during the course of our lives.

Some say that such a matter is outside the realm of the Sunday pulpit, but I find it entirely consistent that He who most desires our happiness would give such wise counsel.

The current counsel of the Church regarding debt is simply, "Avoid debt, with the exception of buying a modest home or paying for education or other vital needs."[1]

A classic quote on the companions of debt and interest was said by Elder J. Reuben Clark in General Conference during the later years of the Great Depression in 1938. "Interest never sleeps, nor sickens, nor dies. It never goes to the hospital, it works on Sundays and holidays. It never takes a vacation, it never visits or travels, it takes no pleasure. It is never laid off work, nor discharged from employment. It never works on reduced hours. . . . It has no love, no sympathy. It is as hard and soulless as a granite cliff. Once in debt, interest is your companion every minute of the day and night. You cannot shun it or slip away from it. You cannot dismiss it. It yields neither to entreaties, demands or orders. And whenever you get in its way, or cross its course or fail to meet its demands, it crushes you."[2]

The Lord commanded Martin Harris to underwrite the publishing of the Book of Mormon in 1830, and then to liquidate the debt and why, when he said, "Pay the debt thou hast contracted with the printer. Release thyself from bondage" (D&C 19:35).

Since just after the opening of the twentieth century, the Church has been free from debt to fund its operations and to pay for its capital expenditures.

In 1996, we finished construction on a new Stake Center in our city and held an open house for the community leaders from other faiths. At the conclusion of the tour, we had a luncheon, and took questions from them. Instead of questions regarding our doctrine, our culture, and our programs, the very first question and the subsequent conversation was, "How do you get your members to pay tithing so you can receive your certificate of occupancy with no debt on the building?" They were amazed that the building was paid for. That is Church policy for all of its capital projects worldwide.

Consumer debts, corporate debts, and public debts are all at dangerous levels today. It seems to be the norm.

President N. Eldon Tanner taught, "Those who structure their standard of living to allow a little surplus, control their circumstances. Those who spend a little more than they earn are controlled by their circumstances. They are in bondage."[3] I'm grateful for that counsel.

Notes:

1. "Family Finances," www.lds.org/topics/finances
2. J. Reuben Clark, *Conference Report,* April, 1938, 103.
3. N. Eldon Tanner, "Constancy Amid Change," *Ensign,* October, 1979.

293. It is my own belief that even prophets live by faith more often than not.

It is not necessary for my faith, to think that the modern day prophets walk and talk with God in the flesh with any frequency, or even at all. Some members speak of the President of the Church, truly the presiding priesthood authority on the earth, as walking and talking with God and Jesus Christ as he would with other close associates. They likewise believe that the other fourteen ordained apostles have such divine communication and association. That they may is entirely plausible and entirely possible, if the Lord so desires. That they must is not a necessity of my faith.

I acknowledge that I am writing about something I know nothing about and about something that is sacred. I suppose it is for this reason, the personal sacred nature of the experience, that even the First

Vision wasn't disclosed by Joseph widely until at least twelve years later. How would you handle such an experience? Think about it.

Likewise, after the marvelous experience on the Mount of Transfiguration, where Peter, James, and John saw Jesus in a glorified and transfigured state, received priesthood keys, heard the voice of God, and saw Moses and Elijah as translated beings, "Jesus charged them, saying, Tell the vision to no man, until the Son of man be risen again from the dead" (Matthew 17:9). This and experiences like it are sacred and apparently of greater worth and purpose than they would have as a mere proselyting tool.

"How does the Savior reveal His will and doctrine to prophets, seers, and revelators? He may act by messenger or in His own person. He may speak by His own voice or by the voice of the Holy Spirit—a communication of Spirit to spirit that may be expressed in words or in feelings that convey understanding beyond words. He may direct Himself to His servants individually or acting in council."[1]

Elaborating on council deliberations, Elder Christofferson said, "It is a process involving both reason and faith for obtaining the mind and will of the Lord [revelation]."[2]

Nephi had to explain the writings of Isaiah to his older brothers and said, among other things, "Behold they were manifest unto the prophet by the voice of the Spirit; for by the Spirit are all things made known unto the prophets, which shall come upon the children of men according to the flesh" (1 Nephi 22:2).

One who has been ordained a prophet, seer, and revelator has developed the ability to discern the promptings of the Spirit and has demonstrated obedience to that Spirit. I don't believe it is common practice for the Lord to commune face-to-face with the presiding authorities or leading councils of His Church, although He may at times. By faith, and by the unmistakable voice of the Holy Spirit, the Lord's will has been and is being carried out throughout the earth.

Consider this, though, as only my opinion. Nor do I feel it would be appropriate to press further on this issue. I am satisfied that the Lord communicates effectively with his servants.

Notes:

1. Elder D. Todd Christofferson, "The Doctrine of Christ," *Ensign,* May, 2012.

2. Elder D. Todd Christofferson.

294. The Church supports the injunction, "In the sweat of thy face shalt thou eat bread."

Speaking at a General Welfare meeting of the Church, attended by leaders from across the earth, President Spencer W. Kimball said, "Those of us in the Lord's work must recognize that work is a spiritual necessity as well as an economic necessity."[1]

In the October, 2012 General Conference, Elder D. Todd Christofferson, quoted from an early Church welfare pamphlet: "A man out of work is of special moment to the Church. . . . The Church cannot hope to save a man on Sunday if during the week it is a complacent witness to the crucifixion of his soul."[2]

Family self-reliance is inextricably tied to our labor to produce, to contribute, to create, and to be compensated for such labor. Calling unemployment a special moment to the Church has proven to be far more than an idle statement.

The Church staffs nearly three hundred LDS Employment Resource Service Centers worldwide that help both members and others with employment, education, and self-employment. Services include job postings, extensive networking, one-on-one coaching, help with resumes and interviewing, internet access, and use of copiers, fax machines, and telephones. It is all free of charge or at cost. These centers are in over twenty countries, and serve people ranging from executives to entrepreneurs, from clerks to cab drivers.

Employment center staff members maintain contacts with local employers who post job openings to an online database. To tap into those jobs that are never posted, there is a Career Workshop offered to teach people how to discover those jobs.

If someone does not have the knowledge or skills to obtain and keep a job, or is underemployed, LDS employment resource centers can often arrange for the needed training. This training varies from area to area, according to local need and economic conditions. In the Philippines, classes are held in basic computer skills; in Ghana, automotive repair; in the Dominican Republic, small appliance repair.

A single mother of two in Guatemala, with no prior work experience, sought help from the local LDS Employment Center. They were aware of a local dentist needing a dental assistant, but the skill set of the young sister did not match the requirements of the job. The deadline for application was three days away. Undaunted, the staff at the center went to work, teaching her basic computer skills, interviewing skills, how to run a fax machine, and more. She applied, interviewed, and got the job! She soon gained the happiness of knowing that she could support herself and her children without the need of help from others.

"If we want to keep the Spirit," said President Ezra Taft Benson, "we must work. There is no greater exhilaration or satisfaction than to know, after a hard day of work, that we have done our best."[3] This program of the Church reaches beyond the Sunday meetings to the whole person. It enables and nurtures our spiritual life.

Notes:

1. Spencer W. Kimball, "Follow the Fundamentals," *Ensign,* May, 1981.

2. *Helping Others to Help Themselves: The Story of the Mormon Church Welfare Program,* 1945, 4.

3. *The Teachings of Ezra Taft Benson,* Salt Lake City: Bookcraft, 1988, 483-484.

295. The writings of Joseph Smith and the revelations of the Lord are discernibly different.

Joseph Smith kept several journals, both by his own hand and by the hand of scribes. The first of these journals, kept very sporadically between 1832 and 1834, was primarily in the handwriting of Oliver Cowdery, Frederick G. Williams, and Parley P. Pratt, with almost half of the entries in Joseph's own handwriting.

The recorded revelations received during that same time period (and they were not the only ones received) are Sections 85-106 (with the exception of Section 99) of the Doctrine and Covenants.

I wanted to see a style difference between Joseph the man and Joseph the revelator when I compared these two sources spanning the same time period. Clearly, there is a difference, although in the diary entries I also see that voice of the Lord on occasion, apparently revelatory, but not canonized.

Twenty-one of the twenty-two sections referred to above are noted as revelations. Of those twenty-one, all but three begin with a variation of "Thus saith the Lord." I found those very words in a journal entry dated November 14-19, 1833, that speak of Sydney Rigdon. It reads like the revelations, unlike the bulk of the journal. In fact, frequently in the journal entries, rather than authoritative and assertive as are the revelations, Joseph is often pleading, seeking the Lord to bless, to redress wrongs, to deliver from temptations, to give wisdom, or to "have mercy on my Brethren in Zion."[1] The difference is like a father and his son, the Father experienced, confident, authoritative, and meting out wisdom, and the son living his comparably mundane life and realizing his need of counsel and direction from one infinitely wiser than he.

Many of the diary entries are simply a dispassionate chronology of everyday comings and goings. "Came from Westfield to Elk kreek (sp) Stayed with Elder Hunt on free cost."[2] Even the excommunication of Jesse Gause, who was a counselor to Joseph for a short time, was recorded as "in the evening Br Jese . . . was excommunicated from the church."[3] No commentary, no expressed feelings were given.

Joseph did use colorful, Biblical type prose on occasion in the journal, such as when he described the eventual fate of Philastus Hurlbut. "the Lord shall destroy him who has lifted his heel against me even that wicked man Doctor P Hrlbert he deliver him to the fowls of heaven and his bones shall be cast to the blast of the wind he lifted his against the Almity (sp) therefore the Lord shall destroy him" (as written by Joseph's hand).[4] Such was a display of Joseph's ability to express himself with some flair.

Yet in the revelations, we see passion (D&C 88:88-91), chastening (D&C 95:2), counsel (D&C 90:18), comfort (D&C 100:15), human nature exposed (D&C 101:8), promises (D&C 100:8), Church procedure (D&C 104:60-78), and eternal doctrine (D&C 93:33-34). All are expressed with power and undisputed confidence.

"In this record [1832-1834 journal], he [Joseph Smith] employed a personal tone quite different from the prophetic voice of his scriptural translations and revelations."[5]

I agree with that summary statement. Joseph Smith was a man called of God. He was given divine utterance as the Lord desired to convey it to certain individuals or more particularly to the Church at large. His recorded diaries and the recorded revelations are from two different sources, one personal and the other divine.

Notes:

1. Dean C. Jesse, comp., *The Joseph Smith Papers: Journals Volume 1: 1832-1839,* entry of January 16, 1834, Salt Lake: The Church Historian's Press, 2008, 24.

2. Dean C. Jesse, entry of March 26, 1834, 36.

3. Dean C. Jesse, entry of December 3, 1832, 10.

4. Dean C. Jesse, entry of April 1, 1834, 37.

5. Dean C. Jesse, 4.

296. Knowledge comes line upon line, precept upon precept, here a little, and there a little.

Isaiah is first recorded teaching this pattern of receiving inspiration (revelation) as written in Chapter 28 verses 10 and 13. Nephi received a similar revelation, and then recorded further clarity and insight when he quoted the Lord as adding, "And blessed are those who hearken unto my precepts, and lend an ear unto my counsel, for they shall learn wisdom; for unto him that receiveth I will give more; and from them that shall say, We have enough, from them shall be taken away even that which they have" (2 Nephi 28:30).

I was surprised that such a beautiful and rational explanation of the pattern of revelation found in Isaiah was seen differently by other writers in a simple Google search. "The phrase appears to be mere gobbledygook, a mockery of the prophet's words."[1] Thereafter follows a lengthy dive explaining that conclusion. This view was not isolated but shared by several others in separate commentaries of Isaiah 28:10, 13.

In truth, Isaiah warns the people, that "in spite of the Lord's instructing Israel through prophets, many of the people apostatized" (Isaiah 28:13, footnote b, LDS edition KJVB). As recorded by

Nephi, revelation received and acted upon brings further revelation. Revelation disregarded will cause the people to "fall backward, and be broken, and snared, and taken" (Isaiah 28:13).

"For he will give unto the faithful line upon line, precept upon precept" (D&C 98:12).

"If thou shalt ask, thou shalt receive revelation upon revelation, knowledge upon knowledge" (D&C 42:61).

"And they shall also be crowned with blessings from above . . . and with revelations in their own time—they that are faithful and diligent before me (D&C 59:4).

"That which is of God is light; and he that receiveth light, and continueth in God, receiveth more light; and that light growth brighter and brighter until the perfect day" (D&C 50:24).

There is a direct correlation—he that is faithful, diligent, inquiring, believing—will receive increasing understanding and light. With some exceptions, (Paul on the road to Damascus, Alma hearing a voice of thunder, and a few others), this is the pattern of our being the recipient of incremental divine tutoring.

"The fundamental doctrines and principles of the restored gospel were not delivered to the Prophet Joseph Smith in the Sacred Grove in a neatly organized binder. Rather, these priceless treasures were revealed line upon line as circumstances warranted and as the timing was right."[2] As with the unfolding of the kingdom in these latter days, so is the deepening of our own understanding and testimony on a personal level, as we cultivate faith and seek knowledge.

"And I, John [the apostle], saw that he [Christ] received not of the fulness at the first, but received grace for grace . . . until he received a fulness" (D&C 93:12-13).

"And Jesus increased in wisdom and stature" (Luke 2:52).

Such is the divine model. We are blessed to have such an understanding of the scriptural wisdom, "precept upon precept; line upon line" (Isaiah 28:10).

Notes:

1. *Precept Upon Precept?* Dialogs and Commentary, www.acts17-11.com/cows_precept.
2. David A. Bednar, "Line upon Line, Precept upon Precept," *New Era*, September. 2010.

297. After Jesus' resurrection, the Father added to His introduction of The Son "in whom I have glorified my name."

In the New Testament, God the Father introduced his Son Jesus Christ at the baptism by John with the words, "This is my beloved Son, in whom I am well pleased" (Matthew 3:17). Later, upon the Mount of Transfiguration, He made the same introduction, adding a binding directive to "hear ye him" (Matthew 17:5). Elder Neal A. Maxwell has referred to these introductions as the Father giving us "Jesus' crucial genealogy."[1]

When the resurrected Christ was introduced to the people of Nephi in the land Bountiful, "it was not a harsh voice, neither was it a loud voice; nevertheless, and notwithstanding it being a small voice it did pierce them that did hear to the center, insomuch that there was no part of their frame that it did not cause to quake; yea, it did pierce them to the very soul, and did cause their hearts to burn" (3 Nephi 11:3).

At first they could not understand the voice, until they "did open their ears to hear it. . . And the third time they did understand the voice which they heard; and it said unto them: Behold my Beloved Son, in whom I am well pleased, in whom I have glorified my name—hear ye him" (3 Nephi 11:5-7).

How is this introduction different from what the Father said at the baptism of Jesus or on the Mount of Transfiguration? It is the addition of the words "in whom I have glorified my name." I find it significant that these words in the Book of Mormon are so sequentially correct when compared to the two previous divine introductions. For at this moment, Jesus had "finished my preparations unto the children of men," by which "glory be to the Father" (D&C 19:19). It also aligns with the declaration of the Father that He "will glorify it [His name through Christ] again" (yet future) (John 12:28).

Four verses later in the record of Nephi, after the Father's introduction, Jesus spoke of his role as the promised Messiah in terms that would have been familiar and confirming to the faithful, "And behold, I am the light and the life of the world; and I have drunk out of that bitter cup which the Father hath given me, and have glorified the Father in taking upon me the sins of the world, in the which I have suffered the will of the Father in all things from the beginning" (3 Ne 11:11).

By His absolute obedience to the Father, including His wrenching suffering for all mankind in Gethsemane and on the cross at Calvary, Jesus glorified the Father. Now as a resurrected being to the Nephites, this significant additional declaration could be made.

This is arguably a small observation, but one that confirms anew my testimony of the divine accuracy of the Book of Mormon.

Notes:

1. Neal A. Maxwell, "Out of Obscurity," *Ensign*, November, 1984.

298. When we say "Visitors Welcome," we really mean it.

Whenever people who are not members of our faith come to our Sunday services, they will likely shake more hands than they have in the past several months combined. It seems to be in our DNA to welcome people who are investigating the Church and to let them know how much we enjoy having them.

Stephen Mansfield, in his book *The Mormonizing of America,* writes of his experience in a BYU classroom as an observer:

> "Feeling the moment, I wanted to say something about how welcoming everyone had been, not just at BYU but at headquarters in Salt Lake City and everywhere I had spoken with LDS scholars, politicians, or believers around the country. That's when I used one of my favorite throwaway lines: 'Will you adopt me?'
>
> "Well, of course we will. Would you like for us to call the missionaries?"
>
> "And the whole class cracked up. They had me. Of course they would adopt me. That's what they're on earth to do. Family. Eternity. Belonging. Connection. Progressing together . . .
>
> "It was the type of warm, human moment in which far more is radiated than anyone tries to describe. I loved it. It was sweet and endearing, and I saw in that instant a bit of the enveloping community that has enabled the Latter-day Saints to do what few religions have in the tumultuous modern world: allow people to belong before they believe."[1]

So was my experience as well when I was an acquaintance of the Church through member friends and as I became an interested investigator of its claim to be the restored gospel of Jesus Christ.

In January 1977, I attended my first semester of college at Southern Utah State College in Cedar City, Utah. I was also an eager investigator of the Church by this time in my life. I attended all three hours of Church on Sunday, went to all the firesides, participated in Mutual activities, and even was a member of the LDS fraternity on campus. I often have said that I was loved into this church by many kind, interested, and caring people. My baptism in April of that same year was attended by what I remember as well over one hundred people. The next day in a Stake Conference, Elder Neal A. Maxwell sought me out to warmly take my hand, look me in the eye, and to say, "Welcome to the Kingdom, brother!" I could sense his earnest interest in me personally.

In a world of so much intolerance among religions, I have found that LDS members truly do allow people to belong before they believe. And more so, if they choose not to believe, as in the case of Stephen Mansfield, that kindness and respect is not diminished. We, all of mankind, truly are brothers and sisters.

Notes:

1. Stephen Manfield, *The Mormonizing of America*, Brentwood: Worthy Publishing, 2012, xi-xii.

299. A personal, unforgettable, mountain top experience.

The first three days of our BYU survival course was referred to as Impact. It is designed to be challenging and difficult in the deserts of Southern Utah. We hiked for three days, night and day, catching sleep as we could at night on huge rocks retaining warmth from the days baking sun or in the quiet morning hours while the sun was rising. We never made a formal camp, had no fires, and cooked no meals. The make-up of the group was diverse by age, physical ability, attitudes, and motivations. Yet we had to move together as a group and as the course instructors led us.

It soon became apparent that water was going to be a problem. What we had brought was gone the first day. It was hot and dusty throughout each day, and we were getting parched. The first waterhole we came upon was low and stagnant. Not drinkable.

I don't remember how many water holes we came to that were dry. I don't remember how many, or if any, we came to that we were able to drink from. But I do remember a thirst that I'd never known.

We eventually came to a muddy river, the Escalante, as I remember. We plunged in, clothes and all, and just sat in this brown/grey river water—drinking, refreshing, smiling—totally contented.

But then, we had to move on. Before us was a mountain (or a good sized hill) we had to scale to come out of the canyon and back up to the high desert. Just short of the top, was a bowl like area where a water source was expected to be. So we set out.

It was a climbing experience more than a trail. Some were not physically able on their own to make this pitch, so I ended up in the rear helping those who needed help. Hoisting, encouraging, pulling, pushing from beneath, finding new routes, carrying their gear, supporting their footholds. It was slow going.

At the top, we encountered a muddy spot where the water hole was supposed to be, so we dug down, let the water fill our holes, and strained the water through bandanas so we could drink. It worked. We had water.

I personally was exhausted. But before I went to seek water, I had this amazing feeling of satisfaction and accomplishment. So much so, that I went off apart, sat on the edge of the cliff, and looked out over the Escalante River in the distance. Everyone had made it. The older woman with the gimp leg, the overweight and the unfit, everyone was now at the top. It was a contentment not to be forgotten. It was pure love, joy, and peace. It was a spiritual moment, only later recognized for what it was.

"But the fruit of the Spirit is love, joy, peace" (Galatians 5:22).

It was one of the first encounters with the sweetness of the Spirit that I can remember. I have felt it many times since. Sometimes it is as a confirmation of truth, other times (as on this occasion) a result of righteous achievement, or at other times as an encouragement toward dreams and future expectations. And at still other times and places, influencing or confirming some of the more common experiences of life, and some that are extraordinary.

My experience on the mountain above the Escalante River is one I shall never forget, and one that became an introduction upon a quest to capture it again and again.

300. The term "unpardonable sin" is coined in the Book of Mormon and clarified by living prophets.

The Book of Mormon is the only place in scripture that uses the term "unpardonable sin" (Jacob 7:19, Alma 39:6), although it was taught by the Savior as blasphemy against the Holy Ghost of which there is no forgiveness (Matthew 12:31, Mark 3:29, Luke 12:10).

Paul described this unpardonable sin as "sin willfully after that we have received the knowledge of the truth" (Hebrews 10:26).

Nephi wrote the words of the Lord, "After ye have repented of your sins, and witnessed unto the Father that ye are willing to keep my commandments, by the baptism of water, and have received the baptism of fire and of the Holy Ghost, and can speak with a new tongue, yea, even with the tongue of angels, and after this should deny me, it would have been better for you that ye had not known me" (2 Nephi 31:14).

Sherem, who publicly and brazenly denied the Christ, later confessed, "I fear lest I have committed the unpardonable sin, for I have lied unto God; for I denied the Christ, and said that I believed the scriptures; and they truly testified of him" (Jacob 7:19). King Benjamin called such a denial of the Spirit of the Lord as "open rebellion against God" (Mosiah 2:37).

Latter-day prophets have helped us to understand that this unpardonable sin is not possible to those whose "seeds [merely] fell by the wayside" (Matt 13:4), "had no root" (Matt 13:6), or even whose testimony was "choked" by thorns (Matthew 13:7). The Prophet Joseph Smith taught that "He has to say that the sun does not shine while he sees it."[1] Joseph Fielding Smith elaborated, "Therefore, he has resigned himself to evil knowingly."[2]

In fact and in essence, the unpardonable sin is "having denied the Holy Spirit after having received it, and having denied the Only Begotten Son of the Father, having crucified him unto themselves and put him to an open shame" (D&C 76:35).

The witness of the Holy Ghost to our soul of eternal truths is undeniable and indelible. Yet it is a personal experience, the intensity of which is only known by the person in receipt of, and by the testator, the Holy Spirit. It is nurtured by experience over time and by refining. Such condemnation where "there is no forgiveness in this world nor in the world to come" (D&C 76:34) is not for the casual or immaturely developed spiritual soul. That is comforting doctrine to us mortals as we navigate this life in view of our eternal life.

Notes:

1. Joseph Fielding Smith, comp., *Teachings of the Prophet Joseph Smith,* Salt Lake City: Deseret Book, 1976, 358.

2. Joseph Fielding Smith, *Answers to Gospel Questions*, Salt Lake City: Deseret Book, 1957, 2:120, 4:92.

301. The image of Boy Scouting dovetails with what the Lord teaches of manhood.

One of the strong iconic symbols of our day is that of a Boy Scout. Such is equated with courtesy, good deeds, clean living, outdoorsmanship, enthusiasm, and cheerful service. That the Church adopted scouting as the activity arm of its program for young men is a really good fit.

Jesus himself stated the lofty goal for our sons, "Therefore, what manner of men ought ye to be? Verily I say unto you, even as I am" (3 Nephi 27:27).

That mental picture of the character of Christ is very much embodied in the scouting movement. Consider the Scout Oath and the Scout Law as you think of the qualities that the Savior would endorse:

> "On my honor, I will do my best, to do my duty to God and my country, and to obey the Scout law; to help other people at all times; to keep myself physically strong, mentally awake, and morally straight."
>
> "A Scout is: Trustworthy, Loyal, Helpful, Friendly, Courteous, Kind, Obedient, Cheerful, Thrifty, Brave, Clean, and Reverent."[1]

The mission of the Boy Scouts of America is "to prepare young people to make ethical and moral choices over their lifetimes by instilling in them the values of the Scout Oath and Law."[2]

In truth, it's the bridge between scouting experiences and priesthood service that make this such a good training ground for the Church. Primary General President Cheryl Lant said, "Scouting prepares boys to become righteous men who hold and honor the priesthood of God. Scout leaders have the responsibility to help each boy connect what he is learning in Scouting to his priesthood preparation and his future as a covenant-keeping missionary, husband, and father."[3]

I've personally slept in a sleeping bag for well over one hundred nights on various camping trips with young scouts. I've witnessed the growth, leadership opportunities, challenge, industry, adventure, discovery, and fun that such experiences create. The hours spent around a campfire in casual conversation, singing, telling jokes, performing skits, or teaching through stories, make memories long to be remembered. Those experiences mold boys into men of good character.

"The Church became the first nationally chartered organization to affiliate with the Boy Scouts of America,"[4] back in 1913. It fits well with our Thirteenth Article of Faith which says in part, "We believe in being honest, true, chaste, benevolent, virtuous, and in doing good to all men. . . . If there is anything virtuous, lovely, or of good report or praiseworthy, we seek after these things" (Articles of Faith, 13). We seek after these things because such things bring us to Christ, whereby we can then bring others to Christ. The scouting program facilitates this for our young men.

Notes:

1. Boy Scouts of America website, www.scouting.org/Home/BoyScouts.aspx.
2. Boy Scouts of America website, www.scouting.org/scoutsource/Media/mission.aspx.
3. Cheryl Lant, Former LDS Primary General President, www.ldsbsa.org/wp-content/uploads/2014/06/May-2006-Entire-Newsletter.pdf.
4. "A Century of Scouting in the Church," *Ensign,* October, 2013.

302. There is a significant difference between curiosity and prayerful seeking.

It was September of 1976. I was staying with CB and Carol Lambert, a family who took me in as their own after my BYU Outdoor Survival experience of the previous year. They lived in Provo and told me that President Spencer W. Kimball would be the devotional speaker at BYU on Tuesday and I ought to go. "He's the current prophet of the Church, right?"

"Yes, he is."

The title of Prophet is not at all common to those who are not members of the Church. To them, prophets are either larger-than-life Biblical legend or modern-day kooks who have assumed that lofty title. This leader of the Mormon Church certainly didn't seem the latter, but rather an intelligent, thoughtful, and well respected man, so I decided to go to the devotional. I was curious.

I went by myself and sat in the upper rows of the very large Marriott Center. I remember that I was particularly interested in seeing the prophet and if I would sense accord to that title.

When I returned from the devotional, Carol asked me what I thought. I think I told her that I was unimpressed. Not disrespectfully, only not moved in any particular way. It was a nice lecture. If I was hoping to feel something, I didn't.

Since joining the Church, I've reflected on that experience on several occasions and wondered why I didn't feel the Spirit bear witness to me that President Kimball was indeed a Prophet. I think I understand now.

I went into that September devotional much like I would have attended any venue for entertainment or for information. I wanted to be acted upon, with no thought to enable that process, and most pointedly, without exercising any faith that I could be moved.

"I would exhort you that ye would ask God, the Eternal Father, in the name of Christ, if these things are not true; and if ye shall ask with a sincere heart, with real intent, having faith in Christ, he will manifest the truth of it unto you, by the power of the Holy Ghost" (Moroni 10:4).

Nephi exercised this pattern to know the truth. "After I had desired to know the things that my father had seen, and believing that the Lord was able to make them known unto me" (1 Nephi 11:1).

In my experience, I was curious, but I wasn't seeking. I was casual in attendance, not eager to know. I was wearing the lens of the world, not the lens of faith.

As my sincerity grew to know if prophets and apostles walked the earth today, coupled with faith that I could know, I did come to know. Two years later, I would receive and reverence a mission call to Mexico from a Prophet of God, even that same Spencer W. Kimball.

303. Gospel truths are often received as confirmation of what we already believed.

As literal children of God, I believe we must have divine DNA within us, so to speak. What I mean by that is that we not only have inherent divine qualities we can and should nurture, but we also possess divine intuitions. Intuition can be defined as the direct perception of truth, independent of any reasoning process or scientific method. In other words, it is things which are true that we just know and seem to have always known.

My wife first heard the missionary discussions while visiting her parents in South Africa, where they were on a work assignment. Her mother had very recently been baptized, and her dad was, at that same time, reactivated after forty years of inactivity. On the plane trip home to Australia, my not-yet-wife pondered what she had been introduced to. She said she never had to wrestle with the doctrines she was taught. It just made sense. As an example, having attended a Church of England boarding school, she was taught that God the Father and Jesus Christ formed two parts of the trinity, and by definition, the trinity was one God. Yet in her own view and practice, she prayed to God the Father and always looked to Jesus Christ as the Savior—two distinct, separate beings.

When taught the commandments and then on that same flight home, she knew the Word of Wisdom was correct doctrine and prayed for the strength to let go of worldly habits to align with what she now knew to be God's will. The commandments were intuitively correct to her, and now she could see a supportive structure aligned with that intuition, in contrast to the voices of marketing and popular culture she had only seen previously.

Recently, I was visiting my dad in Washington State. After many years of observing religion and even experimenting with different Christian faiths, he has adopted the stance that there is no God and there is no life after death. One day over breakfast, he said, "So often I have wished my parents were alive to see this, or that I could share such-and-such an experience with them." Then he said, "I can't explain it, but I've always felt my parents could see, and do know of these experiences, that they were a part of my life still." Even as an avowed non-believer, those intuitions of truth linger within.

I like the adage that "the gospel is simply beautiful and beautifully simple." Likely it is so because the core doctrines of our very identity seem to be implanted within us.

Our missionaries across the earth baptize thousands each month from all backgrounds, nationalities, cultures, economic circumstances, political systems, traditions, and previous faiths. Indeed, as they are introduced to the keystone of our religion, the Book of Mormon, it is "as of one that hath a familiar spirit" (Isaiah 29:4). They hear the voice of the Master, a voice that resonates with the truth within them.

304. Scriptural history is replete with visions and dreams.

"Visions and dreams have constituted the means of communication between God and men in every dispensation of the priesthood. In general, visions are manifested to the waking senses, whilst dreams are given during sleep."[1]

We read with reverence and high regard the revelatory experiences recorded in the Old and the New Testaments. Such experiences are confirming of the dealings of the Lord with His covenant people.

"The word of the Lord came unto Abram in a vision" (Genesis 15:1).

"And when Abram was ninety years old and nine, the Lord appeared to Abram" (Genesis 17:1).

"And the angel of the Lord appeared unto him [Moses] in a flame of fire out of the midst of a bush" (Exodus 3:2).

Gideon rejoiced "for because I have seen an angel of the Lord face to face" (Judges 6:22).

"Daniel had understanding in all visions and dreams" (Daniel 1:17).

The first verse of the books of Isaiah, Ezekiel, Obadiah, and Nahum all refer to the vision they recorded.

Joseph was taught the truth of Mary's conception in a dream (Matthew 1:20-24), and the wise men were "warned of God in a dream that they should not return to Herod" (Matthew 2:12).

Peter received a vision where he was commanded to take the gospel to the Gentiles, a landmark departure from the strict customs of the Jews (Acts 10:9-17, 28). Immediately following this vision, Peter preached to Cornelius, who had been visited by an angel telling him to seek out Peter (Acts 10:3-5).

Saul witnessed a "light from heaven" and conversed with the risen Lord on his way to Damascus, an experience that forever changed him (Acts 9:1-9).

Joseph Smith experienced "a pillar of light . . . above the brightness of the sun" (Joseph Smith History 1:16), from which he, too, was forever changed.

Other heavenly messengers visited the Prophet Joseph to restore priesthood and priesthood keys, to instruct, to direct, to comfort, and to reprove. Heavenly visions, visitations, and voices were not uncommon in the opening scenes of the restoration.

The fact that Joseph Smith had many experiences with angels, visions, dreams, and the very voice of the Lord is, instead of a disqualifier, a bona fide set of experiences for one so called to restore the Church of Jesus Christ to the earth in these latter days. It is entirely consistent with the Biblical record of God's dealings with his servants the prophets.

Notes:

1. James E. Talmage, *Articles of Faith,* Salt Lake City: The Church of Jesus Christ of Latter-day Saints, 1977, 226.

305. "Be in the world, but not of the world" is good, practical, and encouraging counsel.

The LDS community doesn't own this phrase. It is a theme preached from pulpits across the Christian spectrum, but I believe Latter-day Saints live it and identify with it second to none.

As always, Jesus is the model for this injunction. He who is the very Son of God, the only begotten in mortality, walked, ate, drank, socialized, conversed, contended, traveled, attended, and no doubt found enjoyment in the experience of mortal life. Yet, He declared in prayer to His Father, "I am not of the world" (John 17:16). Furthermore, in that same prayer, He framed the basis for the title phrase when he said, "I pray not that thou shouldest take them out of the world, but that thou shouldest keep them from the evil" (John 17:15).

It is interesting and seemingly in contrast that Paul speaks of fitting into the norms of those in our society, "that I might by all means save some" (1 Corinthians 9:22). Paul is acknowledging the need to associate, to contribute, to collaborate—to truly be in the world. He also makes clear that we are not to compromise our covenants with God when he says, "being not without law to God, but under the law to Christ" (1 Corinthians 9:21).

Latter-day Saints who participate prominently in the world form a relatively high percentage of the total LDS population. In business, academics, science, law, politics, sports, the arts—members of the Church are contributing as recognized leaders. If not leaders, they contribute to the ranks of those who make pleasant society what it is throughout the world.

Church members are known for their adherence to keeping the Sabbath day holy, for dressing modestly and not having pre-marital or extra-marital sexual relations, not using foul language, not abusing drugs or alcohol, striving to be honest, maintaining a high success rate in marriages, being loyal and law abiding citizens, defending the traditional family unit, living within their means, serving missions across the earth, and donating at least ten percent of their income to the Lord's work, plus donating to the poor and needy both locally and abroad. Members are certainly not *of* the world.

Any General Conference of the Church will make frequent mention of the disturbing trends of the world and the ever widening gap between the standards of God and the standards of the world. Reference will likely be made as well of preserving that gap between the ways of the world, and the conduct of the Latter-day Saints. That gap is a key indicator of being able to be *in* the world but not *of* the world. And that gap insures that we are on safe ground.

306. Those who knew Joseph Smith best believed him most.

It appears from the very beginning, that young Joseph Smith's family believed his reports of seeing angels, visions, and being appointed to bring forth an ancient record. This is remarkable. It is often the case that parents and siblings will discount the stories of a young family member as the product of an active imagination or the escape to a make-believe world. Yet young Joseph must have possessed such credible honesty that his immediate family, first and foremost, believed him. In the case of his parents and four of his five brothers, they remained faithful all their days to the claims and Church that Joseph was called to restore.

Three and one half years after the First Vision, Joseph received visits of the angel Moroni during the course of one night. The next morning, obedient to the command of the angel, Joseph related the encounter to his Father, whose response was, "It was of God," and to "do as commanded by the messenger" (Joseph Smith History 1:50).

Immediately, Joseph did just that and went to the place where the plates were buried, beheld the plates, and received further instruction from the heavenly messenger. "It was the following evening that Joseph told the rest of the family about the angel and the plates. William said they were "melted to tears, and believed all he said."[1] Two months later, Alvin, the oldest of the Smith boys, dying from a sudden sickness, called the family to his bedside. "He urged Joseph Jr. to be a good boy and do everything that lies in your power to obtain the Record."[2]

Hyrum, Joseph's older brother of five years, is remembered for his legendary loyalty to his brother and to the cause of the Church. His integrity, purity, humility, and personal devotion to the work was sealed along with the blood of Joseph on the fateful day of their martyrdom in 1844. John Taylor said, "In life they were not divided, and in death they were not separated" (D&C 135:3).

Another faithful and intimate witness to Joseph's divine calling was his wife Emma. She participated in the obtaining of the plates, acted as scribe during the translation, prepared the first hymnal for the Church, was the first to preside over the newly created Relief

Society organization, and was a general witness to just about every other scene of the restoration through the Nauvoo period. It was she who preserved the translation of the Bible manuscript and brought them across the Mississippi to Nauvoo because she felt them to be inspired. She believed.

Oliver Cowdery could be called the co-founder of the Church, given his role as a signed witness of the plates, in the translation and publication of the Book of Mormon, in the receipt of the two priesthoods, and in the formal formation of the Church. He shared several visions and heavenly manifestations during the early days of the Church, of which he wrote, "These were days never to be forgotten . . . What joy! . . . I shall ever look upon this expression of the Savior's goodness with wonder and thanksgiving while I am permitted to tarry" (Joseph Smith History, note to vs. 71). Oliver, although separated from the Church for ten years, returned and died in the faith. So far as we know, he never denied his experiences while estranged for those ten years. He was a man of integrity, respected both in and out of the Church.

His family, his wife, his beloved saints. Not a one of them prospered from the endeavor in terms of wealth or popularity. In fact, they suffered in a most undeserved manner, but they stood by the Prophet. They had the fire of testimony that he was a Prophet and that the Lord had restored his Church to the earth once again. "Those who knew Joseph best believed him most."[3]

Notes:

1. Richard L. Bushman, *Rough Stone Rolling,* New York: Alfred A. Knopf, 2005, 46.

2. Richard L. Bushman, 46.

3. Steven C. Harper, *Mormon Scholars Testify,* www.mormonscholarstestify.org/2065/steven-c-harper.

307. Worthy, qualified, capable, willing, and able Saints make a strong bench of leadership for the Church.

Mission Presidents are a rare breed. I mean by that that they are successful, spiritual, committed men, receiving a most awesome trust to preside over 170+ young missionaries. Together with their wives, they mentor, teach, train, assign, direct, guide, protect, encourage, discipline, counsel, support, and lead their young missionaries. They must be able to leave their business or employment for three years, be free from unnecessary debts, and take their family into their called field of labor, either within their own country of residence, to the outer reaches of the globe, or anywhere in between.

A Temple President and Matron oversee the operation of a sacred House of the Lord and hold the keys of the sealing power of Elijah. Their delegated keys enable the continuing injunction of the Lord given to Peter, "And I will give unto thee the keys of the kingdom of heaven: and whatsoever thou shalt bind on earth shall be bound in heaven: and whatsoever thou shalt loose on earth shall be loosed in heaven" (Matthew 16:19).

To staff a temple of average size (about 39,000 sq. ft.) requires approximately 750 volunteers who are called and set apart, temple worthy, and able to participate usually weekly on a given shift. These people accommodate the thousands of temple patrons who attend the temple to perform live or vicarious ordinances each year. Temple Presidents and Matrons also serve for a period of three years, leaving their personal concerns to serve wherever they may be assigned.

Area Seventies serve for a period of three to five years or so, retain their current employment and family responsibilities, and live at home. Our particular Area Authority resides two states away and has oversight for twenty-one stakes in our local area. He is typically on assignment three weekends out of a given month, presiding or assisting with stake conferences. In addition, he trains, coordinates, communicates, guides, and is a first responder to each of the Stake Presidents within his several coordinating councils. Their charge and responsibilities are awesome, indeed, and require men of tremendous faith, ability, and discipline. Remember, they often continue to hold down full time employment as well!

In addition to these Church Authorities, General Presidencies are called and sustained for the Aaronic Priesthood and the four auxiliaries of the Church. Each requires full-time service, usually for a period of five years. They travel the earth training, teaching, and lifting local leaders.

There are currently 418 missions across the earth, 147 operating temples, and approximately 314 serving Authorities and General Presidency members of the Church. A small living allowance, including housing for mission presidents, is made available for those full-time authorities that may need it. Many though are well along in their careers, and financially able to support themselves in their ministry. None of these leadership positions are professional positions receiving a salary.

Such a deep rooted system of service that provides training and support continues to self-perpetuate. Youth are trained from a young age in the home and supported by the priesthood and auxiliary organizations of the Church, as well as in the seminary program. They eagerly look forward to missions and lives of service to their fellows and to rear the rising generation in righteousness.

I am in awe of the caliber of leadership in the Church, the depth of the bench, and the personal discipleship of these willing servants. Such selfless sacrifice is likely unique in all the world. Onward, Christian Soldiers!

308. The conditions that brought about the death of Jesus and Joseph Smith share similarities.

First of all, I want to be clear that the purposes and outcomes that flow from the crucifixion of Jesus Christ and the martyrdom of Joseph Smith, are not herein being compared. Jesus was the Son of God, the Messiah, "slain for the sins of the world" (3rd Nephi 11:14), and Joseph was a great, yet mortal, prophet. However, the similarities surrounding their final days are noteworthy.

- Both had obtained an influence that threatened the status quo of civil and religious affairs. Nauvoo was the second largest city in Illinois, carrying political implications, as well as hosting its own militia in the Nauvoo Legion. More volatile still, both Jesus and Joseph challenged the religionists of their day.
- Both were martyred by intolerant members of the mainstream religion(s) of their day. "Now the chief priests, and elders, and all the council [religious council], sought false witness against Jesus, to put him to death" (Matthew 26:59). Thomas C. Sharp, owner of the local *Warsaw Signal* newspaper, "devoted his entire time to slandering, to lying against and misrepresenting the Latter-day Saints."[1] Mr. Sharp is representative of those who opposed the Latter-day Saints, while maintaining a respected stature in the community.
- Just prior to the final anguished scenes of their lives, both Jesus and Joseph found solace in a hymn. "And when they had sung an hymn, they went out into the mount of Olives" (Matthew 26:30). While imprisoned at Carthage, and at the request of the Prophet, John Taylor sang the plaintive tune we know as "A Poor Wayfaring Man of Grief."[2]
- Jesus had his Judas. Joseph had his several apostates who sought to discredit and inflame the public mind against him.

- Both were sealed to their fate by mob injustice rather than by judicial arraignment.

- Both were paraded before the people by their captors in an attempt to appease the curious and highlight what the captors considered a victory. They tried to humiliate Jesus on his way to Calvary and mock Joseph as he was paraded before the militia in Carthage.

- Jesus was helped on his way to Golgotha by Simon of Cyrene. Although compelled to carry Jesus' cross, I sense that Simon did so with some understanding of the significance and honor of the occasion. To Willard Richards, just prior to entering the jail cell in Carthage, Joseph asked, "if we go into the cell, will you go in with us?" Replied Willard, "Brother Joseph, you did not ask me to cross the river with you—you did not ask me to come to Carthage—you did not ask me to come to jail with you—and do you think I would forsake you now?"[3]

- Both Jesus and Joseph were charged with crimes they either didn't commit or didn't merit. Jesus was charged with blasphemy for declaring Himself as the Son of God, the Christ, and a King (Matthew 26:63-66). It was the truth. Joseph was held on trumped up charges of treason, thereby disallowing bail to insure his custody.

- In both cases, the Governor of the land wanted to placate the mob mentality and mitigate any punishment, but in both cases, they abdicated their responsibility to the more vociferous factions. Pilate declared, "I am innocent of the blood of this just person" (Matthew 27:24) but then "willing to content the people" (Mark 15:15), he delivered Jesus saying "see ye to it" (Matthew 27:24). Governor Ford of Illinois enticed Joseph to come to Carthage and "pledged his faith as Governor, and the faith of the state, that we should be protected, and that he would guarantee our perfect safety."[4] Soon after apprehending Joseph, Governor Ford gave charge to Captain Robert F. Smith "you have the Carthage Greys at your command."[5] He

> might just as well have said as did Pilate, "see ye to it." It was indeed the fox guarding the henhouse.

Both Jesus and Joseph were unjustly brought to their death by religious and civil bigots of their time, with somewhat parallel experiences of note.

Notes:

1. *History of the Church of Jesus Christ of Latter-day Saints,* Salt Lake City: Deseret Book, 1960, 4:489.
2. James Montgomery, "A Poor Wayfaring Man of Grief," *Hymns of the Church of Jesus Christ of Latter-day Saints,* Salt Lake City: The Church of Jesus Christ of Latter-day Saints, 1985, 29.
3. *Teachings of the Presidents of the Church: Joseph Smith,* 2007, 460; see also *History of the Church of Jesus Christ of Latter-day Saints,* Salt Lake City: Deseret Book, 1962, 6:616.
4. "Elder John Taylor's Account of His Meeting With Governor Ford, June 22, 1844," *History of the Church of Jesus Christ of Latter-day Saints,* Salt Lake City: Deseret Book, 1962, 6:544.
5. "Willard Richards' Account of the Arrest and Imprisonment of Joseph Smith, June 22-25, 1844," *History of the Church of Jesus Christ of Latter-day Saints,* Salt Lake City: Deseret Book, 1962, 6:570.

309. Full time missionaries are a standing model for righteous joy.

"I love missionary work SO much!!! I love seeing the Lord's hand (literally) in my life. It's such an honor to represent Him and do His work for Heavenly Father's children. I have NEVER been happier."[1]

"So I'm still loving being a missionary, and I'm so glad we have the chance to be involved in such a great work!"[2]

These are taken from emails home and are typical of the energy, optimism, and expression of happiness these young missionaries experience.

It can't just be by motivational means that they are so pumped up and full of faith. Zone conferences with their Mission President only occur every ninety days, and then they go back to their assigned areas with their companion. This can be many hours away from any motivational influence.

Nor is their joy coming from what would be considered normal twenty-year-old experiences. In fact, their day is loaded with failed appointments, rejection, studying from scripture, planning, wearing a shirt and tie (or dress/skirt for the sisters), and giving community service. They specifically don't call home, don't watch TV or listen to popular music, don't socialize with the opposite sex, and don't go to the latest movies. They have a fixed bedtime and arise before 6:30 am each day.

How is it, then, that they are so happy? To me, it is a testimony of the power of the Spirit in this work and an indication of the environment where the Spirit readily resides.

These missionaries keep the commandments; are obedient to priesthood leaders; lose themselves in the service of others; pray sincerely morning, night, and throughout the day; study the word of God intensely; exercise their faith in Christ; fast; teach true doctrine; and more. Their prayers and planning are focused on the needs of others. Their greatest yearnings are for the welfare of those they teach.

As the Apostle Paul, missionaries endure their own trials and suffering, and not a few.

"This week has been pretty rough for me. . . . Trials can be very difficult, but I know that my trials have helped me draw closer to my Savior Jesus Christ."[3]

Like Paul, they remember, "For as the sufferings of Christ abound in us, so our consolation also aboundeth by Christ" (2 Corinthians 1:5).

True joy takes on a more accurate description as we understand that it is not a synonym for the more temporary and, too often, elusive happiness that the world pursues. True joy is a spiritual sensation, and its attainment requires a spiritual focus and immersion. Missionaries are afforded this singular focus, and those who avail themselves of these opportunities, whether in the mission field or not, know that corresponding joy and peace.

Notes:

1. Email home from Sister Jenna Reeder, serving in the Oregon Salem Mission, (by permission).

2. Email home from Elder Spencer Barr, serving in the Germany Berlin Mission, (by permission).

3. Email home from Elder Bill Kemsley, serving in the Argentina Resistencia Mission, (by permission).

310. As the heavens are higher than the earth, so are my ways higher than your ways.

In my own musings, I sometimes wonder at the unique delivery of the religious experience that exists in the Church. It is unique when contrasted with other Christian churches. In fact, I wonder if to be entirely comfortable with one's church would indicate that it is more a creation of man than of God. Please don't misunderstand me, I am indeed comfortable with The Church of Jesus Christ of Latter-day Saints. But the very fact of its unique doctrinal positions, cultural practices, temple worship, priesthood role, centralized leadership, and a host of other distinguishing doctrines and practices, is a compelling segue into this divine declaration, "For my thoughts are not your thoughts, neither are your ways my ways, saith the Lord. For as the heavens are higher than the earth, so are my ways higher than your ways, and my thoughts than your thoughts" (Isaiah 55:8-9).

We believe that The Church of Jesus Christ of Latter-day Saints is the authorized Kingdom of God on the earth today, restored through the Prophet Joseph Smith by divine intervention. Organized by the living Christ, directed by the living Christ, one would expect the organization to be, well, unique.

Rather than re-packaging traditional doctrines and practices (most of those were postulated by men hundreds of years after the death of Christ), the Lord has revealed His thoughts and His ways anew in these latter days.

Here's an example. Section 76 of the Doctrine and Covenants, given to Joseph Smith and Sidney Rigdon in early 1832, was anything but conventional doctrine. Known simply as "The Vision" at the time of 1832, this revelation is a whole new school of thought and understanding which describes heaven as the three degrees of glory. What was Brigham Young's reaction to this new revelation? "I didn't understand it. . . . I had been so schooled in traditional Christian thought, that I could hardly comprehend it."[1] This revelation was not of man, but of God.

Other doctrines and practices seem counter intuitive or paradoxical when seen through mortal eyes. Examples are the notion of prosperity through tithes and offerings, the eager anticipation of young people to serve two year missions at the prime of their youth, members carving out time to do temple work for the deceased, or serving without pay for five to twenty-five hours per week or more, in various forms of church service. These practices, and so many others, are not the ways of man.

We should revel in the fact that The Church of Jesus Christ of Latter-day Saints stands alone in many of its doctrinal and practical tenets. Just as Isaiah 55:8-9 speaks of a single divine source, so stands a single divine organization revealing His ways and His thoughts.

Notes:

1. "The Vision – Doctrine and Covenants 76 – Episode 32," *The Joseph Smith Papers* Season 2, Audio; www.mormonchannel.org/listen/series/the-joseph-smith-papers-audio.

311. Stay in the mainstream of the gospel.

In 1977, I was in Cedar City, Utah, attending Southern Utah State College. What I was really doing, though, was investigating the Church. I was there in Utah to get a closer look, to know the Saints, to participate in the programs, to see the fruits of the gospel. And ostensibly to begin my college education.

One Wednesday at our Institute activity, the deal was that the boys would stand behind a portable chalk board, pull up their pant legs, and have the girls guess whose legs were whose. When I heard this was to be the activity, my first impression was that this was so juvenile, I wasn't going to participate. I was far too above this silly stuff, or so my thoughts ran. But then I had an impression that I will forever be grateful for, "Cragg, it's the Lord's program, just stay in the mainstream of the Church, and you'll be fine." So I participated and lived through it just fine, probably even enjoyed it.

This mainstream of the Church is safe ground. Practices, procedures, programs, policies, and certainly culture, all may change and evolve over time, but in the main, none of these will ever lead us from the path of salvation.

After the crucifixion of the Savior, the early apostles spent much of their time correcting false doctrines and incorrect practices, and in essence, keeping the Saints in the mainstream of the Church. Here are a few examples:

The books of Romans and Galatians were written in part to those who claimed that obedience to the Mosaic Law was the means to salvation. This explains the strong emphasis Paul gives to the grace of Christ, in contrast to works (the Mosaic Law). This is what these saints needed to understand. Paul taught them to balance the essential doctrines of faith, grace, and good works.

To the Corinthians, Paul gave correction against this background, "There were factions forming in the Corinthian branch with different views regarding moral conduct and doctrine. Some of the converts were assuming a libertine or free thinking attitude with respect to the doctrines . . . which had been taught to them against the old background which had been part of their former conduct and thinking."[1]

In another circumstance, it appears that some early Christians had adopted an early form of Gnosticism and were teaching that Jesus could not have truly come in the flesh, for God is Holy and could have nothing to do with contaminating matter. John wrote in his First Epistle to dispel such notions.

These examples from the writings of the early apostles certainly have more gravity than my simple experience of many years ago. What strikes me most of these experiences, though, is that there is a mainstream. A mainstream of doctrines, principles, and practices. A mainstream of safety founded on the Chief Cornerstone. "And are built upon the foundation of the apostles and prophets, Jesus Christ himself being the chief corner stone" (Ephesians 2:20). I've found that same safety by consciously keeping both feet in this mainstream of light and life.

Notes:

1. Howard W. Hunter, "The Reality of the Resurrection," *Conference Report,* April, 1969.

312. Alma said, "By small and simple things are great things brought to pass" (Alma 37:6).

This morning our stake celebrated fifty years since the Church has been organized in our little city. The mayor pro-tem read a proclamation stating June 29, 2013 as dedicated to The Church of Jesus Christ of Latter-day Saints!

The very growth of the Church at large from six charter members in 1830 to 15,000,000 183 years later is certainly impressive. Since 1977 when I was baptized, the Church has grown at an overall rate of 3.87 percent annually. Extrapolated out at this same rate are some pretty astounding numbers. Pick what time frame you will.

The Lord's model for the building of the kingdom can be planted in any country, climate, culture, geography, or economic condition, usually coupled with some degree of religious freedom. It will grow. Taking the phrase from scriptural language, many refer to the earth as "the Lord's vineyard" (D&C 72:2) and see their locale as a portion of the Lord's vineyard. Members consider that they have a stewardship in their part of the vineyard to nurture faith, watch over the members, and add to the collective Church at large.

In November of 1984, my wife and I moved to this town as newlyweds of one year. Our first child was born that same month. We attended our first Sunday in the newly constructed chapel in the town just south of us. I still remember the sacrament meeting talks that day. A young man had just returned from a mission to England. We learned later that this family were some of the early members here, arriving sometime in the late 1960's. From that first ward and single building, four stakes have been formed, some seven meetinghouses and four stake centers built, and membership within that original ward geographic footprint has gone from about 350 to over 13,000 members. All within thirty years!

"Wherefore, be not weary in well-doing, for ye are laying the foundation of a great work. And out of small things proceedeth that which is great" (D&C 64:33). In a subsequent revelation, the Lord gave us this larger vision, "Let no man count them as small things; for there is much which lieth in futurity, pertaining to the saints, which depends upon these things" [building the kingdom] (D&C 123:15).

"Therefore, dearly beloved brethren, let us cheerfully do all things that lie in our power; and then may we stand still, with the utmost assurance, to see the salvation of God, and for his arm to be revealed" (D&C 123:17). We stand today upon the shoulders of those who lived this counsel, and who, whether living or dead, must enjoy tremendous satisfaction at witnessing the fruits of their labors. And the glory and thanks be to God and to our Savior for such a blessing to experience.

313. The passing of the mantle is real and is spiritually discernible.

In the spring of 2001, I was released from serving as the bishop of our ward after five years of service. The local paper found it newsworthy and carried a short article with a picture of me and the new bishop. Under the photo was written, "Bishop Cragg Rogers passes the leadership mantle to the new bishop, Harlow Hagee." I'm pretty sure the article and this caption were written and submitted by our own public affairs person, Bobbye Fisher, because that language referring to the "leadership mantle" is very much a part of the LDS vernacular.

I like the definition of "mantle" in the Oxford dictionary: "an important role or responsibility that passes from one person to another."[1] It is that, but of greater interest to me is the conscious recognition by others of that role and responsibility. The credence, respect, expectations, and trust that immediately flow to him or her who receives that mantle.

As an example, when a man is called to serve as a bishop, he is set apart to be the presiding high priest of the ward. This same man who was just Brother So-and-So prior to his ordination is now recognized as one who is authorized and will rightfully receive revelation to lead and guide his ward. His counsel will be sought out, not that he has particularly changed overnight, but that he now bears the mantle of the bishop. The Lord will honor that mantle, and the faithful know it.

This is different from being promoted to lead in a business or having authority and power in a political field. Those positions and transfers are usually predictable given the positioning, the grooming, and the degree of tenure or experience. They are more sequential.

Young David was chosen by the Lord through Samuel to be the King of Israel. "But the Lord said unto Samuel, Look not on his countenance, or on the height of his stature . . . for the Lord seeth not as man seeth; for man looketh on the outward appearance, but the Lord looketh on the heart. . . . Then Samuel took the horn of oil, and anointed him in the midst of his brethren; and the Spirit of the Lord [the mantle] came upon David from that day forward" (1 Samuel 16:7, 13).

When Elijah was taken up to heaven, Elisha "took the mantle of Elijah that fell from him . . . And when the sons of the prophets which were to view at Jericho saw him, they said, The spirit of Elijah doth rest on Elisha. And they came to meet him, and bowed themselves to the ground before him" (2 Kings 2:14-15).

President Thomas S. Monson reminds those who serve that "the mantle of leadership is not the cloak of comfort but rather the robe of responsibility."[2] Without exception, I've watched those called to lead and receive this almost palpable mantle approach their calling with humility. They are willing servants, enabled by the mantle given them of the Lord and acknowledged by the people they serve.

Notes:

1. www.oxforddictionaries.com/us/definition/american_english/mantle.

2. Thomas S. Monson, "Sugar Beets and the Worth of a Soul," *Ensign,* July, 2009.

314. Even as a prophet, Joseph Smith was not above chastening from the Lord.

Gladys Clark Farmer has written that "to chasten denotes to make chaste,"[1] in the sense of being refined, tried, purified. I like that definition as it relates to the process of improvement, progress, and course correction. When the Lord chastens his children, it is to bring them to repentance, which is to re-align their course with eternal verities. Adam, Moses, David, Job, Paul, Lehi, the brother of Jared—all were at times chastened of the Lord. I suppose that all the great prophets have been so schooled.

We have a unique perspective, though, when observing the chastening of Joseph Smith, because the chastening came as revelations from the Lord directly to him. "I suppose that another evidence of the Prophet Joseph Smith's humility, his willingness to expose himself and show his vulnerability, was the fact that the revelations that he received, a dozen and a half of them, contained instances where he and his role is diminished. He is reproved by Jesus Christ, his weaknesses are exposed, the call for him to improve shows up."[2]

First to cite are the words of the Lord to Joseph in mid-1828, as a consequence of the loss of 116 pages of manuscript from the first part of the Book of Mormon. Joseph had reluctantly allowed these pages to pass from his custody to that of Martin Harris. "Behold, you have been entrusted with these things, but how strict were your commandments. . . . And behold, how oft you have transgressed the commandments and the laws of God, and have gone on in the persuasions of men. For, behold, you should not have feared man more than God. Although men set at naught the counsels of God, and despise his words—Yet you should have been faithful; and he would have extended his arm and supported you against all the fiery darts of the adversary; and he would have been with you in every time of trouble. Behold, thou art Joseph, and thou was chosen to do the work of the Lord, but because of transgression, if thou art not aware, thou wilt fall" (D&C 3:5-9).

About nine months later, the Lord again chastened Joseph for his conduct and re-visited the same caution, "And now I command you, my servant Joseph, to repent and walk more uprightly before me, and to yield to the persuasions of men no more; And that you be firm in keeping the commandments wherewith I have commanded you" (D&C 5:21-22).

These early experiences were perhaps the forming of Joseph's unyielding obedience to the commandments of the Lord throughout his ministry.

At one point, Joseph received this strong rebuke, "And now, verily I say unto Joseph Smith, Jun.—You have not kept the commandments, and must needs stand rebuked before the Lord" (D&C 93:47).

Impressive to me is that these instances reveal a third party to these very writings. Were it the writings of Joseph, such chastening would not likely be included. It is the gentle and merciful Lord who is molding, mentoring, and coaching his Prophet as he shoulders the opening scenes of this dispensation. It is recognition of Joseph, the man, being tutored of the Lord.

Notes:

1. Gladys Clark Farmer, "Chastening," *Encyclopedia of Mormonism*, 1992, 264.

2. Ronald O. Barney, "The Sermons of Joseph Smith – Episode 40," *The Joseph Smith Papers*, Audio; www.mormonchannel.org/listen/series/the-joseph-smith-papers-audio.

315. You are hereby called to serve as a missionary of the Church of Jesus Christ.

So begins the call letter from the President of the Church to the anxious members who have qualified themselves to serve as a full-time missionary.

The culture within the Church of young people and senior couples serving missions is unparalleled. It is a renewing testimony of the personal witness of the Spirit to individual hearts that the Gospel is true. It follows from such a testimony that we want to share it with others. We see this pattern over and over in the scriptures. Here are just a few examples:

Paul, two verses after the report of his baptism, goes "and straightway he preached Christ in the synagogues, that he is the Son of God" (Acts 9:20).

Enos was converted during a prayerful experience in the forest, and immediately, "I began to feel a desire for the welfare of my brethren, the Nephites; wherefore, I did pour out my whole soul unto God for them" (Enos 1:9).

Alma the younger, following his conversion, "began from this time forward to teach the people" (Mosiah 27:32).

Our young missionaries, prior to receiving that letter of calling, have already complied with initial requirements which include

- Living morally clean

- Completely abstaining from coffee, alcohol, tobacco, and harmful drugs
- Being active in Church meetings and responsibilities
- Living within the laws of the land
- Maintaining good health practices, including having an appropriate level of strength and vitality
- Having developed good literacy skills
- Earning all or a portion of the roughly $10,000 cost of serving for two years
- Meeting frequently with their Bishop and Stake President to discuss their moral worthiness, their motivation for wanting to serve, their depth of testimony, funding for the mission, and other preparatory concerns

And that just gets them qualified to apply to serve a mission.

Most people who are not members of the Church marvel that these missions are paid for by the missionaries and their families. Missionaries are not compensated by the Church for their service. They live frugally while on a mission, which (in the States) is about $180 per month, after housing and transportation costs.

They email or write home once each week, receiving like correspondence from friends and family. They only place a call home on Mother's Day and Christmas! They are expected to live mission rules, arise at 6:30 am, always be in sight of their assigned companion and work until 9:30 at night. They study three to four hours each day from the scriptures, *Preach my Gospel,* and when applicable, their foreign language. They don't watch TV, listen to contemporary music, go to movies, or follow their favorite teams. Although they are young and single, they shun flirtations or relationships with the opposite sex and hold at bay any special somebody that took their heart and time previously. They hold no gainful employment for these years of service.

"As you devote your time and attention to serving the Lord, leaving behind all other personal affairs, the Lord will bless you. . . . Greater blessings and more happiness than you have yet experienced await you as you humbly and prayerfully serve the Lord in this labor of love among His children.[1]

That young people would embark on such a mission is a manifestation of their faith and conviction. I've seen many departing missionaries adopt as their statement of purpose the declaration of the Prophet Moroni, "Behold, I am a disciple of Jesus Christ, the Son of God. I have been called of him to declare his word among his people, that they might have everlasting life" (3 Nephi 5:13). To their discipleship, their actions stand as a living testimony. It is, indeed, a labor of love among His children. It follows a scriptural pattern for those who are truly converted to the gospel of Jesus Christ.

Notes:

1. Excerpt from our son's mission call dated May 7, 2013.

316. Motives matter and are real indicators of integrity.

This morning I sat in a training class for young adults preparing to enter into the mission field. Blake Wassom, a returned missionary and former teacher at the Missionary Training Center in Provo, was the instructor. He drew on the chalkboard a triangular sketch, with a missionary, investigators, and the Godhead at each of the three corners. He then placed a two-way arrow between each of the three, indicating that there is a needed relationship in each instance—the missionary to the Godhead, the missionary to the investigator, and the investigator to the Godhead. And of course, vice-versa in each instance.

He asked which of these three relationships was the most important. Most reasoned that the relationship of a missionary to God would be the most important, so they could lead, teach, and model for their investigators.

The instructor then referred us to the very purpose of a missionary in *Preach My Gospel,* "[My purpose as a missionary is to] Invite others to come unto Christ by helping them receive the restored gospel through faith in Jesus Christ and His Atonement, repentance, baptism, receiving the gift of the Holy Ghost, and enduring to the end."[1]

Going back to the drawing on the chalkboard, Brother Wassom then mapped out the purpose statement as it was relevant to each of the three relationships. Textually, it was like this:

- Missionary to Investigator: Invite, help, baptize
- Investigator to Godhead: Come unto Christ; receive the restored Gospel; develop faith in Christ; repent, desire, and be baptized; receive the gift of the Holy Ghost; remain faithful all of life

It immediately became clear that the most important relationship in this triangle was the investigator to God their Father, their Savior Jesus Christ, and to the feelings and witness of the Holy Ghost. The relationship of a missionary to the Godhead is presupposed in this blueprint. To drive the point home, Brother Wassom made the comment, "This is not about you. You may call it *your mission*, but it is not about you."[2]

Bringing people into the Church is not to see our numbers grow, although that is a gratifying result. It is not to increase the tithing contributions and enrich the Church. It is not to have people believe us and to like us. It is not to prove scriptural points of doctrine by selected supportive verses. It is not to sell copies of the Book of Mormon. It is not to attach investigators to our own personality.

It is, most importantly, to help others come unto Christ—to develop that real, personal, two-way relationship with God, to commit to faithfully follow the commandments, to keep covenants, and to build the kingdom of God on the earth. Then can it be said that the seeds sown "fell into good ground, and brought forth fruit" (Matthew 13:8).

We have the faith that when we can face a person to Christ, the Spirit will bear witness of the truth. Coupled with the knowledge that "the Spirit of Christ is given to every man" (Moroni 7:16), we then have a formula for true conversion for an investigator. It is a reliance on the promises of God and not upon the reasoning of man. It is an anchoring to and an attempt to anchor toward, the only sure foundation, "a foundation whereon if men build, they cannot fall" (Helaman 5:12). It is a pure, altruistic motive.

Notes:

1. *Preach My Gospel,* Salt Lake City: Intellectual Reserve, Inc., 2004, 1.
2. Blake Wassom, Stake Missionary Preparation Class, July 2013

317. The legacy of Martin Harris is a faithful witness to the restoration.

Were it not for Martin Harris, the launch of the restoration in these latter days would have had to take a different course. "What a unique and valuable contribution Martin Harris, one of Joseph's first confidants outside his family, made to the Restoration."[1]

It was late 1827 when Martin Harris first befriended Joseph Smith after hearing of the Gold Bible that was to be translated. As testament to his interest in and hope for this new work, Martin gave Joseph fifty dollars to pay debts and locate to Pennsylvania to begin the translation, a good sum of money in those days. Martin was more than twenty years Joseph's senior and a prosperous farmer in Palmyra.

Sometime in early 1828, Martin carried notations of the characters written on the plates to New York to a Professor Charles Anthon, seeking his professional endorsement as to their authenticity. Subsequent conflicting testimony by Mr. Anthon of this meeting, in contrast to the report of Martin Harris, is still debated. However, from this meeting, Martin was even more enthusiastic about the work, firm testimony to me of the endorsement actually received.

Following the loss of the 116 pages of original translation manuscript, the Lord referred to Martin Harris as a "wicked man" in both sections 3 and 10 of the Doctrine and Covenants. This is of note for at least two observations: 1) Martin was not soured toward the work for such a strong rebuke, and 2) Joseph would not have risked alienating this man of reputation and needed means by such seemingly harsh language.

But it was revelation from God, and He knew Martin's heart. Approximately ten months later, Martin would testify to all the world in writing "that an angel of God . . . laid before our eyes, that we beheld and saw the plates" (The Testimony of Three Witnesses, Book of Mormon).

About two months after that experience, Harris entered into a contract with E.B. Grandin to publish the Book of Mormon, mortgaging his farm as collateral if not paid in full within eighteen months after printing commenced. In fact, Harris was forced to sell 151 acres in a private sale to compensate Grandin.[2]

A few months later, Martin was present when the Church was legally organized and was baptized that same day. He was appointed to the first High Council in 1834, served as a member of Zion's Camp, participated in the United Order, and was one of three appointed and granted authority by the Prophet "to choose twelve men from the Church as Apostles."[3]

Although excommunicated for a time, he was rebaptized and died in the faith. "In 1860 he told a census taker that he was a 'Mormon Preacher,' evidence of his continuing loyalty to the restored gospel."[4]

Here was a man who could have exposed a fraudulent work if it were so, or who could have taken personal offense on several occasions and separated himself from his Mormon associations. It was Martin's faith and his honoring of sacred experiences and promises that will be his legacy and witness of some of the key foundational moments of the restoration.

Notes:

1. Susan Easton Black and Larry C. Porter, "For the Sum of Three Thousand Dollars," *Neal A. Maxwell Institute for Religious Scholarship,* Provo: Brigham Young University, 2005, publications.maxwellinstitute.byu.edu.

2. Black and Porter.

3. Kirtland High Council Minutes, 149; *History of the Church,* 2:186-187

4. Dallin H. Oaks, "The Witness: Martin Harris," *Ensign,* May, 1999.

318. Angels, visions, plates, healings, tongues, and revelation are all divine patterns.

"And Jesus looking upon them saith, With men it is impossible, but not with God; for with God all things are possible" (Mark 10:27). I think that is a good definition of miracles. Miracles are those events and occurrences that we as mortals don't understand, and therefore, label as impossible. When they are observed or experienced as fact, we call them miracles. The Old and the New Testaments are rife with miracles.

"For behold, I am God; and I am a God of miracles; and I will show unto the world that I am the same yesterday, today, and forever; and I work not among the children of men save it be according to their faith" (2 Nephi 27:23).

Too many people who are introduced to the restored gospel of Jesus Christ dismiss it as too far-fetched, too unbelievable, too incompatible with the contemporary times in which we live—a book written on gold plates and buried in what is now New York by an ancient prophet, then brought forth in these days by an angel; priesthood keys being delivered by holy messengers to a modern day prophet in a sacred temple; current revelation from God, recorded and published as scripture; the gathering of Israel; healings, anointing's, blessings, and ordinations.

It is precisely these types of restored practices and occurrences that speak to the authenticity of this work. Let's look at some of the miracles upon which our Judeo-Christian heritage is founded and which are generally accepted as fact amongst believers.

- Moses spoke with God at the burning bush that was not consumed
- Daniel was cast to the lions and protected by an intervening angel
- The Red Sea was parted by the Lord, and the Israelites passed through to the other side on dry ground
- Jesus caught up to his disciples after a night of prayer by walking directly to them on water

My faith is not built on these and the many other supernatural occurrences we call miracles, but I accept these miracles because of my faith in Christ. And I expect similar miraculous intervention to be resident in the Lord's Kingdom today.

There are some instances in our Church history that make us raise our eyebrows today, as if to say, "Really?" No more, though, than Elisha floating an axe or Baalam and the conversation with his donkey. Not being present, we can only take it as written.

"Behold, great and marvelous are the works of the Lord. How unsearchable are the depths of the mysteries of him; and it is impossible that man should find out all his ways. And no man knoweth of his ways save it be revealed unto him; wherefore, brethren, despise not the revelations [and miracles] of God" (Jacob 4:8).

God is omnipotent, unlimited, and almighty. We counsel Him not, nor do we set the parameters of His capabilities, nor the timeline for His marvelous work. His hand was evident yesterday, and His hand is evident today. I believe in a God of miracles.

319. Oliver Cowdery comes into the opening scenes as a scribe and a believer.

Looking back at history as a sequence of events, it all seems logical and almost predictable as a story line, but in the actual unfolding, the next step, that future step, is sometimes entirely unknown.

Immediately upon obtaining the plates, Joseph was badgered by the local folk. Apparently, they had enough belief in the truthfulness of his story that they wanted a piece of the action, particularly lured by the mention of the word gold. To escape that growing harassment, Joseph and Emma moved to Harmony, Pennsylvania to live with Emma's parents in December of 1827. With the hidden plates in their possession, it was Joseph's intention to begin the translation while in Harmony.

Joseph translated a few characters in January, which Martin Harris took to New York City to Professor Charles Anthon and others to seek their professional opinion of the translation.

Then, from mid-April to mid-June of 1828, Joseph translated the first 116 pages, with Martin Harris as his scribe. Those pages were lost by Martin, Joseph was reprimanded by the Lord for the whole fiasco, and his gift to translate was taken from him. By September 22, that gift was restored to Joseph. Emma and perhaps others acted as scribe. But over the winter, it progressed very slowly.

In March of 1829, at the request of Martin Harris, Section Five of the Doctrine and Covenants was received, with this surprising charge, "Behold, I say unto thee Joseph, when thou has translated a few more pages, thou shalt stop for a season, even until I command thee again; then thou mayest translate again. . . . Stop, and stand still until I command thee, and I will provide means whereby thou mayest accomplish the things which I have commanded thee" (D&C 5:30, 34).

Meanwhile, Oliver, as a schoolteacher, boarded with Joseph's parents and learned from the Smith family of the work that Joseph was called to perform. Oliver declared to the Smiths, "The subject upon which we were yesterday conversing seems working in my very bones, and I cannot, for a moment, get it out of my mind . . . I have made it a subject of prayer, and I firmly believe that it is the will of the Lord that I should go [to see Joseph]. If there is a work for me to do in this thing, I am determined to attend to it."[1]

"Two days after the arrival of Mr. Cowdery (being the 7th of April) I commenced to translate the Book of Mormon, and he began to write for me."[2] Together, Joseph and Oliver completed the translation sometime in late June of 1829.

It was March of 1829 when Joseph was told that means would be provided to translate. In April, Oliver Cowdery came upon the scene, having previously received a witness that the work Joseph was doing was true.[3] Joseph could not have known how that revelatory promise would be fulfilled, but he certainly believed that it would. It was, as the Lord said it would, and it was fulfilled in the very capable person of Oliver Cowdery.

Notes:

1. Lucy Mack Smith, *History of Joseph Smith by his Mother*, Salt Lake City: Bookcraft, 1958, 139.

2. *History of the Church of Jesus Christ of Latter-day Saints,* Salt Lake City: Deseret Book, 1964, 1:32-33.

3. *History of the Church of Jesus Christ of Latter-day Saints,* 1:35.

320. Jesus' alleged "sin" was proclaiming a truth that disrupted accepted mainstream doctrine.

In the final mortal hours of Him who is the Savior of all men, Jesus was ultimately accused of blasphemy, because He answered affirmatively to the injunction, "Tell us whether thou be the Christ, the Son of God" (Matthew 26:63). Significantly, the accusation of blasphemy was not made by Pontius Pilate the Governor, nor by Herod Antipas the Tetrarch of Galilee, but by Caiaphas, the Sadducean High Priest and apparently the spiritual leader of the Jews.

This was not the first time Jesus had openly declared His divinity and His role as the promised Messiah. When He declared Himself to be the Messianic fulfillment of Isaiah's prophecy, the people "thrust him out of the city, and led him unto the brow of the hill . . . that they might cast him down headlong" (Luke 4:16-29).

At the time of Christ, the Jews had a bias regard for their progenitor, Abraham. Ostensibly, it took precedence over their looking forward to the coming of the promised Messiah. It became a faith of its own. When Jesus ended a lengthy exchange regarding His divinity with the statement "Before Abraham was, I am," the unbelieving Jews "took they up stones to cast at him" (John 8:58-59).

There is a parallel today in declaring the truth that all people are sons and daughters of God, and by natural extension, can become like

Him. The parallel is in the reaction to that statement by mainstream Christianity, who declare it, likewise, to be blasphemy.

The fifth president of the Church, Lorenzo Snow, said, "As man now is, God once was; as God now is, man may be."[1] That is glorious doctrine and truly fundamental to the very purposes of God "to bring to pass the immortality and eternal life of man" (Moses 1:39). It in no way diminishes the eternal reverence we have toward our Heavenly Father. Nor will He ever cease to be our God. We will worship Him forever and be eternally grateful for His merciful and comprehensive plan of salvation.

I reverence my Heavenly Father. I love His ways. I know Him, and He knows me. I long to be like Him in some way, as the ultimate expression of my worship. And I know that can only be approximated by having an attitude and perspective of humility, awe, and undiminished eternal reverence. As Jesus was summarily dismissed in His day by the appointed High Priest as a blasphemer, I don't expect the accepted doctrinaires of today to embrace this truth regarding our divine identity and our divine destiny. But truth it is.

Notes:

1. Lorenzo Snow, as quoted by Gerald N. Lund, "I Have a Question," *Ensign*, February, 1982.

321. The Doctrine and Covenants demonstrates a divine manner of speaking.

Patterns of language are to some extent like fingerprints, unique to the individual. The Lord spoke to the ancient prophets, and they recorded that communication. Some are chronicled in the Holy Bible. The Lord continues to speak to prophets in these latter days, and much of what was given to the Prophet Joseph Smith is recorded in the Doctrine and Covenants. The divine source of these communications is the Lord Jesus Christ, so we ought to see similar patterns of language. And we do. Let's compare just Section 1 of the Doctrine and Covenants with selected Bible verses.

Doctrine and Covenants	The Holy Bible
D&C 1:1 "Hearken ye people from afar; and ye that are upon the islands of the sea, listen together."	Isaiah 49:1 "Listen, O isles . . . and hearken, ye people, from afar."
D&C 1:10 Unto the day when the Lord will come to recompense unto every man according to his work and measure to every man according to the measure which he has measured to his fellow man.	**Proverbs 24:12, Matthew 7:2** "And shall not he render to every man according to his works?" "And with what measure ye mete, it shall be measured to you again."
D&C 1:15 "For they have strayed from mine ordinances, and have broken mine everlasting covenant."	**Isaiah 24:5** "Because they have transgressed the laws, changed the ordinance, broken the everlasting covenant."
D&C 1:19 "The weak things of the world shall come forth and break down the mighty and strong ones."	**1 Corinthians 1:27** "And God hath chosen the weak things of the world to confound the things which are mighty."
D&C 1:19 "That man should not counsel his fellow man, neither trust in the arm of flesh."	**Jeremiah 17:5** "Cursed be the man that trusteth in man, and maketh flesh his arm."
D&C 1:35 "For I am no respecter of persons."	**Acts 10:34** "Of a truth I perceive that God is no respecter of persons."

D&C 1:38	Matthew 24:34, 35
"And though the heavens and the earth pass away, my word shall not pass away, but shall all be fulfilled."	"This generation shall not pass, till all these things be fulfilled. Heaven and earth shall pass away, but my words shall not pass away."
D&C 1:39 "And the Spirit beareth record, and the record is true."	**1 John 5:6** "And it is the Spirit that beareth witness, because the Spirit is truth."

Section 1 was received by Joseph Smith between sessions of a conference in Hiram, Ohio, on November 1, 1831. Joseph was twenty-five-years old. The revelation was recorded by John Whitmer as it was dictated by Joseph. There was no simultaneous consulting of Biblical text.

This language correlation with the Bible occurs throughout the Doctrine and Covenants and is both evidence of a common divine source and of clarity in the declaration of true principles.

322. Stewardship interviews are a means for accountability, counsel, and renewal.

Here's some good LDS jargon: "Meet me at the stake center with your companion for a PPI concerning your home teaching families, and we can also discuss your priesthood responsibilities as it relates to your calling and to your own family." That is perfectly clear to me and quite common coming from my quorum leader.

A PPI is a Personal Priesthood Interview, although that acronym seems to be in waning use in favor of the more straightforward reference to merely conducting an interview. All priesthood bearers and all Church auxiliary presidents are accountable to an authorized file leader for the discharge of their responsibilities.

We are big believers in responsibility and duty. "Wherefore, now let every man learn his duty, and to act in the office in which he is appointed, in all diligence. He that is slothful shall not be counted worthy to stand" (D&C 107:99-100).

When Jesus gave the parable of the talents in Matthew 25, the rewards went to those who magnified or increased the talents given them. When given responsibility in the kingdom, or as a parent, we likewise seek to "yield fruit . . . and increased; and brought forth, some thirty, and some sixty, and some an hundred" (Mark 4:8).

"When performance is measured, performance improves. When performance is measured and reported, the rate of improvement accelerates."[1]

The notion of stewardship—all we have and receive really comes from and belongs to God—is foundational to how we look at the world. Said the Lord, "For it is required of the Lord, at the hand of every steward, to render an account of his stewardship, both in time and in eternity" (D&C 72:3).

And so we take part in interviews - with our children (formal or informal), our quorum leader, our auxiliary leader, our bishop, and the stake presidency. There are temple recommend interviews, tithing settlement interviews, youth interviews, worthiness interviews, interviews to issue a calling, home teaching interviews, auxiliary interviews, priesthood interviews, personal interviews. Each is designed with the objective to edify, as well as to understand, to express appreciation, to inquire, to assist, to counsel, to instruct. It is also an opportunity to give an accounting, to report on one's responsibility, to follow up on previous interviews, and to discuss the needs and efforts in our ministry to others.

It is a process that blesses at least three people—the interviewer, the person giving an accounting, and the person(s) they are called to serve. It is a continuous focusing activity because interviews occur at every level in the Church, from the Lord to His prophet, to the Quorum of the Twelve, to General Authorities, to Stake Presidents, Bishops, Quorum leaders, Auxiliary leaders, priesthood leaders, priesthood bearers, teachers, husbands and wives and children.

"And the books were opened . . . and the dead were judged out of those things that were written in the books, according to their works" (Revelation 20:12). It is both a privilege and an uplifting experience to give an accounting to one who holds keys or designated authority and is a precursor to when we will one day stand before God.

Notes:

1. Thomas S. Monson, "Thou Art a Teacher Come From God," *Conference Report,* October, 1970.

323. All things must be done by common consent in the Church.

This statement and practice of common consent has always impressed me as a provision for the inclusion of Church membership at large. Not once, but repeatedly, does the Lord stress this practice as an important doctrine. And I believe it is unique to ecclesiastical administration within the LDS Church.

"For all things must be done in order, and by common consent in the church" (D&C 28:13).

"That certain men among them shall be appointed, and they shall be appointed by the voice of the church" (D&C 38:34).

"And all things shall be done by common consent in the church" (D&C 26:2).

"The president of the church . . . is appointed by revelation, and acknowledged in his administration by the voice of the church" (D&C 102:9).

That last quote highlights this practice best. It is both divine revelation and subsequent common consent. Joseph Smith coined the term "Theodemocracy" and defined it, "where God and the people hold the power to conduct the affairs of men in righteousness."[1]

At the very organization of the Church in Fayette, New York, "one of the first orders of business . . . was to ask those participating if they desired to have the church organized. To this they consented by unanimous vote. They were [then] asked if they could sustain Joseph Smith, Jr., and Oliver Cowdery as the presiding officers of the Church. To this they also responded by unanimous vote."[2]

At the first conference of the Church held on June 9, 1830, the "Articles and Covenants [were] read by Joseph Smith, Jr., and received by unanimous voice of the whole congregation."[3]

The law of common consent is rooted in the tenet of unity. "I say unto you, be one; and if ye are not one ye are not mine" (D&C 38:27). The three highest councils in the church are under divine injunction to be one. "And every decision made by either of these quorums must be by the unanimous voice of the same" (D&C 107:27).

Every member of the Church has the opportunity to publicly manifest (sustain) support or not to support those actions that have influence or authority over them as members of the Church. These actions may include general or local Church policy, callings and positions of responsibility, or even the canonization of new scripture.

"Our privilege of sustaining leaders is granted by the Lord. Sustaining makes known to the Church who has authority and enables each of us to show support. We honor all our leaders, both men and women, and are grateful for brothers and sisters so united in this Kingdom of God on earth."[4]

The law of common consent is a practice and a term unique to the Lord's Church. It enables the lay membership to receive their own witness of a particular inspired action and then to express support and loyalty to that action. Indeed, it enables and prepares the Lord's people "to serve him with one consent" (Zephaniah 3:9).

Notes:

1. Joseph Smith, Jr., "The Globe," *Times and Seasons,* April 15, 1844, 510.

2. Doyle L. Green, "April 6, 1830: The Day the Church Was Organized," *Ensign,* January, 1971.

3. *"Minutes of the first Conference held in the Township of Fayette, Senaca [sp] County, State of New York,"* Minute Book 2, June 9, 1830.

4. Russell M. Nelson, "Woman—Of Infinite Worth," *Ensign,* November, 1989.

324. The Church acts with political neutrality.

Our fundamental commonality as members of the Church is our testimony that God is our Father, that Jesus is the Christ, and that the Church has been restored to the earth through Joseph Smith and is governed by an authorized priesthood through living prophets and apostles today. Although we are united and inclusive of all that that testimony entails, from there we, as a membership, are a most diverse body. We differ in our favorite sports teams, our favorite hobbies, the genre of music we listen to, the books we read, and the places we vacation. When it comes to politics, we cover the gamut from right to left and everything in between.

This political diversity is, I believe, as it should be. The official stance of the Church is that "while affirming the right of expression on political and social issues, the Church is neutral regarding political parties, political platforms, and candidates for political office. The Church does not endorse any political party or candidate. Nor does it advise members how to vote."[1]

Jesus displayed lawful adherence to the governmental authorities of his time (see Matthew 17:24-27, 22:17-21). It is a tenet of our faith to be "subject to . . . rulers . . . and sustaining the law" (Articles of Faith, 12). Yet, Jesus also seemed indifferent to their various caucuses. His mission was infinitely more important than such parochial matters. His comment to his disciples regarding Herod the tetrarch on one occasion that Luke recorded is interesting, "Go ye, and tell that fox" (Luke 13:32). I can't define the context or tone of that comment; however, I find it interesting (or at the least, amusing).

Our political diversity is openly displayed and acknowledged in the Church through public figures such as Glen Beck, Harry Reid, Mitt Romney, Jon Huntsman, Orrin Hatch, Ezra Taft Benson and many others. That short list of political figures would never have unanimous consent on issues of politics but would be of one accord in faith and testimony of the gospel.

"As citizens, Church members are encouraged to participate in political and governmental affairs, including involvement in the political party of their choice. Members are also urged to be actively engaged in worthy causes to improve their communities and make them wholesome places in which to live and rear families."[2] And to do that, there are various schools of thought. Each individual can and should act according to his or her own conscience and allow others to do the same.

Notes:

1. *Handbook 2 Administering the Church*, Salt Lake City: The Church of Jesus Christ of Latter-day Saints, 2010, 21.1.29.
2. *Handbook 2 Administering the Church*, 21.1.29.

325. The Mormon Tabernacle Choir conveys the fruit of the Spirit.

I remember visiting a dear friend in Utah before I was a member of the Church. On Sunday, the music in that home changed from the more common popular music to Mormon Tabernacle Choir or classical varieties exclusively. I thought that was odd. If this is such beautiful, enjoyable music that you bring out on Sundays, why not enjoy it the rest of the week as well? I personally found it to be motivational, encouraging, peaceful music. It made me feel good, even happy. To this day, I often enjoy the music of the Tabernacle Choir and only wish they had more recordings out there to scroll through. I continue to feel what I felt years ago as I listen to this beautiful choir and the equally talented orchestra and bells that perform with them.

The apostle Paul wrote, "But the fruit of the Spirit is love, joy, peace, longsuffering, gentleness, goodness, faith" (Galatians 5:22). This is a good summary statement of what flows from the Mormon Tabernacle Choir and is a witness of the source of its inspired work.

The long running program of "Music and the Spoken Word" is a weekly half hour broadcast highlighting a live choir performance, together with the delivery of a short non-denominational Christian message. These messages are of an uplifting, encouraging tone, usually anecdotal, and always with a cheery, reassuring, conclusion. I would say they help to bridge the longsuffering moments of our lives. They inspire faith. They showcase love, gentleness, goodness. They kindle and build a joy within us.

Equally impressive is that the 350 or so members of the choir, and the one hundred or so members of the orchestra, are volunteers without pay! "Members of the Tabernacle Choir [and Orchestra] are selected on the basis of character and musical competence. . . . Choir members sing because they love to share truth and the beauty of music with people everywhere."[1] They perform because of their testimonies of the sacred, their passion for patriotism, their sheer joy of a broad spectrum of music, and the desire to impart that to others as a labor of love.

"The Mormon Tabernacle Choir is dedicated to the universal language of music that has the power to bring joy, peace, and healing to its listeners. . . . This unique music organization transcends cultural and generational boundaries and brings together people from around the world through stirring music. The Choir, the Orchestra at Temple Square, and the Bells on Temple Square act as goodwill ambassadors for The Church of Jesus Christ of Latter-day Saints."[2] It is an organization that bespeaks of faith, hope, and charity. It is recognized and associated with the sacred. It focuses on the noble traits of mankind. It is an inspired organization that engenders love, joy, peace, gentleness, goodness, faith. Paul wrote that these are clear fruits of the Spirit (Galatians 5:22).

Notes:

1. www.utah.com/mormon/tabernacle_choir.htm.
2. www.mormontabernaclechoir.org/about.

326. A lesser man than Joseph Smith wouldn't have held out hope in a system that was often used against him.

Joseph Smith was a party to the law more than two hundred times between the years 1826 and 1844 in the capacity of a defendant, a plaintiff, a witness, or a judge. By sheer quantity of cases brought against Joseph (about forty-eight criminal cases), one would have to conclude that the law became a tool of harassment and duress by his enemies, particularly, in light of the fact that not once was he found guilty of any charges against him! Yet, however unfair and or unresponsive the law had been in Joseph's experience, Joseph placed a firm hope and trust in the lawful system he felt was guaranteed by the United States Constitution. He said, "I am the greatest advocate of the Constitution of the United States there is on the earth."[1]

"Stand by the Constitution of your country."[2] "The Constitution of the United States is a glorious standard."[3]

It would have been an easier conclusion, and perhaps understandable, to expect Joseph to become bitter and jaded by a system that so frequently caused his liberties to be curtailed. To be indicted and arraigned even once in a person's lifetime is usually consuming and certainly traumatic. This occurred repeatedly over an eighteen-year period!

The years between 1840 and 1843 are good examples of the constant legal maneuvering others employed toward the prophet. The timeline below is taken from "Joseph Smith and the Law," Episode 45, *The Joseph Smith Papers* audio series.[4]

- *August 1840:* Charges of treason stemming from the "Mormon War" of 1838-1839 in Missouri are dismissed by Circuit Court Judge Thomas Reynolds of Missouri

- *September 1840:* Governor Boggs of Missouri issued the extradition order to Governor Carlin of Illinois where Joseph was a resident, either unaware of the dismissal by Judge Reynolds one month earlier or in spite of it. Arrest warrant in Illinois could not locate Joseph, and no arrest was made.

- *November 1840*: Thomas Reynolds succeeded Lilburn Boggs as Governor of Missouri

- *June 1841:* Governor Reynolds now appealed to Governor Carlin to arrest and extradite Joseph Smith to Missouri, even though it was Reynolds who dismissed the case back in August of 1840! Joseph was arrested this time and brought before Illinois Judge Stephen Douglas on a writ of habeas corpus. Judge Douglas ruled that the charges were unenforceable. Case closed.

- *May 1842*: Lilburn Boggs was shot and seriously wounded by an attempted assassin. Soon thereafter, Governor Reynolds again sent an extradition writ to

Governor Carlin for Joseph to appear in Missouri. Joseph was arrested in Nauvoo, invoked habeas corpus, and was freed by the Nauvoo courts.

- *November 1842:* Thomas Ford was elected Governor of Illinois. He provided a written statement that the requests from the state of Missouri for extradition were unconstitutional.
- *December 1842:* Joseph submitted himself to the legal process after being in hiding. He went to Springfield, Illinois. The case was referred to a Federal Court under Judge Nathaniel Pope. Pope ruled that the Missouri extradition request was unwarranted and illegal. This affirmed the ruling of the Nauvoo court under the writ of habeas corpus.
- *June 1843:* While Joseph and his family were visiting Emma's family about two hundred miles north of Nauvoo, Joseph was arrested under a Missouri extradition order for treason again. In contrast to his position in November 1842, Governor Ford issued the warrant for Joseph's arrest. Again by writ of habeas corpus, the case was heard in a municipal court in Nauvoo, with the state of Missouri presenting their arguments. The court dismissed the extradition petition. Joseph was a free man, once again.

Joseph N. Walker said of Joseph's legal experiences, "Joseph became noble because of the law. He learned how to forgive others, to find justice, and to look for peace."[5]

It was during the time frame described above that Joseph received significant revelations including the command to build the Nauvoo temple, detailed instructions on baptisms for the deceased and other ordinances, instruction on priesthood organization, the nature of angels, knowledge and intelligence required for salvation, blessings through obedience to divine law, the corporeal nature of God and Christ, marriage status in the celestial world, and more (D&C 124-131).

Joseph remained composed and unflappable during a constant barrage of legal accusations throughout his lifetime. He acted like a man of clear conscience with trust in God, believing that right would prevail over wrong. He possessed a confidence in the very system under which he was hounded. He acted like a man who knew who he was, a Prophet of God.

Notes:

1. *History of the Church of Jesus Christ of Latter-day Saints,* Salt Lake City: Deseret Book, 1962, 6:56-57.

2. Letter addressed to W.W. Phelps dated July 25, 1836, Kirtland, OH, *The Missouri Mormon Experience,* Thomas M. Spencer, ed., University of Missouri Press, 2010, 39.

3. *History of the Church of Jesus Christ of Latter-day Saints,* 3:304.

4. "Joseph Smith and the Law – Episode 45," *The Joseph Smith Papers*, Audio; www.mormonchannel.org/listen/series/the-joseph-smith-papers-audio.

5. "Joseph Smith and the Law – Episode 45."

327. The Aaronic Priesthood has divine duties within the House of Israel.

I especially write this to my grandsons and granddaughters and to their kids and posterity so that they may sense the Biblical, prophetic responsibility we have as stewards over the ordinances and the administration of the Lord's Kingdom in these latter days. It is an awesome honor, blessing, and privilege to bear and officiate in this priesthood and every bit as awesome to sustain, honor, encourage, and inspire its righteous use.

In was May of 1977, when the Aaronic Priesthood was conferred upon me and I was ordained to the office of a priest. I took that seriously and sensed it was an important occurrence. Within days of my baptism and ordination, I headed out alone into Cedar Breaks to backpack for several days and to study. One of the books I took with me was titled *The Aaronic Priesthood Through the Centuries* by Lee A. Palmer, so that I could learn of this priesthood that was conferred upon me.

We call it a preparatory priesthood. You may see that description as a reference to preparing you to receive the Melchizedek Priesthood, and that is true. As you mature through your teen years, you will learn how to magnify your priesthood through administering the sacrament, home teaching, collecting fast offerings, and helping the bishop of your ward in other ways. It is also called the preparatory priesthood because you are helping to prepare the way for the coming of the Lord Jesus Christ a second time. John the Baptist prepared the way for His coming anciently, as he cried repentance saying, "Prepare ye the way of the Lord" (Mark 1:3). John held this same Aaronic priesthood. By being faithful and responsible to your duties in the priesthood, you are both preparing yourself for greater trust and involvement and helping others to prepare for that time when they will "stand before God at the last day" (Ether 5:6).

This priesthood is not a program that Church leaders designed to involve young men and to keep them active in the Church. It is an appendage to the Melchizedek priesthood. "As a result of the failure of the Israelites to observe the gospel law administered by Moses under authority of the Melchizedek Priesthood, the Lord gave an additional law of performances and ordinances and 'confirmed a priesthood also upon Aaron and his seed, throughout all generations' (D&C 84:18) to administer it."[1] This additional law of performances and ordinances was embodied in what we call the Mosaic law. Its purpose was to point the Israelites to the coming of the Messiah. You hold that same priesthood, and when you administer the sacrament and other priesthood duties, you, too, point yourself and others in the ward and in your family to Christ.

When the priesthood is conferred upon you and you are ordained to an office, you have a priesthood lineage that tracks back to the Savior Himself. Ask your dad for your priesthood lineage. You have received the priesthood in the Lord's authorized manner. "And no man taketh this honour unto himself, but he that is called of God, as was Aaron" (Hebrews 5:4).

Do you believe you were called of God? You were. It's common in the Church to receive the priesthood, but never forget that you were placed in this family and called to this work by design. Your charge is anything but common.

You live in the fullness of times. The two priesthoods that existed anciently to preside, effect ordinances, and to direct the Church and Kingdom are upon the earth today. You have a work to do. Be prayerful. Do your duty. This is His work.

Notes:

1. LDS Bible Dictionary, "Aaronic Priesthood."

328. Divine counsel is available for raising a family.

We've all heard the lament, "We get married, have kids, raise a family, and never receive a user's manual on how to do it. I received detailed instructions on how to use and care for my toaster, but kids come, and we just kind of learn as we go!"

For those considering discipleship to the Master, Jesus gave this analogy, "For which of you, intending to build a tower, sitteth not down first, and counteth the cost, whether he have sufficient to finish it" (Luke 14:28)?

Similarly, this could be applied to the young newlyweds who are desirous to have children and are ready to plunge into this new and ever exciting world of parenting. As part of their preparation, they should make themselves aware of what resources they have available to successfully navigate this new adventure and sacred trust and then take advantage of such inspired resources.

In the Church, there is a tremendous focus on the family because it is indeed the fundamental unit of society. The following is a partial list of programs, manuals, booklets and other resources that the Lord has made available to parents and families:

- Counsel to hold a weekly Family Home Evening
- "The Family: A Proclamation to the World"
- "A Parent's Guide," teaching children through their various stages of development
- Living Prophets and Apostles
- Scriptures
- Children's Primary classes from eighteen months of age to age twelve
- Cub Scouting
- Opportunity for Sunday worship as a family
- School day Seminary classes for youth
- "For the Strength of Youth" pamphlet (standards to live by)
- Boy Scouting
- Personal Progress Program for young women
- Opportunities for service as a family

- Annual Stake Youth Conferences
- Annual Stake Girl's Camp
- Annual Father/Son campouts
- Annual High Adventure experiences for young men
- Evening weekly youth activities
- Regular stake dances for youth
- Speaking opportunities in front of an audience from the age of three
- Duty to God program
- Faith in God program
- "A Guidebook for Parents and Leaders of Youth"
- Activity days for young girls
- Relief Society for women and mothers
- Priesthood training for young men from twelve years of age
- Priesthood training for men and dads

All of these writings, counsel, programs, activities, and leaders are to help parents to fulfill their role as parents. Most importantly in a gospel context, the Lord counsels, "And again, inasmuch as parents have children in Zion, or in any of her stakes which are organized, that teach them not to understand the doctrine of repentance, faith in Christ the Son of the living God, and of baptism and the gift of the Holy Ghost by the laying on of the hands, when eight years old, the sin be upon the heads of the parents. . . . And they shall also teach their children to pray, and to walk uprightly before the Lord" (D&C 68:25, 28).

The Lord has not left us on our own as we sail in changing winds across the wide channel of raising a family. He has elevated the parent's responsibility to one of paramount importance. And He has provided inspired counsel to match that responsibility to those who will hear and avail themselves of such insight and opportunities. Collectively, they can be seen as a "Users Manual" of supreme importance.

329. Joseph was destined to prove a disturber and an annoyer of the adversary's kingdom.

In team competition, it's the winning team, the one on top who is likely to draw the most trash talk. All the competitors want to knock that team off the pedestal. That would then give rise to their own ambitions.

Immediately after relating the First Vision to a few contemporaries, Joseph later recorded their reaction in his own history:

> "It seems as though the adversary was aware, at a very early period of my life, that I was destined to prove a disturber and an annoyer of his kingdom; else why should the powers of darkness combine against me? Why the opposition and persecution that arose against me, almost in my infancy? . . . I soon found, however, that my telling the story had excited a great deal of prejudice against me among professors of religion, and was the cause of great persecution, which continued to increase; and though I was an obscure boy, only between fourteen and fifteen years of age, and my circumstances in life such as to make a boy of no consequence in the world, yet men of high standing would take notice sufficient to excite the public mind against me, and create a bitter persecution; and this was common among all the sects – all united to persecute me. It caused me serious reflection then, and often has since, how very strange it was that an obscure

> boy of a little over fourteen years of age, and one, too, who was doomed to the necessity of obtaining a scanty maintenance by his daily labor, should be thought a character of sufficient importance to attract the attention of the great ones of the most popular sects of the day, and in a manner to create in them a spirit of the most bitter persecution and reviling. But strange or not, so it was, and it was often the cause of great sorrow to myself" (Joseph Smith History 1:22,23).

We now are witnesses to the growth from such humble beginnings to a worldwide Church. Accordingly, the devil has had an obsession with seeking to slander, defame, disparage, and if possible, derail this work. The Church's mission is to invite others to come unto Christ, with all the positive behavioral changes that implies. It is a spawning ground for love, forgiveness, compassion, faith, hope, service, family, education, fine arts, tolerance, community, truth, and all other tenets that are "virtuous, lovely, or of good report or praiseworthy" (Articles of Faith, 13).

To have a target figuratively drawn on our backs by him who opposes the light of Christ and is the prince of darkness is a badge of honor. It is also an indication of the eternal importance to the human family that can be effected by the Lords work, instituted once again upon the earth as the Lord's Church restored.

330. The Lord could trust Joseph with spiritual knowledge and sacred experiences.

Today our missionaries teach of the First Vision in the very first discussion. But in the early Church, that wasn't the case. That surprised me when I first learned that fact. In actuality, the account of the First Vision was not first written until 1832, some twelve years after the actual experience, and apparently even that written version was not widely disseminated. It wasn't until 1842 that the First Vision, as we know it today, was published.

Section 76 of the Doctrine and Covenants was received and recorded in February of 1832. It was a doctrinal milestone, declaring that the Father and the Son are distinct individual beings. It expanded on the concept of heaven or hell with clarity about the revealed degrees of glory awaiting in the eternities.

The First Vision was first recorded by Joseph in July of 1832, after the Lord gave section 76. As detailed as is section 76, Joseph declared some years later, "I could explain a hundred fold more than I ever have of the glories of the kingdoms manifested to me in the Vision [section 76] were I permitted, and were the people prepared to receive them. The Lord deals with this people as a tender parent with a child, communicating light and intelligence and the knowledge of his ways as they can bear it."[1]

Giving revelation when people can bear it is illustrated in an early missionary experience in England. Although it was 1837, more than five years after Section 76 was received, Joseph Smith instructed the Elders not to preach of the Vision [section 76] but to stick closely to the first principles of the Gospel, "until such time as the work was fully established, and it could clearly be made manifest by the Spirit to do otherwise."[2] Contrary to this counsel, a young Elder stood to a large congregation and read Section 76 verbatim, immediately changing the proselyting effort from one "with the most flattering prospects" to "which turned the current feeling generally and nearly closed the door in all that region."[3] The doctrine was true, but the people, given the traditions they knew, were not ready to receive it at that time.

When Peter, James, and John had the supernal experience on the Mount of Transfiguration, they were charged by the Savior to tell it to no one until after Jesus' death and resurrection. Here, they saw Jesus transfigured and stood in the presence of Moses and Elias, then heard the voice of God introduce and affirm His beloved Son, Jesus. There is no record that these three apostles violated the charge given to them, even though, no doubt, it would have appeared an excellent endorsement to favor their cause.

Were these apostles obliged to their silence because of the sacred nature of the experience? Or was it that the people weren't in a state to believe? Or was it to try their own integrity? We just don't know.

The early response from having shared the First Vision with one local preacher, perhaps caused Joseph to remain silent on the subject for the many years that followed (Joseph Smith History 1:21). Or perhaps Joseph just felt it too sacred to share widely. It could be that the Lord even commanded Joseph to not share the experience until a later time after that first experience caused such prejudice. We just don't know.

Joseph had many sacred experiences with angels and heavenly messengers that are recorded and likely some that are not recorded. When Joseph said, "were I permitted,"[4] it shows a strict discipline and restraint on his part to be absolutely in alignment with the will of the Lord. Some things, for their ineffable nature, "are not lawful for man to utter" (D&C 76:115, 2 Corinthians 12:4), except in the appropriate time and place. Apparently, Joseph didn't hurry to share all that he experienced but was measured and prudent in his role as a teacher. The Lord could trust Joseph.

Notes:

1. Joseph Fielding Smith, comp., *Teachings of the Prophet Joseph Smith,* Salt Lake City: Deseret Book, 1976, 305.
2. *History of the Church of Jesus Christ of Latter-day Saints,* Salt Lake City: Deseret Book, 1960, 2:492.

3. "History of Joseph Smith," *The Latter-Day Saints' Millennial Star*, Liverpool: Franklin D. Richards, 1854, Volume 16, 55.

4. Joseph Fielding Smith, 305.

331. A Presidency in the Church is unique, unanimous, responsible, and revelatory.

In the Merriam-Webster dictionary, there is a separate definition of presidency pertaining to the LDS Church, which says, "A Mormon executive council of the church or a stake consisting of a president and two counselors."[1] I believe this is a unique arrangement. I believe its original formation, purposes, and existence constitute an inspired order in the Church.

Although the word "presidency" is not Biblical, and the use of "presidents" in the book of Daniel seems to be secular, we see the model of a presidency governing the ancient apostles. To Peter, the Lord said, "And I will give unto thee the keys of the kingdom of heaven" (Matthew 16:19). "Peter was the chief Apostle of his day. It was he who called the Church together and directed the calling of an Apostle to replace Judas Iscariot" (Acts 1:15-26)[2] As preparation for future governing leadership, it was Peter, James, and John who accompanied the Lord and witnessed the transfiguration of Christ and other sacred experiences on the mount. It was here, too, that those promised keys were conferred upon each of the three apostles[3] with Peter as the presiding apostle. It was this presidency of Peter, James, and John who visited the Prophet Joseph Smith and Oliver Cowdery, and conferred upon them those same priesthood keys for the work of salvation in these latter days.

A presidency outside the Church commonly has reference to a single person as president and the collective appointees working under his direction. It also refers to tenure for that specific elected president.

The pattern of inspired governance, that of a president and two counselors, forms a presidency. Today, each local priesthood quorum across the earth will be governed by a presidency. Local and General auxiliary organizations will be governed by a presidency. Wards and stakes are governed by presidencies. Areas, missions, temples, branches, and districts are governed by presidencies. The Church at large is governed by what we refer to as the First Presidency.

A presidency can be seen as a council, presided over by the president. Together they consider, discuss, debate, seek understanding, propose, and prayerfully seek resolution to the concerns of the presidency. And in the end, they are united in their decision, or there is no decision. Unity as a presidency is an imperative. "And if ye are not one, ye are not mine" (D&C 38:27, see also John 17:21-23, 1 Cor 1:10).

That the Lord has inspired and restored the use of presidencies is an administrative light to the field of organizational behavior. Presidencies provide for a broader point of view, a more thoughtful conclusion, a sharing of the load, and a support to the person who presides. It is analogous to the account of Aaron and Hur as they "stayed up his [Moses] hands, the one on the one side, and the other on the other side; and his hands were steady" (Exodus 17:12). Presidencies are truly an inspired form of Church government.

Notes:

1. www.merriam-webster.com/dictionary/presidency.
2. lds.org, *The Guide to the Scriptures,* "Peter."
3. *History of the Church of Jesus Christ of Latter-day Saints,* Salt Lake City: Deseret Book, 1964, 3:387.

332. True disciples know from whence come power, wisdom, and holy influence.

David Whitmer, well into his old age, recalled a story of the Prophet Joseph Smith during the period when the Book of Mormon translation was underway:

> "He [Joseph] was a religious and straightforward man. He had to be; for he was illiterate and could do nothing himself. He had to trust in God. He could not translate unless he was humble and possessed the right feelings towards everyone. To illustrate so you can see: One morning when he was getting ready to continue the translation, something went wrong about the house and he was put out about it. Something that Emma, his wife, had done. Oliver and I went upstairs and Joseph came up soon after to continue the translation, but he could not do anything. He could not translate a single syllable. He went downstairs, out into the orchard, and made supplication to the Lord; was gone about an hour—came back to the house, and asked Emma's forgiveness and then came up stairs where we were and then the translation went on all right. He could do nothing save he was humble and faithful."[1]

That may seem like a small kind of incident to relate, but there is something very important that it brings to light. David Whitmer didn't need to tell this story. He was not likely trying to win converts to the faith, as he himself had disassociated from the Church many years previous. In telling this remembrance, David illustrates an ordinary day in the life of the prophet in the company of but three others, including Emma. Joseph knew that his power to translate came from God. He couldn't continue the translation without the spirit of God, nor would he.

"And if ye receive not the Spirit, ye shall not teach" (D&C 42:14).

My own experience parallels that of Joseph regarding domestic matters. I remember more than once, I would leave home to go to a Church meeting of some sort—either to counsel someone, to give a talk, to teach a class—and for one reason or another, things weren't right between my wife and me. I felt the absence of the Spirit. I realized that I couldn't very well go fill an assignment requiring divine assistance, if I were not humble enough to fix whatever it was between my wife and me. So I turned the car around, went into the house, acknowledged my bad tone or discourteous words or whatever it was, asked forgiveness, and made amends. It was always a sweet ending. Then, I left the home with the company of the Holy Ghost.

This is a spiritual work. One can't fake the conveyance of the Spirit. He just won't be there if the environment is not conducive and inviting for his influence. This little remembrance of Joseph shows he knew from whence came his power and inspiration. To a small audience of three, Joseph matter-of-factly displayed the honesty and integrity that both characterized and enabled his mission.

Notes:

1. Brigham H. Roberts, *A Comprehensive History of the Church of Jesus Christ of Latter-day Saints,* Salt Lake City: The Church of Jesus Christ of Latter-day Saints and Deseret New Press, 1930, 1:131.

333. The tone and delivery of our leaders are of quiet, confident, passionate conviction.

Early on in my young life, one of the characteristics of religious leaders that turned me off was the podium-pounding, high volume, seemingly insincere theatrics that I had on occasion witnessed. Likewise, those who wore their religion on their sleeve, but their actions seemed less about Christian charity than about being an infomercial for their cause. And the glory be to them. It was easy to dismiss religion under those scenarios, because it never moved me to feel of His reality nor to witness the practical blessings that one would expect to flow from having a real divine connection.

I suppose Jesus had a voice that carried well as he preached to multitudes, on occasions several thousand people. But I can't imagine him in scream mode. The Beautitudes, given in the open air, begins, "And he opened his mouth, and taught them, saying . . ." (Matthew 5:2). Thereafter flow some of the most peaceful teachings in all of history, concisely presented and powerfully illustrated in simple speech.

In our Sacrament meeting talks, or in General Conferences, you won't see any theatrics. The talks will be level, conversational in tone, practical, spiritual, and all built around the framework of truth and the cornerstone of Christ. "And we talk of Christ, we rejoice in Christ, we preach of Christ, we prophesy of Christ, and we write according to our prophecies, that our children may know to what source they may look for a remission of their sins" (2 Nephi 25:26).

When a person speaks of truth, testifies of Christ, and all under the influence of the Spirit, the Holy Ghost can testify (confirm) to the hearts of the listeners in an indelible, undeniable way. There is no more powerful nor more efficient communication. "Let all things be done unto edifying," said the apostle Paul (1 Corinthians 14:26). "Wherefore, he that preacheth and he that receiveth, understand one another, and both are edified and rejoice together" (D&C 50:22).

I received some good counsel long ago regarding those who preach. If they ask you to send your money to Jesus and then give you their own address, it probably is more about them than Jesus. I feel likewise about the high octane, over-the-top evangelist. Energy is good, and I am sure the Savior was energetic, passionate, and firm when He cleared the temple of the money changers. But when He taught, there was no need to embellish. His teaching of eternal truths (and by virtue of who He was) confirmed the doctrine to the hearts of the honest hearers.

To the people of Nephi, the voice of Jesus Christ was heard from the heavens, "and it was not a harsh voice, neither was it a loud voice. . . it being a small voice it did pierce them to the center . . . and did cause their hearts to burn" (3 Nephi 11:3). I believe that truth can stand on its own merits. I am grateful for that honest, humble delivery that resonates to the heart of the hearer.

334. We are commanded to repent, to change, to become, and to work out our salvation.

Latter-day Saints are really into improvement, in doing better tomorrow than we did today, in making corrections to our behaviors. I think that desire is rooted in our unique understanding that as children of God, we can and should act as our perfect parents. The goal is to become like them, to the extent that we can while in this mortal experience.

John the Baptist's message to "Repent ye; for the kingdom of heaven is at hand" (Matthew 3:2) was a preparatory message. As the forerunner of the promised Messiah, his message was to call the people to prepare themselves so that when the Savior made himself known, they would recognize Him for who He was.

Our call today to repent is also, in a sense, a preparatory one. We are preparing for the second coming of the King of Kings, the Glorified Christ, the Redeemer of the world, the Hope of Israel. Consider the meaning of these scriptures:

"Beloved, now are we the sons of God, and it doth not yet appear what we shall be; but we know that, when he shall appear, we shall be like him; for we shall see him as he is" (1 John 3:2).

"Wherefore, my beloved brethren, pray unto the Father with all the energy of heart, that ye may be filled with this love, which he hath bestowed upon all who are true followers of his Son, Jesus Christ; that ye may become the sons of God; that when he shall appear we shall be like him, for we shall see him as he is; that we may have this hope; that we may be purified even as he is pure" (Moroni 7:48).

Could the Savior come and we miss the very import of the moment? To imply that we shall see him as he is, suggests that it would be possible to see him for less than he is. Moroni speaks of the necessity to be filled with the love of Christ, and to be pure "even as he is pure" (Moroni 7:48). These are characteristics we must attain to, or at least be gaining ground on, if we are to appreciate his majesty and greatness.

Both Paul and Moroni charge us to "work out your own salvation... with fear and trembling" (Philippians 2:12, Mormon 9:27). To me, this means to reconcile ourselves to God, with great humility. Such a reconciliation is at least a two part process:

1. Our personal efforts to repent, to change, to take upon us the "divine nature" (2 Peter 1:4)

2. Receiving and "relying alone upon the merits of Christ" (Moroni 6:4.) His very Atonement is defined as a means [the only means] to reconcile man to God.[1]

It is embedded within the LDS culture to improve, to progress, to grow, to learn from, to beautify, to qualify, and ultimately to become that "new creature" (2 Corinthians 5:17, Galatians 6:15, Mosiah 27:26). That is, indeed, a worthy goal for which we can find ample scriptural encouragement.

Notes:

1. lds.org, *The Guide to the Scriptures*, "Atone."

335. That was *the* turning point in your life.

Saturday, September 18, 1976, Squaw Peak, Provo Canyon. The statement above is what my dad said regarding the events of that day. I include it as a formative moment of my faith.

At this point in my life, I had been on the BYU survival trip twice and was in the midst of my journey to know of God. I was seeking to know what was true, but there was no real urgency to my quest. I enjoyed what I was learning, but retained my status as a free spirit. I had just come off a month long hitchhiking trip through Colorado and now stayed with the Lambert's, dear friends in Provo.

I draw the following quotations in the narrative from a letter dated just one week later on September 26, which I had written to my parents. "I just went out for a hike one morning, was headed for the top of Squaw Peak. My route was to scale around the outside, just regular walking." At the foothill, I found some rocky places and thrilled at the challenge of being able to scale large boulders with some effort. "I came to a point where I could either climb some more, or go around on solid ground. Looking at the wall before me, I thought it would be a challenge, but it looked stepped off enough so as to be like a 'stairway' with irregular gaps between steps."

I soon realized that you can't go back down as you went up. "I was committed, and my mind was entirely on the goal of the top. Therefore every few feet compounded my predicament. I finally came to a place where it was sheer face and two rocks at arms stretch to try and pull up to and roll up on. By now I was (as I found out later by rope length) 190' up. Insane. Still, I was heavily in tune with making it to the top. Had no other option really. I grabbed those two rocks protruded from the face, my body and legs were dangling. . . . My arms were pretty tired by now. . . . They started shaking and my grip was slipping. . . . Fell for 20 feet, and was stopped on a ledge in a sitting position with my arms behind me, and my legs dangling in air."[1]

I sat on that ledge for about six hours. In the end, I was rescued by Scott Royall and the Sheriff's Department. I had much time to think and to think deeply—about life, about our mortality, about what really mattered, about God.

"Sgt. Jerry Scott said he considered the rescue a 'life and death situation' and indicated he felt that Rogers could not have remained on the ledge overnight."[2]

Whether I was saved by the hand of God, or by sheer chance, I cannot say, but from that experience came a newfound reverence for the Almighty. Life and its very purpose became whittled down to a very few important truths. I came to believe there was more to life than what I had previously given to its value. That belief paved the way for the subsequent light and knowledge that came into my life and led me to the fullness of truth. I will be forever grateful for the safe rescue and for the personal realizations that came into my heart that day, September 18, 1976.

Notes:

1. Handwritten letter dated September 26, 1976, on file.
2. Front Page of *The Daily Herald,* Provo, UT, September 19, 1976.

336. Emma Smith was the first convert who sacrificed all for Joseph's cause.

Joseph and Emma married in January of 1827. It was only eight months later that Emma assisted Joseph in obtaining the gold plates from the Hill Cumorah. Emma's intimate involvement as a first-hand witness and participant in the unfolding of the restoration, shows that when she married Joseph, she embraced his cause as well.

"One of the things that impresses me about this whole marriage is that Emma Smith is the first person to actually have to make a serious commitment as a Latter-day Saint. Joseph implies here that the family [her family] was upset about him continuing to assert that he had had a vision. Emma believes that he has had a vision. But she is the first one that leaves Father and Mother, brother and sister. Emma leaves everything behind but the clothes on her back, to join Joseph Smith. That's the first major commitment that anybody has to make in the restoration, to really put their faith on the line and say 'I believe.' And Emma's the one that makes that commitment."[1]

Emma was very close to the translation of the Book of Mormon. From an interview she had with her sons just months before she died, she related, "The plates often lay on the table without any attempt at concealment, wrapped in a small linen tablecloth which I had given him [Joseph] to fold them in. I once felt the plates as they lay on the table, tracing their outline and shape. They seemed to be pliable like thick paper, and would rustle with a metallic sound when the edges were moved by the thumb, as one does sometimes thumbing the edges of a book."[2]

From that same interview with her sons, Emma affirmed her testimony "My belief is that the Book of Mormon is of divine authenticity. I have not the slightest doubt of it. . . . Though I was an active participant in the scenes that transpired and was present during the translation of the plates. . . . And had cognizance of things as they transpired, it is marvelous to me, a 'marvel and a wonder,' as much as to anyone else. . . . I know Mormonism to be the truth; and believe the Church to have been established by divine direction."[3]

The entire seventeen years of Emma's marriage to Joseph was one of privation, hardship, upheaval, sacrifice and ostracism—a veritable crucible of faith. Her testimony, from such a front row, hands-on, intimate perspective, is evidenced by the faithful companionship she provided for Joseph and the work he was called to restore.

To Joseph who was incarcerated in Liberty, Missouri, in 1839, Emma wrote, "Was it not for conscious innocence, and the direct interposition of Divine mercy, I am very sure I never should have been able to have endured the scenes of suffering that I have passed through . . . but I still live, and am yet willing to suffer more, if it is the will of kind heaven that I should for your sake."[4]

Emma's witness by her faithful life and repeated testimony is perhaps second only to Joseph himself in credibility. If Joseph were a charlatan, she would have been the one to expose him as such, particularly in her later years as the Church moved west and she remained behind in Nauvoo to fare for her family as best she could. She then had no vested interest in perpetuating the story of the restoration—except for the fact it was true—and she knew it. Hers is a great and lasting testimony, that of perhaps the first real convert to the Church in these latter days, and one of sterling integrity.

Notes:

1. Dr. Mark Staker, "Harmony—Episode 8," *The Joseph Smith Papers*, Audio; www.mormonchannel.org/listen/series/the-joseph-smith-papers-audio.
2. "Emma Smith's Last Testimony," February 1879, Interview by Joseph Smith III, Community of Christ Archives; Published in *The Saints' Herald, Official Paper of the Reorganized Church of Jesus Christ of Latter Day Saints,* Plano, Illinois, October 1, 1879, Vol. 26, No. 19.
3. "Emma Smith's Last Testimony."
4. Emma Smith, "Letter, 7 March 1839" in Joseph Smith Letterbook 2, Quincy, IL, 37.

337. The fullness of the everlasting Gospel of Jesus Christ is just that.

This is a phrase that is uniquely LDS, and makes a characterization that is most enlightening. Fullness (spelled "fulness" in the scriptures) is an unambiguous word. Scripturally, among others, it is used as

- "Fulness of joy" (Moses 7:67, Psalms 16:11, 3 Nephi 28:10)
- "Fulness of the blessing of the gospel of Christ" (Romans 15:29)
- "Fulness of iniquity" (Ether 2:10)
- "Fulness of my scriptures" (D&C 42:15)

Latter-day Saints have grown up using the words "the fullness of the gospel" in their phraseology. We find it used in the Book of Mormon and even more so in the Doctrine and Covenants, where it has particular reference to the sharing and receiving of the gospel of Jesus Christ in these latter days.

Let's define "gospel" first. The *Guide to the Scriptures* defines that term as "God's plan of salvation, made possible through the atonement of Jesus Christ. The gospel includes the eternal truths or laws, covenants, and ordinances needed for mankind to enter back into the presence of God."[1]

Furthermore, "This greater priesthood [Priesthood of Melchizedek] administereth the gospel" (D&C 84:19). This is an important piece, for without the authorized greater priesthood, the fullness of the gospel has not been upon the earth. The existence of one presupposes the other.

The fullness of the gospel of Jesus Christ, is the Plan of Redemption, designed to bring about man's immortality and eternal life.[2] In the scriptures is found the fullness of the gospel, specifically named as the Bible and the Book of Mormon, "Thou hast beheld that the book [Bible] proceeded forth from the mouth of a Jew; and when it proceedeth forth from the mouth of a Jew it contained the fulness of the gospel of the Lord" (1 Nephi 13:24).

"Which [Book of Mormon] contains a record of a fallen people, and the fulness of the gospel of Jesus Christ to the Gentiles and to the Jews also" (D&C 20:9).

"And again the elders, priests and teachers of this church shall teach the principles of my gospel, which are in the Bible and the Book of Mormon, in the which is the fulness of the gospel" (D&C 42:12).

Jesus himself spoke of the fullness of the gospel while in the Americas (3 Nephi 16:10, 12, 20:28, 30).

The fullness of the gospel is just that. It includes all truth, laws, doctrines, principles, covenants, ordinances, offices, powers, commandments, injunctions, and more that are essential to salvation. "But I will remember my covenant unto you, O house of Israel, and ye shall come unto the knowledge of the fulness of my gospel" (3 Nephi 16:12). This promise given by the Savior comes by way of the restoration through the Prophet Joseph Smith, bringing back to the earth the fullness of the gospel of Jesus Christ.

Notes:

1. lds.org, *The Guide to the Scriptures*, "Gospel."
2. lds.org, *The Guide to the Scriptures*, "Plan of Redemption."

338. The New and Everlasting Covenant was contained within the first revelation after the Church was organized.

In April 1830, questions arose regarding the need for rebaptism in the newly organized Church if a person had been baptized previously. For the first time in scripture, and as a description of the work now unfolding, the Lord spoke of this "new and everlasting covenant, even that which was from the beginning" (D&C 22:1). Baptism itself wasn't defined as *the* new and everlasting covenant, but rather as *a* new and everlasting covenant.

There is significant scriptural usage of the term "everlasting covenant," particularly in the Old Testament in reference to God's covenant promises to the House of Israel. In the singular reference found in the New Testament, mention is made to the resurrection of Jesus "through the blood of the everlasting covenant" (Hebrews 13:20).

"It [a covenant] is everlasting in the sense that it is God's covenant and has been enjoyed in every gospel dispensation where people have been willing to receive it."[1] Covenants between God and man are intended to be everlasting. The very use of the word "covenant" in the Church will presuppose the word everlasting as its antecedent.

"The new and everlasting covenant is the sum total of all gospel covenants and obligations."[2] Joseph Fielding Smith explained, "It [the new and everlasting covenant] is everything—the fulness of the gospel. So marriage properly performed, baptism, ordination to the priesthood, everything else—every contract, every obligation, every performance that pertains to the gospel of Jesus Christ, which is sealed by the Holy Spirit of promise according to his law here given, is a part of the new and everlasting covenant."[3]

"It is new every time it is revealed anew following a period of apostasy. . . . The new and everlasting covenant was revealed again to men on the earth by Jesus Christ through the prophet Joseph Smith."[4]

Elder D. Todd Christofferson gave a succinct statement that serves well here as a summary: "The new and everlasting covenant is the gospel of Jesus Christ. In other words, the doctrines and commandments of the gospel constitute the substance of an everlasting covenant between God and man that is newly restored in each dispensation."[5]

The full use of the phrase "the new and everlasting covenant" is only used by the Lord in this dispensation, as recorded in the Doctrine and Covenants. I find it interesting that immediately after the organization of the Church, the Lord introduced this most informative phrase to collectively describe the gospel covenants that were coming forth once again to the earth. That moment required the formal clarity that this was a new dispensation and that covenants are initiated by God and are intended to be of eternal, everlasting significance.

Notes:

1. lds.org, *The Guide to the Scriptures*, "New and Everlasting Covenant."
2. Joseph Fielding Smith, *Doctrines of Salvation,* vol. I, Salt Lake City: Bookcraft, 1956, 156.
3. Joseph Fielding Smith, 158.
4. lds.org, *The Guide to the Scriptures*, "New and Everlasting Covenant."
5. D. Todd Christofferson, "The Power of Covenants," *Ensign,* May, 2009.

339. Charity is the pure love of Christ.

Using stunning comparatives, Paul makes clear that acquiring charity is pre-eminent to all else (1 Corinthians 13:1-3, 13). Mormon says we should "cleave unto charity, which is the greatest of all" (Moroni 7:46). Both list the qualities that define charity, Paul expanding on one of them, "vaunteth not itself, is not puffed up," and uniquely including another, "doth not behave itself unseemly" (1 Corinthians 13:4-5). On such a vital subject, though, it is the Book of Mormon that gives particular depth to our understanding.

The phrase, "But charity is the pure love of Christ," is only found in scripture in Moroni 7:47. It speaks volumes. Doctrine and Covenants 45 also lists some of the qualities of charity that embody this pure love of Christ.

"And whoso is found possessed of it at the last day, it shall be well with him" (Moroni 7:47). Mormon is speaking to baptized members of the Church. Apparently, if we can obtain this one virtue, we will be well prepared for the eternities. Have you noticed those elderly souls who truly love—think almost exclusively of others, love truth, believe in Christ, have hope in Christ, and have endured well this life—don't seem to fear their mortal passing? Rather, they seem to have an expectant joy as their days play out.

"Pray unto the Father with all the energy of heart, that ye may be filled with this love, which he hath bestowed upon all who are true followers of his Son, Jesus Christ" (Moroni 7:48). Charity is a gift, a result of true discipleship. It must be desired, and that desire cannot be casual. Its acquisition or lack is a measurement of our level of discipleship.

A result of charity is "that ye may become the sons of God" (Moroni 7:48). We are now sons and daughters of God, so this scripture must have reference to a more intimate relationship with God, perhaps as a reference to living in His presence and immediate influence.

"That when he shall appear we shall be like him, for we shall see him as he is" (Moroni 7:48). Apparently, when the Savior comes, there will be some who don't see Him for who He really is. Those who have given themselves to being His true disciples and have acquired this pure love of Christ will readily receive Him as the promised Millennial Messiah. They will have become like Him.

Moroni links charity with hope, "That we may have this hope" (Moroni 7:48). Hope is centered in the atonement of Christ, the resurrection, and life eternal (Moroni 7:41). It is the most well placed optimism.

Charity makes it possible "that we may be purified even as he is pure" (Moroni 7:48). Joseph Smith clarified, "Charity preventeth a multitude of sins" (JST, 1 Peter 4:8). As our nature changes to become more refined and more Christ like, our baser desires and inclinations recede.

"As important as it is to lose every desire for sin, eternal life requires more. To achieve our eternal destiny, we will desire and work for the qualities required to become an eternal being."[1]

Charity, or the pure love of Christ, may best summarize those qualities required for eternal life. Certainly, it is a characteristic of those who will attain and enjoy the continued presence of God and Jesus Christ. We are fortunate that the Prophet Moroni was inspired to include these deeper insights of his father Mormon on the very important behavioral quality of charity.

Notes:

1. Dallin H. Oaks, "Desire," *Ensign,* May, 2011.

340. Religion must be personal and timeless, not just a belief in traditional lore.

President Spencer W. Kimball, the twelfth president of the Church, was an example of one whose faith was personal, real, and visible in an eternal context. I'll use his example as an illustration of what is in the hearts of faithful members of the Church across the world and throughout time. Those who don't nurture this personal, connective, real, practical religion could be those whom the Savior referred to as those who "have no root in themselves, and so endure but for a time" (Mark 4:17).

The first example of a personal religion is taken from a talk given by President Kimball titled "Peter, My Brother."

> "Some time ago a newspaper in a distant town carried an Easter Sunday religion editorial by a minister who stated that the presiding authority of the early-day church fell because of self-confidence, indecision, evil companions, failure to pray, lack of humility, and fear of man. He then concluded: 'Let us as a people, especially those who are Christians and claim to abide by the Word of God, not make the same mistakes and

> fall as Peter fell.' (Rev. Dorsey E. Dent, *A Message for This Week.*)
>
> "As I read this, I had some strange emotions . . . for Peter was my brother, my colleague, my example, my prophet, and God's anointed. I whispered to myself, 'That is not true. He is maligning my brother.'
>
> "The Savior knew this apostle could be trusted to receive the keys of the kingdom, the sealing and the loosing power.
>
> "Simon Peter was spiritual and prophetic. He received the revelations concerning the Church. Angels accompanied him in and released him from the prison, and a great vision opened the door to millions of honest souls.
>
> "The apostle lives. The weak things of the world confounded the wise. Millions have read his testimony. His powerful witness has stirred multitudes. Through the countless ages of eternity, he will live and extend his influence over the children of this earth. With his brethren, the Twelve, he will judge the nations."[1]

On another occasion, while in Copenhagen, Denmark, President Kimball and others visited the famous Thorvaldsen statues of Christ and the Original Twelve Apostles. Elder Boyd K. Packer tells this story:

> "In Peter's hand, depicted in marble, is a set of heavy keys. President Kimball pointed to those keys and explained what they symbolized. Then . . . he turned to President Benthin (Copenhagen Stake President) and with unaccustomed firmness pointed his finger at him and said, 'I want you to tell everyone in Denmark that I hold the keys! We hold the *real* keys, and we use them every day.'
>
> "Pointing to me, he said, 'Here we have the *living* Apostles. Elder Packer is an Apostle. Elder Thomas S. Monson and

> Elder L. Tom Perry are Apostles, and I am an Apostle. We are the living Apostles.'"[2]

The restoration of the Gospel in these latter-days refreshes the doctrines and practices that the Lord initiated anciently. We sense a connection to the ancients, in a sense more personal than mere traditional lore. Like President Kimball, we become defenders of the faith, and we respect those chosen of the Lord.

Notes:

1. Spencer W. Kimball, "Peter My Brother," *Speeches of the Year*, Provo, Utah: Brigham Young University Press, 1971.
2. Boyd K. Packer, "The Twelve," *Ensign,* May, 2008.

341. The counsel to read, study, ponder, and live by scripture is an anchor in Christ.

We are continuously counseled to read and study the scriptures every day as a family, as a couple, and individually. It is more than a checklist exercise. It is actual sustenance to our spirit, a lifelong course of learning of the things of God. As going without food is to the body, we become spiritually sick and/or weak when we neglect that study.

Jesus was the Master of scriptural understanding. Within the four Gospels, and while ministering among the Nephites, I counted over eighty-five unique references by the Savior to the scriptures! There are another twenty-nine or so references to the scriptures in the narrative. Here are a few examples: "But how then shall the scriptures be fullfilled?" (Matthew 26:54), "not knowing the scriptures" (Matthew 22:29), "search the scriptures" (John 5:39), "well did Esaias prophecy" (Matthew 15:7). Jesus had scriptural knowledge and familiarity. He both modeled and commanded that we acquire it likewise.

I have always liked the following statements from President Spencer W. Kimball and have found them to be applicable in my own life:

> "I find that when I get casual in my relationships with divinity and when it seems that no divine ear is listening and no divine voice is speaking, that I am far, far away. If I immerse myself in the scriptures the distance narrows and the spirituality returns."[1]
>
> "I am convinced that each of us, at some time in our lives, must discover the scriptures for ourselves—and not just discover them once, but rediscover them again and again."[2]

The course of study for the youth seminary program is the scriptures. Not a commentary on, not a visual of, not an animated version, not an entertaining, packaged, summary of them. Students take their scriptures to class and study the inspired words as written by the prophets. And they receive the confirming witness of the Spirit of the truths contained therein and also discover an unending "living" well from which to draw throughout their lives.

The Prophet Moroni, speaking of a process implemented for new converts to the faith, wrote, "Their names were taken, that they might be remembered and nourished by the good word of God, to keep them in the right way, to keep them continually watchful unto prayer, relying alone upon the merits of Christ, who was the author and the finisher of their faith" (Moroni 6:4).

Just pulling up the last General Conference of the Church (October, 2013) on the internet, each of the three senior apostles spoke about the benefits of scripture study with talks entitled "We Never Walk Alone" by President Thomas S. Monson, "The Key to Spiritual Protection" by Boyd K. Packer, "The Doctrines and Principles Contained in the Articles of Faith" by L. Tom Perry.

How grateful I am for the scriptures. They are a bedrock, an anchor, a beacon, a guide, an inspiration, a facilitator for the Spirit, and a comfort. They are living, relevant, and universal. "Search the scriptures;

for in them ye think ye have eternal life: and they are they which testify of me" (John 5:39). We are counseled continuously to follow that admonition of the Master, and are enriched by so doing.

Notes:

1. Spencer W. Kimball, "What I Hope You Will Teach My Grandchildren," an address to Seminary and Institute personnel at Brigham Young University, July 11, 1966.

2. Spencer W. Kimball, "How Rare a Possession—the Scriptures!" *Ensign*, September, 1976.

342. The Judeo-Christian influence has greatly blessed the human experience.

I believe in the Judeo-Christian view of mankind's existence, which begins with Adam and Eve and establishes the House of Israel, a covenant relationship with God, up through the great lawgiver Moses, and on to the ministry of the Savior and His early apostles. I believe in the Judeo-Christian ethical standards as enumerated in the Ten Commandments. I believe in the Judeo-Christian values that all men are created equal. I believe the Judeo-Christian tenets that espouse individual opportunity and accountability, and that promote industry, honesty, civil courtesy, education, patriotism, individual liberties, the rule of law, private property ownership, care of the poor, elderly and the disabled, religious worship, and support of the traditional family. I believe that this covenant relationship with God—and the beliefs, practices and values that create the Judeo-Christian culture—brings light and inspiration to the world and advances the human community.

When we presuppose or accept that there is a divinely ordained people upon the earth, that does not imply that these people have rights to eternal blessings that others do not have. It does say that that people have certain authorities and responsibilities to the human family and certain gifts and understandings to carry out those responsibilities.

"Jews are a famously accomplished group. They make up 0.2 percent of the world population, but 54% of the world chess champions, 27% of the Nobel physics laureates and 31% of the medicine laureates [20% of total Nobel laureates]. Jews make up 2% of the US population, but 21 percent of the Ivy league student bodies, 26% of the Kennedy center honorees, 37% of the Academy Award-winning directors, 38% of those on a recent Business Week list of leading philanthropists, 51% of the Pulitzer Prize winners for nonfiction."[1]

Latter-day Saints make up a similar percentage of the world population as do the Jews; however, they lay no claim to Nobel prizes. Absent that recognition, an impressive list of inventions and discoveries by LDS people have improved the human condition. A partial listing would include the television, stereo sound, digital audio recording, the transistor radio, hearing aids, the first word processor, the traffic light, the odometer, the first repeating rifle and the automatic shotgun, and even the electric guitar. Henry Eyring developed the Absolute Rate Theory of Chemical Reactions, and Wilford Gardner was known as the father of soil physics for his work.

Perhaps some of the greatest LDS contributions to the human family, though, lies at the institutional level, such as family history linking families and generations across the earth, temples promoting moral and ethical uprightness, adherence to local and national law, a generous humanitarian program, a model welfare program for the poor, a perpetual education fund for the disadvantaged, and a university system operating under the banner "Enter to Learn, Go Forth to Serve." Other than the University system, these efforts are largely supported by quiet volunteers.

Of course, the larger population who are not Jewish nor LDS within our Judeo-Christian world make up the larger portion of significant contributions to improve the human condition. The Old Testament directs, "Arise, shine, for thy light is come, and the glory of the Lord is risen upon thee" (Isaiah 60:1). The New Testament says, "Let your light so shine before men" (Matthew 5:16). It is my observation that the Jews and those of Christian influence, including Latter-day Saints, have contributed to the advancement of society and culture in favorable disproportion to their numbers.

Notes:

1. David Brooks, *The New York Times,* January 11, 2010, A23.

343. Faithful saints have hearts like the Master.

What are the qualities and characteristics of Jesus that cause us to want to dwell with Him for the eternities? Jesus was absolutely obedient to his Father, acting in a willing humility that would perhaps seem unnecessary for one of his stature. He loves us, and hence, "we love him, because he first loved us" (1 John 4:19). He is compassionate, understanding, and encouraging. Peace is His environ. His stated purpose is to see that we have a more abundant life (John 10:10). He sees us for who we are inside, not for our photogenic appeal. And He has willingly given His life for our happiness as a witness of His sincerity and devotion.

I see Christlike characteristics among the faithful saints. It is this observation and experience that causes me to want to say, as did Ruth, "Thy people shall be my people, and thy God my God" (Ruth 1:16).

There is a cost to discipleship, and that cost can be measured by those preferential desires, ambitions, and appetites that we are willing to re-direct, or to forego entirely, as the wisdom of the Lord may direct. This is how the Savior lived as He constantly sought to do nothing but the will of His Father, "for I do always those things that please him" (John 8:29). The pure willingness to pay this price is what makes the faithful so attractive.

Since I've been a member of the Church, I've observed and followed five presidents and their administrations—Spencer W. Kimball, Ezra Taft Benson, Howard W. Hunter, Gordon B. Hinckley, and Thomas S. Monson. In these men I see no guile. They have no personal agenda. Their agenda is the Lord's agenda. They love people. Service to mankind, both members of the Church and others, is their mission and ministry.

I look at the Quorum of the Twelve Apostles and see men who have had distinguished careers, yet have set those aside to answer the call to serve. These are strong men, men of decision and action, yet humble and submissive when enjoined of the Lord.

The mission and essence of a true disciple is the same as his Master. For Disciples of Christ, that mission is scripturally encapsulated, "To bring to pass the immortality and eternal life of man" (Moses 1:39). In doing so, that gap referred to in Isaiah about our thoughts and ways is brought nearer to alignment (Isaiah 58:8-9).

I heard a story of an elderly LDS man whose wife passed away on a Saturday, and yet on Sunday, he attended his normal Church services. When asked why he came to Church when his wife had so recently passed, he looked taken aback and answered, "Where else would I go? More than ever, I need the love and support of you my friends and family."

Faithful Saints are not primarily motivated by money. In fact, they give up their own time and money to help and bring another forward. Principles, doctrines, and commandments matter more than personal or popular expediency. Charity, the pure love of Christ, is their watchword and guiding prism. These are the people I want to continue my association with.

344. Nephi's psalm is a formula for hope and renewal and a reminder of our mortality.

One of my favorite verses in all of scripture is the latter half of 2 Nephi 4:19 which says, "Nevertheless, I know in whom I have trusted." Nephi makes this declaration as a pivot from a state of despondency to a crescendo moment concluding the chapter, "Behold, my voice shall forever ascend up unto thee, my rock and mine everlasting God" (2 Nephi 4:19)!

For various reasons, I find a kinship with Nephi in these verses and have used his formula as a sort of launch pad upward from the inevitable down moments we all experience in life. It's nice to know that even a prophet has those moments. In this particular scriptural chronology, it was only five verses earlier that Nephi's father Lehi "died, and was buried" (2 Nephi 4:12). I think this was a factor for the tender exposure Nephi records of his own personal struggles.

We see an emotional outpouring of Nephi's apparently conflicted condition. "Behold, my soul delighteth in the things of the Lord; and my heart pondereth continually upon the things which I have seen and heard" (2 Nephi 4:16). Then in the next verse Nephi exclaims, "O wretched man that I am! Yea, my heart sorroweth because of my flesh; my soul grieveth because of my iniquities. I am encompassed about, because of the sins which do so easily beset me. And when I desire to rejoice, my heart groaneth because of my sins." (2 Nephi 4:17-19).

Then comes the pivotal moment referred to above, "Nevertheless, I know in whom I have trusted. My God hath been my support" (2 Nephi 4:19). From there, Nephi steps from one stone of hope to another, until he is once again renewed in hope and faith. He does that in at least five identifiable steps:

1. He recognizes and remembers past spiritual experiences (2 Nephi 4:20-25).

2. He recognizes that the devil is the source of temptation, and his desire is to destroy our peace, afflict our soul, and cause us to be angry (2 Nephi 4:26-27).

3. He makes a commitment to change. He declares a turning point (2 Nephi 4:28-30).

4. He turns to the Lord in humble and solicitous prayer (2 Nephi 4:31-33).

5. He recognizes and draws upon the power and strength of the Lord, turns from the "arm of flesh," and exercises trust in God (2 Nephi 4:34-35).

This is a workable formula to bring us to higher ground. It can transport us from those momentary setbacks and recurring low valleys to the magnificent mountains of hope and joy. It is a scriptural jewel in my estimation.

345. Similar language in the Book of Mormon and the Bible evidence a common source.

To the Corinthians, Paul at one point wrote of his "infirmities," and that "there was given me a thorn in the flesh" (2 Corinthians 12:7). He even petitioned the Lord to take away that thorn, and records that rather than do so, the Lord said unto him, "My grace is sufficient for thee" (2 Corinthians 12:9).

Then, as I was reading in the Book of Mormon, I saw where the Prophet Moroni was concerned that his weakness in writing would perhaps cause the Gentiles not to believe. The Lord responded to him, "My grace is sufficient for the meek" (Ether 12:26), and in the very next verse, "my grace is sufficient for all men that humble themselves before me" (Ether 12:27).

We see that same language at the conclusion of the Book of Mormon, again through the Prophet Moroni (Moroni 10:32), and then in the Doctrine & Covenants, Sections 17 and 18 dated June 1829, likely the same month the words of Moroni were translated. The very construction of the phrase "my grace is sufficient" is uncommon. Yet, it conveys, in this case, a doctrine that the Lord wants us to understand. So much so, that it was delivered by the Lord soon after His death and resurrection through Paul, then some four hundred years later to Moroni, then in this dispensation through the Prophet Joseph Smith.

The following are other examples of divine language, which are not common everyday phrases, found in both the Bible and in the Book of Mormon:

Bible	**Book of Mormon**
Ephesians 6:4 "the nurture and admonition of the Lord"	**Enos 1:1** "the nurture and admonition of the Lord"
Matthew 9:22 "thy faith hath made thee whole"	**Enos 1:8** "thy faith hath made thee whole"
Ephesians 4:5 "one faith, one baptism"	**Mosiah 18:21** "having one faith and one baptism"
Romans 14:11, Isaiah 45:23 "every knee shall bow to me, and every tongue shall confess" "every knee shall bow, every tongue shall swear"	**Mosiah 27:31** "Yea, every knee shall bow, and every tongue confess"
Isaiah 22:13 "let us eat and drink; for tomorrow we shall die"	**2 Nephi 28:7** "Eat, drink, and be merry, for tomorrow we die"
Job 6:27 "and ye dig a pit for your friend"	**2 Nephi 28:8** "dig a pit for thy neighbor"
1 Corinthians 2:14 "But the natural man receiveth not the things of the Spirit of God"	**Mosiah 3:19** "For the natural man is an enemy to God"

Hebrews 11:1 "Now faith is the substance of things hoped for, the evidence of things not seen"	**Alma 32:21, Ether 12:6** "if you have faith ye hope for things which are not seen" "faith is things which are hoped for and not seen"
Isaiah 28:16 "a precious corner stone, a sure foundation"	**Helaman 5:12** "it is upon the rock of our Redeemer . . . which is a sure foundation"
Hebrews 13:8 "Jesus Christ the same yesterday, and to day, and for ever."	**1 Nephi 10:18** "For he is the same yesterday, today, and forever"
Revelation 21:10 "And he carried me away in the spirit to a great and high mountain"	**1 Nephi 11:1** "I was caught away in the Spirit of the Lord, yea, into an exceedingly high mountain"
Deuteronomy 5:10, Exodus 20:6 "And showing mercy unto thousands of them that love me and keep my commandments"	**Mosiah 13:14** "And showing mercy unto thousands of them that love me and keep my commandments"

By no means are these a thorough list of correlated scripture found in the Book of Mormon and the Bible. It is only a sample of many such instances of similar language used.

I don't believe Joseph Smith had the scriptural background to weave these and many others into the Book of Mormon as common plagiarism. Nor do I read of any evidence that he cross-referenced the Bible during the translation process. Rather, I believe that the source of such divine sayings is one and the same. They are inspired by Him who changes not, and they stand as another testament to the truthfulness of the Book of Mormon.

346. The Church enters into countries by the front door, which is by legal recognition.

On Christmas Day 2012, Elder Russell M. Nelson spoke at a devotional at the Missionary Training Center in Provo, Utah. As part of his remarks, he felt it was important enough to comment on a popular rumor in circulation that our young missionaries were being "called to one area and transferred to open the work in another formerly closed area, such as China." He went on to emphasize, "Such rumors are absolutely false. Refute them!" He then explained in very clear terms the process of gaining legal status in a given country. "Leaders of this Church enter countries new to the Church through the front door. We do not go in through the back door or via the alley. Our relationships are based on honesty, openness, integrity, and complete compliance with local law."[1]

Our relationship with the People's Republic of China over the years is a good example of how the Church is firmly committed to respecting the laws and traditions of other countries. China has not granted permission for our well-known missionary model to be implemented in their country. Yet many Chinese nationals have joined the Church while temporarily living in other nations. Indeed, we have whole Chinese congregations throughout the United States, Britain, Canada, and Australia. So when or if these faithful people (as Latter-day Saints) return to the People's Republic of China, how will they worship? Who is their priesthood leader? Can they openly practice their faith?

The Church created a website specifically to answer questions for Chinese "members outside China and by Church leaders who work around the world with those members."[2] That site states, "In order to observe Chinese laws and directions on religious activities, the Church is blocking access to this website so it cannot be viewed inside China."

"The laws of some nations, such as China, presently forbid foreign missionaries. In other nations, the laws forbid any proselyting by Christians. Some of those barriers will drop when friendship is cultivated and trust is earned. Other barriers will fall because of the blessings of God, whose work this is."[3]

The depth of our Church leaders' respect for the traditions and culture of other nations is captured in a closing comment by Elder Dallin H. Oaks from the same devotional, "People sometimes ask me about what can be done to 'open China.' In response, I state my belief that China is already 'open'—it is we who are closed. We are closed because we expect the Orient to be the same as the West, China to be the same as Canada or Chile. We must open our minds and our hearts to the people of this ancient realm and this magnificent culture. We must understand their way of thinking, their aspirations, and their impressive accomplishments. We must observe their laws and follow their example of patience. We must deserve to be their friends."[4]

The manner in which the Church cultivates and honors international relationships, does not usually result in swift approvals, but it does establish firm and enduring friendships of trust and mutual benefit. "Latter-day Saints . . . believe in being responsible citizens of the nations and communities to which they belong."[5] I am proud to belong to a Church that honors the laws and traditions of other nations and works within the system for legal and authorized recognition.

Notes:

1. Russell M. Nelson, "Elder Russell M. Nelson Urges Missionaries to Refute Rumors," Missionary Training Center, Provo, December 25, 2012; *Church News,* www.lds.org/church/news/elder-russell-m-nelson-urges-missionaries-to-refute-rumors.

2. www.mormonsandchina.org.

3. Dallin H. Oaks, "Getting to Know China," Brigham Young University Devotional, March 12, 1991.

4. Dallin H. Oaks.

5. www.lds.org/topics/citizenship.

347. The Church functions by the frequent use of councils and the synergy of collective, inspired counseling.

Wednesday morning, I got a call asking if our young men's group and I could help to do some tree trimming for a sister who needed some help. "Just bring some gloves, it shouldn't take too long." When we arrived that late afternoon, what I thought was merely tree trimming, translated to removing a very large major branch of a mature tree hanging over the house. My guess is that it weighed 1,500 pounds!

It was too high to reach, so just how were we going to do this? Someone had a plan, so we set to work. When all was roped up and in place to start cutting, we stood back, and the leader asked for concerns we could see that may pose a problem.

One of the young men, an engineering kind of thinker, said that the angle the rope was running from the end of the limb to the "V" in the main trunk was too low, not creating enough angle to really support the limb when cut. So we moved the rope to a higher "V" in the tree. Then, there was concern that when the limb was cut at the trunk, the weight of the branch could cause the branch to fall the distance of the rope from trunk to tied tip. So someone suggested cutting from the bottom in a wedge cut, to allow the branch to bend before an abrupt break. Then, we could reach it from the roof and pare it back with chainsaws.

Other ideas and suggestions adjusted the original plan, and in the end, it worked beautifully, and we spared the roof. There were more than a few of us with some anxiety throughout the process, but each new idea seemed to better insure our success.

This is a long story to illustrate the power of collective counseling which produces a synergy. Definitions and synonyms for synergy are teamwork, harmony, team effort, combined effort, working together, and unity.

The Church has a long history of working in councils to enable and utilize this collective counseling. Joseph Smith was inspired to establish the First Presidency, the Quorum of the Twelve, Councils of Seventy, High Councils, local quorums, and auxiliary organizations, such as the Relief Society. These and other administrative organs have enabled many to have a stake and a voice in the kingdom and certainly have lightened the burden of leadership.

"This is the miracle of Church councils: listening to each other and listening to the Spirit! . . . The best leaders are not those who work themselves to death trying to do everything single-handedly, the best leaders are those who follow God's plan and *counsel* with their *councils*."[1]

This same model is to be used in the family by fathers and mothers and their children to decide together on their legacy purposes and to counsel regularly to stay on course.

The frequent use of council meetings in the Church and in our homes is wise counsel indeed, from Him whose counsel is the object of all such meetings.

Notes:

1. M. Russell Ballard, "Counseling with Our Councils," *Ensign,* May, 1994.

348. What would you say are the most important lessons you've learned on your mission?

I recently asked that question to our sister missionaries, Sister Hadlock and Sister Asay, while they were at our house for dinner. Their response was obedience to God and love of all people. I was immediately struck by the similarity in the response to the question posed to Jesus, "Master, which is the great commandment in the law? Jesus said unto him, Thou shalt love the Lord thy God with all thy heart, and with all thy soul, and with all thy mind. This is the first and great commandment. And the second is like unto it, Thou shalt love thy neighbor as thyself" (Matthew 22:36-39).

Let's look at the sister's first lesson learned, obedience to God. There are at least three reasons to be obedient to God: 1) to receive blessings, 2) to avoid pain and suffering for wrong choices, 3) to show our love for Him. If we are obedient in order to show love to the Savior first, then the other two will be ours as well. The motivation to receive blessings and to avoid pain could exist independently, even at the exclusion of showing love for God.

Jesus connected obedience with love, when He said simply, "If ye love me, keep my commandments" (John 14:15).

To those whose obedience to God is because of their love for God, great scriptural promises are given, "My Father will love him, and we will come unto him, and make our abode with him" (John 14:23).

"Ye shall abide in my love" (John 15:10).

"And showing mercy unto thousands of them that love me and keep my commandments" (Mosiah 13:14, Deuteronomy 5:10, Exodus 20:6).

"Keeping the covenant and mercy to them that love him, and to them that keep his commandments" (Daniel 9:4).

"The Lord thy God shall bless thee in the land" (Deuteronomy 30:16).

And now let's look at the second lesson the sisters learned, love of all people. Paul wrote, "Though I have the gift of prophecy, and . . . though I have all faith . . . and have not charity, I am nothing. . . . And now abideth faith, hope, charity, these three; but the greatest of these is charity" (1 Corinthians 13:2, 13). The Prophet Moroni recorded, "Cleave unto charity, which is the greatest of all. . . and whoso is possessed of it at the last day, it shall be well with him (Moroni 7:46-47). The Lord said, "By this shall men know that ye are my disciples, if ye have love one to another" (John 13:35).

Without consciously knowing it, these good sister missionaries had recited Jesus' summation of all the prophets—to love God and to love our fellows. It is an uncommon response from two twenty-year-old young people, but not entirely unexpected given their devoted discipleship as missionaries. They learned these lessons through the tutelage of the Holy Spirit.

349. The Joseph Smith Papers Project is an ambitious, honest effort for transparency.

"The Joseph Smith Papers project is an effort to gather together all available documents produced by Joseph Smith himself or by others he appointed as scribes... This landmark collection will include 20 volumes organized into six series: Journals, Revelations and Translations, History, Documents, Administrative Records, and Legal and Business Records. All of the more than 2,000 documents will be published electronically on the project's website, and a large number will also be published in print."[1]

Church Historian and Recorder Elder Marlin K. Jensen said, "We believe *The Joseph Smith Papers* will be the most important Church history project of this generation."[2]

Ronald K. Esplin is the managing director of the Joseph Smith Papers project, which is expected to take about twenty years to complete. Here he gives scope and breadth to the project, "The focus of the Joseph Smith Papers is to gather all of the surviving manuscripts and documents that belonged to Joseph Smith by virtue of being part of his office, or that he created by dictation, by his own hand, or in some way set in motion a record that were part of his official responsibilities as President of the Church. . . . There will be no exclusions, no omissions, all of the papers we have access to and can find will be published in their entirety."[3]

Prior to this ambitious effort, and particularly up through about 1980, Richard N. Holzapfel summarizes some of the early Church histories that have created and supported a certain lore about the man Joseph Smith. "Some early Latter-day Saints, and some early efforts by those Latter-day Saints, have, with good intention, tried to provide us a rather sanitized version of the prophet's life, believing that such a telling of the story would serve the Kingdom best. Much like our own efforts at writing our personal diaries and autobiographies . . . [we] tend to downplay conflict, take our own interpretation of events, and as a result, my diary is not as open and honest a record as it should be."[4]

Richard L. Bushman, in the preface to his candid interpretive history of Joseph Smith titled *Rough Stone Rolling*, acknowledges an unavoidable bias both he and all other biographical authors are faced with. "Everything about Smith matters to people who have built their lives on his teachings. To protect their own deepest commitments, believers want to shield their prophet's reputation. On the other hand, people who have broken away from Mormonism . . . have to justify their decision to leave. They cannot countenance evidence of divine inspiration in his teachings without catching themselves in a disastrous error."[5]

This project is not to convince people that Joseph Smith was a Prophet. It is not a project that is controlled, in the sense of contained and approved documents. New documents are being discovered and sought even during the project, and they too will be included and published, just as they are.

On the call and ministry of Joseph Smith, the veracity of the Church stands. His story must be told, unvarnished and unbiased. This scholarly work of publication will surely enable the welcome sentiment from a beloved hymn, "Millions shall know 'Brother Joseph' again."[6] In the end, those of us who believe that Joseph Smith was a Prophet of God, also believe that his life exposed in the first person, will support that view.

Notes:

1. www.mormonnewsroom.org/article/the-joseph-smith-papers.
2. www.mormonnewsroom.org/article/the-joseph-smith-papers.
3. Ronald K. Esplin, "Overview– Episode 1," *The Joseph Smith Papers*, Audio; www.mormonchannel.org/listen/series/the-joseph-smith-papers-audio.
4. Richard Neitzel Holzapfel, "Joseph Smith, the Early Years," in Richard Neitzel Holzapfel, editor, *Joseph Smith's Prophetic Ministry – 1805-1819*, Salt Lake City: Deseret Book, 2009, audio CD.
5. Richard L. Bushman, *Rough Stone Rolling*, New York: Alfred A. Knopf, 2005, xix.
6. William W. Phelps, "Praise to the Man," *Hymns of the Church of Jesus Christ of Latter-day Saints*, Salt Lake City: The Church of Jesus Christ of Latter-day Saints, 1985, 27.

350. In this Church, everyone is or will be a teacher.

In the Church, there is no paid local clergy. We literally teach one another. We teach children, youth, and adults. We teach from the pulpit, in the classroom, at home, around a campfire, in the homes of friends and acquaintances, one-on-one, to specific groups, and to large gatherings. We teach teachers how to be better teachers and instruct leaders of their responsibilities and duties. We teach formally and as occasion allows.

The role of a teacher in the Church is held in high regard for the reach and influence it has. The following statement by Elder Jeffrey R. Holland of the Quorum of the Twelve expresses how Church leadership feels about the role of a teacher:

> "We are so grateful to all who teach. We love you and appreciate you more than we can say. We have great confidence in you. . . . To teach effectively and to feel you are succeeding is demanding work indeed. But it is worth it. We can receive 'no greater call.' . . . For each of us to 'come unto Christ,' to keep His commandments and follow His example back to the Father, is surely the highest and holiest purpose of human existence. To help others do that as well—to teach, persuade, and prayerfully lead them to walk that path of redemption also—surely that must be the second most significant task in our lives. Perhaps that is why President David O. McKay once said, 'No greater responsibility can rest upon any man [or woman], than to be a teacher of God's children.'"[1]

I couldn't begin to count the number of lessons I have heard regarding faith. A lesson on faith, for me, is more a reminder and a rekindling of the hope that is in me, but to a child, those early lessons on faith are carefully placed in the heart to effect a lifetime of hope, optimism, and trust. To a young teenager, that lesson on faith might find application in the halls of high school, where their beliefs are challenged. To a new convert or those investigating the restored gospel, they learn that "even if ye can no more than desire to believe, let this desire work in you, even until ye believe" (Alma 32:27).

As teachers, we are taught in the Church to utilize the following principles:

- Love those you teach
- Teach by the Spirit
- Teach the doctrine; highlight the principles
- Invite diligent, participative learning
- Apply teaching to real needs
- Testify of the truths being taught

Teaching and training is constantly happening at all levels of the Church. It is that vital! We have no formal theological training schools. We learn as we teach, and at some point, we all teach, "till we all come in the unity of the faith, and of the knowledge of the Son of God" (Ephesians 4:13). To attain that perfect unity and that perfect knowledge of the Son of God, teaching and effective teachers will be a continued focus for the Lord's Church.

Notes:

1. Jeffrey R. Holland, "A Teacher Come from God," *Ensign,* May, 1998.

351. Indexing is a visionary effort to bless and connect families.

The Digital Indexing program is a volunteer effort to transcribe valuable information from genealogical records and make that information available to freely search online. These records include birth and death certificates, marriages, baptisms, passenger records from ships, immigration records, census data, conscription listings, and many more.

The first indexing of available documents began in 1921 and was handwritten on index cards that were then filed alphabetically in card catalogues. This initial effort must have seemed almost hopeless given the vision and scope of seeking to account for all available documents throughout history up to that time! Without the knowledge of what technologies would be available to us in the twentieth-first century, they had to start somewhere, and so start they did.

In 1961, this index card system was entered on a punch card computer system.

About 1977, tiny photographic images of historical records were then stored on microfiche and microfilm. These could be read by projection readers and hand recorded onto extraction cards.

1987 opened a new efficiency when volunteers could index from home using printed copies of original records, mailing their work in to Salt Lake City on the old floppy disks.

In 2001, indexing could be done from home using digital images from CD-ROMs.

And then in 2006, the current digital indexing was made available on the internet via FamilySearch.org.

From the humble beginnings of handwriting and typing individual index cards and filing those in drawers, volunteers are now indexing well over a half-million names each day. But the task is staggering. Here are some current facts to give size and context to the job at hand:

- From North and South America and Europe, about 5.3 billion records have been preserved. An estimated ten billion more records need to be digitally preserved from these continents.

- An additional sixty billion records need to be digitally preserved from all other parts of the world
- At the current rate, and because of recent collaboration with other organizations, it is estimated that to index the 5.3 billion records now digitally preserved will require twenty to thirty years. Prior to the recent collaborative agreements, it would have taken two hundred to three hundred years!
- An estimated twenty-eight billion people have lived since AD 1500
- About one billion people's information is preserved in FamilySearch.org's online Family Tree
- About twenty-seven billion people still need to be identified and their information linked online to complete the family tree of mankind since AD 1500.

Why is a Church so involved and committed to what may be seen as a secular pursuit? And what drives the over 350,000 volunteers in over 130 countries to give of their time to this effort? It's our belief that we are all brothers and sisters, children of the same Heavenly Father. It's our belief in the fundamental unit of society, the family. It's our remembrance that we are who we are for the lives of those who have gone on before. It's to provide the saving ordinances vicariously for all of mankind. It's to continue the work that the Savior initiated in 1 Peter 3:19 and D&C 138:18-19, 28-34, when He went to the Spirit World. With the help of friends across the earth who are seeking to discover their own family trees, eventually everyone who has ever lived will be accounted for. It is because all are known to God, and "the worth of souls is great in the sight of God" (D&C 18:10).

352. The Book of Mormon liberally cautions us how we might lose the Spirit of the Lord.

Early on in the course of human history, the Lord declared, "My spirit shall not always strive with man" (Genesis 6:3, Moses 8:17). It was important enough to repeat to the Mulekites, to the Nephites, and through the Prophet Joseph Smith (Ether 2:15, 2 Nephi 26:11, D&C 1:33).

Knowing that all men are born into this life possessing the light of Christ (Moroni 7:16) and that children are without sin until the age of accountability, how is it that there is so much evil in this world? How do men become like an Adolf Hitler, a Pol Pot, Idi Amin, or Josef Stalin, with such disregard and even hatred for the lives of others? Certainly, these men and their like are the extremes when measuring distance from the Spirit of the Lord. But any distance from the Spirit of the Lord will diminish our happiness, or worse, if we don't correct our course.

We know that the Spirit of the Lord, the Holy Ghost, the influence of the Lord will not be in a heart of unbelief, a place or heart of wickedness, and does not dwell in "unholy temples" (Helaman 4:24). "And there were no gifts from the Lord, and the Holy Ghost did not come upon any, because of their wickedness and unbelief" (Mormon 1:14).

Foolishly, we sometimes withdraw ourselves from the Spirit by our own behaviors. "These be they who separate themselves, sensual, having not the Spirit" (Jude 1:19). King Benjamin elaborated on this theme, "After ye have known and have been taught these things, if ye should transgress and go contrary . . . that ye do withdraw yourselves from the Spirit of the Lord, that it may have no place in you to guide you in wisdom's paths . . . therefore he listeth to obey the evil spirit" (Mosiah 2:36-37).

Taking that course, we could arrive at a point of being past feeling, which only accelerates that dangerous direction. "Who being past feeling have given themselves over unto lasciviousness, to work all uncleanness with greediness" (Ephesians 4:19). Moroni describes this state as a result of wickedness and being "without principle" (Moroni 9:20).

Laman and Lemuel had both seen and heard an angel, yet "could not feel his words" because they "were past feeling" (1 Nephi 17:45). Hence, they heard with their ears, saw with their eyes, but entirely missed the import of an angel's personal visit and call to repentance.

When we procrastinate our repentance, live wickedly, harden our hearts, and otherwise are unfit, unholy temples, we are on our own. We come to a point where the Lord says, "I will withdraw my Spirit from them" (Helaman 13:8; see also Helaman 4:24, 6:35, Alma 34:35, D&C 19:20, Mormon 2:26).

When a body of people collectively pursue this course—leaders, nations, armies, cities and peoples—a most terrible state ensues. "For behold, the Spirit of the Lord hath already ceased to strive with their fathers; and they are without Christ and God in the world" (Mormon 5:16; see also 1 Nephi 7:14, Ether 15:19, Moroni 8:28, 9:4).

Saul, through a series of bad choices, quickly descended from favor with the Lord to the situation in which, "the Spirit of the Lord departed from Saul" (1 Samuel 16:14). The Book of Mormon prophets help us to recognize this tragic path and its progressive stepping stones, so we can avoid the state where Saul arrived, and instead "be blessed, prospered, and preserved" (Mosiah 2:36) as a result of keeping the Spirit of the Lord.

353. The Thirteenth Article of Faith is an exuberant declaration for living our lives.

"We believe in being honest, true, chaste, benevolent, virtuous, and in doing good to all men; indeed, we may say that we follow the admonition of Paul—We believe all things, we hope all things, we have endured many things, and hope to be able to endure all things. If there is anything virtuous, lovely, or of good report or praiseworthy, we seek after these things" (Articles of Faith, 13).

What's not to love about that positive statement? It is noble, selfless, interesting, patient, and uplifting. It compels to action, hope, vision, and humility. It inspires art, creation, opportunity, and faith.

Paul recorded much the same, "Finally, brethren, whatsoever things are true, whatsoever things are honest, whatsoever things are just, whatsoever things are pure, whatsoever things are lovely, whatsoever things are of good report; if there be any virtue, and if there be any praise, think on these things" (Philippians 4:8).

Character is "the aggregate . . . traits that form the individual nature . . . particularly of a moral or ethical quality."[1] Over a lifetime, a focus on conducting oneself honestly, of being true to our better self, accepting our duties and responsibilities, living a chaste life in deed and in thought, sharing and giving generously of our time and means to those in need, and seeking the welfare and uplift of our fellows contributes to an improved society, a personal confidence, and a heightened enjoyment. It represents the high road.

The phrase of believing, hoping, and enduring all things is a declaration of faith. It recognizes that the way may not be easy, but the outcome is sure for those who finish the race. It is trust in the Lord, come what may.

"If there is anything virtuous, lovely, or of good report or praiseworthy, we seek after these things" (Articles of Faith 13). And there are so many of those things! To waste time with the tawdry, the inane, and the insipid is to overlook and miss out on the tasteful, the intelligent, and the exhilarating. Art, literature, history, geography, and good music are some things. Travel, education, volunteer service, and career contributions are other noble things. Raising a family, teaching our children, enjoying the company of others are wonderful things. There is no end to these things that we could and should pursue.

Some claim that religion is restrictive, or perhaps, that it inhibits that zest for life that we all want to lean toward. In fact, Jesus summed up his gospel purposes when He said, "I am come that they might have life, and that they might have it more abundantly" (John 10:10).

The Thirteenth Article of Faith is a beautiful, outward, positive tenet of our faith. It has always been a source of satisfaction for me to hold it up as a model of how we approach life. It is an ideal and one that blesses our lives and outlooks.

Notes:

1. www.dictionary.reference.com/browse/character.

354. The Church teaches consistent, reasonable, comprehensive doctrines.

Up until the time I went on a BYU survival program in 1975, religion had always been for other people, and in my mind, was a creation of their making. Historically, some men had worshipped a single god, while others worshipped multiple gods. Those gods had been characterized in the personification of passions, emotions, natural occurrences, states of nature, animals, trees, heavenly bodies, or many other elements of nature. Some worshipped a god of spirit, others a god of form, some a god who spoke, others a god who was silent. God could be angry and vindictive, or easy-going, gentle, and tranquil. Even within given churches, interpretations of the nature of God and their professed doctrines would vary by locale or by preacher. My conclusion on the matter was that god was whatever man wanted or needed him to be. Man creates his god.

So, it was in this attitude that I was immersed with about twenty-seven Mormons and three of us not of the faith on the BYU survival program. We were to be together for twenty-nine days, hike approximately 170 miles, experience snow, extreme heat, thirst, hunger, sickness, and general deprivation. We leaned on one another, encouraged one another, cared about one another. We had a lot of time to talk and get to know one another.

I wanted to know about their faith. It was very apparent that their faith was uppermost in their lives. I watched them pray, make reference to the help of God, and draw upon faith in difficult circumstances. I found them to be a very kind and inclusive people.

I started by asking some people about their God. I was struck by the consistent response I received. "He is our Heavenly Father, and we are made in his image. He loves His children, and you too, are a child of God."

"Who is Jesus then? Are they one and the same?"

"Jesus is our Savior, the only begotten of God in the flesh, and He died for our sins and imperfections, so that we could once again live with Him and God our Father. He was resurrected and is in the presence of God as a separate individual, perfected as is God."

"What is the purpose of this life?"

"To come from our premortal state, gain a physical body, be part of a family, learn to live by faith in Christ, receive the ordinances of the Gospel, and enter into a covenant relationship with Deity."

This record is certainly not the actual text of conversations, I really don't remember such detail, but it is representative of where several conversations went. The interesting part to me was that everyone I asked had the same response. They all understood it the same. And to me, it just felt right. It made sense.

Now, almost forty years later and much more familiar with the doctrines of The Church of Jesus Christ of Latter-day Saints, I have a more certain witness that this is indeed the Church restored by the Lord in these latter days.

It struck me those many years ago, and it continues to move me today that the doctrines of the Church are consistent, reasonable, comprehensive, and scripturally sound.

355. The restored Gospel of Jesus Christ reveals the merciful nature of God.

From the fall of Adam and Eve, there has been this huge gap between the character, the perfections, and the life of God as contrasted to mortal man. Few, if any, would disagree with that assessment. For this gap, mankind is in need of a Savior, who alone has the power and identity to atone for the sins and frailties of our lives.

But how does it happen that every soul that has ever lived will be able to "putteth off the natural man and becometh a saint through the atonement of Christ the Lord" (Mosiah 3:19)? How is it that this huge gap and the only real antidote to that gap are linked in the individual lives of humanity? How is it in the end, fair, impartial, dispassionate, and equitable to all? The Plan of Salvation, also scripturally referred to as the Plan of Happiness, Redemption, and Mercy, provides for all of God's children. It is, in fact, more generous and merciful than many of the prevailing religious philosophies of men. The following saving truths and understandings illustrate that merciful plan and speak to the grace of God towards all of his children.

The Plan of Salvation is universal to all mankind:

- All are born into this world with the light of Christ, or a conscience, to guide them (Moroni 7:16)

- The most elemental objective of mortality is to attain a physical body
- "All little children are alive in Christ, and also all they that are without law" (Moroni 8:22)

Through the Church He organized, Jesus Christ implemented the Plan of Salvation:

- The Gift of the Holy Ghost is a lighthouse to covenant keepers
- Covenant keepers are anxiously engaged in bringing all people, living and dead, unto Christ
- Ordained prophets and apostles guide the faithful and supervise the ordinances of salvation

To see starving kids in hopeless conditions in various parts of the world cause some to lose hope in the existence of God. To understand that obtaining a physical body, in the context of a pre-mortal and a post-mortal life, gives perspective to such distressing situations. Coupled with the fact that they are alive in Christ, we see glorious endings for these and similar mortal plights.

It would be grossly unfair to eternally condemn any person for not accepting something they never even had knowledge of, to condemn one who is unaccountable for their actions through no fault of their own, or to condemn innocent children. Instead, "little children are whole, for they are not capable of committing sin" (Moroni 8:8). To those who never heard the gospel of Jesus Christ in its fullness, "every ear shall hear it" (D&C 88:104). Christ himself initiated the gospel to be "preached to the dead" (D&C 138:30, 1 Peter 3:19). And a great work of teaching the gospel will take place in the millennium, so that those good people can accept or reject His teachings.

In this final dispensation, in order to prepare for the coming of the Lord to the earth in glory, the Church that Jesus organized is charged with the task of taking the gospel to all people, both living and dead.

The Church is to administer the ordinances of salvation and bring all unto Christ and His bridging Atonement. The Gospel is bold, compassionate, and inclusive. It is individual, intimate, and personal. It is the mercy of God to all His children and a witness of His grace to all us imperfect beings. All of us.

356. We trust in the rising generation.

Many would agree that the best way to learn is to do. Our youth take an active part in the work of the kingdom, by delegation, by assignment, by invitation, by calling, by challenge, or of their own initiative. Just today, Sunday, I observed the following:

- Eight kids from seventeen down to about seven-years-old sang a musical number in the sacrament meeting, and they were accompanied on the piano by a young man of fifteen
- A girl of fourteen was the pianist in another sacrament meeting
- A young woman of fifteen spoke for ten minutes in sacrament meeting on faith, hope, and charity
- A young man of eighteen spoke in sacrament meeting prior to his leaving on a mission to California
- The priesthood lesson was taught by three young men ages thirteen to sixteen on virtues and standards to live by as true disciples of Jesus Christ
- An early morning missionary preparation class was held for all high school seniors, where they formed companionships and taught gospel principles to those with predetermined needs.
- Young men ages twelve to eighteen prepared, blessed, and administered the sacrament to the entire congregation. This is the most important, sacred part of our

worship. They also brought the required bread and cleaned up after the services.

The Aaronic Priesthood young men, and the corresponding young women, are led by a presidency of their peers. Scout troops are led by the boy leaders. The office of a Bishop has a special charge and interest to minister to the youth of his ward.

Recently, the youth of the Church have been challenged to research an ancestor and take that name to do ordinance work for them in the temple. In October, 2011, Elder David A. Bednar gave an invitation to the rising generation to get involved in family history work, "You are sons and daughters of God, children of the covenant, and builders of the kingdom. You need not wait until you reach an arbitrary age to fulfill your responsibility to assist in the work of salvation for the human family."[1]

A remarkable show of trust is when a man as young as eighteen or a woman as young as nineteen are set apart to be full-time missionaries. They are recognized in public as authorized representatives of The Church of Jesus Christ of Latter-day Saints. They teach people often much their senior about things requiring wisdom beyond their years. They have been prepared for this service and this trusted call. It works. These young missionaries rise to the challenge.

All of these examples and many more demonstrate the preparing of the next generation to be actively involved in the work of the Lord. The leaders of the Church have confidence in the youth. "The future of the kingdom of God upon the earth will, in part, be aided by your devotion."[2]

These youth will raise righteous, faithful families, and they will accept the covenant responsibilities of membership in the Church. Involvement in the Church that gives personal spiritual experiences from a young age cause this rising generation to sing in unison, "to

God's command, soul, heart, and hand, faithful and true, we will ever stand."[3]

Not only does the leadership of the Church have trust in the rising generation, but also know that these youth can, do, and will receive and teach by the Holy Spirit. That is what families teach them to recognize, to seek, and to nurture. The Church supports our youth by giving them opportunities to participate from a young age and in very significant ways.

Notes:

1. David A. Bednar, "The Hearts of the Children Shall Turn," *Ensign,* October, 2011.

2. Thomas S. Monson, "The Lighthouse of the Lord: A Message to the Youth of the Church," *Ensign,* February, 2001.

3. Evan Stephens, *True to the Faith,* – Hymns of the Church of Jesus Christ of Latter-day Saints, Salt Lake City: The Church of Jesus Christ of Latter-day Saints, 1985, 254.

357. From Moses to Jesus to Joseph Smith, delegation has been the form of leadership.

When I first heard the classic definition of what priesthood authority is and thought that I was ordained to bear that priesthood, I felt very humble indeed. "Priesthood is the power and authority of God. God delegates that power and authority to man to act in all things necessary for the salvation of His children."[1] Wow! That authority is broadly spread; all active, worthy men in the Church, and even our young men, bear this priesthood authority, and have this charge. That delegated authority contrasts with the one or the few who are founding or otherwise charismatic leaders of a given church.

In addition to this grand delegation of priesthood power and authority, delegation of responsibility is taught and practiced at all levels of the Church. "Individual leaders cannot and should not do everything themselves. . . . Leaders should delegate service opportunities to others."[2] The Church handbook lists effective delegation techniques:

- Clearly explain the calling or assignment, with any time-frames and expected follow up
- Keep a written record and follow up on the charges given
- Allow the person called or assigned to fulfill the charge and provide encouragement and assistance as needed
- Receive a report from the person on what they did, and accept this report as their best effort, expressing appreciation for the good things the person has done

We learn of this model of delegation from Moses' experience recorded in Exodus chapter 18, "And when Moses' father in law [said] . . . why sittest thou thyself alone, and all the people stand by thee from morning unto even? . . . Thou wilt surely wear away, both thou, and this people that is with thee; for this thing is too heavy for thee; thou art not able to perform it thyself alone" (Exodus 18:14, 18). He then counseled Moses to select "able men, such as fear God, men of truth, hating covetousness, and place such over them [the people]" (Exodus 18: 21).

Jesus initiated a delegated structure which he called His Church (Matthew 16:18). It included apostles, seventies, evangelists, pastors, teachers, bishops, priests, elders, and other offices of delegated responsibilities.

Joseph Smith restored that church with the priesthood offices and the corresponding delegation of responsibilities and authority. He certainly did not keep priesthood authority or Church governance to himself or even to an appointed few.

Delegation is a principle of God's ways within His Church. It broadens the work of the Lord, deepens the testimony of the participants, and inspires trust. It is a brilliant means to engage men and women to actively take part in the Lord's work and to learn to love what and whom He loves.

Notes:

1. www.lds.org/topics/priesthood.
2. *Handbook 2 Administering the Church*, Salt Lake City: The Church of Jesus Christ of Latter-day Saints, 2010, 3.3.4.

358. Prior to discovery, the Americas were populated by the Book of Mormon remnant people and other American continent civilizations.

I used to explain the Book of Mormon by drawing a simple sketch that showed the old world of Jerusalem and the new world of the Americas with a boat and route of passage of the families of Lehi and Ishmael from Jerusalem to the Americas. Then, as part of the drawing, I would make triangles throughout Central and South America to depict the archeological ruins we now know of and then declare, "These very civilizations are the descendants of these Book of Mormon people." What I meant was that they were *all* descended from the Book of Mormon people.

Similarly, the introduction to the Book of Mormon used to say, "All were destroyed except for the Lamanites, and they are the principal ancestors of the American Indians" (Introduction, Book of Mormon). That has been changed now to read, "And they are among the ancestors of the American Indians" (Introduction, Book of Mormon).

"Most early Latter-day Saints assumed that Near Easterners or West Asians like Jared, Lehi, Mulek and their companions were the first or the largest or even the only groups to settle the Americas. . . . In fact, cultural and demographic clues in its text (the Book of Mormon) hint at the presence of other groups."[1]

We as a people welcome these new findings and understandings. By whatever means the Americas were populated, of which the Jaredites, Lehites, and Mulekites were a part, I welcome and thrill at the evidences that directly confirm or support the Book of Mormon narrative.

"Dr. John Clark of the New World Archeological Foundation has compiled a list of sixty items mentioned in the Book of Mormon. . . . In 1842, only eight (13%) of those sixty items were confirmed by archeological evidence. . . . We find in 2005 that forty-five of those sixty items (75%) have been confirmed."[2]

David G. Calderwood, a member of the LDS Church who lived in South America for many years, has devoted considerable scholarship into understanding ancient America and the Book of Mormon. His interest was in the early Spanish and Portuguese chronicles, archeological discoveries, and art history, with a comparative evaluation of these sources to the Book of Mormon. His work, entitled *Voices From the Dust, New Insights into Ancient America*[3] is a compelling book drawing many parallels from these sources to the Book of Mormon. He notes religious and doctrinal similarities to Jewish customs and understanding, cycles of prosperity and degeneration, weaponry for warfare, and many other confirming historical writings, findings and drawings.

However, speaking for the Church, Elder Dallin H. Oaks observed, "It is our position that secular evidence can neither prove nor disprove the authenticity of the Book of Mormon."[4]

As interesting as the evidences and parallels from confirmed history and diligent scholarship are, (and they are indeed interesting), the Book of Mormon is a record primarily concerned with conveying religious truths, and particularly as a second witness of the mission of Jesus Christ. A witness of its authenticity is promised to all who study the book "with a sincere heart, with real intent, having faith in Christ" (Moroni 10:4). I also see it as narrating some part and portion of the native American civilizations.

Notes:

1. www.lds.org/topics/Book-of-Mormon-and-DNA-studies
2. Michael R. Ash, "Archeological Evidence and the Book of Mormon," *Fair Mormon,* www.fairmormon.org/perspectives/publications/archaeological-evidence-and-the-book-of-mormon.
3. David G. Calderwood, *Voices From the Dust, New Insights into Ancient* America, Austin, TX: Historical Publications, Inc., 2005.
4. Dallin H. Oaks, "The Historicity of the Book of Mormon," in Paul Y. Hoskisson, ed., *Historicity and the Latter-day Saint Scriptures,* Provo, UT: Brigham Young University Religious Studies Center, 2001, 239.

359. Now consider how great this man Melchizedek was.

The apostle Paul, in speaking of Melchizedek, the "king of Salem, priest of the most high God" (Hebrews 7:1) urges us to "consider how great this man was" (Hebrews 7:4).

Alma taught similarly of Melchizedek's preeminence as a priesthood bearer, "Now there were many before him, and also there were many afterwards, but none were greater" (Alma 13:19). Perhaps as the Savior said of John the Baptist, that there was "not a greater prophet" (Luke 7:28), so Melchizedek was that model of a righteous priesthood holder. As a further candid observation of his greatness, President Gordon Little of our Stake Presidency commented, "You just don't get the priesthood named after you for being a fifty percent home teacher!"

Biblical references to Melchizedek are few. Genesis 14 introduces him as a contemporary of Abram who blessed Abram after a victorious battle to rescue Lot, Abram's nephew. Melchizedek then received tithes from Abram (Genesis 14:18-20, Hebrews 7:2). David penned the messianic psalm, "Thou art a priest forever after the order of Melchizedek" (Psalm 110:4). This statement is used by Paul to the Hebrews several times in Chapters Five, Six, and Seven. Melchizedek was referred to as the King of Salem (Jerusalem), priest of the most high God, King of righteousness, King of peace (Hebrews 7:1-2).

The Book of Mormon and latter-day revelation give us much insight to this priesthood namesake, Melchizedek. Such priesthood naming was "because Melchizedek was such a great high priest" (D&C 107:2). We learn of Melchizedek's piety and reverence as he "offered up prayers and supplications with strong crying and tears unto him that was able to save him from death" (JST, MS Hebrews 5:7). We see that even "when a child he feared God" (JST, Genesis 14:26).

The strong and effective priesthood power and leadership of Melchizedek was preached by Alma. "His people had waxed strong in iniquity and abomination; yea they had all gone astray; they were full of all manner of wickedness. But Melchizedek, having exercised mighty faith . . . did preach repentance . . . and they did repent; and Melchizedek did establish peace in the land" (Alma 13:17-18). In fact, Alma tells us to "humble yourselves even as the people in the days of Melchizedek" (Alma 13:14). So complete was their repentance, that "his people wrought righteousness, and obtained heaven, and sought for the city of Enoch which God had before taken" (JST, Genesis 14:34). We also learn from Alma that Melchizedek "did reign under his father" (Alma 13:18).

"Abraham received the priesthood from Melchizedek, who received it through the lineage of his fathers" (D&C 84:14). He was "the keeper of the storehouse of God; him whom God had appointed to receive tithes for the poor" (JST, Genesis 14:37-38).

The priesthood that bears this man's name was formerly called "the Holy Priesthood, after the Order of the Son of God" (D&C 107:3) or "after the order of the Only Begotten Son" (D&C 76:57). What an incredible honor and tribute to a faithful priesthood bearer that "the church, in ancient days, called the priesthood after Melchizedek" (D&C 107:4).

We are blessed to have further insights and understanding into the life of this great prophet through latter-day revelations and translations. The whole of mankind is blessed to have the Lord's authorized priesthood once again on the earth, the priesthood known as Melchizedek.

360. Whoso are faithful are sanctified by the Spirit unto the renewing of their bodies.

These words come from the first verse of what we call the Oath and Covenant of the Priesthood. In full, that verse says, "For whoso is faithful unto the obtaining these two priesthoods of which I have spoken, and the magnifying their calling, are sanctified by the Spirit unto the renewing of their bodies" (D&C 84:33).

This weekend, the Meridian, Idaho Temple was to be dedicated, and Elder L. Tom Perry from the Quorum of the Twelve was to preside. In addition, he would then preside at the Boise West Stake Conference. His responsibilities were a Temple Dedication Saturday morning, a Stake Conference that afternoon and evening, more conference sessions Sunday morning, and no doubt, training of stake presidency members. In summary, he would speak and dedicate the Meridian Temple, speak at all three sessions of Stake conference, then fit in some stake presidency training and reviews. And Elder Perry is ninety-two years old!

Well, it turns out that something came up. Elder Perry asked Elder David A. Bednar to step in for him. Elder Bednar is thirty years his junior, the youngest member of the Twelve.

The presiding leadership of the Church is a living testament to this scriptural promise. They seem to possess energy, vigor, mental acuity, and sound judgment well into their later years. Whereas the average male life expectancy in the United States is around seventy-six years, the average age of the members of the Quorum of the Twelve is seventy-nine years, and going strong!

On a piece for "60 Minutes" aired in 1996, President Gordon B. Hinckley was interviewed by Mike Wallace and had the following exchange during that interview:

Wallace: There are those who say, "This is a gerontocracy. . . . This is a church run by old men."

Hinckley: Isn't it wonderful to have a man of maturity at the head? A man who isn't blown about by every wind of doctrine?

Wallace: Absolutely, as long as he's not dotty.

Hinckley: Thank you for the compliment.

The promise in the scriptures of the renewal of their bodies not only is fulfilled in the lives of these faithful Church leaders, but also in the lives of countless other faithful members of the Church. It is not limited to brethren who bear the priesthood. Those who seek after and honor their covenants while fulfilling their Church responsibilities, receive this renewing of their bodies to enable them to carry out their responsibilities.

President Thomas S. Monson promised, "When we are on the Lord's errand, we are entitled to the Lord's help. Remember that whom the Lord calls, the Lord qualifies."[1] To qualify is "to be fitted or competent for something."[2]

I have observed the "renewing of their bodies," most notably in the leadership of the Church and also in my own personal experience. It is linked to the promise given to the faithful in D&C 89 that they "shall receive health in their naval, and marrow to their bones; And shall find wisdom and great treasures of knowledge . . . and shall run and not be weary, and shall walk and not faint" (D&C 89:18-20). In other words, to be fitted for what we are called to do—physically, mentally, spiritually and emotionally.

Notes:

1. Thomas S. Monson, "Duty Calls," *Ensign*, May, 1996.
2. www.dictionary.reference.com/browse/qualify.

361. The Lamanites are a remnant of the Jews.

A remnant is described as "a fragment . . . usually a small part . . . a trace . . . a remaining."[1]

When He spoke of the Book of Mormon, the Lord declared, "Which is my word to the Gentile, that soon it may go to the Jew, of whom the Lamanites are a remnant, that they may believe the gospel" (D&C 19:27).

Nephi spoke similarly, "And then shall the remnant of our seed know concerning us, how that we came out from Jerusalem, and that they are descendants of the Jews" (2 Nephi 30:4).

In revelations received in September and October of 1830, and later in June and July of 1831, the Lord referred to at least some of the Native American Indians (and perhaps all of them) as Lamanites:

"Behold, I say unto you that it [Zion] shall be on the borders by the Lamanites" (D&C 28:9).

"Thou shalt take thy journey among the Lamanites" (D&C 28:14).

"Build up my church among the Lamanites" (D&C 30:6).

"He shall go with my servants, Oliver Cowdery and Peter Whitmer, Jun., into the wilderness among the Lamanites" (D&C 32:2).

"Take your journey into the regions westward, unto the land of Missouri, unto the borders of the Lamanites" (D&C 54:8).

As an apparently interchangeable term, Jew is used in place of Lamanite when the Lord actually made the much anticipated declaration of Independence, Missouri, as the center place of Zion. "And also every tract lying westward, even unto the line running directly between Jew and Gentile" (D&C 57:4).

What is of interest to me in all of this is that the revelations, the Book of Mormon, and the Old Testament are all in harmony. The tribes of Ephraim and Manasseh were largely among the "lost tribes" of the Northern Kingdom of Israel. However in about 941 BC, "the strangers with them out of Ephraim and Manasseh" (2 Chronicles 15:9) gathered to the Southern Kingdom "in abundance" (2 Chronicles 15:9). Judah and Benjamin were the dominant tribes of this Southern Kingdom, and collectively, it was called the Kingdom of Judah. From this region which included Jerusalem, came Father Lehi and the family of Ishmael, direct descendants of Joseph through Manasseh and Ephraim respectively (Alma 10:3).[2] The lost tribes were led away captive into Assyria in 721 BC. Lehi and Ishmael left Jerusalem, or the Kingdom of Judah, in approximately 600 BC. They were Jews, as these people and their descendants were known by Nephi (2 Nephi 30:4, 33:8) and on down through recorded history.

It is said that Ephraim "hath mixed himself among the people" (Hosea 7:8), and I suppose the same could be said of Manasseh. Hence, this Jewish blood has some place and perhaps prominence amongst the native Americans of North and South America. We, as a Church, have collectively referred to them as the Lamanite people.

Notes:

1. www.dictionary.reference.com/browse/remnant.
2. Erastus Snow, "God's Peculiar People, Etc.," delivered at Logan, UT, May 6, 1882, reported by Geo. F. Gibbs, *Journal of Discourses, vol. 23,* 184.

362. The wrath, anger, indignation, and vengeance of God are mortal traits ascribed to a Perfect, Immortal Being.

Add to the words above, the rage and fury of God, with qualifiers such as "fierceness of" (Nahum 1:6), "fullness of" (Ether 9:20), and "shall wax hot" (Exodus 22:24), and one might conclude that the Lord is grumpy, irritable, and emotionally volatile. No, these are human terms, and although God is a being who indeed feels and expresses emotion (Moses 7:28-40), these terms best describe the inevitable consequences of man's unrighteous choices.

"The 'wrath of God' is a term usually indicating his disapproval of the deeds of the wicked and justifying the inevitable punishments that will befall them if they do not repent. Latter-day Saints believe that His response is a natural application of the law of justice (Mosiah 3:26), which requires that punishments be exacted when God's laws have been violated or the blood of innocent Saints has been shed (Mormon 8:21-41; D&C 77:8)."[1]

Wrath, anger, and indignation all have similar dictionary definitions that could be summarized as a strong feeling of displeasure aroused by a wrong. When speaking as we are of Deity, the word "righteous" should be inserted between the words "strong" and "feeling."

"God's love is so perfect that He lovingly requires us to obey His commandments because He knows that only through obedience to His laws can we become perfect, as He is. For this reason, God's anger and His wrath are not a *contradiction* of His love but an *evidence* of his love."[2]

"Doctrine and Covenants 1:24 tells us, 'These commandments are of me, and were given unto my servants in their weakness, after the manner of their language, that they might come to understanding.' In other words, I believe that the word *anger* is applied the way it is in the scriptures because we understand that language and because it has the clearest, most positive effect on us (see D&C 19:6-7)."[3]

"At this point we should look at our definition of *anger*. I am using it in the sense that it is an emotion that results from judging others unrighteously, wanting to control others, or selfishly wanting our own ends met. I submit that God does not get angry when anger is thus defined—or as we commonly use the word. Anger is a feeling of hostility, resentment, wrath, or ire. None of these feelings was present nor, I believe, ever is present with God. I believe God's actions are *interpreted* at times as arising out of anger because he applies consequences, including punishment, for violation of his laws. But when we look at God's punishment, we find that it is just—there is no element of hostility or revenge."[4]

Joseph Smith and Sidney Rigdon taught that to have real faith, we must have "a *correct* idea of his [God's] character, perfections and attributes."[5] Although our Heavenly Father and the Lord Jesus Christ do indeed have perfectly refined and appropriately expressed emotions, it is entirely elevated from our mortal expressions of anger and wrath. Theirs is not erratic, capricious, impulsive, fickle, or unpredictable. The wrath of God is something we bring upon ourselves as a just consequence of our choices and actions (Mosiah 3:26, 5:5). This understanding of scriptural wording is consistent with a Father in Heaven who is the embodiment of emotional perfection, and who, first and foremost, loves His children.

Notes:

1. Donald B. Gilchrist, *Encyclopedia of Mormonism,* "Wrath of God," New York: Macmillan, 1992, 1598.
2. Dallin H. Oaks, "Love and Law," *Ensign,* November, 2009.

3. Burton C. Kelly, "The Case Against Anger," *Ensign*, February, 1980.

4. Burton C. Kelly.

5. *Lectures on Faith*, Salt Lake City: N.B. Lundwall, Lecture Third, 2-4.

363. As a book of scripture, the Pearl of Great Price is aptly named.

Elder Mark E. Peterson, a member of the Quorum of the Twelve, declared that the Pearl of Great Price "contains some of the greatest revelations of God to man."[1]

I agree with that assessment. The Joseph Smith History is, of course, unique and contains the account of the most important event to occur since the Atonement and the Resurrection of our Lord, the visitation of the Father and the Son to the boy Joseph Smith.

The translation of Matthew 24 describes the Second Coming of the Savior, signs of the times, and the fate of the wicked.

The Book of Moses, a work from the Bible translation, and the Book of Abraham, a translation or revelation from Egyptian papyri, provide what I consider to be doctrinal, historical, clarifying, and expanding narratives from the Lord. They are true nuggets of divine wisdom and knowledge.

Here is a partial compilation of some of those nuggets:

> Moses 1:3-6 – Moses learns his identity and purpose. "I am God. . . . Thou art my son. . . . I have a work for thee. . . . Thou art in the similitude of mine Only Begotten." With that understanding, Moses resisted and cast out Satan. We have that same identity.

Moses 1:39 – "For behold, this is my work and my glory—to bring to pass the immortality and eternal life of man." This is a laser-focus divine mission statement.

Moses 2:26, Abraham 4 – The statement, "Let us make man in our own image," clarifies the "us" in Genesis 1:26 as God the Father and Jesus Christ.

Moses 3:17, 6:56 – This is the first scriptural use of the word "agents" referring to man's ability to choose. "Nevertheless, thou mayest chose for thyself, for it is given unto thee," was said to Adam just following the charge not to eat of the fruit of the tree of knowledge of good and evil.

Moses 4:1-4, Abraham 3:27-28 – The most complete record of how Satan (Lucifer) "was cast down" and became the devil. These verses connect and clarify references in Revelations 12, D&C 29, Isaiah 14, and 2 Nephi 2.

Moses 5:6-8, 6:52-53 – Adam strictly obeyed. He learned that one purpose of sacrifices "is a similitude of the sacrifice of the Only Begottten." Adam and Eve received, participated in, and taught their children the first four principles and ordinances of the Gospel, which are faith, repentance, baptism and the Gift of the Holy Ghost.

Moses 5:10-11 – Rather than remorse, Adam and Eve saw their fall (by their conscious choice) as a blessing to enable the purposes of God, including the birth of the human family. They had hope in "the joy of our redemption" as a remedy to their now mortal condition.

Moses 6:5-6 – These verses provide actual knowledge that Adam and his posterity had developed a written language and kept a book of remembrance. Adam and Eve taught their children to read and write in a "language which was pure and undefiled."

Moses 6:62 – This revelation to Adam is the first recorded use of the term "Plan of Salvation." This plan was from the beginning "unto all men."

Moses 6 & 7 – Much detail is given regarding the character, life, and mission of the Prophet Enoch and his people; for example, "All nations feared greatly, so powerful was the word of Enoch."

Abraham 1:1-5 – We learn of Abraham's character from an early age, as he desired to "keep the commandments of God." The priesthood is identified with the Lord's work, as contrasted to other contemporary gods and forms of worship.

Abraham 2:9, 11 – As part of the Abrahamic covenant, Abraham's descendants would receive the gospel and bear the priesthood, "that in their hands they shall bear this ministry," by which all the families of the earth would be blessed with salvation.

Abraham 3:22 – Clear reference is made to a pre-mortal existence and the doctrine of foreordination, for "among all these there were many of the noble and great ones."

Abraham 3:25 – Fundamental understanding to one of the core purposes of life is provided, "And we will prove them herewith, to see if they will do all things whatsoever the Lord their God shall command them."

"The Pearl of Great Price . . . contains revelations on certain subjects superior to any other scriptures or writings on those subjects found in the world. . . . [It] helps to clarify some of the difficult passages in the other scriptures."[2]

It is, indeed, a pearl of great price.

Notes:

1. Mark E. Peterson, "Know for Yourself," *Conference Report,* April, 1952, 104-107.

2. Milton R. Hunter, "The Modern Scriptures, Our Greatest Aids," *Conference Report,* October, 1955, 64-68.

364. Church leaders encourage intelligent and thoughtful conviction.

"Latter-day Saints are not obedient because they are compelled to be obedient. They are obedient because they know certain spiritual truths and have decided, as an expression of their own individual agency, to obey the commandments of God. . . . There is an obedience that comes from a knowledge of the truth that transcends any external form of control. We are not obedient because we are blind, we are obedient because we can see."[1]

The very Church itself came about by the questioning boy Joseph Smith. Many of the revelations in the Doctrine and Covenants are the result of questions. We are divinely encouraged to seek learning, wisdom, understanding, and knowledge. Over and over, we are scripturally counseled to ask, but we are to "ask in faith, nothing wavering" (James 1:6).

Intelligent and thoughtful conviction to a doctrine, a principle, a prophetic decree, a calling, a practice, or a program requires building on previous proven tenets of belief. Like mathematics. When someone inquires to learn how to solve a quadratic equation, that person knows that the previously learned principles of simple arithmetic cannot be compromised in any real solution.

Asking in faith includes building upon certain spiritual truths that we have already faithfully acquired. These truths include:

- God is our perfect, corporeal, loving Heavenly Father
- Jesus Christ is our perfect, corporeal, loving personal Savior

- We are mortal physical beings, from a pre-mortal spiritual existence, destined for a resurrected post-mortal existence
- All are born into this life endowed with the Light of Christ
- Our freedom to choose our course in life is inviolable to God by His own design
- Prayer is a direct two-way communication with God
- The Holy Ghost teaches and witnesses of truth to honest, humble, penitent souls
- Scriptures, or the teachings of prophets, are the word of God unto salvation
- Priesthood ordinances performed under priesthood keys identify the orderly Kingdom of God on the earth

So with our lens of faith firmly in place, and "with a sincere heart, with real intent" (Moroni 10:4), "you must study it out in your mind, then you must ask me" (D&C 9:8). Thereby, we may receive our own conviction, our own understanding, and our own testimony.

"He [God] wishes the worship, not of blind and dumb slaves, but of intelligent and free women and men."[2]

I am grateful to belong to a Church that encourages its people to think, to reason, to inquire, and to prayerfully seek. I am grateful for bedrock truths which constitute the secure laboratory wherein we can conduct our pursuit of continued learning. I am grateful for a living Father in Heaven who hears and inspires and a resurrected Savior who actively directs His Kingdom.

Notes:

1. Boyd K. Packer, "Agency and Control," *Ensign,* May, 1983.

2. Michael Novak, "The Blind-Obedience Myth," *National Review Online,* Apr 27, 2005; www.nationalreview.com/article/214289/blind-obedience-myth-michael-novak.

Part Five

Core Reason

core , noun - "[OFTEN AS MODIFIER] The part of something that is central to its existence or character." (Oxford Dictionaries Online)

365. My list of top ten doctrines that are clarified, restored, or revealed by Joseph Smith.

My testimony of the divine call to the Prophet Joseph Smith in these latter days is at the core of everything I've written about in this book. I believe he is loved by God and a favored instrument in the hands of the Lord Jesus Christ. He was a man with his own eccentricities, which have become ample fodder for those who see him as a fraud or wish to make their case against the Church he restored. In truth, there are a few claims made of Joseph's behaviors that even I can't reconcile, but there are also some recorded Biblical accounts that I can't reconcile. Someday, though, all those things will be understood by how it really was, because the evidence overwhelmingly convinces me that the Bible is the word of God and that Joseph Smith is a Prophet of God.

"Joseph Smith, the Prophet and Seer of the Lord, has done more, save Jesus only, for the salvation of men in this world, than any other man that ever lived in it," said Elder John Taylor of the Council of the Twelve following the martyrdom of Joseph (D&C 135:3). I list below what I consider ten of the key doctrines for the salvation of men in this world that came through the Prophet Joseph Smith.

1. We are spirit offspring of Heavenly Parents. Jesus Christ was the Firstborn and was chosen to be the Savior of all mankind. Jesus is physically resurrected and on the right hand of God the Father. The Holy Ghost testifies of all truth and participates as the third member of this Godhead. The greatest form of worship to God is to seek to become like Him through our discipleship to His Son.

2. Man existed pre-mortally as a spirit entity and is born into mortality to live by faith in Jesus Christ and to learn to control physical appetites with spiritual resolve, while seeking to obtain the virtues of charity. Earth life is a mortal probation

to learn and to grow in families. Man is free to choose his course.

3. The earth was organized of existing materials, not created of nothing. The fall of Adam and Eve was a noble choice to enable the human race and was not born of a sinful act of ignorance or worse.

4. The Priesthood and its enabling keys were restored to the earth to provide order and authority to administer ordinances and associated covenants.

5. Broad, coherent, confirming, corroborative, enlightening, encouraging, comforting, inspired, scripture has been added to the Bible—about fifty-six percent more of the Word of God, by page count.

6. Essential ordinances and sacred temples have been restored to bind us by covenant to God and to secure marriages and families into the eternities.

7. Christ organized the work of preaching the gospel to the spirits in prison. Postmortal glories await mankind versus the idea of simply a heaven or hell.

8. Salvation will be offered to all, without exception. All will hear of Jesus Christ.

9. The Atonement of Jesus Christ began privately in Gethsemane, was public on Calvary, and culminated with the resurrection of the Master. He suffered for our pains, afflictions, sicknesses, infirmities, sins, and even death.

10. This is the last dispensation prior to the Second Coming. The keys of gathering, sealing, restoring, and all other keys specific to this last dispensation have been conferred. The Church will play a significant role at the Lord's coming.

These are beautiful, inclusive, expansive doctrines, and all are unique to the Church that Joseph Smith founded. I will be forever grateful to that faithful man. "He lived great, and he died great in the eyes of God and his people" (D&C 135:3). "Praise to the man who communed with Jehovah."[1]

Notes:

1. William W. Phelps, "Praise to the Man," *Hymns of the Church of Jesus Christ of Latter-day Saints,* Salt Lake City: The Church of Jesus Christ of Latter-day Saints, 1985, 27.

TOPICAL INDEX
OF RELEVANT CHAPTERS

Bolded chapters are of primary relevance to a particular topic

Raised in San Diego California, converted at 21 years old, served a mission to Mexico, and a graduate of Brigham Young University, Cragg has enjoyed living in Texas for the last 32 years raising five children with me! Now enjoying grandchildren, it is for these people in our lives that this book has been written.

A testimony from Dad, Papa, Bishop, President, Brother Rogers or Cragg as all of you may know him.

Enjoy,

Fiona